HISTORICAL DICTIONARIES OF WAR, REVOLUTION, AND CIVIL UNREST
Edited by Jon Woronoff

Asia

1. *Vietnam*, by William J. Duiker. 1989. *Out of print. See No. 27.*
2. *Bangladesh*, 2nd ed., by Craig Baxter and Syedur Rahman. 1996. *Out of print. See No. 48.*
3. *Pakistan*, by Shahid Javed Burki. 1991. *Out of print. See No. 33.*
4. *Jordan*, by Peter Gubser. 1991
5. *Afghanistan*, by Ludwig W. Adamec. 1991. *Out of print. See No. 47.*
6. *Laos*, by Martin Stuart-Fox and Mary Kooyman. 1992. *Out of print. See No. 35.*
7. *Singapore*, by K. Mulliner and Lian The-Mulliner. 1991
8. *Israel*, by Bernard Reich. 1992
9. *Indonesia*, by Robert Cribb. 1992. *Out of print. See No. 51.*
10. *Hong Kong and Macau*, by Elfed Vaughan Roberts, Sum Ngai Ling, and Peter Bradshaw. 1992
11. *Korea*, by Andrew C. Nahm. 1993
12. *Taiwan*, by John F. Copper. 1993. *Out of print. See No. 34.*
13. *Malaysia*, by Amarjit Kaur. 1993. *Out of print. See No. 36.*
14. *Saudi Arabia*, by J. E. Peterson. 1993. *Out of print. See No. 45.*
15. *Myanmar*, by Jan Becka. 1995
16. *Iran*, by John H. Lorentz. 1995
17. *Yemen*, by Robert D. Burrowes. 1995
18. *Thailand*, by May Kyi Win and Harold Smith. 1995
19. *Mongolia*, by Alan J. K. Sanders. 1996. *Out of print. See No. 42.*
20. *India*, by Surjit Mansingh. 1996
21. *Gulf Arab States*, by Malcolm C. Peck. 1996
22. *Syria*, by David Commins. 1996. *Out of Print. See No. 50.*
23. *Palestine*, by Nafez Y. Nazzal and Laila A. Nazzal. 1997
24. *Philippines*, by Artemio R. Guillermo and May Kyi Win. 1997

Oceania

1. *Australia*, by James C. Docherty. 1992. *Out of print. See No. 32.*
2. *Polynesia*, by Robert D. Craig. 1993. *Out of print. See No. 39.*
3. *Guam and Micronesia*, by William Wuerch and Dirk Ballendorf. 1994
4. *Papua New Guinea*, by Ann Turner. 1994. *Out of print. See No. 37.*
5. *New Zealand*, by Keith Jackson and Alan McRobie. 1996

New Combined Series

25. *Brunei Darussalam*, by D. S. Ranjit Singh and Jatswan S. Sidhu. 1997
26. *Sri Lanka*, by S. W. R. de A. Samarasinghe and Vidyamali Samarasinghe. 1998
27. *Vietnam*, 2nd ed., by William J. Duiker. 1998
28. *People's Republic of China: 1949–1997*, by Lawrence R. Sullivan, with the assistance of Nancy Hearst. 1998
29. *Afghanistan*, 2nd ed., by Ludwig W. Adamec. 1997. *Out of print. See No. 47.*
30. *Lebanon*, by As'ad AbuKhalil. 1998
31. *Azerbaijan*, by Tadeusz Swietochowski and Brian C. Collins. 1999
32. *Australia*, 2nd ed., by James C. Docherty. 1999
33. *Pakistan*, 2nd ed., by Shahid Javed Burki. 1999
34. *Taiwan (Republic of China)*, 2nd ed., by John F. Copper. 2000
35. *Laos*, 2nd ed., by Martin Stuart-Fox. 2001
36. *Malaysia*, 2nd ed., by Amarjit Kaur. 2001
37. *Papua New Guinea*, 2nd ed., by Ann Turner. 2001
38. *Tajikistan*, by Kamoludin Abdullaev and Shahram Akbarzedeh. 2002
39. *Polynesia*, 2nd ed., by Robert D. Craig. 2002
40. *North Korea*, by Ilpyong J. Kim. 2003
41. *Armenia*, by Rouben Paul Adalian. 2002
42. *Mongolia*, 2nd ed., by Alan J. K. Sanders. 2003
43. *Cambodia*, by Justin Corfield and Laura Summers. 2003
44. *Iraq*, by Edmund A. Ghareeb with the assistance of Beth Dougherty. 2004
45. *Saudi Arabia*, 2nd ed., by J. E. Peterson. 2003
46. *Nepal,* by Nanda R. Shrestha and Keshav Bhattarai. 2003
47. *Afghanistan*, 3rd ed., by Ludwig W. Adamec. 2003
48. *Bangladesh,* 3rd ed., by Craig Baxter and Syedur Rahman. 2003
49. *Kyrgyzstan,* by Rafis Abazov. 2004
50. *Syria,* 2nd ed., by David Commins. 2004
51. *Indonesia,* 2nd ed., by Robert Cribb and Audrey Kahin. 2004

Historical Dictionary of Indonesia

Second Edition

Robert Cribb
Audrey Kahin

Historical Dictionaries of Asia, Oceania, and the Middle East, No. 51

The Scarecrow Press, Inc.
Lanham, Maryland • Toronto • Oxford
2004

SCARECROW PRESS, INC.

Published in the United States of America
by Scarecrow Press, Inc.
A wholly owned subsidiary of The Rowman & Littlefield Publishing Group, Inc.
4501 Forbes Boulevard, Suite 200
Lanham, Maryland 20706
www.scarecrowpress.com

PO Box 317
Oxford
OX2 9RU, UK

British Library Cataloguing in Publication Information Available

Library of Congress Cataloging-in-Publication Data

Cribb, R. B.
Historical dictionary of Indonesia / Robert Cribb, Audrey Kahin.— 2nd ed.
p. cm. — (Historical dictionaries of Asia, Oceania, and the Middle East ; 51)
Includes index.
ISBN 0-8108-4935-6 (alk. paper)
1. Indonesia—History—Dictionaries. I. Kahin, Audrey. II. Title. III. Series.
DS633 .C75 2004
959.8'003—dc22 2003025416

∞™ The paper used in this publication meets the minimum requirements of American National Standard for Information Sciences—Permanence of Paper for Printed Library Materials, ANSI/NISO Z39.48-1992.
Manufactured in the United States of America.

Contents

Editor's Foreword

When the first edition of this volume appeared just over a decade ago, it would have seemed almost pointless to ask in which direction Indonesia would turn. Everything seemed perfectly clear. It had a political regime that was, if anything, too stable and an economy that was moving smartly ahead toward a secure status as a newly industrialized country. But now, with the damage caused by the Asian financial crisis and the uncertainty since the fall of Suharto, there are many questions to answer: political, economic, social, and even religious. Will democracy take hold this time, or will instability reign (unless the army intervenes again)? Will industrialization continue and supplement weaker agricultural and mining sectors, and will the states leave more room for private enterprise? Will the many peoples, regions, and classes come together or splinter further? Will Islam cohabit comfortably with other religions, or will the appeal (or fear) of an Islamic state be too strong? This book cannot provide the answers, but it can certainly elucidate the questions and give some idea of where Indonesia is headed at present. So it is of much greater interest for all those concerned about Indonesia, the Indonesians first and foremost, followed by the rest of Southeast Asia and the broader world as well.

This second edition of the *Historical Dictionary of Indonesia* has been thoroughly updated and considerably expanded, partly to round out its overall coverage, and very much also to include information about the many things that have occurred meanwhile. It has a double advantage in examining Indonesia as a country but also looking closely at its numerous components, without which nothing makes sense. Thus, while the chronology and introduction help us see the overall thrust, some of the most useful dictionary entries deal with the specific ethnic groups, islands, and regions, giving their history prior to the creation of the state of Indonesia and even prior to Dutch colonization. Others present the most notable leaders of all periods and important aspects of politics, economics, and social, cultural, and religious life. The bibliography, which is also expanded and updated, has the additional advantage of relating specific works to specific entries, so readers know where to seek further information. And the list of acronyms and abbreviations is virtually indispensable.

This book is the result of a joint effort. It is based on an excellent and much-admired first edition by Robert Cribb, who has written widely about Indonesian history and politics; was professor of Southeast Asian history at the University of Queensland in St. Lucia, Australia; and is now at Australian National University. It has been updated and expanded, while maintaining much of the original text, by Audrey Kahin, who was managing editor of Southeast Asia Publications at Cornell University and coeditor, and then editor, of *Indonesia.* She has also written extensively on Indonesia, including several books, and is presently a freelance editor and writer.

What they both obviously share is an intense interest in the country, where they have traveled frequently and widely, and an ability to convey this interest to others. That may explain why this book is, among other things, written in a style that can be easily read by students while including a wealth of information that is not readily available elsewhere, and certainly not in such an accessible form.

Jon Woronoff
Series Editor

Preface

The *Historical Dictionary of Indonesia* is intended primarily as a convenient reference tool for those whose studies or professional activities demand ready access to reliable information on Indonesia's history to the present. The current edition is an updating and revision of the dictionary prepared by Dr. Robert Cribb and published in 1992. The major changes in the revised version are in the coverage of the last 15 years of Indonesia's history, which have been the most turbulent experienced since the 1960s, or indeed perhaps since the transfer of sovereignty at the end of 1949. In order to devote the necessary space to the events of these years, I have felt it necessary to cut some items from the first edition of the dictionary that, although interesting and useful in themselves, are not of central importance for those seeking to understand the nature of contemporary Indonesia. The original dictionary contained an immense amount of valuable information on the history of Indonesia under the Netherlands East Indies Company (VOC) and the Dutch colonial government, and although it has been necessary to shorten some of these entries in order to keep the volume to a reasonable length, they provide such a useful treasure of information (particularly for English-speaking readers with little access to Dutch sources) that most of them have been retained.

The emphasis in the present edition is, however, on the late Suharto period and on the military, economic, and political forces that helped maintain its power but ultimately led to its downfall. It also covers the transfer of power to a new administration, the disorder and violence that has followed this change, and the often unsuccessful efforts by reformers to push for a new, more democratic state and society. In view of the fact that one of the major problems facing the governments of post-Suharto Indonesia is how to dismantle the centralized administrative structure that has characterized Indonesia since independence without this leading to disintegration, there is also a greater focus in the dictionary on the Indonesian regions outside Java. Although East Timor gained its independence in 1999, there are still several extensive entries dealing with that territory and its relations with Indonesia, for the Suharto regime's invasion of East Timor in 1975 and the struggle leading to its ultimate liberation have had a profound effect on the recent history of the Republic of Indonesia.

Acknowledgments

In revising and updating this *Dictionary,* I have been indebted especially to Dr. Robert Cribb, who compiled the original dictionary and provided me with many of his notes and ideas for a revised version. I am also grateful to him for drawing the maps that appear here. Anyone wishing to follow the text more closely through its geographic context is advised to consult his *Historical Atlas of Indonesia* (Richmond, UK: Curzon, 2000), which has become an indispensable reference for scholars working on Indonesian history.

I am grateful to Scott McCasland-Bodenstein for his computer assistance, to Margaret McCasland for helping me with the technical side of preparing the bibliography, to Kaja McGowen who provided useful advice, and to friends and family who have had to accept the fact that so much of my time over the past couple of years has been occupied in bringing this work to completion.

My thanks also go to Jon Woronoff, who has made useful suggestions and has been patient as I missed several deadlines, and the staff at Scarecrow Press, especially Kim Tabor and Andrew Yoder.

Audrey Kahin

Reader's Note

Several changes have been made in the order of the components in the revised *Historical Dictionary of Indonesia* to bring it into line with other volumes in this series. The following is a brief guide to the main sections comprising the dictionary.

After this reader's note, there is a list of acronyms and abbreviations. This list is by no means exhaustive, as Indonesians seem to have an ongoing inclination to update and introduce acronyms into their language at a spectacular pace. It has also been necessary to retain many of the acronyms that were of importance in earlier decades of Indonesia's history but are no longer in use. As in the first edition of the dictionary, I have followed the rule that where the acronymic origin of a word has become obscure (e.g., Gestapu, Masjumi, Fretilin, Golkar, and PRRI/Permesta), the entry appears under the acronym with a cross-reference from the full name. In the list of acronyms, as in the dictionary as a whole, cross-references to other dictionary entries are usually indicated by the use of bold type. I have attempted to maintain a consistent use of terminology both in the acronym and its translation. In using the dictionary, readers not familiar with an organization's full title or its English meaning will find these in this list.

In the chronology that follows the maps, as in most of the rest of the dictionary, the emphasis is on the more recent period rather than on the early history of the archipelago. The same chronological divisions are used here as in the historical section of the bibliography, so that it should be easy to refer to the literature relating to the different periods. As is the practice throughout the volume, bold type has been used to indicate a cross-reference to the relevant dictionary entries.

The introduction has been expanded to provide a more detailed background of Indonesia's history, especially in the postindependence period, and give a broader context for the entries that follow.

As mentioned in the preface, the greatest change in the dictionary is in its coverage of events of the past 15 years. The entries dealing with political and economic events of the Suharto era have also been expanded, and some of the coverage of colonial history and the Sukarno era condensed. There is more biographical data on people who have played an important role in these recent periods, especially in the political and economic fields. There is probably still inadequate coverage of the arts in Indonesia, and I hope the bibliographical entries in the section on Indonesian culture will lead readers to explore the field more deeply for themselves.

Again, as throughout the volume, cross-references are indicated by bold type. I have also continued Dr. Cribb's practice of numbering the items in the bibliography and noting the number of the relevant bibliographic item within square brackets at the end of most of the dictionary entries. These references are not exhaustive, but they provide an easy way for the reader to find works on which the entry is based and suggestions for further reading on the topic.

The bibliography has been expanded to include a selection of the voluminous literature that has appeared on Indonesia over the past 12 years, and it has been necessary to remove some of the earlier, more ephemeral works in order to make room for them. A more extensive introduction to the bibliography appears immediately preceding it.

As Dr. Cribb noted in his preface to the original dictionary, all works on Indonesian history require an explanation for the spelling. General entries in the dictionary use modern Indonesian spelling (*ejaan yang disempurakan* [EYD], or perfected spelling; *see* INDONESIAN LANGUAGE). Until 1973, Indonesian words followed Dutch spelling conventions, most notable of which were the use of *tj* for the English sound *ch, j* for *y, oe* for *u, dj* for *j,* and *sj* for *sh,* although in the early independence period, some of these conventions had already changed, especially a more common use of *u* instead of *oe.* The Indonesian spelling reform of 1973, which attempted to harmonize usage in Malay and Indonesian, generally brought these spellings closer to English-language usage. The major changes were for *j* now to be rendered as *y, tj* as *c, dj* as *j, nj* as *ny,* and *ch* as *kh.* The greatest confusion with these changes in spelling comes with the rendering of personal names and names of organizations. I have generally followed the convention of retaining the original spelling of names of people or organizations that ceased to exist before the introduction of the spelling changes, while in all other personal names the spelling generally used is either that preferred by, or most commonly employed in referring to, the person. (*See also* entry on NAMES.)

Contemporary Indonesian terminology and spelling are used for place names: thus Kalimantan and Sulawesi, not Borneo and Celebes, although the common English spelling of Sumatra and Java is used instead of the Indonesian Sumatera and Jawa. The recently introduced Papua has been used for Indonesian Western New Guinea, previously known as Irian Jaya (and before that, Irian Barat), as this is now its official name and the name most Papuans prefer, although it is still unclear whether it will be retained in official Indonesian usage.

Acronyms and Abbreviations

Note: The headings under which the terms appear in the dictionary are set in bold type.

ABRI	Angkatan Bersenjata Republik Indonesia, **Armed Forces of the Republic of Indonesia**.
AD	Angkatan Darat, **Army**.
AH	Anno hijrae, Muslim year. *See* CALENDARS.
AJ	Anno Javanicae, Javanese year. *See* CALENDARS.
ALRI	Angkatan Laut Republik Indonesia, **Navy** of the Republic of Indonesia.
AMS	Algemene Middelbare School, General Secondary School. *See* EDUCATION.
ANETA	Algemene Nieuws en Telegraaf Agentschap, General News and Telegraph Agency. *See* NEWS AGENCIES.
APEC	Asia-Pacific Economic Cooperation.
APODETI	**Associação Populár Democrática Timorense**, Timorese Popular Democratic Association.
APRIS	Angkatan Perang Republik Indonesia Serikat, Armed Forces of the Federal Republic of Indonesia. *See* ARMY.
ASEAN	**Association of Southeast Asian Nations**.
ASPRI	Asisten Presiden Republik Indonesia, assistants to the president of the Republic of Indonesia. *See* MALARI.
AURI	Angkatan Udara Republik Indonesia, **Air Force** of the Republic of Indonesia.
BABINSA	Bintara Pembina Desa, NCOs for Village Development. *See DWIFUNGSI.*

BAIS	Badan Intelijen Strategis, Strategic Intelligence Body. *See* INTELLIGENCE.
BAKIN	**Badan Koordinasi Intelijen Negara**, State Intelligence Coordinating Agency.
BAKORSTANAS	**Badan Koordinasi Bantuan Pemantapan Stabilitas Nasional**, Coordinating Body to Assist in Maintaining National Security.
BAPERKI	**Badan Permusyawaratan Kewarga Negaraan Indonesia**, Consultative Body of Indonesian Citizenship.
BAPINDO	**Bank Pembangunan Indonesia**, Indonesian Development Bank.
BAPPEDA	Badan Perencanaan Pembangunan Daerah, Regional Development Planning Board.
BAPPENAS	**Badan Perencanaan Pembangunan Nasional**, National Development Planning Board.
BB	**Binnenlandsch Bestuur**, literally, administration of the interior, the European bureaucracy of the Netherlands Indies.
Berdikari	*Berdiri atas kaki sendiri,* to stand on one's own feet. *See* ETYMOLOGY.
BFO	Bijeenkomst voor Federale Overleg, Federal Consultative Meeting. *See* FEDERALISM.
BIA	Badan Intelijen ABRI, Armed Forces Intelligence Agency. *See* INTELLIGENCE.
BIMAS	Bimbingan Massal, mass guidance. *See* GREEN REVOLUTION.
BKKBN	Badan Koordinasi Keluarga Berencana Nasional, National Family Planning Coordinating Body. *See* FAMILY PLANNING.
BKR	Badan Keamanan Rakyat, People's Security Organization. *See* ARMY.
BKS	**Badan Kerja Sama**, Cooperative Bodies.
BNI	Bank Negara Indonesia, Indonesian National Bank. *See* BANKING.
BPK	Badan Pemeriksa Keuangan, State Audit Board. *See* CONSTITUTIONS.
BPM	Bataafse Petroleum Maatschappij, Batave Petroleum Company. *See* "KONINKLIJKE"; OIL.
BPS	**Badan Pendukung Sukarnoisme**, Body to Support Sukarnoism.

BPS	Biro Pusat Statistik, Central Statistical Bureau; *also* Badan Pusat Statistiek, Central Statistical Body. *See* STATISTICS.
BPUPKI	**Badan Penyelidik Usaha Persiapan Kemerdekaan Indonesia**, Investigatory Body for Preparatory Work for Indonesian Independence.
BTC	Banking and Trading Corporation. *See* STATE ENTERPRISES.
BTI	**Barisan Tani Indonesia**, Indonesian Peasants' Front.
Bulog	**Badan Urusan Logistik Nasional**, National Logistical Supply Organization.
CCP	Chinese Communist Party. *See* CHINA, RELATIONS WITH.
CGI	**Consultative Group on Indonesia**.
CIDES	Center for Information and Development Studies. *See* IKATAN CENDEKIAWAN MUSLIM INDONESIA.
CONEFO	Conference of the New Emerging Forces. *See* NEKOLIM.
CSIS	**Centre for Strategic and International Studies**.
DDII	Dewan Dakwah Islamiyah Indonesia, Indonesian Islamic Preaching Council. *See* ISLAM IN INDONESIA.
DEKON	Deklarasi Ekonomi, Economic Declaration. *See* GUIDED ECONOMY.
DEPLU	Departemen Luar Negeri, Department of Foreign Affairs. *See* FOREIGN POLICY.
DGI	Dewan Gereja Indonesia, Indonesian Council of Churches. *See* PROTESTANTISM.
DI	**Darul Islam**, House of Islam.
DIY	Daerah Istimewa Yogyakarta, Special Territory of Yogyakarta. *See* YOGYAKARTA.
DKI	Daerah Khusus Ibukota, Special Capital Territory. *See* JAKARTA.
DPA	**Dewan Pertimbangan Agung**, Supreme Advisory Council.
DPN	**Dewan Pertahanan Negara**, State Defense Council.
DPR	**Dewan Perwakilan Rakyat**, People's Representative Council.
DPR-D	Dewan Perwakilan Rakyat Daerah, People's Representative Council local assemblies.

DPR-GR	Dewan Perwakilan Rakyat Gotong Royong, mutual self-help.
DPR-S	Dewan Perwakilan Rakyat Sementara, provisional.
DRET	**Democratic Republic of East Timor**.
Drs	Doctorandus. *See* TITLES.
Dt	Datuk. *See* TITLES.
DVG	Dienst voor Volksgezondheid, Public Health Service. *See* HEALTH.
EB	Europees Bestuur, European administration. *See* BINNENLANDSCH BESTUUR.
EC	European Community.
ELS	Europese Lagere School, European Lower School. *See* EDUCATION.
EYD	*Ejaan yang disempurnakan,* perfected spelling. *See* INDONESIAN LANGUAGE.
FALINTIL	Forças Armadas de Libertação Nacional de Timor, Armed Forces for the National Liberation of Timor. *See* FRETILIN.
FBSI	Federasi Buruh Seluruh Indonesia, All-Indonesia Federation of Labor. *See* LABOR UNIONS.
FDI	Foreign direct investment. *See* INVESTMENT, FOREIGN.
FDR	**Front Demokrasi Rakyat**, People's Democratic Front.
FRETILIN	Frente Revolucionária do Timor Leste Independente, Revolutionary Front for an Independent East Timor.
FSPSI	Federasi Serikat Pekerja Seluruh Indonesia, Federation of All-Indonesia Workers' Associations. *See* LABOR UNIONS.
FUII	Front Umat Islam Indonesia, Indonesian Muslim Community Front.
G/30/S	Gerakan Tiga Puluh September, 30 September Movement. *See* GESTAPU.
GAM	Gerakan Aceh Merdeka, Independent Aceh Movement. *See* ACEH.
GANEFO	Games of the New Emerging Forces. *See* NEKOLIM.
GAPI	**Gabungan Politik Indonesia**, Indonesian Political Federation.
GBHN	Garis Besar Haluan Negara, Broad Outlines of State Policy. *See* MAJELIS PERMUSYAWARATAN RAKYAT.

GDP	Gross domestic product.
GERINDO	**Gerakan Rakyat Indonesia**, Indonesian People's Movement.
GERWANI	**Gerakan Wanita Indonesia**, Indonesian Women's Movement.
GESTAPU	Gerakan September Tiga Puluh, September 30 Movement.
GHS	Geneeskundige Hogeschool, Medical School. *See* EDUCATION.
GKI	Gereja Kristen Injil di Tanah Papua, Papuan Church of the Christian Gospel. *See* PAPUA.
GOLKAR	Golongan Karya, Functional Groups.
HAM	Hak Azasi Manusia, **human rights**.
HANKAM	Pertahanan dan Keamanan, (Department of) Defense and Security. *See* ARMED FORCES.
HANSIP	Pertahanan Sipil, Civil Defense. *See* ARMED FORCES.
HBS	Hogere Burger School, Higher Civil School. *See* EDUCATION.
HCS	Hollands-Chinese School, Dutch Chinese School. *See* EDUCATION.
HIR	Herziene Inlands Reglement, Revised Native Regulations. *See* LAW.
HIS	Hollands-Inlandse School, Dutch Native School. *See* EDUCATION.
HKTI	Himpunan Kerukunan Tani Indonesia, Association of Indonesian Peasant Leagues. *See* LABOR UNIONS.
HMI	**Himpunan Mahasiswa Islam**, Muslim Students' Association.
HNSI	Himpunan Nelayan Seluruh Indonesia, All Indonesia Fishermen's Association. *See* LABOR UNIONS.
HVK	Hoge Vertegenwoordiger van de Kroon, high representative of the Crown. *See* GOVERNOR-GENERAL.
IAIN	Institut Agama Islam Negeri, State Islamic Religious Institute. *See* EDUCATION, ISLAMIC.
IBRA	Indonesian Bank Restructuring Agency. *See* BANKING.
ICMI	**Ikatan Cendekiawan Muslim Indonesia**, All Indonesia League of Muslim Intellectuals.
IEV	Indo-Europees Verbond, Indo-European Union. *See* INDO-EUROPEANS.

IGGI	**Inter-Governmental Group on Indonesia**.
IMET	International Military Education and Training Program. *See* UNITED STATES, RELATIONS WITH.
IMF	International Monetary Fund.
INDRA	Indonesian Debt Restructuring Agency. *See* DEBT, FOREIGN.
INPRES	Instruksi Presiden, presidential instruction.
IPKI	**Ikatan Pendukung Kemerdekaan Indonesia**, League of the Supporters of Indonesian Independence.
Ir	Ingenieur. *See* TITLES.
ISDV	**Indische Sociaal-Democratische Vereeniging**, Indies Social Democratic Association.
JABOTABEK	Jakarta-Bogor-Tanggerang-Bekasi. *See* JAKARTA.
JI	Jemaah Islamiah, Islamic community. *See* ISLAM IN INDONESIA, ISLAMIC STATE.
KABIR	Kapitalis birokrat, bureaucratic capitalist. *See* CLASS ANALYSIS.
KADIN	Kamar Dagang dan Industri, Chamber of Commerce and Industry.
KAMI	**Kesatuan Aksi Mahasiswa Indonesia**, Indonesian Students' Action Front.
KAMMI	Kesatuan Aksi Mahasiswa Muslim Indonesia, National Front of Indonesian Muslim Students.
KAPPI	Kesatuan Aksi Pemuda dan Pelajar Indonesia, Indonesian Youth and School Students Action Front. *See* KESATUAN AKSI MAHASISWA INDONESIA.
KASAD	Kepala Staf Angkatan Darat, army chief of staff. *See* ARMY.
KASI	Kesatuan Aksi Sarjana Indonesia, Indonesian Graduates' Action Front.
KKN	**Kolusi, Korupsi, dan Nepotisme**, corruption, collusion, and nepotism.
KNI	**Komite Nasional Indonesia**, Indonesian National Committee.
KNIL	**Koninklijk Nederlandsch Indisch Leger**, Royal Netherlands Indies Army.
KNILM	Koninklijk Nederlands-Indische Luchtvaartmaatschappij, Royal Netherlands Indies Air Company. *See* AIR SERVICES.

KNIP	**Komite Nasional Indonesia Pusat**, Central Indonesian National Committee.
KNPI	Komite Nasional Pemuda Indonesia, Indonesian National Youth Committee.
KODAM	Komando Daerah Militer, Regional Military Command. *See* DEFENSE POLICY; *DWIFUNGSI.*
KOGA	Komando Siaga, Readiness Command. *See* KOMANDO OPERASI TERTINGGI.
KOGAM	Komando Ganyang Malaysia, Crush Malaysia Command. *See* KOMANDO OPERASI TERTINGGI.
KOKAR	Korps Karyawan, Employees' Corps. *See* KORPS PEGAWAI REPUBLIK INDONESIA.
KOMNAS HAM	Komisi Nasional Hak Azasi Manusia. National Committee for **Human Rights**.
KOPASSANDHA	Komando Pasukan Sandi Yudha, Secret Warfare Commando Unit. *See* KOMANDO PASUKAN KHUSUS.
KOPASSUS	**Komando Pasukan Khusus**, Special Commando Unit.
KOPKAMTIB	**Komando Operasi Pemulihan Keamanan dan Ketertiban**, Operational Command for the Restoration of Security and Order.
KORPRI	**Korps Pegawai Republik Indonesia**, Government Officials Corps of the Republic of Indonesia.
KOSGORO	Koperasi Serba Guna Gotong Royong, Multipurpose Cooperative for Gotong Royong.
KOSTRAD	Komando Cadangan Strategis Angkatan Darat, Army Strategic Reserve.
KOTI	**Komando Operasi Tertinggi**, Supreme Operational Command.
KOTOE	Komando Tertinggi Operasi Ekonomi, Supreme Operational Command for the Economy. *See DWIFUNGSI.*
KOWILHAN	Komando Wilayah Pertahanan, Regional Defense Commands. *See* DEFENSE POLICY.
KPM	**Koninklijke Paketvaart Maatschappij**, Royal Packet Service Company.
KPU	Komisi Pemilihan Umum, General Elections Committee. *See* ELECTIONS.
KRISMON	Monetary crisis. *See* FINANCIAL CRISIS.

KUHAP — Kitab Undang-Undang Hukum Acara Pidana, procedural code for criminal law. *See* LAW.

KUHP — Kitab Undang-Undang Hukum Pidana, criminal code. *See* LAW.

LBH — Lembaga Bantuan Hukum, Legal Aid Bureau. *See* LEGAL AID SERVICES.

LEKRA — **Lembaga Kebudayaan Rakyat**, Institute for People's Culture.

LEMHANNAS — Lembaga Pertahanan Nasional, National Defense Institute. *See* DEFENSE POLICY.

LIPI — Lembaga Ilmu Pengetahuan Indonesia, Indonesian Academy of Sciences.

LKBN — Lembaga Kantor Berita Nasional, National News Agency Institute. *See* ANTARA.

LKBN — Lembaga Keluarga Berencana Nasional, National Family Planning Institute. *See* FAMILY PLANNING.

LKMD — Lembaga Ketahanan Masyarakat Desa, Institute for Village Community Resilience. *See DESA*.

LMD — Lembaga Musyawarah Desa, Village Consultative Council. *See DESA*.

LNG — Liquefied natural gas. *See* GAS.

MAHMILLUB — **Mahkamah Militer Luar Biasa**, Extraordinary Military Tribunal.

MALARI — Malapetaka 15 Januari, Disaster of 15 January.

MANIKEBU — **Manifes Kebudayaan**, Cultural Manifesto.

MANIPOL — **Manifesto Politik**, Political Manifesto.

MAPHILINDO — Malaya, Philippines, and Indonesia.

MASJUMI — Madjelis Sjuro Muslimin Indonesia, Consultative Council of Indonesian Muslims.

MIAI — **Majelis Islam A'laa Indonesia**, Supreme Islamic Council of Indonesia.

MMI — Majelis Mujahidin Indonesia, Council of Indonesian Defenders of the Faith. *See* ISLAMIC STATE.

MONAS — Monumen Nasional, National Monument. *See* JAKARTA.

MPR (S) — **Majelis Permusyawaratan Rakyat** (Sementara), (Provisional) People's Deliberative Assembly.

Mr — Meester in de Rechten. *See* TITLES.

MUI — Majelis Ulama Indonesia, Council of Indonesian Islamic Scholars. *See* ISLAM IN INDONESIA.

MULO	Meer Uitgebreide Lagere Onderwijs, Broader Lower Education. *See* EDUCATION.
NASAKOM	Nasionalisme, Agama, Komunisme; nationalism, religion, communism.
NEFIS	Netherlands Forces Intelligence Service. *See* POLITIEK INLICHTINGEN DIENST.
NEFO	New Emerging Forces. *See* NEKOLIM.
NEKOLIM	Neo-Kolonialis dan Imperialis, neocolonialists and imperialists.
NGO	Nongovernmental organization.
NHM	**Nederlandsche Handel Maatschappij**, Netherlands Trading Company.
NIAS	Nederlands-Indische Artsenschool, Netherlands Indies Doctors' School. See HEALTH.
NICA	**Netherlands Indies Civil Administration**.
NII	Negara Islam Indonesia. *See* DARUL ISLAM.
NIROM	Nederlandsch-Indische Radio Omroep Maatschappij, Netherlands Indies Radio Broadcasting Company. *See* RADIO.
NIT	**Negara Indonesia Timur**, State of East Indonesia.
NTB	**Nusatenggara** Barat, Western Lesser Sundas.
NTT	**Nusatenggara** Timur, Eastern Lesser Sundas.
NU	**Nahdlatul Ulama**, Revival of the Religious Scholars.
OLDEFO	Old Established Forces. *See* NEKOLIM.
OPEC	Organization of Petroleum Exporting Countries. *See* OIL.
OPM	**Organisasi Papua Merdeka**, Free Papua Movement.
OPSUS	**Operasi Khusus**, Special Operations.
ORBA	Orde Baru, **New Order**.
ORI	Oeang (i.e., Uang) Republik Indonesia, **currency** of the Indonesian Republic.
ORMAS	Organisasi Massa, **mass organizations**.
OSVIA	Opleidingsschool voor Inlandsche Ambtenaren, Training School for Native Officials. *See* EDUCATION.
PAI	Persatuan Arab Indonesia, Indonesian Arab Union. See ARABS.
PAN	**Partai Amanat Nasional**, National Mandate Party.
PANGAB	Panglima Angkatan Bersenjata, commander in chief of the armed forces. *See* ARMED FORCES.

PANGESTU Paguyuban Ngèsti Tunggal, Association for Striving towards Harmony with God.

PARAS Partai Rakyat Sosialis, Socialist People's Party. *See* PARTAI SOSIALIS.

PARI Partai Republik Indonesia, Party of the Indonesian Republic. *See* TAN MALAKA.

PARINDRA **Partai Indonesia Raya**, Greater Indonesia Party.

PARKINDO **Partai Kristen Indonesia**, Indonesian Christian Party.

PARMUSI **Partai Muslimin Indonesia**, Indonesian Muslims' Party.

PARSI Partai Sosialis Indonesia, Indonesian Socialist Party. *See* PARTAI SOSIALIS.

PARTINDO **Partai Indonesia**, Indonesia Party.

PBB **Partai Bulan Bintang** (Moon and Stars Party).

PBI **Partai Buruh Indonesia**, Indonesian Labor Party.

PBI **Persatuan Bangsa Indonesia**, Association of the Indonesian People.

PDI **Partai Demokrasi Indonesia**, Indonesian Democratic Party.

PDI-P **Partai Demokrasi Indonesia—Perjuangan**, Indonesian Democratic Party of Struggle.

PDRI **Pemerintah Darurat Republik Indonesia**, Emergency Government of the Republic of Indonesia.

PELNI Perusahaan Pelayaran Nasional Indonesia, Indonesian National Shipping Company. *See* SHIPPING.

PEMILU Pemilihan Umum, general elections. *See* ELECTIONS.

PEPUSKA Pemilikan Pusat Kapal-Kapal, Central Shipowning Authority. *See* SHIPPING.

PERMESTA Piagam Perjuangan Semesta Alam, Universal Struggle Charter. *See* PRRI/PERMESTA REBELLION.

PERSIS **Persatuan Islam**, Islamic Union.

PERTAMINA Perusahaan Tambang Minyak Nasional, National Oil and Gas Mining Corporation.

PERTI **Persatuan Tarbiyah Islamiyah**, Islamic Education Association.

PESINDO **Pemuda Sosialis Indonesia**, Indonesian Socialist Youth.

PETA **Pembela Tanah Air**, Defenders of the Homeland.

PETRUS Pembunuhan/ Penembakan Misterius, mysterious killings/shootings.

PI — **Perhimpunan Indonesia**, Indonesian Association.

PID — **Politiek Inlichtingen Dienst**, Political Intelligence Service.

PIR — **Persatuan Indonesia Raya**, Greater Indonesian Association.

PK — **Partai Keadilan**, Justice Party.

PKB — **Partai Kebangkitan Bangsa**, Rise of the People Party.

PKI — **Partai Komunis Indonesia**, Indonesian Communist Party.

PKK — Pembinaan Kesejahteraan Keluarga, Family Welfare Development. *See DESA.*

PKN — **Pakempalan Kawula Ngayogyakarta**, Yogyakarta People's Party.

PKP — Partai Keadilan dan Persatuan, Justice and Unity Party. *See* PARTIES, POLITICAL.

PKRI — Persatuan Katolik Republik Indonesia, Catholic Union of the Republic of Indonesia. *See* PARTAI KATOLIK.

PN — Perusahaan Nasional, **state enterprise**.

PNI — **Partai Nasional Indonesia**, Indonesian National Party.

PNI-Baru — New PNI. *See* PENDIDIKAN NASIONAL INDONESIA.

PP — **Persatuan Perjuangan**, Struggle Union.

PPBI — Pusat Perjuangan Buruh Indonesia, Indonesian Workers' Struggle Center. *See* LABOR UNIONS.

PPKI — Panitya Persiapan Kemerdekaan Indonesia, Committee for the Preparation of Indonesian Independence. *See* BADAN PENYELIDIK USAHA PERSIAPAN KEMERDEKAAN INDONESIA.

PPKI — Persatuan Politik Katolik Indonesia, Indonesian Catholic Political Union. *See* PARTAI KATOLIK.

PPKJ — Pakempalan Politik Katolik Jawi, Political Association of Javanese Catholics. *See* PARTAI KATOLIK.

PPMI — Persaudaraan Pekerja Muslim Indonesia, Indonesian Muslim Workers' Brotherhood. See LABOR UNIONS.

PPP — **Partai Persatuan Pembangunan**, Unity Development Party.

PPPKI	**Permufakatan Perhimpunan Politik Kebangsaan Indonesia**, Confederation of Indonesian Political Organizations.
PRC	People's Republic of China. See CHINA, RELATIONS WITH.
PRD	**Partai Rakyat Demokrasi**, Democratic People's Party.
PRRI	Pemerintah Revolusioner Republik Indonesia, Revolutionary Government of the Republic of Indonesia. *See* PRRI/PERMESTA REBELLION.
PSI	**Partai Sosialis Indonesia**, Indonesian Socialist Party.
PSII	**Partai Sarekat Islam Indonesia**, Indonesian Islamic Association Party.
PT	Perusahaan Terbatas, limited liability company.
PUSA	Persatuan Ulama Seluruh Aceh, All-Aceh Ulama Association. *See* ACEH.
PUSKESMAS	Pusat Kesehatan Masyarakat, Center for Society's Health (see HEALTH).
PUTERA	**Pusat Tenaga Rakyat**, Center of the People's Power.
PWI	Persatuan Wartawan Indonesia, Indonesian Reporters' Association. *See* NEWSPAPERS.
R.	Raden. *See* TITLES.
R.A.	Raden Ajeng. *See* TITLES.
REPELITA	**Rencana Pembangunan Lima Tahun**, Five-Year Development Plan.
RHS	Rechtshogeschool, law school. *See* EDUCATION.
RIS	**Republik Indonesia Serikat**, Republic of the United States of Indonesia.
RMS	**Republik Maluku Selatan**, Republic of the South Moluccas.
RPKAD	**Resimen Para Komando Angkatan Darat**, Army Paracommando Regiment.
RR	Regeringsreglement, Government Regulating Act. *See* CONSTITUTIONS.
RRI	Radio Republik Indonesia, Radio of the Republic of Indonesia. *See* RADIO.
RUSI	Republic of the United States of Indonesia. *See* REPUBLIK INDONESIA SERIKAT.
SARA	Suku, Agama, Ras, Antar-golongan; ethnicity, religion, race, intergroup relations.

SARBUPRI	Serikat Buruh Perkebunan Republik Indonesia, Union of Plantation Workers of the Republic of Indonesia. *See* SENTRAL ORGANISASI BURUH REPUBLIK INDONESIA.
Satgas Papua	Satuan Tugas Papua, Papua Task Force. *See* PAPUA.
SBG	Serikat Buruh Gula, Sugar Workers' Union. See SENTRAL ORGANISASI BURUH REPUBLIK INDONESIA.
SBSI	Serikat Buruh Sejahtera Indonesia, Indonesian Prosperous Workers' Union. *See* LABOR UNIONS.
SEATO	Southeast Asia Treaty Organization.
SESKOAD	Sekolah Staf dan Komando Angkatan Darat, Army Staff and Command School. *See* ARMY.
SH	Sarjana Hukum. *See* TITLES.
SI	**Sarekat Islam**, Islamic Association.
SIT	Surat Ijin Terbit, publication license. *See* CENSORSHIP.
SIUPP	Surat Ijin Usaha Penerbitan Pers, permit to operate a press company. *See* CENSORSHIP.
SMP	Satgas Merah Putih, Red and White Task Force. *See* PAPUA.
SOBSI	**Sentral Organisasi Buruh Seluruh Indonesia**, All-Indonesia Federation of Labor Organizations.
SOKSI	**Sentral Organisasi Karyawan Seluruh Indonesia**, All-Indonesia Federation of Employee Organizations.
SPSI	Serikat Pekerja Seluruh Indonesia, All Indonesia Workers' Union. *See* LABOR UNIONS.
St.	Sutan. *See* TITLES.
STICUSA	Stichting voor Culturele Samenwerking, Institute for Cultural Cooperation. *See* LEMBAGA KEBUDAYAAN RAKYAT.
STOVIA	School tot Opleiding van Inlandsche Artsen, School for the Training of Native Physicians. *See* EDUCATION; HEALTH.
SUPERSEMAR	Surat Perintah Sebelas Maret, Executive Order of 11 March.
TABANAS	Tabungan Pembangunan Nasional, National Development Savings Scheme. *See* BANKING.
TAPOL	***Tahanan politik,*** political prisoners.
THS	Technische Hogeschool, Institute of Technology. *See* EDUCATION.

TKR	Tentara Keamanan Rakyat, People's Security Army. *See* ARMY.
TNI	Tentara Nasional Indonesia, Indonesian National Army. *See* ARMED FORCES; ARMY.
TPN	Tentara Pembebasan Nasional, National Liberation Army. *See* PAPUA.
TRI	Tentara Republic Indonesia, Army of the Republic of Indonesia. *See* ARMY.
TRIKORA	Tri Komando Rakyat, People's Triple Command. *See* PAPUA.
TRIP	Tentara Republik Indonesia Pelajar, Student Army of the Indonesian Republic.
TRITURA	Tri Tuntutan Rakyat, Three Demands of the People. *See* KOMANDO AKSI MAHASISWA INDONESIA; MALARI.
TVRI	Televisi Republik Indonesia, Television of the Republic of Indonesia. *See* TELEVISION.
UDT	**União Democrática Timorense**, Timorese Democratic Union.
USDEK	Undang-undang '45, 1945 Constitution; Sosialisme a la Indonesia, Indonesian socialism; Demokrasi Terpimpin, guided democracy; Ekonomi Terpimpin, guided economy; and Kepribadian Indonesia, Indonesian identity. *See* MANIFESTO POLITIK.
UUD	Undang-Undang Dasar, Constitution. *See* CONSTITUTIONS.
VFR	Voorlopige Federale Regeering, Provisional Federal Government. *See* SUCCESSION.
VOC	Vereenigde Oost-Indische Compagnie, United East Indies Company. *See* DUTCH EAST INDIES COMPANY.
VSTP	Vereeniging van Spoor- en Tramweg Personeel, Union of Rail and Tramway Personnel. *See* LABOR UNIONS.
ZOPFAN	Zone of Peace, Freedom, and Neutrality. *See* ASSOCIATION OF SOUTHEAST ASIAN NATIONS.

Maps

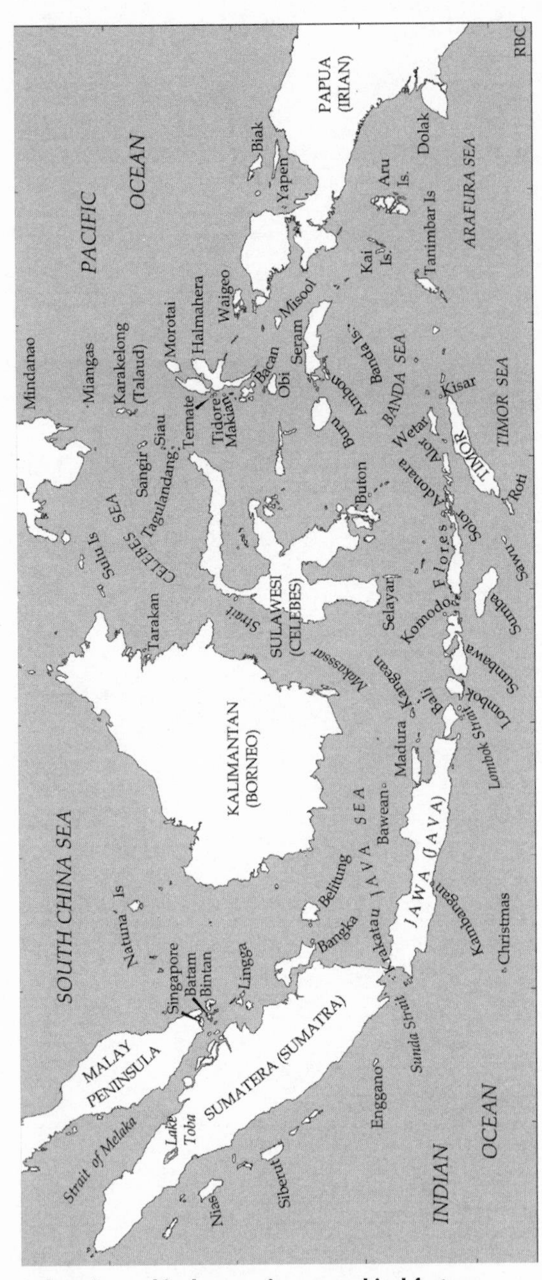

Map 1: The Indonesian archipelago: main geographical features

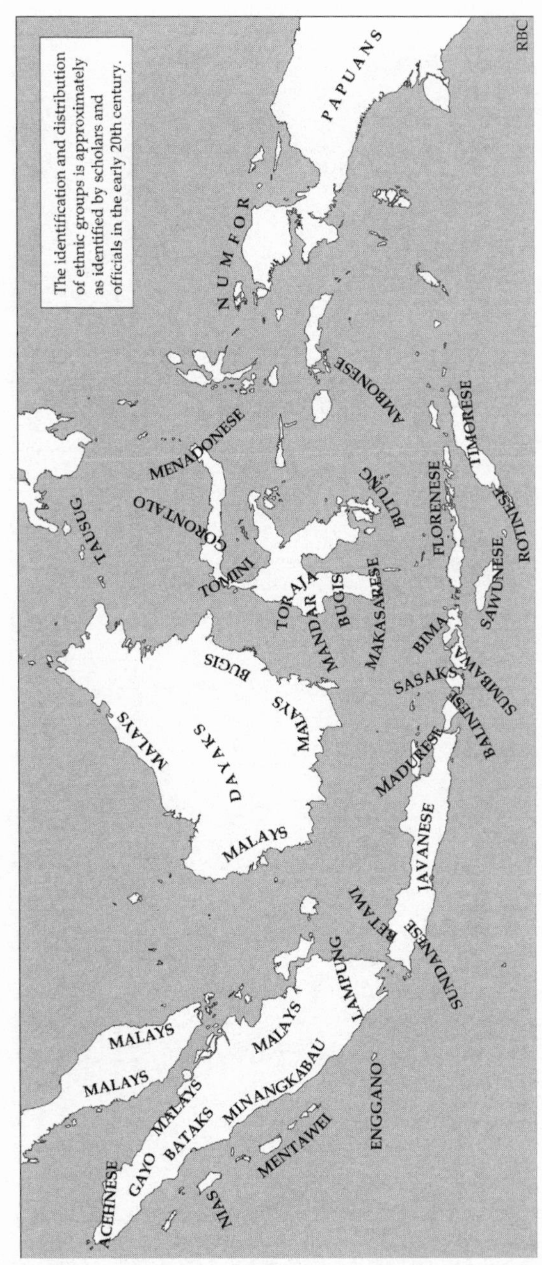

Map 2: The Indonesian archipelago: traditional distribution of ethnic groups

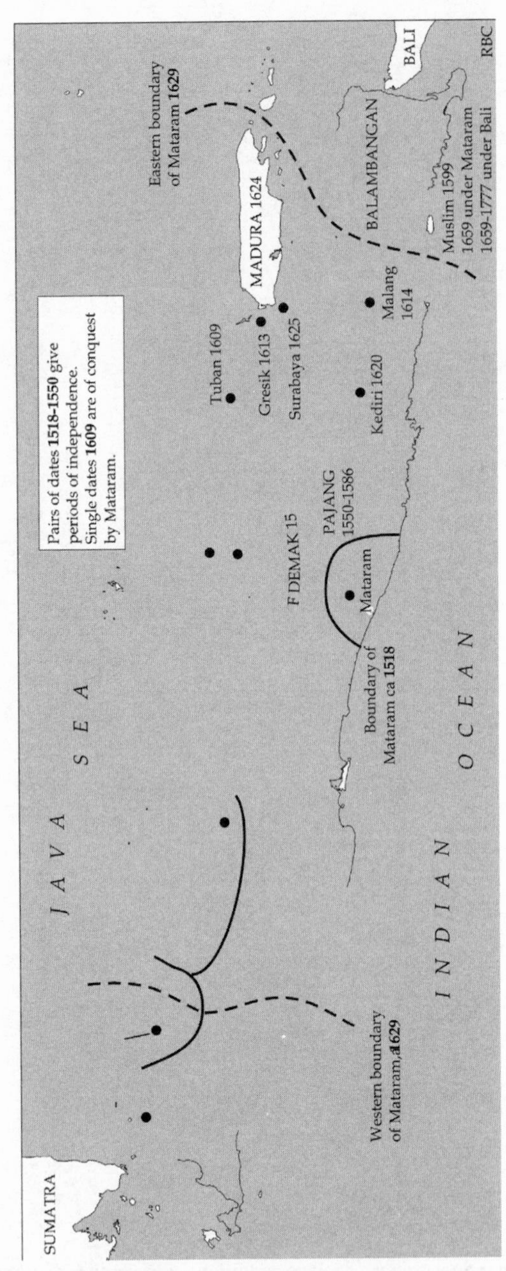

Map 3: Java in the 16th and 17th centuries: the expansion of Mataram

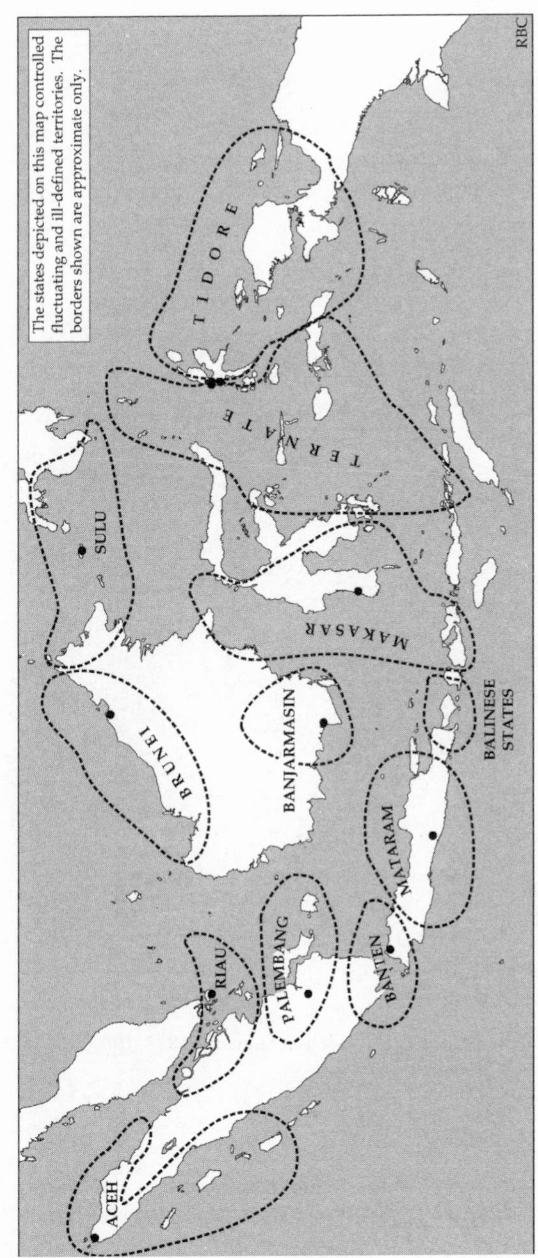

Map 4: Indonesia in the 17th century: major states

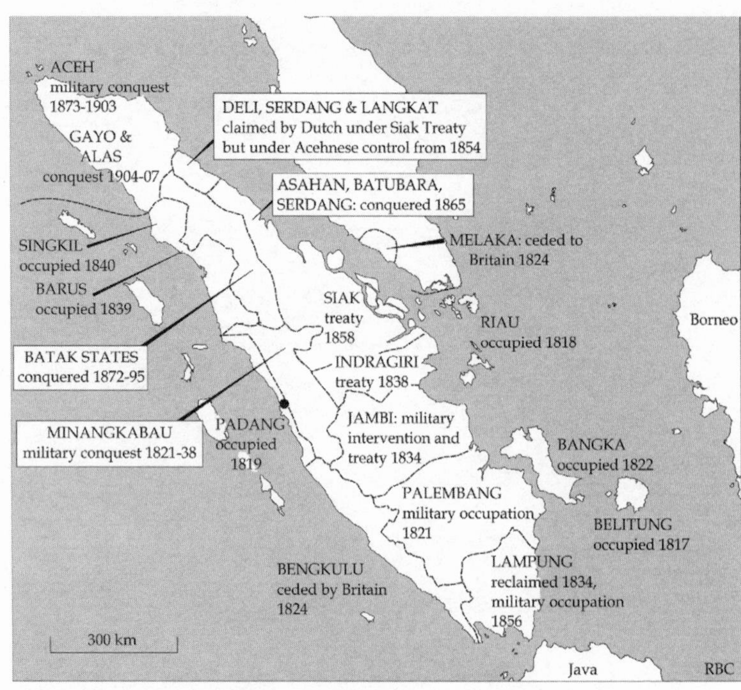

Map 5: Dutch territorial expansion in Sumatra, 1817–1907

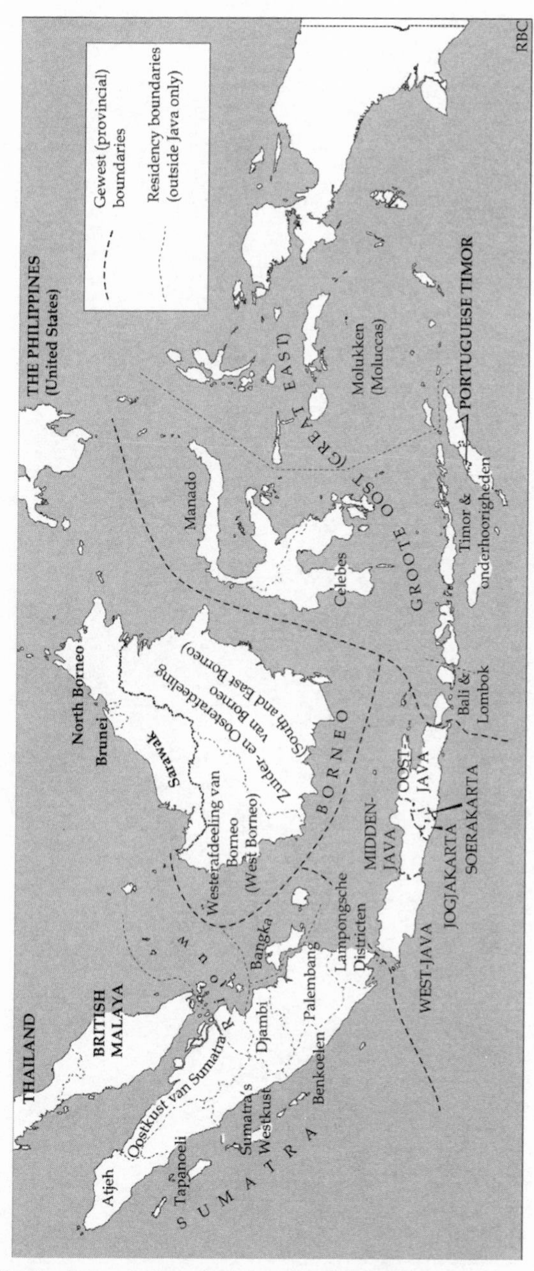

Map 6: Netherlands East Indies: administrative divisions in 1940

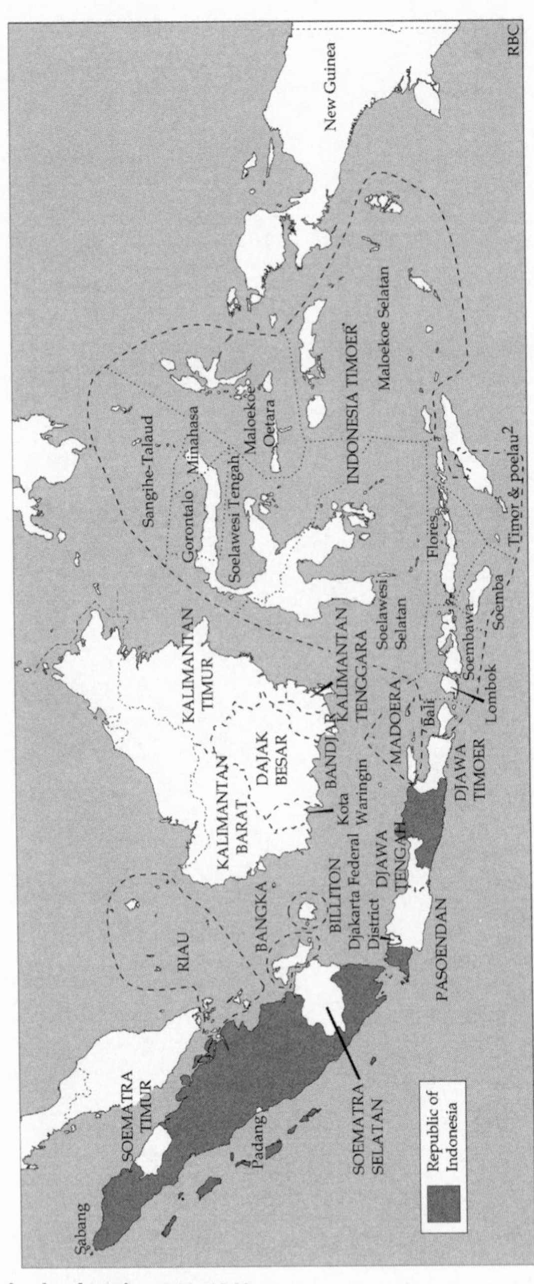

Map 7: Federal Indonesia, 1948–1949

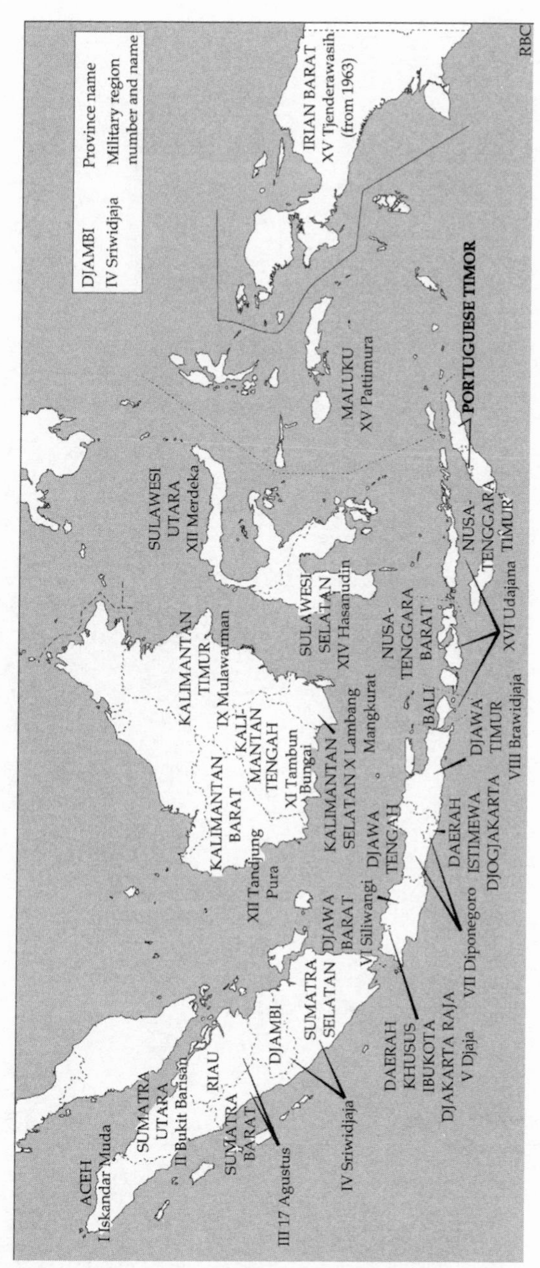

Map 8: Indonesia: provinces and military regions, 1958–1959

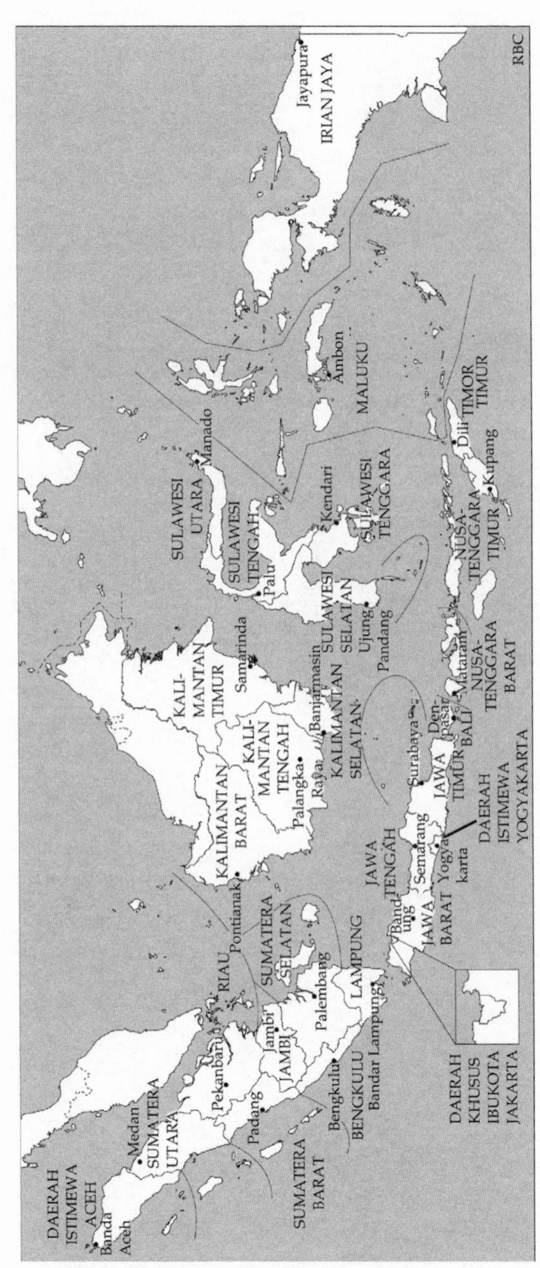

Map 9: Indonesian provinces and their capitals, 1976–1999

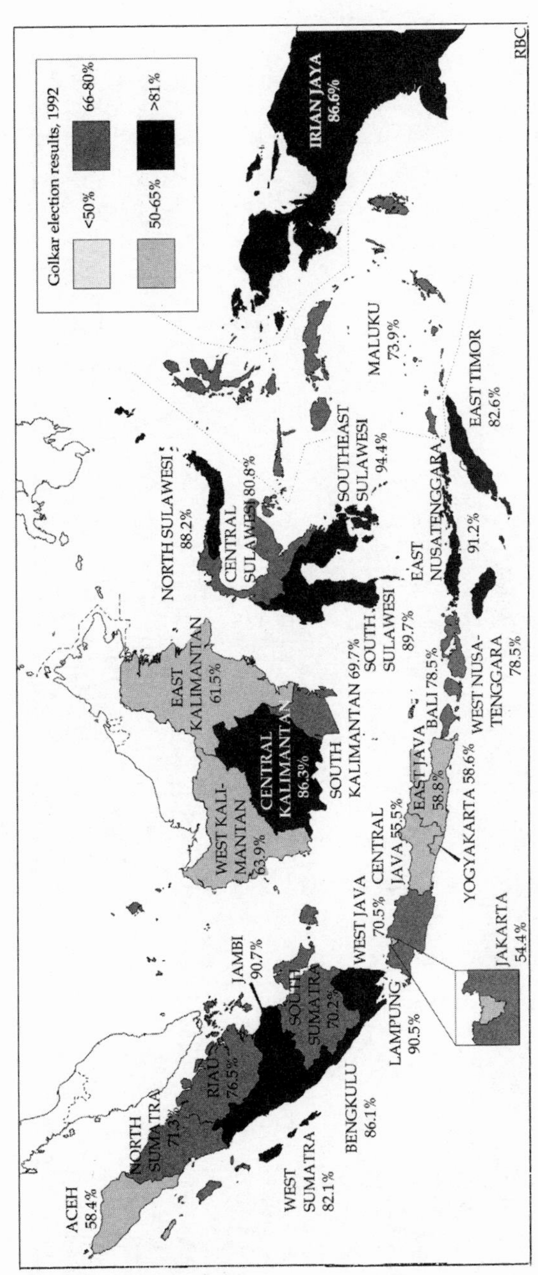

Map 10: Golkar in the 1992 elections

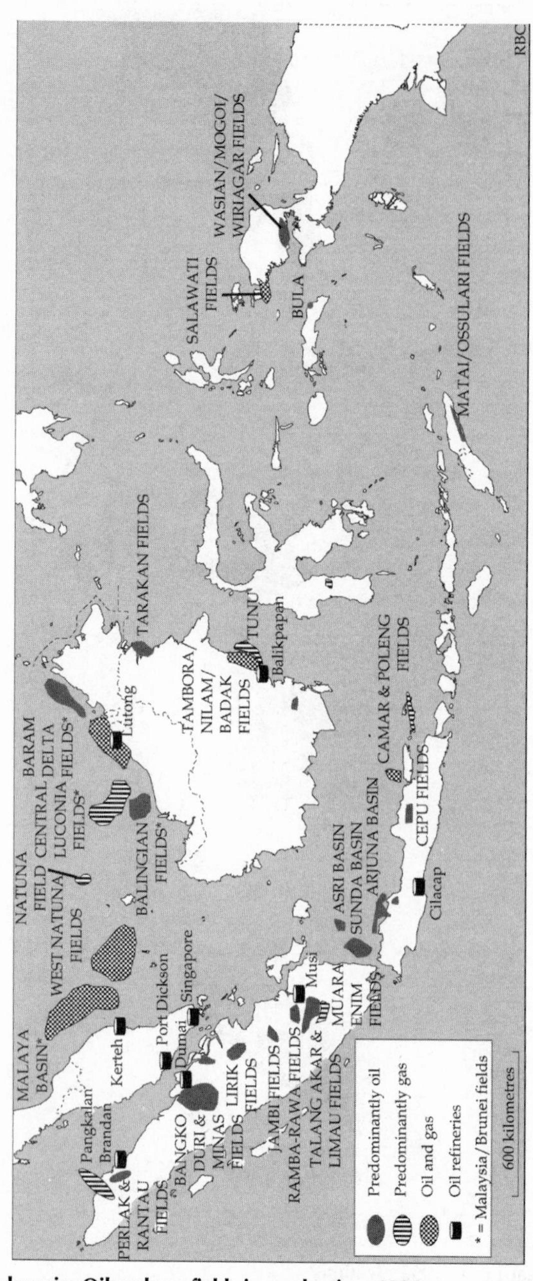

Map 11: Indonesia: Oil and gas fields in production, 1994

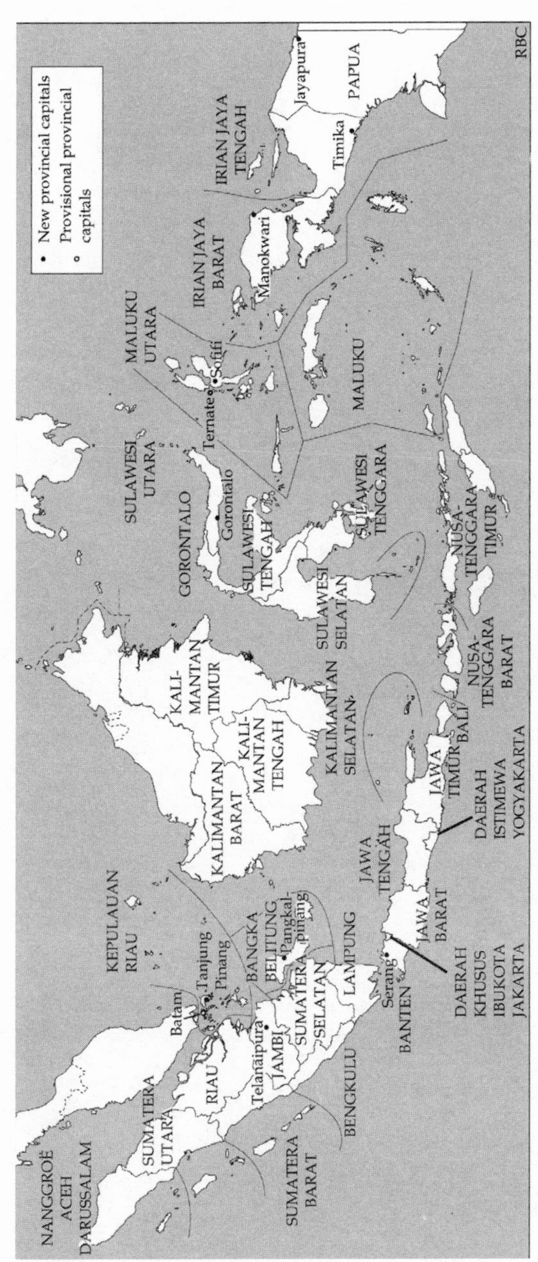

Map 12: Indonesian provinces, 2003 (with new provincial capitals)

Chronology

Early History (to c. 1400)

1.9 million years ago Hominids *Pithecanthropus* and *Meganthropus* lived in Java (*see* **PREHISTORY**).

40,000 years ago Wajak Man (*Homo sapiens*) lived in Java.

15,000–8,000 years ago Sea levels rise, separating Java, Sumatra, and Kalimantan from the Asian mainland and New Guinea from Australia.

c. 3000 B.C. Austronesian peoples begin moving into Indonesia from the Philippines (*see* **MIGRATIONS**).

c. 1000 B.C. ***Kerbau*** introduced to Indonesia.

c. 400 A.D. Hindu kingdoms of **Tarumanegara** and **Kutai** emerge in West Java and East Kalimantan.

c. 675 Rise of **Srivijaya** in Sumatra.

c. 732 Emergence of **Mataram** under Sanjaya.

c. 760 Construction of Sivaitic temples at Dieng.

c. 824 Construction of **Borobudur** begins.

c. 840 Construction of **Prambanan** begins.

860–c. 1000 Golden age of Srivijaya.

Before 929 Political center of Java moves to East Java.

914–1080 First known Hindu kingdom on **Bali**.

1006 Srivijaya attacks Java.

1019–c. 1045 **Airlangga** rules Java.

1023–1068 Chola raids on Sumatra.

c. 1045 According to legend, Airlangga divides his kingdom into **Kediri** and Janggala.

1222 Ken Angrok founds **Singasari**.

1292 Civil war in Singasari; Jayakatwang kills Kertanegara; Mongol invasion of Java.

1293 Wijaya founds kingdom of **Majapahit** and rules (1293–1309) as Kertarajasa.

c. 1297 Sultan Malek Saleh of **Pasai**, first known Muslim ruler in the archipelago.

c. 1330–1350 Adityavarman rules in **Minangkabau**.

1331–1364 **Gajah Mada** is prime minister of Majapahit.

1387 Founding of **Banjarmasin**.

Islamic States and the Expansion of the VOC: 1400–1800

1402 Kingdom of **Melaka** founded.

1406, 1408, 1410, 1414, 1418 Expeditions by **Zheng He** (Cheng Ho) to Southeast Asia.

c. 1478 **Demak** becomes first Muslim state on Java.

1511 Portuguese seize Melaka.

1522 Portuguese build fort in **Ternate**.

1527 Sultanate of Demak defeats Majapahit.

1552–1570 **Banten** rises as independent state under Sultan Hasanuddin.

1570 Revolt against the Portuguese in Ternate.

1575–1601 Senopati rules **Mataram**.

1596 First Dutch ships under **de Houtman** arrive in Banten.

1605 Dutch seize **Ambon**.

1607–1645 Rise of **Aceh** under Sultan **Iskandar Muda**.

1613–1645 **Sultan Agung** rules Mataram.

1619 Dutch establish base in Jayakarta (later **Batavia**).

1621 Dutch seize control of **Banda** islands.

1623 **"Amboyna Massacre."** Mataram subjugates Gresik and **Surabaya**.

1629 Sultan Agung unsuccessfully attacks Batavia.

1641 Dutch capture Melaka from Portuguese.

1641–1675 Aceh ruled by Queen Taj al-Alam.

1663 Treaty of Painan establishes Dutch influence in Minangkabau.

1667 **Makassar** falls to Dutch and **Bugis** forces; Treaty of Bungaya; **Dutch East Indies Company (VOC)** wins control of north coast of Java.

1671–1679 Revolt of **Trunojoyo** on Java.

1704–1708 First Javanese War of Succession.

1719–1723 Second Javanese War of Succession.

1723 Forced delivery of **coffee** to Dutch by regents of **Priangan** begins.

1740 Revolt of the **Chinese** in Batavia.

1746–1755 Third Javanese War of Succession.

1755 Treaty of **Giyanti**.

1778 **Bataviaasch Genootschap van Kunsten en Wetenschappen** founded.

1790–1820 **Gold** rush in West Kalimantan (*see* ***KONGSI*** **WARS**).

1795 **Batavian Republic** founded; first **census** conducted on Java.

1799 VOC bankrupt.

Colonial Rule and the Nationalist Movement: 1800–1942

1800 **1 January:** VOC Charter allowed to lapse; company properties taken over by the Dutch state.

1803–1837 Paderi Wars in Central Sumatra.

1808–1811 **Herman Willem Daendels** governs the Dutch Indies.

1811 **August–September:** British conquest of Java.

1811–1816 **Thomas Stamford Raffles** is lieutenant-governor of Java.

1812 British seize **Bangka** and **Belitung** from **Palembang**.

1813 First **land rent** introduced; Sultanate of Banten abolished.

1815 Eruption of **Tambora**.

1816 Dutch restored to their Indonesian possessions.

1817 **Botanical gardens** at Bogor founded; revolt by Pattimura in Ambon.

1821 **Cholera** reaches Indonesia.

1824 **Anglo-Dutch Treaty**; founding of **Nederlandsche Handel Maatschappij**.

1825–1830 **Java War**.

1828 Dutch settlement at Lobo in **Papua**.

1830 **Cultivation system** introduced.

1846 Commercial **coal** mining begins in South Kalimantan.

1854 Revised Regeeringsreglement (**Constitution**) of the Netherlands Indies promulgated.

1859–1863 War of Succession in **Banjarmasin**.

1863 **Tobacco** cultivation begins in **East Sumatra**.

1864 First **railway** established.

1870 **Agrarian Law**; start of **Liberal Policy**.

1871 Undersea telegraph cable laid between Java and Australia.

1873–1904 Aceh War.

1877 End of ***batig slot*** (budgetary surplus) transfers to Dutch treasury.

1878 Coffee plantations devastated by disease.

1880 **Coolie Ordinance** introduced.

1883 Eruption of **Krakatau**.

1886 First **oil** discovery at Pangkalan Brandan.

1888 Anticolonial uprising in Banten.

1891 Tooth of **Java Man** discovered in East Java.

1894 Dutch conquest of **Lombok**.

1901 Start of **Ethical Policy**.

1902 **Transmigration** begins.

1905 Dutch occupy Tapanuli, North Sumatra; **decentralization** measure introduced in Dutch territories.

1905–1906 Dutch conquest of **Bone**.

1908 **Budi Utomo** founded; antitax rebellion in West Sumatra; Dutch conquer southern Bali.

1910 Outbreak of bubonic **plague** on Java; **Sarekat Islam** and **Indische Partij** founded.

1912 **Muhammadiyah** founded.

1914 **Indische Sociaal-Democratische Vereniging** (Indies Social Democratic Association) founded.

1916 **Volksraad** installed.

1917 Rebellion in **Toraja** land.

1918 Influenza pandemic.

1920 **Partai Komunis Indonesia** (PKI, Indonesian Communist Party) founded.

1923 Communists expelled from Sarekat Islam.

1925 **November: Algemene Studieclub** founded.

1926 **November:** Communist uprising in Banten; internment camp established at **Boven Digul**. **31 December: Nahdlatul Ulama** (NU, Revival of the Religious Scholars) founded.

1927 **January:** Communist uprising in West Sumatra. **June: Tan Malaka** establishes **Partai Republik Indonesia** (PARI, Indonesian Republican

Party) in Bangkok. **July: Partai Nasional Indonesia** (PNI, Indonesian Nationalist Party) founded.

1928 October: Youth Pledge.

1929 December: Sukarno jailed.

1931 April: PNI dissolves itself; **Pendidikan Nasional Indonesia** (PNI, Indonesian National Education; also called PNI-Baru, New PNI) and **Partai Indonesia** founded.

1933 February: Mutiny on the ***Zeven Provinciën***. **Mid**: Dutch impose assembly ban (*vergader verbod*) on several political parties. **August:** Sukarno jailed and exiled.

1934 February: Hatta, **Sjahrir**, and other political leaders jailed and exiled.

1935 December: Partai Indonesia Raya founded.

1936 July: Sutarjo Petition.

1937 May: Gerakan Rakyat Indonesia founded. **Antara** news agency founded.

1941 July: Netherlands Indies stops exports of oil, **tin**, and **rubber** to **Japan**.

War and Revolution: 1942–1949

1942 27–28 February: Battle of the **Java Sea**. **9 March:** Dutch forces on Java capitulate to Japan at Kalijati. **27 March:** Dutch forces on Sumatra surrender unconditionally.

1943 June: Japanese order establishment of volunteer armies (**Peta** on Java, **Giyu gun** on Sumatra).

1944 September: Japanese Prime Minister Kuniaki Koiso issues declaration promising Indonesian independence.

1945 March: Japanese set up Investigatory Body for Indonesian independence. **June:** Sukarno formulates **Pancasila**. **15 August**: Japan surrenders. **17 August:** Indonesia declares independence. **18 August:** Constitution promulgated and Republic of Indonesia established. **29 September:** First Allied landings in Jakarta. **5 October:** Formation of Indonesian **army**. **10 October:**

Allied troops land in Medan and **Padang**. **1 November: Manifesto Politik** of the Indonesian Republic issued. **10 November:** Battle of Surabaya. **14 November:** First parliamentary cabinet formed under Sutan Sjahrir.

1946 January: Tan Malaka establishes **Persatuan Perjuangan**. **March:** Tan Malaka and followers arrested. **April:** First formal negotiations begin between Indonesians and Dutch. **15 November: Linggajati Agreement** initialed; British forces leave Indonesia. **24 December: Negara Indonesia Timor** founded.

1947 March: Komité Nasional Indonesia endorses Linggajati agreement. **21 July:** First of Dutch **"Police Actions"** launched.

1948 17 January: Renville Agreement signed. **September: Madiun** rebellion launched and suppressed. **19 December:** Second of Dutch "Police Actions." **22 December: Pemerintah Darurat** established on Sumatra.

1949 14 April: Republican leaders and Dutch begin talks. **7 May: Roem–van Roijen** agreement reached. **6 July:** Republican government returns to Yogyakarta. **13 July:** Emergency government returns its mandate. **7 August: Darul Islam** movement declares an Islamic state. **23 August: Round Table Conference** begins in The Hague. **27 December:** Transfer of Sovereignty except for West New Guinea (Papua).

Sukarno Era: 1950–1966

1950 23 January: Attempted coup by **R. P. P. Westerling** in Bandung. **April: Benteng Program** launched; **Andi Aziz** affair; Declaration of the **Republik Maluku Selatan** (Republic of the South Moluccas). **17 August**: Reestablishment of unitary state (*see* **FEDERALISM**). **26–29 September:** Indonesia joins **United Nations**.

1952 17 October: Army challenges Sukarno, demanding dissolution of parliament and holding of **elections**.

1953 Java Bank nationalized (*see* **BANKING**). **September:** Aceh revolt begins.

1955 18–24 April: Asia-Africa Conference held in Bandung. **29 September:** General elections.

1956 8 May: Indonesia unilaterally abrogates Netherlands Indonesian Union. **4 August:** Indonesia repudiates international **debt** to the Netherlands.

1 December: Hatta resigns as vice president. **20 December:** Banteng council proclaimed in West Sumatra.

1957 **9 April:** Sukarno commissions first Business Cabinet (Kabinet Karya). May: **Dewan Nasional** founded. **29 November:** United Nations refuses to act on the West Irian dispute. **30 November:** Cikini assassination attempt against Sukarno. **3 December:** PNI and PKI unions begin seizure of Dutch businesses in Indonesia (*see* **NATIONALIZATION**). **5 December:** Justice Ministry orders expulsion of 46,000 Dutch citizens. **13 December: Nasution** announces that army will manage seized enterprises; **Mohammad Natsir** and other Masjumi leaders flee to Sumatra.

1958 **15 February:** Pemerintah Revolusioner Republik Indonesia proclaimed in Bukittinggi, West Sumatra. **12 March**: Nasution begins military operations against Sumatra rebels. **10 May:** Government forces begin operations against rebels in Sulawesi. **18 May:** Government forces shoot down American plane flying over Ambon in support of the rebels and capture its pilot.

1959 **14 May:** Alien Chinese banned from trading in rural areas. **5 July:** Restoration of 1945 Constitution. **17 August**: Sukarno outlines the **Manifesto Politik** (*see* **GUIDED DEMOCRACY**).

1960 **5 March:** Sukarno dissolves parliament.

1961 First postindependence **census**. **April–September:** Surrender of most of the **PRRI/Permesta** rebel leaders. **19 December:** Sukarno announces military campaign against Dutch in Irian (*see* **PAPUA**).

1962 **15 August:** Dutch hand authority in Irian to United Nations.

1963 **March:** Sukarno's *Deklarasi Ekonomi* (*see* **GUIDED ECONOMY**). **1 May:** United Nations hands Irian to Indonesia. **31 July–5 August:** Sukarno attends Manila summit on Malaysia (*see* **MAPHILINDO**). **23 September:** Sukarno announces plans to crush Malaysia (*see* **CONFRONTATION**). **October: Manifes Kebudayaan**.

1964 **17 August:** Sukarno gives his "Year of Living Dangerously" speech.

1965 **2 January:** Indonesia withdraws from the United Nations. **30 September–1 October: Gestapu** coup attempt. **2 October:** General **Suharto** takes responsibility for restoring "security and order." **Late 1965–1966:** Mass killings of PKI members and associates. **13 December:** 1,000 rupiah (Rp) devalued to Rp 1 (*see* **CURRENCY**).

1966 13 February: First post-Gestapu **Mahmillub** trial begins. **11 March:** Sukarno issues **Supersemar** order, transferring full executive authority to Suharto. **12 March:** PKI and associated organizations banned. **11 August:** Relations with **Malaysia** normalized, end of Confrontation. **September:** Indonesia rejoins United Nations.

Suharto Era: 1967–1998

1967 12 March: Majelis Permusyawaratan Rakyat—Sementara (MPR-S) strips Sukarno of presidency and appoints Suharto acting president. **April:** Indonesia rejoins **World Bank**. **8 August:** Formation of **Association of Southeast Asian Nations (ASEAN)**.

1968 20 February: Partai Muslimin Indonesia (Parmusi, Indonesian Muslims' Party) founded. **27 March:** MPR appoints Suharto president. **6 June:** Suharto forms first Development Cabinet.

1969 1 April: Launch of first Five-Year Development Plan. **15 July–2 August:** Kabupaten councils in Papua opt for integration with Indonesia in "Act of Free Choice." **2 October:** Attorney General Sugiharto announces plans to settle alleged communist detainees on **Buru**.

1971 17 March: Treaty of Friendship with Malaysia. **3 July:** Second general elections. **23 August:** Indonesia and Malaysia claim territorial rights over the Strait of Melaka.

1973 5 January: Partai Persatuan Pembangunan (PPP, Unity Development Party) formed. **10 January: Partai Demokrasi Indonesia** (PDI, Indonesian Democratic Party) formed. **12 February:** Indonesia signs border agreement with **Papua New Guinea**.

1974 15 January: Malari affair.

1975 11 March: Indonesia reaches border agreement with Philippines. **29 July:** Indonesia recognizes Provisional Revolutionary Government of South Vietnam. **26 August:** Portuguese colonial government abandons **East Timor**. **28 November: Fretilin** declares **Democratic Republic of East Timor**. **7 December:** Indonesian forces invade Dili, capital of East Timor.

1976 3 March: Ibnu Sutowo, director of state oil company **Pertamina**, dismissed. **22 September:** Government authorities claim to have uncovered coup plot by **Sawito Kartowibowo**.

1977 2 May: Third general election. **May:** Paratroops dropped in the central valley of Papua to crush rebellion by **Organisasi Papua Merdeka** (OPM, Free Papua Movement).

1978 16 January: Bandung students issue **White Book** criticizing New Order performance. **22 March:** MPR reelects Suharto as president. **15 November:** Rupiah devalued (*see* **CURRENCY**).

1979 July–December: Ten thousand political prisoners released.

1980 February: ABRI Masuk Desa program introduced (*see* ***DWIFUNGSI***). **5 May: Petition of Fifty** signed.

1981 28 March: Radical Muslims hijack Garuda DC-9 en route from Palembang to Medan. **25 February:** Malaysia recognizes Indonesia's **Archipelagic Concept**.

1982 4 May: Fourth general election. **December:** Law of the Sea Convention in Jamaica effectively recognizes Indonesia's Archipelagic Concept.

1983 30 March: Rupiah devalued. **April:** "Mysterious killings" of criminals begins (*see* **PETRUS**). **October: Sudharmono** and Sarwono Kusumaatmaja take over leadership of **Golkar**; Golkar restructuring begins.

1984 20–22 August: First national congress of Pertai Persatuan Pembangunan (PPP) accepts Pancasila as its sole basic principle. **12 September:** Tanjung Priok affair (*see* **WHITE PAPER**). **Early December: Muhammadiyah** adopts Pancasila as its sole basic principle. **Mid-December: Nahdlatul Ulama** adopts Pancasila as its sole basic principle, but withdraws from PPP.

1985 21 January: Bomb explosion on **Borobudur**. **5 July:** Resumption of direct trade with **China**. **18 August: H. R. Dharsono** placed on trial for subversion. **August–November:** 1,600 people dismissed, mainly from the oil industry, for alleged links with the PKI. **August:** First of a series of executions of PKI members detained after the 1965 **Gestapu**. **December 1985–August 1986:** International oil price drops from US$25 to $12 per barrel.

1986 8 January: H. R. Dharsono sentenced to 10 years of jail for subversion. **May:** Legislation passed requiring **mass organizations** to adopt the Pancasila as their sole basic principle. **12 September:** Rupiah devalued by 31 percent. **October:** Treaty of Mutual Respect, Friendship, and Cooperation with Papua New Guinea. **9 October:** Newspaper *Sinar Harapan* banned.

1987 4 February: Plans announced to privatize some of Indonesia's **state enterprises**. **21 April:** Fifth general election. **14 December:** Suharto calls for nuclear weapons free zone in Southeast Asia. **24 December:** Major reduction announced in government regulation of imports, exports, foreign investment, and tourism.

1988 5 January: 1988–1989 budget allocates 36 percent of prospective foreign income to service international **debt**. **10 March:** Suharto reelected as president, Sudharmono elected vice president. **22 September:** KOPKAMTIB abolished. **27 October:** Deregulation of the banking sector (*see* **BANKING**). **November:** Indonesia recognizes state of Palestine.

1989 6–8 February: Violent clashes in **Lampung** between troops and local people. **24 February:** Indonesia and China agree to restore diplomatic relations. **April:** Student protests over dispossession of small farmers for development projects. **8 June:** Suharto receives United Nations Population award for Indonesia's **family planning** program. **11 December:** Indonesia signs Timor Gap agreement with Australia.

1990 17 January: 150 students demonstrate before U.S. ambassador on a visit to East Timor. **3 February:** Lampung rebels sentenced. **15 February:** Four political prisoners, jailed since 1965, executed. **February:** Netherlands refuses to sign aid agreement because of execution of the four detainees. **16 April:** Indonesian army kills five Acehnese. **August:** Government lifts ban on strikes. **8 August:** Diplomatic relations officially restored between China and Indonesia. **16 September:** Dharsono released from jail. **October-November:** Public outcry over poll in newspaper *Monitor* that ranked Mohammad below political figures; its editor arrested. **December: Ikatan Cendekiawan Muslim Indonesia (ICMI)** formed.

1991 1 January: Indonesia joins **Human Rights** Commission. **3 April:** Forum Demokrasi established under **Abdurrachman Wahid**, League for Restoration of Democracy formed under Ponke Princen. **8 April:** *Monitor* editor sentenced to five years in jail. **4–5 July:** Army kills seven suspected rebels in Aceh. **November:** Massacre at Santa Cruz cemetery in Dili, East Timor; Indonesian military arrest **Jose Alexandre "Xanana" Gusmão**.

1992 **10 June:** Sixth general election. **September:** Abillo Jose Osorlco Soares becomes governor of East Timor.

1993 **January–February:** ABRI and PDI propose **Try Sutrisno** for vice president. **27 February:** Edi Sudrajat replaces Try as panglima. **17 March:** Sixth Development Cabinet announced; **Benny Murdani** dismissed as minister of defense.

1994 **February–March:** Government publishes White Paper on events in 1965. **10 February: Mochtar Pakpaham** and other **labor** leaders arrested. **14 April:** Labor demonstrations in Medan and elsewhere. **29 April:** Government arrests more labor leaders. **June:** Philippines president Fidel Ramos bans non-Filipinos from participating in Manila conference on East Timor. **17 June:** U.S. Senate passes bill banning use of U.S. equipment in East Timor. **21 June:** Government closes news magazines *Tempo, Detik,* and *Editor.* **October:** Labor activist **Muchtar Pakpahan** on trial. **6 October:** Foreign Minister Alatas meets with East Timorese in New York. **November:** APEC summit held in Jakarta. **10 November:** Indonesia's first **aircraft** christened by Suharto. **14 November:** UN recognizes Indonesia's archipelagic status.

1995 **January:** Army kills three East Timor civilians. **May:** State Administrative Court says government acted unlawfully in closing *Tempo.* **19 July: Pramoedya Ananta Toer** awarded Magsaysay prize. **August:** Netherlands Queen Beatrice visits Indonesia. **17 August:** Indonesia celebrates 50 years of independence.

1996 **Early January:** Rebels in **Papua** seize British, Dutch, and Indonesian prisoners. **April:** Death of Suharto's wife (Siti Hartinah "Tien"). **April–May:** Sri Bintang **Pamungkas** sentenced to 34 months in jail. **20 June: Megawati Sukarnoputri** excluded from Partai Demokrasi Indonesia (PDI) party congress held in Medan, and Suryadi endorsed as party head. **19–20 June:** Over 100 injured in protest demonstrations. **June:** Ten churches burned or ransacked in Surabaya. **27 July:** Government supporters attack and occupy Megawati's party headquarters. **30 July:** Muchtar Pakpaham detained. **7 August:** Suharto accuses **Partai Rakyat Demokrasi (PRD)** of being like PKI. **9 August:** Megawati appears at police headquarters with other PDI members. **11–12 August:** Budiman Sudjatmiko arrested. **13 August:** Suharto accuses PRD of trying to topple the government. **11 October:** Bishop **Belo** and **Jose Ramos Horta** awarded Nobel

Peace Prize. **October:** Several churches burned near Situbondo, East Java. **21 December:** Churches ransacked in Tasikmalaya.

1997 **30 January:** Anti-Christian/Chinese violence in Rengadengklok. **January–March:** Dayak Madurese violence in West Kalimantan leaves hundreds dead. **29 May:** In national elections, Golkar wins 74 percent of the vote, PDI 3 percent, and PPP 23 percent. **June–October:** Jakarta **stock exchange** falls over 30 percent. **14 August:** Rupiah floated. **September:** Race riots in Sulawesi. **11 September:** Parliament approves a new labor law. **September–October:** Forest fires rage in Kalimantan and Sumatra. **19 October:** Suharto announces he will run again as president. **20 October:** Central bank cuts interest rates. **31 October:** First International Monetary Fund (IMF) package announced. **November:** Government closes 16 banks.

1998 **6 January:** 1998–1999 budget announced, ignoring IMF recommendations. **5–8 January:** Rupiah plunges. **January:** IMF creates Indonesian Bank Restructuring Agency (IBRA) to reform Indonesian banking system. **15 January:** Suharto accepts IMF reform package. **22 January:** Rupiah falls to record low of Rp 17,000 to US$1. **February: Wiranto** replaces Feisal Tanjung as army commander. **3 March:** Student protest demonstrations begin in Yogyakarta, Surabaya, Padang, Ujung Pandang (Makassar), and other cities. **6 March:** IMF delays further Indonesian financing. **10 March:** Parliament selects Suharto for seventh term as president, with **B. J. Habibie** as vice president. **14 March:** Suharto announces new cabinet, which includes family members and cronies. **24 March:** IMF and United States delay aid to Indonesia, but United States allows emergency food and fuel subsidies. **March:** Megawati questions U.S. military aid and training. **8 April:** Third IMF agreement. **15 April:** Student protest marches at dozens of campuses. **1 May:** Suharto says reforms must wait until 2003. **6 May:** Prices of fuel and electricity raised. **9 May:** Suharto flies to Cairo for G-15 summit. **12 May:** Army kills several student demonstrators at Tri Sakti University in Jakarta. **13 May:** Students buried as martyrs; riots erupt in Jakarta. **14 May:** Riots continue, particularly against Chinese businesses and Suharto cronies; over 500 killed. **15 May:** Suharto returns early from Cairo. **16 May:** Faction of Golkar removes support from Suharto. **18 May:** Students drive to Parliament; Harmoko calls on Suharto to resign. **19 May:** Students occupy Parliament building. **20 May:** Suharto rejects calls to resign and proposes new elections; army clamps down in Jakarta; **Amien Rais** calls off mass protests. **21 May:** Suharto resigns in favor of Vice President Habibie.

Post-Suharto: 1998–Present

1998 22 May: President Habibie pledges to dedicate himself to democratization; a Development Reform Cabinet (Kabinet Reformasi Pembangunan) announced.

23 May: Prabowo Subianto replaced as head of **Kostrad**; army removes students from Parliament building. **25 May:** Habibie promises early elections and frees political prisoners Muchtar Pakpahan and Sri Bintang Pamungkas. **28 May:** Government takes over Bank Central Asia. **30 May:** IMF relaxes deadlines for austerity measures. **2 July:** Hundreds of Papuan tribesmen raise "Free Papua" flag in Biak. **6 July:** Indonesian marines kill Free Papua supporters. **August:** Indonesia withdraws 1,000 troops from East Timor, but other forces replace them. **4–5 August:** Portugal and Indonesia agree to discuss autonomy plan for East Timor. **September:** Government proposes electoral reforms. **6 October:** *Tempo* relaunched. **8–10 October:** Partai Demokrasi Indonesia (PDI) congress held in Bali. **10–13 November:** Parliament meets to establish legal framework for reform. **13 November:** Student demonstrations result in at least 16 deaths. **22 November:** At least 14 Christians killed by Muslims in Ketapang, Jakarta. **4 December:** Habibie sacks Pertamina's president.

1999 19 January: Street brawl in **Ambon** sparks religious violence leading to hundreds of deaths. **27 January:** Habibie proposes independence for East Timorese if they don't accept autonomy. **27 February–3 March:** Government closes 38 of Indonesia's sickest banks and nationalizes seven others. **4 March:** Government announces 48 political parties qualified to contest elections. **Mid-March:** Dayak anti-Madurese violence kills 165 by 24 March. **1 April: Police** made independent of armed forces; ABRI renamed Tentera Nasional Indonesia (TNI). **17 April:** Prointegration militias crack down on independence supporters in East Timor. **23 April:** Parliament approves law on intergovernmental fiscal relations, diverting funds to regions. **3 May:** Military in Aceh kills 45 civilians. **10 May:** Golkar formally nominates Habibie as its presidential candidate. **May:** Wiranto announces staged return to pre-1980s 17 Kodam from current 11 Kodam. **15 May:** Kodam XVI Pattimura (Maluku) established. **7 June:** Nationwide elections held. **21 June:** Formal announcement of election results. **23 July:** Army kills more than 50 people in Aceh. **31 July:** Bank Mandiri (encompassing Banks Dagang Nagara, Bumi Daya, Exim, and Bapindo) opens. **8 August:** Vote on independence scheduled for East Timor. **9 August:** In Parliament, "Central Axis" group nominates Abdurrachman Wahid for president. **18–20 August:** Intervillage fighting begins in northern **Halmahera**. **30 August:** East Timorese vote in UN-supervised referendum. **31 August:** Three members of UN staff killed in East Timor. **3 September:** Pro-Jakarta militias rampage in East Timor. **4 September:** East Timor referendum results announced: 78.5 percent vote for independence. **5 September:** At least 100 Timorese killed around Dili. **6 September:** Bishop Belo's home burned and 6,000 refugees taken to West Timor. **7 September:** State of military emergency imposed in East Timor. **12 September:** Habibie accepts plans for international force in East Timor. **15 September:** UN authorizes an international force to enter East Timor. **27 September:** Indonesian military formally transfers authority in East Timor to multinational force. **20–21 October:** Parliament elects Wahid president. **21 October:** Megawati Sukarnoputri accepts vice presidency. **24 October:** Renewed violence in Halmahera, spreading to Ternate and Tidore. **27 October:** Wahid appoints National Unity Cabinet, including State Ministry for Regional Autonomy. **31 October:** Wahid withdraws Kostrad and Kopassus troops from Aceh. **November:** Thousands of Christians evacuated from Maluku to Minahasa.

2000 **17–18 January:** Muslims riot in Lombok. **28 January:** Wahid visits Middle East seeking economic aid. **Mid-February:** Wahid suspends Wiranto as coordinating minister for security. **April:** Military announces trial abolition of military presence at village level in Jakarta and Surabaya. **24 April:** Wahid dismisses two other ministers. **12 May:** Cease-fire agreed to in Aceh. **16 May:** Wiranto formally resigns. **28 May:** Riots in Poso, Central Sulawesi, kill at least 100. **4 June:** Papuan Congress asserts rights of sovereignty and calls for dialogue with Jakarta. **27 June:** State of civil emergency declared in Maluku. **1 July:** National police separated from TNI and placed directly under president's control. **20 July:** Wahid defends ministers' firings before Majelis Permusyawaratan Rakyat (MPR). **9 August:** Wahid agrees to share power with Megawati. **August:** Government abolishes Ministry of Regional Autonomy. **28 August:** Parliament begins investigation of financial scandals involving Wahid. **6 September:** Indonesian militias kill three UN aid workers in West Timor. **19 December:** Wahid visits Banda Aceh. **24 December:** Christmas Eve church bombings throughout Java and Sumatra.

2001 **3 January:** Parliament censures Wahid over Bulog and Sultan of Brunei scandals. **5 January:** Government declares it will control **mining** for five years. **22 January:** Wahid refuses to answer Parliament's accusations and denies wrongdoing. **1 February:** Parliament censures Wahid over financial scandals. **February-March:** Student demonstrations call for Wahid's resignation. **28 March:** Wahid rejects Parliament's censure. **30**

April: Parliament censures Wahid a second time. **20 May:** Kostrad soldiers pledge loyalty to Constitution. **28 May:** Attorney general clears Wahid of wrongdoing. **30 May:** Wahid rejects second censure; Parliament to meet to initiate impeachment of Wahid; police reject Wahid's firing of police chief. **1 June:** Wahid reshuffles cabinet. **9 July:** Wahid threatens state of emergency on 20 July if charges not dropped against him. **13 July:** Amien Rais says he will call impeachment vote if Wahid declares state of emergency. **20 July:** Parliament announces intention of convening session to oust Wahid. **22 July:** Two Christian churches bombed in Jakarta. **23 July:** Parliament votes to dismiss Wahid; Megawati Sukarnoputri sworn in to replace him as president. **24 July:** Separatist leaders and human rights lawyers arrested in Aceh. **26 July:** Parliament elects Hamzah Haz of Partai Pembangunan Persatuan (PPP) as vice president. **16 August:** In her first state of the union address, Megawati apologizes for military abuses. **September:** Election held in East Timor for de facto parliament and to draft new constitution. **13 December: Supreme Court** declares Tommy Suharto must serve 11 months in jail. **17 December:** Suharto hospitalized.

2002 **10 January:** Reestablishment of separate military command for Aceh. **22 January:** Abdullah Syafei, commander of Gerakan Aceh Merdeka (GAM), killed together with six others. **February:** Coordinating minister for political and social affairs given authority to resolve Aceh situation. **2 March:** On Sulawesi, Moluccan Christian and Muslim leaders sign peace accord (Malino II) formally ending hostilities on Ambon. **March:** Tommy Suharto arrested. **28 April:** 14 Christians killed in clashes in Maluku. **1 May: Laskar Jihad** leader Ja'afer Umar Thalib arrested on charge of inciting Muslims to attack Christians. **20 May:** UN Secretary-General Kofi Annan cedes governing authority to newly independent Democratic Republic of East Timor with Jose Alexandre "Xanana" Gusmão as president. President Megawati Sukarnoputri attends ceremony. **5 June:** Indonesian security agents arrest and extradite Omar Al Faruq (allegedly al Qaeda's Southeast Asia representative). **June:** Eurico Guterres and six other pro-Jakarta militia leaders charged with crimes against humanity for violence after Timor's 1999 independence vote. **29 June:** Aceh rebels kidnap nine crew members of an ExxonMobil boat. **July:** President Gusmão visits Jakarta to discuss Indonesia–Timor relations. **August:** U.S. State Department urges federal court to dismiss human rights suit against ExxonMobil. **1 August:** Malaysia law calls for imprisonment and caning of illegal workers, forcing thousands of migrants to flee back to Indonesia. **3 August:** MPR votes to approve direct elections for president and vice president and to abolish military seats in parliament by 2004, defeats proposal for introduction of Islamic law (*syariah*). **15 August:** Human rights court clears six army and police officers of crimes against humanity in East Timor. **31 August:** Gunmen attack jeep near **Freeport** mine in Papua, killing two Americans and an Indonesian. **September:** Akbar Tanjung, Golkar head and speaker of Parliament, sentenced to three years in jail for misusing $4 million of government funds. He appeals. **30 September:** Army–police clash over marijuana trade near Medan leaves eight dead and over 20 wounded. **12 October:** Bomb blast destroys nightclub in Bali, killing 202 people, about half foreign, 88 of them Australian tourists. **Mid-October:** 1,000 members of Laskar Jihad return to Java from Ambon; their leader Ja'far Umar Thalib states that they have disbanded. **18 October:** Indonesia issues emergency decree on terrorism. **Late October:** Government orders arrest of Abu Bakar Ba'asyir, allegedly spiritual leader of Jemaah Islamiah; despite being in hospital, he is taken into detention. **5 November:** Police arrest Amrozi bin Nurhasyim, who allegedly bought and transported the bombs used in the Bali bombings. **9 December:** Indonesian government and Acehnese rebel negotiators sign a peace agreement. **17 December:** The World Court awards the small Celebes Sea islands of Ligitan and Sipadan to Malaysia. **December:** East Timor's parliament ratifies a treaty with Australia on production, profit sharing, and distribution of royalties and taxes from oil and gas reserves.

2003 January: Lt. Col. Sujarwo, former army commander in East Timor, is convicted of failing to prevent attacks on home of Bishop Belo; Jakarta High Court upholds jail sentence against Akbar Tanjung; government raises prices for fuels, electricity, and communications, sparking large protest demonstrations in many Indonesian cities; a presidential instruction (***inpres***) proposes dividing Papua into three provinces; FBI links Indonesian soldiers to the 31 August 2002 killing of two Americans near the Freeport mine in Papua; in response to public opposition, government repeals many of the price hikes on fuel and other items. **2 February:** Police arrest terrorist suspect Selamat Kastari, accused of complicity in terrorist attacks. **February:** Megawati confirms that she will run for reelection in 2004. **25 February:** United Nations indicts General Wiranto and other officers for crimes against humanity during East Timor's independence vote in 1999. **March:** Indonesia states it will ignore the UN's arrest warrants for Wiranto and the others accused. **13 March:** Former East Timor commander Brig. Gen. Noer Moeis sentenced to five years in jail. **26 March:** Megawati addresses meeting of Non-Aligned Movement in Kuala Lumpur, and Indonesia formally requests UN Security Council to convene an emergency meeting on Iraq. **31 March:** Hundreds of thousands participate in antiwar protests against U.S.-led war in Iraq. **4 April:** Government declares severe acute respiratory syndrome

(SARS) a national epidemic threat; three GAM fighters killed in Pidië, Aceh; bill proposed transferring development powers from **Bappenas** to Ministry of Finance; Organisasi Papua Merdeka (OPM) attacks weapons warehouse in Wamena Papua, killing two TNI soldiers. **14 April:** Charges of treason officially filed against Abu Bakar Baa'syir, chiefly in connection with the Christmas Eve 2000 church bombings. **23 April:** Trial of Abu Bakar Baa'syir begins. **24 April:** Peace talks between the government and GAM break down. **27 April:** Bomb explodes at Jakarta airport, injuring 11. **5 May: Nurcholish Madjid** expresses his willingness to run for president in 2004. **12 May:** Amrozi bin Nurhasyim is first defendant to go on trial for the Bali bombings. **18 May:** Peace talks in Tokyo to extend the cease-fire in Aceh between GAM and Indonesian government collapse. **19 May:** Megawati declares martial law in Aceh, and some 50,000 government soldiers and police launch full-scale invasion. **21 May:** U.S. Senate Foreign Relations Committee withholds $400,000 for training military officers in the United States until allegations of army complicity in killing of Americans in Papua are resolved. **Late May:** Imam Samudra goes on trial as mastermind of Bali bombings. **5 August:** An explosion outside the Marriott Hotel in Jakarta kills 10 people and wounds about 150. **7 August:** Amrozi found guilty in Bali bombing case and sentenced to death. **12 August:** Riduan Isamuddim (Hambali), alleged head of Jemaah Islamiyah, arrested in Thailand. **Mid-August:** Maj. Gen. Adam Damiri found guilty for crimes against humanity in East Timor and sentenced to three years in prison. **25 August:** Province of Papua split into three with inauguration of new provinces of Central Irian Jaya and West Irian Jaya. **2 September:** Court acquits Abu Bakar Baa'syir of terrorist charges, but sentences him to four years in jail for sedition. **10 September:** Imam Samudra sentenced to death for his role in the Bali bombing. **18 September:** Ali Imron sentenced to life imprisonment for his role in the Bali bombings. **October:** Landslide disrupts production at Freeport's Grasberg mine in Papua. **2 October:** Ali Gufron (Mukhlas) sentenced to death for authorizing the Bali bombings. **9–12 October:** Attacks on Christian villages in central Sulawesi leave 13 villagers and six suspects dead. **December:** Abu Bakar Baa'syir's jail sentence reduced to three years for immigration and forgery charges; second major landslide hits Freeport mine in Papua. **7 December:** General Elections Commission announces 24 parties eligible to contest 2004 elections. **29 December:** Political parties submit their candidate lists for elections.

2004 **4 February:** The Supreme Court overturns the corruption conviction of Golkar head Akbar Tanjung.

Introduction

A wide-flung archipelago lying between the Pacific and Indian Oceans, Indonesia is the world's most populous Islamic country. For over 2,000 years, it was a crossroads on the major trading route between China and India, but was not brought together into a single entity until the Dutch extended their rule throughout the Netherlands East Indies in the early part of the 20th century. Declaring its independence from the Dutch in 1945, the Republic of Indonesia was ruled by only two regimes over the next half century—the nonaligned parliamentary and Guided Democracy of the flamboyant Sukarno and the Western-oriented authoritarian military rule of General Suharto. Neither regime was able to realize the country's potential either economically or politically, and after Suharto's resignation in 1998 his successors have struggled in varying degrees to introduce a more democratic and representative structure of government. They have been faced on the one hand with separatist movements and widespread ethnic and religious violence and on the other with a military eager to reassert its dominance of the state. At the same time, there have been formidable economic challenges to be overcome in the aftermath of the Asian financial crisis of the last years of the 20th century.

LAND AND PEOPLE

Lying between the Asian and Australian continents and between the Indian and Pacific Oceans, the Indonesian archipelago straddles the Equator, between 6°08'N and 11°15'S and between 94°45'W and 141°05'E. The Republic of Indonesia shares land borders with Papua New Guinea, Malaysia, and Australia. There are three official time zones, 7–9 hours ahead of Greenwich mean time.

The country is 2,027,087 square kilometers (sq. km) in area, plus 3,166,163 sq. km in territorial waters. It is 5,100 km long on its east-west axis and 1,888 km broad on its north-south axis. It consists of approximately 13,669 islands the size of a tennis court or larger; the exact number changes frequently due to siltation and volcanic eruptions. About 6,000 islands are named, and about 1,000 are inhabited. Indonesian annexation of the Portuguese overseas territory of East Timor never received full international recognition, and East Timor gained its independence in 1999. The islands are customarily grouped into four regions: the Greater Sundas (Sumatra, Java, Kalimantan, and Sulawesi); the Lesser Sundas or Nusatenggara (the chain of islands running from Bali eastward to Timor); the Moluccas, or Maluku, between Sulawesi and New Guinea (Papua); and Papua. Over 80 percent of Indonesia's land area is accounted for by its five largest islands: Kalimantan, Sumatra, Sulawesi, Java, and the western portion of New Guinea, now named Papua.

The Greater Sundas Islands and part of Nusatenggara sit on the Sunda shelf, a southeastern extension of the Asian continental plate partly covered by shallow seas. A zone of volcanic activity along the southern rim of this shelf has created a chain of volcanoes that forms the spine of Sumatra and Java. Papua sits on the Sahul shelf, a geologically stable extension of the Australian continental plate. Between these two shelves, Maluku is an area of extreme geological instability, with volcanic mountains and deep sea trenches. Australia is still moving north, and the mountains of Papua rise 4 to 5 cm per century. The highest is the snowcapped Puncak Jaya in Papua at 5,030 meters.

As Indonesia lies in the tropics, temperatures are determined primarily by the time of day and by elevation. The maximum recorded temperature range in Jakarta is 18° to 36° C. There are permanent, but receding, snowfields in the Maoke mountains of Papua. Rainfall is generally heavy, with all of Kalimantan and most of Sumatra and Java, eastern and southern Sulawesi, Maluku, and Papua receiving an average annual rainfall of 200 cm or more. Timor and Sumba, which lie in Australia's rain shadow, receive 100 to 150 cm per year. In recent times, it has been recognized that the El Niño Southern Oscillation regularly changes rainfall patterns to produce a pronounced dry season in much of the archipelago.

High temperatures and heavy rainfall generally work to encourage chemical weathering, which impoverishes tropic soils. In much of Indonesia, especially Kalimantan, this process was sidestepped by the growth of tropical rain forest, rooted in a shallow layer of topsoil from which nutrients are rapidly recirculated. As this rain forest layer is lost due to the extensive logging that has taken place over the past three decades, soil degradation has been rapid. In Java and West Sumatra, basic andesitic volcanic materials ejected from volcanoes are responsible for the high levels of fertility in those regions. There are approximately 829 active volcanoes in Indonesia today.

Indonesia's population is predominantly mixed Austronesian-Austromelanesian in origin, with the Austromelanesian component becoming stronger in the east. There has always been a basic cultural division between the coastal peoples and the upland interior groups (such as the Bataks of Sumatra and the Dayaks of Kalimantan), who until recently depended on shifting slash-and-burn agriculture. Over the centuries, there has been considerable admixture of Chinese and Arab elements, and a large Chinese minority exists throughout the archipelago mainly in urban areas. The population is estimated in the 2000 census at 206.3 million, of whom the majority live on Java. Islam is the principal religion, but there are significant Christian (Protestant and Catholic), Hindu, and Buddhist minorities.

EARLY HISTORY

Although the first human settlement in the archipelago has been dated from 1.9 million years ago, the ancestors of most modern Indonesians arrived from the north from about 3000 B.C. Hindu and Buddhist kingdoms emerged in many parts of the western archipelago from the fifth century A.D. In the early centuries of the Christian era, trading ships from India began to ply the Melaka Strait, and it was perhaps two centuries later that direct trade began between the western archipelago and China. Indian culture, in particular, exerted a powerful influence on the character of the states that developed in the archipelago. By the seventh century, there were two principal types of political units: the maritime trading states along the coasts of Sumatra, North Java, Kalimantan, Sulawesi, and some of the other eastern islands, and the rice-based inland kingdoms, particularly those in East and Central Java.

Predominant among the maritime states was Srivijaya, a Mahayana Buddhist kingdom on Sumatra's southeast coast, which, by the late seventh century, was a center of trade with India and for several centuries monopolized much of China's commerce with the Malacca Strait and the western archipelago. Several rice-based Hindu-Buddhist kingdoms developed in the interior of Java between the eighth and 14th centuries, including the Hindu kingdom of Mataram, which flourished on Central Java's Dieng Plateau in the early eighth century; the mid-ninth-century Mahayana Buddhist kingdom on the nearby Kedu Plain, which left the massive Buddhist temple of Borobudur; and a near-contemporary Hindu kingdom that left extensive Sivaite monuments in nearby Prambanan. When the center of power shifted to East Java during the succeeding centuries, the kingdoms that developed there—under Sindok (r. 929–947) and Airlangga (r. 1019–c. 1045)—united with Bali and relied more on trade with the outside world. By the 13th century, the kingdom of Singasari, under the Tantric Buddhist king Kertanagara (r. 1268–1292), was asserting its ascendancy over areas of Sumatra formerly controlled by Srivijaya.

The Mongols under Kublai Khan attacked Java in 1292, killing Kertanagara, but his successor, Wijaya, expelled a subsequent Mongol invasion, founding Majapahit, the greatest of the Javanese empires, in 1293. Majapahit claimed sovereignty over much of the archipelago and parts of the Malay Peninsula.

Before the end of the 13th century, merchants from South India and Gujarat were successfully propagating Islam among some of North Sumatra's coastal trading states. However, until the early 15th century and the rise of Melaka, Islam spread only gradually through the archipelago. An entrepôt on the west coast of the Malay Peninsula, Melaka came to dominate the strait and thus the trade route between the Spice Islands of the eastern archipelago and India. By 1436 it had become the major emporium for the trade that had grown in response to the rising European demand for spices. At the same time, it was the major center spreading Islam to the other trading kingdoms of the archipelago. The North Javanese coastal kingdoms that converted to Islam exerted commercial and military pressure on the Javanese kingdom of Majapahit, contributing to its virtual disappearance by the early 16th century.

INTRUSION OF THE WEST AND THE COLONIAL STATE

From the early 16th century, the trading states of island Southeast Asia faced growing pressure from the Portuguese, British, Spaniards, and Dutch, all of whom were seeking to profit from the European demand for spices. The Portuguese made a major effort to wrest the spice trade from the local Islamic states. They conquered the Sultanate of Melaka in 1511, and from there attempted to exclude all competitors from the trade to Europe. In response, the local powers strove to establish alternative trading routes. The most powerful of the competing trading states was Aceh, which by the 16th century dominated much of northern Sumatra, controlled the pepper ports down Sumatra's west coast, and ultimately extended its influence to some of the sultanates on the Malay Peninsula. There were other strong Islamic states: Makassar on Sulawesi, Banten in West Java, and the Islamic Mataram in Central Java, which grew in importance in the second half of the 16th century and absorbed many of Java's maritime principalities during the first half of the 17th century.

After the founding of the Netherlands' United East India Company (VOC) in 1602, the Dutch soon replaced the Portuguese as the dominant outside power in the region. Jan Pieterszoon Coen established a base in Sunda Kelapa on the northwest coast of Java, which he named Batavia, and moved to isolate the archipelago's interisland network from international commerce. After capturing Melaka from the Portuguese in 1641, the Dutch also attempted to impose a monopoly on the spice trade, restricting cultivation of cloves to Ambon and of nutmeg and mace to the Banda islands.

Over the next century, although continuing to dominate the trade of the eastern archipelago, the Dutch shifted their attention from the Spice Islands to Java. They introduced coffee and other export crops to the island and worked with amenable collaborators from among the local aristocrats and the growing numbers of Chinese they had encouraged to immigrate to Java in extracting these export crops. In other parts of the archipelago, however, the VOC played an exceedingly limited role. During the 18th century, as the company attempted to expand its territorial control, the increased administrative costs, combined with a decline in the spice trade, led it to bankruptcy. Its charter was allowed to lapse in December 1799, and the Dutch government took over its debts and assumed direct responsibility for administration of its possessions in the East Indies.

In the Napoleonic wars, Herman Willem Daendels was sent to organize the defense of Java against the British, but was recalled in 1811 when the Netherlands was incorporated into the French Empire. Dutch areas of the archipelago came under a brief British interregnum (1811–1816), during which Thomas Stamford Raffles attempted to centralize and reform the administration of Java. Shortly after their resumption of power, the Dutch were forced to expend massive sums in suppressing a rebellion (1825–1850) led by the Javanese prince Diponegoro. They then annexed extensive areas of Central Java, and in 1830 Governor-General Johannes van den Bosch instituted the "Cultivation System" (Cultuurstelsel), whereby peasants had to devote a percentage of their land (officially one-fifth but usually far more) to cultivating government-designated export crops instead of rice. Although extremely profitable for the Dutch, the system was partly responsible for the widespread famine that swept parts of Java in the 1840s and 1850s.

Concurrently, Dutch power was spreading over other parts of the archipelago. Their forces intervened in West Sumatra against the reformist Muslim Paderi movement, finally defeating and exiling its leader, Tuanku Imam Bonjol, in 1837. In the 1850s they annexed Sumatra's northeast coast principalities and the tin-mining island of Belitung (Billiton). Finally, after 30 years of warfare, Dutch forces subdued Aceh and Bali in 1908 and 1909 and continued to bring regions of Sulawesi, Maluku, the Lesser Sundas, and most of Kalimantan under firmer control.

A bitter campaign by Dutch liberals against the Cultivation System succeeded by the 1870s in removing some of its harsher aspects, though forced deliveries of coffee continued until 1919. Oil, tin, and rubber, coming mostly from the newly acquired areas of Sumatra and Kalimantan, began to replace coffee, sugar, and tobacco as the main exports to Europe. At the beginning of the 20th century, the Dutch introduced their "Ethical Policy" in part as a response to domestic criticisms of government policies in the Indies, but also as a means of training a local workforce to help run the expanding state bureaucracy. Infrastructure of the archipelago was expanded through the development of railways, roads, and interisland shipping, and more health and educational facilities were provided for the local people.

Although this change had very limited results, with only a few thousand Indonesians receiving even a secondary-level Western education, the policy did help create two new social elements in the archipelago: a small Western-educated intelligentsia, particularly on Java, which served the colonial regime (mostly in clerical roles); and an even smaller group of entrepreneurs and smallholders on some other islands, who began to compete with a still predominantly Chinese commercial class. In time, both elements became resentful of a colonial structure that denied them a role commensurate with their education and abilities.

NATIONALIST MOVEMENT AND THE ACHIEVEMENT OF INDEPENDENCE

Local entrepreneurs formed the basis of the first major anti-Dutch nationalist movement, the Sarekat Islam (SI, Islamic Union), established in 1912, which grew out of an association of batik merchants formed in an attempt to contain competition from Chinese entrepreneurs. By 1918 it claimed a membership of more than 2 million, with branches throughout the Netherlands East Indies. Responding in part to the SI's calls for self-government, the Dutch established a Volksraad (People's Council) at the end of World War I, but the few indigenous members of this advisory body had little influence.

Other organizations questioning Dutch rule also developed during the 1910s, the strongest being the Indies Social Democratic Association (ISDV), made up largely of intellectuals—Dutch, Eurasian, and Indonesian—who saw socialist teachings as directly relevant to the colonial situation they faced in the Indies. At that time it was possible to hold membership in more than one political party, so these radicals also constituted an influential component of the SI. In 1920 the ISDV became the Communist Association of the Indies, which developed into the Communist Party of Indonesia (PKI). Conflict grew between the communist and Islamic streams within the Sarekat Islam, until the communists were expelled from all branches of the party in 1923. Severely weakened by this struggle, the Sarekat Islam never regained its coherence, size, and unity. A deep schism also developed within the Communist Party, and an effort to mount a nationwide anticolonial revolution planned for 1926 resulted in only a few scattered outbreaks, mainly in Banten and West Sumatra. The Dutch easily suppressed these uprisings and then took harsh steps to eradicate the influence of the communists and other anticolonial groups from the Indies.

From then on, the anti-Dutch political movement in Indonesia was headed by leaders who were not identified closely with either communism or Islam. Sukarno, Mohammad Hatta, and Sutan Sjahrir emerged as the foremost nationalist leaders. Sukarno founded the Indonesian National Party (PNI) in 1927, an organization that demanded complete independence from the Dutch. In October 1928, a youth congress articulated Indonesian aspirations in the slogan "Indonesia, one people, one language, one motherland" and adopted Indonesian as the national language.

Alarmed by the strength of Sukarno's following, the Dutch arrested him, together with seven other party leaders, at the end of 1929. The remaining leader of the PNI dissolved the party and adopted more cautious policies. Although Sukarno was released from jail in 1931, he was arrested again two years later and sent into exile until the Japanese released him in 1942. Mohammad Hatta and Sutan Sjahrir, who saw Sukarno's 1929 arrest as proof of their contention that mass parties under charismatic leadership were very vulnerable to Dutch counterattack, sought instead to train a small cadre of potential leaders in many parts of Indonesia. But this effort also failed and both leaders were arrested in 1934, remaining in exile until the eve of the Japanese occupation.

After these arrests, more moderate leaders and parties emerged who were willing to work within the parameters set by the colonial administration. They based their party programs on cooperation with the Dutch and gradual achievement of self-government but attracted only a small following. The Netherlands government rejected even such modest proposals as the Volksraad's request for an Indonesian parliament and the Soetardjo petition (mid-1936) calling for evolutionary development toward self-government. Only in 1941 after Germany overran the Netherlands did the Dutch queen promise some postwar devolution of political authority.

The Japanese dealt a humiliating defeat to the Dutch in early 1942, and three and a half years of Japanese occupation dismantled the Dutch power structure, dividing the archipelago into three separate military administrations. Of these, the Japanese regime on Java was most sympathetic to the Indonesian nationalists, allowing Sukarno, Hatta, and other prewar leaders freedom to address large audiences in return for their help in mobilizing Indonesian support for the Japanese war effort. Outside Java, the Japanese military authorities were extremely repressive, permitting the nationalists no more latitude than had the Dutch.

From September 1943, the Japanese established "volunteer" militias in Java, Bali, Sumatra, and Kalimantan to help repel expected Allied landings. In October 1944, in an effort to muster support against these anticipated attacks, the Japanese promised independence to Indonesia and partially relaxed controls over the nationalist leaders' activities on Java; but prior to their surrender to the Allies on 15 August 1945, they paid little more than lip service to their promise of self-government.

On 17 August 1945, Sukarno and Hatta proclaimed Indonesia's independence, and the following day members of a Japanese-sponsored preparatory committee for independence elected them president and vice president of the new Republic of Indonesia. By late September, when British forces on behalf of the Allied command began to land in Java and Sumatra to accept the Japanese surrender, a functioning Republican administration already existed in much of these two islands. When the British attempted to take over the administration on behalf of the Dutch, they met with fierce resistance in many parts of Java and Sumatra. But in the eastern archipelago, Australian forces had already established themselves in New Guinea and parts of Kalimantan before the Japanese surrender, and they were able to restore Dutch authority with comparative ease to most of these areas. The relative strength of the Republic in Java and Sumatra and of the Dutch in the eastern archipelago was reluctantly acknowledged by both sides. Thus, before their withdrawal in November 1946, the British were able to persuade the Dutch as well as the Indonesians to initial the Linggajati agreement recognizing de facto authority of the Republic in only Java and Sumatra and planning for the establishment of a federal system for the whole of Indonesia.

The British departure precipitated a direct military and diplomatic struggle between the Republic and the Dutch. From 1946, the Dutch began to set up autonomous territories in the areas they controlled that were to form part of a projected Federal State of Indonesia with strong ties to the Netherlands. The Dutch attempted to reimpose their rule over Republican-controlled areas through two major military operations, euphemistically termed "police actions," in July 1947 and December 1948. In the second of these, they overran the Republican capital at Yogyakarta and arrested most of the Republic's top leaders, including Sukarno and Hatta. But the vigor of Republican guerrilla resistance and pressure from the international community ultimately forced the Dutch toward accommodation, and after talks culminating in the Roem–van Roijen agreement, Sukarno and Hatta were allowed to return to Yogyakarta in July 1949. A "Round-Table conference" was convened in The Hague the following month. Negotiations among the Netherlands, the Dutch-sponsored states, and the Republic culminated in the Netherlands government agreeing to transfer sovereignty over all of Indonesia at the end of 1949, with the exception of western New Guinea (Papua), to a federal Republic of the United States of Indonesia (RIS or RUSI) consisting of the Republic and the Dutch-sponsored states.

THE SUKARNO ERA

The newly independent government of Indonesia, launched in January 1950, faced immense problems in its attempts to create a viable state out of the archipelago's disparate peoples and cultures. It inherited a country devastated by nearly a decade of war, an enormous debt from the Dutch, and a poorly educated population, with many of the small components of educated civilians discredited by their collaboration with the colonial government. The federal state was tarnished by its identification with the Dutch divide-and-rule policy, and by August 1950 it had been replaced by a Unitary State of Indonesia, with its capital on Java and with a form of government likely to feed outer-island fears of Javanese dominance. There was a brief revolt in Sulawesi and Ambon against the unitary state and in favor of a South Moluccan Republic (RMS), but the Indonesian National Army (TNI) easily crushed the rebellion, with many of the rebel soldiers fleeing with their families to the Netherlands.

Suspicions between the center of power on Java and the other islands were exacerbated by views with regard to Islam's role in the new state. In 1945 the formateurs of the Constitution had established the Pancasila, or Five Principles—belief in the one God, humanitarianism, nationalism, democracy, and social justice—as the ideology on which the state would rest. The lack of a specifically Islamic religious orientation created dissatisfaction, particularly in the strongly Muslim areas of the Outer Islands and West Java, a dissatisfaction that soon led to serious rebellions by the Darul Islam (House of Islam) especially in West Java, Aceh, and South Sulawesi.

There was also a severe rift between the new state's civilian and military sectors. Most army officers regarded themselves and their forces as the major component in Indonesia's achievement of independence. They viewed with contempt the faction-torn, ineffective, and often corrupt governments that followed each other in rapid succession during the early 1950s. The nationwide elections finally held in 1955 did little to resolve the country's problems, for there was no clear winner. Four parties emerged with substantial support—the National Party (PNI), the modernist Islamic Masjumi, the traditionalist Islamic NU, and the Indonesian Communist Party (PKI). Only one of these parties, the Masjumi, had a major following outside Java.

Outer-island disillusionment with political developments was further strengthened by the insufficient funds allocated to economic development of regions outside Java, despite their providing most of the country's export earnings. Responding to this dissatisfaction, regional military commanders, particularly in Sumatra and Sulawesi, began large-scale smuggling in copra and rubber, using the profits for themselves, their soldiers, and their regions. In a series of largely bloodless coups between December 1956 and March 1957, army-led councils seized power from the local civilian authorities in several regions of Sumatra and Sulawesi. The dissidents in Sumatra were joined in December 1957 by several top Masjumi party leaders forced to flee Jakarta by increased harassment from leftist mobs in the aftermath of an assassination attempt against Sukarno at the end of November. Emboldened by support from these civilian political leaders, the dissident colonels in Sumatra and Sulawesi challenged the government in Jakarta by proclaiming a competing Revolutionary Government of the Republic of Indonesia (PRRI) on 15 February 1958. Despite arms and covert paramilitary assistance to the insurgents from the United States and Taiwan, Jakarta's army soon defeated the major rebel forces on Sumatra, though it took longer for government troops to gain the upper hand in Sulawesi. Guerrilla activity against the central government continued on both islands until 1961.

At the center, Sukarno had answered the crisis of confidence in Indonesia's postrevolutionary governments by calling for an overhaul of the party system and proposing instead a system of "Guided Democracy" based on a return to the 1945 Constitution, under which the president's powers would be expanded and functional representation in parliament would be added to that of the political parties. After Guided Democracy replaced parliamentary democracy in 1959, Sukarno strove to implement his concept of Nasakom (nationalism, religion, and communism), a fusion of what he viewed as the major streams making up Indonesia's political culture. He also struggled to maintain a balance between the two strongest competing forces in the society at that time—the army and the Communist Party.

In the international arena, he was also conducting an activist foreign policy. In the late 1950s, he challenged the Dutch over their continued retention of West Irian (Papua) until under U.S. pressure an agreement was finally reached in 1962 whereby the United Nations took over administration of the territory until May 1963, when it was handed over to Indonesia. In return, Indonesia agreed to provide the Papuans with the opportunity before 1969 to register whether or not they wished to continue under Indonesian rule. Sukarno led Indonesia in its policy of "confrontation" with the new federation of Malaysia, which incorporated the north Borneo territories of Sabah and Sarawak, bordering on Indonesian Kalimantan. Beginning in late 1963, this confrontation involved two years of sporadic Indonesian attacks, mostly into Sarawak.

Knowing of U.S. involvement in the PRRI rebellion and suspecting its involvement in assassination attempts against him, Sukarno hardened his anti-Western stance during the early 1960s. He criticized American actions in Vietnam, withdrew Indonesia from the United Nations, and proposed establishment of an anti-imperialist axis stretching from Beijing to Jakarta.

In early August 1965, widespread rumors of a "Generals' Council" plotting to overthrow Sukarno intensified and were intermingled with warnings of Sukarno's imminent demise as he suffered the resurgence of a kidney complaint. The period of rumor and uncertainty broke on 30 September 1965 when Lieutenant Colonel Untung of Sukarno's palace guard led an action in which six top generals were kidnapped and brutally murdered. Forces under General Suharto crushed the movement within 24 hours. The dynamics and real instigators of this so-called Gestapu (Gerakan Tiga Puluh September, 30 September Movement) have remained obscure and are the subjects of intense controversy. Whoever was responsible, it was Suharto who, after successfully crushing the Untung forces, took control of the army and eventually maneuvered Sukarno into surrendering effective presidential power to him on 11 March 1966. The army alleged PKI responsibility in the Gestapu, and, despite Sukarno's efforts to prevent the bloodshed, during 1965–1966 army units together with some Muslim organizations and others launched massacres of communists and supporters of their mass organizations, with estimates of the dead ranging between 300,000 and 1 million. The PKI was banned on 13 March 1966, and the army arrested hundreds of thousands of people accused of having ties to the party.

At the end of the Sukarno era, Indonesia was left with an economy close to collapse. Sukarno's renunciation of Western aid had exacerbated the country's parlous economic situation and expanded its debt. Budget deficits were nearly half of the country's gross domestic product, exports had declined drastically, and inflation had risen to an annual rate of almost 600 percent.

THE SUHARTO ERA

When he assumed power, Suharto initiated basic changes in the government's ideological and political orientation and in its economic policies, but he also made use of the authoritarian legislation that accompanied the introduction of Guided Democracy to impose a militarily enforced "bureaucratic authoritarian regime" that dominated Indonesia over the next 30 years. His so-called New Order government abandoned Indonesia's confrontation with Malaysia, deemphasized party politics, and laid its main stress on economic rehabilitation. "Development" became its slogan, and the regime opened the country to foreign investment while also pursuing a generally pro-Western foreign policy.

Needing to legitimize its rule for both a domestic and foreign audience, the new regime prepared for parliamentary elections but was reluctant to hold them until it could ensure the result. To do this, it built up the already existing General Secretariat of Functional Groups (Sekber Golkar) as an instrument to dominate the political process, and then moved to emasculate the existing political parties. The eight political parties that remained after the 1971 elections were forced to consolidate into two groupings, which eventually became the Partai Demokrasi Indonesia (PDI), incorporating the secular and Christian parties; and the Partai Persatuan Pembangunan (PPP), incorporating the Islamic parties. Golkar's success in all subsequent elections was guaranteed, for not only did all government employees, including teachers, have to vote for Golkar, but it also controlled voter registration and was the only contender allowed to organize at the village level. Through constant manipulation, the government was able to ensure that Golkar's share of the vote never fell below 62 percent. By the 1987 elections when Golkar achieved a record 73.2 percent of the vote, it seemed that Suharto had effectively turned the political parties into nonoppositional bodies.

But although the government was successful in eliminating any challenge in the political arena, particularly from Islamic organizations, critics of the regime, lacking a legitimate spokesperson, had little option but to oppose the government in less legitimate ways. Eruptions of discontent surfaced periodically throughout the New Order, from the Malari of 1974 to the violent demonstrations that eventually removed Suharto from power in 1998.

The Suharto regime also perceived maintenance of national integration as a basic problem, and to preserve the country's unity the government employed a policy of militarization and centralization. In 1969 Suharto reorganized the armed forces into a system of regional commands in which Javanese dominated all top echelons of the army hierarchy, especially in the regions outside Java. Through the army's territorial structure, the regime was able to exert political pressure at every level of society, monitoring and largely controlling political and social developments. It expanded the concept of the army's dual function (*dwifungsi*), originally developed by former army commander A. H. Nasution in the 1950s, asserting the army's duty to participate as a "social-political force" throughout the society. The firmness of central military control was successful in preventing any serious challenge to Jakarta from any of the previously volatile regional commands.

At the same time, Jakarta utilized one of the major components of Indonesia's development policy, the transmigration program, to strengthen its control over potentially dissident areas, transferring people from the densely populated provinces of Central and East Java to Sumatra, Kalimantan, and Sulawesi as well as East Timor and Irian Jaya (Papua). But this program also increased fears of Javanese colonization in these areas, and the ecological damage inflicted by many of these settlements strengthened opposition to the policy and led to international criticism. In the final years of the Suharto regime, the policy was reduced drastically.

These measures were insufficient to prevent, and indeed may have encouraged, strong disaffection in three major regions: East Timor, Papua (Irian Jaya), and Aceh. Indonesia's invasion of East Timor at the end of 1975 was never accepted by the people of that territory and led to a long, drawn-out, bloody, and brutal war in which perhaps a third of East Timor's population died. Similarly in Papua, after the Dutch finally relinquished control via the United Nations, Jakarta had to wage a "secret war" against stubborn resistance from a number of Papuan groups, the largest being the Organization for a Free Papua (OPM), which were increasingly supported by local dissatisfaction at the exploitation of their region's resources and the brutal repression that accompanied this. In Aceh, too, local outrage at Jakarta's exploitation of the region's oil and gas resources and the brutal policies used to enforce this succeeded in turning what began as a weak, locally based Free Aceh Movement (Gerakan Aceh Merdeka, GAM) into a potent force enjoying considerable popular support throughout the province.

Between Suharto's accession to power in 1966 and the early 1990s, Indonesia experienced rapid economic development that contributed to a rising standard of living for its population. Between 1965 and 1996, its economy grew at an annual rate of about 7 percent, a growth underpinned in large part by foreign investment. This economic growth was accompanied by a decline in the incidence of absolute poverty and by marked improvement in both education and health care. During these years there was a striking shift from agriculture to industry, in large part based on the processing of petroleum and natural gas. By 1993 the World Bank characterized Indonesia as a "high-performing Asian economy." But its development during these years had been built in large part on loans negotiated at the beginning of the Suharto era, and by the late 1980s Indonesia had the largest foreign debt in Southeast Asia, with the burden of servicing this debt accounting for 37 percent of all government expenditures. In Suharto's final years, moreover, his economic achievements were undermined by the widespread corruption that increasingly permeated all parts of his government. Together with the economy's growing ties to global capital markets, this corruption rendered it vulnerable in the aftermath of the collapse of the Thai currency and the onset of the Asian financial crisis in 1997.

This financial crisis, along with the perception that the Suharto regime was riddled with corruption and the perception of an alternative as Megawati Sukarnoputri emerged at the head of the revitalized PDI, all contributed to a growing crisis that engulfed the regime in early 1998 and forced Suharto's resignation in May of that year. His unexpected and rapid capitulation to the forces confronting him opened the way for Vice President B. J. Habibie's accession to the presidency.

THE *REFORMASI* ERA

The relatively smooth transfer of power in May 1998 left almost all of the New Order structure in place, impeding efforts to implement the *reformasi* that had been the battle cry of the forces opposing Suharto. Although viewed as weak and mercurial, B. J. Habibie instituted policies that had a significant effect on Indonesia's future course, most notably by initiating steps that ultimately enabled East Timor to gain its independence and by introducing a decentralization law dismantling the centralized structure that had characterized the Indonesian state since independence. Habibie also oversaw a remarkably successful and peaceful election process, the first fair election held since 1955. Megawati Sukarnoputri's Democratic Party of Struggle (Partai Demokrasi Indonesia—Perjuangan, PDI-P) emerged from the election with a plurality of the vote. Golkar and the PPP came in second and fourth, and longtime NU head Abdurrachman Wahid's new Rise of the People Party (Partai Kebangkitan Bangsa, PKB) took third place. Wahid's political maneuvering enabled him to succeed Habibie as president, but through his erratic behavior and apparent inability to confront the country's major problems, he squandered the opportunity offered him. He antagonized both parliament and the military and was ultimately impeached in July 2001, with Megawati voted in as his successor.

The government under both Wahid and Megawati continued to be plagued by the corruption that had characterized the Suharto regime, especially in its later years. Although the implementation of the decentralization law proceeded much more smoothly than had been anticipated, it did not stem the ethnic and religious violence that had broken out in many parts of the archipelago, especially Kalimantan, Maluku, and Sulawesi, in the wake of Suharto's resignation. In addition, the heavy-handedness of the Indonesian military response to the separatist movements in both Aceh and Papua exacerbated the disaffection in those two provinces. Under Megawati, the armed forces were given a much freer hand, particularly in Aceh, to crush the rebels by whatever means necessary. The all-out military operation against the rebels in Aceh further exacerbated opposition there to the central government, as the government's division of the province of Papua into three smaller provinces antagonized the disaffected population there.

These problems were rendered only more intractable by the terrorist movements that emerged in many parts of the world in the wake of the September 11, 2001, attacks on New York and Washington, DC. Pressure on the Indonesian government to take strong action against radical Islamic elements came not only from the United States but also from Indonesia's neighbors, Malaysia and Singapore. Finally, in response to a disastrous bombing attack in Bali in October 2002 that killed over 200 people, Megawati's government cracked down on suspected members of the shadowy organization, the Jemaah Islamiyah (JI, Islamic Community), which

Singapore and Kuala Lumpur accused of responsibility. Indonesian authorities arrested and tried a number of suspects in the Bali bombings and sentenced three of the alleged leaders to death and several to life imprisonment.

In the closing months of 2003 preparations accelerated for nationwide legislative and presidential elections scheduled for 2004. In December 2003, the Electoral Commission published the names of the 24 parties that had met the criteria for contesting these elections. The first elections were to be held on 5 April 2004 for the national parliament (Dewan Perwakilan Rakyat) and for regional parliaments (Dewan Perwakilan Rakyat Daerah, DPRD) at the provincial and district levels, as well as for the new Regional Representative Council (DPD) set up under the constitutional changes of 2002. These elections promised to be challenging for the voters who would be required to select both a party and individual candidates for most of the legislative bodies.

Parties that emerged from these elections with three percent of the seats or five percent of the votes could then nominate a candidate for the presidency. The leading presidential contenders were likely to be Megawati Sukarnoputri (nominated by the PDI-P), either Akbar Tanjung or Wiranto (from Golkar), Abdurrachman Wahid (PKB), Hamzah Haz (PPP), Amien Rais (PAN), and perhaps General Susilo Bambang Yudhoyono (Partai Demokrat, PD, or possibly PKB), Professor Yusril Mahendra (PBB), and even Suharto's daughter Siti Hardijanti (Tuti) Rukmana (Partai Karya Peduli Bangsa, PKPB [Concern for the Nation Party]) should their parties gain sufficient support to nominate a candidate. The presidential election was to be held on 5 July 2004, and if no single candidate emerged with more than 50 percent of the vote, the top two vote-getters would then compete in a run-off election to be held on 20 September. The process was scheduled to be completed before 20 October. Though in early 2004 Megawati Sukarnoputri was still the leading presidential candidate, her popularity had drastically declined over the previous two years and it was not inconceivable that one of the other contenders would provide a strong challenge should she fail to gain a majority in the first round.

As they approached the elections the Indonesian electorate evidenced little of the hope and excitement that characterized the first post-Suharto elections in 1999. Disillusionment at the extent of the corruption in the *Reformasi* period and cynicism at the ineffectiveness of the new political actors dominated the national and local scene, along with nostalgia in some quarters for the security and order of the Suharto era, a sentiment on which the Golkar party and some candidates from the New Order period hoped to capitalize.

At the same time, there was a slow but steady improvement in Indonesia's economic situation, as the rupiah strengthened and inflation was curbed. Foreign investment remained sluggish in the aftermath of the terrorist attacks, but the economic outlook for 2004 was relatively good with an anticipated growth rate of between 4 and 5 percent. In October 2003 the International Monetary Fund (IMF) praised the government's handling of the economy, approving a final loan in the program set up in the late 1990s to help Indonesia recover from the Asian financial crisis. The Indonesian government intended to end the loan program at the end of 2003, thus freeing itself from IMF conditions that it felt were not in tune with Indonesia's social and economic needs.

The Dictionary

– A –

ABANGAN (from Javanese *abang,* red)**.** Term popularized by American anthropologist Clifford Geertz to describe Javanese Muslims in East Java whose religion, sometimes called *kejawen* (Javanism) or ***kebatinan,*** encompasses many non-Islamic elements, especially mysticism and respect for local spirits. Followers of *kejawen* insist that their religious commitment is different from, not less than, that of orthodox ***santri*** Muslims. *See also ALIRAN*; ISLAM. [1239, 1351]

ABDURRACHMAN WAHID (1940–)**.** Born in Jombang, East Java, and grandson of the founder of **Nahdlatul Ulama (NU)** Kyai Hasyim Asyari, Wahid studied in Cairo and Baghdad and then taught at the Hasyim Asyari University in Jombang. He was elected chairman of the NU in 1984 and withdrew it from formal politics when the **Suharto** government decreed that all political parties and organizations had to acknowledge the **Pancasila** as their *azas tunggal* (sole foundation). Under his chairmanship, NU was the first Islamic mass organization to accept this decree. His closeness to Suharto at this time led to a strong challenge being mounted against him at the NU's 1989 national congress, where the president came to his support, though this alliance between them was short-lived.

Known by the affectionate nickname of Gus Dur, Wahid gained enormous stature during the 1990s not only among his NU followers but also throughout the society, where he played an active role despite severe physical weaknesses that left him nearly blind and despite infirmity due to diabetes and a series of strokes. As an early leader of the prodemocracy movement, he preached tolerance of other religions and was a founding member of the Forum Demokrasi in 1991 and an opponent of the religious intellectuals' organization **Ikatan Cendekiawan Muslim Indonesia (ICMI)**, which he accused of being a tool of the Suharto administration. The president's supporters then led a campaign against him in the Muslim community, and he moved closer to the **Partai Demokrasi Indonesia (PDI)**, particularly to **Megawati Sukarnoputri**, with whom he formed an ad hoc alliance in the mid-1990s. During the closing months of Suharto's rule, he played a controversial role, again meeting with Suharto and campaigning with the president's daughter Siti Hardijanti Rukmana (Tutut) in behalf of **Golkar** in areas previously loyal to the **Partai Persatuan Pembangunan (PPP)**. He played no direct part in Suharto's ouster. During the subsequent opening of the political process, he founded the **Partai Kebangkitan Bangsa (PKB)** and became its head. Although his party only came in third in the 1999 **elections** (with 12.7 percent of the vote), he was able to maneuver Megawati (whose **PDI-Perjuangan [PDI-P]** came in first) out of the presidency, garnering sufficient support in **parliament** to become Indonesia's president in October of that year. He arranged for Megawati to be elected as his **vice president**.

Wahid's stormy tenure lasted less than two years, and after a long struggle to prevent his impeachment by parliament, he was replaced by Megawati Sukarnoputri. He had proved himself to be an erratic and autocratic administrator, never coming to grips with the enormous economic and political problems his country faced. Despite the minority position of his party, he treated parliament with contempt and alienated his longtime ally and vice president, Megawati. He did not build sufficiently on his natural strength among the Muslim community in confronting the secessionist threat in **Aceh** or easing the interreligious tensions in eastern Indonesia, passing over responsibility for the eastern provinces to Megawati. Instead he spent much of his time in travel abroad, ostensibly to raise urgently needed aid. Although not himself suspected of corruption, he tolerated corrupt practices amongst his closest associates, losing the moral high ground he had occupied when he first assumed office.

When he realized that his power was crumbling, Wahid resorted to arbitrary measures, firing his police chief and openly confronting the army, driving it into a closer alliance with Megawati. When his impeachment seemed imminent, he declared a state of emergency and ordered security forces to shut down the legislature. The **army** refused to obey the order and sent in reinforcements to protect parliament. The assembly voted unanimously to remove Wahid as president, and Megawati was immediately sworn in as his replacement on 23 July 2001.

After his ouster, Wahid remained as advisory chairman of the PKB and in 2003 dismissed two of the party's leaders because of their support two years previously for his impeachment, a dismissal that was upheld by the Jakarta High Court. [0771, 0760, 1029]

ACÇÃO NACIONAL POPULÁR (ANP, National Popular Action). Founded by António Salazar in 1930 as the União Naçional, the ANP was the sole legal political party in Portugal and its overseas provinces, including **East Timor**. It was abolished in 1974 after the armed forces coup in Portugal. Many of its former members in East Timor later joined the conservative **União Democrática Timorense**. [0806]

ACEH. Muslim state in the northernmost part of **Sumatra**, founded in the 15th century by rulers of the state of Lamuri after their expulsion by **Pedir**. Sultan Ali Mughayat Syah (r. 1514–1530) was able to draw many Muslim traders to his port of Banda Aceh (Kuta Raja) after the fall of **Melaka** to the Portuguese in 1511, transforming it into a major emporium for **trade** in **pepper** and Indian cloth. With European weapons purchased from the profits of this trade, he conquered much of northern Sumatra, including **Pasai** and Pedir. Under Sultans Alauddin Riayat Syah al-Kahar (r. 1537–1571) and **Iskandar Muda** (r. 1607–1636), Aceh fought a protracted war with the Portuguese and with the sultanate of Riau-Johor (*see* **RIAU**). Sultan Alauddin sought with partial success to concentrate the pepper trade in Kuta Raja and turned his court into a major regional center of Islamic law and learning. He was patron to the writers **Hamzah Fansuri** and Syamsuddin of Pasai. Iskandar Muda used revenue from taxation and his own personal trade to build a strong centralized state that was able to subdue the Acehnese commercial nobility (*orang kaya*) as well as the feudal rulers of the interior (*uleëbalang*). He pushed Acehnese rule southward along both coasts of Sumatra as far as **Padang** and **Nias** in the west and **Aru** in the east, as well as dominated Pahang, Kedah, and Perak on the **Malay Peninsula**. He launched major but unsuccessful attacks on Riau-Johor in 1613 and 1623 and on Melaka in 1614 and 1629, losing most of his navy in the latter campaign.

After the fall of Melaka to the Dutch and the shift of trading activity to **Batavia** and the Sunda Strait, Aceh was ruled by a succession of four queens, beginning with Taj al-Alam (r. 1641–1675) in coalition with the *orang kaya,* but state power declined under Dutch military pressure and the rise of *uleëbalang* power based on the growing rice trade. At the same time **Islam** became more and more firmly established, leading to the rise of powerful Islamic scholars, or ***ulama,*** whose influence ended the tradition of female rule. The **Anglo-Dutch Treaty** of 1824 guaranteed Aceh's independence, but in 1871 the British authorized the Dutch to invade to avoid possible French annexation. The Dutch annexed Aceh in 1874, but the ferocious Aceh War lasted from 1873 to 1903 and the Dutch won only because of the advice of **Snouck Hurgronje** that they should support the *uleëbalang* against the sultanate and because of their vigorous military action led by **Joannes Benedictus van Heutsz**. According to official estimates, 100,000 Acehnese and 12,000 Dutch were killed in the operations. Guerrilla warfare, led mainly by *ulama,* continued until 1914, by which time the Dutch had been able to crush the opposition and install an administration headed by the *uleëbalang.*

A reformist religious revival under the *ulama* began in the late 1920s and culminated in formation of the Persatuan Ulama Seluruh Aceh (PUSA, All-Aceh Union of Ulama) in 1939 headed by the most prominent of the religious leaders, **Muhammad Daud Beureu'eh** from Pidië (Pedir). Under their occupation, the Japanese used PUSA leaders for propaganda purposes but maintained the Dutch administrative system with the *uleëbalang* carrying out such tasks as collecting the rice crop and organizing forced labor.

In 1945, after the Japanese surrender, the *ulama* declared for the Indonesian Republic and launched a social revolution in which most *uleëbalang* were killed or deposed. Aceh became one of the most loyal Republican regions, being its most staunch financial supporter. Except for the island of Pulo Weh (Sabang), the Dutch made no effort to retake Aceh during the **Revolution**. After his return to Yogyakarta in July 1949, **Sukarno** appointed **Sjafruddin Prawiranegara** as deputy prime minister, with power to decree government regulations for Sumatra, and Sjafruddin established Aceh as a separate **province**. In 1950, however, this decree was rescinded and Aceh became part of the province of North Sumatra. When the government then tried to deprive PUSA of its control over the civil administration, army, and economy and to erode Aceh's effective autonomy, a revolt broke out in September 1953. This was led by Daud Beureu'eh and was affiliated with the more general **Darul Islam** uprising. The designation of Aceh as a province in 1957 and as a *daerah istimewa* (special territory) with greater autonomy in religious and educational matters in 1959 largely ended the revolt.

Under the **Suharto** regime, many of the attributes of autonomy disappeared as the government canceled the region's control over religion, education, and law. Hopes for maintaining any degree of autonomy disappeared after massive reserves of natural **gas** were discovered in 1971 in Lhokseumawe in northern Aceh, and by 1977 a liquefied natural gas

(LNG) refinery had commenced production. These discoveries did not benefit the local people. By the end of the 1980s, the province was contributing 30 percent of Indonesia's **oil** and gas exports, but nearly all of the profits and taxes were channeled directly to the central government. Establishment of an industrial zone around Lhokseumawe displaced much of the local population and removed their source of livelihood.

As early as 1976, anti-Jakarta feeling in the region had sparked a new rebel movement known as the Gerakan Aceh Merdeka (GAM, Free Aceh Movement), which called for the creation of an independent state of "Aceh-Sumatra." Headed by Hasan di Tiro, who had been born in Pidië but had mostly lived abroad since the early 1950s when he served in the Indonesian mission to the United Nations, the GAM at this time was weak, and Indonesian government forces were able fairly easily to suppress it and kill or exile most of its leaders. However, its remnants continued recruitment; and when by 1989 local resentment had grown at the central government's exploitation of Aceh and its people, GAM reemerged and mounted a far stronger challenge to central authority. The Indonesian military responded brutally, deploying about 12,000 troops in counterinsurgency operations in 1990 and killing an estimated 2,000 mostly civilian Acehnese by mid-1991 when the government appeared again to have crushed the movement.

The rebellion resumed in late 1998 after the government had begun to withdraw some of its forces in the wake of Suharto's resignation. In response, the military redeployed hundreds of troops to the area and began another major counterinsurgency campaign. This was accompanied, however, by the **Abdurrachman Wahid** government's resumption of negotiations with the GAM beginning in 2000. The following year (9 August 2001), Wahid's successor, **Megawati Sukarnoputri**, signed a law providing again for special autonomy for the Province of Nanggroe Aceh Darussalam. Under this law the province was granted special powers, including permission for its legal system to be based on Islamic law. Also under the new **decentralization** law, Aceh could begin to receive 70 percent of the net income from the vast ExxonMobil oil and gas fields near Lhokseumawe, though its share of proceeds from gas exploitation was less than had been negotiated by **Papua** regarding its fields. Despite these moves the level of violence continued high, with more than 1,700 people being killed in 2001 alone and widescale **human rights** abuses carried out by both sides.

In January 2002 a separate military command (KODAM), the Iskandar Muda command, was again established for Aceh. But on the 21st of that month, Indonesian troops killed GAM's military commander, Abdullah Syafei, who was one of two GAM leaders invited for peace talks scheduled to be held in Geneva the following week. It seemed that the government had chosen to emphasize a military solution when in July 2002 the military commander requested six more infantry battalions (a total of about 4,000 soldiers) in addition to the **army** and **police** forces of about 25,000 already in the territory.

Nevertheless, efforts continued toward a peaceful settlement and negotiations resumed in Geneva between representatives of the GAM and central government, who signed a peace agreement on 9 December 2002. This provided for regional autonomy, control over the province's natural resources, and elections for an Acehnese legislature, but it contained no provision for disarmament or demilitarization. By the time the accord was signed, it was estimated that 12,000 people had died in the conflict during the previous decade. The agreement provided only a temporary respite. On 24 April 2003 further talks between the two parties failed, leading to a breakdown of the truce. Megawati declared martial law in the province, and some 50,000 soldiers and police launched a major attack to crush the GAM rebels. *See also* TJIK DI TIRO; UMAR, TEUKU. For list of rulers of Aceh, *see* APPENDIX C. [0529, 0568, 0660, 0777, 0808, 0818, 0820, 0827, 0946, 1258, 1261]

"ACT OF FREE CHOICE." *See* OPERASI KHUSUS; PAPUA.

ADAT. Arabic term literally meaning "custom," as distinct from **law** laid down in the Qur'an and other texts. *Adat* has come to denote all indigenous customary law in Indonesia, as opposed to the codified civil and criminal law of the colonial and Republican governments, as well as, more narrowly, the body of customary law as recorded in the late 19th and early 20th century by Dutch scholars, notably **Cornelis van Vollenhoven**, **Snouck Hurgronje**, and G. A. Wilken and given the name *adatrecht* ("adat law"). The compilers identified 19 *adatrechtskringen* or *adat* law zones of similar legal tradition. This codification was undertaken to allow the partial application of "traditional" law to the indigenous peoples of the regions as part of a more general policy of indirect rule. *Adat* law, as codified, has tended to emphasize the collectivist aspects of traditional practice, in which crimes committed by an individual against another are seen as committed by and against the whole community. *See also* ISLAM; LAW; *ZELFBESTUREN*. [0479, 1075, 1082, 1083, 1084]

ADONARA. *See* SOLOR ARCHIPELAGO.

AFFANDI (1910–1990)**.** Painter with a vigorous style described as impressionist and reminiscent of van Gogh. He was a founder of Pelukis Rakyat (People's Painters) and a member of **Lembaga Kebudayaan Rakyat (Lekra)**, but later in life became less sympathetic to the notion that art should have a social purpose. In 1955 he was elected to the **Constituent Assembly** under **Partai Komunis Indonesia (PKI)** sponsorship but sat in the assembly's sessions as a nonparty member. *See also* CULTURE, DEBATE ON THE ROLE OF. [0159, 0202]

AFRICA, HISTORICAL LINKS WITH. Although Austronesians probably touched the east coast of Africa en route to **Madagascar** (*see* **MIGRATIONS**) and although that coast was raided by Southeast Asian pirates, perhaps Indonesian, in the 10th century, Indonesia has had little influence on the African continent, except perhaps in the field of **music**. A. M. Jones has argued that several features of African traditional music have an Indonesian origin. The principal **trade** route that took Indonesian cinnamon, **cloves**, and other spices to the Mediterranean in classical times probably ran via East Africa, and Africa was also the source of an important number of cultivated plants used in the archipelago, especially kapok and **oil palm**.

The Dutch settlements in South Africa were formally under the **Dutch East Indies Company (VOC)**, though independent of **Batavia** for most practical purposes, and an important "Malay" community exists in South Africa, the descendants of slaves and political exiles from the VOC's East Indies possessions. The first of these arrived in 1667, and there was a substantial import of slaves from 1715 to 1767, when the trade was banned by the **Raad van Indië**. Troops were recruited in Dutch settlements on the coast of Guinea in west Africa for service in the colonial army (**Koninklijk Nederlandsch Indisch Leger**, **KNIL**) until the loss of those colonies in 1872.

From December 1962 to April 1963 an Indonesian unit, the Pasukan Garuda, served in the Congo as part of the **United Nations** (UN) forces there. Some intellectual links existed between the liberation movements in Portugal's African colonies and **Fretilin** in **East Timor** (*see also* **EXILE**), and those former colonies, along with Portugal, led international resistance to Indonesia's annexation of the colony in 1976. [0165, 0527]

AGRARIAN LAW OF 1870. More correctly the Agrarian article of the Regeeringsreglement or **Constitution**, this marked a major change in colonial agrarian policy. Under the **Cultivation System**, villages had been the owners of **land** but acquired with ownership the obligation to provide land and **labor** for government purposes, while Europeans were largely prohibited from acquiring land. Under the 1870 law, Western companies were at last allowed long-term leases over land, though the ban on freehold sale of land to non-Indonesians was strengthened. The law provided that leases should be for no longer than 75 years on "unused" land and 21 years on village land, and that leases could not infringe traditional rights of indigenes. It also declared all "unclaimed" land to be government property, though it recognized indigenous usufruct rights on such lands. The law removed the right of nonresident noncitizens to lease land. Except for the provision on unclaimed land, it applied only to **Java** and **Madura**. *See also BESCHIKKINGSRECHT*; INDO-EUROPEANS; LIBERAL POLICY; RACE. [0484, 0638]

AGRICULTURAL INVOLUTION. Term coined by American anthropologist Clifford Geertz for the process, beginning under the **Cultivation System**, by which **land** tenure arrangements on **Java** allegedly became steadily more complex and intertwined with systems of credit, lease, and usufruct as population grew. It was allegedly able to emerge because the cultivation of **rice** permitted steadily greater labor inputs with only slightly diminished productivity per capita. A consequence of agricultural involution, in Geertz's view, was the absence of a clearly defined landlord class and a set of social obligations on both rich and poor, which hindered capital formation. This hampered the development of a vibrant entrepreneurial **economy** such as that of **Japan**. Presented originally as a hypothesis rather than as a fully elaborated theory, the idea of agricultural involution generated abundant research, much of which tended to disprove its conclusions. In particular, research has shown enormous regional variation and numerous examples of capital and class formation in rural Java. *See also BESCHIKKINGSRECHT*; CLASS ANALYSIS; *DESA*; SHARED POVERTY. [0328, 0349]

AGRICULTURE. Wet-**rice** cultivation (*sawah*) based on an intricate irrigation system has characterized the agricultural techniques of Indonesia's most populous areas, notably on **Java** and **Bali**. A dry agricultural method based on shifting cultivation (***ladang***) has been more prevalent in the upland regions of the **Outer Islands** of **Sumatra**, **Kalimantan**, and **Sulawesi** and is still common, especially in parts of Kalimantan. Under the **Dutch** in the late 18th and early 19th century, the colonial government sponsored a major expansion of wet-rice agriculture, expanding irrigation, clearing **land**, and beginning a program to breed improved varieties. At the same time, plantation agriculture came to the fore as the Dutch invested their capital in such crops as **sugar**, **tobacco**, **coffee**, **tea**, and later **rubber**, leading to the development of a dual economy (*see* **DUALISM**), wherein the plantations produced crops for export and indigenous farmers supported themselves with subsistence crops. At the same time Indonesian smallholders competed with the plantations, especially with such items as coffee that could be easily developed as a cash crop. Smallholder production in such areas as south Sumatra and Sulawesi competed with estate exports, both under the Dutch and in subsequent periods, especially at times when international prices were high. In the mid-1800s the expansion of the **cultivation system**, under which villagers had to devote one fifth of their land to crops for the government, brought huge profits to the Dutch, with the production and export of valuable tropical crops financing the administration of the colony and contributing to the Dutch coffers.

After independence, efforts to redistribute land under the 1960 Basic Law on Agriculture (Undang-Undang Pokok Agraria)—passed at the urging of the **Partai Komunis Indonesia (PKI)** and applying mainly to Java—aimed to assist smallholders who had lost or were in danger of losing their land because of indebtedness. (*See* **LAND REFORM**.) Although the law was never rescinded, there were few efforts to implement it.

From the mid-1960s the **green revolution** brought a rapid increase in agricultural production, particularly of rice, with *sawah* output rising by more than 250 percent between 1966 and 1991. In 1985 Indonesia became for a while self-sufficient in rice, before drawbacks in the system reversed some of these advances and the droughts of 1991 and 1997 forced the government again to begin importing rice. Under the **Suharto** regime, cash crop production did not increase at a similar rate. One notable exception was **oil palm**, and plantations cultivating this crop began to replace the forests in many parts of Sumatra and Kalimantan as Indonesia aimed to become the world's largest palm oil producer. For other cash crops, output growth has been slow and erratic, in large part dependent on the rise and fall of international prices for these products. During the closing decades of the 20th century, Indonesia's economy was transformed from one based mainly on agriculture to one based mainly on industry, with agricultural output shrinking from 56 to 17 percent of gross domestic product (GDP) between 1965 and 1995, while industrial output rose from 13 to 42 percent. [0318, 0319, 0330, 0340, 0348, 0730, 0761]

AGUNG, SULTAN (r. 1613–1646)**.** Ruler of **Mataram**, Agung came to the throne amid a sustained campaign by his father Seda ing Krapyak to defeat the port cities of Java's north coast, especially **Surabaya** and Tuban. Agung conquered **Sukadana** in **Kalimantan** in 1622 and **Madura** in 1624, and he finally starved Surabaya into submission in 1625. His campaigns devastated much of the countryside, causing severe food shortages and badly damaging Java's overseas **trade**. However, they established, for the first time since **Majapahit**, a single city (around Agung's court at Karta, near modern **Yogyakarta**) as the center of Javanese culture. In 1629 he attempted unsuccessfully to capture the Dutch fortress of **Batavia**, but was able to conquer most of East **Java** in a series of campaigns from 1635 to 1640, in honor of which he took the Islamic title sultan in 1641. [0560]

AIDS. Since the human immunodeficiency virus (HIV) was first identified in Indonesia in 1985, AIDS has spread rapidly in Indonesian society. By 2001 an estimated 80,000 to 120,000 Indonesians were living with HIV, and according to the Indonesian government cumulative HIV/AIDS cases jumped 60 percent from 2000 to 2001, with 635 AIDS cases and 1,678 HIV infections reported from January to September 2001. An estimated 3,856 AIDS deaths had occurred through 2000, and a further 274 AIDS deaths were reported between January and September 2001. The first infections were probably brought by Western tourists to **Bali**, but at least since the early 1990s the main conduits of infection have been sailors and fishermen from Thailand and India, and long-distance truck and bus drivers in Indonesia itself. Ignorance of the cause of infection, religious objection to the use of condoms, widespread extramarital sex by men, and routine reuse of needles in medical procedures have all contributed to the spread of the disease. In 1987 the government launched a National AIDS Control Commission (NACC) and in 1994 created a ministerial AIDS Prevention and Control Commission. The campaign to limit the spread of AIDS has concentrated on the "family values" of fidelity and chastity rather than on "safe sex." *See also* HEALTH; PROSTITUTION; SEX. [1205, 1206]

AIR FORCE (Angkatan Udara Republik Indonesia, AURI)**.** Founded in 1945 with a few former Japanese trainer aircraft, the air force contributed to the revolution mainly by using its planes to import war materials. Its operations were plagued by crashes, in one of which its first commander, Halim Perdanakusuma, was killed. Air Commodore Suryadi Suryadarma

(1912–1975) became chief of staff in 1946. Especially dependent on modern technology, the air force received extensive supplies from the **Soviet Union** in the 1960s and was the most left wing of the armed forces, especially from January 1962 under Air Vice-Marshal Omar Dhani (b. 1924). Some of the events of the **Gestapu** coup took place at Halim Air Force Base; Dhani was jailed, and the force itself was heavily purged. Under the **New Order**, the separate identity of the air force was gradually submerged in that of the **Armed Forces**. [0714, 0727]

AIRCRAFT INDUSTRY. Although the Netherlands airline KLM was established in 1919 partly to provide air links with the Indies, regular services did not begin until the founding of the Koninklijk Nederlandsch-Indische Luchtvaartmaatschappij (KNILM) in 1927, with a subsidy from the colonial government. Since 1950, international air services have been provided by **Garuda**. In 1976 **B. J. Habibie**, with **Suharto**'s backing, established an indigenous aircraft industry, the Industri Pesawat Terbang Nurtanio (IPTN, Nurtanio [later Nusantara] Aircraft Industry) in **Bandung**, which by the early 1980s was assembling helicopters and other light aircraft under license from Western corporations. IPTN reached a contract with Boeing Corporation in 1982, under which it became a qualified supplier of aircraft components for Boeing and General Dynamics. The first Indonesian air show was held in 1986, and until 1988 Nusantara enjoyed a monopoly of light aircraft sales to Indonesia's 55 domestic airlines. In the mid-1980s IPTN entered into a joint venture with Spain's Construcciones Aeronauticas SA (CASA) to manufacture a twin-turboprop commuter transport plane, the CN-235, several of which were sold to overseas airlines. In 1989 it began a project to develop a domestically produced commuter aircraft, the 64–68-seat N250, which was unveiled at the end of 1994. In early 1998 during the **financial crisis**, the International Monetary Fund (IMF) barred future subsidies for aircraft manufacturing at a time when the N250 still lacked certification. Thereafter the debt-ridden IPTN concentrated on marketing its turboprop CN-235 and acting as a subcontractor for aircraft parts, engineering designs, and computer technology. [0414]

AIRLANGGA (Erlangga; 991–1046)**.** Of Javanese and Balinese royal descent, Airlangga was at the court of the king of **Java** in 1006 to be married to the king's daughter, Dharmawangsa, when the court was abruptly attacked by forces from **Srivijaya**. Alone of the royal family, Airlangga escaped and established his rule over an attenuated kingdom in East Java and **Bali**. After the fall of Srivijaya in 1024–1025, he expanded his power on Java, creating a network of alliances and vassalages centered on the Brantas river valley. Although regional chiefs (***bupati***) remained powerful, Airlangga's kingdom was more centralized than any before that time. He built irrigation works in the Brantas delta, which controlled flooding and enabled a major expansion in the cultivation of **rice**, which was exported through the new deepened harbor of **Surabaya** to other parts of the archipelago. He is also credited with increasing the Javanese content of court culture and with diminishing its Indian elements. In about 1045, according to legend, Airlangga abdicated to become an ascetic after having divided his kingdom between his two sons to form the kingdoms of **Kediri** and **Janggala**. [0509, 0512, 0516, 0520]

AKSI SEPIHAK (direct action)**.** *See* LAND REFORM.

ALANG-ALANG (*Imperata cylindrica* Poaceae)**.** A hardy grass that is an early colonizer in cleared rainforest areas, its matted root system makes it difficult to eradicate. Its spread is traditionally one of the factors prompting shifting cultivators to move. It is intolerant of shade, and so gradually gives way to tree species, but where repeated fires hamper the growth of broad-leafed plants, it may form extensive fields resistant to forest succession, leading to the so-called Green Desert, something of a misnomer, since many communities do return *alang-alang* fields to cultivation. Shifting cultivators are commonly blamed for the spread of the grass, but it seems that some of the largest areas of infestation were caused by extensive cultivation of **pepper** and gambier in the 19th century. [1148]

ALGEMENE RECHERCHE. *See* POLITIEK INLICHTINGEN DIENST.

ALGEMENE STUDIECLUB (General Study Club)**.** The club was founded in November 1925 on the model of study clubs organized by **Dr. Sutomo** to bring together young Indonesian intellectuals to discuss politics and philosophy. The Algemene Studieclub in **Bandung** included **Sukarno** and was openly political. After the banning of the **Partai Komunis Indonesia (PKI)** in 1927, the club became the core around which the **Partai Nasional Indonesia (PNI)** was formed. *See also* NATIONALISM. [0888]

ALI-BABA FIRMS. They had their roots in the cooperation between **Chinese** smugglers and Indonesian officials during the **Japanese occupa-**

tion and particularly during the revolutionary war, when the Republic sanctioned the trading of local products in exchange for hard cash or military supplies, using Chinese businessmen. In the 1950s establishment of such firms was an effort to circumvent legislation encouraging ***pribumi*** business at the expense of the Chinese. In practice firms were still run by a Chinese ("Baba"), with an Indonesian ("Ali") as nominal head, sometimes providing political protection. *See also CUKONG*; INDONESIANIZATION. [1045, 1068]

ALI SASTROAMIJOYO (1903–1975)**.** Nationalist politician, prominent in the **Perhimpunan Indonesia** in Holland, and after independence leader of the left wing of the **Partai Nasional Indonesia (PNI)**. As prime minister from July 1953 to July 1955, he sponsored the **Asia-Africa Conference** and abrogated the Netherlands Indonesian Union. His cabinet fell after the **army** refused to accept his nominee for chief of staff. Ali formed a second cabinet in March 1956, which was also dogged by scandals and regional rebellions. Its resignation on 14 March 1957 marked the end of parliamentary democracy. He remained party leader during **Guided Democracy**, but was purged in 1966. [0695, 0706, 0841]

ALIRAN (lit., "stream" or "current")**.** In Indonesian usage this term is applied to any group characterized by adherence to similar ideas or ideals, for example, *aliran sosialis.* In Western social science, following the work of American anthropologist Clifford Geertz, it denotes the two major cultural-religious traditions in Muslim Javanese society: the syncretist ***abangan*** and the orthodox ***santri***. A third *aliran* identified by Geertz, the ***priyayi,*** is now commonly regarded as a class category, referring to the aristocratic aspect of the *abangan aliran* (and sometimes extended to part of the *santri* elite). *Aliran* structure has been said to resemble the *verzuiling* ("pillarization") of Dutch society, with most people belonging in the 1950s and 1960s to *aliran*-specific (rather than national, regional, or class-based) political, social, and other organizations. Organizational life in **Java**, however, has always been far more fragmented than this would imply. The 1955 **election** results, for instance, suggested the existence of at least four *aliran* at that time. In many regions the classification is subethnic, *santri* coming from the ***pasisir*** and *abangan* from the interior of Java. The classification is made more problematic by the fact that some *santri* Muslims, especially of the **Nahdlatul Ulama**, draw a good deal of their thought from non-Islamic Javanese traditions. *See* ISLAM; *KEBATINAN*. [0700, 0703, 1239, 1343]

ALISYAHBANA, SUTAN TAKDIR (1908–1994)**.** Novelist and philosopher, born in North **Sumatra**. He studied **law** in **Batavia** and worked as editor for the **Balai Pustaka** before founding the journal *Poedjangga Baru* with Armijn Pané and Amir Hamzah. He played a major role in developing the **Indonesian language** as a tool for sophisticated intellectual and technical usage, especially through his editing of the journal *Pembina Bahasa Indonesia.* [0636, 0890]

ALOR. Island and archipelago in **Nusatenggara**. The mainly animist population still produces cast bronze drums whose cultural origin is uncertain. *See also GAMELAN.* [1219]

AMANGKURAT I (r. 1646–1677)**.** Son and successor to Sultan **Agung**, he sought to consolidate his father's empire by gathering all authority in the land to himself, but in doing so he alienated both court officials and regional lords. In 1647 he lost control of the **Balambangan** region; most of **Mataram**'s former vassals in **Sumatra** and **Kalimantan** also fell away. He forbade his subjects from leaving **Java** and in 1652 banned the export of **rice** and timber, though his aim seems to have been to gain control of the **trade**, especially with the **Dutch East Indies Company (VOC)**, for himself. His authoritarian rule precipitated the revolt of the Madurese prince **Trunojoyo** in 1671, in the course of which Amangkurat was driven from his capital in 1677 to die in exile. [0484, 0560]

AMBON (Amboina)**.** Island and city in **Maluku** (formerly the Moluccas), originally a part of the sparsely populated hinterland of **Ternate** and **Tidore**. The Portuguese established a fort in 1574, but in 1605 the **Dutch East Indies Company (VOC)** seized the island, made it the center of their operations in the east of the archipelago under **Cornelis de Houtman**, and planted extensive **clove** orchards. For most of the 17th century, the Dutch struggled to exclude other foreigners (*see* **"AMBOYNA MASSACRE"; ENGLISH EAST INDIA COMPANY**) and to establish a monopoly on the spice **trade** (*see* **HONGI RAIDS**). British forces seized the island during the Napoleonic Wars (1796–1802, 1810–1817), and the restoration of Dutch rule was followed by a revolt on the nearby island of Saparua in 1817, led by Thomas Matulesia (1783–1817), also known as Pattimura.

In the latter part of the colonial period, the Ambonese gained a reputation for strong loyalty to Dutch rule. This was partly because service in the colonial army or **Koninklijk Nederlandsch Indisch Leger (KNIL)** was one of the few employment opportunities available to Ambonese, and they were posted widely through the archipelago (though the military category "Ambonezen" also included many from the **Minahasa** and **Timor**). Christian Ambonese had European legal status (*see* **LAW**; **RACE**), though seldom enjoyed practical legal equality. In 1930, Protestant Christians formed around 67 percent of the Ambon population, with the balance Muslims.

Ambon was the scene of heavy fighting between Japanese and Australian troops in 1942, and it was bombed by the Allies in 1945. It became part of the **Negara Indonesia Timur (NIT)** in 1946, and after the transfer of sovereignty in 1949 became a base of the separatist **Republik Maluku Selatan (RMS)**.

In the years after independence, there was an influx of Muslim migrants, mostly from **Sulawesi**. The Buginese in particular came to dominate Ambon's commercial life, eroding the power of the Christians. An Ambonese Muslim became governor of the island in the early 1990s, and Christian resentment of Muslims increased with the downturn in the **economy** and the collapse of clove prices. In October 1998, there was a rumor that the governor intended to replace all top civil servants with Muslims. Interreligious violence broke out early the following year and continued through 1999, with Jakarta apparently powerless to end it. It was exacerbated by an influx of Muslim volunteers from **Java**, particularly members of the **Pemuda Pancasila** and **Laskar Jihad**. By the end of the year, Muslims controlled approximately 40 percent of Ambon city and Protestants 60 percent, and the economy was in ruins.

In early 2000 the violence spread to the islands of **Banda**, **Buru**, **Ternate**, and **Halmahera**. By June more than 2,500 people had been killed in Ambon, and tens of thousands of Bugis and other Sulawesi migrants had fled. Altogether, between January 1999 and mid-2001 more than 6,000 people died in the Moluccan Islands before the violence petered out.

In March 2002 the government flew Christian and Muslim representatatives to Sulawesi to sign the Malino II Agreement, which brought a formal end to hostilities on Ambon and called for the disarming of **militia** groups and an investigation into the origins of the violence. Some of the 150,000 refugees began to return, but there was a further outbreak of violence on 28 April when masked gunmen slaughtered 14 Christian villagers. About 400 Laskar Jihad members remained on Ambon until October, when they returned to Java after the **Bali** bombing and announced that their organization had been disbanded. [0025, 0491, 0559, 0781, 0784, 0967]

"AMBOYNA MASSACRE." In 1623 **Dutch** authorities on **Ambon** executed 10 English merchants and 10 Javanese alleged accomplices on charges of conspiring to seize the local Dutch fort. Dutch writers have cited the affair as an example of English perfidy, with British writers complaining in turn that the governor of Ambon had reneged on his promise to protect the merchants. The massacres hastened the withdrawal of British interests from the archipelago to India. *See also* ENGLISH EAST INDIA COMPANY. [0491]

AMERICAS, HISTORICAL LINKS WITH THE. Tropical America was a major source of plants cultivated in the Indonesian archipelago from the 17th century. These included chili, **cinchona**, **pepper**, **rubber**, sisal, soursop, vanilla, pawpaw, and pineapple. The disease **syphilis** probably also derives from the Americas.

AMIEN RAIS. *See* RAIS, AMIEN.

AMIR SJARIFUDDIN (1907–1948)**.** Nationalist politician. Born in Medan, he graduated from the faculty of **law** in **Batavia** in 1933. He was deeply involved in the nationalist movement and helped to establish the **Gerakan Rakyat Indonesia (Gerindo)** in 1937, arguing strongly that Japanese fascism was an even greater danger to Indonesia than Dutch colonialism. When **Japan** attacked, he accepted *f*25,000 from the Dutch to set up an underground resistance against the Japanese. As a result of his underground activities, he was arrested by the Japanese in January 1943 and condemned to death, but his life was spared through the intercession of **Sukarno**. After independence, he cofounded the **Partai Sosialis (PS)** with **Sutan Sjahrir**, becoming deputy prime minister and defense minister in the Sjahrir cabinets. He cooperated closely with **A. H. Nasution** and with the **Pemuda Sosialis Indonesia (Pesindo)** and was one of the architects of the Indonesian conventional **army**.

Amir became prime minister on 3 July 1947 and headed the Indonesian delegation in negotiations leading to the controversial **Renville Agreements** of January 1948. Discredited by his role in these agreements, he was forced to resign and joined the radical opposition to the Sukarno/**Mohammad Hatta** government, forming a **Front Demokrasi Rakyat (FDR)** in February of that year. When **Partai Komunis Indonesia (PKI)** leader **Musso** returned from Moscow in August 1948, Amir allied his FDR with the Communist Party, announcing that he had been a communist since before the war (a claim then widely doubted). In September he joined the unsuccessful **Madiun** uprising against the Sukarno/Hatta government and was captured in late October. He was summarily shot by government troops at the start of the second Dutch **"Police Action"** on 19/20 December 1948. [0478, 0674, 0858, 0865, 1117]

AMUK. A temporary derangement that leads an individual (normally male) to wild and directionless violence, usually against other people. It is not clear whether *amuk* has any strictly clinical causes; most observers attribute it to a reaction against the extreme suppression of personal feelings allegedly demanded in many Indonesian societies, but it may have developed, like the Viking *berserk,* as a technique for inspiring terror in enemies during battle and could apparently be encouraged by the use of **cannabis** or **opium**. *See also LATAH*; WARFARE.

ANAK BUAH. Literally, "fruit child." Protégé, client. *See BAPAK.*

ANGKATAN BERSENJATA REPUBLIK INDONESIA (ABRI)**.** *See* ARMED FORCES OF THE REPUBLIC OF INDONESIA.

ANGKATAN '45; ANGKATAN '66. *See* GENERATIONS.

ANGLO-DUTCH TREATY. Signed on 17 March 1824, it revised British and **Dutch** colonial holdings in western Indonesia. The British, ceding **Bengkulu** to the Dutch and receiving **Melaka** in exchange, confined themselves to and were given exclusive rights on the **Malay Peninsula**, where they immediately established the port of **Singapore**. The Dutch were given a free hand on **Sumatra** but agreed to guarantee the independence of **Aceh**. The treaty permanently split the territories of the sultanate of **Riau-**Johor. It explicitly permitted the British to retain their interests in northern Borneo and to **trade** in areas not annexed by the Dutch. *See also* BELITUNG; NETHERLANDS INDIES, EXPANSION OF; RAFFLES, THOMAS STAMFORD. [0583]

ANSOR (from Arabic *al-ansar,* followers of the Prophet)**.** Youth organization founded in 1934 and affiliated with the **Nahdlatul Ulama (NU)**, known for its participation in massacres of communists, especially in East Java, in 1965–1966. *See also* MASSACRES OF 1965–1966.

ANTARA ("between")**.** Founded on 17 December 1937 by R. M. Sumanang and A. M. Sipatuhar, it was developed by **Adam Malik** and others as a private, nationalist **news agency**. During the **Japanese occupation**, it was merged with the Japanese agency Domei but became Indonesia's official news agency in 1945. Several agencies were merged with Antara in 1963 to form the Lembaga Kantor Berita Nasional (LKBN, National News Agency Institute), but the name Antara is retained for daily use. [1304]

ANTASARI. *See* BANJARMASIN.

ARAB WORLD, RELATIONS WITH. Trade in spices linked Indonesia and the Arab world even before the emergence of **Islam**, but it is the ***haj***, or pilgrimage to Mecca, and the study of Islam in general that have taken the largest number of Indonesians to the Middle East. **Arabs** have always been prominent in the archipelago as traders and mercenaries. Some 10,000 Indonesians (so-called *mukim*) lived semipermanently in Arabia in the late 19th century. From the early 20th century, many Indonesians studied at Al-Azhar University in Cairo.

In November 1946 the Arab League recommended recognition of the Indonesian Republic, and Egypt and Syria in June 1947 were the first states to officially recognize it. In the 1950s, Indonesia joined Arab and other states in Asia and Africa to form the Non-Aligned Movement (*see* **ASIA-AFRICA CONFERENCE**). Muslim organizations, especially the modernist Dewan Dakwah Islamiyah Indonesia (DDII, Indonesian Islamic Preaching Council) founded in 1967 by former **Masjumi** leaders, received donations from such countries as Saudi Arabia, Kuwait, and Egypt for social and educational programs. During the 1970s and 1980s they established hundreds of schools and mosques, and increased their contacts with the Arab world, sending hundreds of students to centers of learning in the Middle East. Also, since 1987 the number of Indonesians working in the Middle East has increased substantially. Indonesia has no diplomatic relations with Israel but recognized the state of Palestine only in November 1988. Jemaah Islamiyah, the group accused of complicity in terrorist activities, including the **Bali** bombing, reportedly receives financial support and military training from Al Qaeda forces in the Middle East and has sent volunteers to train with them in Afghanistan. *See also* TURKEY, HISTORICAL LINKS WITH. [0084, 0543, 0774, 1031, 1039, 1363]

ARABS. Coming especially from Hadramawt, Arabs settled in Indonesia in small impermanent trading communities from perhaps the fifth century, and Arab adventurers founded the kingdom of **Pontianak**; other dynasties had Arab ancestry. As with the **Chinese**, Arab communities absorbed much local culture, some disappearing altogether and others forming distinctive ***peranakan*** communities. The greatest immigration took place in the second half of the 19th century, when large communities settled especially on the north coast of **Java**. Sharing **Islam** with most Indonesians, the Arabs were often better able than the Chinese to be accepted as part of the nationalist movement. In 1934 A. R. A. Baswedan founded the Persatuan Arab Indonesia (PAI, Indonesian Arab Association) in **Semarang** to encourage the allegiance of *peranakan* Arabs to Indonesia. The PAI joined the **Gabungan Politik Indonesia (GAPI)** in 1939–1940. An Indo-Arabische Beweging (Indo-Arab Movement) founded in 1939, on the other hand, argued for continued separate status. After independence Arabs were generally accepted as Indonesians, and in the 1990s several Indonesians of Hadrami descent were cabinet ministers, notably long-serving foreign minister Ali Alatas.

The modernist Al Irsyad organization, established in 1913 by Arab Indonesians, is among the most active proponents of the introduction of Islamic law and establishment of an **Islamic state**. It runs a network of schools and colleges, including a school in Solo founded and headed by Abu Bakar Ba'asyir as well as about 140 missions and several hospitals. Its chief, Faisal Buasir, is also a prominent leader in the **Partai Persatuan Pembangunan (PPP)**. After the unification of Yemen in 1990, growing numbers of Indonesian young people traveled there each year to study at religious schools. The Arab community came under suspicion in the wake of the terrorist attacks in New York (2001) and **Bali** (2002) as several of the prominent Islamic militants in Indonesia (including Abu Bakar Ba'asyir and **Laskar Jihad** head Ja'afar Umar Thalib) are of Arab descent. [0480, 1041, 1057, 1069]

ARCHEOLOGY. The earliest serious archeological work in the archipelago was conducted by the **Bataviaasch Genootschap van Kunsten en Wetenschappen**, while in the early 19th century **T. S. Raffles** did some work on the antiquities of **Java**, such as the excavation and partial reconstruction of **Borobudur**. Extensive archeological work, however, did not begin until the foundation of the Commissie in Nederlandsch-Indië voor Oudheidkundig Onderzoek op Java en Madoera (Netherlands Indies Commission for Investigation of Antiquities on Java and **Madura**) in 1901 under J. L. A. Brandes. Headed successively by N. J. Krom (1910–1916), F. D. K. Bosch (1916–1936), and W. F. Stutterheim (1936–1942), and becoming the Oudheidkundige Dienst (Archeological Service) in 1913, it was active in investigating and protecting the archipelago's antiquities, though it paid greatest attention to the Hindu-Buddhist relics of Java. The postindependence Dinas Purbakala dan Peninggalan Nasional (National Archeological and Remains Service, now Pusat Penelitian Arkeologi Nasional, National Center for Archeological Research) under H. R. van Heekeren (to 1956) and then Sukmono continued this work while giving greater attention to the archeology and prehistory of the other islands. [0112–0124, 0507]

ARCHIPELAGIC CONCEPT (*Wawasan Nusantara*)**.** On independence, Indonesia inherited a three-mile territorial waters limit around each of its (then) 13,677 islands. Largely for security reasons, this was expanded by a declaration of 13 December 1957 and an Act of 18 February 1960 to 12 miles, measured from a straight baseline drawn from the outermost points of each island, thus covering the entire archipelago. The 1973 Act on Indonesia's Continental Shelf claimed seabed resources but required the reaching of seabed agreements with **Malaysia** (1969, 1971, 1981), Thailand (1971, 1975, 1977), **Australia** (then including **Papua New Guinea**) (1971, 1972, 1973), **India** (1974, 1977), **Singapore** (1973, 1978), and Papua New Guinea (1980). A further treaty was signed with Australia in 1988, establishing a marine border in the so-called Timor Gap, covering the territorial waters of former Portuguese Timor. Overlapping claims with **Vietnam** and **China** in the South China Sea remain unresolved, the most troubling for Indonesia being Beijing's unilaterally declared boundary that in 1995 included Indonesia's rich Natuna Island **gas** field. The principle, argued by Indonesia since the 1958 Convention on the Law of the Sea, that an archipelagic nation is entitled to claim all waters between its islands as internal waters was upheld by the **United Nations** International Convention on the Law of the Sea in 1982, though the **Sunda** and **Lombok** straits are recognized as international waterways. On 21 March 1980 Indonesia claimed a 200-kilometer Exclusive Economic Zone around its outer perimeter, and this was formalized by law in 1983. In 1994 Indonesia's claim to archipelagic status was recognized under the United Nations Law of the Sea Convention, giving Indonesia an additional 3 million square km of territorial waters and jurisdiction over another 3 million square km Economic Exclusion Zone. *See also* CONTINENTAL DRIFT; PIRACY. [1108]

ARCHITECTURE. Austronesian migrants to Indonesia in circa 3000 B.C. apparently brought with them techniques for building thatched communal dwellings (*see* **MIGRATIONS**) of a kind still seen among the **Dayaks**. In later times, however, smaller dwellings for individual (extended) families became more common, and the typical house throughout much of the archipelago was a light, impermanent structure built of palm and bamboo materials, with a steep roof against tropical rains and constructed on poles as a protection against flooding. Royal palaces adopted the same style on a grander scale. In **Java**, the characteristic structure of royal palaces is the *pendopo,* consisting of a steep roof with decorated ceiling supported on pillars over a raised floor, with no walls.

Foreign influences may have registered first in religious architecture: **Hindu** and **Buddhist** temples were often of stone and brick, and many examples still survive especially on Java (*see* **ARCHEOLOGY**; **BOROBUDUR**; **KRATON**). The style of mosque most common in Indonesia, especially Java, is also distinctive, being square, with four supporting pillars and a veranda (*serambi*) facing east. European trading companies used brick and stone extensively for their trading posts, partly for defensive reasons, and their early dwelling houses were closely modeled on European styles. A distinctive Dutch colonial architecture emerged in the early 19th century, with high ceilings, marble or tiled floors, deep verandas, neoclassical pillars, living areas opening directly onto the garden, and separate pavilions for cooking, bathing, and the like. This style declined in the 20th century with a return to European urban models. Since independence, many Indonesian architects have endeavored to incorporate traditional forms and motifs in their work. While the **Suharto** government was often suspicious of manifestations of regional ethnic identity in matters such as **language**, it expressly encouraged the preservation of the strikingly different characteristic architectural styles of Indonesia's many ethnic groups; this official sanctioning is seen perhaps most clearly in Jakarta's Taman Mini Indonesia Indah (Beautiful Indonesia in Miniature theme park). [0125–0131, 0536]

ARISAN. A rotating credit association, typically of 10–20 persons, common on **Java**. Members meet regularly to pay fixed contributions, the entire kitty at each meeting being taken by one member, chosen by lot or prior agreement. The *arisan* ends when all members have drawn from it. *See also* PAWNSHOPS.

ARMED FORCES OF THE REPUBLIC OF INDONESIA. Until 1999 (when its name was changed and the police separated from it), the armed forces was named Angkatan Bersenjata Republik Indonesia (ABRI) and encompassed the **army** (Angkatan Darat), **navy** (Angkatan Laut), **air**

force (Angkatan Udara), and **police** (Polisi Negara or Angkatan Kepolisian). In 1962 **Sukarno** created ABRI as a central body over the previously separate individual forces, mainly as a device to remove General **A. H. Nasution** from command posts. Until the advent of the **New Order**, therefore, the central armed forces command had little power over the separate services. After the abolition of separate service ministries in 1967, however, the armed forces, except the police, were gradually integrated within a single command structure under the Ministry of Defense and Security (Hankam, Departemen Pertahanan dan Keamanan). From 1967 to 1983, the posts of defense minister and ABRI commander were always held by the same man. In 1988 the armed forces consisted officially of 284,000 personnel, with a further 800,000 in "reserves," which included the village guards (Hansip, Pertahanan Sipil).

In April 1999 the armed forces were renamed Tentara Nasional Indonesia (TNI, Indonesian National Army), the name they had held during most of the **Revolution** and the 1950s. On that same date the police were formally separated from the armed forces, although this order was not implemented until the following year. In 2000 the armed forces comprised 300,000 men in the army, air force, and navy. Armed Forces Day is celebrated on 5 October.

For a list of armed forces commanders, *see* APPENDIX E. *See also* DEFENSE POLICY; *DWIFUNGSI*; "FIFTH FORCE." [0037, 0714, 0930, 0968, 0972, 0974, 0975]

ARMY (Angkatan Darat, AD). The Indonesian army dates its founding to 5 October 1945, when the new national government announced the creation of a Tentara Keamanan Rakyat (TKR, People's Security Army) and gave a mandate for the actual formation of an army to Urip Sumoharjo, a retired major from the Dutch colonial army (**Koninklijk Nederlandsch Indisch Leger [KNIL]**). The government had previously (on 22 August) created a quasi-military Badan Keamanan Rakyat (BKR, People's Security Organization), responsibility for which was largely devolved to regional national committees (**Komité Nasional Indonesia, KNI**); BKR units in general formed the basis of the TKR.

The new army drew its officer corps principally from former soldiers and officers of the KNIL and the Japanese-sponsored **Pembela Tanah Air** (Peta) on **Java** and **Giyugun** on **Sumatra**. For about 40 years, the army remained under the domination of the so-called Generation of '45 (*see* **GENERATIONS**) who first made their mark and obtained command posts during the national **Revolution**. The ranks of this generation were thinned in later years by the exclusion and self-exclusion of many fundamentalist Muslims and leftists so that the social base of the officer corps could increasingly be described as conservative, ***abangan***, and from the small town elites of Java.

After 1945 a gradual centralization of military authority took place. Initially most army units depended financially and logistically on local civilian governments, and regional commanders enjoyed extensive autonomy from the center. Senior officers met in **Yogyakarta** on 12 November 1945 and elected **Sudirman** as army commander, relegating the government's choice, Urip, to the post of chief of staff. The **navy** and **air force** were separate organizations under the Ministry of Defense. Hierarchy was further weakened by the existence of numerous armed organizations outside the army (*see* **BADAN PERJUANGAN**; **HIZBULLAH**; ***LASYKAR***). Gradually, however, military authority was concentrated in the general staff, dominated by former KNIL officers. With the help of the Ministry of Defense under **Amir Sjarifuddin**, irregular armed units were disbanded or incorporated, Sudirman's authority was gradually diminished, and "reliable" officers were gradually placed in key positions. In this process the TKR changed its name to Tentara Keselamatan Rakyat (TKR, 1 January 1946), Tentara Republik Indonesia (TRI, 24 January 1946), and Tentara Nasional Indonesia (TNI, June 1947). In 1949 the Republic's armed forces were merged with the KNIL to form the APRIS (Angkatan Perang Republik Indonesia Serikat, **Armed Forces of the RIS**), becoming APRI in August 1950.

The postrevolutionary army was overlarge (perhaps 500,000 in late 1949) and deeply segmented. Divisional commanders, especially of the Siliwangi, Diponegoro, and Brawijaya divisions in West, Central, and East Java respectively, enjoyed great autonomy, while the regional commanders in **East Sumatra** and **Minahasa** maintained major smuggling operations. The high command was unable to meet army financial needs and the following decades saw a gradual movement toward reduction of size and centralization of authority, promoted particularly by **A. H. Nasution** as minister of defense. This process included the creation of elite commando-style units (**Komando Cadangan Strategis Angkatan Darat [Kostrad]**, **Resimen Para Komando Angkatan Darat [RPKAD]**, and Banteng Raiders) directly under central command and an expansion of formal military training both at the Army Staff and Command School (Seskoad, Sekolah Staf dan Komando Angkatan Darat) in **Bandung** and at Fort Leavenworth in Texas. In 1952, Nasution began a program of transferring regional commanders away from their power bases.

When the officers mobilized parliamentary support against the transfers and demobilizations, Nasution and others organized demonstrations in **Jakarta** on 17 October, calling for the dissolution of parliament. Sukarno refused and Nasution was suspended from duty for three years, leaving the high command much weakened.

With his reinstallation as chief of staff in November 1955, Nasution resumed his transfer program, which sparked the regional military coups preceding the regional rebellions. Martial law was instituted throughout the country. Dismissals after the **PRRI/Permesta rebellion** and an expansion of the army to 330,000 for the West Irian **(Papua)** campaign increased the power of the high command, headed from 1962 by **Ahmad Yani**. During **Guided Democracy**, President Sukarno, suspicious of army power, promoted the distinctive identities of the navy, air force, and police, but in 1967–1970, after General **Suharto** became president, the four separate ministries were reabsorbed into the Defense Ministry.

Under President Suharto, the role of the army expanded into all levels of the administration when ***dwifungsi***, the official doctrine authorizing the armed forces' extensive participation in politics and government introduced in 1960, was expanded and implemented. During the early years of the **New Order**, the top positions within the army were still dominated by the 1945 generation of officers, but by the early 1980s these officers were gradually retiring from active service to be replaced by a new "professional" generation graduated from the Military Academy, established in Magelang in 1957. With this development there was a decline in the importance of affiliation with the historic territorial divisions (**Siliwangi**, Diponegoro, and so on) of the Revolution, and greater emphasis was placed on technical service specializations (infantry, artillery, engineers, and the like). Javanese dominance of the officer corps continued, however, into the early 1990s, with between 60 and 70 percent of senior officers of Javanese origin, a proportion that lessened to approximately 55 percent by the end of the New Order. By 1988, all members of the '45 generation had retired.

During the 1980s, under **Benny Murdani** (who held the post of commander in chief of the armed forces from 1983 to 1988), the army's influence expanded throughout all sectors of the state and society. In 1985–1986 there was a major reorganization of the armed forces, whereby the 16 regional commands instituted in the late 1950s were reduced to 10 (*see* map 8). Power within the army was further centralized within the hands of Commander in Chief Murdani, and roles previously held by the navy and air force were taken over by the army. The aims of the reorganization were primarily to emphasize the importance of internal security vis-à-vis that of external threat. In 1988 army personnel officially numbered 215,000. Murdani's strengthening grip on the military, however, drew the suspicion of the president, leading to his abrupt removal from his position as commander in chief in February 1988 (though he was appointed minister of defense and held onto his post as **Kopkamtib** commander) and replacement by army chief of staff and former Suharto aide, **Try Sutrisno**.

From that point on, particularly after Murdani's later dismissal from his post as minister of defense in 1993, it became clear that Suharto was attempting to strengthen his personal control over the army, a situation reflected in the rapid personnel changes in the top army leadership throughout the mid-1990s. The growing strength of Suharto's connection to Muslim organizations and the resultant increase in the influence of Muslim officers, together with a shift in the army's relations with **Golkar** and the increasing influence of Suharto family members, such as the president's son-in-law **Prabowo Subianto** in the army and his daughter Siti Hardijanti Rukmana (Tutut) in Golkar, led to increasing schisms within the officer corps and a resultant weakening of its power.

As dissension grew with the **financial crisis** and collapse of the rupiah in late 1997 and early 1998, Suharto made efforts to protect himself by placing officers of undisputed loyalty in key positions around the nation's capital, but the army became incapable of decisive action. This was clear in May 1998 when Suharto called on the military to defend him and, instead, Armed Forces Commander in Chief **Wiranto** was one of those who advised the president to abdicate in favor of his vice president **B. J. Habibie**.

Immediately after Suharto's resignation Prabowo, as Kostrad commander, made an effort to replace Wiranto but was instead himself dismissed. Subsequently Wiranto moved to remove or transfer officers closely allied with Prabowo from influential positions and subsequently announced a program of military reforms reducing the army's political role in Indonesian society. On Armed Forces Day (5 October) 1998, he announced the separation of the national **police** from the armed forces and the reversion of the armed forces' name to Tentara Nasional Indonesia (TNI), publicly cutting the army's ties to Golkar and declaring its neutrality in the forthcoming electoral campaign. He also agreed to the TNI's representation in parliament being reduced from 75 to 38 seats, and he drastically reduced the numbers of army personnel seconded to nonmilitary governmental positions. It was subsequently announced that the army's territorial structure would revert to the pre-1984 system of 17 rather than 10 Kodam (four each in **Sumatra**, Java, and **Kalimantan**, two in **Sulawesi**, and one each in **Nusatenggara**, **Maluku**, and Irian [**Papua**]).

But the army was discredited by its reactions to the unrest in **Aceh** and its role in sponsoring **militias** involved in the 2001 massacre in **East Timor**. Wiranto had been replaced as armed forces commander in chief by his deputy Admiral Widodo Adisutjipto (1944–) in November 1999, being appointed instead to the position of coordinating minister for political and security affairs, and then forced to resign from that position in May 2000. The new president **Abdurrachman Wahid** overrode many of Wiranto's policies, particularly in Aceh, and publicly disagreed with his plans for reorganizing the military's territorial structure. Subsequent fierce infighting among the officer corps was exacerbated by investigations into **human rights** abuses by military elements in East Timor and other restless areas. President Wahid's interference in military affairs alienated much of the officer corps, who established close ties with his vice president, **Megawati Sukarnoputri**. Army Chief of Staff Endriartono Sutarto (1947–) refused to back President Wahid when he tried to proclaim a state of emergency and dissolve parliament in early 2001; instead, the army supported moves in parliament to impeach the president.

When Megawati replaced Wahid as president, she seemed intent on appointing Army Chief of Staff Sutarto as armed forces commander in place of Admiral Widodo, though he was not due for retirement until 2004. Lieutenant-General Ryamizard Ryacudu (1950–), head of the Army Strategic Reserve, replaced Sutarto as army chief of staff. Both Sutarto and Ryamizard have close links not only to Megawati but also to her husband Taufik Kiemas and the **Partai Demokrasi Indonesia—Perjuangan (PDIP)**, and Ryamizard is also the son-in-law of Try Sutrisno. Despite its close alliance with the president, however, the military seemed unlikely to resume a major parliamentary role—with its current representation of 38 appointees scheduled to end in 2004. Former defense minister Juwono Sudarsono criticized its forces for acting as mercenaries in their general policy of collecting protection money from large and small businesses—a practice that had been common since the late 1970s when the state cut the army budget, but one that gained publicity with the killings of Americans near the **Freeport** mine in August 2002. The army began making attempts in early 2003 to supersede civilian control in the event of a national emergency, introducing a provision to a TNI bill before parliament authorizing the armed forces chief to deploy troops when he determines the well being of the state is at risk, needing only to inform the president 24 hours after so doing. Such a provision would directly contravene the Indonesian **Constitution** as well as the 2002 Defense Act, which stipulates that the sole authority to declare a national emergency rests with the president.

Despite calls by reformers wishing to dismantle the territorial system, the current army leadership is apparently trying to expand the number of territorial units. They see such an expansion as strengthening their political power at both the national and local level while helping ease their financial difficulties. For a list of army commanders, *see* APPENDIX E. *See also* DEFENSE POLICY; MILITARY BUSINESS OPERATIONS; WARFARE. [0668, 0669, 0709, 0714, 0727, 0731, 0733, 0877, 0968, 0972, 0973, 0981, 1005]

ARTS, ARTISTS. Indonesia's prehistory yielded works of durable materials like stone, metal, and sometimes clay, which are still preserved today. Other art forms are still perpetuated, although often in a new medium. These include dance, the ***wayang*** (shadow play), and the classical dance drama of **Java** and **Bali**. Parallel to traditional art forms are contemporary painting and sculpture. Portuguese sources indicate that there were experts in painting at the court of **Majapahit** in the early 16th century, and Western influences on indigenous art may have begun with pictures brought by agents of the **Dutch East India Company (VOC)** as gifts to local rulers in the 17th century.

Modern Indonesian painting has its roots in the 19th century when a number of Dutch and other European artists lived in the Indies. The first Western-trained Indonesian painter of significance was **Raden Saleh** (1816–1880). Following him, the "Beautiful Indies" school of painting, with its emphasis on naturalistic landscapes and portraits, was prevalent in the early decades of the 20th century. The modern Indonesian art that emerged in the late 1930s was characterized by its growing emphasis on the individual and its increasing experimentation with new approaches to painting. After independence in 1945, two fine arts departments were established in Indonesia modeled on Dutch academies—the Faculty of Fine Art and Design in **Bandung** "espousing aesthetic formalism" and the Indonesian Academy of Fine Art (ASRI) in **Yogyakarta**, practicing "an art rooted in social realities." Both schools played important roles in the development of modern Indonesian art. In Bali the tradition of painting and sculpture provided the foundation for modern artists (for example, Agus

Djaja [Djajasuminta]), while in Java the artists drew largely on Western influences (for example, **Affandi**, Basoeki Abdullah, **Hendra Gunawan**, and Anton H. Sudjojono).

In 1965 the overthrow of the **Sukarno** regime and the resulting massacres silenced many of the socially engaged artists, especially those who had been affiliated with the **Lembaga Kebudayaan Rakyat (Lekra)**. It was not until the mid-1970s that a group of young artists, calling themselves the New Art Movement, challenged the more established artists in the academies and tried to bring their art closer to Indonesian life. In the closing decades of the 20th century, according to Astri Wright, "Official Indonesian definitions of modern art to a large degree cluster around the old Javanese philosophical values *halus* and *kasar,*" with *halus* referring to the "'universalist' aesthetic adhered to by many senior artists" and *kasar* represented by younger artists seeking to view society "from an ant's perspective" and focusing on the less refined and more disturbing aspects of modern Indonesian society. *See also* CULTURE, MUSIC. [0150, 0159, 0172, 0201, 0202]

ARU. Malay-Batak kingdom on the east coast of **Sumatra**, near modern **Deli**. Seldom fully independent, it was occupied by Javanese forces from **Majapahit** in 1350, became briefly independent around 1460, and was later contested by the Muslim rulers of **Aceh** and **Riau**. It fell to Aceh in about 1600 but during the 17th century reemerged as the independent sultanate of Deli. [0818]

ARU ISLANDS. Archipelago in southeastern Indonesia with a largely Melanesian population. The islands were formally annexed by the **Dutch East Indies Company (VOC)** in 1623 as a source of **pearls** and **birds of paradise**, but there was little active Dutch presence and they were effectively under **Bugis** and Makassarese domination until Dutch administration was established in 1882. Commercial pearl fishing expanded in the early 20th century. [0032]

ARUNG PALAKKA (1634–1696)**.** Prince of the **Bugis** state of Soppeng in southern **Sulawesi**. After rebelling against Sultan Hasanuddin of **Makassar** in 1660, he took refuge with his followers on **Buton** before they served as mercenaries for the **Dutch East Indies Company (VOC)** in Batavia in 1663. He joined the VOC attack on Makassar in 1666–1667 and as a reward was made commander in chief and later (1672) Arumpone, or king, of **Bone**. He assisted the VOC against **Trunojoyo** on

Java in 1678. His autocratic rule in South Sulawesi prompted an exodus of Bugis to other parts of the archipelago. [0549]

ASAHAN. Malay-Batak and Acehnese sultanate on the east coast of **Sumatra**, founded 1695 and formerly subordinate to **Siak**. It was annexed by the Dutch in 1865 and the sultan exiled to **Riau**, but in 1885 he was returned with reduced powers to provided a legal and political basis for the expansion of European **tobacco** cultivation, later replaced by **rubber**. In 1932 Dutch firms involved in the mining of **bauxite** on Bintan made plans for an alumina plant powered by hydroelectricity from the Asahan River, which flows out of Lake Toba. War and other concerns delayed plans and not until July 1979 did work begin on the so-called Asahan project, a joint venture with Japanese investors that opened in February 1982 and involved the construction of a hydroelectric dam on the Asahan River to supply power for an aluminum smelter at Kuala Tanjung. Since that time, however, the water level in Lake Toba has dropped two meters as a result of declining rainfall in the catchment area, and the factory has at times had to cease production. [0818]

ASIA-AFRICA CONFERENCE (Bandung Conference)**.** Held in April 1955 on the initiative of the **Ali Sastroamijoyo** cabinet and attended by the leaders of 29 Asian and African states, including Zhou Enlai of **China**, Jawaharlal Nehru of **India**, Prince Norodom Sihanouk of Cambodia, and Gamal Nasser of Egypt. The conference endorsed Indonesia's claim to West Irian (*see* **PAPUA**) and helped to establish **Sukarno**'s credentials as a major Non-Aligned Bloc leader. *See also* FOREIGN POLICY. [0695, 1102, 1122]

ASLI ("original")**.** Term widely used to describe cultural elements and traditions believed to predate Muslim, Christian, and often **Hindu-Buddhist** influence. Several small tribal groups—the **Badui** (West **Java**), Tenggerese (East Java), Bali Aga (**Bali**), Buda (**Lombok**), and Donggo (**Sumbawa**)—are believed to preserve the traditional culture of their respective regions. (*See also* **SAMIN MOVEMENT**. [0487])

Asli is also an ambiguous term for indigenous people, often used in the context of some form of discrimination against foreigners. *Asli* may mean "born in Indonesia"—the 1945 **Constitution** prescribes that the **president** shall be *asli* and seems to be based on the article of the U.S. constitution, which requires the president to be native-born—or it may refer more narrowly to ethnicity, thus excluding descendants of **Chinese**, **Arabs**, and Europeans. *See also PRIBUMI*.

ASMAT. Ethnic group inhabiting the swampy lowlands of southeastern **Papua**. Their skilled woodcarving attracted much attention from collectors and ethnographers, but since the 1970s Asmat society has been seriously disrupted by labor recruitment for the timber industry and by the relocation of communities for this purpose. [0803, 1230]

ASSOCIAÇÃO POPULAR DEMOCRÁTICA TIMORESE (APODETI, Timorese Popular Democratic Association)**.** Formed in Portuguese Timor in 1974 by Arnoldo dos Reis Araujo to press for the colony's integration into Indonesia as an autonomous province, APODETI drew its rather meager support from the small Muslim community and from people in border areas. It received substantial financial aid from **Badan Koordinasi Intelijen Negara (Bakin)** and the Indonesian consulate in Dili. It allied with the **União Democrática Timorese (UDT)** in July 1975, just before the UDT coup, and many of its leaders were jailed by **Fretilin** in the subsequent civil war. It disappeared as a party after the Indonesian invasion of December 1975, but many of its followers were appointed to posts in the new provincial government after 1976. [0806]

ASSOCIATION OF SOUTHEAST ASIAN NATIONS (ASEAN)**.** ASEAN was founded on 8 August 1967 and comprised at that time Indonesia, **Malaysia**, the **Philippines**, **Singapore**, and **Thailand**. The ASEAN secretariat is in **Jakarta**, and **H. R. Dharsono** was the first secretary-general. Its members saw their principal security threats as internal and aimed to avert these by promoting economic development through regional cooperation. Brunei joined ASEAN in 1984, soon after achieving independence from **Britain**; **Vietnam** became the seventh member in 1995; Laos and Burma (Myanmar) were admitted to full membership in 1997; and **Cambodia** became its 10th member in 1999. ASEAN formally aimed to create a Zone of Peace, Freedom and Neutrality (ZOPFAN) in Southeast Asia, but its members commonly disagreed on the extent to which great powers should be a part of this goal. Little economic integration has been achieved, as became evident during the 1997–1998 **financial crisis**, but on occasions ASEAN successfully operated as a unit in international affairs, especially in the achievement of a Cambodia settlement. *See also* FOREIGN POLICY. [0001, 1101, 1103]

ASSOCIATION PRINCIPLE. Doctrine, linked with the **Ethical Policy** and especially **Snouck Hurgronje**, which argued that colonial rule should aim to assimilate the Indonesian elite to modern Western secular culture by means of **education** and the opening of government positions to qualified Indonesians. It was opposed both by conservatives who saw in it an end to colonial rule and by the proponents of ***adat***, who believed it would rob Indonesians of their own culture. *See also* DJAJADININGRAT, ACHMAD; MUIS, ABDUL.

ASTRA. Founded in 1957 by William Soeryadjaya (Tjia Kian Liong), Astra became Indonesia's largest **automobile** producer. Unlike other manufacturers, it retained considerable autonomy from the **Suharto family** and was the main partner of Toyota in the car-manufacturing subsidiary, Toyota Astra Motor. As the most visible symbol of **Japanese** influence in Indonesia, its showroom was burned down by demonstrators in the **Malari** riots (1974). Astra International was also active in **banking**, insurance, **mining**, food crops, and plywood manufacturing. In 1992 the company collapsed because of mismanagement at Bank Summa and was taken over by a group of ethnic **Chinese** businessmen, led by Prajogo Pangestu and **Liem Sioe Liong**. Astra borrowed extensively in the mid-1990s, and after defaulting on its debt it signed a debt restructuring plan in 1999, which involved selling assets to help the company pay off its losses. It was forced to ask for debt relief again in 2002 as, with little faith in Indonesia's economic recovery, few foreign investors were willing to buy Indonesian assets. In December 2002, Astra's major creditors agreed to a new restructuring, forgiving part of its debt and stretching out the repayment schedule to 2009. Toyota in a joint venture with Astra announced in March 2003 that it planned to make an investment of $180 million in expanding the production of utility vehicles, an investment that would give it a 95-percent stake in the joint venture. [0313, 0402, 0745, 0748]

AUSTRALIA, HISTORICAL LINKS WITH. Up to about 3000 B.C., much of Australia and the Indonesian archipelago seem to have formed a single cultural region inhabited by Austro-Melanesian (Australoid) people who reached the area 50,000–100,000 years ago, perhaps earlier. This continuity was broken by the arrival of Austronesians in the archipelago (*see* **MIGRATIONS**); although the Austronesians certainly reached the Australian coast from time to time, there is no trace of permanent settlement.

In the 17th century, Dutch authorities in **Batavia** sent expeditions to the south to look for trading opportunities, but these explorers reported nothing of commercial advantage there. The Dutch technique of sailing to Indonesia by heading directly east from the Cape of Good Hope led a number of vessels to sight and run against the western Australian coast. In the 18th century the exhaustion of trepang (beche de mer) fields in the archipelago brought Indonesian fishing fleets of up to 2,000 vessels, mainly from **Makassar**, to the northern coast of Australia, where some cultural influences on Aborigines are still visible.

During the first years of British settlement in eastern Australia in the late 18th century, the Dutch settlements in Indonesia were the nearest point of European civilization; and during the 19th century, Australian produce found something of a market there. There were also important scientific connections between the two colonies in the field of tropical **agriculture**. A **telegraph** link between Banyuwangi on **Java** and Darwin, Australia, was laid in 1871. Australian **tourism** to Indonesia began in the early 20th century, and Australian commercial interests became involved in eastern Indonesia, especially in the **pearl** industry of the **Aru Islands**.

During the 19th century, the Dutch colonial authorities became increasingly worried by the possibility of Australian imperialist expansion in the eastern archipelago, and well-founded Dutch suspicion of Australia's intentions hampered cooperation in the defense of the Indies against Japan, although the two countries were joined with Britain and America in the so-called ABDA (American-British-Dutch-Australian) command. During the **Japanese occupation of Indonesia**, the colonial rulers formed a government-in-exile in Australia and attempted to stave off Australian ambitions to establish some form of hegemony in **Papua** (Irian) and **Timor**. [1116]

AUSTRALIA, RELATIONS WITH. At the close of World War II, Australian forces accepted the Japanese surrender and restored Dutch rule in eastern Indonesia, despite Australian ambitions in the region. The Indonesian struggle, however, quickly attracted the sympathy of the Left in Australia, where dockworkers organized strikes against Dutch shipping, the first tangible sign of international support for the Republic. Australian policy makers, historically unsympathetic to the Dutch and keen to cultivate good relations with prospective neighbors, increasingly sided with Indonesia in international forums, and Australia was Indonesia's nominee on the **United Nations** Good Offices Committee in 1947–1948.

Relations with Indonesia deteriorated in the late 1950s over Indonesia's continued claim to West Irian (**Papua**), which was seen in Australia as expansionist, and in the early 1960s Australian troops fought Indonesians in northern Borneo during **Confrontation**. Relations were good during the first decade of the **New Order** as Australia increasingly sought friends in Asia while Indonesia looked for Western aid, but the Indonesian invasion of **East Timor** in 1975, including the killing of five journalists from Australia and later including what Indonesia has seen as persistently hostile press reporting soured relations, which reached a nadir in 1986 after a report in the *Sydney Morning Herald* (10 April) on the **Suharto** family's wealth.

From then on, Indonesia's policy in East Timor was a continuing thorn in its relationship with Australia, reaching a climax in 1999. In April of that year, Australia pressed for introduction of an international peacekeeping force to oversee the planned plebiscite on independence, it opened a consulate in Dili on 8 June, and it strongly protested Indonesian support of prointegration **militias** in their continuing violent campaigns. Australia was the first country to pledge troops toward an international peacekeeping force when widespread violence followed the 31 August vote, and it headed the force that was dispatched to East Timor from Darwin on 20 September. Australian leaders condemned the Indonesian militias for their continuing violence against the Timorese, with some Australians boycotting Indonesian goods and services, while Indonesians responded with anti-Australian demonstrations. Relations remained cool, and in December 2000 Indonesia protested Australia's role in the secession of East Timor while Australia was concerned about the potential refugee problem. In 2001 the Indonesian foreign minister visited Australia, and the two countries agreed on joint measures to combat terrorism and on introducing measures on a regional basis to reduce illegal migration to Australia from Afghanistan and south Asia, via Indonesia.

In the aftermath of the **Bali** bombings of October 2002 in which 89 Australian tourists lost their lives, relations between the two countries underwent a further change when they signed an agreement allowing the Australian Federal Police (AFP) to participate in the investigation. But fears were raised in Indonesia when Australian Prime Minister John Howard declared in December that his government was willing to launch preemptive attacks on terrorists in neighboring countries. In 2002 total trade between Australia and Indonesia reached a record high of A$7.4 billion, with Indonesia's exports to Australia at A$4.3 billion. [0479, 1107, 1112, 1114, 1116, 1133]

AUSTRONESIANS. *See* LANGUAGE; MIGRATION; RICE; TARO.

AUTOMOBILE INDUSTRY. The domestic automobile industry grew up in the 1970s. The two major car manufacturers were **Astra**, which took up more than half the market, and the **Salim Group**. In 1996 **Suharto** announced that a company, PT Timor Putra Nasional, owned by his son, Hutomo (Tommy) Mandala Putra, would be allowed to develop a "national car," to be named the Timor, in conjunction with Kia Motors of South Korea. In fact, the company imported duty-free Timors made wholly in South Korea, an arrangement denounced both by Indonesian competitors and the **World Bank**. In July 1997, the Suharto government pressured Indonesia's biggest state and private banks to finance a Timor factory east of Jakarta, but in January of the following year, an agreement with the International Monetary Fund (IMF) led Suharto to end tax breaks for the national car. *See also* INDUSTRIALIZATION; SUHARTO FAMILY. [0313, 0402]

AZAS TUNGGAL ("sole principle"). *See* PANCASILA.

AZIZ, ANDI ABDUL. Captain in the **Koninklijk Nederlandsch Indisch Leger (KNIL)** who seized control of **Makassar** in a limited coup on 5 April 1950, partly to prevent the landing of Republican troops who, he feared, might begin to dismantle the **Negara Indonesia Timur (NIT)**, partly out of frustration at the slow progress made in integrating former KNIL troops into the **Republik Indonesia Serikat (RIS)** armed forces. The Aziz affair ended when the NIT government failed to back him, and he was arrested in **Jakarta** on 18 April. The resemblance of the affair to the abortive coup by **R. P. P. Westerling** in **Bandung** was an important element in discrediting the NIT. [0699, 0784]

– B –

BABAD. Javanese verse chronicles commonly written to describe and glorify the rise or rule of a particular king, though some deal exclusively with mythical tales. The term *babad* also means "to clear forest," suggesting that these chronicles were associated with the founding of kingdoms; they appear to be an indigenous development, though all known *babad* were written after the conversion of **Java** to **Islam**. [0497, 0502, 0505]

BABAD TANAH JAWI. Babad celebrating the power of 17th-century **Mataram**, probably composed in the court of **Sultan Agung**, though all known manuscripts date from the 18th and 19th centuries.

BACAN. Island in northern **Maluku**. Its people probably came originally from **Halmahera** but now include a sizeable Christian community of part-**Portuguese** descent. The Portuguese founded a fort there in 1558, which fell in 1609 to the **Dutch**, who placed Bacan under the sovereignty of **Ternate**. [0026, 0032]

BADAN INTELIJEN NEGARA (BIN). *See* BADAN KOORDINASI INTELIJEN NEGARA (BAKIN).

BADAN INTELIJEN STRATEGIS (Bais, Strategic Intelligence Body). *See* INTELLIGENCE.

BADAN KEAMANAN RAKYAT. *See* ARMY.

BADAN KERJA SAMA (BKS, Cooperative Bodies). Formed in 1957–1958 to allow coordination between the **army** and party **mass organizations** (*organisasi massa*) under the general idea, strongest in the army, that the military should play a guiding role in directing national energies. The largest of these bodies, the BKS Bumil (*Buruh-Militer,* Labor-Military) and the BKS Tamil (*Tani-Militer,* Peasant-Military), were formed in October 1957 and September 1958 respectively. **Partai Komunis Indonesia (PKI)** mass organizations that were initially involved soon withdrew, and the BKS became clearly anticommunist coordinating bodies. In December 1962, they were dissolved into the **Sentral Organisasi Karyawan Seluruh Indonesia (SOKSI)**. *See also DWIFUNGSI*. [0714]

BADAN KOORDINASI BANTUAN PEMANTAPAN STABILITAS NASIONAL (Bakorstanas, National Stabilization and Coordination Body). A security organization formed on 5 September 1988 to replace **Komando Operasi Pemulihan Keamanan dan Ketertiban (Kopkamtib)**. Its responsibilities were vague but included monitoring security matters and giving advice to the government. President **Suharto** was formal head of the organization (unlike Kopkamtib, which was in a technical sense independent of the presidency), and General **Try Sutrisno** was the effective commander, but Bakorstanas boards at each level included civilian as well as military officials. Under President **Abdurrachman Wahid**, Bakorstanas was abolished in March 2000.

BADAN KOORDINASI INTELIJEN NEGARA (Bakin, State Intelligence Coordinating Body)**.** A nominally civilian intelligence organization, separate from military intelligence structures and reporting directly to the president. It was established in 1967, and its functions overlapped substantially with those of **Komando Operasi Pemulihan Keamanan dan Ketertiban (Kopkamtib)** and included surveillance of civilian dissent. Bakin was headed from January 1974 to late 1989 by Lieutenant-General Yoga Sugama (1925–2003). Under **Abdurrachman Wahid**'s presidencey, Bakin was reorganized in January 2001 and renamed Badan Intelijen Negara (BIN, State Intelligence Agency), with **police** intelligence as its operational arm. When **Megawati Sukarnoputri** became president, BIN's influence expanded and its head, Hendro Priyono, was appointed to the cabinet. After the **Bali** bombins BIN was appointed sole coordinator for all intelligence activities in Indonesia, and local branches were established throughout the archipelago. *See also* INTELLIGENCE SERVICES.

BADAN PENDUKUNG SUKARNOISME (BPS, Body to Support Sukarnoism)**.** Founded in September 1964 by a group of journalists, including **Adam Malik**, opposed to the **Partai Komunis Indonesia (PKI)** in an attempt to distinguish publicly between Sukarnoism and communism and to separate **Sukarno** from the PKI. It was banned by Sukarno as an alleged CIA plot on 17 December 1964. [0727]

BADAN PENYELIDIK USAHA PERSIAPAN KEMERDEKAAN INDONESIA (BPUPKI, Investigatory Body for Preparatory Work for Indonesian Independence)**.** In March 1945, the **Japanese occupation** authorities on **Java** set up the BPUPKI following Prime Minister Kuniaki Koiso's promise of eventual independence for the region. Membership included most of the better-known prewar nationalists and represented most streams of thought. The body met in **Jakarta** from 28 May 1945 and was the forum to which **Sukarno** presented his speech outlining the **Pancasila** on 1 June. It also drafted a **Constitution** for independent Indonesia (10–17 July) and decided that Indonesia should include the **Malay Peninsula**, northern Borneo, and **East Timor**, though this was later rejected by the Japanese. On 7 August, the BKUPKI was replaced by a 21-member **Panitia Persiapan Kemerdekaan Indonesia (PPKI)**. *See also* ISLAMIC STATE, DEMANDS FOR AN; SUCCESSION. [0644, 0647, 0663]

BADAN PERENCANAAN PEMBANGUNAN NASIONAL (Bappenas, National Development Planning Board). Indonesia's principal economic planning body, founded in 1963 by **Sukarno** but later the stronghold of the group of **New Order** economic policy makers known as the "technocrats" or "Berkeley Mafia" (many of them having studied at the University of California, Berkeley). The group included **Widjojo Nitisastro**, Ali Wardhana, Emil Salim, Mohamad Sadli, and Barli Halim; it had the patronage of **Sumitro Djojohadikusumo** and was initially strongly influenced by the International Monetary Fund (IMF) view that the economic difficulties faced by the country under Sukarno's **Guided Economy** could be remedied by sober financial policies, looser economic controls, and an opening of the country to foreign **investment**. It lost much of its influence in the late 1980s and 1990s with the rise of **B. J. Habibie** and the expanding role the **Suharto family** and cronies played in the Indonesian **economy**.

In 2003 an effort was made to further erode the role of Bappenas in shaping Indonesia's development policies. A bill was proposed transferring the drawing up of short- and medium-term economic development programs from Bappenas to the Ministry of Finance, which would no longer have to coordinate with Bappenas over the country's fiscal policies. Until then, Bappenas participated actively in drawing up macroeconomic targets, yearly state budget figures, and the five-year national development program (now called Propenas) (*see* **RENCANA PEMBANGUNAN LIMA TAHUN**). Under the proposal, Propenas would be replaced by the Medium-Term Expenditure Framework (MTEF), which would provide guidance for three, rather than five, years. *See also* CENTRE FOR STRATEGIC AND INTERNATIONAL STUDIES; DEVELOPMENT IDEOLOGY. [0295, 0353]

BADAN PERJUANGAN (struggle organizations). These sprang up widely in 1945 as an expression of popular will to defend the Indonesian Republic against the returning **Dutch**. Often untrained and armed only with bamboo spears, they were outside the control of the regular **army**, and in early 1946 the government moved to consolidate them into better-organized ***lasykar***, incorporate them within the army, or disband them. *See also* SURABAYA. [0643, 0674, 0681]

BADAN PERMUSYAWARATAN KEWARGA-NEGARAAN INDONESIA (Baperki, Consultative Body on Indonesian Citizenship). A political organization of Indonesian **Chinese**, founded by Siauw Giok

Tjhan (1914–1980) on 13 March 1954 to succeed the Partai Demokrat Tionghoa (Party of Democratic Chinese). It encouraged Chinese to accept Indonesian citizenship but defended the right of Chinese to retain their culture as citizens. This attitude was opposed by the proassimilation Lembaga Pembinaan Kesatuan Bangsa (Institute for Developing National Unity). Baperki was banned in 1966. [1045, 1063]

BADAN URUSAN LOGISTIK NASIONAL (Bulog, National Logistic Supply Organization). Established in 1967 as a government purchase agency, Bulog expanded its role in the 1970s to supervise and stabilize the distribution and price of basic commodities such as **rice**, **sugar**, and flour, partly as an aid to political stability. It was sharply criticized for **corruption** in the allocation of distributorships by the Commission of Four.

Despite deregulatory packages instituted by the **Suharto** government in 1995 and 1996, Bulog retained its monopolies, including the exclusive right to import wheat and sugar. It attempted to stabilize rice prices in 1996. In 1997 it came under attack from the International Monetary Fund (IMF), which tied further financial assistance to a substantial deregulation of the domestic food market; as a result, Bulog's monopoly of the importation of all commodities with the exception of rice was ended. Under the presidency of **Abdurrachman Wahid**, its deputy chairman was jailed for providing the president and his associates with considerable funds they had requested without issuing a decree. [0761, 0763]

BADUI. Tribe of southern **Banten**, widely believed to be descendants of pre-Muslim Sundanese who refused to convert to **Islam**, but probably of much greater antiquity. They worship *lelembut,* ancestral spirits who dwell near the source of the rivers Ciujung and Cisemet. Only 40 Badui families, the "Inner Badui," are permitted by custom to inhabit this sacred area, and these are forbidden all contact with the outside world. The remainder, the Outer Badui, are permitted some contact but are forbidden to make use of introduced technology such as horses, **writing**, vehicles, and beds. *See also ASLI.*

BAHASA INDONESIA. *See* INDONESIAN LANGUAGE.

BAJAU. Also known as Sea People (*orang laut*) or Sea Gypsies, the Bajau are a seafaring Malay people of eastern Indonesia and the southern Philippines, typically living aboard boats or in small settlements of temporary houses on stilts over the sea. Their dispersal from a presumed home in southern **Sulawesi** may date from the fall of **Makassar** to **Dutch** and **Bugis** forces in 1667 or to the commercial opportunities offered by trepang collection. During the 18th–19th centuries, Bajau fleets ranged as far as **Australia** in search of trepang for the **China trade**. [0549]

BALAI PUSTAKA. The government commission for literacy and popular publication, founded in 1917 as the Comite (later Kantoor) voor de Volkslectuur (Committee, Office for Popular Literature). It published cheap reading material in Malay, Sundanese, and Javanese (both original works and translations from Dutch, including the letters of **Raden Ajeng Kartini** in 1921); maintained libraries; and provided court interpreters. [0219, 0231, 0234]

BLAMBANGAN. The last **Hindu** kingdom on **Java**, controlling the eastern end of the island (Besuki and Probolinggo) after the fall of **Majapahit**. It was fought over by **Mataram** and the Balinese state of Gelgel in the early 17th century, but flourished as an independent kingdom from 1670 to 1690. In 1697 it was attacked once more by Mataram and the Balinese rulers of Buleleng. Mataram transferred its claim over the region to the **Dutch East Indies Company (VOC)** in 1734, and the company subdued it in a major campaign in 1771–1772. Constant warfare and the piratical raids of Madurese severely depopulated the region, and further destruction was caused by an eruption of Mt. Ijen in 1817. In the 19th century, the area was extensively settled by Madurese. The name now refers to the forested peninsula on Java's southeast corner rather than to the former territory of the kingdom. [0502, 0577]

BALI. Although the culture and society of Bali have been studied extensively, until recently relatively little was written on the island's history. Probably **Hindu** from the eighth or ninth century (the first Hindu inscriptions record a king Warmadewa in the ninth century), Bali was ruled at least in part by the Javanese king **Airlangga** in the early 11th century and was conquered by **Majapahit** in 1334. A period of intensive Javanization followed, and contemporary Balinese sometimes refer to themselves as *wong Majapahit* (people of Majapahit). There is said, too, to have been considerable migration of Javanese Hindus to Bali following the fall of Majapahit to the ***pasisir*** states in 1527. The island remained divided between nine or so independent states—Klungkung, Karangasem, Mengwi, Badung, Bangli, Tabanan, Gianyar, Buleleng, and Jembrana—though the rulers of Klungkung, whose territory included the temple of Besakih on Mt. (Gunung) Agung and who were known as the Dewa Agung, were sometimes regarded as overlords. Slaves were a major export in the 17th and 18th centuries, the average annual export being 1,000–2,000. This **trade** was in the hands of the rajas. Balinese formed an important element in the **Betawi** communities around **Batavia**. Balinese mercenaries also fought in various wars in **Java**.

Dutch political interest in the island began in the 19th century. To exclude other Europeans, the Dutch obtained acknowledgments of sovereignty from Badung, Klungkung, Karangasem, and Buleleng in 1841 and launched a series of military operations on the island in 1846, 1848, and 1849. The Dutch were also keen to stop Balinese **piracy** and plunder of shipwrecks, and they attempted to intervene to control practices such as **slavery** (common) and widow-burning (very uncommon). Buleleng and Jembrana were brought under closer control in 1853, and Karangasem and Gianyar were conquered in 1882. The plunder of a Dutch shipwreck in 1904 provided the pretext for full military operations on the island against Badung in 1906 and Klungkung in 1908. In the final battles of each campaign, the respective royal families committed collective suicide (*puputan*), walking into the guns of the Dutch forces. After a period of direct rule by the Dutch, during which Singaraja on the north coast was the island's capital, the former kingdoms were restored in 1929 to their former rulers as ***zelfbesturen*** (self-governing territories under Dutch authority) in a massive ceremony at Besakih.

The **Japanese** military administration continued the Dutch system of indirect rule but coupled this with an increasingly harsh system of surplus extraction. Under their rule, existing conflicts intensified especially as the Japanese attempted to mobilize the Balinese behind their war effort. When Dutch forces landed in March 1946, they encountered strong military opposition that continued until 1948. Using pro-Dutch Balinese elements, however, they incorporated the island into the Dutch-sponsored federal state of East Indonesia (*see* **FEDERALISM; NEGARA INDONESIA TIMUR [NIT]**) in 1946. After the NIT was dissolved in 1950 many of the old power arrangements remained more or less intact, the kingdoms being converted into *kabupaten* and the rajas, or members of their families, generally taking the office of ***bupati***.

Head of the region (*kepala daerah*) and from 1958 governor of the province was Anak Agung Bagus Suteja (?–1965). Close to **Sukarno** and officially nonparty, Suteja played an important role in increasing the representation of the **Partai Komunis Indonesia (PKI)** and other leftists in the island's administration and legislative bodies. Social tensions mounted during the early 1960s, partly as a result of a **land reform** campaign by the PKI, and apprehension mounted especially after several thousand people died in an eruption of Mt. Agung in 1963. In the aftermath of the **Gestapu**, Suteja's authority weakened, and after he was removed to Jakarta in late November 1965 troops began to arrive from Java and the massacre began. Perhaps 60,000 people were slaughtered as alleged communists or leftists in 1965–1966.

Bali had been a significant tourist destination in the early 1930s, but under the **New Order**, the island became a major international tourist center, with its attraction expanding exponentially in the 1990s and accounting for about a third of Indonesia's revenue for **tourism**. After **Suharto**'s fall, about 1.5 million foreigners were visiting the island annually, for it was seen as a place largely immune to the ethnic and religious violence that was plaguing other parts of the archipelago. This impression was shattered on 12 October 2002, when powerful bombs destroyed a nightclub in the Kuta Beach tourist district, killing about 202 people, 89 of them Australians. *See also* HINDUISM; LANGE, MADS JOHANSEN; MASSACRES OF 1965–1966. [0091, 0205, 0711, 0819, 0824, 0825, 0832, 1214, 1216, 1382]

BANDA ISLANDS. Small archipelago in **Maluku**, known especially for the cultivation of **nutmeg**. Dependent on **Java** for **rice**, Banda came under the rule of **Majapahit** in the 14th century and attracted a **Portuguese** fleet under d'Abreu in 1511. **Dutch trade** in the islands began in 1599, and the **Dutch East Indies Company (VOC)** under **Jan Pieterszoon Coen** annexed them in a bloody campaign from circa 1609 that left the islands largely depopulated, perhaps 15,000 Bandanese being killed. The islands were divided into nutmeg "groves" or *perken,* each *perk* being under a VOC *perkenier* with slaves to work for him. *Perkeniers* were obliged to deliver their produce to the company and, later, the colonial government at fixed prices. With abolition of the monopoly in 1864, the *perkeniers* became immensely wealthy until the depression of 1894.

During the late colonial period, Banda Neira, the main island in the group, became a place of exile for prominent Indonesian nationalist leaders, including **Tjipto Mangoenkoesoemo**, exiled there in 1928; Iwa Kusumasumantri (1899–?), who arrived in 1930 (both Mangoenkoesoemo and Kusumasumantri were permitted to leave in early 1941); and **Sutan Sjahrir** and **Mohammad Hatta**, who were transferred there from **Boven Digul** in 1936 and were only allowed to return to Java when the **Japanese** invaded in January 1942.

During the 1980s, the islands were developed for **tourism** by Des Alwi (whom Sjahrir had adopted during his exile on the island), but their popularity declined markedly during the interethnic violence following the fall of **Suharto**, which engulfed the Maluku islands. [0087, 0491]

BANDITRY. Crime is presumably as old as human society in Indonesia, but the earliest known form of organized crime in the archipelago is rural banditry, along with its marine counterpart, **piracy**. The plundering of travelers and the raiding of outlying settlements is often difficult to distinguish from early state building, and a number of rulers of parts of **Java**, notably **Ken Angrok**, began their careers as rural criminals. Criminal gangs generally formed around a single leader and did not survive his death or loss of prestige. Leaders commanded not only martial arts (*pencak silat*) but also magical powers such as the ability to confer invulnerability, invisibility, or inaudibility on their followers. The extent of rural banditry is always difficult to estimate, since there are ample reasons for both exaggeration and underreporting, but many areas of Java had a reputation as "unsafe" throughout the colonial period.

Bandit gangs frequently took part in peasant uprisings against the colonial power and in the 20th century came into contact with nationalist groups. **Sarekat Islam (SI)** and the **Partai Komunis Indonesia (PKI)** in particular valued the bandits both as a source of potential armed strength and as a representation of the strength of the mass of the people. Gangs provided some of the armed support for the PKI's uprising in the **Jakarta** region in 1926, but were generally ineffective against the colonial police.

During the **Revolution**, gangsters in the Jakarta region and elsewhere joined nationalists in armed resistance organizations (***lasykar***), but they were generally unsuccessful in holding back the **Dutch** and most were suppressed by the Republic's own **army** in the course of the Revolution. In the chaotic years that followed the transfer of sovereignty, rural banditry was rife in many regions, though it was often associated with political dissent. Under the **New Order**, greatly increased social control in the countryside diminished the incidence of banditry there, though urban crime remained rampant. In the 1982 **elections**, in particular, figures associated with the government were said to be employing urban criminals both to intimidate the other parties and as agents provocateurs. The elections were followed by a dramatic upsurge in violent crime, perhaps encouraged by this rumor of approval, which was suppressed, however, by the government's program of extrajudicial killings known as ***Petrus*** (*penembakan misterius*), beginning early 1983, which claimed several thousand victims. *See also* PEMUDA PANCASILA. [0485, 0734, 0743, 1228]

BANDUNG. Major city in the **Priangan**, developed by the **Dutch** after 1810 as a center for the region's plantation industry. It was the capital of the Priangan from 1864 and grew rapidly after the arrival of the **railway** in 1880. The colonial Department of War transferred there in 1916, and the city was proposed as an eventual capital of the Netherlands Indies. In 1946, the southern part of the city was burned by Indonesian nationalists forced to evacuate by the Allies. [0561, 0681]

BANDUNG CONFERENCE. *See* ASIA-AFRICA CONFERENCE.

BANGKA. Large island off the southeast coast of **Sumatra**, site of major **tin** mines since 1710, operated at first by the sultan of **Palembang**, who began to introduce laborers from **China**, **Siam**, and **Vietnam**. British forces seized Bangka in 1806 and abolished the sultanate in 1816, but the island was restored to the **Dutch**, who continued tin mining as a government enterprise. The island also became a major exporter of white **pepper** in the 19th century, producing 90 percent of the world supply. After falling to the **Japanese** in World War II, Bangka was reoccupied by the Dutch in early 1946. The Dutch exiled **Sukarno**, **Mohammad Hatta**, Haji Agus Salim (1884–1954), and other Republican leaders to the island after their second **"Police Action"** of 19 December 1948. [0658, 0801]

BANGSA INDONESIA **("Indonesian nation").** Ambiguous ethnic term that may refer simply to those born in Indonesia; more commonly, however, it describes ethnicity and excludes citizens of European, **Chinese**, Indian, **Arab**, and other exogenous ancestry. *See also ASLI*; *PRIBUMI*.

BANJARMASIN. Kingdom on the Barito River in southern **Kalimantan**, reputedly founded by Empu Jamatka in 1387. It quickly became an important source of diamonds, bezoar stones, and dragon's blood (a plant exudate) but was dependent on **Java** for the supply of **rice** and was tributary in succession to the Javanese states of **Majapahit**, **Demak**, and **Mataram**. Its ruler converted to **Islam** in circa 1520, and the sultanate received many refugees from the north coast of Java after the fall of **Surabaya** to Mataram in 1625. In the 17th century **pepper**, gambier,

gold, and **rattan** became major trading commodities, attracting **Chinese** traders as well as the **Dutch** and **English East India Companies**. Large areas of ***alang-alang*** grassland in the region today are a legacy of the indiscriminate clearing of forest for pepper and gambier cultivation in this period. Both the Dutch and the British attempted to enforce monopolies in the port, but successive agreements with sultans were unenforceable as economic and political power collected in the hands of powerful pepper planters. The sultan of Banjarmasin formally ceded sovereignty to the Dutch in 1786–1787, though he retained his throne and continued to rule with little interference.

Governor-General **Herman Willem Daendels** abandoned Dutch holdings in Banjarmasin in 1809, but in 1857 the Dutch reasserted their right to appoint the deceased sultan's successor and imposed a half-Chinese son of the previous sultan on the unwilling aristocracy. A full-scale war of succession ensued (1859–1863), the anti-Dutch party, strongly Islamic, being led by a junior prince, Pangeran Antasari (1797–1862), and a peasant leader, Sultan Kuning. The Dutch formally abolished the sultanate in 1860. Sporadic fighting continued beyond the formal end of major hostilities until 1905.

The area was a site of tough resistance to the Dutch by guerrillas under Hasan Basry in the period 1945–1949, and much of the hinterland remained in Republican hands, though, to the indignation of local leaders, it was not recognized formally as Republican territory in the **Linggajati** or **Renville Agreements**. In January 1948 the Dutch established a federal state, the Daerah Banjar, to be a constituent of the Indonesian federal republic (*see* **FEDERALISM**), but this was dissolved in March 1950. Resentment against central government policies led to a local uprising under Ibnu Hajar, which became associated with the **Darul Islam** and lasted until 1963. [0811, 0693]

BANK PEMBANGUNAN INDONESIA (Bapindo, Indonesian Development Bank)**.** State owned, the bank employed thousands of employees, and when it lost half its capital in a loan scam by one of its clients, Eddy Tansil, which was revealed in 1994, **Suharto** refused pressure from Finance Minister Mar'ie Muhammad to liquidate the bank. (Tansil was accused of diverting to his private use a US$420 million Bapindo loan intended to fund a West Java petrochemical project.) In the resulting trials, four of Bapindo's directors were sentenced to 4–8 years in jail. Eddy Tansil was sentenced to life imprisonment but escaped and fled the country in 1996. [0761]

BANKING. The **Dutch East Indies Company (VOC)** initially drew its capital from the Netherlands and, having a monopoly of **trade** in the archipelago, had no wish to allow local credit facilities for others. In 1746, however, Governor-General Gustaaf Willem, baron van Imhoff (1705–1750), established a Bank van Leening (Lending Bank) in Batavia for the support of trade enterprises. This minor retreat of Dutch capital from direct investment to the financing of others was continued in the 19th century by the **Nederlandsche Handel Maatschappij**, which began as a trading company and ended as a largely banking operation. Other major banks in the Netherlands Indies were the Nederlandsch-Indische Handelsbank (established 1863), the Nederlandsch-Indische Escompto-Maatschappij (established 1857), and the Koloniale Bank. The Java Bank (Javasche Bank) was established in 1828 as a semiprivate, semigovernment bank of circulation (issuing currency), while the Algemene Volkscredietbank (founded 1934) undertook small-scale loans to and from the public.

During the **Japanese occupation**, commercial banking was taken over by the Yokohama Specie bank while the Syomin Ginko replaced the Volkscredietbank, becoming Bank Rakyat after independence. When the Indonesian Republic nationalized the Java Bank in 1953, turning it into the Bank Indonesia, the Bank Industri Negara (originally the Bureau Herstel Financiering, established by the **Dutch** in 1948) was made responsible for financing industrial development, while the BNI financed imports and exports. Other Dutch banks were nationalized in 1958, Escompto becoming the Bank Dagang Negara (State Trading Bank), which subsequently especially financed **mining**. In 1965 the various state banks were merged into the BNI, but they separated again in December 1968. A National Development Savings Scheme (Tabanas, Tabungan Pembangunan Nasional) was introduced in 1971. On 27 October 1988 Indonesia announced a major deregulation of the banking sector, including easier availability of foreign exchange licenses and permitting **state enterprises** to deposit funds with private banks.

As a result, the number of banks increased from 112 in 1988 to 239 in 1996, many of which were not financially sound, as they had been mismanaged or exploited by their owners. There was an immense volume of uncollectable credits that had often been used to finance property projects run by other companies under the aegis of a bank's owners. The central bank (Bank Indonesia) had to come to the assistance of the failing banks, and there was a growing number of financial scandals (*see* **BANK**

PEMBANGUNAN INDONESIA [BAPINDO]). There were also charges of **corruption** against Bank Indonesia, and in December 1997 it fired four of its seven directors. In 2003, after a one-year trial, three of its former directors were sentenced to jail sentences ranging from two and one-half to three years for abuse of power in disbursing liquidity support funds totaling US$1.1 billion.

In November 1997 in accordance with International Monetary Fund (IMF) recommendations, the finance minister closed 16 private banks considered insolvent. Two bankers, both members of the **Suharto family**—Bambang Trihatmodjo of Bank Andromeda and Probosutedjo (Suharto's brother-in-law) of Bank Jakarta—refused the order, but ultimately both had to yield. By January 1998, the public had lost all faith in the banking system and was withdrawing and transferring massive amounts to foreign banks. During the Asian **financial crisis**, the Indonesian government had to extend approximately US$13 billion in emergency loans to shore up local banks, and it struck a deal for these loans to be repaid in four years. An Indonesian Bank Restructuring Agency (IBRA) was set up in 1998, as a result of the IMF's US$76 billion bank bailout. Under measures passed in November 1998 and May 1999, banking laws were amended to allow foreign-owned banks to acquire up to 100 percent of shares in existing banks, including the former state banks.

Under President **Abdurrachman Wahid**, oversight of IBRA came under the Ministry of Finance, and when **Megawati Sukarnoputri** succeeded him as president she switched this oversight to the Ministry of State-Owned Enterprises. IBRA experienced manifold difficulties, being unable to meet its targets for asset sales and having six different heads in the 30 months leading up to August 2001. However, in 2002 it proposed extending the debt repayment deadline by six more years and cutting the interest rate on the outstanding debt. It remained reluctant to institute criminal prosecution against prominent debtors, including the eldest daughter of former President Suharto, and in August 2002 the appeals court overturned a corruption conviction imposed in March on the central bank governor, Syahril Sabirin, stemming from the 1999 Bank Bali scandal. With IBRA scheduled to terminate in February 2004, the government planned to set up a temporary banking guarantee implementation unit (UP3) under the Ministry of Finance to implement the government's guarantee on bank deposits until a deposit guarantee agency (LPS) could be set up. *See also* CURRENCY; PAWNSHOPS. [0057, 0381, 0382, 0384 0315, 0390, 0394, 0479, 0761]

BANTEN (Bantam)**.** On the northern coast of West **Java**, Banten was seized by Muslims of the sultanate of **Demak** in 1527. It rapidly expanded during the 16th century, and under Fatahillah conquered the **Pajajaran** port of Sunda Kalapa in the early 1520s. After Banten defeated a **Portuguese** fleet in Sunda Kalapa harbor in 1527, the city was renamed Jayakarta. Banten emerged as the dominant entrepôt and outlet for **pepper** from West Java and South **Sumatra**. It was in continual conflict with **Mataram** over control of the **Priangan**. In 1601 ships of the **Dutch East Indies Company (VOC)** defeated a Spanish-Portuguese fleet in Banten harbor. The city began to decline after the foundation of **Batavia** in 1619. **Thomas Stamford Raffles** abolished the Banten sultanate in 1813. In 1888 a major anticolonial uprising took place in Banten, and in 1926 it was one of three regions where the **Partai Komunis Indonesia (PKI)** uprising broke out.

During the **Revolution**, it was not reconquered by the **Dutch** until their second **"Police Action"** and was one of the few regions not drawn into Dutch federalist projects. There was friction between local leaders and the Republican government throughout the Revolution, and in 1949 the Republic crushed a revolt against its authority.

As result of the post-**Suharto decentralization** policies, Banten, now a **province**, gained power to regulate activities at some of its ports that handle the export of the products of Krakatau steel to the **United States**, Europe, and other parts of Asia. [0822, 0836, 0660]

BANTENG (*Bos javanicus*)**.** Bovine similar to **cattle**, occurring wild or feral on many islands and elsewhere in Southeast Asia, recognizable by a white disk on the buttocks. First known to have been domesticated in Thailand before 3500 B.C., it is valued for its agility, its easy trainability, and more recently its low-fat meat. Most "cattle" on **Bali** and **Timor** are in fact banteng, while the cattle of **Madura** appear to be a stable banteng-zebu cross that was developed circa 500 A.D. A banteng's horned head represents national unity on the Indonesian coat of arms and was adopted as symbol by the **Partai Nasional Indonesia (PNI)** and subsequently **Partai Demokrasi Indonesia (PDI)**. It is sometimes confused by Westerners with the buffalo (***kerbau***), to which, however, it is not closely related. [1154]

BAPAK ("father")**.** Common term of deferential address for superiors, believed to promote a collectivist, familial attitude to society. Often abbreviated to "Pak." Under the **New Order**, it largely replaced the more egalitarian "*bung*" as a term of address for political leaders. In 1981, **Suharto**

accepted the title *Bapak Pembangunan* (father of development). *Bapak* also denotes a patron who protects, sponsors, and otherwise assists protégés (***anak buah***). *See also* PATRIMONIALISM. [1391]

BARISAN PELOPOR (Vanguard Corps, from Dutch *voorloper,* pioneer). Youth wing of the **Jawa Hokokai**, formed in August 1944 initially to conduct propaganda, but in May 1945 becoming a paramilitary brigade of about 80,000, though training was limited. At the outset of the **Revolution**, with the dissolution of the **Pembela Tanah Air (PETA)**, it took the name Barisan Banteng (**Banteng** Corps) and was the only quasi-military force at the disposal of Republican leaders. It was not incorporated into the **army** and became one of the more important ***lasykar*** units. [0643]

BARISAN TANI INDONESIA (BTI, Indonesian Peasants' Front). Founded in November 1945 and affiliated soon after with the **Partai Komunis Indonesia (PKI),** the BTI aimed initially at improving conditions on state-owned lands and in forest areas. From the mid-1950s, however, it began to work more widely in rural areas, organizing peasants and using its party contacts to remedy injustices. Despite a shortage of cadres, it reached a claimed membership of 16 million by 1965. It was the main agent by which the PKI promoted **land reform** and conducted direct action (*aksi sepihak*) in the villages, and it aroused great hostility among landowners. It was banned in 1966. [0994, 0997]

BARUS. Port on the west coast of **Sumatra**, north of Sibolga, and probably the entry place for Indian influences penetrating the **Batak** interior. The hinterland of Barus was an important source of **camphor** and benzoin, and the port was possibly the one known as "P'o-lu" in Chinese records of the seventh to eighth centuries. It was certainly the "Fansur" mentioned as an important source of camphor in Arabic records of the ninth century onward. By the early 16th century when it appears in the *Suma Oriental* of **Tomé Pires**, it was a rich and busy port. Apparently the **Minangkabau** rulers exerted influence over the region, but Acehnese territorial influence spread there and by the late 16th century **Aceh** controlled the **trade** of Barus along with that of other west Sumatran ports. [0793]

BATAKS. The Batak can be regarded as a single people incorporating several ethnic and linguistic subgroups. The largest of these, the Toba Batak, inhabit mountain valleys near Lake Toba. To their north were the Pakpak (Dairi), Karo, and Simalungun, and to their south the Angkola and

Mandailing—all of whom speak Batak dialects, some mutually unintelligible. The Bataks were traditionally organized in villages (*huta*), the patrilineal kinship system was dominant, and all knew the *marga* or exogamous patrilineal clan. A line of priest kings called **Sisingamangaraja** played a unifying spiritual role. Ancestor worship was at the center of traditional religion, though there was some recognition of a creator god, Mulajadi na Bolon. Contacts with the outside world were limited at first to **trade** in benzoin and **camphor** through **Barus** on the west coast; Batak legend also acknowledged some allegiance to **Aceh**, **Minangkabau**, and Ayudhya (**Siam**). In general, however, the Batak uplands were isolated until the mid-19th century when Protestant missionaries, the **Dutch** government, and the lowland plantation agriculture encroached simultaneously.

Dutch rule was gradually established in the period up to 1907, when Dutch troops shot Sisingamangaraja XII. Most Karo and Simalungun were administratively incorporated into the East Coast Residency, while the others were included in Tapanuli. About half the Toba became Christians, as did numbers of Simalungun and other North Tapanuli Bataks. The southern Angkola and Mandailing are largely Muslim, having been converted by the Paderi (*see* **MINANGKABAU**) in the 1820s. Many Batak, however, remained animist. (The 1930 **census** recorded 345,408 Muslims, 299,000 Christians, and 512,327 "pagans" among the Batak.) Under Dutch rule the position of traditional leaders steadily weakened, though the colonial authorities made some attempt to bolster them by forming a Tapanuli Council in 1938.

Before 1940 members of ruling lineages held most positions of prestige, but peasants largely repudiated their legitimacy during the **Revolution**, when there was widespread violence among Batak of both Tapanuli and East Sumatra. In its aftermath there were massive migrations, particularly of Toba, to the former plantation lands of East Sumatra. *See* DECENTRALIZATION. [0282, 0660, 0793, 0804, 0901, 1260, 1262]

BATAM. Island in the **Riau** archipelago opposite **Singapore**. In 1970 it became a base of **oil** and **gas** operations in Indonesian waters and from 1971 was developed under **Pertamina** as a port to compete with **Singapore**. The project was suspended in 1976 after Pertamina's bankruptcy but was revived by Technology Minister **B. J. Habibie** to play a more complementary role with Singapore. In 1974 **Suharto** had first proposed the possibility of Batam becoming a free **trade** zone, and in the late 1980s Singapore suggested the possibility of it forming part of a "triangle of growth" with Johor and Singapore within the **Association of Southeast Asian Nations (ASEAN)**. In 1989 Singapore, together with the Johor government and the Indonesian businessman **Liem Sioe Liong**, began to invest directly in an industrial estate on the island. Habibie was pivotal in promoting the island's development. In the 1990s Singapore investment in the island grew, and by 1995 its value was US$649 million, a little under 50 percent of approved foreign **investment**. *See also* GROWTH TRIANGLES. [0362, 0366, 0369]

BATAVIA. Capital city of the Netherlands Indies, site of a **Dutch East Indies Company (VOC)** post from 1610, and founded in 1619 by **J. P. Coen** as regional headquarters for the VOC, on the site of the **Banten** port of Jayakarta. It was first constructed as a **Dutch** city, complete with canals and walls to resist attack from **Mataram**, and much of the surrounding countryside was cleared of its inhabitants to create a kind of cordon sanitaire around the city. Batavia became a major center of settlement by **Chinese**, who lived within the city under their own laws. Tension between the Dutch and the Chinese led to a massacre of Chinese in 1740. The social composition of the city was also influenced by a large slave community, much of it Balinese in origin (*see* **SLAVERY**), who formed the basis for a constantly evolving mestizo culture. By the 19th century, observers identified the **Betawi** as a distinct ethnic group. (*See also* **PARTICULIERE LANDERIJEN**.)

Chronic health problems as a result of waterborne diseases, especially **malaria**, led the colonial authorities in 1810 to shift the center of administration to Weltevreden (the area around the Koningsplein, the present Medan Merdeka). Further government offices shifted to **Bogor** and **Bandung**. A modern harbor was completed at Tanjung Priok in 1886. In 1905, as part of more general administrative reforms, the city was made a *gemeente* (municipality) with limited autonomy (*see* **DECENTRALIZATION**). The city's **population** in the 1930 **census** was 435,000. In 1942, Batavia was occupied by **Japanese** forces, and its name was changed the following year to **Jakarta**. *See also* HEALTH. [0491, 0584, 0585, 0609]

BATAVIAASCH GENOOTSCHAP VAN KUNSTEN EN WETENSCHAPPEN (Batavian Society of the Arts and Sciences)**.** Founded in 1778 by J. C. M. Radermacher (1741–1783) to conduct linguistic, geographical, and anthropological research in the archipelago. Its library formed the nucleus of the National Library of Indonesia collection. *See also* ARCHEOLOGY. [1196]

BATAVIAN REPUBLIC (Bataafsche Republiek). In 1794–1795 French revolutionary troops joined "patriots" (*patriotten*) in overthrowing the conservative Dutch Republic, founding the Batavian Republic, which survived until its incorporation into the French Empire in 1806. Among the various reforms undertaken by the new state was to replace the **Dutch East Indies Company (VOC)**'s Heeren XVII (Seventeen Gentlemen) in 1795 with a Comite tot de Zaken van de Oost-Indische Handel en Bezittingen (Committee for the Affairs of the East Indies Trade and Possessions) and to take possession of the VOC on 17 March 1798. When the VOC charter, which governed Indies affairs, lapsed at the end of 1799, the republic set up a Raad van Aziatischen Bezittingen en Etablissementen (Council for Asian Possessions and Establishments) and in 1803 promulgated a colonial charter, preserving most of the existing system by making the colonial government responsible for the first time to the metropolitan government. In 1806 the charter was replaced by a more liberal "Reglement op het Beleid der Regeering enz." The effect of these measures was limited, however, by the Napoleonic Wars and the occupation of the Indies colonies by **Britain**. The Republic ceased to exist when the Netherlands was occupied by France in 1811. *See also* DAENDELS, HERMAN WILLEM; NETHERLANDS, CONSTITUTIONAL RELATIONSHIP WITH INDONESIA.

BATIG SLOT (budgetary surplus). From 1799 to 1903, the treasury of the Netherlands Indies was part of that of the Netherlands. From the inception of the **Cultivation System** in 1831 until 1877, regular *batig slot* transfers were made to the Dutch treasury from the Indies, totaling *f*823 million over the four decades. *See also* "EERESCHULD, EEN"; *INDIË VERLOREN, RAMPSPOED GEBOREN*.

BATIK. Method of cloth dyeing by wax-resist, first reliably reported from **Java** in the 17th century. Traditionally, beeswax is applied with a metal pen (*canting*), but in the late 19th century metal stamps (*cap*) were introduced widely, as were German aniline dyes to replace the traditional vegetable pigments. Since the 1970s silkscreen prints of fine batik motifs have become widespread. Batik motifs have symbolic significance, specific designs formerly being reserved for particular social groups and occasions. In the early 20th century, Pekalongan became the center for a batik style incorporating European motifs. Batik "painting"(smaller batiks for display rather than wearing) emerged in the 1960s and in the closing decades of the century became an accepted **art** form, distinguished from oil painting in that most batik painters employ craftspeople to do the waxing and dyeing, based on the artist's specifications. Batik has generally been seen as socially conservative, though after independence **Sukarno** promoted a bright pattern called "batik Indonesia." The Solo designer Mohamad Hadi incorporated left-wing motifs in **cloth**s in the early 1960s.

The time-consuming work of fine batik production is commonly the work of **women**, both in villages and in the courts. Village producers were generally dependent on *bakul* (suppliers of cloth and materials), and much batik trading came into **Chinese** hands in the early 20th century, prompting a struggle between indigenous and Chinese merchants that contributed to the emergence of **nationalism** (*see* **SAREKAT ISLAM**). A number of successful **trade** cooperatives emerged in the 1920s and 1930s to keep the industry in indigenous hands. Recent dramatic price rises for high-quality batik have allowed the reemergence of indigenous batik entrepreneurs. At the same time, modern mass production has introduced a new range of motifs and patterns, drawing on the decorative style of non-batik-making cultures. [0144, 0173, 0202, 1403]

BAUXITE. Has been mined on Bintan Island in **Riau** since the 1920s. Most of the product has been exported to **Japan**, but since 1982 some processing to alumina has taken place in the Inalum plant at **Asahan**. **Mining** operations were taken over by the state firm, PT Aneka Tambang. In the late 1970s extensive deposits were found in West **Kalimantan**, but they were judged not feasible for exploitation. [0413]

BAWEAN. Volcanic island in the Java Sea. Settled by Madurese in the 14th century, it was at first an independent state and was later ruled by **Mataram**, until it was conquered by the **Dutch East Indies Company (VOC)** in 1743 and was administered from **Surabaya**. The population is predominantly Muslim with a strong tradition of ***merantau***. Baweanese formed an important trading minority on **Java** in the 19th century. [0007]

BECAK. Three-wheeled pedicab, mostly with the driver at rear, introduced in 1936 but becoming a common form of urban and rural public transport (especially on **Java**) only during and after World War II. In 1971 *becak*s were banned from some main roads in **Jakarta**, partly to reduce congestion, partly because they were considered demeaning to the drivers. Since then the ban has been extended to other roads and cities, and *becak*s have been replaced partly by three-wheeled motorized *bajaj*. [0469, 0470, 0585]

BELITUNG (Billiton)**.** Large island between **Sumatra** and **Kalimantan**. It was formerly under the sultanate of **Palembang**, but in 1812 was seized by the British along with **Bangka** as reparations for the so-called massacre of Palembang. It was disputed by **Britain** and the Netherlands until 1824, and remained barely occupied until 1851, when the Billiton Maatschappij began **mining** there. Extensive immigration of **Chinese** laborers began in 1852.

BELO, BISHOP CARLOS FILIPE XIMENES (1948–)**.** Born near Baucau in **East Timor** in 1948, Belo went to Portugal in 1968 to study for the priesthood. He returned to East Timor in 1974 after the overthrow of the **Portuguese** dictatorship but then went back to Portugal, where he was ordained to the priesthood in 1980. He left Portugal again for East Timor in 1981; was named apostolic administrator, the head of East Timor's Catholic Church, in 1983; and in 1988 was appointed bishop. In the early 1980s he began condemning Indonesian military atrocities in East Timor and in 1984 wrote to the **United Nations** secretary-general calling for a democratic referendum in the region. Pope John Paul II visited East Timor in October 1989 and spoke out on **human rights**. After the Santa Cruz massacre in 1991, hundreds of demonstrators sought refuge in Bishop Belo's home. He continued to speak out for human rights and was increasingly seen as "the voice of the voiceless." He was awarded the Nobel Prize for Peace in 1996, together with **José Ramos Horta**. During the violence following the 1999 referendum on independence, many East Timorese again sought sanctuary in his home, but this time Indonesian-supported **militias** stormed the house and seized hundreds of these refugees, transporting them to West Timor.

After East Timor gained its independence, Bishop Belo went to Portugal for medical treatment, announcing in November 2002 that he would be retiring from his position for health reasons. [0855]

BENGKULU (Benkulen, Bencoolen)**.** Town and region on the southwestern coast of **Sumatra**, formerly subject successively to **Minangkabau**, **Banten**, and the **Dutch East Indies Company (VOC)**. The **English East India Company** founded a settlement there, Fort Marlborough, in 1685 after the **Dutch** had forced them out of Banten. In 1760 the British named Bengkulu capital of their West Sumatran Presidency, and it was their only major region of influence in the archipelago until their expansion during the Napoleonic Wars. **Pepper** was the principal **trade** good, but the colony was seldom more than marginally profitable, being hampered especially by a poor harbor. After a brief period under the energetic rule of **Thomas Stamford Raffles**, who tried to expand the production of **nutmeg**, **cloves**, and cassia, Bengkulu was ceded to the Dutch in the **Anglo-Dutch Treaty** of 1824. But the Dutch did not move to subdue the region, which became a center of **piracy**, until 1868. It never reemerged as a major trading center. It was **Sukarno**'s place of exile from 1938 to 1942, and it became capital of the newly reconstituted province of Bengkulu in 1967. [0491, 0780]

BENTENG PROGRAM. Measures introduced in 1950 to provide ***pribumi*** entrepreneurs with import licenses in order to hasten the development of an indigenous business class. In 1956, however, the program's formal discrimination against **Chinese** was ended, and it was abolished by **Juanda Kartawijaya** in 1957. *See also* ALI-BABA FIRMS; INDONESIANIZATION; SJAFRUDDIN PRAWIRANEGARA. [0313]

BERAU. State in east **Kalimantan**, founded in the 17th century. It was initially subject to **Banjarmasin** but became independent in circa 1750 under Sultan Hasanuddin and dominated the neighboring states of Bulungan and Sumbaliung. Some authorities believe that it was the model for Patusan in *Lord Jim* by **Joseph Conrad**. A Dutch protectorate was established there in 1906.

BERI-BERI. Disease caused by lack of vitamin B1 (thiamine). In the 1870s it became a major health problem in the plantation regions of North **Sumatra**, where workers were fed with mechanically husked **rice**. The idea of deficiency disease was then unknown, and many medical researchers attributed the disease to fungal contamination. In the 1880s C. Eijkman in **Batavia** showed that beri-beri was a consequence of eating hulled rice, but not until 1909 did G. Grijns develop the specific idea that a substance was lost in the milling process.

"BERKELEY MAFIA." *See* BADAN PERENCANAAN PEMBANGUNAN NASIONAL.

BESCHIKKINGSRECHT (right of disposal or allocation)**.** With the strengthening of village (***desa***) structure on **Java** in the 19th century, the colonial government acknowledged the collective right of villages to allocate land to their own members or to other purposes, such as ***tanah bengkok,*** according to circumstances. Under the **Liberal Policy**, this right enabled village elites to allocate **rice** land to **sugar** companies on rotating leases. The different growing cycles and irrigation methods of the two crops worked against rice production. The term *beschikkingsrecht* also applied to the right of the colonial government to allocate *woeste* or wasteland, that is, areas not under active cultivation, to European companies, for sugar production, as forest reserve, or for other purposes, though **Cornelis van Vollenhoven** argued in the 1920s that this practice should not permit villages to be deprived of their usufruct rights over nonagricultural land. *See also* AGRARIAN LAW OF 1870.

BETAWI ("Batavians"). An ethnic group that emerged in **Batavia** from among the many Indonesian residents of the city and the surrounding countryside (*ommelanden*). In a broad sense, the term applied to all of the many Indonesian mestizo cultures that emerged there, but it applies most strictly to a group that first became apparent in the 19th century. The Betawi proper spoke Malay with heavy Balinese and Chinese influence and considered themselves strongly Islamic (though they were less than orthodox in practice). Because of the dominating presence of the colonial establishment and Indonesian immigrant communities, and because of the influence of the ***particuliere landerijen***, Betawi seldom flourished in their own city: they had an unusually high illiteracy rate and played little role in the administrative or political life of the capital. Muhammad Husni Thamrin (1894–1941) founded a political organization called Kaum Betawi in 1923. *See also* MARDIJKERS. [0585]

BETEL. The seed or "nut" of the palm *Areca catechu* (Arecaceae), *jambe,* or *pinang,* native to the region. It has been reported that it was chewed as early as the seventh century, generally in combination with other substances: commonly lime, pepper leaf (*sirih*), and gambier, and occasionally **opium**, amomum, **cloves**, **camphor**, **nutmeg**, and/or **tobacco**. Seeds were exported to **China** in the 13th century. Betel chewing is addictive and leads to loss of appetite, excessive salivation, and general deterioration. Although partially displaced by tobacco smoking from the 16th century, the custom of betel chewing remains widespread, especially in rural areas. [0576]

BEUREU'EH, TEUNGKU MUHAMMAD DAUD (c. 1900–1987). Acehnese Muslim scholar and leader, one of the founders of the anticolonial Persatuan Ulama Seluruh Aceh (PUSA, All-Aceh Union of Ulama) in 1939. In August 1947 Daud Beureu'eh became military governor of **Aceh**

and was governor of the short-lived Aceh province from January to August 1950. Hostile to the inclusion of Aceh in North **Sumatra** province along with the Christian **Bataks**, disappointed at the failure of the central government to adopt **Islam** as the basic principle of the state, and alarmed by the arrest of PUSA activists in August 1951 (at a time when communists were being arrested elsewhere in Indonesia), he joined the **Darul Islam** in circa September 1953, declaring Aceh to be part of the Islamic State of Indonesia and launching a general revolt throughout the region. The rebels never controlled more than half the province and failed to capture the capital, Banda Aceh, but they were well entrenched in the countryside, especially in the north. Beureu'eh headed both civil and military commands for the Islamic state in Aceh and in January 1955 was appointed vice president next to **Sekarmaji Marijan Kartosuwiryo**, but there was little effective coordination with the rebellion elsewhere. As the rebellion dragged on, many on both sides began feeling their way toward a compromise, but it was only after Beureu'eh's followers deposed him in a bloodless coup in March 1959 that a settlement was reached, Aceh receiving the status of a Daerah Istimewa (Special Territory). Beureu'eh then briefly formed an alliance with remnants of the **PRRI/Permesta rebellion** now formed into the Republik Persatuan Indonesia (RPI), but ceased resistance in May 1962.

After the advent of the **Suharto** regime, Beureu'eh was appointed to the regime-sponsored Indonesian Council of Ulama (MUI), but was removed two years later, possibly because of his independent stance. He did not officially support the Gerakan Aceh Merdeka (GAM), reportedly because it had not adopted Islam as its ideology, but the government was fearful enough that he might sympathize with it that they removed him to **Jakarta** in 1978. In the early **elections** of the **New Order**, he supported Islamic parties in the elections, but in the final year of his life he gave his "blessing" to a **Golkar** victory in the province of Aceh. [0808, 0820, 0827, 1258]

BHARATAYUDDHA ("War of the Bharatas"). Old Javanese *kakawin* (poem) based on the **Mahabharata** and composed in 1157 by Mpu Sedah and Mpu Panuluh under the patronage of **Joyoboyo** of **Kediri**. It describes the 18-day battle that ends the war between the Kurawa and Pandawa. [0132, 0159]

BHINNEKA TUNGGAL IKA (Old Javanese "They are many, they are one," usually translated as "Unity in diversity"). Phrase reputedly coined by Empu Tantalar in the 15th century and adopted on 17 August 1950 as Indonesia's national motto. *See also* GARUDA.

"BIG FIVE." The five major **Dutch** trading houses in late colonial Indonesia, which also held a dominant place in the export **economy** until they were nationalized in 1957. They were the Internationale Crediet en Handelsvereeniging Rotterdam (Internatio), Jacobson van den Bergh, Borneo Sumatra Maatschappij (Borsumij), Lindetevis Stokvis, and Geo. Wehry. *See also* NATIONALIZATION. [0315]

BILLITON. *See* BELITUNG.

BIMA. Kingdom on the eastern half of the island of **Sumbawa**, founded in perhaps the 11th century from when there are signs of **Hindu** influence. It was a vassal of **Makassar** in the early 17th century and converted to **Islam** in circa 1640. Although the **Dutch East Indies Company (VOC)** assumed suzerainty in 1667, the Bima sultanate remained a powerful regional kingdom into the 19th century, creating Bimanese settlements in **Flores** and **Sumba**. Effective Dutch control was not established until the late 19th century. After independence, the sultanate was challenged by young Islamic reformers loyal to the Republic and opposed to the sultan's cooperation with the Dutch in the federal movement. Most of the Bima aristocracy, however, was able to retain its influence and formed the major part of the new bureaucracy. [0574]

BINNENLANDSCH BESTUUR (BB, internal administration)**.** The generalized administrative corps of the Netherlands Indies. Until the 19th century, the term meant little more than the body of **Dutch East Indies Company (VOC)** officials in the colony, especially those posted to represent the governor-general outside the capital, **Batavia**. The BB emerged as a distinct structure on **Java** in the early 19th century under **Herman Willem Daendels**, who divided the island into prefectures and created a relatively ordered bureaucratic hierarchy. This structure was somewhat modified by **Thomas Stamford Raffles**, who replaced the prefects with residents, and by the **decentralization** program of the early 20th century.

Administrative dualism was a central principle of the BB. The organization was divided into the *Europeesch Bestuur,* or European administration, and the ***Inlandsch Bestuur,*** or native administration, the latter supervising the former, so that, according to the aims of the system, all contacts by the Indonesian masses with their rulers would be through fellow Indonesians. In 1865 the *Europeesch Bestuur* on **Java** numbered only 175 men, backed of course by the colonial **army**. On Java, the rank of *controleur* was paired with that of ***bupati*** in the *Inlandsch Bestuur* as a putative advisory "elder brother" to the Indonesian ruler. In time the *Europeesch Bestuur* developed an extended hierarchy running (from below) *adspirant controleur*, *controleur*, *assistent resident*, *resident,* and *gouverneur,* and holders of senior posts were generally recruited from lower ranks in the hierarchy.

In the 19th and 20th centuries, the role of the BB was diminished by the emergence of distinct specialist branches of government, beginning with finances in 1854. By the end of the colonial era, departments of justice, finances, **education** and religion, economic affairs, transport and water affairs, war, and naval affairs had emerged alongside the BB, all of them open at all levels, unlike the EB, to Indonesians. [0479, 0604]

BIRDS OF PARADISE (*cenderawasih*)**.** Birds of the family *Paradisaeidae*, found principally on the island of New Guinea (**Papua**) and adjacent regions. The males are often spectacularly plumed and have been used by people of the island for adornment since early times. The first pelts to reach Europe were sewn so as to conceal the feet, and the belief grew that the birds never rested but always flew as if in paradise. **Trade** in bird of paradise pelts was underway in the 16th century and is probably much older. **China** was the principal market at first, but it was displaced by Europe in the 19th century. In 1911, 43,000 pelts were exported from **Ternate**. Concern over the effect of this trade helped to prompt the first nature **conservation** measures in the Netherlands Indies.

BOEKE, JULIUS HERMAN (1884–1944)**.** Prominent economic advisor to the colonial government and professor at Leiden University. Influenced by the writings of M. K. Gandhi, he proposed the notion of **dualism**, rejecting the application of Western economic theory to the Asian village and urging a dualistic economic policy that would protect and even restore what he saw as traditional communal village life while providing general welfare for the Westernized sections of society. He was interned in Buchenwald 1941–1944 for anti-Nazi activities. *See also DESA*; DEVELOPMENT IDEOLOGY. [0292]

BOGOR. Formerly Buitenzorg, city in the foothills of Mt. Salak south of **Jakarta**. Governor-General Gustaaf Willem, baron van Imhoff established a private house there in 1745 and the official residence of the governor-general was gradually transferred there. The city was the site of an agricultural research station that became the basis of the Landbouwkundige Faculteit, subsequently the Bogor Agricultural Institute (Institut Pertanian Bogor; *see* **EDUCATION**) and of a **botanical gardens**.

BONE. Bugis state in southern **Sulawesi**, founded in the 14th century and the main rival of **Makassar**, which conquered it and converted it to **Islam** in 1611, though it was left autonomous. Bone was awarded by the Dutch to **Arung Palakka** under the Treaty of Bungaya in 1667. The Bone kingdom became a centralized state, and it was at this time that Buginese and Makassarese began migrating from its authoritarian rule to establish themselves in other regions of the archipelago. The rulers of Bone took advantage of the opportunity offered by the British interregnum in the Indies during the Napoleonic Wars to repudiate the treaty of Bungaya, and in 1824 they launched a war on local **Dutch** garrisons. Though defeated by Dutch and Makassarese forces from Gowa in 1825, Bone continued to resist the Dutch during the **Java War** and accepted the renewed treaty only in 1838. The power of the Bone kingdom declined in the 19th century, and its weakening centralized system opened the way for aristocrats to conduct **trade** activities and commercialized **agriculture**. In 1859 the Dutch sent an expedition against Bone, deposing its queen and formally making the kingdom a subject, rather than an ally, of the Dutch. A further expedition in 1905 captured the capital, Watampone, and deposed the ruler, who was not replaced until 1931. [0502, 0529, 0549]

BOROBUDUR. Buddhist monument in Central **Java**, constructed circa 800 A.D. under the **Sailendras**. It is in the form of a massive stupa, with seven terraces. The quadrangular four lower galleries of reliefs tell the life story of the Buddha and other **Buddhist** teachings such as the Jatakas. One gallery of lower reliefs was later covered with earth to prevent collapse of the structure. Three circular upper terraces are bare but for 72 small stupas containing statues of the Buddha. A single larger stupa is at the center. The overall form of the monument is also a representation of Buddhist philosophy, the crowded lower terraces symbolizing the distractions of daily life, the bare upper terraces the achievement of detachment. The reliefs are carved in the Indian style and show a mixture of Indian and Javanese motifs: elephants, for instance, which are not native to Java (though formerly they were imported from **Sumatra**), and a cockatoo, which is not found in **India**.

Borobudur was damaged by earthquakes and buried by volcanic ash some time after its construction and was first reexcavated by **Thomas Stamford Raffles** in 1814. A full-scale reconstruction was undertaken by the colonial archeological service under Theodor van Erp in 1907–1912, and a further restoration occurred under the auspices of UNESCO from 1973 to 1983, costing US$60 million. In 1985 an explosion of uncertain origin damaged the upper part of the monument, though this was subsequently repaired. *See also* ARCHEOLOGY. [0113, 0116]

BOTANICAL GARDENS ('sLands Plantentuin, Kebun Raya)**.** Founded in **Bogor** (Buitenzorg) in 1817 by Caspar Georg Carl Reinwardt (1773–1854) and directed successively by Carl Ludwig Blume (1796–1862), Melchior Treub (1851–1910), and others, the gardens became one of the finest tropical plant collections in the world. In 1860 a branch was established in Cibodas. Until the establishment of a separate conservation section in the Department of Agriculture in 1951, the gardens had primary responsibility for **conservation** of nature in the Netherlands Indies and Indonesia. [1194, 1195]

BOTH, PIETER (?–1615)**.** First **governor-general** of the Netherlands Indies. He expelled the Spaniards from **Tidore** and the **Portuguese** from Fort Henricus on Solor, opened **Dutch East Indies Company (VOC)** offices in **Java** at Sunda Kelapa (later **Batavia**) and Japara, and sent the first **Dutch** mission to the court of **Mataram**. [0491]

BOVEN DIGUL (Tanah Merah)**.** Detention center on the upper Digul River in West New Guinea (**Papua**), established in 1926 primarily for those accused of involvement in the 1926–1927 **Partai Komunis Indonesia (PKI)** uprisings. Some 1,308 alleged communists and nationalists were detained there in May 1930, a number that declined to about 446 in 1937. Among those held there under the so-called *exorbitante rechten* of the governor-general (*see* **EXILE**) were **Mohammad Hatta** and **Sutan Sjahrir**, both of whom were transferred to Banda Neira in 1936. In 1943 the camp was closed and the remaining detainees were removed to **Australia**, where they were later released under pressure from Australian labor unions. *See also TAHANAN POLITIK*. [0634, 0865]

BRITAIN, HISTORICAL LINKS WITH. The **English East India Company** was the main agent for British involvement in the archipelago during the 17th and 18th centuries. In 1800, after the **Dutch** colonial administration had recognized the pro-French **Batavian Republic**, British forces occupied **Melaka**, West **Sumatra**, and Dutch possessions in **Maluku**. A British fleet appeared before **Batavia** but lacked forces to take the city. The colonies were restored under the Treaty of Amiens in March 1802.

In August and September 1811, after French forces had occupied the Netherlands in 1810, company forces from British India conquered **Java** and other Dutch possessions in the archipelago (**Ambon**, **Minahasa**) in order to remove French influence, and they established an interim administration on Java under **Thomas Stamford Raffles** as lieutenant-governor, with an advisory council of Dutch and British. Hoping to retain the island for Britain, Raffles undertook major reforms there, but he was unable to convince the company's directors that the colony would be worthwhile, and it was restored to the Dutch in August 1816 under the terms of an Anglo-Dutch convention signed in 1814. British policy was also that the Kingdom of the Netherlands in Europe (then including Belgium) should be bolstered as a powerful bulwark against possible French expansion, and Britain saw the revenues from Indonesia as playing some role in Dutch power. Britain retained its existing settlements in **Bengkulu** until 1824.

From this time on, however, Dutch rule in the colony remained to some extent at British sufferance. The **Anglo-Dutch Treaty of 1824** allowed the Dutch extensive holdings in the archipelago, but Britain acquiesced in this arrangement partly because the Netherlands had ceased to be a major European power and thus played a useful role for Britain in keeping French and later German political influence out of the region. Britain's **Singapore** naval base, established in 1921, became the keystone of Dutch **defense policy** in the colony. At the same time, the Dutch felt constrained to allow considerable British commercial investment there as a further guarantee of their tenure. British investments in the Netherlands Indies in 1929 were valued at *f*277.9 million, second only after that of the Netherlands. Only in a few cases, such as the **shipping** industry, did the Dutch discriminate actively against British interests (*see also* **TELEGRAPH**). [0077, 0083, 0818, 0583]

BRITAIN, RELATIONS WITH. British and **Dutch** forces cooperated with those of the **United States** and **Australia** in the defense of the region against the **Japanese** in 1941–1942; and after the Allied counterattack began, **Sumatra** was included in the predominantly British South East Asia Command under Lord Louis Mountbatten. On 16 August 1945, this command was extended to cover the entire Netherlands Indies, thus giving the British primary responsibility for accepting the Japanese surrender, evacuating Allied prisoners-of-war and internees, and restoring the colonial government. By the time British forces arrived in **Jakarta** in late September, however, the Indonesian Republic was relatively firmly established. Unwilling to fight a major colonial war to restore Dutch control (especially since Britain was in the process of withdrawing from **India**), the British attempted to play a mediating role between the Dutch and the Republic, sponsoring first informal contacts and then negotiations that ultimately led to the **Linggajati Agreement**. Britain's formal postsurrender responsibilities ended on 30 November 1946.

During the 1950s Indonesia became suspicious of British intentions in retaining the **Singapore** naval base, and relations declined sharply as Britain's formula for granting independence to its Southeast Asian possessions involved creation of a Malaysian federation, including Singapore and the north Borneo territories, without giving up its Singapore base. In response, in September 1963 **Sukarno** instituted a policy of **Confrontation** against **Malaysia**. In May 1965 he claimed, on the basis of a letter said to be from the British ambassador Sir Anthony Gilchrist, that Britain was plotting with **army** groups to overthrow him.

After **Suharto**'s accession to power, Confrontation was ended and relations between Britain and Indonesia improved markedly. Within the context of the **Inter-Governmental Group on Indonesia (IGGI)**, British loans to Indonesia totaled more than US$736 million and further sums were pledged during the 1990s within the framework of the **Consultative Group on Indonesia (CGI)** and in accordance with a series of so-called UK–Indonesia Concessional Loan Arrangements (CLA), which financed projects in such sectors as power, transportation, broadcasting, higher **education**, and **forestry**. [0478, 0661, 0726, 1120]

BROAD OUTLINES OF STATE POLICY. *See* MAJELIS PERMUSYAWARATAN RAKYAT.

BUBONIC PLAGUE (*Pasteurella pestis*)**.** It is possible that parts of Indonesia were affected by the plague pandemics of the sixth and 14th centuries, but evidence suggesting this is slender. The disease is first known definitely to have reached **Java** in 1910 aboard a **rice** ship from Burma, and outbreaks continued on the island until the 1940s. The death toll from the disease in the period 1911–1939 is officially given as 215,000, but was almost certainly many more. Fears of the virulence of the disease led the colonial government, through its Dienst der Pestbestrijding (plague control service), founded in 1915, to undertake a massive control program, which included extensive quarantine, the destruction and fumigation of property, the reconstruction of 1.25 million houses to rat-proof designs, and, from 1934, an extensive vaccination program in which 7 million people were vaccinated or revaccinated. The common method of diagnosing plague deaths, by puncturing the spleen of the deceased, was strongly resisted by Muslims, who saw it as a violation of the dead. *See also* ETHICAL POLICY; HEALTH. [0576, 1204]

BUDDHISM. Theravada Buddhism was probably established briefly in southern **Sumatra** in the fifth century, but was soon replaced by Mahayana Buddhism. **Srivijaya** became a major center of Buddhist studies in the seventh century, having close ties with Nalanda in Bihar. In later centuries, strong influences from Tantrism were felt. The massive stupa of **Borobudur** was succeeded by Hindu rather than Buddhist temples, but Buddhism seems to have survived as an aspect of **Hinduism** rather than being displaced. The religion of **Majapahit** was Hindu and Buddhist, but formal adherence to Buddhism largely ceased among indigenous Indonesians with the conversion to **Islam** in the 13th–16th centuries, though Buddhism remains an important element in Hindu religious practice on **Bali**.

In colonial times Buddhism was largely a religion of **Chinese in Indonesia**, but in the 1930s, under influences from theosophy, Buddhism underwent a revival among Europeans in the colony. After independence, Buddhist leaders made determined efforts to recruit indigenous Indonesian members, forming the Perbuddhi (Perhimpunan Buddhis Indonesia, Indonesian Buddhist Association) in 1958. Buddhists now constitute approximately 4.5 percent of the population. Under the **New Order**, the insistence of the **Pancasila** on "Belief in God" led some Buddhists to revise their philosophy to include a single supreme deity, Sang Hyang Adi Buddha. Vesak Day (celebrating the birth of Buddhism's founder) has been a national holiday in Indonesia since 1983. *See also* RELIGION AND POLITICS. [0487]

BUDGETS. Suharto's **New Order** based its economic philosophy on the slogan of a balanced budget, which proved to be an effective political device to prevent recurrence of the economic disasters of the early 1960s. By ensuring that expenditure was determined by revenue, the government was able to control political pressures that demanded larger expenditure levels. However, the immense international loans on which the New Order's **economy** was based complicated the situation. In the 1980s as **oil** revenues declined, **debt**-servicing obligations rose to 30.3 percent of government expenditures in 1987, necessitating sharp reductions in government subsidies in fields such as **rice**, fertilizer, and pesticides. After 1990 the need to maintain a balanced budget was increasingly subordinated to political concerns until the financial collapse of the late 1990s. *See also* CORRUPTION; DEBT; ECONOMY; FINANCIAL CRISIS. [0301, 0730]

BUDI UTOMO ("Noble Endeavor")**.** Society founded on 20 May 1908 by Dr. Wahidin Sudiro Husodo (1857–1917), **Dr. Sutomo**, and Gunawan Mangunkusumo and regarded as the start of Indonesia's national awakening (*kebangkitan nasional*). It aimed at first to promote the study of Javanese culture and to improve access to Western **education**, but slowly became more political, arguing in 1914, for instance, for an Indies militia. Dominated by the lesser ***priyayi*** of the colonial civil service, it was always conservative and was viewed with approval by the colonial government as a positive result of the **Ethical Policy**. As a result, it was somewhat distrusted by other nationalist parties. In 1935 it dissolved itself into the **Partai Indonesia Raya (Parindra)**. *See also* ASSOCIATION PRINCIPLE; NATIONALISM. [0625]

BUFFALO. *See KERBAU.*

BUGIS. Ethnic group in southern **Sulawesi**, forming in 1979 approximately half of the region's people (3.5 million out of 7 million). Like the neighboring Makassarese, the Bugis were traditionally divided into many small states, but their kingdom of **Bone** became increasingly powerful in the 16th century until it was conquered by **Makassar** and converted to **Islam** in the early 17th century. Led by **Arung Palakka**, many Bugis joined the **Dutch East Indies Company (VOC)** against Makassar in the campaigns of 1660, 1666–1667, and 1668–1669, but in the late 17th century, following the defeat of Makassar, many Bugis fled the area and settled widely on **Sumatra**, **Kalimantan**, and the **Malay Peninsula**, founding the last dynasty of the sultans of **Aceh**. Such communities feature in several works of **Joseph Conrad**. Bugis troops were often used as mercenaries. Bugis are the major inter-island trading community of eastern Indonesia, establishing a dominance in the archipelago's sea-trading network. The regional rebellions of the 1950s triggered further Bugis migration, this time to Indonesia's eastern islands, and as the **Suharto** regime strengthened control over **East Timor** and Irian Jaya (**Papua**), Bugis merchants followed the military forces. As immigrants and Muslims, they became one of the major targets of attack in the interethnic, interreligious violence in **Maluku** and Timor in the late 1990s, many being forced to return to South Sulawesi. *See also* RIAU. [0461, 0549, 1245, 1246]

BUITENZORG. *See* BOGOR.

"BUNG." Common term of address (for males) during the **Revolution**, derived from Javanese *abang* ("brother") and implying revolutionary equality; it is now seldom used except to refer to leaders of the Revolution, especially Bung Karno (**Sukarno**). The Sundanese equivalent, "Bang," is routinely adopted by governors of Jakarta as a populist gesture. *See also BAPAK.*

BUPATI. In precolonial **Java**, the *bupati* was a local chief generally in a vassal relationship with a nearby king or senior chief. His authority was over households, or *cacah* (and thus men-at-arms), rather than over territory and was likely to fluctuate widely with the vagaries of war and economic change. There was a natural tendency for the domain of a *bupati* (*kabupaten*) to coincide with economic and geographical boundaries, so that although the political geography of Java was always in flux, the boundaries of *kabupaten* remained historically relatively stable.

Under **Dutch** rule, the fealty of the *bupati* was shifted from the royal courts to the **Dutch East Indies Company (VOC)**, and they were tied increasingly to specific areas of **land** rather than to scattered households, though they retained something of the character of allies, rather than officials, of the company. They were obliged only to organize the delivery of crops demanded by the VOC and were left in full control of internal administration of their territories. Under **Herman Willem Daendels** and **Thomas Stamford Raffles**, however, the *bupati* became unambiguously officials of the colonial administration (***Binnenlandsch Bestuur***), with the title *regent.* The Dutch also reduced the number of *bupati* dramatically in some regions, placing each *bupati* at the head of a native hierarchy within his *kabupaten* or regency (*see* ***INLANDSCH BESTUUR***).

Restraining, and at times reversing, this trend toward bureaucratization was the need of the colonial government to employ the traditional authority of the *bupati* as a key to the control of the Javanese peasantry. Under Daendels, and later under the **Cultivation System**, the *bupati* were primarily responsible for mobilizing **labor** in service of production for the colonial state, and colonial authorities sought from time to time to bolster the position of the *bupati* as small-time kings or princes, especially by making the office hereditary. In 1913 a conservative Regentenbond (Regents Society) was formed.

The *bupati* were largely retained in office during the **Japanese occupation** as *ken-cho.* On independence, the Indonesian Republic retained the *kabupaten,* headed by a *bupati,* as a major administrative unit, and it has now been extended throughout Indonesia as the principal administrative division below the province, known formally as *Daerah Tingkat II* (second-level region). Between 1957 and 1959, *bupati* were elected to office. Under the **decentralization** policies in the post-**Suharto** era, the *kabupaten* became the principal unit of administration and was no longer dependent on the province for its budget and direction. *See also DESA*; *PRIYAYI*. [0479, 0636]

BURU. Mountainous island in **Maluku**, originally inhabited by the highland Alfurs. From circa 1520 it was under the rule of **Ternate**, which converted the coastal areas to **Islam**, and it was an important **clove**-producing area until **Dutch East Indies Company (VOC) hongi raids** in 1652 destroyed the plantations. Local resistance to the **Dutch** in 1657 gave the VOC the excuse to move the indigenous population to the area around Kayeli Bay. In the early 19th century, the island became a major center for the production of *kayuputih* oil. After the **Gestapu** coup of 1965, many thousands of political prisoners (***tahanan politik***) were detained in prison camps on the island, with the last of these prisoners released only in December 1979. [0025, 0253, 0736, 1189]

BUTON (Butung)**.** Muslim sultanate established in 1540, based on the earlier kingdom of Wolio and covering the islands off the southeast arm of **Sulawesi**. It was conquered by **Ternate** in 1580, and successive sultans thereafter tried to play off **Ternate**, **Makassar**, and the **Dutch East Indies Company (VOC)**. With the fall of Makassar, the kingdom came definitely within the **Dutch** sphere of influence. They weakened the political base of the kingdom, however, by exporting slaves on a large scale. After a Dutch military expedition in 1906, the sultan signed the

Korte Verklaring in 1912. The sultanate was abolished in 1960. Asphalt has been mined on Buton since 1926. *See also ZELFBESTUREN*. [0446]

– C –

CALENDARS. Numerous traditional calendars have been employed in the archipelago at various times. The Muslim calendar is lunar, with a year of 354 or 355 days divided into 12 months. The counting of years commenced in 622 A.D. with Muhammad's flight (*hijrah*) to Medina, and Muslim dates are commonly denoted in English by A.H. (*anno hijrae*), in Indonesian by H (years according to the Christian calendar being marked with M for *Masehi*). The year 1410 A.H. commenced on 3 August 1989 A.D. The Javanese calendar, also lunar with 354–355 days per year, was adopted by **Sultan Agung** of **Mataram** using much Muslim terminology but with a somewhat different division of months and arrangement of leap years and a base year of 78 A.D., the putative start of the Hindu-Javanese era. Years are now commonly denoted with the initials A.J. (*anno Javanicae*). For agricultural purposes, the Javanese also used sun-years (*mangsa*), but these were not counted. The year 1922 A.J. commenced on 3 August 1989 A.D.

During the **Japanese occupation**, the traditional Japanese system of counting years from the founding of the imperial dynasty was used; 1942 thus became 2602. [0032]

CAMBODIA, RELATIONS WITH. The precolonial Javanese state of **Majapahit** claimed ties with Cambodia in the 14th century. But there was little interaction between the two regions throughout the colonial period, when Cambodia formed part of French Indochina. After World War II, growing ties developed between their two leaders, **Sukarno** and Prince Norodom Sihanouk, both of whom were struggling to maintain their countries as neutralist states and leading members of the Non-Aligned Movement. Sihanouk attended the 1955 **Asia-Africa Conference** in **Bandung**. After the fall of Sukarno, when Indonesia entered the Western camp, relations between Sihanouk and Indonesian president **Suharto** were not warm. The Indonesian government acceded to American requests that anti-Sihanouk Cambodian troops be trained in Indonesia. After the 1970 coup against Sihanouk the **United States** encouraged Indonesia to help in Cambodia, but Foreign Minister **Adam Malik** headed off these efforts. He criticized the American/Vietnamese incursion into Cambodia and convened the Djakarta Conference on

Cambodia held in May 1970, which succeeded in keeping Indonesia neutral in the dispute.

Indonesia played a mediating role in Cambodia when in July 1988 it hosted the first round of negotiations between Cambodian groups and interested regional states, and subsequently it was instrumental in getting the warring Cambodian factions to agree to **United Nations**–sponsored **elections** in 1993.

Cambodia was admitted to the **Association of Southeast Asian Nations (ASEAN)** in April 1999, and in July 2002 direct trading links were established between Jakarta (Tanjung Priok) and Sihanoukville. At that time, Indonesian exports to Cambodia had reached US$72 million in value compared with less than US$1 million in imports from Cambodia. Indonesia expressed an interest in importing **rice** from Cambodia, while Cambodia wished to import **oil** and fertilizer. [0748, 0751, 1125, 1144]

CAMPHOR (from Malaysian *kapur*)**.** Aromatic crystalline substance collected from cavities in the trunks of felled *Dryobalanops aromatica* (Dipterocarpaceae) trees, especially in northern **Sumatra**. It was used in incense and medicines and for the preservation of corpses, and from the sixth century it was traded extensively from **Kalimantan** and from North Sumatra through the west coast port of **Barus** to **China**, **India**, the **Arab** world, and the Mediterranean. Collection was done in great secrecy, and collectors developed a secret language to conceal their activities. **Trade** with China declined after techniques were developed to extract camphor from the East Asian tree *Cinnamomum camphora. Dryobalanops* is now more important as a timber tree. [0527, 0543, 0793]

CANNABIS (*Cannabis sativa* Cannabaceae, *ganja*)**.** Native to the area around the Caspian Sea but reported from **Java** in the 10th century, cannabis was used both for its fiber and as an intoxicant, though its use never approached that of **betel**, **opium**, or **tobacco**. Its use was banned in 1927, but it is still found wild in northern **Sumatra** and has been the subject of a government antinarcotic campaign since the late 1970s. In the 1990s sections of the Indonesian military reportedly developed a strong interest in the illegal cannabis trade from **Aceh**. [0331, 0332]

CATHOLICISM. Although the Franciscan Odoric of Pordonone preached in **Java**, **Sumatra**, and **Kalimantan** in circa 1324, formal Catholic missionary activity in Indonesia began only after the **Portuguese** captured **Melaka** in 1511 and established outposts in **Maluku**. Francis Xavier worked in **Ternate** and **Ambon** 1546–1547, and significant conversions were made in Ambon, Ternate, **Flores**, **Timor**, and the north coast of Java. Militarized Dominican friars claimed much of the islands of Flores and Timor for Portugal in the mid-16th century and were the principal agents of Portuguese domination there until the early 19th century. They were expelled by the Portuguese government in 1834.

The **Dutch East Indies Company (VOC)** banned the promotion of Catholicism, and though formal freedom of religion was allowed with the fall of the company in 1800, many practical restrictions remained. The Catholic Church continued to be banned from certain regions, notably the **Batak** regions of northern Sumatra and the **Toraja** areas of **Sulawesi**, but in the mid-19th century was allocated Flores and Timor as mission areas as part of an agreement with the Portuguese over jurisdictions in east **Nusatenggara**. The present Catholic population of about 5 million is concentrated on Flores and Timor and to a lesser extent in Central Java, where it has been adopted by many **Chinese** Indonesians. Albert Sugiyopranoto (1896–1963) was the first Indonesian to be appointed bishop.

Youth organizations tied to the Catholic Party (**Partai Katolik**) played a large role in the **student** demonstrations that brought **Suharto** to power, and their leaders developed close ties to **Ali Murtopo**, joining with him in the establishment of the **Centre for Strategic and International Studies (CSIS)**, which had a substantial influence on shaping the policies of the early **New Order** government. Under the Suharto regime, Catholics then came to play a policy and media role in Indonesian life disproportionate to their numbers. The Catholic-owned Kompas-Gramedia group published the respected daily newpaper *Kompas* and weekly magazine *Tempo,* and by the mid-1990s dominated the publishing industry. *See also* CHRISTIANITY; MEDIA; RELIGION AND POLITICS. [0835, 1341]

CATTLE (*Bos taurus* and *B. indicus*)**.** Cattle were abundant on **Java** from the 10th century, and dried meat was exported to **China** in the 19th century. There was little traditional use of milk in the archipelago except in parts of **Sumatra** and for ritual purposes. Dairies, however, were established by the **Dutch East Indies Company (VOC)** in **Ambon** and the **Batavia** region in the 17th century, and milk became a luxury especially associated with European ways of life. From 1880, condensed milk was imported from Europe and **Australia**, and use of milk began to spread increasingly to Indonesians. The colonial **agriculture** department began systematic improvement of cattle strains in 1904. The first hygiene regulations for milk were issued in 1920. Under the **New Order**, attempts were made to develop the cattle industry as consumer demand for meat and milk grew. *See also BANTENG*; *KERBAU*; PASTEUR INSTITUTE.

CELEBES. *See* SULAWESI.

CENDANA GROUP. General term for those business interests associated with **Suharto**'s presidential palace, notably the holdings of his wife Siti Hartinah (Tien) Suharto (especially the charitable organization Yayasan Harapan Kita); her brother-in-law Probosutejo (especially the Mercu Buana group); her sons Tommy (Mandala Putra Hutomo), Sigit Harjojudanto, and Bambang Trihatmojo; and her daughter Siti Hardiyanti Rukmana (Tutut); and with President Suharto's banker **Liem Sioe Liong**. *See also* CLOVES; SUHARTO FAMILY. [0313, 0373]

CENSORSHIP. Until 1815 the **governor-general** had absolute right to restrict or ban the circulation of publications in the Indies, though this right was exercised mainly in the centers of European settlement. Although the free circulation of Netherlands publications was guaranteed by the **Regeeringsreglement** (**constitution**) of the Netherlands Indies in 1815, local and foreign publications were subject to censorship. The 1856 Reglement op de Drukwerken (Regulation of Publications) provided for prepublication censorship, and the governor-general had the right, in consultation with the **Raad van Indië**, to ban local periodicals on grounds of agitation or the undermining of state authority. Like the **exorbitante rechten**, this power was not subject to judicial appeal or review. In 1906 postpublication censorship was introduced: all publications had to be submitted to the censor within 24 hours and could be suspended. From 1914 prosecution was also possible under the so-called *haatzaai* articles (*see* **SUBVERSION**). Revised regulations for press muzzling (*persbreidel*) were introduced in 1931, and in the following five years 27 nationalist **newspapers** were restricted. Prepublication censorship was restored under the **Japanese**.

In the first years of independence, there was virtually no censorship, but control was restored in 1957 with the imposition of martial law. Publications were censored by prepublication government instructions, by bans on distribution, by the blacking out of offending articles (especially in the case of foreign publications), and by withdrawal of a publication's Surat Ijin Terbit (SIT, publication license), introduced in 1958. Heavy press restrictions were introduced in 1965–1966, when 46 newspapers were banned and the Indonesian Journalists' Association (Persatuan

Wartawan Indonesia) was purged. Restrictions were formalized in a new Press Law of December 1966, intended officially to ensure that the press would be "free but responsible."

Under the **New Order**, newspapers, magazines, popular music, and particularly films were controlled through censorship codes designed to protect state security and social harmony. In the film industry, a Badan Sensor Filem (BSF) carried out this censorship. Literature, popular fiction, and magazines were subject to standard censorship procedures—all book titles had to be cleared by the Attorney-General's Department, and magazines required a publishing license subject to recall by the Department of Information. Another Press Law in September 1982 replaced the SIT with a Surat Ijin Usaha Penerbitan Pers (SIUPP, Permit to Operate a Press Company), withdrawal of which could stop publication not just of the offending publication but of all other business operations associated with it. One characteristic of the censorship under **Suharto** that influenced the nature of what appeared was the fact that the censors evaluated publications after they appeared, not before, which invited writers to test the limits of censorship but also to employ self-censorship and avoid open criticism of the governing regime.

In August 1990 the government announced that there would be no more banning of newspapers, but after a period of "openness" (*see* ***KETERBUKAAN***) over the next few years, it reimposed harsh censorship in June 1994, banning the popular news magazines *Tempo* and *Editor,* together with the political tabloid *Detik. Tempo*'s editor, Goenawan Mohammad, challenged the ban in court, but after initial favorable findings the **Supreme Court** upheld the government's actions. Throughout this period, the plays of **Willibrordus S. Rendra** and the novels of **Pramoedya Ananta Toer** were consistently banned. Although much of the censorship was lifted after the end of the Suharto regime, some restrictions remained, with authorization of the attorney general required before a book could be published. *See also* MEDIA. [0756, 0761, 1304, 1306.]

CENSUSES. Most rulers in Indonesia have required some form of **population** count for **taxation** purposes, and Alfred Wallace describes an ingenious method of counting attributed to the ruler of **Lombok**. Most commonly, however, households rather than individuals were counted and the association with taxation makes early figures, which are not common in any case, highly unreliable. S. C. Nederburgh conducted the first census of **Java** in 1795, and the **Dutch** conducted a partial count of the population of the Indies in 1905, a more extensive count in 1920, and a full census in 1930. A further census planned for 1940 was canceled because of the war. The first census in independent Indonesia was held in 1961 but was incomplete, and many of the detailed results have since been lost. Full censuses were held in 1971, 1980, 1990, and 2000. In 2000 the census bureau was more ambitious than in previous censuses and attempted to administer a full questionnaire, involving, in addition to a complete enumeration of the population on such common topics as name, sex, and age, more detailed information on such matters as relationship to head of household, marital status, socioeconomic characteristics, **education**, fertility, mobility, and housing conditions. [0069, 0071, 0072, 0075, 1318]

CENTRE FOR INFORMATION AND DEVELOPMENT STUDIES (CIDES). An Islamic think tank set up in 1993 by the **Ikatan Cendekiawan Muslim Indonesia (ICMI)** as a counterweight to the Christian-led think tanks, especially the largely Catholic-led **Centre for Strategic and International Studies (CSIS)**. CIDES was the brainchild of **B. J. Habibie**, then minister for science and technology; under his chairmanship, CIDES'S major focus was on development issues. Its influence declined after Habibie lost the Indonesian presidency. [0756]

CENTRE FOR STRATEGIC AND INTERNATIONAL STUDIES (CSIS). A research center established in 1971 and associated with Lieutenant-General **Ali Murtopo** (1924–1984) and **Operasi Khusus (Opsus)**. CSIS played a major role in developing a political format for **New Order** Indonesia, especially a number of important tools for political control such as the principle of ***monoloyalitas*** for civil servants and the notion of the **"floating mass."** In economic policy making, it has taken a somewhat similar corporatist view, generally arguing against the "internationalist" views of the technocrats (*see* **BADAN PEREN CANAAN PEMBANGUNAN NASIONAL**) and for close coordination between government and business as in Japan, with the state setting investment priorities and encouraging import-substitution **industrialization**. CSIS was close to the head of **Pertamina**, Ibnu Sutowo, and **oil** revenues provided Indonesia with a degree of financial independence that made some of the CSIS policies possible. It has always been active in regional and international issues, especially in **U.S.**–Indonesia relations and in relations with the other **Association for Southeast Asian Nations (ASEAN)** states. Major figures in CSIS have been the conservative Catholic Chinese Liem Bian Kie

(Jusuf Wanandi), Jusuf Panglaykim, and Harry Tjan Silalahi. With the death of its highest political sponsors and the establishment of **Ikatan Cendekiawan Muslim Indonesia (ICMI)**'s think tank, the **Centre for Information and Development Studies (CIDES)**, in the early 1990s, the influence of CSIS declined somewhat, but it maintained its reputation as an institution producing important research and information in the policy and international fields. Even after **Suharto**'s fall, it retained influence especially with respect to Indonesia's relations with the United States. *See also* KOMITÉ NASIONAL PEMUDA INDONESIA. [0313, 0733, 0756]

CERAM. *See* SERAM.

CHAERUL SALEH (1916–1967). One of the youth leaders who pressed **Sukarno** and **Mohammad Hatta** to declare independence in August 1945, Chaerul Saleh later moved close to the radical position of **Tan Malaka** and briefly joined a ***lasykar*** unit in West **Java** in 1949 to press for a less accommodating settlement with the **Dutch**. Twice arrested by the **army**, he was exiled to Holland in 1952 but returned in 1955. He was close to, but not a member of, the **Murba** and soon became close to Sukarno, entering the first *kabinet karya* in 1957. In 1963, after the death of **Juanda Kartawijaya**, he became one of three deputy prime ministers (with **Subandrio** and **Johannes Leimena**) and was increasingly seen as a possible leftist successor to Sukarno, though he was popular with neither the army nor the **Partai Komunis Indonesia (PKI)**, which tried to have him "retooled" (i.e., removed) in 1964 after he had promoted the **Badan Pendukung Sukarnoisme**. He remained close to Sukarno after the **Gestapu** and was jailed by the new government in 1966, dying the following year. [0643, 0695, 0879]

CHAIRIL ANWAR (1922–1949). Poet. Though his total output was tiny, Chairil Anwar is credited with enormously widening the scope of Indonesian poetry from the formal style of the ***kakawin*** and ***pantun*** to a terse, personal style. *See also* GENERATIONS; JASSIN, H. B. [0225, 0228, 0234]

CHENG HO. *See* ZHENG HE.

CHERIBON. *See* CIREBON.

CHINA, HISTORICAL LINKS WITH. Trade created the earliest links between China and the Indonesian archipelago. The Strait of Melaka was also an important staging post on trade routes between **India** and China (*see* **SRIVIJAYA**). This early trade was the basis for a political relationship between China and Indonesian states that is still not clear. Until the 10th century, trade seems to have been largely in the hands of local traders whose large vessels took spices and forest products to the ports of South China and carried Chinese goods, especially ceramics and **silk**, back to Southeast Asia for local consumption and onward trade. These traders were permitted to operate in Chinese courts only if their rulers acknowledged Chinese suzerainty and paid tribute to China. Much trade, in fact, was conducted within this framework, goods from Southeast Asia being delivered as "tribute" with Chinese goods being returned as imperial "largesse." Imperial sale of goods obtained in this fashion was an important source of state revenue, especially during the Sung period, and in 1381 an imperial edict forbade Southeast Asian "envoys" from using their "diplomatic" status to trade privately. Some rulers, on the other hand, seem to have courted Chinese imperial favor to mark their seniority over neighboring kingdoms, and a few requested diplomatic and military assistance against enemies in a way that suggests true vassal status (*see* **"HO-LO-TAN"**). No practical Chinese assistance, however, ever appears to have reached the archipelago.

Between the 10th and 12th centuries, the tributary trade was gradually displaced by so-called private trade, in which Chinese traders came for the first time to Southeast Asia. The manufacture of ceramics for the Southeast Asian market was a major industry in southern China during the Southern Sung (1127–1179) and Yuan (1279–1368) dynasties. In the 13th century, the **Mongol** rulers of China misinterpreted the China–Indonesia relationship to assume a much closer vassalage. Their effort to assert this authority on **Java** in 1292, however, was a failure (*see* **MAJAPAHIT**). Under the first Ming emperor, the tributary trade was restored, and Chinese exports dramatically declined. With the rise of the **Dutch East Indies Company (VOC)**, relations were dominated by the question of China's responsibility for and to the local Chinese community, and policy varied from outright rejection to enthusiastic espousal of local Chinese interests. *See also* CHINESE IN INDONESIA; ZHENG HE. [0543, 0544, 0545]

CHINA, RELATIONS WITH. Relations between Indonesia and China since 1945 have been dominated by the question of China's relationship with Chinese residents in Indonesia. Indonesia recognized the People's Republic of China (PRC) in June 1950 but sought to keep relations at a low level to minimize official Chinese contact with local Chinese. Relations improved after **Sukarno** visited China in 1956, and China granted Indonesia credits of US$11.2 million for **rice** and textiles in 1958. They cooled again when China opposed the 1959 law expelling Chinese traders from the countryside (*see* **CHINESE IN INDONESIA**). China's global anti-imperialist policy, however, fitted well with Sukarno's activist foreign policy and in 1961 the two countries signed a treaty of friendship and cooperation. By 1964 there was talk of a Jakarta–Peking anti-imperialist axis. Initially the **Partai Komunis Indonesia (PKI)** kept some distance from the Chinese Communist Party (CCP) in order to avoid appearing to take sides in the Sino-Soviet dispute, but by 1964 most observers considered the PKI to be pro-Beijing rather than pro-Moscow. After the 1965 coup, however, China was accused of having abetted the PKI, especially by allegedly importing 100,000 small arms for use by the **"Fifth Force"** under PKI control. Demonstrators attacked the Chinese embassy, and in October 1967 Indonesia officially broke off relations. Diplomatic contacts resumed in 1973 and direct **trade** in 1985, but did not until 1990 the two countries normalized relations after a 23-year break. A 1980 citizenship law in China removed all recognition of dual nationality. Indonesia and China have disputed claims to areas of the South China Sea, especially over the portion that includes the Natuna **gas** field.

After **Megawati Sukarnoputri** became president in 2001, relations between the two countries warmed as Indonesia sought to become China's major source of **oil** and gas supplies. Chinese oil companies invested in Indonesia's oil and gas fields, looking to double China's oil supply over the next decade. Although Indonesia lost out to **Australia** over a contract to supply $13 billion worth of liquefied natural gas (LNG) to China over the next 25 years, China began negotiations with Jakarta with respect to the Pertamina LNG field in **Papua**, and on 26 September 2002 the China National Offshore Oil Corporation (CNOOC) signed a long-term contract worth $12.5 billion (over 25 years) for Indonesia to supply China with 2.6 million metric tons of gas a year from this Tangguh field. CNOOC would participate with British Petroleum (BP) in developing the field. At the same time, other Chinese companies pledged investments in Indonesia of more than $2 billion, including a preliminary accord to construct a gas pipeline linking Kalimantan and Java. [1130, 1139, 1145]

CHINESE IN INDONESIA. The earliest known Chinese residents of the archipelago were the **Buddhist** pilgrims, Fa Xien (414) and I Jing

(689–692), who spent time studying in **Srivijaya** on their way to or from major monasteries in **India**. Chinese traders arrived from approximately the 10th century, forming enclave settlements in the coastal **ports**. The initial position of these Chinese was in many ways analogous to that of Hindu-Buddhist and later Islamic traders. They represented an advanced culture from which local rulers found it useful to borrow culturally and politically, though the political influence of Chinese thought in Indonesia was never more than superficial. A few traders thus entered court life, reaching high rank as ministers if they were especially able, while the majority remained as temporary residents, living in Chinese quarters similar to those of the Indonesian trading groups. The number involved was never large, and in adopting local culture and customs they lost their Chinese identity. Many married local women, and their descendants merged with the indigenous population. Muslims from the Chinese empire (especially Yunnan) formed a significant community in northern **Java** in the 15th century, but claims that one or more of the Nine Walis (*see* ***WALI SONGO***) credited with converting the island to **Islam** were Chinese remain controversial.

Under the **Dutch East Indies Company (VOC)**, the Chinese first began to emerge as a distinct intermediary class in Indonesia. But they found the VOC racially and culturally more exclusive and bureaucratically more rigid than the indigenous courts of Java and **Sumatra**, and they found the most profitable employment on the fringes of VOC activity, as farmers (*see* ***PACHT***) for the collection of tolls and market **taxes** and the sale of **salt** and **opium**. In the 19th century, Chinese were important in the operation of **pawnshop**, opium, and gambling farms. There thus emerged a Chinese community that was economically powerful but excluded from access to political power in the colony, a state of affairs that has applied ever since. Chinese communities were typically organized as semiautonomous corporations under Chinese "officers," with ranks such as captain and major, who were responsible for taxation and for maintaining order in their communities. In the 19th century, the separation of the Chinese from the remainder of society was formalized with the creation of the legal category of Foreign Oriental (*see* **RACE**). Resident Chinese continued to adopt local ways at the expense of their Chinese customs and a distinct local Chinese culture, called Baba or ***peranakan***, emerged, mainly on Java. *Peranakan* Chinese in general retained Chinese names and religion but spoke Malay and adopted many other elements of Malay culture, such as the use of **batik**.

During the 19th century, however, *peranakan*s were joined by large numbers of new arrivals, generally called *totoks* or *singkeh,* often impoverished men from the southern provinces of Guangdong, Fujien, and Guangxi (ethnically described as Hokkien, Hakka, Tiuchiu, Cantonese, and so on). Many of these came initially as laborers, the earliest coming in the mid-18th century to the **gold** mines of West **Kalimantan** (where there were 50,000 Chinese miners by the middle of the 19th century; *see* **PONTIANAK**) and to the **tin** mines of **Bangka** and **Belitung**, and later as indentured laborers on the plantations in **East Sumatra**. The Chinese population of Indonesia in 1860 is estimated to have been 222,000. In Kalimantan, many later settled down as peasants. More, however, moved into **trade** and, with family connections in other parts of Southeast Asia, were able to build up powerful regional trading networks. *Singkeh* tended to dominate big capital and small trade, while *peranakan* were most often found in credit, agricultural production, and the professions.

The economic power of the Chinese communities led the **Dutch** to see them from time to time as dangerous. In 1740 Dutch fears of a Chinese coup led to a massacre of the Chinese in **Batavia** and to restrictions on Chinese residence, and in West Kalimantan to the ***kongsi* wars** of the mid-19th century and the destruction of the independence of the *kongsi* in the region. Until 1904 Chinese were banned from residence and **travel** in rural areas. Under the **Ethical Policy**, they were excluded from the revenue farms that had previously been their mainstay, and they moved into retail trade and credit, especially in rural areas. In the early 20th century, Chinese interests began to move into the manufacture of batik and ***kretek***.

The status of Chinese in Indonesian **nationalism** was always ambiguous. Unlike local **Arabs**, they did not generally share Islam with the local population. Even before the emergence of Indonesian nationalism, the political resurgence of nationalism in **China** drew strong support from the *totok* community in Indonesia, and the Guomindang (Kuomintang, Nationalist Party) was active in the colony. In the independence struggle against the Dutch, most Chinese attempted to remain neutral although many of them fought alongside the Republic. **Sukarno** and **Mohammad Hatta** appointed several Chinese to prominent positions in the Republican government. Nevertheless, many Indonesians suspected that the Chinese harbored pro-Dutch sentiments, and there were several local anti-Chinese massacres. In response the Chinese formed local "self-protection forces" (Pao-an tui) to protect their communities.

In 1946 all resident Chinese were offered citizenship retrospective to 17 August 1945 unless they specifically repudiated it, and a similar provision was made under the transfer of sovereignty in 1949. Under Chinese law, however, all such Chinese retained dual nationality. In 1954 the foreign ministers of both countries, Sunario and Zhou Enlai, signed a treaty (ratified in 1958) requiring all with dual nationality to choose one or the other by December 1962. Under the **New Order**, Indonesia repudiated this treaty unilaterally in April 1969, thus voiding citizenships taken out under it and leaving about 80,000 Chinese stateless. There are presently some 5 million people in Indonesia identified as "Chinese," of whom about two thirds are Indonesian citizens and 1 million are citizens of the People's Republic of China (PRC). Procedures for resident Chinese to obtain citizenship were simplified in 1980, but **corruption** and obstruction by officials and reluctance on the part of Chinese slowed the acceptance rate.

In August 1958 the Guomindang was banned and the **army** took over the property of pro-Taiwan Chinese. Then, on 14 May 1959, a government order revoked the licenses for alien Chinese to operate in retail trade in rural areas, affecting an estimated 83,783 out of 86,690 traders. This led to an exodus to the cities. Some 119,000 left Indonesia for the PRC and 17,000 for Taiwan. Other restrictions on Chinese Indonesians since 1965 have included the abolition of the Chinese-language press, except for the government-controlled bilingual *Warta Indonesia;* a ban on the import of Chinese-language materials; encouragement for Chinese to take "Indonesian" (commonly Sanskritic or Muslim) names; and a 2 percent limit on the proportion of Chinese enrollments at most state tertiary educational institutions (and a 30 percent limit in private institutions). Still, however, Chinese are widely perceived as being privileged, especially because of the position of ***cukong***, and anti-Chinese violence has broken out on many occasions. Particularly extensive riots took place in Central Java in November 1980.

New Order policy initially tended to equate Chinese culture with communist influence, and the government pressured the overseas Chinese community to assimilate. After 1966, all remaining Chinese-language schools had to adopt Indonesian as the sole language of instruction and a national curriculum. All purely Chinese organizations, whether or not they were political, were forbidden, as was the use of Chinese characters even on shop signs. A presidential decree in 1980, which applied to certain areas of Indonesia with large numbers of ethnic Chinese (including North Sumatra, **Riau**, Bangka, Belitung, parts of West Java, and West Kalimantan), greatly loosened the restrictions on Chinese becoming Indonesian citizens, and a large proportion of the resident Chinese community in these areas took advantage of the opportunity.

The growing ties between top Chinese businessmen and the **Suharto** family during the closing years of Suharto's rule made the Chinese community, and small businessmen in particular, a natural target for protesters at the collapsing **economy**. The final years of the New Order were marked by increasingly frequent disturbances in parts of Java in which Chinese houses, businesses, and churches were targeted. Evidence of coordination in these attacks suggested that they were not always a result of spontaneous mob anger, but rather had been "turned on" to pressure Chinese communities to pay for protection from the security forces. During the riots of 1998 that accompanied Suharto's overthrow, Chinese businesses were among those that were looted and burned, but the extent of anti-Chinese activity did not approach that in the previous change of regime. *See also* CONFUCIANISM. [0024, 0050, 0277, 0285, 0552, 0630, 0801, 1043, 1045, 1048, 1049, 1052–1056, 1059–1068, 1072–1074, 1286]

CHRISTIANITY. Scattered, evanescent communities of foreign-born Christians, mostly Armenian and Persian Nestorians, existed in the archipelago from perhaps the fifth century, but there was no significant conversion to Christianity in the archipelago until the arrival of **Catholic** priests with the **Portuguese** in the early 16th century. Francis Xavier visited **Maluku** in 1546, converting the wife of the sultan of **Ternate**, and by 1559 there were reputedly 8,000 Catholics on that island and a similar number on **Ambon**. Dominican missionaries were the first to enter **Nusatenggara**, building a fort on **Solor** and spreading Catholicism throughout the eastern archipelago. By the end of the century, there were reported to be about 100,000 Catholics in the region. With the coming of the **Dutch**, Portuguese influence waned, and Catholicism was largely confined to **Flores** and parts of **Timor**.

Under Dutch rule, **Protestant** missionary activity began and strong Christian communities emerged among the **Bataks** in northern **Sumatra** (largely proselytized by German missionaries) and among the people of **Minahasa** on Sulawesi. The largest shift to Christianity occurred after the **massacres of 1965–1966**, when probably at least 1.5 million people (about 1.5–2 percent of the **population**), most from communist strongholds in Central and East **Java**, converted to Christianity under government pressure for all Indonesians to profess a sanctioned religion. By the late 20th century, Christians in the country numbered at least 15 million, about half of whom were Catholic.

After the fall of **Suharto**, religious tensions rose. While under Suharto there had been an average of a dozen attacks a year on churches in Indonesia; in the four years following his fall more than 400 churches were razed, bombed or ransacked. *See also* RELIGION, POLITICAL SIGNIFICANCE OF. [1003, 1399]

CHUO SANGI-IN (Central Advisory Councils)**.** Consultative bodies established by the **Japanese** military authorities on **Java** and **Sumatra** in

October 1944. Their membership drew on the Indonesian nationalist establishment, but they had few powers, their duties being largely limited to offering advice and suggestions in response to questions from the Japanese. Regional councils (Shu Sangi-kai), set up in September 1944, seem to have played a similar, limited role. [0661, 0663]

CINCHONA (spp. Rubiaceae)**.** A tree from the Andes regions of South America, the bark of which is processed to produce quinine, the major medicine for preventing and treating **malaria**. In 1852 the colonial government sent Justus Karl Hasskarl (1811–1894) to South America to collect seeds and plants. These were brought to **Java** in 1854, and after some experiments were planted successfully at Cibodas in West Java. Under the vigorous direction of **Franz Wilhelm Junghuhn**, the strain was improved and commercial plantations were laid out. In 1930 Java produced 11,900 tons of kina (cinchona bark), most of the world's supply. [0331, 0332, 0347]

CIPTO MANGUNKUSUMO. *See* TJIPTO MANGOENKOESOEMO.

CIREBON (Cheribon)**. Port** city on **Java**'s north coast, founded in the 16th century by Sunan Gunung Jati (?–1570) (*see* **ISLAM IN INDONESIA**). From 1640 to 1677 it was vassal to **Mataram** and in 1681 came under **Dutch East Indies Company (VOC)** rule, but it remained a major center of ***pasisir*** culture. From 1662 sovereignty was shared and the territory of the state divided between three royal families, Kanoman, Kesepuhan, and Cirebonan. Today the principality is characterized by its almost equal number of Javanese and Sundanese speakers and by the relatively high position of its **Chinese**, or *peranakan,* minority. *See also* PRIANGAN. [0491, 0595]

CITIES. In contrast with the great European cities, many of which have been major centers for millennia, the location of Indonesian cities has tended to change with time, and most of the large cities of the modern archipelago were not important centers 500 years ago. This was partly due to the custom of traditional rulers shifting their capitals, partly due perhaps to the impermanence of much traditional **architecture** and partly due to the fact that ritual, rather than monument, was the essential feature of royal display. (*See also* **PORTS**.)

Modern urban growth began in the 1870s with the expansion of **Batavia**, **Surabaya**, **Bandung**, **Yogyakarta**, **Surakarta**, and **Se-**

marang on **Java** and **Medan** and **Palembang** on **Sumatra**. The term "city" was first given administrative meaning with the creation of municipalities under the **decentralization** of 1903. Urbanization was 3.8 percent in 1930 but grew to 14.8 percent in 1961. In 1930 half the indigenous **population** of the cities of Batavia, Bandung, and Surabaya were born outside the cities, though all **census** figures are inaccurate to the extent that the administrative divisions used for counting fail to reflect the actual extent of urbanization. The 49 municipalities formed by the **Dutch** have been retained by the Republic as Kotamadya, with a status analogous to that of the *kabupaten* (Daerah Tingkat II). Newly important towns requiring some form of distinct administration are now designated *kota administratif* (administrative towns) within *kabupaten;* there were 29 of these in 1987. The 1990 census showed that over 50 million people were living in urban areas, a number that increased to over 86 million in 2000, when 42 percent of the population, as against 30.9 percent in 1990, were living in urban areas. [0069, 0539, 0751, 1388, 1389]

CLASS ANALYSIS. Before 1925, even Marxists rarely used class categories in analyzing Indonesian society, many believing that the Indonesian-**Dutch** conflict transcended class divisions within Indonesian society (*see also* **NATIONALISM**). Most class analysts have acknowledged the existence of an aristocratic class or classes. Debate has focused rather on the existence and nature of the commercial bourgeoisie (middle class) and the identification of potential allies of the proletariat.

Since early times, extensive commerce has taken place in the coastal regions of Indonesia, but no indigenous capitalist bourgeoisie emerged to seize state power. This has been attributed variously to culture (*see* **DUALISM**; **SHARED POVERTY**), **religion**, and the fact that **taxation** in various forms prevented traders from accumulating investment capital. Colonial policies in turn inhibited the rise of an Indonesian bourgeoisie that would compete with Dutch interests and instead allowed middle levels of the **economy** to be dominated by the **Chinese**. Although the Chinese constituted a bourgeoisie in some senses, they were precluded from gaining political power because they did not assimilate culturally. In independent Indonesia, the state itself seized Dutch investments (*see* **NATIONALIZATION**), restricted Chinese business, and sought to foster an Indonesian middle class. The **Partai Komunis Indonesia (PKI)** described those who administered **state enterprises** and profited from government patronage as "bureaucratic capitalists" (*kapitalis birokrat*, *kabir*), but few of these seemed able to accumulate significant investment capital. Under the **New Order**, however, the scale of capital accumulation by groups close to the **Suharto** regime and the extent of their investments within Indonesia suggested to some that they were acquiring attributes of the bourgeoisie. (*See also* **CENDANA GROUP**; **INDONESIANIZATION**.)

A separate but related issue has been the relative absence of a class of large landowners, especially in the countryside of Java, at least until the late Suharto period. Most observers have noted that, although there are clear differentiations of wealth and power within Javanese villages, control of **land** is not concentrated in a small number of wealthy families as, say, in the Philippines. This has been attributed both to cultural features of Javanese rural society (*see* **AGRICULTURAL INVOLUTION**; ***DESA***; **DUALISM**; **"SHARED POVERTY"**) and to policies of the Dutch, which limited the opportunities for capital accumulation in the countryside (*see* **INDIË VERLOREN**; **RAMPSPOED GEBOREN**) and encouraged the traditional aristocracy of **Java** to remain or become primarily agents of the state rather than landowners in their own right (*see* ***CULTIVATION SYSTEM***, ***LIBERAL POLICY***). Under the impact of the **Green Revolution**, there was evidence that a class of wealthy agricultural businessmen was developing in many parts of Java. Along with them, in the late Suharto period high-ranking military and civilian associates of the regime began to constitute a new group of large landowners, forcibly acquiring huge tracts of land both for investment and for use as resorts and golf courses.

The Indonesian proletariat (working class), whether strictly or loosely defined, has always been small, and revolutionaries have consequently sought class allies for it. From the 1920s debate focused on whether the so-called bourgeois nationalists were appropriate allies. This debate, which reflected similar discussion in Marxist circles elsewhere, was never satisfactorily resolved. Until the 1950s peasants were seldom considered, partly because of romantic ideas of village life (*see* ***DESA***), partly because of Marx's Asiatic Mode of Production model. The PKI under D. P. Aidit (1923–1965) suggested that peasants as a class were oppressed by feudalism and (neo)colonialism and thus could also be revolutionary, but the party was seldom able in practice to identify clear class divisions in rural areas. In the 1980s some observers noted a widening gap between rich and poor as a result of the Green Revolution and suggested that a rural bourgeoisie and proletariat were emerging. Such a development was complicated by the wide-scale appropriation of rural land in the late Suharto period both by the state and by speculators from the urban areas. *See also* MARHAEN; PATRIMONIALISM. [0313, 0373, 0399, 0895, 0904, 0921]

CLOTH. The earliest cloth in the archipelago was made of felted bark in a style still found in parts of **Kalimantan**, **Sulawesi**, **Seram**, and **Papua**. With the arrival, however, of **cotton**, weaving became a major activity, symbolic of creation and preeminently the work of **women**, as **metalworking** was the work of men. Many traditional cultures of the archipelago use ritual cloths, such as the famous ship cloths of **Lampung**, to celebrate rites of passage. Indonesian cloth manufacture is best known for its dyeing techniques, especially *ikat,* in which the threads are tie-dyed before weaving, and **batik**. Traditional dyes were **indigo**, *soga* (a brown dye from plant roots), and the red *mengkudu.* The complexity of the production process made cloth a rare commodity and until the 14th century most people continued to wear clothes of bark and plaited vegetable fiber. Large quantities of Indian **cotton** cloth and smaller amounts of **Chinese silk** began to arrive in the 14th century, partly to pay for spices purchased in the archipelago, and the *sarung* became a common item of clothing, though local weaving continued in many areas and the finest of cloth, such as the *songket* of Islamic Sumatra with its **gold** and silver thread, continued to be made in the archipelago.

In the 20th century, **Japanese** cloth strongly penetrated the Indonesian market, leading the colonial government to apply quotas in the 1930s. This encouraged an expansion of domestic production dominated by indigenous entrepreneurs such as **A. M. Dasaad**. Within a few years, however, the industry was largely in the hands of **Chinese** businessmen. Automated weaving began in the 1960s and 1970s, and Japanese industrial cloth production expanded after 1965. [0147, 0151, 0439]

CLOVES (*cengkeh*)**.** The dried immature flower buds of *Syzygium aromaticum* (Myrtaceae), used widely in food, medicine, and perfume. Originally found only on **Ternate**, **Tidore**, and adjacent islets, cloves were traded to **China** from circa 500 B.C. to **India** from circa 200 B.C. and perhaps to **Africa**. Until the 16th century, Javanese merchants were prominent in the **trade**, but they were partly displaced by the **Portuguese**, who expanded production on **Ambon** and surrounding islands. On gaining hegemony in **Maluku**, the **Dutch** restricted production outside Ambon and destroyed trees in order to keep the price high (*see*

***HONGI* RAIDS**). In 1789, however, a tree was smuggled to Mauritius in French territory and from there spread to Penang and Zanzibar, breaking the Dutch monopoly.

Cloves form an important ingredient in Indonesian ***kretek*** cigarettes and were imported from Zanzibar for this purpose until 1987, when domestic production rose dramatically. Production was concentrated in East **Java**, and by the 1990s the industry supported an estimated 4 million people. In 1968 a lucrative monopoly of clove imports had been granted to P. T. Mercu Buana (owned by President **Suharto**'s half-brother Probosutejo) and P. T. Mega, owned by the president's banker, **Liem Sioe Liong** (*see also* **CENDANA GROUP**). Culinary clove production for export became well established on Java and other islands.

In the late 1980s, after failing in their effort to control the domestic clove market, a group of spice traders, with Tommy Suharto as their front man, proposed setting up a government-sanctioned monopoly in cloves. President Suharto designated cloves an "essential commodity" that needed to be regulated by the state, and in 1991 a Clove Support and Marketing Agency (Badan Penyangga dan Pemasaran Cengkeh, or BPPC) was set up with Tommy as chairman. The result was declining sales in cloves and great resentment from farmers and *kretek* makers. In 1998 under the International Monetary Fund (IMF)–backed reform program, Suharto had to agree to end the monopoly, and it was abolished in May of that year. *See also* SUHARTO FAMILY. [0313, 0331, 0332, 0527, 0751, 0760, 0896]

COAL. With the development of steamships in the 19th century, the coal deposits of the archipelago became important as a source of fuel, especially for the **navy**. The first coal reserve was discovered in Pengaron, **Kalimantan**, and a mine was opened there in 1848, but eventually failed. Two other coalmines were launched during the 19th century in Kalimantan and were developed by both private enterprise and the **Dutch** colonial government. A major coal deposit of what proved to be the best quality of coal in the archipelago was found in West **Sumatra** in 1868, and a second major deposit was found at Bukit Asam in South Sumatra shortly thereafter. The Ombilin mine at Sawahlunto in West Sumatra began production in 1892 as a **state enterprise**, employing both open-cast and underground mining. Production at this mine reached over 600 tons in 1924, falling to less than 500 tons as a result of miners' strikes in 1925 and 1926. Total coal production in the Netherlands East Indies reached a peak in 1930 of nearly 1.9 million tons.

Under the **Japanese occupation**, subsidiaries of the Mitsui Company were allowed to exploit the Bukit Asam and Ombilin coalmines, with other Sumatran mining areas exploited by other private Japanese companies. The Japanese also constructed a **railway** to Sumatra's east coast to transport coal from the Ombilin mine. But in the later years of the occupation, production declined drastically as mining companies were forced to help the Japanese war effort with men and supplies.

In postindependence Indonesia, the government's poor financial state impeded its rehabilitation of the mining companies, and coal also faced growing competition from **oil** as an energy source. By 1962 coal production had fallen to under 500,000 tons. Determined to increase coal production, Jakarta carried out repairs and rehabilitation of the Ombilin and Bukit Asam mines and explored for new coal deposits in **Kalimantan**.

Under the **New Order**, development of coalmines was neglected for nearly a decade. The Ombilin, Bukit Asam, and Mahakam mining companies were merged into one state-owned company, but coal production steadily decreased to less than 200,000 tons a year. After the oil crises of the 1970s, however, the government was forced to rethink its energy policy and put more emphasis on coal production. In the late 1980s, open-cut production in East Kalimantan was expanded for export and reached full production in 1993–1994, as the availability of oil for export diminished. Although the PT Kaltim Prime coalmine was the largest mine there, its disputes with local landowners meant that it experienced huge losses in mid-2001. Between 1986 and 1990 Indonesian coal production rose from 2 million tons to 11.2 million tons, of which 42 percent was exported. According to *Far Eastern Economic Review* yearly figures, Indonesia produced 58.3 million metric tons of coal in 2000. [0407, 0411, 0413, 0416]

COCONUT (*Cocos nucifera* Arecaceae)**.** This widespread and versatile palm tree supplies food, clothing, and building materials in tropical coastal regions. There is much debate about its origins, but most evidence suggests that it originated and was domesticated in the western Pacific. It is closely related to human settlement and most commonly spreads by planting. Coconuts became a commercial crop only in the mid-19th century with a rise in demand for copra for soap making. Extensive plantations were established in this period, but smallholders accounted for 95 percent of production, especially in **Minahasa**. With 112 million trees in 1918, Indonesia was the world's largest prewar producer. In 1938 copra exports reached a high of 556,500 tons. Production declined in the 1970s and 1980s due to disease and the need to remove old trees for replanting.

For some producers, **sugar** production from coconut flowers is now more lucrative than copra. [0331, 0332, 0449]

COEN, JAN PIETERSZOON (1557–1629)**.** Founder of **Dutch** power in the Indies. As fourth **governor-general** from 1619 (though he was appointed in 1617), he established a trading post at **Sunda Kelapa** in 1610 and a fort there in 1618, which later became **Batavia** and which he turned into the headquarters of the **Dutch East Indies Company (VOC)** operations in the east. In 1621 he brutally conquered the **Banda Islands**. His term of office ended in 1623, but he was persuaded by the Heeren XVII (Seventeen Gentlemen) to resume it in 1627 and defended Batavia against two unsuccessful attacks by **Mataram**. [0491]

COFFEE (*Coffea* spp. Rubiaceae)**.** Native to the Middle East, coffee plants were brought to Indonesia by the **Dutch East Indies Company (VOC)** in 1696. The company encouraged planting by the ***bupati***s in **Priangan** in the early 18th century, and it was soon taken up as a cash crop by the local population. The first **Java** coffee was sold in Amsterdam in 1712, and in 1725 production exceeded that of the previous market leader, Yemen; after 1726, the VOC controlled 50–75 percent of the world's coffee **trade**. Cultivation was initially free, but in 1725 came under a VOC monopoly and became one of the major crops of the West Java Preangerstelsel (forced cultivation system). Production of *C. arabica* in central and eastern Java expanded greatly, especially under **Herman Willem Daendels**, so that Java coffee dominated world markets by 1811. Coffee then became one of the principal crops of the **Cultivation System**, and a government monopoly of production on Java was maintained until 1915. Estate production of coffee began in East Java in 1870. In 1878, the coffee leaf disease *Hemileia vastatrix* devastated plantations on Java, leading to a shift to *C. robusta* in the late 19th century and an expansion of cultivation in southern **Sumatra**, **Bali**, **Timor**, and **Sulawesi**, but coffee's share of the total value of Indies exports never recovered, standing at 2.27 percent in 1938 and declining further after World War II. Production in 1950 was 12 percent of that before the war, but expansion of cultivation, especially by transmigrants in **Lampung**, made Indonesia the world's third largest producer, with 7 percent of global production and export. The smallholder cultivation of coffee has always been linked to the crop's price on the international market, and it surged in the late 1970s.

The **financial crisis** of 1997–1998 stimulated a further spurt in coffee production as prices for this export crop multiplied to six or seven times those of the precrisis period. In the uplands of South Sumatra and Sulawesi, migrants joined the local people in planting coffee trees, converting **rice** land to coffee cultivation, and attempting to maximize their yield. The subsequent drop in prices reversed the trend. [0331, 0332, 0340, 0765, 0797]

COKROAMINOTO, HAJI UMAR SAID. *See* TJOKROAMINOTO, HAJI UMAR SAID.

COLIJN, HENDRIKUS (1869–1944)**.** Dutch prime minister. Colijn joined the **Koninklijk Nederlandsch Indisch Leger** (**KNIL**) as a young man and took part both in the conquest of **Lombok** and, as adjutant to **J. B. van Heutz**, in the **Aceh** War from 1895 to 1904. On his return to the Netherlands, he entered politics and business, becoming director of the Bataafse Petroleum Maatschappij (*see* **OIL**) and, in 1923, minister of finance. He was prime minister in 1925–1926 and from 1933 until 1939. During the **Depression**, he was a major spokesman for free trade. He died in German internment during World War II.

COLONIES, NETHERLANDS MINISTRY OF. With the dissolution of the **Dutch East Indies Company (VOC)**, the Netherlands government established its formal authority over the Indonesian possessions through a colonial department that went through various names until finally becoming the Ministry of Colonies (Ministerie van Koloniën) in 1848. The ministry's task was preparing general policy lines and handling relations between the colony and the Netherlands, rather than direct administration, and no minister of colonies visited the Indies until 1941. In the 20th century, however, ministers were generally technical specialists with Indies experience; nine of the 25 held the post of **governor-general** before or after. In February 1945, the ministry's title was changed to Overseas Territories (Overzeese Gebiedsdelen). For successive names of the ministry and a list of ministers, *see* APPENDIX B. *See also* NETHERLANDS, CONSTITUTIONAL RELATIONSHIP WITH INDONESIA.

COMMISSIONER-GENERAL. Under the **Dutch East Indies Company (VOC)**, commissioners (*commissarissen-generaal*) were occasionally appointed as representatives of the Netherlands government in the East. From 1814 to 1819, three commissioners-general—C. T. Elout (1767–1841), G. A. G. P. van der Capellen (1778–1848), and A. A. Buyskes (1771–?)—governed the Indies with the tasks of resuming control of the colony from

Britain and establishing a new colonial administration, a complex constitutional and technical task after the fall of the **Dutch East Indies Company (VOC)** and the interregna under French and British rule. Van der Capellen was also **governor-general** (executive head of the government) and continued in this post as sole commissioner-general until 1826. His successors B. du Bus de Gisignies (1780–1848) and J. van den Bosch (1780–1839) also held the post briefly alongside the governor-generalship to 1834. In 1946–1948 Willem Schermerhorn, Max van Poll, and Feike de Boer were commissioners-general for the purpose of negotiating a settlement with the Indonesian Republic. [0659]

COMMUNICATIONS. *See* MEDIA; POSTAL SERVICE; RAILWAYS; ROADS; SHIPPING; TELEGRAPH.

COMMUNISM. *See* MARXISM; PARTAI KOMUNIS INDONESIA.

CONFRONTATION (*Konfrontasi*)**.** Indonesia's opposition to the creation of **Malaysia** as a federation of Malaya, **Singapore**, and British colonies in northern Borneo was first expressed as "confrontation" by **Subandrio** in January 1963 after Malay and British forces had crushed a rebellion in the north Borneo sultanate of Brunei, but a compromise was reached between Indonesia, the **Philippines**, and Malaya's prime minister Tunku Abdul Rahman at the **Maphilindo** conference held at the end of July 1963. This compromise called for the **United Nations** to send a team to the north Borneo territories to ascertain whether their people wished to be included in the new Malaysia federation. Before the UN secretary-general could publish the results of this exercise, the Malay prime minister and British foreign minister announced that Malaysia would be formed on 16 September irrespective of the results of the UN ascertainment. In response, **Sukarno**, on 23 September, announced that Indonesia would *ganyang* (literally, "gobble raw," but generally translated as "crush") Malaysia. Initially, Indonesia was joined less vociferously in its opposition to Malaysia by the Philippine government.

Aside from their objections to Malaysia itself, Indonesian political forces had their own reasons for Confrontation: the **army** wished to retain its privileged position and access to funds after the recovery of West Irian **(Papua)**; the **Partai Komunis Indonesia (PKI)** wished to engage key army units away from the centers of power of **Java** and enhance its nationalist status; and Sukarno wished to maintain the momentum of popular mobilization he had begun during the Irian campaign. To increase pressure on Malaysia, the army's **Komando Operasi Tertinggi (KOTI)** command was reorganized and border incursions began into Sarawak, where Indonesian troops were largely unsuccessful against British Commonwealth forces. In August and September 1964, small-scale landings took place on the **Malay Peninsula**. Army enthusiasm for the conflict soon diminished, partly because they did not want to deploy capable forces away from the centers of power on Java, and partly because Confrontation was one of the grounds for left-wing arguments in favor of a worker-peasant **"Fifth Force."** From mid-1965, even before the rise to power of **Suharto**, the **intelligence** officers **Benny Murdani** and **Ali Murtopo** were maintaining contacts with Malaysia, and in May 1966, shortly after the **Supersemar** order gave Suharto executive power, negotiations with Kuala Lumpur began. Relations were normalized on 11 August 1966. [0478, 1120, 1123, 1126]

CONFUCIANISM (*Konghucu*)**.** The general term given to traditional Chinese religion in the archipelago, though what is practiced is an eclectic blend of Confucianism with **Buddhism** and Taoism rather than Confucianism proper despite a Confucian revival in the late 19th century. Like other recognized **religions**, Confucianism in Indonesia has been under pressure to conform to official notions of what constitutes a religion and has tended increasingly to treat Tien (Heaven) as a deity and Confucius as a prophet and to identify Confucian classics as holy scripture. [1335, 1369]

CONRAD, JOSEPH (1857–1924)**.** Conrad visited the archipelago as a sailor between 1883 and 1888 and set several of his novels there, especially *Almayer's Folly* (1895), *An Outcast of the Islands* (1896), and *Lord Jim* (1899–1900). Much of his writing describes the venality of European activity in the region. [0243, 0629]

CONSERVATION, NATURE. The director of the Bogor Botanical Gardens, Melchior Treub, suggested creation of a nature reserve on Mt. Gede, near **Bogor**, in 1889. Ordinances to protect the **bird of paradise** were first issued in 1905 and were revised in 1909 to include the **rhinoceros**, elephant, and **orangutan**. The first nature reserves (*natuurmonumenten*) were gazetted in 1916 at the urging of the Nederlandsch-Indische Vereeniging tot Natuurbescherming (Netherlands Indies Society for Nature Preservation), founded in 1912 by S. H. Koorders and K. W. Dammerman. By 1942 natural monuments and game reserves covered

130,000 hectares (ha) (55 reserves) on **Java**, about 500,000 ha on **Sumatra**, and over a million ha on Borneo. Andries Hoogerwerf was appointed nature protection officer in 1935.

In 1951 Kusnadi was appointed head of the Nature Protection Division of the Agriculture Department. In the mid-1970s, Indonesia cooperated with the World Wildlife Fund in developing a national conservation strategy that resulted in the declaration of the country's first five national parks in 1980 and a further 11 in 1982. By the late 1980s, national parks and reserves covered approximately 6 percent of the country.

The rapid expansion of the logging industry under the **Suharto** regime caused widespread deforestation throughout Indonesia, especially in **Kalimantan** and **Sumatra**, together with loss of rainforest and genetic erosion. Several approaches have been suggested to conserve remaining forests and regenerate hardwood species, including trying to involve international bodies in funding local measures toward environmental conservation. One of the most hopeful of these was the U.S. Tropical Forest Conservation Act, whereby debtor nations can obtain a 40 percent cut in certain debts in return for carrying out conservation measures. **Germany** also offered a similar act. *See also* DEPOK; ENVIRONMENTAL PROTECTION; FORESTRY; KOMODO; UJUNG KULON. [0013, 0730, 0943, 1154]

CONSTITUENT ASSEMBLY (*Konstituante*)**.** Elected in December 1955 to draft a **Constitution** to replace Indonesia's provisional 1950 Constitution, the composition of the assembly largely followed that of the 1955 parliament, though there were more independent members. The assembly convened in November 1956 but was unable to reach agreement on the question of whether **Islam** or **Pancasila** should be the foundation of the state. This deadlock was among the factors leading **Sukarno** to dissolve the assembly and restore the 1945 Constitution by decree on 5 July 1959. [0695, 0982]

CONSTITUTIONS. Until the establishment of crown rule in 1815, the charter of the **Dutch East Indies Company (VOC)** and the various treaty arrangements with individual states in the archipelago were all that passed for a constitution. In 1815 the Dutch government promulgated a *Regeeringsreglement* (RR, Government Regulating Act), which functioned as the constitutional basis for the state of the Netherlands Indies. Reissued in various forms up to 1854, the RR of that year, though modified in 1925 and renamed the *Wet op de Staatsinrichting van Nederlandsch-Indië*, remained in force until the end of **Dutch** rule. (*See also* **GOVERNOR-**

GENERAL, OFFICE OF THE; NETHERLANDS, CONSTITUTIONAL RELATIONSHIP WITH INDONESIA; SUCCESSION.)

The first Constitution (*Undang-Undang Dasar*, UUD) of the Republic of Indonesia was adopted on 18 August 1945 by the **Panitia Persiapan Kemerdekaan Indonesia (PPKI)** and was based on a draft prepared by the **Badan Penyelidik Usaha Persiapan Kemerdekaan Indonesia (BPUPKI)** established by the **Japanese** in March 1945. This Constitution was intended to be provisional and replaced by a document prepared by a **constituent assembly**. The preamble (*pembukaan*) established the **Pancasila** as Indonesia's national philosophy, omitting the **Jakarta Charter**. The Constitution provided for four branches of government—the president, the **Dewan Perwakilan Rakyat (DPR)**, the Audit Board (Badan Pemeriksa Keuangan, BPK), and the **Supreme Court** (Mahkamah Agung)—but in fact it concentrated powers in the hands of the president. Under the original terms, the president was not accountable to the DPR, only having to give an accounting at the end of his term to the **Majelis Permusyawaratan Rakyat (MPR)**, consisting of members of the DPR, and delegates of the regions and other groups. Under Article IV, until the DPR and MPR were formed the president held supreme executive and legislative power. A series of subsequent measures, however, broadened political participation in government and weakened the authoritarian character of the Constitution. Most important, Article IV of the transitional provisions of the Constitution was abolished, and the legislative power of the DPR and MPR was given to the **Komité Nasional Indonesia Pusat (KNIP)** until those bodies could be formed. In November 1945 the KNIP's working group initiated a number of measures whereby the presidential cabinet was replaced by a parliamentary cabinet, with ministers accountable to the KNIP rather than to the president.

A second Constitution, federal in structure, was drafted at the **Round Table Conference** and came into force with the creation of the **Republik Indonesia Serikat** on 27 December 1949. This Constitution provided for a prime ministerial system and gave extensive constitutional protection to the federal states (*see* **FEDERALISM**). With the dissolution of the states in 1950, however, it was replaced on 14 August by a provisional third Constitution, unitary in structure but retaining the prime ministerial system. According to the 1949 Constitution the government could not be toppled by parliament, and according to the Constitution of 1950 parliament could not be dissolved by the president, although it could topple the government. The 1950 Constitution continued the structure of parliamentary government with the president mainly holding a ceremonial function.

After **elections** in 1955, a **Constituent Assembly** attempted unsuccessfully to agree on a new Constitution. On 5 July 1959, **Sukarno** restored the 1945 Constitution by presidential decree. Parliamentary democracy was thereby replaced by a system drastically redistributing state power, with both executive and legislative powers concentrated in the hands of the president. The DPR became a largely consultative body, with functional groups added to the elected representatives. The **Suharto** government retained the 1945 Constitution but concentrated power even further in the hands of the president. The 1945 Constitution was apotheosized as a sacred pillar of the national identity. Whereas, for example, it authorized changes to itself by a two-thirds majority of the MPR, in 1983 the sitting MPR renounced this right and prescribed that any change must be referred to the people by referendum and must be approved by at least 90 percent of the voters in a turnout of at least 90 percent.

After the fall of Suharto, the parliament instituted measures to amend the 1945 Constitution to prevent it being used again to justify an authoritarian regime. In October 1999 the president and **vice-president** were limited to two terms in office and the MPR authorized itself to hold annual sessions to review presidential performance. More extensive amendments in August 2000 gave a constitutional basis for **decentralization** (by requiring governors, *bupati*, and mayors to be elected), established a bill of rights for all citizens and brought the security forces under closer control and scrutiny of parliament. In protecting citizens from retroactive legislation, however, it also shielded members of the Indonesian **armed forces** from legal accountability for atrocities committed in **East Timor** and elsewhere. In August 2002 further amendments were introduced. The MPR's powers were limited to specific functions and it was to consist entirely of elected representatives from the DPR and a new regional chamber, the Dewan Perwakilan Daerah (DPD, Regional Representative Council). The president and vice president were to be elected by direct popular vote from 2004, and a president's tenure was limited to two five-year terms. In the legal field a Constitutional Court was to be established, separate from the **Supreme Court**, and a Commission of Judiciary was to be formed to propose candidates for appointment to the Court. Constitutional backing was also given to the principles of regional autonomy, and **human rights** provisions were added to the Constitution. At the same time, the MPR rejected an effort to amend the Constitution to allow the full imposition of Islamic law (*syariah*) for all Indonesian Muslims, and it voted to end military and police representation in the parliament as of 2004. [0643, 0647, 0674, 0982, 0989]

CONSULTATIVE GROUP ON INDONESIA (CGI). Successor to the **Inter-Governmental Group on Indonesia (IGGI)**. This body was formed after **Suharto** disbanded the Dutch-led IGGI in March 1992, when the **Netherlands** suspended aid to Indonesia in the aftermath of the Dili massacre (*see* **EAST TIMOR**). The CGI was headed by the **World Bank** and in July 1992 allocated US$4.94 billion in new grants and low-interest loans to Indonesia. This amount held relatively steady throughout the rest of the Suharto years, but in 1999 the consortium undertook to extend loans worth a total of US$7.9 billion. At the meeting held in Tokyo in October 2000, Indonesia committed itself to accelerating the privatization of **state enterprises** and of **debt** restructuring, and it emphasized that despite implementation of **decentralization** the central government would remain the responsible authority for all development assistance. It also undertook to institute an equitable and sustainable **forest** management system. [0748, 0760]

CONTINENTAL DRIFT. The present general topography of Indonesia is largely a result of the breaking up of the former great southern continent Gondwana and the separate northward movement of several of its parts into the southern flank of the old Laurasian landmass. One section of Gondwana, bearing what is now **Nusatenggara**, parts of **Maluku**, western **Sulawesi**, **Java**, **Kalimantan**, **Sumatra**, the **Malay Peninsula**, Thailand, and Burma, seems to have begun to move north around 200 million years ago. Initially, this landmass formed an east-west belt bulging northward over the Tropic of Capricorn, but the northward movement of the Indian plate during the Cretaceous period (about 136 million years ago) pushed its western end northward, creating the present oblique northwest-southeast alignment of Sumatra and Malaya. **Australia**, New Guinea, and eastern Sulawesi broke from Gondwana about 90 million years ago, pushed northward at about 10 cm per year, and collided violently with the rest of what is now Southeast Asia about 19–13 million years ago. The mountains of New Guinea were thrust up, the Nusatenggara island chain was twisted north to create much of Maluku, and eastern Sulawesi and the island of Sula were thrust into western Sulawesi, opening the gulf of **Bone** and twisting the northern arm around to form the gulf of Tomini. *See also* PREHISTORY; SUNDA SHELF; WALLACE'S LINE. [1174, 1186]

CONTROLEUR. Lower-level **Dutch** administrative official, abolished on **Java** in 1922. *See also BINNENLANDSCH BESTUUR.*

COOLIE ORDINANCE (*Koelieordonnantie*). Until 1880 contract laborers brought from South **China** and later from **Java** to work in the plantations of **East Sumatra** could be held to their contracts only by indirect social controls (*see* **GAMBLING**; **OPIUM**) and by the civil legal process, which was often ineffective. From 1880 the Coolie Ordinance gave government sanction to the contracts, allowing imprisonment of laborers who broke their contracts under the so-called *poenale sanctie* (penal sanction). Employers in turn were required to provide defined levels of wages, accommodation, health care, general treatment, and repatriation, but conditions were very bad. *De millioenen uit Deli* (1902), a report by J. van den Brand, increased pressure for change under the **Ethical Policy**, leading to the formation of a **Labor** Inspectorate in 1907 and legislation from 1911 to phase out the penal sanction. The coolie ordinance was strongly criticized in the **United States** as a form of disguised **slavery** enabling Sumatra **tobacco** to compete unfairly with that of America, and the threat of import bans hastened the sanction's disappearance. By this time, however, labor was abundant and employers had little need to use the sanction. During the **Depression**, many laborers hired under contract were released and reemployed at lesser rates. The sanction was largely abolished in 1936. [0320, 0433, 0817, 0830]

COOPERATIVES. A form of social and economic organization based ideologically on notions of traditional village collectivism (*see* ***DESA***), cooperatives were first promoted by the Sarekat Dagang Islam, the forerunner of the **Sarekat Islam (SI)**, in 1913 but encountered little success. In 1920 the Netherlands Indies government established an official Commission for Cooperative Societies to investigate how to introduce cooperatives to Indonesia. In 1927 a "Regulation on Indonesian Cooperative Societies" was promulgated, providing cooperatives with a legal basis and enjoining the government to aid in their formation. In 1929 the **Partai Nasional Indonesia (PNI)** sponsored a Cooperative Congress stimulating the establishment of cooperatives throughout **Java**, though again they were short-lived. The government continued to sponsor their formation, and by the early 1940s there were 574 cooperative societies in operation in Indonesia with 52,555 members. Even before Indonesia achieved independence, the idea of cooperatives was embraced especially by **Mohammad Hatta**, who saw them as an alternative to both colonialism and indigenous capitalism. Hatta favored a restructuring of the **economy** by the creation of production, consumption, and credit cooperatives. Cooperatives thus prospered in the early years of independence, and by 1956 they numbered 12,090, with nearly 2 million members. Most cooperatives, however, have been racked by inefficiency and **corruption**, and their history since then has generally been depressing. [0298]

COPPER. Found in West **Sumatra**, West **Java**, and **Timor**, copper was mined since early times for the production of bronze, often with a high lead content (*see also* **TIN**). Production was never extensive and declined with the large-scale import of Chinese copper cash from the 15th century and Dutch copper *doit* in the 18th century. A huge mine in the Carstensz Mountains of West Irian (**Papua**) was opened by **Freeport** Minerals Inc. in April 1967 to mine the copper and **gold** existing there. Its impact on the people and resources of the area was a major factor in mobilizing support for the separatist **Organisasi Papua Merdeka (OPM).** *See also* CURRENCY; MINING.

COPRA. *See* COCONUT.

COPYRIGHT. The Dutch copyright law was retained after independence, but Indonesia withdrew from membership in the Berne Convention on copyright protection in 1958. By the 1980s, unauthorized copying was widespread and so-called pirate tapes dominated an estimated 70–90 percent of the domestic market for books, videotapes, computer software, records, and cassette tapes. By 1985 an estimated 1–2 million pirated Western tapes were being produced every month for the domestic market, with another 1 million tapes a month being exported to the Middle East and Italy. In September 1987, however, following negotiations with European recording companies, Indonesia passed a law protecting most European material and in April 1988 signed an agreement with the European Community (EC) for reciprocal protection of sound recordings. A bilateral copyright treaty with the United States was signed on 22 March 1989, going into effect on 1 August of that year. *See also* MUSIC. [1142]

"CORNELL PAPER." A preliminary analysis of the origins and details of the **Gestapu** coup of 30 September 1965 prepared immediately after the event by Benedict Anderson and Ruth McVey at Cornell University. The report cast doubt on the then generally accepted view that the coup was the work of the **Partai Komunis Indonesia (PKI)**, arguing that it was most probably the work of junior **army** officers and provided an excuse for elimination of the PKI. The report was circulated confidentially to a small number of scholars but was soon leaked to the wider world, where its then-unorthodox view challenging the **Suharto** government's version of events earned its authors the enmity of the regime. [0690]

CORRUPTION. A phenomenon most easily recognizable in bureaucratic structures, where employees are expected to carry out their duties efficiently and dispassionately for a fixed, regular salary paid by the employer. It makes little sense to talk of corruption in Indonesia before the arrival of the bureaucratically organized European trading companies, since there were no general, formal standards laying down how much and under what circumstances officials might obtain money or other benefits from their positions.

Under the **Portuguese** and the **Dutch East Indies Company (VOC)**, "corruption" consisted largely of infringing official monopolies of **trade**, though the fact that salaries of VOC officials were ludicrously low gave employees little alternative but to engage in illicit activities of one sort or other. Senior VOC officials deplored corruption both for its effects on company profits and for the fact that money-making activities distracted lower officials from their administrative tasks; the later **governor-general** G. W. van Imhoff went as far as suggesting in 1746 that the VOC trading monopoly be abolished in order to eliminate corruption. This was not done, and it is widely accepted that corruption made a major contribution to the VOC's insolvency and collapse at the end of the century.

Only under **Herman Willem Daendels** and his successors was the notion of bureaucratic propriety taken seriously and attempts made to control the outside activities of officials. Considerable attention was given to the question of whether the demands of the ***bupatis*** on their subjects could and should be limited. The polemic novel *Max Havelaar* argued that the *bupati*s' exactions were corrupt and unjust, and this view gradually became orthodox, though the colonial government remained extremely reluctant to discipline officials on these grounds except in the most extreme cases.

The extent of corruption grew dramatically during the **Japanese occupation** (1942–1945), partly because salary payments to officials became increasingly inadequate as the occupation currency depreciated in value, partly because Japanese attempts to regulate the **economy** (requiring permits, for instance, for the transport of food from one *kabupaten* to another) increased the number of opportunities for officials to demand illicit payment. During the Indonesian **Revolution** (1945–1949), it became difficult once more to speak unambiguously of corruption: bureaucratic salaries were paid with such irregularity and at such a depreciated rate that many officials, and especially sections of the **armed forces**, were forced to levy the population for their own survival. Though there was a number of cases in which officials and military personnel enriched themselves unduly, the significance of "corruption" in this period was the habits and contacts it formed, rather than its direct effect on public welfare.

During the 1950s and 1960s, corruption became part of an administrative vicious circle, in which lack of revenue led to inadequate salaries for officials, in turn diminishing government performance and reducing both the contribution of the state to general economic welfare and the state's capacity to collect revenue. These problems remained acute under the **New Order**. In 1970 a presidential inquiry, known as the Commission of Four, investigated corruption in the **Badan Urusan Logistik Nasional (Bulog)**, **Pertamina**, the Department of **Forestry**, and the state **tin** company, P. N. Timah. Such investigations typically caught a number of small offenders while leaving the most corrupt unscathed. The **oil** boom of the 1970s led to even more extravagant instances of corruption in upper levels of the government.

In the 1980s a trend toward administrative deregulation diminished for a while some of the opportunities formerly available for corruption. In 1985, for instance, the government contracted the Swiss firm Société Générale de Surveillance to undertake customs inspections on its behalf, thus bypassing the notoriously corrupt state customs service. Customs officials were suspended on full pay but with dramatically diminished income (*see also* **SHIPPING**).

However, in the 1990s, as members of the **Suharto family** and their close associates solidified control over the most lucrative sectors of Indonesia's economy, corruption became endemic in all sections of the country's economic life. In 1993 Indonesia was nominated as the most corrupt of 10 Asian countries by the Hong Kong–based Political and Economic Risk consultancy. The extent of the corruption was a major focus of the protests against the **Suharto** regime during the **financial crisis** of the late 1990s and was a major reason for the overthrow of the New Order government. Antigovernment demonstrations protested against "Corruption, Collusion, and Nepotism" (**KKN, Korupsi, Kolusi, dan Neopotisme**). But the corruption was so deeply engrained in the society that it survived the change in regime, and **Abdurrachman Wahid**'s tolerant attitude toward it was a major element in his impeachment in 2001. Nor did matters improve under his successor, **Megawati Sukarnoputri**, with news reports asserting in early 2003 that 20 percent of **World Bank** and other foreign loans were being siphoned off, and accusations being made that the situation was even worse than under Suharto, because then "only Suharto's cronies were able to commit corruption" while all politicians under Megawati participated in it. [0297, 0748, 0763, 0961, 1398]

CORVÉE LABOR. *See HERENDIENSTEN.*

COTTON (*Gossypium* spp. Malvaceae)**.** Introduced to Indonesia around 300 B.C. from India, cotton was extensively grown in **Java**, **Bali**, and **Nusatenggara** for the local **cloth** industry, though never in sufficient quantity or quality to supplant imported cloth (*see* **DUTCH EAST INDIES COMPANY**; **INDIA, HISTORICAL LINKS WITH**). In the late 18th century, production contracted under pressure from Indian imports. **Palembang** and **Semarang** were the main areas of production. From 1858 the colonial government attempted to extend production, especially for the **Dutch** cotton mills in Twente, but largely without success. [0331, 0332]

COUNCIL OF THE INDIES. *See* RAAD VAN INDIË.

COUPERUS, LOUIS (1863–1932)**. Dutch** author, raised on **Java**. His novel *De stille kracht* (The Silent Force, 1900) was a psychological exploration of Dutch society in the Indies, stressing the exoticism of the Indies environment and the impossibility of Dutch assimilation to it. [0209, 0248]

CREDIT. *See* BANKING.

***CUKONG*.** A **Chinese** businessman who receives protection and privilege from a powerful, often military, patron in exchange for business assistance and/or a share of the profits. The largest *cukong* in **New Order** Indonesia were **Liem Sioe Liong** and William Suryajaya (Tjia Kian Liong, 1922–).

Although Chinese businessmen once made their way primarily on the basis of their business acumen, under the **Suharto** regime significant economic success was not possible without patronage from within the state. All or most successful Chinese businessmen were thus *cukong* to some degree, and this appearance of favor led to much resentment. *Cukong* were a major target of hostility in the so-called **Malari** riots of 1974. The riots led the government to apply some formal restrictions to *cukong* activities, but these were seldom enforced. *Cukong* were also a major target in the overthrow of the Suharto regime; and in the early period of ***reformasi***, many were forced out of the country's economic life. *See also* ALI-BABA FIRMS. [0313, 0373, 1045]

CULTIVATION SYSTEM (*Cultuurstelsel*, once commonly but inaccurately translated as Culture System)**.** In 1830 the state finances of the

Netherlands (which included those of the Netherlands Indies) were in crisis following the Belgian secession and the **Java War**. To save the budget, Governor-General Johannes van den Bosch (1780–1844) introduced a system of agricultural deliveries that operated in theory as follows: the villages of **Java** were invited to use one fifth of their **land**s and approximately 66 days (or one fifth of a year's work) to grow crops designated by the government—principally **sugar cane** and indigo, but also **coffee**, **tobacco**, and **tea**—in exchange for exemption from land **tax**, then levied at 40 percent of the market value of the **rice** crop. Villages taking part in the Cultivation System were also to be freed from other tax-like obligations, such as corvée labor service (***herendiensten***); were to be paid the difference in value between the **land rent** and the value of produce they had delivered; and were indemnified against crop failures beyond their control. By 1836 the direct connection between land rent and product delivery was broken; land rent was levied in full, and suppliers received payment in full for produce delivered. In 1847, it was estimated that 60–70 percent of crop payments returned to the colonial government as tax.

For the **Dutch**, the system thus was a great success. Valuable tropical crops were produced in abundance and not only were the costs of governing the colony readily paid but, under the unified budget system, a substantial budget surplus (***batig slot***) was also transferred to the Netherlands each year, paying off the country's international **debt** and financing the national **railway** system. In the 1850s these transfers comprised 31 percent of the Dutch national income. Private investors in Java, including the later minister of colonies I. D. Fransen van de Putte, made huge profits, especially from the sugar factories that processed government cane. The Dutch royal family profited handsomely through the **Nederlandsche Handel Maatschappij (NHM)**, now ABM-AMRO Bank.

The effect of the system on the Javanese is less clear. Undisputed are the following: villages close to factories were often required to plant far more than one fifth of their land with the designated crops, peasants were never indemnified against crop losses, ***bupati*** and other indigenous officials continued to demand extensive **labor** services, and full payment for the value of the crops was seldom received by the peasants entitled to it. The system was blamed for widespread epidemics and famines on the island in the 1840s. It also certainly strengthened the position of the ***priyayi*** on Java, since they received until 1868 a percentage of production under the system and their quasi-royal status was enhanced as a matter of Dutch policy. Some scholars have argued that the lucrative income to be had from acting as agents of the state discouraged the *priyayi* from moving into land ownership and agricultural production themselves and therefore averted the formation of a powerful class of rural landowners (*see* **CLASS ANALYSIS**).

The system began to be dismantled around 1850, initially because of a hostility in the Netherlands, under the new more democratic **constitution** of 1848, to the favored position of the sugar contractors and the NHM, and later because of growing interest in larger-scale private interest in the Indies and because of political indignation over the oppressive practices linked with the cultivation system, especially as described in the novel ***Max Havelaar*** (*see* **CORRUPTION**). The **Agrarian Law of 1870**, which formally abolished forced cultivation, is generally regarded as the end of the Cultivation System in Java, though some forced cultivation continued to 1890 and vestiges of the system lingered on into the 20th century in the form of the coffee monopoly, which was not abolished until 1915. The Cultivation System was not restricted to Java and was introduced as the Forced Delivery system into other regions of the archipelago, including **Sumatra**. In West Sumatra it was introduced in 1847 in an attempt to monopolize coffee production, relying on peasants to plant, grow, and deliver coffee at low fixed prices to government warehouses. It was profitable for a while before falling into irreversible decline. Nevertheless, it lasted longer than on Java before being largely abolished in the early years of the 20th century. It was one of the factors sparking the dissidence that led to the 1908 rebellion there. *See* MINANGKABAU. [0421, 0601, 0603, 0605, 0797, 0838]

CULTURE, DEBATE ON THE ROLE OF. A long-running debate (*Polemik Kebudayaan*, polemic on culture) took place in Indonesia on the nature of modern Indonesian culture and its relation to society. It was instituted in 1935 by **S. Takdir Alisyahbana** with the argument, echoing the beliefs of **Tjipto Mangoenkoesoemo**, that modern Indonesian culture should incorporate in some essential way the best of Western culture and should accept the need to move beyond traditional culture in the process of becoming part of a universalist world culture. This view was challenged by Ki Hajar Dewantoro, Sanusi Pané, and many others, who argued that Western culture was characteristically materialist, intellectual, and individualist and thus essentially both undesirable and hostile to indigenous Indonesian culture (*see also* **POLITICAL CULTURE**). The latter position was formally ratified in 1959 with the promulgation of **Sukarno**'s **Manipol-USDEK** doctrine, of which the final principle,

Kepribadian Nasional or national identity, asserted the cultural autonomy of Indonesia. It proved nonetheless difficult to specify the nature of a modern Indonesian culture that contained no Western influences. **Artists** of the "internationalist" Seni Rupa school of **Bandung**, for instance, argued that painters of the ostensibly "nationalist" Yogya school were influenced by impressionism and other Western schools.

During the 1950s the terms of the debate shifted somewhat. The universalists, led by **H. B. Jassin** and allegedly exemplified by the (then deceased) poet **Chairil Anwar**, were attacked not by traditionalists but also by the Left, especially members of the **Lembaga Kebudayaan Rakyat (Lekra)** who, in rejecting universalist culture, argued that art should reflect local social conditions and should serve to promote social consciousness. Art should be "for the people" and should resist portraying individualist or bourgeois values. The debate was reignited in 1995 when **Pramoedya Ananta Toer**, a leading member of Lekra in the early 1960s who had been imprisoned for 14 years on **Buru**, was awarded the Ramon Magsaysay Award. *See also* MANIFES KEBUDAYAAN. [0159]

CURRENCY. The use of **gold** and silver coinage in West **Sumatra** and Central and East **Java** dates from at least the eighth century, the earliest coins being gold *masa* of 2.42g stamped with a simple sesame seed design and silver coins of a similar weight stamped with a stylized sandalwood flower. The source of the metal is not certain, but early accounts speak of gold and silver production on both islands and it is reasonable to assume that some of this went into coinage. These relatively high-value coins were probably not in day-to-day circulation but were used for storing wealth and for ritual purposes. Although there is some evidence of an iron bar currency called *iket wsi* in use in the late eighth century, the general use of coins in daily life did not apparently begin until the 11th century, with the appearance of a number of smaller denominations (*kupang* = 1/4 *masa*) in **port** areas, presumably in response to a greater marketization of the **economy**. By the 13th century, gold coins were used extensively for the payment of salaries, debts, and fines. In **Burton (Butung)**, in southeast **Sulawesi**, small squares of **cloth** were reportedly used as currency.

Large quantities of low-denomination Chinese **copper** and copper-lead cash, or *picis,* began to appear on Java in the late 12th century, prompting local imitations in **tin**, copper, and silver and displacing the older currency for most purposes by 1300. *Picis* became the standard currency of **Majapahit** and their use spread to Sulawesi, **Kalimantan**, and Sumatra, though from the 14th century several Islamic states on Sumatra minted their own gold and tin coins. *Picis* were carried about in strings of fixed numbers from 200 to 100,000. Leaden and tin-lead *picis,* worth much less than copper, were fragile and often broke or disintegrated after a few years' use; copper coins, by contrast, were often taken from circulation for ceremonial purposes. So great was the flow of copper coins to Indonesia that the Chinese government banned their export for many years. The widely available *picis* led to a greater monetarization of the economy than before, allowing traders, often **Chinese**, to deal directly, for instance, with the hill people who provided pepper to **Banten** and encouraged the use of credit facilities. Leonard Blussé argues that the perishable nature of the *picis* also encouraged people to spend them quickly, thus promoting the circulation of money.

From circa 1580, silver coinage in the form of Spanish *reals,* minted from Peruvian and Mexican silver, became increasingly abundant, especially as extensive imports of lead by the **Dutch** and other Europeans in the 17th century drove down the value of the *picis.* The **Dutch East Indies Company (VOC)** also produced silver rijksdaalders and from 1733 copper *doit,* though *picis* remained in circulation in many places into the 18th century. In the 19th century, locally minted tin currency was the dominant currency in much of Sumatra.

From 1782 the VOC in **Maluku** issued promissory notes in denominations of 25 to 1,000 rijksdaalders; though bearing interest at 6 percent, these also acted in some respects as paper currency and continued in circulation into the early 19th century, as did bonds issued in 1810 by the Dutch authorities in East Java on security of 1 million rijksdaalders due in silver over 10 years from a Chinese ***pacht*** holder in Probolinggo. This confused currency situation was somewhat regularized by the issue in 1815 of Netherlands Indies guilder (*gulden*) currency notes with handwritten serial number and signature. In 1851 the Java Bank took on the production of bank notes (backed by gold reserves), though the colonial government continued to issue low-value currency notes. Later in the century plantations companies, especially in **East Sumatra**, often issued their own currency notes (*muntbiljetten*) for the payment of workers.

During the **Japanese occupation**, the military authorities initially provided currency notes, but in March 1943 bank notes were issued by the Nanpo Kaihatsu Kinko (Southern Regions Development Bank). This currency rapidly depreciated in value, but it was retained in circulation by both the Allies and the Indonesian Republic after the Japanese surrender. Postwar Netherlands Indies currency notes were not issued on

Java until March 1946, and Republican *rupiah* (ORI, *Oeang,* i.e., *Uang Republik Indonesia*) were first issued only in November. Separate local emergency Republican currencies were later issued in several parts of Sumatra and Java. In 1950 a new federal rupiah was issued, and previous Dutch and Republican currencies were exchanged for it at various rates. Dutch colonial authorities in West New Guinea (**Papua**) issued separate New Guinea notes from 1950, while various rebel governments such as that of the **PRRI/Permesta** rebels overprinted Republican currency for internal circulation.

In January 1950 US$1.00 purchased Rp 3.80. A devaluation on 13 March 1950 took this to Rp 7.60; a system of multiple exchange rates complicated the picture, but most observers argue that the rupiah was overvalued in this period, thus encouraging imports and discouraging exports. After a period of sustained inflation in the late 1950s, the currency was drastically reformed on 28 August 1959, with the freezing (i.e., demonetization) of notes of Rp 25,000 and above and the reduction of other currency to one tenth of its nominal value (i.e., Rp 1,000 became Rp 100). Further depreciation of the currency under **Guided Democracy** led to a similar measure on 13 December 1965, Rp 1,000 becoming Rp 1. In the early 1970s the exchange rate stabilized at US$1.00 = Rp 415, but this jumped to Rp 625 in late 1978, to Rp 970 in 1982, to Rp 1,700 in the late 1980s, and to Rp 2,600 in mid-1997.

The devaluation of the Thai baht in July 1997 sparked a **financial crisis** throughout Southeast Asia and had a devastating effect on the value of the rupiah, which plumetted to more than Rp 10,000 to US$1.00 by January 1998. Over subsequent years it rarely dropped below Rp 8,000 to US$1 and occasionally rose as high as Rp 16,000. In 2001 it started the year at Rp 9,450 and ended it around Rp 11,000. During 2002, with austerity measures being introduced, the rupiah began to strengthen, dipping to below the 9,000 mark in the middle of the year, and by mid-2003 it was one of Asia's strongest currencies. *See also* BANKING; SJAFRUDDIN PRAWIRANEGARA. [0057, 0379, 0391, 0398, 0479]

– D –

DAENDELS, HERMAN WILLEM (1762–1818). Dutch general, lawyer, and administrator. After gaining military experience in the forces of the Dutch "Patriotten" who established the **Batavian Republic** in the Netherlands in the late 18th century, Daendels was sent to Indonesia in

1807 by King Louis Napoleon of the Netherlands as **governor-general** (1808–1811) with the task of organizing the defense of **Java** against the British. In addition to constructing defensive works on the north Java coast, including the first **road** along the entire length of the island, he introduced many internal reforms, especially to combat **corruption** among European officials and to reform the **army**. He also reduced the power of the ***bupati*** on Java, placing them under nine regional prefects or *landrost.* He was recalled in 1811 when the Netherlands was incorporated into the French Empire, and he died as governor of Dutch possessions on the Gold Coast (now Ghana). [0491]

DANGDUT. Style of modern popular **music** employing electric guitars, drums, and voices with a sinuous melody line and a heavy irregular beat. *Dangdut* first emerged in about 1972 as a blend of Western, Middle Eastern, and ***kroncong*** elements. Its chief exponent has been Rhoma (Oma) Irama (1947–), who employed it for both political comment and the promotion of **Islam**. After some years of decline in the early 1980s, it became hugely popular again, with widespread broadcasts and booming cassette sales. In addition to the usual themes of love and loss, *dangdut* continued its moralist tone, protesting the gap between rich and poor and the neglect of Islamic morality. Although maintaining its character as the voice of the "little people," in recent years *dangdut* became a matter of controversy because of the rise in popularity of Inul Daratista, who was criticized by conservatives because of the sensuous dancing that accompanied her singing. [0149, 0154]

DANI. Ethnic group in **Papua**, inhabiting the Baliem Valley of the interior highlands, "discovered" only in the 1930s. They construct terraced, irrigated fields. [1230]

DANISH EAST INDIA COMPANY. *See* SCANDINAVIA, HISTORICAL LINKS WITH.

DARTS. Propelled from blowpipes and often smeared with poisons such as ***upas,*** they were the classic weapon of hunting in Indonesian jungles, especially **Kalimantan**, where room to move was limited and projectiles were not often deflected by winds. *See also* WEAPONS.

DARUL ISLAM (DI, House of Islam)**.** General name for the Muslim revolutionary movement launched in West **Java** in 1948 by **S. M. Karto-**

suwiryo with the twin aims of establishing an **Islamic state** and vigorously prosecuting the war of independence against the Dutch. The movement arose immediately after the Indonesian Republic had agreed, under the January 1948 **Renville Agreement**, to withdraw its **armed forces** from West Java. In March 1948 the Darul Islam decided to establish its own administration in the region, but stopped short of a total break with the Republic. It formally repudiated the Republic on 7 August 1949, after the final cease-fire between **Dutch** and Republican forces, by declaring an Islamic state, the Negara Islam Indonesia (NII).

The movement attracted not just those who wanted the implementation of Islamic law in independent Indonesia but also many who opposed the strength of Dutch influence in the new **Republik Indonesia Serikat (RIS)**, and the DI spread in varying degrees to most Muslim parts of the archipelago, encompassing the rebellion in **Aceh** under **Daud Beureu'eh**, the rebellion of **Kahar Muzakkar** in South **Sulawesi**, and that of Ibnu Hajar in **Banjarmasin**. From the start the **Masjumi** was ambivalent toward it, sympathetic toward its aims but rejecting its methods. West Java was always the core of the movement, and fighting was especially fierce there although DI forces occasionally reached the outskirts of **Jakarta**. The movement largely crumbled after Kartosuwiryo was killed in 1962. In an attempt to discredit opposition to the **Suharto** government in the 1977 **elections**, the Darul Islam was reactivated by General **Ali Murtopo** in the mid-1970s and given the name **Komando Jihad**. [0693, 1019, 1031]

DATUK. *See* TITLES.

DAYAKS. A collective term for the indigenous peoples of **Kalimantan**, comprising at least 20 different ethnic groups. They are generally divided into three groupings: the Dusun and Murut in the north; the Kenyah, Kayan, Kayang, and Iban in the center; and the Ngaju in the center and south. Dayaks traditionally practice shifting **agriculture** (*swidden*) and hunting, and live in multifamily longhouses up to 180 meters long. Political leadership is ephemeral as power relationships change within family groups. In precolonial times, headhunting was said to be common as a means of accumulating "life force." Tension between Dayaks and the Muslims of **Banjarmasin** led in 1958 to the creation of the province of Central Kalimantan.

Governments have traditionally been uneasy over the way of life of the Dayaks, seeing it as unsettled, destabilizing, and, in recent times, ecologically destructive (*see* ***ALANG-ALANG***), and there have been many attempts to encourage Dayaks to establish permanent settlements, take up commercial crops such as **cloves** and **pepper**, and convert to a major **religion**. Over the years many Dayaks did convert to **Islam**, the religion of the Malay inhabitants of the island's coastal regions. In 1980, however, the traditional Dayak religion was recognized under the name **Kaharingan** as a branch of **Hinduism**.

The Dayaks became victims of two of the major policies of the **Suharto** government—**transmigration** and exploitation of the **forests**. Between 1980 and 1985 more than 100,000 non-Dayaks were moved into west and central Kalimantan under the transmigration program, and the numbers were increased by voluntary migrants, especially from **Madura**. (The Dayaks came to constitute only approximately 40 percent of West Kalimantan's population and 60 percent of Central Kalimantan's.) At the same time, Dayaks were forcibly removed from their land in favor of concession holders who from the 1980s felled an estimated 233,000 hectares of the rainforest every year. Traditional Dayak leaders and institutions were stripped of their authority and replaced by bureaucrats appointed by Jakarta. Sporadic clashes with the immigrants began in 1979. After the huge forest fires of 1997, violence broke out and spread and intensified as Dayak tribesmen attacked Madurese settlements northwest of **Pontianak**, killing about 450 and forcing about 20,000 to flee. In early 1999, with the erosion of the central government's authority after Suharto's fall, the scale of the violence exploded. Dayak tribesmen attacked Madurese in Sambas (north of Pontianak), leaving more than 100 dead and forcing thousands more to flee, many to **Sulawesi** and others to Madura. Dayaks reoccupied land abandoned by the refugees, and especially in West Kalimantan took over occupations from which they had previously been excluded and began to revive their traditional culture. [0329, 0766, 0811, 1217]

DEBT, INTERNATIONAL. In the colonial period, large amounts of money were transferred annually to the **Netherlands** as the so-called budgetary surplus (***batig slot***), though this did not constitute a true international debt. Following World War II the Netherlands claimed *f*25,000 million in reparations from **Japan** for losses and destruction during the occupation; of this, however, only *f*130 million was received, most of it by the expropriation of Japanese property in Indonesia itself. After independence, Japan paid a further US$223 million in reparations to Indonesia. Under the terms of the **Round Table Conference** of 1949, Indonesia took over a total debt of approximately *f*4,6 billion (US$1.7 billion) from the former Netherlands Indies. This was a source of considerable resentment, since it included some of the costs of the colonial war against the Republic and represented a drain on independent Indonesia's program of economic development. The **Ali Sastroamijoyo** government repudiated 85 percent of this debt on 4 August 1956, by which time, however, only $171 million of the debt was still outstanding. Under **Sukarno**, Indonesia acquired a debt of US$2.4 billion (of which $990 million was to the **Soviet Union** and its allies).

In facing the crisis of the late 1960s, the **Suharto** government was helped by the **Inter-Governmental Group on Indonesia (IGGI)**, set up in 1967, which provided more than 75 percent of development expenses during the regime's early years. As a result of these and other loans negotiated at the beginning of the Suharto era, Indonesia in early 1988 had the largest foreign debt in Southeast Asia, totaling US$43.2 billion. In 1988 debt servicing accounted for 37 percent of all government expenditure and was estimated to total about $6.3 billion for the year. In 1995 total **trade** and foreign debt were 52 and 57 percent of GDP and GNP respectively. By the end of 1997, the volume of short-term debts was US$20 billion, with the total debt in November 1997 estimated by Minister of Finance Mar'ie Muhammad at US$65 billion. At the end of December, a Private Foreign Debt Settlement Team (TPULNS, Tim Penanggulangan Utang Luar Negeri Swasta) was formed, and its head, Radius Prawiro, estimated the total of private foreign debts to be US$74 billion, with the debt of the government and state companies at well over US$60 billion. In 2002 the debt was running at 90 percent of GDP and if the government were to reduce it to its targeted 60 percent of GDP by 2004 there would need to be an annual growth rate in the economy of 6 percent (rather than an actual 3.3 percent).

On 12 April 2002 the group of creditor nations known as the Paris Club agreed to reschedule the $5.4 billion of the Indonesian debt that fell due between 1 April 2002 and 31 December 2003, agreeing to forgo both principal and interest. Indonesia was granted 20 years to repay foreign development aid loans, and other official foreign aid would be repaid over 18 years. Nevertheless, Indonesia's external debt burden remained crushing at $140 billion—nearly 100 percent of its GDP, a figure that dropped to just over 70 percent by the beginning of 2003. Goals set in restructuring agreements signed by some of the companies most seriously in default (e.g., Asia Pulp & Paper, which defaulted on $14 billion in debts in 2001) were rarely met. To appease international lenders,

Megawati Sukarnoputri's government raised prices for fuel, electricity, and phone calls in January 2003 on the eve of a major donors' conference, which agreed to a $2.7 billion loan request to help the government plug the budget deficit and repay debt. In August 2003 the cabinet decided not to extend the IMF special program when it expired at the end of the year. *See also* WORLD BANK. [0353, 0378, 0387, 0760]

DEBT OF HONOR. *See* "EERESCHULD, EEN."

DECENTRALIZATION. Until 1903, all government officials and organizations in the Indies were formally agents of the **governor-general** for the administration of the colony and were entirely dependent on the central administration for their budgets. A Decentralization Law in 1903, however, established a limited degree of financial and administrative autonomy in 32 municipalities (*gemeenten*), mainly on **Java**, and 15 territories (*gewesten*) throughout the colony. This was followed in 1922 by a so-called *bestuurshervorming* (administrative reform), under which the *gemeenten* became *stadsgemeenten* ("city municipalities"), and the island of Java was divided into three provinces, West, Central, and East, in 1926, 1930, and 1927 respectively. The **Vorstenlanden** on Java continued to be administratively separate as *gouvernementen.*

The situation in the **Outer Islands** remained complicated. **Dutch** rule in most regions was based on treaty relations with local rulers (***zelfbesturen***). In 1922 Dutch authority was represented by three governors (in **Aceh**, **East Sumatra**, and Celebes [**Sulawesi**]), 15 residents, and one assistant resident. The 1922 reform provided for the creation of *gouvernementen* of **Sumatra**, Borneo, and the "Great East" (*Groote Oost*), though for financial reasons these were not implemented until July 1938, except for a *proto-gouvernement* of the Great East, covering **Maluku** and Irian (**Papua**), formed in 1926. As a further measure, the Dutch established so-called ***adat***-law communities (*adatrecht gemeenschappen*) in **Minangkabau** and **Banjarmasin** in 1938 and in **Palembang** in 1941.

The distinctive feature of all these new units was the presence of representative councils that played some role in the formulation of regulations and the allocation of **budgets**. They generally consisted of members elected (under a restricted franchise) and appointed by the governor-general from the three racial groups. Europeans were invariably overrepresented in relation to Indonesians, but the representation of each group varied to some extent in proportion to its share of the **population**. From 1924 all regency councils on Java had an Indonesian majority. The head of the local administration was both chairperson of the council and chair of its College van

Gecommitteerden or Gedeputeerden (College van Burgemeester en Wethouders in the case of *stadsgemeenten*), the executive body for daily administrative matters of the council. It was these local councils that chose the elected members of the **Volksraad**.

The Indonesian Republic's Law no. 22 of 1948 established **provinces** (*daerah tingkat I*), *kabupaten* (*daerah tingkat II*), and villages as the key levels of government. Law no. 1 of 1957 increased the number of provinces from nine to 15 and gave local assemblies (Dewan Perwakilan Rakyat Daerah) the power to elect regional heads (***bupati*** and governors), but **Sukarno** rescinded this law in September 1959. Under **Guided Democracy** and to an even greater extent under the **New Order**, the degree of centralization increased, despite a regional autonomy law in 1974 (Law No. 5/1974) establishing regional development planning boards (Bappeda) at the provincial and *kabupaten* level. Nevertheless, the president appointed all local officials and further strengthened this control with military secondments to the bureaucracy (*see also* ***DWIFUNGSI***). The **Jakarta** government exerted tight control over the whole administrative and financial structure of the country down to the village level (*see* ***DESA***), retaining all power at the center and channeling the regions' wealth to Jakarta (*see* **TAXATION**). It did, however, take a tentative step toward decentralization in 1995 when it launched a two-year district autonomy pilot project transferring selected functions from central and provincial levels to 26 districts, but without making any adjustment to local government finance.

After **Suharto** resigned in May 1998, the regions demanded a fairer distribution of wealth and a greater voice in their own affairs. The government of **B. J. Habibie** took steps to assuage regional discontent by introducing a new decentralization law (Law No. 22/1999), which was passed by the parliament on 23 April 1999, to go into effect over a two-year implementation period. It promised extensive autonomy to Indonesia's regions in all matters except foreign, defense, judicial, religious, and monetary affairs, relinquishing to the regions responsibility for **health**, **education**, land rights, and investments. It was not to the provincial governors that these powers were devolved but to the country's over 300 district heads (*bupati*) and mayors. The law provided for these officials to be elected by their local parliaments, and it ended the practice of military officers holding posts in the bureaucracy. At the same time, a law (Law No. 25/1999) was passed under which regional governments were given so-called equalization funds (*dana perimbangan*) in the form of block grants that they could allocate according to local needs. They were also allowed to keep 80 percent of the revenue from **mining**, **forestry**, and **fisheries** in their territories, as well as 30 percent from natural **gas** and 15 percent from **oil**. Only 40 percent of tax income would be paid to the central government. This arrangement tended to favor the resource-rich regions, such as **Riau**, East **Kalimantan**, Aceh, and Papua. Jakarta later had second thoughts about aspects of the program. In August 2000 it abolished the Ministry of Regional Autonomy responsible for implementing the policy and in January 2001 announced that the mining industry would remain under the central government's control for up to five years.

In many parts of Indonesia, however, implementation of the decentralization laws led to a more fluid and dynamic situation, with greater pressure for establishment of new **provinces**, districts, and **cities**. By 2003 parliament had approved the creation of four new provinces and 106 new districts and cities. (Two more provinces were added in August 2003, when parliament voted to divide Papua into three provinces.) *See also* FEDERALISM. [0397, 0472, 0591, 0638, 0937, 0948, 0950, 0963]

DEFENSE POLICY. For most of the 19th century, after **Britain** restored the Indies to the **Dutch** in 1816, the principal task of the colonial **army**, the **Koninklijk Nederlandsch Indisch Leger (KNIL)**, was extending colonial power throughout the archipelago and guarding against rebellion in areas already controlled. External threats were few and were met by diplomatic rather than military precautions. In the late 19th century the rise of German, Japanese, and Russian sea power aroused Dutch alarm, but colonial defense policy focused on the defense of **Java** by land forces. During World War I, extensive debate took place over the desirability of an Indies militia, and in 1923 military service was made compulsory for Dutch citizens (thus excluding the majority of Indonesians). Possible expansion of the colony's naval defenses was also much discussed, but not until 1936 did naval expenditure significantly increase.

Army officers of the Republic after 1945 initially disagreed sharply on questions of military strategy. In general, former KNIL officers favored construction of a compact, Western-style, disciplined army that might defeat the Dutch on their own terms, while former **Pembela Tanah Air (Peta)** officers advocated a larger armed force whose strength would lie in its confidence and commitment to an independent Indonesia. Both, however, thought in terms of frontal warfare, and only after a long series of setbacks, beginning with the battle of **Surabaya** in November 1945, in which Indonesian forces offered heavy resistance to arriving Allied troops at great cost, did ideas of guerrilla **warfare** gradually spread. Military thinkers, especially **A. H. Nasution**, developed the idea of total people's war, central to which was the principle that national defense depended on close cooperation between a guerrilla army and the people. Though this strategy was never fully implemented during the **Revolution**, it became the basis for the army's territorial defense structure in which considerable operational autonomy was given to regional military commanders. The names and scope of these regional military commands have varied from time to time. During the Revolution, the term Wehrkreis (pl., Wehrkreise) was used on a fairly ad hoc basis within a separate Java Command. In 1950 these were replaced by seven Teritorium dan Tentara (T & T, Territory and Army) commands, covering the entire country. T & T commanders developed deep local roots, often at the expense of subordination to the High Command. Between 1957 and 1959 these were gradually replaced by 16 (17 with Irian **[Papua]**) military regions (Komando Daerah Militer, Kodam), along with three overarching Inter-Regional Commands (Komando Antar Daerah, Koanda), covering **Sumatra**, **Kalimantan**, and Eastern Indonesia. In 1963 the Kodam were replaced by Penguasa Pelaksana Dwikora Daerah (Pepelrada, Regional Authorities for the Implementation of Dwikora). They were restored in 1967 only to be replaced in 1969 by six Komando Wilayah Pertahanan (Kowilhan, Regional Defense Commands) that had authority over air, naval, and army units.

In 1985 the Kowilhan were abolished and again replaced by Kodam, then numbering 10. In May 1999 it was announced that there would be a phased return to the earlier system of 17 Kodam, and the first move was taken on 15 May when KODAM XVI Pattimura covering **Maluku** was established. No timetable was set for establishment of the other new Kodam.

From the late 1950s, the territorial strategy was reinforced with the notion of ***dwifungsi***, asserting among other things that the military role in administration contributes to national resilience. In practice, however, there was some retreat from this broad defense strategy, greater emphasis being placed under the **New Order** on technically sophisticated strike forces such as **Komando Pasukan Khusus (Kopassus)** and on domestic **intelligence** functions. The importance of domestic intelligence agencies stemmed from the contention, prevalent during the Cold War, that the military needed to counter communist penetration by emphasizing surveillance against domestic subversion. Defense policy was based on the assumption of a perpetual state of national insecurity and a continuing widespread threat to political stability. The focus on intelligence as the major tool to combat domestic subversion reached its apogee in the late 1980s under Armed Forces commander and head of **Kopkamtib Benny Murdani**, in a campaign that was widely seen as targeting political **Islam** even more than the earlier predominant communist threat. After the fall of the **Soviet Union**, perceived threats to national security were broadened to include globalization, which was portrayed as introducing foreign values that threatened the harmony of the **Pancasila** state. Such a stance was used in the closing years of the **Suharto** regime to justify its repressive policies in quashing political dissent and democratic movements. Such movements as those advocating **human rights**, greater democracy, and **environmental protection** were grouped with former communist organizations under the rubric of *organisasi tanpa bentuk* (OTB, formless organizations) and subject to national vigilance and military suppression. It was under such a rubric that the armed forces in 1996 cooperated with and directed paramilitary groups in crushing the supporters in the **Partai Demokrasi Indonesia (PDI)** of **Megawati Sukarnoputri**.

After Suharto's fall, there was great pressure for the military to return to the barracks, stemming from its identification with the more brutal policies of the **New Order** regime, including its destruction of opposition forces and its human rights abuses, especially in **East Timor** and **Aceh**. But with the communal and ethnic violence that plagued many parts of the archipelago and with East Timor's separation from Indonesia, the major task of Indonesia's armed forces came to be perceived as the maintenance of national unity vis-à-vis regional dissidence and violence, especially in Aceh and Papua. Combating "Islamic terrorism" was added to Indonesia's major defense needs after the September 2001 terrorist attacks on New York and Washington and especially after the **Bali** bombing of October 2002. But many of the measures in this "war on terrorism" were conducted under the auspices of the newly independent **police** forces.

Strengthened under the presidency of Megawati, the armed forces in March 2003 made a renewed effort to expand their role drastically when they introduced a legislative provision removing the authority to declare a national emergency from the hands of the president to those of the chief of the armed forces. This proposed new legislation would abrogate a measure in the **Constitution** and in the 2002 Defense Act and would give the armed forces unilateral authority to deploy troops in the event of a national emergency. The armed forces chief would be the one to determine that the well being of the state was at risk and would only need to inform the president 24 hours after forces were deployed. Although the measure was unlikely to pass, it signaled the renewed confidence of the armed forces in the face of civilian authorities' perceived failure to maintain the security of the state. For a list of defense ministers, *see* APPENDIX E. [0668, 0714, 0731, 0966, 0972, 0974]

DELI. Sultanate in **East Sumatra**, successor state to the kingdom of **Aru**, emerging in the 16th century as an object of struggle between **Riau** and **Aceh**, which finally won suzerainty only to lose it to **Siak** in a long contest for power beginning in 1710. Deli was included in the Siak territories that submitted to the **Dutch** in 1858 but was acquired by the Dutch from Siak in 1884. [0818]

DEMAK. The first Muslim state on **Java**, founded probably by a **Chinese** Muslim trader in the late 15th century. This trader's grandson, Sultan Tranggana (1504?–1546), conquered **Majapahit** in circa 1527 and extended his influence to south **Sumatra** and **Banjarmasin**, attacking **Melaka** in 1512. The kingdom was exhausted, however, in a major campaign in **Balambangan** in 1546, and after Tranggana's death it was rapidly eclipsed by Pajang and **Mataram**. *See also PASISIR*. [0560]

DEMANG. *See INLANDSCH BESTUUR.*

DEMOCRATIC REPUBLIC OF EAST TIMOR (DRET)**.** This state was proclaimed in Dili on 28 November 1975, while Indonesian forces were invading the **Portuguese** colony from the west, with Francisco Xavier do Amaral as president and Nicolau Lobato as prime minister. Portugal's insistence that it retain sovereignty over **East Timor** was one of the few diplomatic levers against the Indonesian presence during the 1980s and 1990s. Do Amaral surrendered to Indonesian forces in 1978 and was succeeded by Lobato, who was killed in battle later the same year. *See also* FRETILIN; GUSMÃO, JOSE ALEXANDRE "XANANA." [0806]

DEPOK. Village south of **Batavia**. In 1714, the ***particuliere landerij*** here was bequeathed by Cornelis Chastelein to his liberated Christian slaves and their descendants in perpetuity, and for around two centuries the "Depokkers" formed a distinct indigenous Christian community on the outskirts of Batavia. Chastelein also instructed that part of the land never be cleared, and this area was handed over in 1913 as a nature reserve to the Netherlands Indies Society for Nature Protection. *See also* CONSERVATION, NATURE.

DEPRESSION OF THE 1930s. The Great Depression struck the Netherlands Indies severely, halving the colony's exports and forcing dramatic cuts in the budget. Austerity measures effectively ended the **Ethical Policy**'s program of government expenditure, leading on the one hand to the mutiny on the vessel ***Zeven Provinciën*** and on the other to the formation of the *Stuw* group of progressive colonial officials. Unemployment rose and **taxes** increased. In an effort to preserve the Western-dominated large **rubber** plantations, the government placed heavy restrictions on smallholder production in **Sumatra**.

DESA (village)**.** According to common belief, the *desa* was the main unit of social organization in rural **Java** in precolonial times. Villages are said to have been geographically distinct entities comprising **rice** fields (*sawah*), orchards, and dwellings, often in a single cluster, sometimes distributed among two or more hamlets (*kampung*). Village life, under an elected head, or *lurah,* was said to be a model of Indonesian democracy, decisions being taken by a process of exhaustive deliberation (***musyawarah***) producing a consensus (*mufakat*) articulated by the *lurah.* A sense of common destiny gave the villagers collective responsibility so that while the interests of an individual would always be subordinate to those of the *desa,* the community as a whole took an active interest in the welfare of all its members. This led to the habit of ***gotong royong*** or mutual self-help and, according to Clifford Geertz, ultimately to "shared poverty" (*see* **AGRICULTURAL INVOLUTION**). This view of village life influenced leaders searching for Indonesian forms of democracy; **Guided Democracy** was explicitly an attempt to implement village democratic forms at the national level.

Recent research has cast doubt on this view of the precolonial village and suggests that rural society was organized in much smaller households (*cacah*) that were not geographically clustered and that were in patron–client relationships with local officials who acted as intermediaries between rulers, especially ***bupati,*** and households. The collectivist enclosed village seems to have become an article of government faith first under **Thomas Stamford Raffles**, who saw the village as an alternative unit of administration to the *bupati.* Villages were convenient administrative units for the levying of taxes and the mobilization of corvée labor, and British and Dutch policies on **land rent** and **labor** did much to create a communal village life.

The process was reinforced by romantic views of traditional village life, which helped to crystallize notions of a village culture and philosophy distinct from that of the courts or the trading cities (*see* ***ALIRAN***; **DUALISM**). Whether original or constructed, however, the collectivist nature of the village was breached by the penetration of the money economy, especially through **taxation** and the commercialization of **agriculture**. (*See* **GREEN REVOLUTION**.)

Since the time of Raffles, the *desa* has been one of the main administrative units on Java, headed by a *desahoofd* or *lurah* (now *kepala desa*). In 1979 new regulations aimed at standardizing local administration throughout Indonesia established the *desa* as the lowest administrative unit, replacing the various village configurations outside Java. Each *desa* was to have a Village Consultative Council (LMD, Lembaga Musyawarah Desa) and an Institute for Village Community Resilience (LKMD, Lembaga Ketahanan Masyarakat Desa), headed by the *lurah,* which was to promote development, inculcate the **Pancasila**, and see to matters such as **family planning** and local security and order. Irrespective of the size of its population or territory, each *desa* would receive the same amount of development funds from the central government. At the same time, though village communities were able to nominate the village heads, government officials appointed them, and these village officials became salaried civil servants. By 1987 there were 61,439 *desa,* plus 4,952 urban *kelurahan*. After **Suharto**'s resignation, this *desa* law was a major target for reform and many traditional local administrations outside Java reverted to their earlier forms. *See* DECENTRALIZATION. [0335, 0596, 0752, 0807, 0977, 1007, 1386]

DEVELOPMENT IDEOLOGY. The notion of macroeconomic development as a manageable process bringing eventual greater prosperity for all emerged in **Germany** in the second half of the 19th century and influenced **Dutch** colonial thinking by the end of the century. Most thinkers tied the possibility of self-sustaining growth to the viability of capitalism. Followers of **J. H. Boeke** (*see* **DUALISM**), believing that the indigenous **economy** would remain permanently precapitalist, saw Western enterprise as an essential part of such development, while others sought to use quasi-traditional institutions such as **cooperatives** to bring the indigenous economy into the capitalist world.

At the declaration of independence, many Indonesians felt strongly that colonial economic policies and the ravages of war had left the country economically backward and that a major program of development (*pembangunan*) was necessary, but it was only under the **New Order** that *Pembangunan,* conceived as a long-term process of perhaps 25 years, was elevated to become a central pillar of government policy. The precise nature of this program was always under debate, especially between the advocates of a more free-market economy and proponents of import-substitution industrialization, and more quietly over the extent to which true national prosperity (*kemakmuran*) could be divorced from justice (*keadilan*). During its early decades the economic policies of the New Order were responsible for massive economic growth, and in 1983 President **Suharto** assumed the title *Bapak Pembangunan* ("father of development"). *See also* BADAN PERENCANAAN PEMBANGUNAN NASIONAL; CLASS ANALYSIS. [0299, 0353, 0358, 0364, 0738, 0914, 0928]

DEWAN NASIONAL (National Council)**.** Formed by **Sukarno** in May 1957 as an assembly of 41 functional group representatives to advise the cabinet after the fall of the second **Ali Sastroamijoyo** cabinet. It was dissolved in June 1959 with the return to the 1945 **Constitution**. *See also* GUIDED DEMOCRACY. [0706, 0859]

DEWAN PERTAHANAN NEGARA (DPN, State Defense Council)**.** Established on 6 July 1946 under State of Emergency regulations, and comprising the prime minister, senior cabinet ministers, the **army** commander, and ***lasykar*** leaders, the DPN became a central decision-making body of the Indonesian Republic during the **Revolution**.

DEWAN PERTIMBANGAN AGUNG (DPA, Supreme Advisory Council)**.** A respected but powerless council of senior and retired government figures that can offer proposals to the government on matters of national importance as well as opinions on matters raised by the **president**. The Republic's first DPA, formed in 1945, was merged with other bodies into the parliament of the **Republik Indonesia Serikat (RIS)**. The council was reestablished in July 1959 just before the return to the 1945 **Constitution**. *See also* DEWAN PERWAKILAN RAKYAT.

DEWAN PERWAKILAN RAKYAT (DPR, People's Representative Council)**.** Indonesia's principal legislative body, constitutionally subordinate to the **Majelis Permusyawaratan Rakyat (MPR)**, to which all DPR members automatically belong. Though prescribed by the 1945 **Constitution**, its role was taken during the **Revolution** by the **Komité Nasional Indonesia Pusat (KNIP)**. The unicameral parliament of the **Republik Indonesia Serikat (RIS)** was called the DPR and consisted of members of the two chambers of the RIS parliament, together with the members of the 1945 Republic's **Dewan Pertimbangan Agung (DPA)** and the Working Committee of the KNIP. Members of parliament elected in 1955 took their seats in March 1956. In 1959 members of this elected parliament became, with a few exceptions, members of a provisional DPR under the restored 1945 Constitution. **Sukarno**, however, suspended this DPR in 1960 after it refused to pass his budget and installed instead the DPR–Gotong Royong, whose members were appointed by him and which could be dissolved at his will. The DPR-GR was purged of its **Partai Komunis Indonesia (PKI)** and other left-wing members in October and November 1965.

Under the **New Order**, **elections** in 1971 reconstituted the DPR, then numbering 460, of whom 360 were elected and 100 appointed, 75 from the **armed forces** and 25 from other groups. In 1987 membership was increased to 500, with 100 appointed from the armed forces. Although constitutionally empowered to initiate legislation and monitor government actions, the DPR was a very weak institution during the New Order period. Government manipulation of the political process ensured that its membership was overwhelmingly progovernment.

The situation changed dramatically with the resignation of **Suharto**, the movement for ***reformasi***, and the 1999 elections. After these elections, the 500-member body was constituted as follows: **Partai Demokrasi Indonesia—Perjuangan (PDI-P)**, 153 seats; **Golongan Karya (Golkar)**, 120; **Partai Persatuan Pembangunan (PPP)**, 58; **Partai Kebangkitan Bangsa (PKB)**, 51; **Partai Amanat Nasional (PAN)**, 34; with the remaining parties sharing 46 seats and the armed forces retaining only 38 seats. (Thus, Golkar's percentage of the seats fell from 76 percent in 1997 to 26 percent in 1999, and the allocation to the armed forces was cut by half from the preelection number of 75 seats.) Although **Abdurrachman Wahid** was able to manipulate the parliament to win the presidency despite his party's poor showing in the elections, his lack of a majority base was partly responsible for the DPR moving so consistently toward his impeachment in July 2001 and for his replacement by **Megawati Sukarnoputri**, whose PDI-P party held the largest bloc of seats. Constitutional changes introduced in 2002 created a new legislative body, the Regional Representatives Council (DPD), that, together with the DPR, forms the reconstituted MPR. The DPD, however, is a largely advisory body and cannot veto legislation adopted by the DPR. Despite Megawati's close relations with the **army**, the MPR passed a measure in 2002 whereby the military would relinquish all its seats in the DPR in 2004. [0695, 0756, 0765]

DEWANTORO, KI HAJAR. *See* SUWARDI SURY ANINGRAT, R. M.

DHARMA WANITA (The Duty of Women)**.** Official association of the wives of government employees (there was no such association for husbands). Under the **New Order**, membership was compulsory and the organization's hierarchy closely followed that of the bureaucracy; that is, the wife of a section head was automatically head of the section's Dharma Wanita. The function of Dharma Wanita is to separate the bureaucratic corps socially from other parts of the community in the interests of detaching the bureaucracy from supposedly extraneous interests. Dharma Pertiwi is the equivalent organization for wives of military personnel. *See also* KORPS PEGAWAI REPUBLIK INDONESIA; *MONOLOYALITAS*; WOMEN AND MEN.

DHARSONO, MAJOR GENERAL HARTONO REKSO (1925–1996)**.** One of the key officers who helped **Suharto** restore order and seize power after 30 September 1965. He was commander of the Siliwangi Division (Kodam VI) of West **Java** from 1966 to 1969 and became Indonesia's ambassador in Bangkok and later secretary-general of the **Association of Southeast Asian Nations (ASEAN)**. He later turned against Suharto and in 1978 openly called for the **New Order** to return to its original ideals, urging Suharto to share power or step down. As a result, the president removed him from his position. He became a leading member of the **Petition of Fifty**. In 1984 he was jailed for speaking out against the brutal suppression of the Muslim riots at Tanjung Priok, north of **Jakarta** (*see* **WHITE PAPER**). He was released from prison in 1990. [0733, 0751]

DIEMEN, ANTHONY VAN (1593–1645)**. Dutch East Indies Company (VOC)** director-general of **trade** under **J. P. Coen** from 1627 to 1629 and Coen's successor as **governor-general** from 1636 to 1645. He presided over the period of the company's greatest expansion, when it seized **Melaka**, Formosa, and Ceylon and ordered the drafting of the Bataviaasche Statuten, which formed the basic **law** of the colony until 1848. [0491]

DIGUL. *See* BOVEN DIGUL.

DIPONEGORO, PANGERAN (1785?–1855)**.** Javanese prince, son of Sultan Hamengkubuwono III of **Yogyakarta**. After being passed over for the succession to his father, Diponegoro withdrew to his estates and cultivated his reputation as a spiritual leader. He led the **Java War**

(1825–1830) against the Dutch but was captured by the Dutch General Hendrik Merkus Baron de Kock while under guarantee of safe conduct for negotiations and was exiled to **Makassar**, where he died. [0597]

DIPTEROCARPS (Dipterocarpaceae, *meranti*, *kruing,* and other local names)**.** Common rainforest trees in western Indonesia, characteristic of the flora inherited from the ancient supercontinent of Laurasia (*see* **CONTINENTAL DRIFT**). Valued for their tall, straight trunks, they have been felled extensively for timber since 1966. Since many species flower and fruit for the first time up to 60 years after germination, long after they reach marketable girth, the regeneration of some dipterocarp forests is in doubt. *See also* FORESTRY; WALLACE'S LINE. [1148]

DIVORCE. *See* MARRIAGE, POLITICAL SIGNIFICANCE OF.

DJAJADININGRAT, PANGERAN ARIA AHMAD (1877–1943)**.** Son of a ***bupati*** family and one of the first of the Javanese elite to receive a Western education under the **Association Principle**. The novelty of this idea is indicated by the fact that when he enrolled at a Dutch primary school in **Batavia**, he used the name Willem van Banten, implying that he was an illegitimate **Indo-European**, rather than his own, aristocratic Javanese name (*see also* **NAMES**). He became a protégé of **Snouck Hurgronje** and after completing secondary school succeeded his father as *bupati* of Serang. As later *bupati* of Batavia, member of the **Volksraad**, technical adviser to the Dutch delegation at the League of Nations, and member of various government commissions, he was one of the most senior Indonesians in the colonial government. [0626, 0636]

DOUWES DEKKER, EDUARD (Multatuli; 1820–1887)**.** Author of the celebrated novel ***Max Havelaar*** (1860) based on his own experiences as assistant resident in Lebak in West **Java**. There, having accused the local ***bupati*** of extortion and **corruption**, he was himself dismissed in March 1856. [0624]

DOUWES DEKKER. E. F. E. (Setiabudi)**.** *See* INDISCHE PARTIJ.

DUALISM. 1. Concept formulated by the Dutch economist **J. H. Boeke** to describe the existence within a single political order of a Western capitalist sector and an indigenous precapitalist one. Accepting much of the prevailing colonial view of the communal village (*see* ***DESA***), Boeke argued that the indigenous **economy** was not driven by wages, prices, and capital but by mutual social obligations. He saw this precapitalist economy as an unchanging feature of the society (*see* ***GOTONG ROYONG***; **SHARED POVERTY**), partly because modern capitalism was too advanced to offer the indigenous economy a point of entry. Boeke's ideas were criticized in the volume *Indonesian Economics.* [0292, 0299, 0304]

2. Characteristic of traditional Indonesian religions identified by Dutch structural anthropology and described as the symbolic union of opposites, such as man-woman, earth-sky, and left-right, within a whole. **Hinduism** and **Buddhism** are seen as dual aspects of a single truth. [0019, 0480, 1222]

3. Dualism was also used to refer to the division of the ***Binnenlands Bestuur*** **(BB)** into European and native services. [0479]

DURIAN (*Durio zibethinus*, Bombacaceae)**.** Massive thorny fruit, probably native to **Kalimantan**. The specific epithet means civet-like, and refers to the fruit's strong smell, described by **A. R. Wallace** as that of custard passed through a sewer. Devotees, however, regard it as the world's finest fruit. [0100, 1148, 1189]

DUTCH EAST INDIES COMPANY (VOC, Vereenigde Oost-Indische Compagnie, lit., United East Indies Company)**.** Formed in 1602 by the merger of several separate companies founded in the 1590s for **trade** in the Indian Ocean (*see* **LINSCHOTEN, J. H. van**), it was a joint-stock company, that is, the separate holdings of the shareholders were not distinguished in the operations of the company, and profit and loss were shared equally according to stock holdings. Under its charter from the States-General, the company had an official monopoly of all **Dutch** trade east of the Cape of Good Hope and west of the Magellan Straits and the right to exercise sovereignty in that region on behalf of the Dutch state. General company policy was set by the Heeren XVII (Seventeen Gentlemen), who met in turn in the different provincial cities of the Netherlands and appointed a **governor-general** to govern the company in Asia. From 1619 the company's headquarters in Asia was at **Batavia** (*see* **COEN, JAN PIETERSZOON**).

The VOC aimed from the start to gain a monopoly of the spice trade in **Maluku**, using military force to impose restrictive treaties on indigenous states, to exclude foreign competitors, and to destroy spice trees outside Dutch territories (*see* **"AMBOYNA MASSACRE"**; **ENGLISH EAST INDIA COMPANY**; ***HONGI*** **RAIDS**). In 1641 the company seized **Melaka** from the **Portuguese** and in 1666–1669 conquered **Makassar** to deny it as a base for competitors, while in 1682 it successfully excluded foreign traders from **Banten**. The VOC also sought to control the so-called inter-Asiatic trade, especially between the archipelago and **India**; it established major interests in Bengal and on the Coromandel coast for the purchase of **cotton** cloth to be exchanged for spices. **Java** became important for the supply of **rice** and wood.

Throughout the 17th and 18th centuries, the VOC expanded its territorial holdings in the archipelago, making use of wars of succession, especially on Java, to extend its control. In the 18th century, however, the spice trade declined and with it the company. The increased costs of administering a land-based empire, together with rampant inefficiency and **corruption**, led the company to bankruptcy, and the States-General allowed its charter to lapse on 31 December 1799. All debts (some *f*140 million) and possessions were taken over by the Dutch government. *See also* BATAVIAN REPUBLIC. [0456, 0491, 0552, 0553, 0565, 0571]

DUTCH IN INDONESIA. Dutch traders arrived in Indonesia first as temporary visitors, but the growing scope of the operations of the **Dutch East Indies Company (VOC)** soon led Dutchmen to settle in the archipelago for extended periods. In addition to serving as employees of the company and as officials, sailors, and soldiers, some entered the service of indigenous rulers. Although attempts were made in the 17th century to establish settler colonies in **Ambon** and **Banda**, these were soon abandoned. Until the 19th century, therefore, Indies Dutch society was predominantly one of VOC employees, the elite made up of senior officials in **Batavia**, the mass consisting especially of European soldiers and sailors sharing the universal culture of bars and barracks.

Because few Dutch **women** migrated to the colony before the 19th century, most Dutch men had permanent or semipermanent liaisons with Indonesian or other Asian women and gave European status to their children (*see* **RACE**) even if not to their consorts. Dutch colonial society, therefore, especially in Batavia, was mestizo in character, and visitors frequently commented on the apparent readiness with which the Europeans had adopted Indonesian dress, food, and customs such as **betel** chewing. With the opening of the Suez Canal in 1869, more Europeans reached the colony, staying there for briefer periods, and more European women arrived as semipermanent residents. A sharper social distinction began to emerge between Europeans and **Indo-Europeans**, as well as between *trekkers,* who planned to return to the Netherlands at the end of their period of service, and *blijvers,* who planned to retire in the Indies. Colonial society was governed by a strict social hierarchy, with government officials at the top, followed then by military officers, businessmen, and churchmen. In 1930 the European population of Indonesia was about 240,000, of whom 70 percent were Indo-European. Half the European population was concentrated in nine **cities** (37,200 in the Batavia-Meester Cornelis conurbation). In the *sociëteiten* (clubs) a strong jazz tradition developed, and the Europeans of the colony produced an extensive literature. Political activity, such as it was, was focused on the Netherlands rather than on the colony, and a branch of the Nederlandsche Vereeniging voor Vrouwenkiesrecht (Netherlands Association for Female Suffrage) was founded in 1908. Only with the rise of Indonesian **nationalism** did serious local politicking begin, especially through the Vaderlandse Club, formed in 1929. During the **Depression**, the Dutch Nazi party, NSB, won considerable support in the colony, and some NSB members were interned after the fall of Holland in 1940.

As the Japanese approached, the **governor-general** instructed the European population of Indonesia to stay put and share the fate of the Indonesians, and approximately 100,000 were interned for the latter part of the **Japanese occupation**. Approximately one in six died in the substandard conditions, and many were detained by Indonesian revolutionary groups after 1945 as hostages for Dutch good behavior; some were not released until 1947. Dutch citizens were permitted to stay in Indonesia under liberal conditions after the transfer of sovereignty, but many chose to leave and on 5 December 1957 the remaining 45,000 were expelled over the Netherlands' retention of West Irian (**Papua**). *See also* COUPERUS, LOUIS. [0248, 0491, 0584, 0608, 0622, 0659, 1407, 1425]

DWIFUNGSI ("dual function")**.** The official doctrine of the Indonesian **armed forces** under **Guided Democracy** and the **New Order** regime, stating that the function of the military involves both national defense and participation in the country's social and political affairs. The **army**'s territorial structure, a military hierarchy distinct from the combat commands and running parallel to the civilian bureaucracy from the provincial (Komando Daerah Militer [Kodam, Regional Military Command]) to village (Bintara Pembina Desa [Babinsa, NCOs for Village Development]) level, provided military personnel with day-to-day involvement in the running of the country. The typical career pattern of an officer was alternating stints in the territorial and combat commands, followed by "retirement" at age 55 into a post in the civil bureaucracy.

Military involvement in administration began during the **Revolution**, with the creation of the part-military **Dewan Pertahanan Negara (DPN)**. In 1948 several military governors (some of them civilians) were appointed in various parts of the Republic, and **A. H. Nasution** developed his theory of "Total People's Defense" (*see* **GERILYA**), under which the civilian administration was, as it were, put at the disposal of the armed forces for the purpose of fighting the **Dutch**. In the early 1950s civilian politicians attempted to restrict the army's political involvement; in 1954 armed forces were forbidden to campaign in uniform and senior officers were banned from election. In March 1957, following a seizure by military officers of the administration in several provinces, martial law was declared, formalizing the army's political intervention. In 1960 five army officers were appointed as provincial governors. In early 1962 several civilian officials, including **Subandrio**, received titular military rank within the Komando Tertinggi Operasi Ekonomi (Kotoe, Supreme Operational Command for the Economy) in order to have authority over military officers serving within government departments and **state enterprises**.

Only with the advent of the **New Order** did the doctrine of military participation in civil affairs become officially known as *dwifungsi,* claiming a permanent role for the army in both the defense and sociopolitical fields. The armed forces were represented formally in parliament and in provincial and district legislatures by means of a bloc of reserved seats—one fifth of the total until 1995, when their number in the **Dewan Perwakilan Rakyat (DPR)** was reduced to 75 from the previous 100. (On the basis of this representation, serving military personnel were not permitted to vote in **elections**.) During the 1970s the army's continued domination of the state was justified on the grounds that civilians still needed the strong leadership that only the army could provide. In February 1980 the government announced a program called *ABRI masuk desa* ("ABRI enters the villages"), in which armed forces personnel were posted in the villages ostensibly to familiarize themselves with village life and problems and to improve their public profile by helping village development. *Dwifungsi* was first enshrined in legislation only in February 1988.

Tensions between **Suharto** and the army leadership in the early 1990s led to questioning of the *dwifungsi* doctrine, with the army suspecting that the president was unwilling to protect their corporate interests. There was a steady reduction in the number of officers and former officers in the cabinet, and the armed forces' activities in **East Timor** together with significant **budget** constraints after the collapse of **oil** prices produced increased pressure for a smaller, leaner armed forces with correspondingly fewer resources to devote to politics and government. With Suharto's fall some military officers hoped that the army's *dwifungsi* role would again be strengthened, but the revelations of the army's abuses under the late New Order regime led to public demands for the elimination of military involvement in civilian affairs. Under President **Abdurrachman Wahid** and his defense minister, Juwono Sudarsono, there was a strong effort to exert civilian control over the military, and the military formally abandoned the policy of *dwifungsi.* General **Wiranto** felt obliged to apologize to the people of **Aceh** for abuses of the system, and he agreed to the reduction (and eventual elimination) of the armed forces' seats in the legislative bodies. But with **Megawati Sukarnoputri**'s accession to the presidency and her close ties to the military, it seemed likely that they would continue to play an important role in many aspects of political life. *See also* DEFENSE POLICY; "MIDDLE WAY" FOR THE ARMED FORCES. [0714, 0727, 0731, 0733, 0736, 0872, 0972, 0978]

– E –

EAST INDONESIA. *See* NEGARA INDONESIA TIMUR.

EAST SUMATRA (*Sumatra's Oostkust*)**.** A lowland area around the modern city of Medan. In early times it was occupied by **Batak** communities, who were later conquered and partly displaced by Malay kingdoms and sultanates. Disputed by **Aceh**, **Siak**, and **Riau**, it finally emerged as a distinct region through the phenomenal development of its plantation sector in the late 19th and early 20th centuries. **Tobacco** was introduced there in 1863, and **coffee**, **coconuts**, **rubber**, sisal, and **oil palm** somewhat later. The region was the site of the first major expansion of private **investment** in the Indies after the government controls of the **Cultivation System** were lifted. The Deli Maatschappij was formed in 1869 and by the end of the century it dominated the region along with three other companies, Senembah, the Deli-Batavia Maatschappij, and the Tabak Maatschappij Arendsburg. **Labor** was obtained from southern **China** (to 1931) and later from **Java** (*see* **COOLIE ORDINANCE**). There was also much immigration by Bataks from the interior, and by 1930 the Malays comprised only 20 percent of the **population**. As the power of

Western enterprises grew, that of the original rulers of the region—the sultans of **Deli**, **Langkat**, and **Serdang**, as well as Asahan, Batubara, and others—was steadily eroded, though they were compensated by vast incomes from rents. Politically, the East Sumatra planters were influential in colonial circles, J. T. Cremer of the Deli Mij becoming minister of colonies for a time. Administratively, however, the region was always rather independent of **Batavia**.

In March 1946 a social revolution broke out against the sultans and rajas who had leased land to Western enterprises and who were seen as agents of **Dutch** colonial rule and exploiters in their own right; many were killed or driven out. Although the area was formally part of the Republic, Medan was soon occupied by Allied forces, and the remainder of the region was carved up between warlords of various allegiances. The Dutch reconquered much of the area in July 1947 and formed the federal Negara Sumatra Timur (NST, State of East Sumatra) on 25 December 1947, though this was dissolved in August 1950 and was incorporated in the Indonesian province of North Sumatra. *See also* SUMATRA. [0348, 0460, 0673, 0817, 0818, 0830, 0828]

EAST TIMOR (including the enclave of Oécusse)**.** East Timor became clearly defined as a **Portuguese** colony only in 1859, though the Portuguese presence dated from the 16th century (*see* **TIMOR**). Until 1896 the colony was ruled directly from Macau, but even after gaining a separate administration it remained a neglected corner of the Portuguese empire, exporting little more than **coffee** and horses. An indigenous uprising by Dom Boaventura was crushed in 1910–1912, but by 1928 only 200 civilian officials and 300 troops were sufficient to maintain Portuguese rule. Business and government in the capital, Dili, were dominated by a mestizo and **Chinese** elite, while in the countryside local chiefs, or *liurai,* acted as deputies for the colonial rulers. A third of the population was **Catholic**, the rest animist, the most widespread language being Tetum.

At the outbreak of World War II, Portugal declared its neutrality. Portuguese Timor, however, was briefly occupied in December 1941 by a joint Dutch-Australian force, with the idea of keeping it out of Japanese hands. **Japanese** troops occupied the territory from February 1942, and until 1945 the colony was under Japanese army rule although Japan also formally recognized Portuguese neutrality. Australian troops fought a guerrilla war against the Japanese in the hinterland from March to December 1942. During the war, approximately 40,000 Timorese died of famine.

Under the 1953 Organic Law on Overseas Territories, East Timor formally became a province of Portugal, divided into 13 districts called conçelhos (councils) under Portuguese administrators. Below these were 58 *postos,* of which 60 percent were headed by Timorese. An anti-Portuguese uprising, which apparently had some Indonesian backing, was suppressed in 1959.

After the Armed Forces coup in Portugal in April of 1974, the new authorities announced three possibilities for the future of East Timor: independence, continued association with Portugal, and integration with Indonesia. Three political groups—**União Democrática Timorense (UDT)**, **Frente Revolucionária do Timor Leste Independente (Fretilin)**, and **Associação Popular Democrática Timorese (APODETI)**—formed to promote these possibilities respectively. In June 1975 the Portuguese government announced firm plans for a three-year transitional period to full independence for the territory, including a general **election** in October 1976.

Popular support for Fretilin was now such that it was likely to win a full majority in elections, and UDT sought to forestall this by staging a coup in Dili on 11 August 1975 with the help of the police force. Fretilin, supported by Timorese sections of the colonial army, resisted the UDT move, and full civil war quickly broke out. Fretilin forces soon seized power in the major centers, but UDT and APODETI supporters fled across the border into Indonesian Timor, where they regrouped along with Indonesian "volunteers" in what was called "Operasi Komodo" and began a gradual invasion of East Timor, in the course of which five journalists from **Australia** were killed. On 11 October Fretilin formed a "transitional" government and on 28 November declared the independence of the Democratic Republic of East Timor. On 30 November, Portugal requested **United Nations** help in regaining control of the territory.

With the acquiescence of the **United States**, Indonesian **armed forces** mounted a full-scale attack on Dili on 7 December 1975, deploying an estimated 20,000 troops in East Timor by the end of the month. They soon extended their control to all major population centers at the cost of extensive casualties among the civilian population. UDT, APODETI, and other anti-Fretilin groups formed a provisional government under Indonesian auspices, and on 31 May 1976 an Indonesian-sponsored "People's Representative Council" requested integration with Indonesia as its 27th **province**; this took place on 15 July. The United Nations never recognized Indonesian sovereignty.

Fierce resistance by Fretilin continued. Widely reported atrocities carried out by Indonesian forces in the attack on Dili and continued systematic violence by the occupation forces alienated much of the population, and relative security in the territory was only established after major military operations from September 1977 to March 1979 and by means of resettling parts of the population into strategic hamlets. The disruption of **agriculture** associated with the military pacification efforts led to a major famine. Some 200,000 Timorese died during the Indonesian occupation (of an original population of 650,000), most as a result of starvation.

The Indonesian **army** maintained close control of the province, and **military business operations** dominated the coffee and **sandalwood** industries. The Indonesian government lifted formal restrictions on visits to the province on 1 January 1989, believing that Fretilin forces had been reduced to less than 200 rebel soldiers who no longer posed a serious military threat. In November 1990 they arrested the foremost Fretilin leader, **Jose Alexandre "Xanana" Gusmão**, sentencing him in May 1993 to life in prison, a sentence later reduced to 19 years and eight months.

The situation changed dramatically in November 1991 with the so-called Santa Cruz massacre in Dili, when Indonesian soldiers gunned down scores of Timorese **human rights** demonstrators, killing somewhere between 50 and 270 of them. This sparked international protests, with the U.S. Congress cutting its military aid to Indonesia and the UN passing a resolution condemning Indonesia's actions.

Over the following years international aid to East Timor expanded, and Indonesia agreed that much of it could go directly to Timor-based groups and **Catholic** Church–run charities, with the United States alone committing over US$ 4 million in 1994. During the 1990s a new generation of East Timor dissidents became active, in part in reaction to the flow of mostly Muslim migrants into the territory from other parts of Indonesia (in the mid-1990s, a reported 25,000 a year). International attention was again focused on the situation when 29 Timorese scaled the walls of the U.S. embassy in **Jakarta** during the Asia-Pacific Economic Cooperation (APEC) summit in November 1994 and spent two weeks camped in the embassy grounds. Dissidence was further encouraged by Jakarta's unwillingness to bring to justice the military officers responsible for the Santa Cruz massacre, **Suharto**'s refusal to consider a special administrative status for the "province," and suspicion that the Indonesian military was sponsoring an influx of masked vigilantes into Dili who attacked and beat up Timorese known to be opposed to Indonesia's occupation. In January 1995 Indonesian soldiers allegedly murdered six unarmed Timorese civilians. Timorese Catholic Bishop **Carlos Ximenes Belo** became more outspoken in his criticisms of the Indonesian occupation, and he and proindependence advocate **Jose Ramos Horta** were awarded the Nobel Peace Prize in 1996.

After Suharto's resignation, Jakarta finally proposed granting a special status to East Timor and in August 1998 withdrew 1,000 troops from the territory (though many of these were replaced). UN-brokered talks began in late 1998 between Portuguese and Indonesian representatives focusing on a plan for "autonomy with special status" for East Timor. President **B. J. Habibie** shocked all sides on 27 January 1999 when he raised the prospect of offering the territory independence if its people rejected the proposals for autonomy coming out of these negotiations. The UN supervised a referendum on independence on 31 August, but left security in the hands of the Indonesians rather than introducing a UN peacekeeping force, and the Indonesian military began arming pro-Indonesian **militia** groups. In the referendum 98.5 percent of East Timor's voters went to the polls, with 78.5 percent of them voting in favor of cutting ties with Indonesia. When the results were announced on 3 September, the Indonesia-supported militias went on a rampage, causing some 2,000 deaths (including UN staff members), driving more than 200,000 from their homes, burning down Bishop Belo's home, and taking more than 6,000 refugees who had sought sanctuary there into West Timor. On 6 September Indonesia declared martial law in East Timor. Only after a week of threats from the International Monetary Fund (IMF), the **World Bank**, the United Nations, and Washington did Indonesia agree to allow an international force to enter the territory to restore order. A 7,500-soldier UN-backed International Force for East Timor headed by Australia began to land on 20 September.

The UN set up a transitional government in the territory and together with foreign governments spent about US$2.2 billion to rebuild the infrastructure after its destruction in the postreferendum violence. An estimated 120,000 East Timorese remained in refugee camps in West Timor, and the continuing tension broke into open violence with the murder of three UN workers on 6 September 2000 on the West Timor side of the border. In September 2001 an election was held for a de facto parliament to draft a constitution for East Timor. The following year Xanana Gusmão, who had been released from jail in September 1999 and returned to Timor the following month, was elected president. On 20 May 2002 the UN secretary general ceded governing authority to the newly independent Democratic Republic of East Timor in a ceremony attended by Indonesian President **Megawati Sukarnoputri**. The East Timor government immediately signed the Timor Gap **oil**-and-**gas** agreement with Australia. Under this agreement, which was ratified by the East Timor parliament in December and would allow foreign oil companies to begin extracting oil from the Timor Gap, East Timor receives 90 percent of total proceeds, which could, beginning in 2005, earn it $6 billion over 20 years. The World Bank predicted that oil revenues would rise from $21.3 million in 2003 to $76.4 million in 2006. Twenty-nine countries attended a mid-May donor conference and pledged $440 million to help the country over the next three years, and the United States also was running a $25 million annual aid program. Until the oil revenue began to come in, coffee remained East Timor's most important export earner, worth on an average about $10 million per year.

In February 2003 the United Nations indicted General **Wiranto**, together with six other military officers and a civilian official, for crimes against humanity during East Timor's independence vote in 1999. They were charged with financing, training, and arming the pro-Indonesia militias who, together with the Indonesian military, carried out the slaughter. The Indonesian government refused to accept the indictments. The following month a special **human rights** court in Jakarta sentenced Brigadier General Noer Muis, Indonesia's last commander in East Timor, to five years in jail for gross human rights violations in not preventing the attacks. (He was not immediately imprisoned.) Previously the court had acquitted 12 defendants and sentenced two lower-ranking officers and two civilians to jail. [0765, 0799, 0806, 0814, 0855, 0941, 0959, 1140, 1296]

ECONOMY. In 1950 Indonesia's inherited **debt** from the Dutch had a debilitating effect on the new nation's economy. Although most of its leaders favored a modified socialist system with a large **cooperative** component for the economy, many of the country's major plantations and industries remained in the hands of the Dutch and other foreign companies. In 1958 **Sukarno** nationalized Dutch property and during the period of **Confrontation** also expropriated British and American firms, rejecting American aid in 1964. During the closing years of Sukarno's rule there was increasing inflation, growing debt, and declining exports, while foreign reserves shrank to zero.

When **Suharto** assumed power, he appealed for economic support from the West and brought into his government a number of American-trained economists, the so-called Berkeley Mafia headed by **Widjojo Nitisastro**. At their urging, in 1967 the **Inter-Governmental Group on**

Indonesia (IGGI) was set up, and it, together with the **World Bank** and International Monetary Fund (IMF), provided more than 75 percent of development expenses during Suharto's early years. As a result, the inflation rate fell from about 600 percent in 1966 to 22 percent for the years 1969–1972. In the government's first five-year development plan (**Rencana Pembangunan Lima Tahun**), which began in April 1969, major attention focused on **agriculture**, and by the mid-1980s Indonesia was self sufficient in **rice**. At the same time the country was opened to foreign **investment**. New discoveries of **oil** and the dramatic surge in oil prices during the 1970s further boosted the economy. This boom was threatened in 1975 by the crisis in the state-owned oil enterprise, **Pertamina**, but through project cancellations and further foreign help Jakarta was able to salvage the situation by late 1977.

The Indonesian economy was hit hard by the collapse in oil prices in the mid-1980s, and in response the government inaugurated an austerity program and devalued the rupiah by 31 percent in the fall of 1986, attempting to diversify Indonesia's exports and increase its non-oil domestic revenues. Between 1969 and 1994, GDP expanded at an average yearly rate of 6.8 percent and during the early 1990s averaged 8 percent. At the same time after the mid-1980s inflation was kept to single digits, being 6 percent in 1997. But at the same time, Indonesia's economy was undermined by its huge foreign debt.

The forest fires and drought of 1997 combined with the Asian **financial crisis** to plunge Indonesia in the second half of the year into a severe recession, with the rupiah falling to a rate of Rp 10,000 to US$1. In October 1997 the government announced it would seek help from the international financial organizations and under strong pressure from the IMF Suharto finally signed his agreement to the terms of the fund's $33 billion bailout plan. The government held down prices of rice and fuel, hoping to avoid the riots that would break out in the face of the austerity measures in the plan, but it continued to protect banks owned by **Suharto**'s **family** and friends. When the president then refused to carry out the measures he had agreed to with the IMF and openly defied it by appointing loyalists and cronies to his new cabinet, the Indonesian economy was on the brink of collapse.

After Suharto resigned, the chaos continued with the rupiah dropping to Rp 16,500 to US$1 by June 1998 and foreign capital fleeing the country. President **B. J. Habibie** committed himself to implementing the IMF's policies, recalled Widjojo Nitisastro to an advisory role in the government, and launched attempts to reform the entire **banking** and corporate structure. His successor **Abdurrachman Wahid** continued efforts to implement economic reforms, promising to address the problem of **corruption** and the wealth of the Suharto family, but his government, too, became embroiled in corruption scandals.

In 2001 **Megawati Sukarnoputri** brought in a new economic team headed by former ambassador to the United States, Dorodjatun Kuntjoro-Jakti. Although hoping eventually to restore a 7 percent GDP growth rate, during 2001 they reached only 3.3 percent (compared with 4.8 percent in 2000) instead of the 6 percent or higher that would be needed to reduce Indonesia's debt from a current 90 percent to a targeted 60 percent by 2004. However, the rescheduling of the debt by the Paris Club of lenders in mid-April 2002 had a positive impact, particularly on the strength of the rupiah to the dollar, and inflation levels also fell. The IMF had instituted a four-year, $5.2-billion economic recovery program for Indonesia in 1999, and this was embraced by Megawati's economic team, which began to institute unpopular measures, such as increasing prices for fuel, electricity, and communications as well as selling Indonesian assets to foreign companies. Indonesia's economy expanded at a rate of 3–4 percent in 2002, with poverty rates declining to 16 percent by January 2003. Indonesia's average growth between 1998 and 2002 had dropped to –0.1 percent from 7.6 percent between 1987 and 1996. Total exports fell from $62.1 billion in 2000 to $57 billion in 2002.

The economy improved markedly in 2003, despite the falloff in foreign investment as a result of the terrorist bombings in **Bali** and Jakarta. In July the government announced that it would not renew its program with the IMF once it expired at the end of 2003. By October, it had used up $4.7 billion of the loan and the IMF approved a further $493 million. By then the government had succeeded in curbing inflation to a yearly rate of 5.3 percent and maintaining a stable **currency**, but the IMF recommended that it increase its efforts to attract foreign investment and curb the still-endemic corruption. In response to the IMF's optimistic assessment of Indonesia's economic policies, the stock market rose to a three-and-one-half-year high, and economic growth in 2004 was forecast at between 4 and 5 percent. *See also* CURRENCY; FORESTRY; INDUSTRIALIZATION; TRADE. [0290, 0294–0296 0301–0303, 0312, 0313]

EDUCATION, GOVERNMENT SCHOOLS. This entry is concerned mainly with formal, Western-style training (*see also* **EDUCATION, PRIVATE AND ISLAMIC**), but what follows should be read with the understanding that home-based education traditionally played an important role in Indonesia and was probably responsible, for instance, for a high level of literacy in precolonial times (*see* **WRITING SYSTEMS**).

Under **Dutch East Indies Company (VOC)** rule, schools were small, locally based, and mostly religiously oriented. The company distrusted the effects of education on its indigenous subjects and gave schools little encouragement, and from 1648 to 1778 the giving of any kind of lessons required a government license. Only after the company's fall did extensive, government-sponsored education begin. A Dutch-language primary school was set up in **Batavia** in 1816 followed by a three-year public elementary school in 1849 and a teacher training school in 1852. From 1864 the colonial state maintained so-called Europeesche Lagere Scholen (ELS, European Lower Schools), offering a seven-year, Dutch-language course, though it was not until 1867 that a Department of Education was established. Western education at this time was intended primarily for Europeans, and it was expected that the children of Dutch residents would return to the Netherlands for more advanced studies if desired. The ELS, however, were opened to "qualified" Indonesians, and some 1,870 were enrolled by 1900. From 1860 the colonial government began to establish Hogere Burger Scholen (HBS, Higher Civil Schools), rigorous secondary schools following the Dutch metropolitan curriculum and so qualifying graduates for admission to Dutch universities.

General education for Indonesians was taken up on a large scale first by the Nederlandsch Zendelinggenootschap (*see* **PROTESTANTISM**) from 1830. In 1848, the state set up 20 "regentschapscholen" (regency schools) to teach the children of the ***priyayi***, but general education for Indonesians was not provided until 1907, when **J. B. van Heutsz** established Volksscholen (*dessascholen*) offering a three-year course in local languages with indigenous teachers. In 1940, about 45 percent of children received some education at this level, though graduation rates were low. In 1908 Hollandsch-Chineesche Scholen (HCS) and in 1914 Hollandsch-Inlandsche Scholen (HIS) were established to provide more advanced primary education to **Chinese** and Indonesians. The curriculum was much the same as that of the ELS, but the first years were taught in Chinese or Malay/Indonesian. From 1914, a kind of lower secondary education was provided by the Meer Uitgebreide Lagere Onderwijs (MULO, Broader Lower Education), which fed in turn into the Algemene Middelbare Scholen (AMS, General Secondary Schools) from 1919, intended to prepare MULO graduates for tertiary education. The interlinking of the lower education system was completed in 1921 with the creation of so-called *schakelscholen* (bridging schools) to prepare Volksschool graduates for the MULO. The rise of **nationalism**, however, led to Dutch complaints that overeducation was producing a kind of intellectual proletariat ripe for disruptive ideas, and from the mid-1920s the provision of Dutch-language education was reduced. (*See also* **ASSOCIATION PRINCIPLE**.)

University-level education began much later in the Netherlands Indies than in British **India** or French Indochina; the few Indonesians and Chinese who received it commonly went to the Netherlands for tertiary education along with Europeans. Quasi-tertiary education was offered by the Opleidingschool voor Inlandsche Ambtenaren (OSVIA, Training school for native civil servants) and the School tot Opleiding van Inlandsche Artsen (STOVIA, School for the training of native physicians), both founded in 1900. A veterinary school offering advanced secondary training was founded in **Bogor** in 1907 and a secondary law school in Batavia in 1909. Resident Europeans formed an Indische Universiteitsbeweeging (Indies University Movement) in 1910, but the authorities argued that there were too few high school graduates to support a full university. Instead, a series of tertiary colleges were established, beginning with the Technische Hogeschool (THS, Institute of Technology) in **Bandung** in 1920 and followed by the Rechtshogeschool (RHS, Law School) in 1924, the Geneeskundige Hogeschool (GHS, Medical School) in 1927, and a Literaire Faculteit (Faculty of Letters) in 1940, all in Batavia. A Landbouwkundige Faculteit (Agricultural Faculty) was founded in Bogor in 1941. A few days before the Japanese landed on Java, the **Volksraad** passed a resolution merging these faculties into a single university. An estimated 230 Indonesians possessed tertiary education qualifications by 1942. All tertiary institutions were closed by the **Japanese** at the start of the occupation, but in April 1943 a medical school, the Ika Daigaku, was reestablished (*see* **HEALTH**). The Dutch opened a "Nooduniversiteit" (emergency university) in **Jakarta** in January 1946, with faculties of medicine, arts, **law**, and **agriculture**, merging these with the other prewar faculties in 1947 to create the Universiteit van Indonesië.

From about January 1946, Republicans conducted limited tertiary education in Jakarta at various Perguruan Tinggi (tertiary colleges); in December 1949 these were merged into Gadjah Mada University in **Yogyakarta**. In 1950 national literacy was estimated at 10 percent, and a massive expansion of both public and private education at all levels took place. Foreign-language schools for Indonesians were banned in 1958.

The **Suharto** regime set a basic educational strategy in 1969 that inaugurated a dramatic expansion in the educational system over the next three decades. In 1974 it launched a nationwide building program to expand primary education, and between 1973–1974 and 1990–1991 the number of primary schools increased from 65,910 to 146,558. In 1984 five years of primary school education became compulsory for all Indonesian children between the ages of seven and 12. The number of primary pupils enrolled doubled from 13.1 million in 1973–1974 to 26.5 million in 1990–1991. In 1994–1995 compulsory education was expanded to encompass three years of lower secondary/junior high school. In tertiary education the Suharto government enacted a policy whereby at least one university was to be established in each province, with the total number of public tertiary institutions reaching 78 in 1994, while student enrollment in both public and private advanced educational institutions rose from 815,000 in 1984 to 1.61 million in 1994.

It has, however, been argued that the growth in school enrollment has been accompanied by a decline in the quality of the education offered and that there has also developed a great discrepancy in standards among the regions and between rural and urban areas (with the highest quality education being offered in a few urban centers in **Java**). The poor quality of education was probably exacerbated by the Suharto government's use of educational institutions to impart government propaganda, with **Pancasila** values being incorporated into all school curricula from the late 1970s and influencing in particular the teaching of such subjects as history, Indonesian language and literature, and religious education. Other factors influencing the quality of education were its cost and the poor teaching standards. In part to offset the latter deficiency, the government introduced a new curriculum for primary and secondary schools in the 1994–1995 school year and during the 1990s also attempted to involve private companies in education to help fit the skills acquired by graduating students to the needs of the job market. Nevertheless, a disproportionate number of students continued to graduate with nontechnical skills and were faced with a resulting lack of job opportunities. [0069, 0353, 0479, 0576, 0626, 0756, 1277, 1278, 1280, 1286, 1287, 1289]

EDUCATION, PRIVATE AND ISLAMIC. The classic traditional educational institution in Indonesia, derived from **Indian** models, was the *asrama,* a residential school where pupils gathered to receive largely religious instruction from a *guru* or teacher. This model of instruction was retained after the arrival of **Islam** in the form of ***madrasah, pesantren,*** or *surau*. As in the West, this relatively formal education helped to define for both sexes a period of youth between childhood and adolescence.

The emerging Indonesian nationalist movement realized the importance of education in inculcating values and increasing national self-confidence, and from the 1920s members of the ***pergerakan*** founded large numbers of so-called *wilde scholen* (wild schools), whose diplomas were not recognized by the colonial government. Best known of these were the *sekolah rakyat* (people's schools) of the **Sarekat Islam**, the **Taman Siswa**, and the **Kartini** schools. On **Sumatra** the most known were the modernist Islamic Thawalib and Diniyah network of schools and the vocational INS in West Sumatra. In September 1932 the colonial government attempted to restrict the operation of these schools by issuing a "wild schools ordinance" that required private schools to have government permission, although financial support of government schools was being reduced because of the **Depression**. A national campaign against the ordinance, led by Ki Hajar Dewantoro of Taman Siswa and Mohammad Sjafei of the West Sumatran INS, succeeded in having the ordinance withdrawn. The number of wild schools reached 2,200 by the late 1930s with an estimated enrollment of 142,000 pupils.

State support for Muslim education began only in 1937, when the colonial government subsidized the establishment of a **Muhammadiyah** MULO in Yogyakarta; Muhammadiyah schools already established in other regions also received financial subsidies from the Dutch government, but most other private religious schools refused such subsidies.

In 1904 Dewi Sartika had established Sekolah Isteri (Women's Schools) in West Java to provide education for **women**; and in 1911 Rohana Kudus (1884–1972, a sister of **Sutan Sjahrir**) founded a school for women (Kerajinan Amai Setia, or KAS) in Kota Gedang in West Sumatra. Probably the most popular school for girls was Diniyah Putri school, established in Padang Panjang, West Sumatra, by Rahmah El Yunusiah (1900–1969) in 1923, which attracted students not only from the East Indies but also from the **Malay Peninsula** and reached an enrollment of 500 in 1939. The school is currently still active.

After independence, the government allowed the emergence of a full Muslim educational system, run by the Department of Religion, alongside the national, secular system under the Department of Education. Primary and secondary schools are classified as *madrasah,* providing 70 percent secular and 30 percent religious education, whose diplomas are considered equivalent to those of secular schools; *diniyah,* in which the proportions are reversed and which qualify students mainly for religious and quasi-religious careers; and Pendidikan Guru Islam (Islamic teachers' colleges), teaching 50 percent secular and 50 percent religious material. Islamic education at all levels expanded under the **New Order**. The number of pupils in the lower secondary system increased to 1.8 million by 1997–1998. The tertiary religious institutions, the Institut Agama Islam Negeri (IAIN, State Islamic Institutes) first established in 1960 by the Ministry of Religious Affairs, had 14 branches throughout the country by the 1990s. Religious education is also compulsory in secular schools. *See also* ISLAM; RELIGION AND POLITICS. [0627, 0807, 1273, 1274, 1279, 1282, 1283, 1288]

"EERESCHULD, EEN" ("a debt of honor")**.** Title of an August 1899 article by the **Dutch** lawyer Conrad Theodor van Deventer (1857–1915) in *De Gids,* arguing that the millions of guilders received by the Netherlands state under the **Cultivation System** and by Dutch companies since 1870 had left the Dutch with a "debt of honor" to Indonesia, an obligation to raise living standards and bring about economic development. The article contributed to the emergence of the **Ethical Policy**, but only two capital transfers from the Netherlands took place. In 1905 *f*40 million was transferred on condition that it was used for the economic improvement of the Javanese and Madurese, while in 1936 *f*25 million was transferred as compensation to the Indies for reserving part of their market for the Netherlands during the **Depression**. *See also BATIG SLOT.*

EGYPT, RELATIONS WITH. *See* ARAB WORLD, RELATIONS WITH.

ELECTIONS. These were first held in the Netherlands Indies in 1903 for members of municipal councils. Although the franchise was highly restricted and Europeans dominated the councils, with reserved seats for each racial group, these elections provided Indonesia with its first experience of electoral competition (*see* **DECENTRALIZATION**). Members of the **Volksraad** were elected by members of these councils.

During the **Revolution**, village elections were held in many parts of Republican territory in early 1946 and in **Yogyakarta** in 1948. Indonesia's first general elections after the transfer of sovereignty were not held until 1955. Voter turnout was 91 percent. Using proportional representation with effectively a single electoral district for the entire country, they produced what many saw as an inconclusive result, the **Partai Nasional Indonesia (PNI)** gaining 57 seats with 22.3 percent of the vote, **Masjumi** 57 seats (20.9 percent), **Nahdlatul Ulama (NU)** 45 seats (18.4 percent), and the **Partai Komunis Indonesia (PKI)** 39 seats (16.4 percent) in a parliament of 257. Twenty-four other parties, including independents, were represented. General elections due for 1959 were never held, partly because a substantial gain in PKI votes seemed likely.

Under the **New Order**, government-controlled elections were held in 1971, then every five years in 1977, 1982, 1987, 1992, and 1997 (for detailed results, *see* **APPENDIX**). In all these elections, with the exception of the first, only the government electoral organization **Golongan Karya (Golkar)** and the two officially sponsored political parties, **Partai Demokrasi Indonesia (PDI)** and **Partai Persatuan Pembangunan (PPP)**, were allowed to participate, and campaigning was restricted to a period of 60 days before polling day. All parties had to submit their candidates and campaign slogans to the security authorities for approval. Challenging the **Pancasila** or the **Broad Outlines of State Policy** and criticizing racial, social, or religious groups (*see* **SARA**) were not permitted.

Civil servants normally had to vote at their offices and were expected, under the doctrine of ***monoloyalitas***, to vote for Golkar. In the villages, too, Golkar drew extensively on support from the **army** and the bureaucracy, sometimes banning campaigning by nongovernment groups on the grounds that the residents had already decided to vote for Golkar. In the New Order elections it was not possible for any party but Golkar to win overall, and government rhetoric portrayed the occasion as one of danger when the social antagonisms of the 1950s and 1960s risked being revived.

After 1971 elections used proportional representation by province, the provincial allocation of seats being weighted to ensure that the provinces on **Java**, with two thirds of the voters, nonetheless elected only half the members of parliament. The final election under the New Order, that of May 1997, was the bloodiest ever. Divisions within the PDI and government attempts a year earlier to suppress the faction headed by **Megawati Sukarnoputri** led many of the party's faithful supporters either to boycott the election or vote for another party. As a result PDI received only 3 percent of the vote, and the election as a whole lacked even the legitimacy of the previous ones.

The 1999 election was the first free election since that of 1955. Of the more than 140 parties that were registered, 48 were allowed to contest the election (for the results, *see* APPENDIX F). Megawati's Indonesian Democratic Party of Struggle (**PDI-P**) received the most votes (35,589,073), with Golkar coming in second (23,741,758), and the three largest Islamic parties, **Partai Kebangkitan Bangsa (PKB),** PPP, and **Partai Amanat Nasional (PAN)**, taking the next three positions. Twenty-four parties met the criteria laid out in the Law on General Elections (No. 12/2003) for participating in the general elections scheduled for 5 April 2004. In these elections voters were to elect party candidates for the national, provincial and district legislatures (DPR and DPRD) and also individual candidates for the new Regional Representative Council (DPD). Law No. 23/2003 provided for the direct election of the **president** and **vice president**. Nomination of candidates for these offices was limited to political parties that won at least 3 percent of the seats or 5 percent of the votes in the April 2004 general election (in later elections the limit would be raised to 15 percent of the seats or 20 percent of the votes). If no presidential candidate received more than 50 percent of the votes in the 5 July 2004 presidential election, a run-off between the top two vote-getters was be held on 20 September.

The final number of eligible voters for the 2004 elections was 145,701,637, a 23-percent increase over the 118.15 million voters in the 1999 legislative elections. *See also* PARTIES, POLITICAL. [0695, 0739, 1004–1015]

ENGLISH EAST INDIA COMPANY. Chartered by Queen Elizabeth I in 1600, this was, like the **Dutch East Indies Company**, a joint-stock company enjoying a national monopoly of **trade** in the region. The company's first expedition to **Java** in 1601 brought back so much **pepper** that the market was glutted and the company began to diversify. It established bases in **Banten**, **Aceh**, **Makassar**, **Maluku**, and Masulipatam (southern India) in the first decades of the 17th century, but by the end of the century had been driven out of the archipelago by the **Dutch**, except for the West **Sumatra** colony of **Bengkulu**. (*See also* **"AMBOYNA MASSACRE."**) The company was taken over by the British crown in 1858 after the Indian Mutiny. *See also* BRITAIN, HISTORICAL LINKS WITH. [0491]

ENVIRONMENTAL PROTECTION. Three issues have dominated environmental concerns in the Indonesian archipelago since the late 19th century: the preservation of unique animal and plant species (for which *see* **CONSERVATION, NATURE**), the maintenance of a stable water regime by maintaining forest cover and preventing erosion, and the control of pollution.

Forest protection for environmental reasons (rather than from illicit collectors of forest products) became an element of **Dutch** colonial policy only late in the 19th century, though in the middle of the century **F. W. Junghuhn** had suggested that areas above 500 meters should not be cleared. It was realized already that rainfall and runoff were more regular on forested slopes and that the agricultural prosperity of **Java** depended in part on leaving areas of the island with their forest cover intact, though the preservation of forests for timber production was also a major consideration. Under the **New Order** regime, there was large-scale indiscriminate clearing in the 1970s. Protests against this caused the government to pay attention to protection of forests, reforestation (*reboisasi*), and afforestation (*penghijauan*), but efforts in this direction lost out generally to the perceived needs of the timber industry. (*See also* **FORESTRY**; **HASAN, MUHAMMAD "BOB"**.)

To deal with the environmental consequences of economic growth, President **Suharto** appointed Emil Salim (1930–) as the first minister for the environment in 1978, with the mandate to find a way of combining economic development with protection of the environment. Salim lacked the authority to be effective in this task. An environmental nongovernmental organization (NGO), the Indonesian Environmental Forum (Wahana Lingkungan Hidup, Walhi), was established in October 1980 as an umbrella organization for groups and individuals interested in protecting the environment. It played an important role in drafting environmental laws, especially the basic law of 1982, and it brought several lawsuits against corporations negligent in implementing environmental regulations. Domestically it has worked with other influential NGOs and has close ties with environmental groups and NGOs in other **Association of Southeast Asian Nations (ASEAN)** countries, through the Southeast Asian Coalition (SEACON) established in 1990. It has not yet, however, developed an autonomous organization and is dependent on funding from other agencies. In 1990 the government set up the Environmental Impact Management Agency (Badan Pengendalian Dampak Lingkungan, Bapedal), and in the early 1990s the minister of the environment also launched the Clean Rivers Project (Prokasih), which had limited success in compelling industrial polluters to install sewerage treatment facilities. It also established an Environmental Achievements Award (Kalpataru), which helped spread environmental awareness. *See also* WERENG. [0730, 0756, 0763, 0943, 1160, 1169, 1183]

ETHICAL POLICY. Common name given to **Dutch** colonial policy in the first decades of the 20th century, following a speech from the throne by Queen Wilhelmina in 1901 announcing: "As a Christian power, the Netherlands is obliged to carry out government policy in the Indies in the consciousness that the Netherlands has a moral duty to the people of these regions." This policy was expressed in a new willingness of government to involve itself in economic and social affairs in the archipelago in the name of rational efficiency. It was a time of improved **health** care, extended **education**, expansion of communications facilities, irrigation and other infrastructure, and the commencement of **transmigration** measures that brought benefits to Western commercial interests as much as to the Indonesians themselves. The **Depression** of the 1930s led to budget cuts in most of these areas, effectively ending the Ethical Policy, which has been criticized most sharply for its paternalist approach. The sharp contrast between the growing indigenous Indonesian capacity to manage a modern state and **economy** and the persistent Dutch supervision was one of the factors that strengthened the nationalist movement. *See also* "EERESCHULD, EEN"; NATIONALISM; *STUW, DE.* [0620]

ETYMOLOGY. Vocabulary in the Indonesian **language** changes rapidly, and the derivation of words has taken on some political significance from time to time. The reforming role of the brief British occupation of **Java**, for instance, has been emphasized at the expense of the **Dutch** by folk legend, which attributes many Indonesian words to **Thomas Stamford Raffles**. Since independence, there has been some attempt to reduce the number of words in Indonesian that are derived from Dutch, while a growth in the number of formerly Javanese words has been seen as a sign of **Javanization**. *Anda* was introduced as a neutral form of the pronoun "you" in 1957. The Komisi Bahasa Indonesia coined about 7,000 new words during World War II, and its successor, the Komisi Istilah (Terminological Commission), had coined or ratified 321,710 new terms by 1970, seeking words first from Malay, second from other Indonesian languages, third from Arabic and Sanskrit, and fourth from European languages. Since the 1970s, however, the **media** have played a dominant role in the coining of words.

Many new words emerge from acronyms; *raker,* for instance, from *rapat kerja,* means working meeting. **Sukarno** was especially well known for such coinages, one of his best known being *berdikari*, from *berdiri di atas kaki sendiri*, "to stand on one's own feet."

EURASIANS. *See* INDO-EUROPEANS.

EXILE. A common technique in both the Netherlands Indies and Indonesia for the removal of politically troublesome people. From 1854, under the so-called *exorbitante rechten,* the **governor-general** could, in the interests of peace and order, expel from the colony anyone with European or Foreign Oriental status and could exile any Indonesian within the colony. This was an administrative right, not subject to judicial appeal or review, and was employed 1,150 times in the period 1855–1920. **Diponegoro** was exiled to Manado, **E. F. E. Douwes Dekker** to Surinam, **Sukarno** to **Flores** and **Bengkulu**, and **Mohammad Hatta**, **Sutan Sjahrir**, and many others to **Boven Digul** in West New Guinea and to **Banda**. For others, going on the ***haj*** to Mecca was a means of voluntary exile. After independence, figures such as **Chaerul Saleh** were informally exiled abroad on study tours, while under the **New Order** many senior army officers have been *didubeskan* ("ambassadored off"). In 1961 Sukarno resumed the right to place citizens under internal exile, and this right was reaffirmed by the **Suharto** government in 1969. Though the inherited provisions of the *exorbitante rechten* have not been used in New Order Indonesia, the enforced residence of political prisoners (***tahanan politik***) on **Buru** amounted to much the same thing. The **Portuguese** practice of exiling dissidents from their African colonies to **East Timor** contributed to the radicalization of political opinion there. [0634, 0865]

EXORBITANTE RECHTEN. *See* CENSORSHIP; EXILE; GOVERNOR-GENERAL, OFFICE OF THE.

– F –

FAMILY PLANNING. In colonial times, the publication of information on birth control techniques was a criminal offense. **Sukarno**'s view that a large **population** was a sign of national power helped ensure that this remained so after independence, though limited promotion of family planning was carried out from 1952 by the Yayasan Kesejahteraan Keluarga (Foundation for Family Prosperity). The first family planning clinic was established in **Jakarta** in 1956, followed by the Perkumpulan Keluarga Berencana Indonesia (PKBI, Indonesian Family Planning Association) in 1957, though both were limited by the technical illegality of their work. Indonesia's population policy was primarily one of **transmigration** from more to less densely settled areas.

Only after the advent of the **New Order** did family planning become a part of public policy; in 1966 **Ali Sadikin**, governor of Jakarta, made the city available for a pilot project by the PKBI. In 1967 the **Suharto** government signed the **United Nations** Declaration on Population and in 1970 established the Badan Koordinasi Keluarga Berencana Nasional (BKKBN, National Family Planning Coordinating Body), which began an extensive program on **Java** and **Bali** to spread information on family planning and to provide free contraceptive services. Much of the earliest family planning work was done, however, by the semigovernmental Lembaga Keluarga Berencana Nasional (National Family Planning Institute), founded in 1968. From 1974 the campaign was extended from Java and Bali to other islands. The program concentrated on providing information and free contraceptives and was conducted largely without coercion but with a good deal of community pressure; it resulted in high acceptor rates (24 percent by 1977), which in turn contributed to falling birth rates. Total fertility fell from an average of more than six children per mother in the 1960s to less than three children per mother in the 1990s, when the government reported that half of all married women of childbearing age were using some form of contraception. In 1991 the most common techniques used by married women were reported as pills, IUDs, injections, implants, and tubectomies in that order (use of condoms was apparently much less frequent). *See also* WOMEN AND MEN. [0761, 0990, 1202]

FEDERALISM. The notion that Indonesia's many ethnic groups might coexist more happily in a relatively decentralized federal state than in a centralized unitary one was a matter of relatively uncontentious discussion by Indonesian nationalists before World War II. Figures such as **Mohammad Hatta** could then be proponents of a federal system for independent Indonesia without in any way compromising their **nationalism**. The Dutch *bestuurshervorming* law of 1922 (*see* **DECENTRALIZATION**) might have encouraged this trend if it had been earlier and more extensively implemented.

In 1946, however, in the midst of the national **Revolution**, **Dutch** authorities proposed a federal system as part of their political alternative to the independent Indonesian Republic. Conceived originally as a means of easing the reunification of the country, which had been administratively divided since 1942, federalism soon became a part of Dutch plans to isolate and ultimately to suppress what they saw as the radicalism of the Indonesian Republic. By playing on outer-island fears of **communism** and of Javanese domination, they established a series of federal states (*negara*) in the territories they controlled. They hoped thereby to entrench a conservative coalition of bureaucrats, aristocrats, **Hindus**, and Christians in the **constitution** of independent Indonesia and so ensure continuing political and economic Dutch influence. Thus the first of the federal states, the **Negara Indonesia Timur (NIT)**, covered the entire, ethnically diverse eastern end of the archipelago (except West New Guinea [**Papua**]) and was intended as a powerful counterweight to the Indonesian Republic.

During the late 1940s, however, federalism became less a vehicle for political conservatism and more a format for ethnic separatism. Plans were abandoned for a *negara* in **Kalimantan** because of the island's ethnic diversity, and the *negara* **Pasundan**, formed in 1948, was explicitly a state of the Sundanese people of West Java. Within the NIT itself, several semiautonomous ethnically based regions were established from 1947. From July 1948 the federal states and protostates were assembled in a permanent Bijeenkomst voor Federale Overleg (BFO, Meeting for Federal Consultation), and it was the BFO with which the Republic of Indonesia fused to form the **Republik Indonesia Serikat (RIS)**, which gained independence in 1949. The official recognition of ethnic subnationalism, however, later encouraged the revolt of the **Republik Maluku Selatan (RMS)** and provided a basis for the Dutch to retain control of West New Guinea after the transfer of sovereignty in 1949.

This Dutch experiment wholly compromised the idea of federalism in the eyes of Indonesian nationalists, and the federal *negara* were quickly dissolved after the transfer of sovereignty, the last disappearing on 17 August 1950. After that, advocacy of a federal state was viewed as tantamount to treason, and it compromised the chances of success for any movement aimed at creating either a decentralized or federal state.

In March 1960, after government troops had defeated the major forces of the **PRRI/Permesta rebellion**, its leaders on **Sumatra** proclaimed the establishment of a federal system, the Republik Persatuan Indonesia (RPI, United Republic of Indonesia), consisting of 10 component states (incorporating the regions under rebel control on Sumatra and **Sulawesi**, together with those in which the **Darul Islam** was active). According to the RPI's constitution, each of these states would form individual governments in accordance with the culture and wishes of their peoples. This RPI really existed only on paper and disappeared with the surrender of the rebels.

Only after the fall of **Suharto** was the issue of federalism again tentatively raised in the context of the 1999 **decentralization** law, when some form of federal relationship seemed to offer a possible rubric for maintaining the loyalty of such dissident regions as **Aceh** and **Papua**. After **Megawati Sukarnoputri** became president, however, her adherence to the idea of the unitary state seemed to preclude the possibility of any moves toward federalism. *See also* NATIVE TROOPS; PROVINCES; SUCCESSION. [0563, 0674, 0679, 0695, 1146]

FEDERASI BURUH SELURUH INDONESIA. *See* LABOR.

"FIFTH FORCE" (Angkatan Kelima)**.** During Indonesia's **Confrontation** with **Malaysia**, **Sukarno** called at one point for 21 million volunteers to fight Malaysia. This idea was taken up in a smaller way by the leaders of the People's Republic of China (PRC), who in November 1964 offered Indonesia 100,000 small arms for the new force, and by the **Partai Komunis Indonesia (PKI)**, which pointed to Article 30 of the **Constitution** ("Every citizen shall have the right and duty to participate in the defense of the state") and argued that victory in the struggle demanded the arming of the workers and peasants. In May 1965 Sukarno described such a body as a "fifth force" alongside the four existing **armed forces** (**army**, **navy**, **air force**, and **police**) and ordered the existing armed forces to prepare plans for it. Zhou Enlai repeated China's offer of arms in April 1965, and in July the air force began training some 2,000 PKI civilians at Halim Air Force Base. The army saw this as a PKI attempt to gain weapons for an insurrection and its leaders resisted the proposal strenuously, except for General Ahmad Jusuf Mokoginta in North Sumatra, who made use of the directive to arm his own force of workers and peasants. In the weeks before the **Gestapu** coup of September, extensive rumors circulated of a clandestine shipment of arms from the PRC to equip the force, though the truth of these rumors was never proven. [0714, 0807, 0859]

FILM. Indonesia's film industry began before World War II, with several local studios, especially Tan Brothers, producing a range of films, mainly on romantic and adventure themes. The 1925 Filmordonnantie (revised in 1940) gave the colonial government power to ban films on moral or social grounds, and films were thus little used by the nationalist movement, although the **Gerindo** leader **A. K. Gani** starred in some productions. Films from the **United States** were widely shown during the 1950s, though **Chinese** and Indian films also held an important share of the market. This sparked a hostile reaction that criticized both the effect of foreign films on the domestic industry and the allegedly corrupting effect of displaying Western lifestyles. During the early 1960s, the campaign against Western film was spearheaded by the left-wing cultural organization **Lembaga Kebudayaan Rakyat (Lekra)** while local filmmakers produced a number of left-oriented films. After the **Gestapu** coup of 1965, the Indonesian film industry was thoroughly purged and many films of the early 1960s were destroyed. Film **censorship** was strict and most contemporary filmmakers concentrated on romantic and historical topics, eschewing any social criticism. When these films dealt with recent history, they hewed closely to the government's propaganda, the most notable example being *Pengkhianatan G30s/PKI* (The Treason of GESTAPU/PKI, 1984). *See also* MEDIA. [0188, 0189, 1306]

FINANCIAL CRISIS (*krismon*)**.** The devaluation of the Thai baht in July 1997 began the economic crisis in East and Southeast Asia. Initially Indonesia experienced only moderate effects, but the country soon entered into a severe recession. During the second half of 1997 the value of the rupiah plunged, and by January 1998 only 22 of Indonesia's 286 publicly listed companies remained solvent. In October 1997 the government announced it would seek help from the international financial organizations and postponed or put under review 76 projects planned by government ministries or state companies. The value of foreign **debts** was enormous. Under strong pressure from the International Monetary Fund (IMF), **Suharto** finally signed his agreement to the terms of the fund's $33 billion bailout plan. The government, however, continued to hold down prices of **rice** and fuel, hoping to avoid the riots that would break out in the face of the austerity measures the plan demanded. At the same time, it continued to protect the banks and other business interests owned by member of the **Suharto family** and cronies. The crisis was one of the major factors in Suharto's forced resignation in May 1998. *See also* BANKING; CURRENCY. [0396, 0455, 0760, 1316]

FISHERIES. Fishing has been a major industry in the archipelago since early times, and salt fish was always a major **trade** item between the coast and inland regions, controlled by **Chinese** middlemen rather than by the fishermen themselves. Fish still provide over 60 percent of the protein intake of most Indonesians and the industry employs approximately 1.3 million, though fishermen are traditionally one of Indonesia's poorest groups and **Partai Komunis Indonesia (PKI)** fishermen's organizations were strong before 1965. Major technological change took place after 1965 with the introduction of trawlers and later purse seines by Chinese entrepreneurs. This modern sector, which in 1980 accounted for 23 percent of the catch but only 2 percent of the fishing fleet, aroused much resentment among traditional fishermen, leading to violence in many areas. Trawling was banned by the government off **Java** and **Sumatra** in 1980 and elsewhere except the Arafura Sea in 1983. For years commercial fishing was also discouraged because, in order to protect the domestic shipbuilding industry, Jakarta imposed high tariffs on the import of fishing boats, making them too expensive for most fishermen to buy. The government relaxed these restrictions to some extent in 1996, but not enough to allow much expansion.

One result was the rapid growth in aquaculture where shrimp and milkfish were farmed in ponds along the coasts of North **Java**, East

Sumatra, and **Bali**. Although these farms provided a profitable export trade, especially in shrimp, they necessitated removal of vast areas of mangrove and other swamp forests, the traditional spawning grounds for the larvae and breeding grounds for other marine life. [0403, 0408, 1175]

FLAG. The national flag of red over white (*merah-putih*) was formally adopted by the ***pergerakan*** at the second Youth Congress in 1928.

"FLOATING MASS." Policy formulated in the 1975 Law on Political Parties and **Golkar**, separating the populace, especially in the rural areas, from political activity except during **elections**. It was intended to ensure that the masses remained fully responsive to government direction ostensibly for the sake of national development. *See also* DEVELOPMENT IDEOLOGY; *MONOLOYALITAS*. [0736]

FLORES (from Portuguese *labo de flores,* cape of flowers). Island in **Nusatenggara**. In the 13th century, the kingdom of Larantuka came under rule of **Majapahit**, but a century later **Makassar** was the dominant power. **Portuguese** missionaries arrived in 1613, though extensive conversion to **Catholicism** did not take place until the 19th century. In the 17th century the island was dominated by the Topasses (*see* **SOLOR ARCHIPELAGO**; **TIMOR**). After Makassar submitted to the **Dutch East Indies Company (VOC)** in 1660 and 1667, the **Dutch** regarded Flores as within their domains, and in 1838 and 1856 they sent military expeditions to suppress **slavery** and the plundering of shipwrecks. The island was not fully conquered until 1907–1908. It was the first place to which the colonial government exiled **Sukarno** in the 1930s. [1241]

FOREIGN INVESTMENT. *See* INVESTMENT, FOREIGN.

FOREIGN POLICY. Indonesia's foreign policy was originally formulated as an adjunct to the struggle for independence in the 1940s, during which two persistent principles in Indonesian foreign policy making were established. First was a deep suspicion of foreign intentions toward Indonesia. Indonesian policy makers see their country as wealthy and strategically located but politically and economically vulnerable to foreign adventurers. The chief focus of these suspicions has varied: in the 1950s and early 1960s it was the **United States** and the **Netherlands**; later it was **China** and, to a lesser extent, **Vietnam** for political reasons and **Japan** for economic ones. **Australia** and the **Arab World** have also come under suspicion. Second, while eschewing formal military alliances as incompatible with an "active and independent" foreign policy, Indonesia has sought international friends in a variety of forums: the **South East Asia League** in 1948; the Non-Aligned Movement in the 1950s and early 1960s, and to a lesser extent in the late **Suharto** and post-Suharto eras; the Conference of the New Emerging Forces (Conefo) and the brief Jakarta–Hanoi–Peking axis (*see* **NEKOLIM**) of the mid-1960s; and, since 1967, the **Association of Southeast Asian Nations (ASEAN)**.

The best-remembered elements of Indonesian foreign policy, however, have had less to do with these general principles than with questions of national security. Indonesia's long-running conflict with the Netherlands over the province of West Irian (**Papua**) was an attempt to recover what it saw as part of the national territory; **Confrontation** with **Britain** and **Malaysia** was partly over the continued presence of British bases close to Indonesian territory and over the right of Indonesia, as the largest regional power, to be consulted on matters of regional political development; the brutal annexation of **East Timor** was, at least ostensibly, an attempt to forestall the emergence of a left-wing government on Indonesia's borders; and Indonesia's often tactless handling of **Papua New Guinea** is related to the threat it sees from **Organisasi Papua Merdeka (OPM)** guerrillas in Papua. Because of this security dimension, foreign policy is often effectively negotiated between the Departments of Foreign Affairs (Deplu) and Defense (Hankam). For a list of foreign and defense ministers, *see* APPENDIX E. *See also* ARCHIPELAGIC CONCEPT; DEFENSE POLICY; PHILIPPINES; SOVIET UNION; UNITED NATIONS. [1102, 1103, 1123, 1125, 1140, 1144]

FORESTRY. From early times, forest products were major items of **trade** in the archipelago, while the **teak** forests of **Java** were an important economic resource for the island's rulers for housing, shipbuilding, and firewood. A government forestry service (Dienst van het Boschwezen) was established on **Java** under **Herman Willem Daendels** and with it emerged a category of forest villages exempt from other forms of **taxation** in exchange for carrying out the often difficult and onerous tasks of forest management. The colonial government introduced German experts to give training and advice from 1849 and laid down comprehensive forest laws in 1865. Patrols of the state forests began in 1880. During the **Japanese occupation**, large areas of forest were cleared both for firewood and construction and to release land for the planting of other crops, and a shortage of fuel during the **Revolution** led to further cutting. In the early 1960s the **Partai Komunis Indonesia (PKI)** often took the side of peasants in the vicinity of state forests in claiming **land** or the right to collect firewood.

In 1967 under the **New Order**, the Basic Forestry Law (BFL, Undang-Undang Dasar Kehutanan) established state control over forests on the islands outside Java. Logging then became a major area of foreign **investment**, since the allocation of logging permits and the clearing of tropical forests required relatively little economic infrastructure. Between 1967 and 1980 logging rights over 4 million hectares were given to state-owned forestry enterprises. Typically concessions were granted to joint operations between large Western firms such as Weyerhaeuser and Indonesian sleeping partners who contributed no capital to the venture and were members or friends of the ruling elite. On Java and **Madura**, forestry was managed by the state-owned Perum Perhutani (State Forestry Corporation). Timber became the country's second largest export after **oil**, and in 1973 Indonesia exported 18 million cubic meters of tropical timber.

In 1975 the Indonesian government began to encourage loggers to process timber in Indonesia rather than exporting raw logs. In 1980 each company's export of raw logs was limited to 32 percent of its total output, and on 1 January 1985 all export of unprocessed logs was banned. This policy led many Western firms such as Weyerhaeuser to withdraw from Indonesia, but their place was taken by Japanese and Korean firms and a dramatic expansion of plywood production occurred. With **Suharto**'s backing, **Muhammad "Bob" Hasan** transformed the Indonesian Wood Panel Processors Association (Asosiasi Produsen Panel Kayu Indonesia, Apkindo) into a cartel controlling the trade practices of 111 plywood producers. Indonesia became the world's largest exporter of plywood, with annual exports totaling US$1 billion in value. In 1988 Hasan formed a joint venture with a Japanese trading company to become **Japan**'s sole importer of Indonesian plywood.

By the late 1980s there was growing concern that after 15 years of intensive logging in **Kalimantan** and **Sumatra**, a great part of their forests had been degraded. The government instituted a "sustainable forestry" policy to rehabilitate the degraded forests and increase the yield from other forestland. This, however, led to even greater clear-cutting, especially in Kalimantan, as money from the reforestation fund was used to finance establishment of state-owned plantations, especially of **oil palm**.

The collapse of the Suharto regime was soon followed by a huge upsurge in illegal logging. Between 1995 and 2000 Indonesia's forest cover fell from 162 million hectares to only 98 million hectares, and deforestation rates in 2001 were in excess of 1.7 million hectares a year even by official government figures. This situation led Indonesia's largest environmental nongovernmental organization (NGO) to call for a complete moratorium on logging for two to three years. An unpublished report from the **World Bank** predicted that all the lowland forests in Sumatra would be extinct before 2005 and in Kalimantan by 2010. To help control the worst effects of the destructive large-scale logging, an independent working group of local NGOs and academics had formed an Indonesian Ecolabeling Institute (LEI), which in 2000 signed a Joint Certification Protocol with the Forest Stewardship Council (FSC), an international nonprofit organization promoting responsible forestry, to issue certificates for Sustainable Forest Management, an internationally recognized labeling system for timber products. But their efforts seemed unable to counter the growth in illegal logging, exacerbated by the new **decentralization** legislation under which local authorities in the regions began granting thousands of small logging concessions to companies to take over local forest areas. In 2002 Indonesia placed a temporary ban on log export, and in June **Malaysia** banned import of logs from Indonesia.

The disastrous forestry policies were a major factor in the fires that engulfed many of the forests of Kalimantan and Sumatra in late 1997 to 1998 and again in subsequent years, spreading a pall of smog over Indonesia's neighbors, especially Malaysia, **Singapore**, and **Thailand**, and costing an estimated $9 billion in damages to health, **tourism**, transport, and agricultural losses. The dry conditions returned in 2002, again sparking widespread forest fires, particularly on Kalimantan. *See also* CONSERVATION, NATURE; ENVIRONMENTAL PROTECTION. [0329, 0343, 0375, 0404, 1173, 1379]

FREEPORT. Freeport Indonesia is 81 percent owned by Freeport-McMoran Copper and Gold Inc. of the **United States** and has been active in the **mining** of **copper** and **gold** in southern Irian Jaya (**Papua**) since 1966. It signed its first contract with the Indonesian government in 1967, and this was renewed in 1976. Its current 30-year contract was signed in 1991. The Indonesian state's share in the company is only 9.4 percent. From the beginning, Freeport's operations provoked widespread opposition from the local Amungme people. Local landholders were removed to make way for the mining operations, receiving compensation only for disruptions to current gardens but no **land** rent or royalties. Subsequent mining caused surface degradation, river water pollution, and destruction of wildlife, and it helped fuel local resistance in association with the **Organisasi Papua Merdeka (OPM)**. In 1977 the local people, assisted by the OPM, sabotaged the mine's operations by blowing up the pipeline carrying the copper concentrate to the coast. In response the Indonesian military carried out reprisals, killing hundreds, perhaps thousands, of villagers and forcibly resettling the people in lower altitudes. By 1980 epidemics swept through the resettled villagers, killing more than 20 percent of their infants.

In an effort to gain local support, Freeport claimed to have spent more than $150 million to build schools, houses, places of worship, a modern hospital, and community facilities over the 1990s. After the fall of **Suharto** when the company became an increased target for dissidents, including the OPM, the share price of Freeport's stock fell drastically (from around $35 in 1998 to $7.50 in 2000).

Freeport provides the Indonesian **armed forces** with approximately $6 million a year to pay for a 550-man task force to guard the company's properties in Papua. At the end of August 2002, gunmen fired on vehicles near the Freeport mine, killing two Americans and an Indonesian and injuring 12 others. It was later discovered that this incident had probably been carried out by members of the Indonesian **army** and was blamed by them on the OPM. FBI investigators were sent to Papua to determine whether this was in fact the case. Landslides in October and December 2003 disrupted Freeport's operations, cutting its daily extraction of copper ore by more than a half, down to approximately 100,000 metric tons a day in the early months of 2004. *See also* UNITED STATES, RELATIONS WITH. [0730, 0754, 0755, 0760]

FRETILIN (Frente Revolucionária do Timor Leste Independente, Revolutionary Front for an Independent East Timor). Founded on 22 August 1974 as the **Associação Social Democrática Timorense (ASDT)**, Fretilin was a grouping of young **East Timor** intellectuals and civil servants, many of them Portuguese-Timorese, who pressed for the territory's immediate independence after the **Portuguese** coup of 1974. Liberation movements in **Africa** influenced not only the choice of the name Fretilin but also the party's program, which included literacy classes, the establishment of **cooperatives**, and the creation of a multitude of affiliated mass organizations for **women**, farmers, **students**, and the like.

Fretilin defeated a coup in Dili by the conservative **União Democrática Timorense (UDT)** in August 1975 and began to establish an administration, but it did not declare independence in the form of the

Democratic Republic of East Timor until November 1975, when the Indonesian invasion from the west was already underway. Driven from Dili and other centers in December 1975, Fretilin retained control of most of the countryside until September 1977 to 1979, when a series of Indonesian operations shattered both its political leadership and its army, the Forças Armadas de Libertação Nacional de Timor (Falintil, Armed Forces for the National Liberation of Timor). During the 1980s, under the leadership of **Jose Alexandre "Xanana" Gusmão**, Fretilin and Falintil were reorganized, with Falintil becoming a largely guerrilla force divided into small mobile groups linked to networks of civilian resistance, and a broader alliance of nationalist groups inside and outside East Timor was constructed. Gusmão was captured by the Indonesians in November 1990 and jailed by them until his final release in mid-September 1999 after the East Timorese had voted overwhelmingly for independence from Indonesia.

Fretilin was the largest party registered under the **United Nations** Transitional Administration, and in the election of 30 August 1991 it won 57 percent of the vote, gaining 55 seats in East Timor's 88-seat Constituent Assembly. [0799, 0806, 0814, 0941, 0959]

FRONT DEMOKRASI RAKYAT (FDR, People's Democratic Front)**.** A coalition of left-wing parties (**Partai Komunis Indonesia [PKI]**, **Partai Buruh**, **Partai Sosialis**, and **Pemuda Sosialis Indonesia [Pesindo]**), formerly part of the **Sayap Kiri**, established in January 1948 following the fall of the **Amir Sjarifuddin** government. Until 1948 the left-wing parties had been in government and generally pursued a line of negotiation with the **Dutch** and accommodation, in the short term, with Western business interests, but the formation of the FDR marked a radicalization of their policy and a shift to promotion of armed struggle and rejection of foreign **investment**. The FDR dissolved on 1 September 1948 when the parties merged into the PKI. *See also* MADIUN AFFAIR. [0661, 0674, 0683, 0684, 1128]

– G –

GABUNGAN POLITIK INDONESIA (Gapi, Indonesian Political Federation)**.** Assembly of Indonesian **nationalist** organizations formed in May 1939 on the initiative especially of M. H. Thamrin of the **Partai Indonesia Raya (Parindra)** and including **Gerakan Rakyat Indonesia**

(Gerindo) and **Partai Sarekat Islam Indonesia (PSII)**. It called for Indonesian self-determination and an elected parliament, using the slogan *Indonesia berparlemen* ("Indonesia with a parliament"). In December 1939 it sponsored a Kongres Rakyat Indonesia (Indonesian People's Congress), which called unsuccessfully for cooperation between Indonesians and **Dutch** in the face of the deteriorating world situation. *See also* SUTARJO PETITION. [0586]

GAJAH MADA. Prime minister of **Majapahit** from 1330 to 1364. As a young man he helped defeat rebels against King Jayanegara, but later had Jayanegara killed after he had stolen Gajah Mada's wife. Under Queen Tribuwana, he rose to become prime minister and under her and her successor Hayam Wuruk (Rajasanagara r. 1350–1389) was effective ruler of the kingdom until his death. He resumed the expansionist military program of King Kertanegara and is said to have sworn not to consume ***palapa*** until the Outer Islands (***Nusantara***) had been conquered. Majapahit maintained a powerful fleet, but it is not certain that it had any real control beyond the shores of **Java**. Gajah Mada's *palapa* oath was widely publicized by **Muhammad Yamin** as an early manifestation of **nationalism**. [0484, 0515]

GAMBLING. Gambling existed in Indonesia in many forms from early times, with contests such as boat races and cockfights, and it was soon recognized as a useful source of state revenue. **Thomas Stamford Raffles** organized a lottery to help pay for the postal road along the northern coast of **Java**. Gambling farms were allocated on the ***pacht*** system and were commonly operated by **Chinese**. On the plantations in **East Sumatra**, gambling became an important means for planters to keep their workforce tied by bonds of indebtedness. The Netherlands Indies government ran a state lottery that was taxed at 21 percent (20 percent for the government, 1 percent for the poor). Although the **Sarekat Islam (SI)** and other religious and nationalist parties campaigned strongly against government promotion of gambling, governments after independence have found the sponsoring of lotteries and casinos a convenient and lucrative source of finance. Religious and social organizations have consistently objected to it, especially on the grounds of its effects on the poor. Gambling was formally banned throughout the country in 1981, but in 1985 the government introduced soccer pools, called *porkas* ("forecast"), to finance sport. Tickets purchased in the *porkas* are formally designated as donations to social projects, with prizes, though even this is banned in **Aceh**. The net revenue from the *porkas* in 1988 was approximately Rp 962 billion. *See also* SADIKIN, ALI. [0576]

GAMELAN. Traditional gong-chime **music** of Indonesia. Neolithic lithophones (stone slabs tuned to a seven-note scale) have been found in **Vietnam**, and these may have been part of a general Southeast Asian musical tradition represented in Indonesia by (wooden) xylophones that have not survived. The first reliable traces of music in the archipelago, however, are cast bronze gongs resembling kettle drums, which reached Indonesia in about 300 B.C. with the spread of Dongson culture from Vietnam. They were probably used first for signaling in battle but soon took on a ceremonial significance. The so-called Moon of Pejeng in **Bali** is one such "drum." Shortly afterward the first Indonesian gongs were produced on **Java** and were probably cast and hammered, rather than directly cast like the Dongson instruments (*see* **METALWORKING**). By the second or first century B.C., these gongs, large kettle-like objects with a raised boss suspended horizontally on cords, were made with specific pitches in three-note *gamelan* ensembles. (*See also* **ALOR**.)

From this basis, the Javanese *gamelan* elaborated into a great variety of form and more complex instrumentation. A five-tone scale (*slendro*) was in use probably by the sixth or seventh century, and the seven-tone *pelog* by the 12th century. The *gong agung,* a larger, flatter, vertically suspended gong with a deep pitch and resonant voice, appeared in the 10th century. The *saron,* or metallophone, was added in the sixth or seventh century and may have been based on traditional xylophones. These instruments create interlocking strata of rhythms, said by some to derive from the rhythm of mortars used to husk rice. Bamboo flutes (*suling*) and spike fiddles (*gending* or *rebab*) were in use by the eighth century, the plucked zither (*celempung* or *kecapi*) by the 14th century, and the oboe (*serunai*) perhaps a century later; all these instruments, and later the voice, added a melodic line of a kind not possible on the basic *gamelan.* This complexity turned the drum (*kendang*) into the pivotal instrument of the ensemble as rhythm-giver. Nonetheless, no true solo tradition has developed; the basic instruments of a *gamelan* cannot be tuned and are manufactured as a single entity rather than as a fortuitous assembly of instruments. Most players are expected to be able to shift easily from one instrument to another.

Bronze *gamelan* ensembles reached Bali around the 10th century, generally displacing traditional wind and string instruments. Around 22 distinct *gamelan* types are still in use on Bali. During the **Majapahit** era (13th–16th centuries), gongs and *gamelan* ensembles were apparently exported extensively from Java and Bali to other parts of the archipelago and to the Southeast Asian mainland, though development of distinctive local styles was rapid.

Gamelan on Java has become "high" art associated with the courts and with ritual (one scholar has described it as "music not to listen to"), but it is nonetheless played on a great number of occasions, though increasingly the use of cassettes is reducing demand for musicians. On Bali, *gamelan* remains much more popular, partly because of the importance of musical offering in **Hindu** ceremonies, partly because musicians have consciously developed brighter rhythms and more exciting forms. *Kebyar* style on Bali now recognizes individual musicians, composers, and dancers as artists.

Gamelan has attracted considerable attention among Western musicians. Claude Debussy was inspired by *gamelan* performances at the Paris Exposition of 1896 to include *gamelan* motifs in his composition, while Olivier Messiaen has also made extensive used of *gamelan* themes. *See also DANGDUT*; *KRONCONG*. [0091, 0135, 0159, 0174, 0175, 0177, 0179, 0183, 0184, 0204]

GANGSTERS. *See* BANDITRY; MILITIAS.

GANI, ADNAN KAPAU (1905–1958)**.** Indonesian nationalist and businessman from South **Sumatra**, trained as a physician. In the prewar period, he starred in various quasi-nationalist romantic **films**, such as *Asmara Murni* (Pure Passion, 1940) but was also active in politics, being one of the leaders of the **Gerakan Rakyat Indonesia (Gerindo)**. At the end of the **Japanese occupation**, he was one of the two foremost nationalist spokesmen on **Sumatra** and enjoyed close relationships with **Sukarno**, **Sutan Sjahrir**, and **Amir Sjarifuddin**. He was a founder of the **Partai Nasional Indonesia (PNI)** on Sumatra and was appointed coordinator and organizer of the **armed forces** on that island, though he failed in his ambition to become Sumatran governor. He was appointed the Republic's minister of prosperity (*menteri kemakmuran*) in November 1946, in which position he continued to play an important role in conducting "**oil** diplomacy" and in developing an economic program for both Sumatra and the Republic as a whole. After independence he built up a fortune trading **rubber** and **pepper** from South Sumatra. *See also* PALEMBANG. [0661, 0839]

GARIS BESAR HALUAN NEGARA (GBHN, Broad Outlines of State Policy)**.** *See* MAJELIS PERMUSYAWARATAN RAKYAT.

GARUDA. 1. Mythological eagle, the vehicle of the god Vishnu, and the conqueror of serpents in **Hindu** mythology. In 1951 it was chosen as the Republic's official coat of arms, with a symbolic representation of the **Pancasila** on a shield around its neck and the motto ***Bhinneka tunggal ika***. 2. Garuda is also the name of Indonesia's international airline, formed on 31 March 1950. Initially a joint venture with KLM, it became wholly Indonesian in 1954. After a period of declining standards and profitability in the late 1950s and early 1960s, and the loss of many staff in the purges of 1965–1966, Garuda improved its position during the 1970s. Wiweko Suparno, appointed by **Suharto** to head the airline in 1968, expanded the fleet of wide-bodied jets as well as its domestic routes, though at the cost of a considerable accumulation of **debt**. By 1980 Garuda had the second largest fleet of planes in Asia. Merpati Nusantara Airlines was founded in 1962 to operate domestic flights and became a Garuda subsidiary in 1978. In 1989 Garuda faced its first real competitor when Tommy Suharto and **Bob Hasan**'s Sempati air challenged its monopoly on the use of jet engine aircraft and flying international routes; three years later Suparno was fired from his job as the airline's president apparently because of his unwillingness to accommodate the needs of the **Suharto family**. During the **financial crisis** of the late 1990s, Garuda was faced with bankruptcy and had to abandon six of its 10 routes to Europe and return several of its leased aircraft. *See also* AIRCRAFT INDUSTRY; INDONESIAN AIRWAYS. [0467, 0748, 0760]

GAS (LNG, liquefied natural gas)**.** Indonesia's first major natural gas reserves were found in the 1970s in the waters around Natuna Island in the South China Sea (*see* map 11), where gas fields contained reserves of an estimated 45 trillion cubic feet. Liquefied natural gas (LNG) was also found in **Aceh** and East **Kalimantan**. The fields in Arun in north Aceh (an estimated 17 trillion cubic feet) began exporting LNG in 1978. These reserves were expected to run out by 2012–2014, though they still generated $1.2 billion a year in exports in 2001. In 1982 Indonesia's LNG exports were valued at US$2.6 billion. In the early 1990s new fields were discovered in east Aceh (with an estimated 24 trillion cubic feet of natural gas), and during that decade Indonesia became the world's largest exporter of natural gas. Acehnese gas exports to **Japan** and Korea were interrupted by violence from armed militants in March 2001, and

ExxonMobil was forced to stop production at its **oil** and gas fields until August of that year. After the plant reopened, more than 3,000 Indonesian troops patrolled its perimeter. Local villagers filed a lawsuit in **United States** federal court against ExxonMobil in July 2001 alleging it ignored the brutality of these troops, a suit that the U.S. State Department urged the court to dismiss.

Huge fields were also opened up in East Kalimantan at the Bontang natural gas facility, giving **Pertamina** flexibility in managing its exports to north Asia. Further exploration began at Tangguh natural gas field in the Birds Head region of western Irian Jaya (*see* **PAPUA**), where British Petroleum (BP) planned to use a low-impact program in developing the reserves of an estimated 24 trillion cubic feet. It was hoped that these enormous deposits would fill the supply gap after the Acehnese fields ran out or if guerrilla activity in that area forced suspension of operations there. In 2002 Pertamina signed a $12.5 billion deal to supply gas to **China** from the Tangguh field over 25 years.

GAYO. Ethnic group in the highland areas of central and southern **Aceh**, culturally intermediate between the Acehnese and **Batak** peoples. Muslim since the 17th century, the Gayo were incorporated into the Acehnese kingdom by **Iskandar Muda** and were annexed to the Netherlands Indies in 1904. Strong local resistance continued until 1913 and during the late colonial period the Indonesian **nationalist** movement was strong in the area. There is a tradition of ***merantau***. Many from the region joined in the **Darul Islam** rebellion of the 1950s, and resentments fueled by the rebellion led to the killing of many people accused of communist affiliations in 1965 (*see* **MASSACRES OF 1965–1966**), with estimates ranging from 800 to 3,000 deaths. [0783]

GELIJKSTELLING. *See* RACE.

GENERATIONS. Because of the succession of dramatic political changes in 20th-century Indonesia, the notion of generational groups has been a strong one in Indonesian historiography. The term *Angkatan '45* (Generation of '45) was originally applied by **Hans Baguë Jassin** in 1951 to writers active immediately after the declaration of independence, notably **Chairil Anwar** and **Idrus**, who transformed the literary use of the Indonesian **language**, but the expression soon became general for the former ***pemuda***, that is, the young people who had fought for independence after 1945. *Angkatan '45* remains the name of the official organization of veterans of the **Revolution**. The **students** who helped to topple **Sukarno** after 1965 referred to themselves as *Angkatan '66,* while later student activists have sometimes identified themselves as *Angkatan* '74, '78, and so on. Some historians have identified generations of '08, '26–'27, or '28 associated with **Budi Utomo**, the uprisings of the **Partai Komunis Indonesia (PKI)**, and the **Youth Pledge**. It is in the Indonesian **army** that the notion of generation is perhaps most apt, since senior positions were occupied from the 1940s to the 1980s by men regarded as members of the *Angkatan '45* (*see* **NASUTION, A. H.**; **SUHARTO**). The term *angkatan* also means "force" as in Angkatan Kelima, or **"Fifth Force."**

GERAKAN ACEH MERDEKA (GAM, Free Aceh Movement)**.** *See* ACEH.

GERAKAN RAKYAT INDONESIA (Gerindo, Indonesian People's Movement)**.** Left-wing nationalist party formed 24 May 1937 to succeed the Sukarnoist **Partindo** and in opposition to the conservative **Parindra**. Its leaders included **A. K. Gani**, **Amir Sjarifuddin**, and **Muhammad Yamin**. More strongly antifascist than anticolonialist, it attempted to cooperate with the colonial government against the **Japanese** threat but received little attention. Yamin left the party in mid-1939, and its activities were severely curtailed from May 1940 by the declaration of a State of War and Siege. [0586]

GERAKAN WANITA INDONESIA (Gerwani, Indonesian Women's Movement)**.** Left-wing **women**'s movement, founded on 4 June 1950 as Gerakan Wanita Indonesia Sedar (Gerwis, Movement of Aware Indonesian Women), primarily to lobby for women's interests in the government. In March 1954 it took the name Gerwani, becoming increasingly close to, though never formally affiliated with, the **Partai Komunis Indonesia (PKI)**. It worked for equal rights of women and men in **marriage** and greater penalties for rape and abduction, as well as establishing kindergartens and midwifery and literacy courses. In 1961 it claimed 9 million members. In the suppression of the Left in Indonesia after 1965, special attention was given to the destruction of Gerwani, on the grounds that it allegedly encouraged women to abandon their duties within the family and promoted sexual promiscuity. *See also* SEX, POLITICAL SIGNIFICANCE OF. [0994, 1430]

GERILYA (guerrilla warfare)**.** The period following the Second **"Police Action"** during which the **Dutch** overran all the major population centers of the Indonesian Republic and a **Pemerintah Darurat Republik Indonesia** (PDRI, Emergency Government of the Republic of Indonesia) under **Sjafruddin Prawiranegara** was established in central **Sumatra**. The Republic's **armed forces** remained under General **Sudirman**, who led the struggle in the Javanese countryside. This period came to an end with the restoration of **Yogyakarta** to the Republic and the release of **Sukarno** and **Mohammad Hatta** in July 1949. *See also* DEFENSE POLICY; ROEM-VAN ROIJEN AGREEMENT. [0668, 0686, 0714, 0877]

GERMANY, LINKS WITH. In the 17th and 18th centuries, Germans were prominent amongst the European inhabitants of the Indies. The scientists **F. W. Junghuhn**, C. G. C. Reinwardt, and Carl Ludwig Blume conducted important research; many Germans served in the colonial army; and German **Protestant** missions were active in the region. German industrialization in the 19th century made Germany a major market for Netherlands Indies products, and major German commercial penetration began under the **Liberal Policy**, the shipping and trading interests of Norddeutscher Lloyd becoming most important. The Straits-und-Sunda-Syndikat, founded in 1911, took major interests in **trade**, plantations, and **mining**, and by 1912 German investment had reached 120–180 million marks, ranking fourth after **Dutch**, British, and Franco-Belgian capital. Germany's late unification (1871) left it little chance for annexation of indigenous states in the region, and **Britain**'s naval power repeatedly thwarted any German ambitions to seize Portuguese **Timor** and part or all of the Netherlands Indies. German business thus aimed at greater access to the colony through commercial penetration of the Netherlands. Germany's respect for Dutch neutrality in World War I was aimed partly at preserving its investments and coaling facilities in the Indies from seizure by Britain. German citizens in the Netherlands Indies, including the painter Walter Spies (1895–1942), were interned after the German occupation of the Netherlands in 1940, partly to forestall a Vichy-style claim to the colony, but many were released under the **Japanese**.

During **B. J. Habibie**'s period of influence in the 1980s and 1990s, economic ties between Germany and Indonesia were strong. When he was minister of research and technology, many German firms won contracts in the strategic industries he controlled, including one for military helicopters and a controversial deal in 1994 when Indonesia purchased 39 warships from the former East German navy. By 1997, 150 German firms operated in Indonesia and German direct investment stood at US$4.5 billion.

GESTAPU (*Gerakan September Tiga Puluh,* G-30-S, September 30th Movement)**.** Late on the evening of 30 September 1965, **army** units led by Lieutenant-Colonel Untung launched a limited coup in **Jakarta** ostensibly to remove a Council of Generals (Dewan Jendral) said to be plotting against **Sukarno** with the help of the **United States** and **Britain**. They killed six leading generals (**Ahmad Yani**, Suprapto, S. Parman, Haryono, Sutoyo Siswomiharjo, and D. I. Panjaitan), seized state **radio** and telecommunications facilities, and declared a revolutionary council (Dewan Revolusi). General **A. H. Nasution** escaped the plotters, though his daughter and an aide were killed in the melée. A lesser coup took place in Central **Java** involving units of the Diponegoro Division. The coup was crushed within 24 hours by **Komando Cadangan Strategis Angkatan Darat (Kostrad)** forces under General **Suharto** (who had not been targeted by the plotters) and Siliwangi Division units. These events (most of them on 1 October rather than 30 September) laid the basis for Suharto's gradual seizure of power and the installation of the so-called **New Order**. The security organization **Komando Operasi Pemulihan Keamanan (Kopkamtib)** was put in place to suppress remnants of the coup, the **Partai Komunis Indonesia (PKI)** was banned for its alleged role, and left-wing elements were purged from the bureaucracy, the **armed forces**, and society in general by imprisonment and massacre (*see* **MASSACRES OF 1965–1966**). Untung, other direct participants in the coup, and senior left-wing figures were put on trial in the special tribunal **Mahkamah Militer Luar Biasa (Mahmillub)**. For many years, from November 1973, Kopkamtib required citizens to obtain a certificate of noninvolvement in the coup (*Surat Bebas G-30-S*) in order to travel or to obtain certain kinds of work. This was later substituted by a general requirement that those holding sensitive posts (including in the **education** system and the **oil** industry) come from a clean (*bersih*) social environment.

Conservative forces and public opinion in general attributed the coup immediately to the PKI, and the Suharto government rigidly enforced that view; G-30-S/PKI became the common official term for both the coup and the party. Evidence of direct PKI involvement in planning the coup, however, was slender and was mainly based on dubious confessions and on testimony concerning a so-called *Biro Khusus* (Special Bureau) of the PKI formed to recruit military officers for the party. Those arguing that the party is unlikely to have planned the coup point to its failure to follow up on the actions of the 30 September Movement in Jakarta. Outside Indonesia, some academics have suggested that the coup was the work of a group of middle-ranking army and senior **air force** officers patriotically concerned over their superiors' hostility to Sukarno and that Sukarno himself may have inspired them. Some have speculated that Suharto planned or contributed to the affair in a Machiavellian plot to remove Sukarno, his commanding officers, and the PKI, a view that was openly propagated after Suharto's fall. That no orthodox scholarly interpretation has yet emerged is due partly to the formidable problems of evidence and plausibility, and partly to the difficulty of conducting research on the event during the New Order period in Indonesia, when many of the participants had been killed or jailed, and it was difficult for impartial scholars to query the official version of events. The official interpretation was only allowed to be questioned within Indonesia after Suharto's resignation in 1998, when several members of Sukarno's government were released from jail and some began to publish their own versions of what occurred in 1965. *See also* "CORNELL PAPER"; GUIDED DEMOCRACY; SUPERSEMAR. [0689, 0690, 0692, 0702, 0712, 0714, 0715, 0857]

GIYANTI, TREATY OF. Signed in 1755 by the **Dutch East Indies Company** and the rebel prince Mangkubumi, it partitioned the rump of the kingdom of **Mataram** into the Sunanate of **Surakarta** under Pakubuwono III and the Sultanate of **Yogyakarta** under Mangkubumi, who took the name Hamengkubuwono I. [0577]

GIYUGUN. People's armies formed in accordance with a **Japanese** general policy directive of 29 June 1943 that indigenous volunteer armies should be established in **Java**, **Sumatra**, North Borneo, and Malaya to assist Japanese forces in defending the region against an anticipated Allied counterattack. On Sumatra, indigenous officers for the Giyugun were drawn frequently from prewar Islamic nationalist youths. *See also* PEMBELA TANAH AIR. [0660, 0675]

GOA. *See* MAKASSAR.

GOLD. Ancient Indian texts vaguely refer to Southeast Asia as Suvarnadwipa ("Land of Gold") and in his *Guide to Geography,* Claudius Ptolemy (?90–168) described a "Golden Chersonese" or peninsula in the Southeast Asian region, which many scholars have identified as **Sumatra** and/or the **Malay Peninsula**. It seems, however, that major exports of gold from the archipelago did not begin until the first century A.D., after the emperor Vespasian banned the export of gold from the Roman empire. At various times **Banjarmasin** and **Minangkabau** were major centers of the gold **trade**. Gold coins were minted in the region from the eighth century (*see* **CURRENCY**). Major gold extraction began in western **Kalimantan** in the 1740s, largely in the hands of **Chinese** (*see* ***KONGSI*** **WARS**), and in the mid-19th century the same area was covered with concessions to around 150 European **mining** companies, most of which failed within a few years. In 1987 a further gold rush began in the interior of East Kalimantan. Since the 1960s PT **Freeport** has mined the gold in **Papua**, which has the largest-known gold reserve of any single operating mine in the world. [0413, 0526, 0538, 0540, 0791, 1048]

GOLKAR (Golongan Karya, Functional Groups, formerly Sekber, i.e., Sekretariat Bersama [Joint Secretariat], Golkar). Golkar was formed in October 1964 by **army** leaders to succeed the **Badan Kerja Sama** as a coordinating body for and later a federation of anticommunist social organizations, a number of which were themselves federations, especially **Sentral Organisasi Karyawan Seluruh Indonesia (SOKSI)**, **Koperasi Serba Guna Gotong Royong (Kosgoro)**, and Musyawarah Kekeluargaan Gotong Royong (MKGR). In 1967 the **Suharto** regime announced that Golkar would be the regime's parliamentary vehicle, and the **New Order** used it after 1971 to reshape Indonesia's electoral system. Although the organization itself remained a federation of social groups, it was dominated by the army and to a lesser extent the bureaucracy. In general **elections** civil servants were obliged to vote for Golkar, and the government controlled the system so completely that Golkar could rely on a consistent vote of over 60 percent of the electorate.

Over the years attempts to make Golkar a more independent organization foundered on President Suharto's reluctance to permit any revitalization of the political system and the large military contingent in its membership. In October 1983, when state secretary **Sudharmono** became chairman of Golkar, he attempted to lessen its dependence on the executive but ran into determined opposition from both Suharto and the military. The army succeeded in pushing him out of the chairmanship in 1988 in favor of Wahono (1925–), a military man who had been Suharto's assistant in **Komando Cadangan Strategis Angkatan Darat (Kostrad)** in 1965. Wahono served as chairman until 1993, when Suharto ensured that Information Minister Harmoko (1939–) should succeed to the post, and two of Suharto's children (Siti Hardijanti Rukmana and Bambang Trihatmodjo) were appointed to Golkar's executive board.

In May 1998 Harmoko's announcement of his lack of support for Suharto's leadership was one of the critical factors in the president's downfall, but subsequently other Golkar leaders pressed for Harmoko's removal from office, and in the Golkar congress of July 1998, Akbar Tanjung (former chairman of **Himpunan Mahasiswa Islam [HMI]** and close to Suharto's successor, **B. J. Habibie**) was elected to head the party.

In the 1999 elections Golkar came second behind **Megawati Sukarnoputri's Partai Demokrasi Indonesia-Perjuangan (PDI-P)** and Akbar Tanjung became speaker of parliament. In September 2002 Tanjung was sentenced to a three-year jail term for allegedly embezzling $4.5 million in state funds meant for the poor and channeled through the **Badan Urusan Logistik (Bulog)**. The sentence was upheld by the Jakarta High Court in January 2003, but overturned on appeal by the **Supreme Court** on 12 February 2004. Throughout the process Tanjung refused to resign his leadership position in Golkar and was expected to be a leading contender for the party's nomination in the July 2004 presidential election. Its organizational strength throughout the country and the widespread popular disillusionment with the PDI-P augured well for Golkar to achieve a strong showing in the April 2004 general elections. See also *DWIFUNGSI*; *MONOLOYALITAS*. [0736, 0748, 0760, 0998, 0999]

GORONTALO. City and kingdom in northern **Sulawesi**. The Suwawa kingdom was founded here in the eighth century, but its links with the 14th-century trading kingdom of Gorontalo are unknown. **Ternate** dominated the area in the 15th and 16th centuries, and the vassal King Matolodulakiki declared **Islam** the state religion in the 16th century. A federated kingdom of Lima Pohalaa emerged in 1673.

GOTONG ROYONG. "Mutual self-help" was said to be the principle inspiring village life throughout Indonesia, especially on **Java** (*see* ***DESA***). While the existence of social differentiation in the village was acknowledged, under *gotong royong* all members of the village had a right and a duty to participate in the economic activities of other villagers. Thus, for instance, if a house were to be built, all would join in the construction; if a field were to be harvested, all had a right to take part and to receive a share of the crop as their reward. The share a harvester received was intended to be in proportion to the amount she or he had collected, but as the number of harvesters grew with the village **population**, the share of the crop received by the harvesters en masse tended to grow in accord with the principles of *gotong royong*. Landlords, however, have often tried to restrict access to the harvest to smaller groups of privileged workers, sometimes entirely from outside the village, in order to increase their own crop share and to ensure a more docile workforce.

The concept was also discredited during World War II when **Japanese** authorities instructed village officials to use it in extracting forced **labor** from the villagers in projects for the Japanese war effort. Similarly under the **Suharto** administration, people outside Java in particular viewed *gotong royong* as a method by which the government sought local cooperation in imposing its centralizing policies. *See also* LAND REFORM; RICE.

GOVERNOR-GENERAL, OFFICE OF THE. Post created in 1610 by the directors of the **Dutch East Indies Company (VOC)** to centralize control over the company's **trade** operations in the East and to organize its military operations. The governor-general was also in charge of the administration of **law** in the colony. Headquarters of the governor-general were first on **Ambon** but shifted under **Jan Pieterszoon Coen** to **Batavia**. From 1815 to 1848 the governor-general was appointed personally by the Dutch king and thereafter by the Crown on the advice of cabinet. From 1815 to 1836 and from 1854 to 1925, the governor-general (also known as the *Landvoogd*) ruled jointly with the **Raad van Indië**, but he remained the sole official point of contact between the colonial government and the metropolitan power: all instructions and requests from The Hague passed formally through the governor-general. A lieutenant governor-general was occasionally appointed, and under **Hubertus Johannes van Mook**, when no governor-general was appointed, this was the highest administrative post in the colony. In November 1948 the post of governor-general was abolished and replaced by that of *Hoge Vertegenwoordiger van de Kroon* (HVK, high representative of the Crown). For a list of the governors-general, *see* APPENDIX A. *See also* COMMISSIONER-GENERAL; NETHERLANDS, CONSTITUTIONAL RELATIONSHIP WITH INDONESIA. [0491, 0638]

GOWA. *See* MAKASSAR.

GREEN REVOLUTION. General term for the dramatic increase in **agricultural** production, especially of **rice**, begun in the mid-1960s. The program started as an agricultural extension program in the Karawang area of West **Java** in 1963 and from 1964 was extended to the rest of the island under the name Bimbingan Massal (Bimas, Mass Guidance), covering 462,000 hectares (ha) by 1966 and over 2 million ha by 1969. The program included the introduction of new high-yielding varieties (HYV) of rice and new cultivation techniques, especially with machinery, extended irrigation, and the use of pesticides and fertilizer, that allowed up to five crops in two years. It is said to have nearly doubled production on Java between 1968 and 1985. It was supported by the international chemical producers CIBA and Hoechst. Problems with the program have included the vulnerability of HYVs to disease and weather variation, the high cost and unreliability of seed and chemical supplies, the poisoning of fishponds and rivers by pesticides and fertilizers, **corruption**, and the fact that the continual cultivation of rice fails to break the life cycle of insect pests such as the **wereng**. [0319, 0333, 0341]

GROWTH TRIANGLES. Indonesia has been involved in three regional "growth triangles" in which adjacent regions in three different countries are given a special association on the basis of complementary economic strengths. The **Singapore**–Johor–**Riau** (Sijori) growth triangle covers Singapore, the Malaysian state of Johor, and the Indonesian provinces of Riau and West **Sumatra**. It was proposed by Singapore in December 1989 as a measure to complement the developing relationship between Singapore and the Indonesian island of **Batam**. Private companies in Singapore provided capital for establishing **labor**-intensive industries on the territory of its partners, with the local governments providing manpower and facilities. Trilateral agreements establishing the growth triangle were signed in December 1994, but connections between Johor and the Indonesian provinces remain meager.

An Indonesia–Malaysia–Thailand Growth Triangle (IMTGT) covering the Indonesian provinces of **Aceh**, North Sumatra, Riau, and West Sumatra, together with the Kedah and Langkawi in **Malaysia** and the southern part of **Thailand**, was formalized in 1993. In the following year, 1994, the Brunei–Indonesia–Malaysia–Philippines Eastern ASEAN Growth Area (BIMP-EAGA) was established, but both it and the IMTGT have yet to show significant results. [0362, 0363]

GUIDED DEMOCRACY (*Demokrasi Terpimpin*). General term for the years 1959–1965, in which Indonesia was dominated politically by **Sukarno** and during which enormous political tension arose between the

army and the **Partai Komunis Indonesia (PKI)**. Guided Democracy was initially a reaction to the apparent mendacity and divisiveness of parliamentary governments in the 1950s, and to the fact that the parties were unable to agree on a cabinet after the fall of the second **Ali Sastroamijoyo** cabinet in 1957 or on a **constitution** to replace the provisional 1950 Constitution. Parliamentary democracy was further discredited by the inability of the central government to maintain control in the provinces and by the participation of members of the **Masjumi** and **Partai Sosialis Indonesia (PSI)** in the **PRRI/Permesta rebellion**. The transition to Guided Democracy began with a declaration of martial law and Sukarno's appointment of himself as prime minister, and it ended with Sukarno's restoration of the country's original 1945 Constitution on 5 July 1959.

The rhetoric of Guided Democracy was both radical and conservative; on the one hand, Sukarno dedicated the nation to completing the unfinished **Revolution** and incorporated Marxist ideas extensively in his numerous ideological statements, especially **Nasakom** (Nasionalisme, Agama, Komunisme). He praised the PKI, attempted to protect it from army hostility, and promoted its participation in the institutions of the state. On the other hand, Sukarno consistently eschewed class conflict, promoting instead a corporatist view of the state in which there were no fundamental conflicts of interest between different social groups. He argued especially against what he described as the Western notion of 50 percent + 1 democracy, which enabled a tyranny by the majority. (*See also* **MANIFESTO POLITIK**.)

Institutionally, too, the picture was confused: the PKI made use of Sukarno's protection and the favorable ideological climate to expand its membership dramatically, while, as a result of martial law and the **nationalization** of **Dutch** property, the **armed forces** became firmly established in government and the **economy**. It became common to speak of a political triangle consisting of Sukarno, the army, and the PKI, but the strengths of each were very different and uncertainty over where Guided Democracy was leading the country contributed to growing tension in the 1960s, which culminated in the **Gestapu** coup attempt of 30 September 1965. *See also* GUIDED ECONOMY. [0696, 0697 0704, 0706, 0850, 0859]

GUIDED ECONOMY (*Ekonomi Terpimpin*). **Sukarno**'s vision of a political reconstruction of Indonesia under **Guided Democracy** was paired with plans for a thoroughgoing restructuring of the country's **economy**. Whereas parliamentary governments in the 1950s had generally aimed at

Indonesianization of the economy by encouraging indigenous entrepreneurs, Sukarno proposed massive state direction of and intervention in the economy by means of regulation and direct state involvement. In Sukarno's view, much of Indonesia's economic difficulty stemmed from its subordination to economic imperialism, and he aimed by means of state investment both to do without foreign capital **investment** and to create an industrial base that would lessen Indonesia's import of manufactured goods. These plans were laid down in an Eight-Year Plan announced in August 1960 and were restated in the Economic Declaration (*Deklarasi Ekonomi,* Dekon) of March 1963.

The **nationalization** of **Dutch** enterprises in 1957–1958 provided the state with control of major parts of the economy, and government controls on other sectors tightened considerably. The money for reinvestment, however, was not there. Nationalized businesses, many of them in military hands, were milked for funds both corruptly and to cover shortfalls in the government **budget**. Plantations in particular, already badly neglected in the 1940s and short of funds in the 1950s, were starved of reinvestment capital needed for replanting. Production declined steadily, leaving the budget steadily less able to meet government commitments. Inflation reached 500 percent a year by late 1965 as the government covered expenditures by printing money and the balance of payments steadily declined.

GUSMÃO, JOSE ALEXANDRE "XANANA" (1946–). Born in a small town on the north coast of **East Timor**, Gusmão attended a seminary in Baucau in the early 1960s. He fulfilled national service in the **Portuguese** army from 1968 to 1971. He joined the **Frente Revolucionária do Timor Leste Independente (Fretilin)** leadership shortly before the 1975 Indonesian invasion and fought with them against the Indonesian assault. After fleeing to the mountains in late 1978 he assumed leadership of both the party and its military army Falintil after the death of its guerrilla leader, Nicolau Lobato, at the end of that year. Gusmão changed Fretilin's strategy in the mid-1980s, constructing a broad alliance with nationalist groups inside and outside East Timor under an umbrella group Conselho Nacional da Resistencia Timorense (CNRT), of which he became chairman. In the late 1980s he urged Fretilin to establish contacts with urban young people and begin a campaign of nonviolent resistance. Indonesian forces captured Gusmão in 1992 in a house on the outskirts of Dili, and in May 1993 he was sentenced to life in prison, a term later cut to 19 years and eight months.

On 10 February 1999, President **B. J. Habibie**'s government transferred Gusmão from prison to house arrest in **Jakarta**, and he was finally released in mid-September, returning to East Timor the following month. After initially participating in the territory's interim parliament, he quit in April 2001, stating that the internal squabbling was hampering East Timor's transition to independence. Despite initial reluctance, he announced in August that he would run for president, and he was overwhelmingly elected in the presidential elections of April 2002 with approximately 80 percent of the vote. He presided over the ceremony of independence on 19 May and became the first president of the independent Republic of East Timor.

– H –

HAATZAAI ARTIKELEN. *See* SUBVERSION.

HABIBIE, BACHARUDDIN JUSUF (1936–). Born in Pare Pare, South **Sulawesi**, Habibie became acquainted with **Suharto** in the early 1950s when Suharto was serving in South Sulawesi and regularly visited the Habibie family. He was educated at the **Bandung** Institute of Technology (1954–1955) and graduated from Aachen Institute of Technology in **Germany** in 1960. After working in Germany, Habibie was appointed in 1973 as technology and aeronautics advisor to Suharto and adviser to **Pertamina**. In 1978 he became minister of research and technology, and he founded and chaired the Badan Pengkajian dan Penerapan Teknologi (BPPT, Body for the Management of Strategic Industries) and the Dewan Riset Nasional (DRN, National Research Council). Habibie helped found the **Ikatan Cendekiawan Muslim Indonesia** (**ICMI**) in 1990 and became its chairman. In 1992–1993 he was also director-general of PT PAL, the state naval dockyard in **Surabaya**; of PT Pindad, the **army** industrial company for the manufacture of arms and ammunition; and of the state-owned Industri Pesawat Terbang Nusantara (IPTN, National **Aircraft** Industry) founded in 1976. Suharto also gave him control over the economic development of eastern Indonesia and **Batam** and of the exploitation of the Natuna **gas** field in the South China Sea. In March 1998 Suharto chose him as his **vice president**. He succeeded Suharto as president on 19 May 1998 and served until defeated in the election of May 1999.

Despite his short and rather erratic tenure as president, Habibie instituted basic changes in the government of Indonesia, the most significant being his willingness to allow **East Timor** to move along the path to independence and his approval of measures for decentralizing the Indonesian political and economic structure. [0760, 0761]

HAJ. The Muslim pilgrimage to Mecca, one of the five pillars of **Islam**. The steady stream of Indonesian pilgrims was and remains one of the important channels of political and cultural contact between Indonesia and the **Arab world**. Already itself a sign of faith, the *haj* tends to increase the conviction of those who undertake it and for this reason the **Dutch** feared it as a potential source of political unrest. From 1825, therefore, they tried to discourage pilgrims by requiring them to obtain a passport and to pay a **tax** of *f*110. They also encouraged the local tradition that seven pilgrimages to **Demak**, site of the first Muslim state on **Java**, were equivalent to one to Mecca. The tax, however, was abolished in 1852, and numbers began to increase, raising Dutch fears and leading to increasing surveillance of those making the *haj.* Until the early 20th century, most pilgrimages were arranged by so-called pilgrim sheikhs, who organized tickets, accommodation, and often finance for the journey. From 1922, however, the *haj* came under state control under the so-called Pelgrimsordonnantie, which regulated shipping, passports, vaccination, quarantine, and the welfare of Dutch subjects in Arabia. In 1926–1927, 52,412 pilgrims traveled from the Netherlands Indies to Arabia, the largest group from any country.

After independence the government maintained tight control over the *haj* for similar reasons and also to preserve Indonesia's foreign exchange and to prevent people from selling **rice** lands to finance the pilgrimage. Under the **New Order**, the **Suharto** government removed the subsidy to those undertaking the *haj* and in 1969 forbade pilgrims from using any programs except those organized by the government. In 1989 the number of pilgrims was 57,903, and this number increased to 205,000 by 2001. President Suharto made the *haj* in 1991, and in the 1990s many government officials also undertook the pilgrimage as Islam became an acceptable part of the political scene. [0627, 0637, 0641, 0983]

HALMAHERA (Gilolo, Jailolo)**.** Large island facing **Ternate** and **Tidore**. The coastal people are largely Malay, with aboriginal tribes ("Alfurs") in the interior. A sultanate of Jailolo briefly emerged in the 17th century but was conquered by Ternate. **Christian** conversions under the **Dutch** were largely confined to northern Halmahera, while the southern regions remained mostly Muslim. The sultans of Ternate and Tidore competed for influence in the area, with the Ternate sultan drawing his major support from Christians in the north, while the Tidore sultan's basis of support was largely among Muslims in the center and south.

In the early 1990s as Muslims made political gains in **Jakarta**, tension arose between the religious communities in Halmahera. When the government of **B. J. Habibie** created a new province of north Maluku conflict was renewed, fueled by competing claims to the proceeds of a local **gold** mine between Muslims and Christians allied with the two sultans. At the end of 1999 violence broke out in northern Halmahera, with at least 907 people killed by early January 2000. [0026, 0570, 0781, 1341]

HAMENGKUBUWONO IX (1912–1988)**.** Sultan of **Yogyakarta**. After studying Indology in Leiden, he became sultan on 18 March 1940, steering the sultanate to slightly greater autonomy under the **Japanese** from 1942. He is best remembered, however, for siding immediately with the Indonesian **Revolution** in 1945 and for putting his domains at the disposal of the Republic. Yogyakarta became first de facto and then formal capital of the Republic and the sultan, as minister of state and general in the Republican **army**, took part in the senior counsels of the Republic, especially in 1948–1949. His refusal to cooperate with the **Dutch** after the fall of Yogyakarta in December 1948 helped to force the Dutch to restore Republican government in July 1949. Hamengkubuwono held the Defense Ministry in 1949–1950 and 1952–1953 and was governor of the Yogyakarta Special Territory until his death. He reentered the cabinet in 1963 as head of the State Audit Board (Badan Pemeriksa Keuangan). In the early **New Order** he emerged as a prominent figure in the **Suharto** regime, becoming deputy prime minister for economics, finance, and development in March 1966 and **vice president** in 1973–1978. [0643, 0695, 0854]

HAMKA (Haji Abdul Malik bin Abdulkarim Amrullah) (1908–1981)**.** Muslim writer and journalist. His best known work was the biography (*Ajahku*) he wrote of his father, the renowned modernist *ulama,* Haji Abdul Karim Amrullah (better known as Haji Rasul), but he was also a prolific and widely read novelist. He was active in the **Muhammadiyah** throughout his life and was one of the most influential Islamic leaders in **New Order** Indonesia, becoming head of the leadership council of the Majelis Ulama Indonesia (MUI, Indonesian Council of Islamic Leaders) in 1975. In the 1960s he had been the subject of a virulent attack by the **Lembaga Kebudayaan Rakyat (Lekra)** on the basis of alleged plagiarism. [0234, 0847, 0848, 0863]

HAMZAH FANSURI (fl. late 16th century?). Poet born in the west Sumatran **camphor** port of **Barus** (also called Fansur). He lived for a time in Ayudhya in **Siam** and may have joined the mystic Islamic Wujudiyyah sect there. He also spent time in Baghdad. His poems, especially "Sharab al-ashiqin" (The Lovers' Beverage), were highly regarded in the court of **Iskandar Muda** but were later strongly criticized by **Nuruddin Raniri** as heretical.

HARAHAP, BURHANUDDIN (1917–?). **Masjumi** leader and from August 1955 to March 1956 prime minister in a Masjumi-**Partai Sosialis Indonesia (PSI)** coalition government. His government oversaw the first general **elections** in September 1955 in which the Masjumi did less well than expected and the PSI was devastated. Although Harahap carried out the dissolution of the Netherlands Indonesian Union in February 1956, he was deeply suspicious of the trend to radicalism in Indonesian politics and joined the **PRRI/Permesta rebellion** in February 1958, for which he was jailed 1962–1965. [0695]

HASAN, MUHAMMAD "BOB" (1931–). Born The Kian Sing in **Semarang**, he was adopted by Central Java **Army** commander Gatot Soebroto and became a Muslim. In the mid-1950s Subroto was **Suharto**'s supervisor, and Suharto and Hasan became friends and, after Suharto was named to the Diponegoro Central Java command in 1955, business partners. During Suharto's presidency, Hasan became head of a vast and diversified business empire, including the Nusantara Ampera Bhakti (Nusamba) group—in which he and Suharto's son Sigit Harjojudanto each held a 10 percent share—a number of **banks**, and most notably a large number of **forestry** concessions. He headed Masyarakat Perhutanan Indonesia (MPI, Indonesia Forestry Society) and, as head of the Asosiasi Panel Kayu Indonesia (Apkindo, Indonesian Wood Panel Association), he controlled all plywood exports from Indonesia and fixed their prices.

After the death of Mrs. Tien Suharto, he became an even closer confidant of Suharto and his family. In March 1998 he was appointed minister of trade and industry in Suharto's Seventh Development Cabinet, a direct challenge to the International Monetary Fund (IMF), which had called for the abolition of Apkindo. **B. J. Habibie** dropped Hasan from his "Development and Reform cabinet" two months later. Hasan was later convicted and jailed for **corruption**, being released in 2004 after serving four of his sixty-year sentence. *See also* SUHARTO FAMILY. [0404, 0760]

HATTA, MOHAMMAD (1902–1980). Political leader, born in West **Sumatra**, where he came early under the influence of modernist Islamic teachers. He studied economics in Rotterdam 1923–1932 and was active as chair of the **Perhimpunan Indonesia (PI)**. In 1927 he was arrested and tried with three others on charges of promoting resistance to **Dutch** rule in Indonesia on the basis of articles he wrote for the PI journal *Indonesia Merdeka,* but he was acquitted for lack of evidence. Struck by the ease with which the Dutch were able to break up **Sukarno**'s **Partai Nasional Indonesia (PNI)** by arresting its top leaders, Hatta founded with **Sutan Sjahrir** the **Pendidikan Nasional Indonesia (PNI Baru)** as part of a long-term plan to build cadre for the nationalist movement. On his return to Indonesia in August 1932, he quickly became prominent among the noncooperating nationalists. In 1934, however, he was sent into internal **exile** to **Boven Digul** from where he was transferred to **Banda** in 1936, being allowed to return to Java only in January 1942 at the time of the **Japanese** invasion.

Hatta was released by the Japanese and agreed to work for them as political advisor, along with Sukarno. Though the two leaders were kept from direct organizational contact with the masses in this period, their public prominence confirmed them as the two dominant nationalist leaders. Together with Sukarno, Hatta was involved in negotiations with the Japanese over independence for Indonesia and after the Japanese surrender the two declared independence on 17 August 1945. Hatta became the country's first **vice president** on 18 August. (*See also* **NATIONALISM**.)

Though the vice presidency held no executive power, Hatta was prominent in economic and administrative policy making in the early **Revolution** and was a consistent advocate of negotiation with the Dutch. He was the leader who had the greatest influence in the regions, especially on Sumatra, and was resident in West Sumatra from July to December 1947. Sukarno appointed him prime minister on 31 January 1948 after the fall of the **Amir Sjarifuddin** cabinet, and Hatta then set out to implement the unpopular **Renville Agreement** and to dismantle the power of the Left, especially after the **Madiun Affair** of September–October 1948. He was captured by the Dutch in the second **"Police Action"** and exiled with other Republican leaders to **Bangka.** He headed the Republican delegation at the **Round Table Conference** and signed the transfer of sovereignty in December 1949 on behalf of the Republic. He resigned as prime minister in September 1950.

Hatta's influence shrank sharply in the 1950s. He differed with Sukarno over the relative emphasis to be given to economic reconstruction and to political goals such as the recovery of West Irian (**Papua**) and on 26 July 1956 he resigned as vice president (effective 1 December). Many saw him as a possible focus for opposition to Sukarno and to **Guided Democracy**, but he was unwilling to join openly with the dissidents, being always reluctant to break the unity of the Republic.

Under the **New Order** he initially became an advisor to **Suharto**, but the president thwarted his plans to create a new political party (Partai Demokrasi Islam Indonesia), and during his final years Hatta became increasingly critical of the new government, lending his name to various movements that were trying to change its political path, including the **Sawito** affair and the **Petition of Fifty**, though he did not live long enough to see the latter presented to the government.

Hatta's ideology was complex. Though strongly influenced by both **Islam** and **Marxism**, and immensely knowledgeable of both, he was suspicious of Islamic radicalism and opposed **communism**. He wished to promote a moral capitalist **economy** in which prosperity could be achieved without exploitation, and he saw **cooperatives** as a path to this goal. He was willing to accept extensive foreign investment in the advanced sectors of the economy but was especially hostile to smaller **Chinese** businesses, which he saw as exploitative. [0613, 0661, 0643, 0849, 0869, 0875, 0884]

HAYAM WURUK. *See* GAJAH MADA; MAJAPAHIT.

HEALTH. The early history of health and disease in the Indonesian archipelago is difficult to reconstruct because of generally vague descriptions of ailments. It seems likely that diseases such as **malaria**, dysentery, and hookworm have long been established in the region, while **bubonic plague**, cholera, influenza, **smallpox**, and **syphilis** are more recent introductions. **Beri-beri** is a product of recent technological change. During the 18th century **Batavia** especially had a reputation for unhealthiness, and during the Napoleonic Wars Governor-General P. G. van Overstraten suggested that in the event of attack, **Dutch** forces should weaken the enemy by letting them capture Batavia and thus contract the diseases occurring there. (*See also* **PIG**.)

Epidemic diseases that struck the workforce and the **armed forces** first drew the attention of colonial authorities, and the earliest public health care was in the form of smallpox vaccination and the treatment to sufferers of syphilis. Batavia became a major center for research into tropical diseases. In 1910 a Civil Medical Service was established separate from that of the military, and from 1925 the Dienst voor Volksgezondheid (Public Health Service) conducted major campaigns emphasizing public hygiene (drainage, sanitation, and so on). Nonetheless, in 1938 the colonial government provided only 116 hospitals, with 17,976 beds, for the entire colony. A further 38,122 beds were provided by private, often mission-based, hospitals, which created unease in Muslim communities who, often correctly, saw provision of medical care as an attempt at conversion.

The earliest official medical training was of smallpox vaccinators and midwives from circa 1817. In 1857 midwifery training was abandoned, but from 1849 a school for paramedical *dokter Djawa* (Javanese doctors) was attached to the hospital in Batavia. A full European-style medical course was offered from 1875, and in 1898 the School tot Opleiding van Inlandsche Artsen (STOVIA, School for the Training of Native Doctors) was founded. The Nederlandsch-Indische Artsenschool (NIAS, Netherlands Indies Doctors' School) was established in **Surabaya** in 1913 and a medical college (Geneeskundige Hogeschool) in Batavia in 1927. (*See also* **EDUCATION**.)

The need for an extensive system of health care for the villages of Indonesia was realized from the time of independence, and a public health education program was launched in 1954. These early efforts, however, were hampered by lack of personnel and by poor coordination between government departments. One of the major aims of the **New Order** government was to provide universal basic health services, an important aspect of which was an innovative **family planning** program. In 1968 a new plan was developed for village health centers or Pusat Kesehatan Masyarakat (Puskesmas, Centers for Society's Health), and since the 1970s these have played a central role in bringing health care to most Indonesians. In the late 1980s the government launched a control plan to limit the spread of HIV/**AIDS**, and in April 2003 it declared the severe acute respiratory syndrome (SARS) a national epidemic threat. [0576, 1197–1206, 1420]

HEEREN XVII (Seventeen Gentlemen)**.** *See* DUTCH EAST INDIES COMPANY.

HEIHO. Indonesian paramilitary units recruited for auxiliary service by the **Japanese** forces in Indonesia from mid-1943. Some saw action against the Allies in eastern Indonesia, and their experience was later welcome in the Republican **army**. Unlike the **Pembela Tanah Air**

(Peta) and **Giyugun**, the Heiho trained no Indonesian officers, but their forces numbered 25,000 by the end of the war and provided many troops of the postwar Republican army. [0661, 0663]

HENDRA GUNAWAN (1918–1983)**.** One of the "fathers" of modern Indonesian painting, Hendra was born in **Bandung** and came under the influence of **Affandi** in 1939. After fighting in the **Revolution**, he was one of the founders of the Pelukis Rakyat (People's Painters) in **Yogyakarta** and also taught at the Akademi Seni Rupa Indonesia (ASRI). A member of the central committee of the **Lembaga Kebudayaan Rakyat (Lekra)**, he was jailed for 13 years following the 1965 **Gestapu** coup. After his release in 1978, he spent most of his remaining years in **Bali.**

In his early work his constant theme was ordinary people at work and play, often depicted in profile and with exaggerated facial features recalling characters of the ***wayang***. During the early 1960s he turned to nationalistic subjects, returning to this subject, usually in the context of the historical anti-**Dutch** struggle, after his release from jail. His prison paintings, however, are more personal and emotional, Astri Wright describing them as "filled with themes of longing, intimacy and togetherness remembered."

Although Hendra borrowed certain stylistic elements from the West, he synthesized these with his indigenous experience to become one of Indonesia's greatest pioneers of modern **art** and one of its most versatile painters. [0159, 0202]

HERENDIENSTEN (services to the lord)**.** Alongside the allocation of revenue farm rights (*see* ***PACHT***), corvée, or compulsory, **labor**, was a major "income" source for traditional rulers in the archipelago and was the means by which many tasks of the state, such as **road** maintenance, were carried out. The demand for **labor** went under a wide variety of names, but *herendiensten* was probably the most common and important. Tension arose over the issue of *herendiensten* in the 19th century when the colonial government sought to channel **taxation** as far as possible to itself. In 1882, several categories of *herendiensten* on **Java** were replaced with an annual poll tax (*hoofdgeld*) of *f*1, but the institution remained in place in some ***zelfbesturen*** until 1942. A form of compulsory labor service remains in force today as *kerja bakti,* "voluntary labor" required for development works and community services. *See also* SLAVERY.

HEUTSZ, JOANNES BENEDICTUS VAN (1851–1924)**.** Professional soldier, from 1898 civil and military governor of **Aceh** and from 1904 to

1909 **governor-general**. His extensive military campaigns, especially in Aceh and eastern Indonesia, marked the final stage of **Dutch** territorial consolidation.

HIMPUNAN MAHASISWA ISLAM (HMI, Muslim Students' Association). Large Muslim student organization, formed in 1947. It was close to the modernist Muslim party **Masjumi** but survived the party's banning in 1960 to become one of the most vocal opponents of the **Partai Komunis Indonesia (PKI)** under **Guided Democracy**. It was a major element in the so-called **New Order** coalition of military, **students**, and Muslims, and initially it favored the program-oriented policies of the **Suharto** regime. In the early 1970s it was dominated by the so-called renewal group, under **Nurcholis Majid**, who headed HMI from 1966 to 1971, which argued in favor of secularization. In 1983 it resisted government attempts to impose the **Pancasila** as its sole basic principle. [0927]

HINDERORDONNANTIE. Regulation issued in 1926 requiring permission from the local authorities for the establishment of any factory or enterprise that might cause damage or danger in the immediate environment. *See also* ENVIRONMENTAL PROTECTION. [0045]

HINDUISM. Hinduism arrived in Indonesia along with **Buddhism** in about the fourth to fifth centuries A.D. (*see* **INDIA, HISTORICAL LINKS WITH**), and merged with traditional beliefs to become the folk religion of much of **Java** and the coastal regions of the western archipelago. Saivism was the dominant form of Hinduism, though Buddhism often also became an aspect of Hinduism in Indonesian practice. A class of priests (*pedanda*) conducted rituals, and local belief emphasized the importance of *dharma* (destiny, duty), but the Indian class and caste system was only weakly transferred. With the penetration of **Islam**, however, Hindu belief was restricted to **Bali** and isolated pockets elsewhere such as **Tengger** in the mountains south of Pasuruan in East Java, though much of Balinese "Hinduism" pays attention to pre-Hindu local deities rather than to the philosophical principles derived from India. Balinese Hinduism was studied and to some extent protected by **Dutch** colonial officials, and after independence **Sukarno**, who was half Balinese, played a similar role. The Muslim-dominated Ministry of Religion, however, was reluctant to recognize it since it was not monotheist and had no sacred book and no prophet, these being regarded as the characteristics of true religions; it classified Hinduism with animism, thus opening Bali officially to Muslim and **Christian** missionary activity. In response, Balinese Hindus formed the Parisada Dharma Hindu Bali (PDHB) in 1959 both to lobby in favor of Hinduism in government circles and to standardize, define, and democratize Hindu doctrine and practice on Bali. Arguments that Hinduism recognized a single supreme god in the form of Sang Hyang Widi resulted in the religion's formal recognition by the ministry in 1962. In 1964 the PDHB changed its name to Parisada Hindu Dharma.

In 1963 Hindu authorities celebrated the ritual of Eka Dasa Rudra, a two-month-long cleansing ceremony needed once a century but previously held probably in the 18th century. On 18 February 1963, three weeks before the climax of the ritual, the volcanic Mt. Agung erupted, causing extensive destruction and loss of life on Bali. The eruption was taken by many Balinese as a sign that much was wrong on the earth, and some scholars have argued that the mass killing of **Partai Komunis Indonesia (PKI)** members on Bali in 1965–1966 was seen by many Balinese as a necessary cleansing operation (*see* **MASSACRES OF 1965–1966**). The ceremony was repeated without volcanic intervention in 1979.

Since 1965, Hinduism has grown dramatically outside Bali. Growth took place first on Java, where from 1967 many ***abangan*** Muslims, appalled by the ***santri*** role in the massacres there and by the prospect of stricter enforcement of Islamic religious law, and driven also by the government insistence that all citizens adhere to a religion, turned instead to Hinduism as the religion of **Majapahit**. In other parts of Indonesia, moreover, Hinduism provided a convenient rubric for government recognition of the traditional beliefs of communities such as the **Toraja** and the **Dayaks**. *See also* RELIGION AND POLITICS. [0536, 1229, 1345, 1364, 1371]

HIZBULLAH ("Army of God")**.** Paramilitary force founded by the **Japanese** in West **Java** in December 1944 affiliated with the **Masjumi**, as a Muslim counterpart to the **Pembela Tanah Air (Peta)**. At the end of the occupation, it had around 500 members and was in no way strong enough to press for an **Islamic state**. During the **Revolution**, however, the name Hizbullah was adopted by armed groups affiliated with the Muslim political party Masjumi and with local Muslim leaders. After 1948 many Hizbullah members joined the **Darul Islam (DI)**, partly because of belief in an **Islamic state**, partly because of fear of demobilization. *See also* ARMY; *LASYKAR*; SABILILLAH. [0661, 0693]

HOGENDORP, DIRK VAN (1761–1882)**. Dutch East Indies Company (VOC)** official on **Java** from 1791 to 1798. He sharply criticized VOC rule on the island for its "feudal" exactions from the **population**, and he proposed extensive changes to the structure of government and finance there, including property rights for the Javanese, transforming the ***bupati*** into a salaried bureaucracy and reforming the **taxation** system, many of which foreshadowed the ideas of **Herman Willem Daendels** and **Thomas Stamford Raffles**. In 1798 he was jailed for these views by the conservative Commissioner-General S. C. Nederburgh but in 1799 escaped to the Netherlands where he continued his campaigns in a series of polemic brochures. [0491]

"HO-LO-TAN." Chinese transcription of the name of an otherwise unknown kingdom on the north coast of West **Java**. It sent seven tributary missions to **China** from 430 to 552, that on 436 from King Vishamvarman requesting diplomatic and military assistance against internal and external enemies. The kingdom may have been conquered by **Tarumanegara** soon after 552. *See also* "KAN-T'O-LI". [0538, 0542, 0543]

HONGI ("fleet") **RAIDS.** Named for the war canoes, or *kora-kora,* of eastern Indonesia but referring generally to **Dutch** naval operations in the 17th century to destroy spice plantations in **Maluku** outside their areas of control in order to ensure their own monopoly of the lucrative **trade**. *See also* DUTCH EAST INDIES COMPANY. [0491, 0565]

HORTA, JOSE RAMOS (1949–)**.** Born of a Portuguese father and East Timorese mother, he went through the colonial school system and became a journalist in 1969. His reports on the colonial government led to his exile to Mozambique in 1971. After returning to **East Timor** Horta became chief of external affairs and information for **Fretilin**, traveling to **Jakarta** in 1974 and receiving an explicit promise from Foreign Minister **Adam Malik** that Indonesia would respect the integrity and independence of East Timor. In early 1975 he pushed for Fretilin to go into coalition with **União Democrática Timorense (UDT)** in the interests of achieving independence, and in November of that year was a member of a diplomatic delegation that went to New York to appeal to the **United Nations**. After the Indonesian invasion he remained in exile and became East Timor's most effective spokesman in the UN and elsewhere and a personal representative of **Jose Alexandre "Xanana" Gusmão**. He was awarded the Nobel Peace Prize in 1996, together with Bishop **Carlos Filipe Ximenes**

Belo. When East Timor achieved its independence, he was appointed the country's foreign minister.

HOUTMAN, CORNELIS DE (c. 1565–1599)**.** Houtman commanded the first **Dutch** commercial expedition to Indonesia in 1595–1597, which demonstrated the possibility of direct **trade** with the Indies. He was, however, authoritarian and tactless and was murdered on orders of the sultan of **Aceh** on his second voyage to the Indies. His brother Frederik (1571–1627) was imprisoned in Aceh for two years and made important early linguistic and astronomical studies there. Frederik later became the first governor of **Ambon** (1605–1611) and governor of **Maluku** (1621–1623) and is commemorated by Houtman's Abrolhos off the West Australian coast. [0491]

HUMAN RIGHTS. Human rights became an important issue in Indonesia in the 1990s after the end of the Cold War, when the Western donor nations began to tie human rights standards to the granting of aid. Indonesia came under particular pressure at the end of 1991 after the Dili massacre in **East Timor**. Indonesian spokesmen, like those of other Asian nations, stressed the importance of maintaining a balance between individual or community rights and the people's "fundamental right to economic and social development." Meeting in **Jakarta** in September 1992, the Non-Aligned Movement declared that disputes over human rights should be settled in a "spirit of cooperation, not confrontation" while accepting "in principle" the "universality of human rights." Indonesia had joined the **United Nations** Commission on Human Rights in early 1991, and in 1993 it established a Komisi Nasional Hak Asasi Manusia (Komnas HAM, National Committee for Human Rights) by presidential decree. Despite its origin, the Komnas HAM has acted as a largely independent body, gaining the people's trust by its effective handling of several cases of human rights abuses.

In February 1999 the government submitted a Human Rights Act, which was passed that September, calling for the establishment of a human rights tribunal. In the aftermath of the massacres in East Timor following the September 1999 referendum, the issue of human rights became inextricably tied to the government's willingness and ability to try those responsible for these massacres, particularly from the military. In November 2000 parliament accepted an Act on Human Rights Tribunals that stipulated that past human rights abuses could be tried by an ad hoc tribunal, approved by parliament and the **president**. Under this act, high-ranking officers and civilians could be held responsible for crimes committed by their subordinates. The maximum sentence was a prison term of 25 years. In February 2002 international prosecutors indicted 17 pro-Jakarta militiamen and Indonesian **students** for crimes against humanity allegedly committed in East Timor in 1999, including a leader of the youth wing of the **Partai Demokrasi Indonesia—Perjuangan (PDI-P)**. In June the government charged pro-Jakarta **militia** leader Eurico Guterres and six others with crimes against humanity for violence that killed more than 1,000 people in East Timor during its 1999 independence referendum. Ten of the Indonesian security officers tried for crimes against humanity in these killings were acquitted by the Indonesian human rights court—six of them in August and four more in December 2002. Two civilians, both from East Timor, were found guilty of related charges. The military was also opposed to investigations into the Trisakti incident and the shooting of student protesters in May 1998.

In February 2003 the United Nations indicted General **Wiranto**, six other military officers, and a civilian for crimes against humanity during the independence vote in East Timor in 1999, but the Indonesian government refused to carry out the arrests. The following month a special human rights court in Jakarta sentenced Brigadier General Noer Muis, Indonesia's last commander in East Timor, to five years in jail for not preventing the attacks. Previously the court had acquitted 12 defendants and sentenced two lower-ranking officers and two civilians to jail sentences. *See also* UNITED STATES, RELATIONS WITH. [0748, 0760]

HUNTING. This was an important source of food for many peoples of the archipelago, though vegetables, both cultivated and collected, were always a more important source of protein and starch. In areas of intensive **rice** cultivation, the purpose of hunting was principally to protect crops and human and animal lives, rather than for food. **Tigers** were hunted for use in public fights, elephants for ivory, and **rhinoceros** for their horns and bezoar stones. Hunting was also a popular sport of the European community in the late colonial period. *See also* CONSERVATION, NATURE.

– I –

IDRUS (1921–1979)**.** Author known especially for his "Surabaya" (1947) and other short stories of the **Japanese occupation** and Indonesian

Revolution, many of which dwell on the brutal and grubby aspects of the events described. His terse style is reminiscent of the poetry of **Chairil Anwar**. [0234]

IKATAN CENDEKIAWAN MUSLIM INDONESIA (ICMI, All Indonesia League of Muslim Intellectuals). Founded in December 1990 and chaired by then minister of research and technology, **B. J. Habibie**, ICMI was essentially a body set up by President **Suharto** to maintain his control over the political system and to press his development and financial policies that were being opposed by the technocrats on whom he had previously relied. But despite the fact that its major officeholders were presidential appointees and that it was backed by the Suharto government, ICMI attracted several opposition Muslim leaders, including **Sri Bintang Pamungkas**, though not **Abdurrachman Wahid**, Deliar Noer, or Ridwan Saidi, who accused it of being merely a vehicle for the president's reelection and of being used by Habibie for his own political ambitions and by the government to co-opt **Islam**. Its supporters, however, contended that the organization strengthened the Islamic devotion of the middle class and government officials. It established a think tank, the **Centre for Information and Development Studies (CIDES)**, in September 1992 (with prominent liberal Islamic intellectuals Adi Sasono and Dewi Fortuna Anwar on its steering committee), which embraced **human rights** issues and became a major competitor to the other longtime think tank established in the 1960s by **Ali Murtopo,** the **Centre for Strategic and International Studies (CSIS)**, which was accused of being dominated by **Catholics**. [1030, 1033, 1328]

IKATAN PENDUKUNG KEMERDEKAAN INDONESIA (IPKI, League of the Supporters of Indonesian Independence). Political party formed in May 1954 by supporters of **A. H. Nasution**, who attributed the country's postindependence malaise to selfish politicians. They called themselves a movement, rather than a party, and were strongest in West **Java**, where Nasution's old **Siliwangi** Division was based, though they obtained only 1.4 percent in the 1955 **elections**. Initially in favor of **Guided Democracy**, which they saw as a way of ending party politics, they turned against it when it appeared that **Sukarno** intended to leave them out of his **Dewan Perwakilan Rakyat—Gotong Royong (DPR-GR)**. Some branches joined the **PRRI/Permesta rebellion** and were banned, but the party survived Guided Democracy to be merged in 1973 into the **Partai Demokrasi Indonesia (PDI)**. [0695, 0714, 0872]

IMAM BONJOL, TUANKU (1772–1864). A second-generation **Minangkabau** religious leader (*tuanku*) of the Paderi movement, which spread reformist **Islam** through central **Sumatra**. After remnants of the anti-Paderi aristocracy asked for **Dutch** help and transferred the region to Dutch sovereignty in exchange, Imam Bonjol became the major military leader resisting the Dutch in the so-called Paderi War (1821–1834). He was captured by the Dutch in 1834, shortly after the fall of his stronghold at Bonjol in the Minangkabu highlands and was exiled first to West **Java** and **Ambon** and finally (in 1841) to Manado. [0791]

INDEPENDENCE, DECLARATION OF. Indonesia's declaration of independence was made by **Sukarno** and **Mohammad Hatta** in the grounds of Pegangsaan Timur 56 in **Jakarta**, on the morning of 17 August 1945. Within a more extensive statement, the independence text read: "We the Indonesian people hereby proclaim the independence of Indonesia. All matters concerning the transfer of power etc. will be carried out in an orderly manner and in the shortest possible time. In the name of the Indonesian people, Sukarno-Hatta." Since 1945, 17 August has been celebrated as independence day and has been the occasion for a major speech by the **president**. *See also* SUCCESSION. [0643, 0662, 0663]

INDIA, HISTORICAL LINKS WITH. Indian civilization fused with indigenous cultural traditions to produce a distinctive Southeast Asian Hindu-Buddhist civilization that, in various forms, dominated the archipelago as far east as the coast of New Guinea from the fifth century until the arrival of **Islam**. The principal historical sources for studying this process of "Indianization" or "Hinduization" are Sanskritic inscriptions found in various parts of the archipelago (*see* **TARUMANEGARA**), archeological discoveries of Indian **trade** goods, and the accounts of **Chinese** travelers, none of which have been adequate to demonstrate the nature or extent of the process. Historians have been unable to agree on whether the primary initiative for the spread of Indian culture came from Indians or Indonesians, whether it was Indonesian rulers who sent traders to the ports of India and summoned Hindu priests to their courts to provide details of Hindu ritual for royal glorification, or whether missionary, commercial, and imperial motives brought Indians themselves to the archipelago. It now appears likely that all these processes played a role, though the movement was more one of ideas than of people. Trade between the archipelago and India began in the first or second century A.D., but there is no evidence of major Indian settlement in the region, and the 11th-century raids of the Cholas on **Srivijaya** were the only significant military excursions across the Bay of Bengal.

It is clear, nonetheless, that most influence was exercised by Brahmans (most Sanskrit vocabulary in Indonesian languages is religious, and there is no sign of an Indian-influenced traders' pidgin), while the courts of local rulers were the major channel for Indian influence. The growth of trade with India and **China** from early in the Christian era must have significantly changed that distribution of power and wealth in local societies. Rulers saw in Hindu-Buddhist cosmology a means of exalting their own positions (*see* **KEDIRI**; **MATARAM**; **SAILENDRAS**). As adopted in Indonesia, **Hinduism** and **Buddhism** argued for an analogy between the state and the cosmos, the ruler analogous to the supreme god, and often a temporary incarnation (*avatar*) of a Hindu deity. From this followed the construction of palaces (***kraton***) that physically resembled the cosmos and the entrenchment of the ruler's right to demand corvée **labor** from his subjects. Scholars have differed over the extent to which Indian cultural influence reached beyond the court. J. C. Van Leur argued that it was never more than a "thin and flaking glaze" over powerful indigenous traditions, but more recent scholars have held that influence went rather deeper and that "culturally Southeast Asia became nearly as 'Indian' as parts of India" (I. W. Mabbett). (*See also* **MEGALITHS**.)

Hindu-Buddhist Indonesia maintained close cultural contact with India, especially through the Buddhist monastery at Nalanda in Bihar, where a Sailendra ruler of **Java** helped to endow a monastery and which received many pilgrims from Srivijaya. The use of the zero, though an Indian invention, is recorded earlier in Java (732) than in India itself (870).

The early Indonesian **nationalist** movement was inspired to some extent by the successes of the older Indian movement. **Partai Indonesia (Partindo)** in particular adopted the principle of *swadeshi* (use of locally made products) at its foundation in 1931, and a few figures were impressed by Gandhi's philosophy of nonviolence, but on the whole direct influence was sparse. *See also* MAHABHARATA; RAMAYANA; WRITING SYSTEMS. [0518, 0521, 0539, 0540, 0543, 0544]

INDIA, RELATIONS WITH. When Indonesia declared independence in 1945, India was still a British colony, but large areas of government had been devolved to Indians and full independence was in the offing. Jawaharlal Nehru's insistence that the Indian troops, who formed a large percentage of the British forces sent to accept the **Japanese** surrender, should not be used to suppress an Asian nationalist movement was one of the factors leading **Britain** to attempt to balance **Dutch** and Indonesian interests in 1945 and 1946, and India later assisted Indonesia with supplies of **cloth** (in exchange for **rice**) and with diplomatic support. In 1948–1949, shortly before the so-called second **"Police Action,"** Nehru unsuccessfully attempted to send in a plane to evacuate **Sukarno** and **Mohammad Hatta** from **Yogyakarta**, and India, together with other Asian states, later hampered the Dutch military effort by denying them overflight rights. In March–April 1949 India invited Indonesian delegates to the Asian Relations Conference in New Delhi. The two countries signed a treaty of "perpetual peace and unalterable friendship" on 3 March 1951, and Sukarno was, with Nehru, a prominent figure in the Non-Aligned Movement. The two countries drifted apart, however, in the closing years of Sukarno's tenure as Indonesia grew closer to **China** in the early 1960s, and relations became even more distant under **Suharto** when Indonesia aligned more closely with the Western powers. *See also* FOREIGN POLICY. [0661, 1104]

INDIË VERLOREN, RAMPSPOED GEBOREN ("The Indies lost, disaster follows")**.** Title of a 1914 pamphlet by C. G. S. Sandberg, deploring the gradual constitutional separation of the Netherlands Indies from the Netherlands (*see* **NETHERLANDS, CONSTITUTIONAL RELATIONSHIP WITH INDONESIA**) but taken up later as a slogan, especially during the Indonesian **Revolution**, by those in the Netherlands who believed that **Dutch** prosperity depended on continuing colonial rule of Indonesia. They pointed especially to the return on Dutch investments in Indonesia, to Dutch markets there, and to the supply of materials for Dutch industry, as well as to the calculations of 1938 that the colonies contributed 13.7 percent of Dutch national income, arguments that reinforced the nationalist view that Dutch rule was the source of Indonesia's major problems. The example of the **Cultivation System**, which had rescued the Dutch **economy** after 1830, was certainly influential here. A subsidiary argument was that possession of Indonesia gave the Netherlands world power status and that without it they would be reduced to "the rank of Denmark." Recent scholars have shown, however, that Dutch investment in Indonesia at the close of the colonial period (40 percent of the country's external investment) was lower in proportion than that of **Britain** in its empire (50 percent), and that returns on that investment were modest (3.9 percent in 1938). After 1945, a powerful counterargument to the *rampspoed geboren* proposition was the likely enormous cost of postwar reconstruction, though this argument was not widely made. *See also BATIG SLOT*; "EERESCHULD, EEN." [0589]

INDIGO (*Indigofera* spp., Fabaceae)**.** Dye plant introduced to Indonesia from the Middle East and widely found in the archipelago by the 17th century. It was traded from **Java** to **China** in the 18th century. Production declined after the late 19th century with the development of German aniline dyes. [0331, 0332]

INDISCHE PARTIJ (Indies Party)**.** Founded in 1911 by the Eurasian E. F. E. Douwes Dekker (1880–1950), the party initially reflected a growing feeling in parts of the **Indo-European** community that their primary ties were with Indonesia rather than the Netherlands. It was, however, soon joined by the Javanese intellectuals **Suwardi Suryaningrat** and **Tjipto Mangoenkoesoemo** and became one of the first political organizations explicitly to transcend ethnic, religious, and regional divisions within the colony and to call for the independence of the Indies ("Indië los van Holland") from **Dutch** rule. The party collapsed in 1913 after the government refused it official recognition and sent its leaders into **exile**, though a few members continued party activities, first in the Nationale Indische Partij (1918) and from 1937 under the name **Insulinde**. Douwes Dekker was interned by the Indies government in 1941 and exiled to **Surinam**. He returned to Indonesia in 1946, joining the Republic and taking the name Danudirja Setiabudi. *See also* NATIONALISM. [0887]

INDISCHE SOCIAAL-DEMOCRATISCHE VEREENIGING (ISDV, Indies Social Democratic Association)**.** Founded in May 1914 by Henk Sneevliet (1883–1942) and others as the first Marxist organization in Indonesia. Initially European in its membership and orientation, it soon began recruiting Indonesians, including Semaun, **Tan Malaka**, and Alimin Prawirodirdjo. Sneevliet was sent into **exile** in December 1918, and on 27 May 1920 the association transformed itself into the Perserikatan Komunis di Hindia (Communist Association of the Indies), later the **Partai Komunis Indonesia (PKI)**. [0621]

INDO-EUROPEANS. During the first two centuries of the **Dutch** presence in Indonesia, few European **women** reached the colony and through concubinage and casual liaisons between European men and Indonesian women there emerged a large community of people of mixed descent, many with official European status (*see* **RACE**). The extent to which such people were socially accepted as equal to other Europeans varied from time to time (*see* **DUTCH IN INDONESIA**), but with the arrival of large numbers of European women in the 20th century, the mixed race group became increasingly sharply demarcated as a distinct social group, called Indo-Europeans (with the derogatory abbreviation "Indo"), occupying subaltern positions in society as clerks, petty officials, and NCOs. Nevertheless, if legally recognized by their fathers, the offspring of Dutch men and Indies women were officially classified as "European." This European status excluded them from the purchase of **land** (*see* **AGRARIAN LAW OF 1870**), though in 1904 the government began to lease small plots to individuals for gardens.

This separation, accompanied by increasing racial discrimination, led to two divergent tendencies: on the one hand, Indo-Europeans came to see Indonesia as their primary home and to downplay the connection with the Netherlands; the **Indische Partij** was at first a strong sign of this. On the other hand, especially with the growth of Indonesian **nationalism**, many Indo-Europeans became worried by the threat to their still-privileged position in relation to Indonesians, and they became strong supporters of the colonial order. The Indo-Europese Verbond (IEV, Indo-European Association), founded in 1919, sought to defend Indo-European interests in the **Volksraad** and argued for economic assistance and social emancipation. Among the Dutch motives for retaining the province of Irian (**Papua**) after 1949 was as a possible place of settlement for displaced Indo-Europeans, and about 6,000 went there in a largely unsuccessful settlement scheme.

About 100,000 Indo-Europeans left Indonesia for Holland shortly after independence, only a little over 10 percent taking Indonesian citizenship at once, partly because they were subject to similar restrictive regulations as **Chinese** Indonesian citizens. In 1951, the IEV became the Gabungan Indo Untuk Kesatuan Indonesia (GIKI, Indo Association for Indonesian Unity) and restricted its membership to citizens. There was a further exodus of Indo-Europeans during the West New Guinea dispute in 1957–1958 when the Indonesian government repatriated all nonessential Dutch nationals to the Netherlands. Indo-Europeans made up a large portion of the 35,000 Dutch citizens who reached the Netherlands by September 1958. [0480, 0584, 0608, 0639, 1046]

INDONESIA (from Greek *indos,* India, and *nesos,* island)**.** The fixing of a clear terminology for the region now called Indonesia has been bedeviled by changing political realities and changing understandings of the cultural and biological character of the region. Southeast Asia (itself a relatively recent term) was once referred to commonly as Further India, the East Indies (*Oost Indië* in Dutch), the Indian or Malay Archipelago, or simply the Indies, in recognition of the Indian cultural influences there. The **Dutch** possessions were thus simply called Netherlands India, the Netherlands Indies, or occasionally Tropical Netherlands. Attempts, mainly by anthropologists, to differentiate the predominantly Malay, Muslim world of island Southeast Asia from the **Buddhist** realms of the mainland led to the coining of the words Malesia, **Insulinde**, **Nusantara**, **Malaysia**, and Indonesia, the latter being initially used by a British anthropologist, J. R. Logan, in 1850, in analogy with Polynesia, and popularized by the German anthropologist Adolf Bastian in his book *Indonesien* (1884). The Malay term for the region was at first simply *Hindia Timur* (East India), but in 1917 Indonesians in the Netherlands formed the Indonesisch Verbond van Studeerenden (Indonesian Students Society) and in 1922 the Indische Vereeniging (Indies Association) in the Netherlands adopted the name Indonesische Vereeniging, or **Perhimpunan Indonesia**. In 1928 the nationalist movement formally adopted the name Indonesia to designate the future nation, its citizens, and its language. This was long rejected by the Dutch as implying a false unity of the colony's ethnic groups, but in their 1948 **constitution**, the Dutch formally adopted the term Indonesië for the colony.

"INDONESIA RAYA." Indonesia's national anthem, composed in 1928 by Wage Rudolf Supratman (1903–1938) for the All-Indonesia Youth Congress. *See also* MUSIC; YOUTH PLEDGE.

INDONESIAN AIRWAYS. Commercial airline established in Burma in late 1948 to obtain funds for Republican representatives abroad during the latter part of the **Revolution**. It operated first with a single Dakota and flew primarily under contract for the government of Burma. Wiweko Suparno was managing director. *See also* GARUDA.

INDONESIAN LANGUAGE (*Bahasa Indonesia*)**.** The national language, derived from Malay, the language of the coastal regions of eastern **Sumatra**, the **Riau** archipelago, and the **Malay Peninsula** (*see also* **LANGUAGES**). From the 17th century, Malay became increasingly the lingua franca of the archipelago, and it was adopted by the **Dutch East Indies Company** (which called it *Maleis,* Malay) in its dealings with indigenous authorities. The **Balai Pustaka** was influential in promoting

Malay as a literary language. Malay was preferred by **nationalists** over Javanese especially because it was not associated with any major ethnic group and because it has no formal levels of speech as does Javanese, which was thus considered to be a "feudal" language. On 28 October 1928 a nationalist youth congress adopted it as the national language (*see* **YOUTH PLEDGE**). Use of Indonesian for administrative purposes increased during the **Japanese occupation** when the use of Dutch was banned. Although spelling authorities have tried to reduce the influence of European languages on Indonesian vocabulary (*see* **ETYMOLOGY**), European influence on Indonesian syntax has been strong, for instance in the use of prefixes such as *pra-* (pre-) and *tuna-* (without) and the use of *dari* (Dutch, *van*) to mean "of."

A spelling system for Indonesian was formalized by Ch. A. van Ophuijsen in 1901, but this was altered after independence, first by the substitution of *u* for *oe* (introduced by Suwandi in 1947) and then by a more extensive set of changes under an Indonesian-Malaysian Language Agreement signed in August 1973, which provides for the harmonization of the two countries' versions of Malay. The 1973 spelling, known as *ejaan yang disempurnakan* (EYD, perfected spelling), changed *tj* to *c*, *dj* to *j*, *j* to *y*, and *ch* to *kh*, and it removed the distinction between *e* and *é*. Vocabulary and grammatical change in Indonesian are rapid, and the two versions of the language remain distinct. An earlier agreement to harmonize the two languages, Melindo, reached in 1959, was never implemented because of **Confrontation**. *See also* MALAYSIA, RELATIONS WITH. [0262, 0267, 0271, 0275, 0277, 0280, 0281]

INDONESIANIZATION. General term applied to programs of Indonesian governments in the 1950s to place a greater share of the **economy** in the hands of Indonesian (by which was generally meant ***pribumi***) businessmen. It was in many ways a continuation of the philosophy of the colonial **Liberal** and **Ethical Policies**, under which government sought to create a conducive environment for economic activity without being a major entrepreneur itself. The **Benteng** (Fortress) program, begun in 1950, aimed to help indigenous businessmen accumulate capital by giving them privileged access to lucrative import licenses. In practice, however, much of the money and most of the licenses went to political and bureaucratic associates of the government or to **Ali-Baba** firms. In 1951 an Economic Urgency Program, formulated by **Sumitro Djojohadikusumo**, aimed at using state funds to set up viable enterprises for later transfer to **cooperatives** or private ownership. From 1956 these programs were abandoned, and Indonesianization began to be replaced by a program of direct state intervention in the economy and regulation of indigenous business. *See also* GUIDED ECONOMY; NATIONALIZATION; STATE ENTERPRISES. [0315, 0313]

INDRAPURA. It emerged as a sultanate on the southern edge of the **Minangkabau** realm in the early 16th century, after the fall of **Melaka** to the **Portuguese** diverted Muslim traders to the western coast of **Sumatra**. A major exporter of **pepper**, Indrapura was conquered by the **Aceh**nese forces of **Iskandar Muda** in 1633. With the decline of Acehnese power, it rose again but was wracked by disputes between the sultans and regional lords, in which the **Dutch** and **British East Indies Company** became heavily involved. Sultan Muhammad Syah was forced to abdicate in 1696, and thereafter Indrapura was under Dutch domination. [0564]

INDUSTRIALIZATION. For most of the colonial period, Indonesia was for the Netherlands primarily a market and a source of raw materials, and local industrialization was not encouraged. This policy was reversed during World War I when it was realized how vulnerable dependence on manufactured imports had made the colony; under the **Ethical Policy**, too, the colonial government wished to provide more employment opportunities for the growing **population**. In 1915 a Commissie tot Ontwikkeling van de Fabrieksnijverheid in Nederlandsch-Indië (Commission for the Development of Industry in the Netherlands Indies) was formed to encourage industrial development; its major but modest achievement was a paper factory in **Bandung** established in 1923.

After independence, import substitution industrialization became a strong element in economic policy. With the coming of the **New Order**, **investment**, especially foreign investment, was seen as the major tool for growth of the capitalist **economy**. Industrial activity was centered in and around the major urban centers, especially in **Java**, and the factories attracted large numbers of workers from the rural areas. The factories stimulated a parallel growth of service industries for their **labor** forces. In the mid-1970s, the government began an aggressive program to promote high-technology industralization, under the direction of **B. J. Habibie.** There was an influx of new technologies from abroad, and large-scale capital-intensive investments stimulated industrialization in fields from military hardware to electronics. Between 1965 and 1995, industrial output expanded rapidly from 13 percent to 42 percent of Indonesia's gross domestic product (GDP). After 1985 there was a striking increase in manufactured exports, which between 1985 and 1991 grew at an annual rate of 30 percent. Although initially many of the industries contributing to this expansion were based on the processing of petroleum (*see* OIL) and natural **gas**, by 1995 these two activities accounted for less than one tenth of total manufacturing output. They were replaced by such industries as **automobile**, garment, footwear, and electronic manufacturers. Plywood constituted an ever-larger proportion of Indonesia's export production (*see* **FORESTRY**). **Mining** accounted for less than 7 percent of GDP growth during the period. During these years, Java's share of manufacturing output and employment declined steadily. *See also* AIRCRAFT INDUSTRY; BADAN PERENCANAAN PEMBANGUNAN NASIONAL; IRON; RENCANA PEMBANGUNAN LIMA TAHUN. [0295, 0353, 0409, 0417, 0479, 0730]

"*INLANDER*" ("native"). The legal category into which all indigenous subjects of the Netherlands Indies were placed. Though this was a subordinate category, with distinctly fewer privileges than that of the Europeans, the shared status it gave contributed to the development of an Indonesian identity. *See also* LAW; NATIONALISM; RACE.

INLANDSCH BESTUUR ("Native Administration"). In the directly ruled territories of **Java** and **Madura**, the colonial administration (***Binnenlandsch Bestuur***) was divided into distinct European and native (*inlandsch*) corps. This situation arose out of the manner of **Dutch** expansion on Java, in which the **Dutch East Indies Company (VOC)** took over the fealty of ***bupati*** from the rulers of **Mataram**, but the system was preserved after the reforms of **Herman Willem Daendels** and **Thomas Stamford Raffles** so that colonial officials dealing directly with the Indonesian **population** would as far as possible be drawn from the traditional elites and would thus enjoy greater authority. The Inlandsch Bestuur, accordingly, was not subject to the same demands for expertise and competence as the Europeesch (European) Bestuur.

Its precise role in successive eras, however, varied considerably. Both Daendels and Raffles introduced administrative reforms to bypass the Inlandsch Bestuur for the sake of more efficient government. In the early 19th century, on the other hand, the Dutch reemphasized the traditional authority, especially of the *bupati,* encouraging them to assume the status of minor royalty (the correspondence of **Raden Ajeng Kartini**, daughter of a *bupati,* was published as *Letters of a Javanese Princess*) and generally ignoring their abuses of power (*see* ***MAX HAVELAAR***). From 1870 the Dutch placed greater emphasis on developing the administrative and technical expertise of the Inlandsch Bestuur. The most senior rank in it was the *bupati.* His deputy was normally the *patih* and he presided over a hierarchy of regional officials: the *wedana, camat,* and, at the head of the village or ***desa,*** the *lurah.*

In the directly ruled territories outside Java and Madura, no uniform system was in force, though in general the colonial government sought to preserve the so-called *Inlandsche gemeenten* (native communities) as the basic unit of government. In many parts of **Sumatra**, the colonial government installed *demang* and assistant-*demang* as regional links between the European and traditional governments. In Java and elsewhere, the participation of the Inlandsch Bestuur in Dutch rule was often resented, and there were violent social revolutions against it in many areas at the start of the **Revolution**. *See also PAMONG PRAJA; PRIYAYI*; TIGA DAERAH. [0479, 0636, 0638]

INPRES (*Instruksi Presiden*)**.** Annual development funds granted by presidential authority under the **Suharto** government to provincial and lower levels of administration to finance such activities as schools, meeting halls, **roads**, bridges, and other infrastructure. [0397, 0730]

INSULINDE (from Latin *insula,* island, *Inde,* India)**.** Poetic term for the Indonesian archipelago, coined by Multatuli in ***Max Havelaar*** in 1860. The name was adopted in 1913 for remnants of the **Indische Partij** and was displaced in poetic usage (except in French) by **Nusantara**. *See also* INDONESIA. [0887]

INSULTING THE HEAD OF STATE. *See* PRESIDENT, POSITION OF; SUBVERSION.

INTELLIGENCE SERVICES. The Republic's first postindependence intelligence agency, Badan Istimewa (Special Agency), was headed by **Zulkifli Lubis**, who had received intelligence training from the **Japanese** during their occupation. In early 1946 its name was changed to Badan Rahasia Negara Indonesia (BRANI, Indonesian State Secret Agency), which had a Field Preparation (FP) training unit.

After the transfer of sovereignty, the intelligence section of the Ministry of Defense (Intelijen Kementerian Pertahanan, IKP) was still headed by Lubis, and he established the Armed Forces Information Bureau (Biro Informasi Angkatan Perang, Bisap) to prepare strategic information for defense and military leaders. Later in the 1950s, when internal struggles within the **armed forces** compelled Lubis to flee to join the regional **PRRI/Permesta rebellion**, IKP lost its influence. Under **Guided Democracy, Subandrio** was put in charge of the Central Bureau of Intelligence (Badan Pusat Intelijen, BPI), which claimed authority over intelligence units of the three services, the **police**, the prosecutor's office, and Hankam (Ministry of Defense and Security).

Another intelligence organization, **Operasi Khusus** (Opsus), had been formed in 1961. It was headed by **Ali Murtopo** and Soedjono Hoemardani (1919–1986), and was used to establish covert contacts with the Malaysian government during **Confrontation**. Opsus later helped ensure progovernment votes in the 1969 "Act of Free Choice" in West Irian (**Papua**) and in Indonesia's general **elections** in 1971 and after. It was also believed responsible for the political party manipulation in the aftermath of these elections, whereby the political party opponents of the **Golkar** were reduced to only the **Partai Persatuan Pembangunan (PPP)** and the **Partai Demokrasi Indonesia (PDI)**. In 1974 competition between the heads of the three intelligence services—Ali Murtopo; Soemitro, head of **Komando Operasi Pemulihan Keamanan dan Ketertiban (Kopkamtib)**; and Sutopo Juwono (1927–), chief of **Badan Koordinasi Intelijen Negara (Bakin, State Intelligence Coordinating Agency)**—came to a head. That same year, **Benny Murdani** was transferred to Hankam and began to take over control of much of Indonesia's intelligence operations when he became intelligence assistant to **armed forces** headquarters and in 1977 was also appointed chief of Pusat Intelijen Strategis (Pusintelstrat, Center for Strategic Intelligence). In addition, in the early 1980s, Murdani became deputy chief of Bakin and chief of Kopkamtib intelligence task force. In 1983 Pusintelstrat became Badan Intelijen Strategis (Bais, Body for Strategic Intelligence), which Benny continued to head after being appointed armed forces commander. Kopkamtib affairs were gradually handed over to Bais. The first two Bais operations were **Petrus** (*pembunuhan/penembakan misterius,* mysterious killings) and Operasi Woyla, the freeing of the hijacked **Garuda** airliner in March 1981.

In January 1994, Bais was replaced by Badan Intelijen ABRI (BIA, Armed Forces' Intelligence Body) under ABRI chief of staff for governmental affairs, Lieutenant General H. L. Mantiri. This change was a result of Suharto's attempts to dismantle Murdani's personal networks and undermine any autonomous military powers outside the president's control; but the intelligence body eventually reverted to its old name, and after the fall of **Abdurrachman Wahid** in 2001 it was again strengthened. When the police were separated from the military in 1999–2001, Bakin was reorganized, assuming the name Badan Intelijen Negara (BIN, State Intelligence Agency), with police intelligence as its operational arm.

The importance of the intelligence services increased in 2001–2002, as the **United States** and other countries pressured Indonesia to more actively pursue groups suspected of being tied to the al Qaeda organization. After the October 2002 bombings in **Bali** President **Megawati Sukarnoputri** appointed BIN as the sole coordinator for all intelligence activities in the country, and assigned its director, Hendro Priyono, to lead the bombing investigation under the antiterrorism legislation adopted on 18 October 2002. In early 2004 Hendro Priyono disclosed plans to establish BIN branches at the provincial, district and municipal levels throughout the country. *See also* POLITIEK INLICHTINGEN DIENST (PID); SUBVERSION [0731, 0972]

INTER-GOVERNMENTAL GROUP ON INDONESIA (IGGI). Established in 1967 as a forum for discussion of the socioeconomic conditions in Indonesia and the coordination of foreign economic aid. The **Netherlands** chaired the organization, which also included **Australia**, **Britain**, **France**, **Japan**, the **United States**, Austria, Belgium, Canada, West **Germany**, Italy, New Zealand, Spain, and Switzerland, along with the **World Bank**, the International Monetary Fund, the Asian Development Bank, and the **United Nations** Development Program. In the early years of the **New Order**, the IGGI had great influence on Indonesia's economic policies, emphasizing the rehabilitation of infrastructure, **currency** stabilization, guarantees for **foreign investment**, and limits on the role of the state in the **economy**. The IGGI provided 60 percent of Indonesia's development budget under the first five-year plan. In 1989 Indonesia received US$4 billion in aid via the IGGI, of which $1.4 billion was provided by Japan. An International Non-Governmental Group on Indonesia (INGI, also Inter-NGO Conference on IGGI Matters) was formed in Amsterdam in 1985 to discuss issues raised at the annual IGGI meeting and to marshal alternative information to influence IGGI decision making.

When the Dutch suspended aid to Indonesia in the aftermath of the Dili massacre in **East Timor**, **Suharto** responded by disbanding the IGGI. A new aid group, the **Consultative Group on Indonesia (CGI)**, which was headed by the World Bank, replaced it. The consortium's yearly commitment to supporting Indonesia's economy was some $5 billion by the mid-1990s. *See also* BADAN PERENCANAAN PEMBANGUNAN NASIONAL; RENCANA PEMBANGUNAN LIMA TAHUN. [0295, 0371, 0748, 0896, 1136]

INTERNATIONAL DEBT. *See* DEBT, INTERNATIONAL.

INVESTMENT, FOREIGN. This primarily denotes the employment of foreign capital in productive operations such as plantations and factories. Direct foreign capital investment remained at a low level for much of the colonial period. The colony was opened to European private enterprise in the 1870s under the so-called **Liberal Policy**, but most capital was generated locally by the reinvestment of profits rather than by imports. Only after the **sugar** crisis of 1884 and during the 1890s and 1900s, when many estates contracted debenture loans, did significant capital transfer take place (*see also* ***BATIG SLOT***). Few restrictions, however, were placed on foreign investment in colonial times, partly because the **Netherlands** wished to involve the great powers, especially **Britain** and the **United States**, in the defense of the colony.

During the **Japanese occupation**, existing enterprises were first taken over by the occupation authorities and then parceled out both to government departments in lieu of **taxation** revenue and to Japanese private companies, but there was no significant introduction of capital. At the start of the Indonesian **Revolution**, the Republic issued a Political Manifesto guaranteeing the security of foreign investments, partly to facilitate an agreement with the Dutch and partly to reassure the United States and Britain. The final settlement between the Republic and the Dutch in 1949 provided for protection of foreign investments against **nationalization** and excessive taxation, but many foreign firms, such as the **Koninklijke Paketvaart Maatschappij (KPM)**, found their economic room to maneuver heavily constricted by foreign exchange and **labor** regulations, and began to disinvest. The nationalization of Dutch investments in 1957 further discouraged foreign investment, as did the seizure of some British and American interests in 1963. Under **Guided Democracy**, a number of production-sharing agreements were concluded, especially with Japanese companies, for production of **oil**, **tin**, and timber.

Restoration of a favorable climate for foreign investment was a major part of **New Order** economic policies from 1966 (*see* **BADAN PERENCANAAN PEMBANGUNAN NASIONAL**), and a law on Foreign Investment Capital (*Penanaman Modal Asing*) was passed in January 1967, giving a renewed guarantee against nationalization, a three-year tax holiday, freedom to repatriate profits, full authority to select management, and some exemption from import duties to foreign firms willing to invest in the country. **Japan** became the largest foreign investor, with virtually all its investments in such industries as textiles, machinery, printing, **banking**, transportation, and **automobiles** being in **Java** while its projects in the outer islands centered on such sectors as **agriculture**, **fishing**, **mining**, and logging (*see* **FORESTRY**). **Freeport** from the United States and Inco from Canada soon arrived to mine **copper** in **Papua** and dig nickel in **Sulawesi**. These two firms remained the largest individual investors (other than in the oil and **gas** industry) in 1996.

Total foreign investment had reached a value of US$4.72 billion in 1989, but at that time foreign investment was restricted by more stringent conditions than in some other Asian countries. This changed in March 1992 when the government announced that investors could start up enterprises under their full control, with a few limitations, especially with respect to minimum size. In June 1994 it virtually eliminated the requirement to divest so that foreigners could not only own 100 percent of a company from the start but could also retain 99 percent over time. As a result there was a new influx of foreign investment proposals and approvals.

In the post-**Suharto** period, the situation changed again as the power of labor unions increased, and they succeeded in obtaining better conditions for workers and establishing and raising the minimum wage. In response, foreign corporations began to shift their businesses to other Asian countries with fewer worker protections. The footwear industry was especially hard hit, with such companies as Nike severely cutting back their presence in the country. Reluctance of foreign countries to invest in Indonesia was exacerbated by the growing ethnic and religious violence and by uncertainty over the effect of **decentralization** on foreign operations in Indonesia. This affected in particular the mining industry, with total investment in it falling from US$9.15 billion in 2000 to US$4.13 billion in 2001.

Total foreign investment fell from an approved US$34 billion in 1997 to US$9 billion in 2001 and plunged a further 39 percent in the first eight months of 2002, compared with the same period in 2001, to US$3.5 billion. After the **Bali** bombings of October 2002 the situation deteriorated even further, with Sony, for example, announcing in late November that it would close an audio equipment factory in West Java (reportedly transferring it to **Malaysia**), while Japanese investment was totaling about US$380 million for 2002 (only 7 percent of 1997 levels). One exception was **China**, which began to invest on a large scale in developing the Tanggung gas field in **Papua** and pledged investment of more than US$2 billion, including an accord for construction of a gas line between **Kalimantan** and Java and a projected bridge between Java and Madura. [0409, 0730, 1147]

IRIAN. The word Irian, derived from a Biak phrase meaning "shimmering land," can be used for the whole of the island of New Guinea or, up to 2001, for its western, Indonesian portion, covering the province of **Papua**, formerly Irian Jaya ("Victorious Irian"), the territory of West New Guinea under the Dutch.

IRON. Traditionally imported from **China** and the Ryukyus and mined and locally smelted in West **Sumatra**, West **Kalimantan**, **Bangka**, **Belitung**, and Central **Sulawesi**, iron was used for the manufacture of agricultural and fishing tools, household goods, and **weapons**. Iron exports may have been the basis of the **economy** of **Luwu** in Sulawesi. It was exported from Kalimantan and Sulawesi to **Majapahit** in the 14th century, but from the late 18th century imports from outside the archipelago dominated the market. **Dutch** plans for a steel industry in Central Sulawesi in 1917 were abandoned, though a small-scale industry was established in the Banjarmasin area in the 1920s. *See also* INDUSTRIALIZATION. [0576, 1272]

ISKANDAR MUDA (c. 1581–1636)**.** Iskandar Muda came to power as sultan of **Aceh** in circa 1607 and, like his contemporary **Sultan Agung** on **Java**, launched a campaign of military expansion, using a navy of heavy galleys and an army that included corps of elephants and Persian horses as well as artillery. He briefly conquered **Riau** in 1613 and pushed Acehnese control far down the east and west coasts of **Sumatra**. His only major defeat was the destruction of several hundred ships in an abortive attempt to seize **Melaka** from the **Portuguese** in 1629. Iskandar Muda's military power was based on his success in controlling the **pepper trade**, which he centralized in the capital Kutaraja (now Banda Aceh), but he always had difficulty controlling the hinterland, where his rule was based on an uncertain alliance with regional war leaders or *uleëbalang*. He seems to have kept his courtiers in a state of fear through frequent purges—he had his own son killed—but his court became a center of learning, patronizing for instance the poetry of **Hamzah Fansuri**. The experience of Iskandar Muda's rule, however, led the Acehnese elite after his death to prefer a line of more pliable queens as rulers. [0484]

ISLAM IN INDONESIA. The roots of Islam in Indonesia go back to at least the 11th century, but extensive conversion did not begin until the 14th century when the Sumatran port city of **Pasai** converted, followed by **Melaka** on the **Malay Peninsula** in the 15th century; **Aceh**, **Banten**, and the Java ***Pasisir*** in the 16th century; and **Makassar**, **Minangkabau**, and Central **Java** in the 17th century. The reasons for conversion are complex, varied, and not wholly clear, though trading contacts usually formed an integral part. Muslim authorities stress the missionary element, especially the role of the so-called Nine Walis (**Wali Songo**) on Java (*see also* **CHINESE IN INDONESIA**). Islam first attracted sizeable numbers of Indonesians in the form of Sufism, whose mystical elements fitted easily with the existing blend of **Hinduism**, **Buddhism**, and traditional religion on Java. Political and economic factors, however, also seem to have been important. The fall of the sultanate of Melaka dispersed Muslims to other parts of the archipelago. Especially under threat from the **Portuguese**, rulers found that conversion to Islam brought valuable alliances; there is no evidence of Islamic revolutions from below playing any role in the conversion of states. Several kingdoms, such as **Pontianak**, were founded as Muslim states; in others, such as Aceh and Minangkabau, Muslim hegemony was established or strengthened at various times by civil war. Perhaps more important, Islamic commercial **law** provided a sounder framework for conducting **trade** than did traditional and Hinduistic law, while individual traders found that conversion made them part of an extensive trading diaspora within which they could more easily obtain credit, information, and other facilities; they perhaps also found that it released them from otherwise costly community responsibilities that made capital accumulation difficult. Those who had made the ***haj*** to Mecca were often well placed to use contacts made there to commercial advantage, and in parts of Java the word *haji* became more or less synonymous with "wealthy trader."

The term "Islamic traditionalism" is generally applied to followers of the four traditional schools of Sunni jurisprudence. Although sultans were the protectors of **religion**, religious authority lay with Islamic scholars, called *ulama* and *kyai,* who devoted their lives to studying not just the Qur'an and Hadiths but also the enormous body of supplementary literature, and to teaching in Islamic schools, called ***pesantren*** or *surau.* Indigenous traditional law (***adat***) in many cases became entwined with this corpus of religious and legal doctrine, so that pious Islamic observance was often combined with acceptance of customs not recognized in the Islam of the Middle East, such as the matriliny of the Minangkabau. Within this category are various groups influenced by successive waves of Islamic reformism, especially Wahhabism.

From the early 20th century, Islamic traditionalism was challenged by the rise of Islamic modernism. In religion, modernism asserted the primacy of the Qur'an and Hadiths and the need for direct individual study of these texts. The modernists also emphasized the importance of the community (*ummat*) of believers and discounted the religious authority of the *ulama* and *kyai,* at least as far as it was based on the exhaustive study of other texts. In much Western writing, the term "Islamic modernism" is used primarily for a variety of Islam that shares many features of Western Christian humanism, such as tolerance of religious diversity, compassion for the socially disadvantaged, enthusiasm for democracy and for technological developments, and moral conservatism. Historically, this stream of modernism saw the heavy weight of traditionalist learning as a barrier to the mastery of modern science and the development of a democratic society; its adherents have often been compared to European Christian democrats and are sometimes described as "Islamic socialists." Though apt in the context of the anticolonial struggle, this comparison is somewhat misleading in later periods, since it ignores the commitment by most modernists to the introduction of Islamic law (*syariah*) and by many of them to an **Islamic state** as prescribed by the Qur'an and Hadiths. In general, the Islamic socialists accept the Indonesian Republic as an appropriate framework within which to promote Islam into the foreseeable future. Ever since the achievement of independence, there have been extralegal Muslim organizations arguing for a more rapid transition to an Islamic state to replace the Indonesian Republic, if necessary through armed struggle. The potency of the call became especially marked in the late **Suharto** period, after many Muslim leaders fled repression to **Malaysia** and the Middle East, some of them joining with other radical Islamic movements and being influenced by teachings of prominent scholars in the Middle East.

Formal Muslim organizations date only from the 20th century. The modernist **Muhammadiyah**, founded in 1912, and the traditionalist **Nahdlatul Ulama (NU)**, founded in 1926, are the most important social organizations of Indonesian Islam. Muslim political organizations have been more ephemeral. **Sarekat Islam**, founded in 1909 as an extended traders' cooperative, was for a time the main vehicle for Indonesian **nationalism** but suffered badly from internal division and **Dutch** restriction. The **Masjumi** party during the early **Revolution** was the major Muslim political party, but it was essentially a marriage of convenience among traditionalists and modernists, and the **Partai Sarekat Islam Indonesia (PSII)**, the successor of the Sarekat Islam, never joined it. Soon after independence was achieved, the Nahdlatul Ulama split from it, becoming a party in its own right, and in 1961 **Sukarno** outlawed the Masjum and arrested several leaders.

After allying with Muslim organizations in 1965–1966 in destruction of the Communist Party (**Partai Komunis Indonesia**), Suharto throughout the 1970s and 1980s sought to depoliticize Islam, amalgamating all the Muslim parties within the **Partai Persatuan Pembangunan (PPP)** in 1973. The government also aroused strong opposition from Muslim groups in that year when it unsuccessfully attempted to introduce a **marriage** law that Muslims considered to be contrary to Islamic principles of marriage. Not allowed to assume a Muslim name, and in the 1977 elections being denied its traditional campaign symbol of the ka'bah, the PPP could only in a very limited sense be described as a Muslim party. In 1984 all organizations, including religious bodies, had to adopt the **Pancasila** as their sole foundation. Denied any legal political expression, some Muslims turned to fundamentalism and militancy (*see* **PALEMBANG**; **WHITE PAPER**), while others, associated previously with Masjumi and with the **Persatuan Islam** (Persis), turned to social and educational activities tied particularly to the Dewan Dakwah Islamiyah Indonesia (DDII, Indonesian Islamic Preaching Council), an association established by former Masjumi leaders in 1967 that had contacts with and some funding from Saudi Arabia and other Middle Eastern countries.

From the mid-1980s the government began to court middle-class Muslims, a policy reflected especially in the establishment of **Ikatan Cendekiawan Muslimin Indonesia** (ICMI) as an acceptable mouthpiece for these members of the Muslim community. At the same time the Suharto regime supported religious education, the building of mosques, and the implementation of Islamic law in matters concerning family and marriage.

After Suharto's resignation, in the 1999 **elections** parties were established representing every shade of Islamic teaching. The **Partai Kebangkitan Bangsa (PKB)** and **Partai Amanat Nasional (PAN)**, headed by the two best-known Muslim leaders, **Abdurrachman Wahid** and **Amien Rais**, explicitly appealed to consituencies wider than their Islamic base. They came in third and fifth respectively (Partai Persatuan Pembangunan [PPP] was fourth) in the election behind the nondenominational **Partai Demokrasi Indonesia—Perjuangan (PDI-P)** and **Golkar**. Although PKB head Abdurrachman Wahid held the presidency for the first two years after the elections, in general the splitting of the

Muslim vote among so many parties lessened the potency of Islam as a political force, especially after **Megawati Sukarnoputri** became president in 2001.

In the immediate aftermath of Suharto's fall, religious tensions between Muslims and **Christians** exploded into violence in many parts of the archipelago. Several of these outbreaks were spontaneous, but some were instigated or supported by forces of an organization called the **Lasjkar Jihad**, whose members were often drawn from graduates of modernist Islamic schools. The violence was also allegedly often the work of Jemaah Islamiah (JI, Islamic Community), a militant group set up in Malaysia in the mid-1990s aimed at establishing an Islamic State. On 24 January 2002, under pressure from the **United States**, Indonesian authorities detained and questioned Abu Bakar Ba'asyir (b. 1938), a leading Muslim cleric and follower of **S. M. Kartosuwiryo** and his **Darul Islam** who was alleged to have links to the al Qaeda terrorist group. Principal of the Al Mukmin school in Surakarta (Solo), which he established after graduating from the Gontor school in East Java, Ba'asyir was and is a proponent of an Islamic state. He had been jailed by Suharto in the 1980s and had then fled to Malaysia, returning to Indonesia in 2000. **Singapore** and Malaysia believed him to be a leader of JI, and Singapore handed over evidence suggesting the existence of JI operational cells in Indonesia.

In September 2002 Singapore authorities arrested 21 men accused of involvement in JI, but it was only after the October **Bali** bombings that the Indonesian government moved against suspected members of the organization, issuing an emergency decree granting legal authority to deal with terrorist suspects and again detaining Ba'asyir and other prominent figures. Ba'asyir was brought to trial in April 2003 on charges of plotting to topple Indonesia's legitimate government. He was acquitted in September of terrorist charges though sentenced to four years in jail for sedition. The sentence was later reduced to three years for immigration offenses. The government also arrested a number of JI members believed to be responsible for the Bali attacks. Imam Samudra, Amrozi, and ali Ghufron (Muklas) were sentenced to death, and Ali Imron to life imprisonment. In August, the alleged head of JI, Riduan Isamuddin (Hambali), was arrested in Thailand. *See also* ARAB WORLD, HISTORICAL LINKS WITH; *KEBATINAN*. [0004, 0039, 0577, 0627, 0791, 0983, 1016–1040, 1052, 1207, 1326, 1328–1329, 1336–1339, 1342–1344, 1346–1352, 1354–1356, 1358, 1359, 1361–1363, 1366, 1373–1375]

ISLAMIC LAW. *See* LAW, ISLAMIC.

ISLAMIC STATE, DEMANDS FOR. The creation of an Islamic state, which will administer and enforce Islamic **law** (*syariah*), is one of the central political demands of **Islam**. This demand was satisfied in many parts of precolonial Indonesia by sultanates, states in which the sultan acted as protector of Islam and appointed officials to enforce Islamic law. The extent to which Islamic law was actually enforced varied considerably from place to place, but the imposition of colonial rule was a major step backward in Muslim eyes from the ideal state of affairs. A number of anticolonial revolts attempted to restore Islamic rule by (re)establishing sultanates, but especially in the 20th century many Muslims were reluctant to return to this autocratic form and proposed instead an Indonesian Islamic state, probably in the form of a republic.

Closer definition of what a modern Islamic state might mean was hampered by division within the Islamic community over such matters as the proper role of Islamic scholars and by the fact that Indonesia, wherever its borders might be drawn, was bound to contain substantial non-Muslim minorities as well as Muslims to whom Islamic law was uncongenial. An Islamic state, therefore, was never part of the platform of the **nationalist** movement, and arguments for an Islamic state were rejected during the drafting of the 1945 **Constitution** by the **Badan Penyelidik Usaha Persiapan Kemerdekaan Indonesia (BPUPKI)** on grounds that this would discriminate against non-Muslim minorities. A compromise requiring Muslims alone to follow Islamic law (the Jakarta Charter, Piagam Jakarta) was agreed on for the preamble but omitted from the final version. After **Sukarno** in 1953 publicly rejected the possibility of an Islamic state, the Islamic case was argued again in the 1957–1959 **Constituent Assembly** but foundered once more on the problem of the non-Muslim minorities, though the reluctance of ***abangan*** Muslims was probably a more important barrier. The **New Order** argued that the **Constitution**'s recognition of both religion and "belief" precludes a religious state. Since 1948 several groups have pursued an Islamic state by armed means, notably the **Darul Islam** and the **Komando Jihad**, and after the fall of **Suharto** the Jemaah Islamiyah (JI, Islamic Community). The JI is allegedly a network of Islamic radical groups, set up in **Malaysia** in January of 1993 largely by Indonesian Muslims who had fled Suharto's repression. It is reportedly willing to employ violent means to establish an Islamic state embracing not only Indonesia but also Malaysia, the **Philippines**, and Islamic regions of southern **Thailand**.

In the post-Suharto period, increasing numbers of Muslims espoused introduction of an Islamic state, or at least of Islamic law. Groups ranged from the illegal Jemaah Islamiyah to the Majelis Mujahidin Indonesia (MMI), a group founded in August 2000 by Abu Bakar Ba'asyir, but most of whose leadership consisted of moderate Muslim intellectuals working for the introduction of Islamic law through parliamentary means. A 2001 survey by *Tempo* magazine found that 58 percent of respondents supported establishment of an Islamic state.

In 2002 it became clear that several of Indonesia's autonomous provincial and district governments were attempting to skirt the Constitution and introduce Islamic law into their areas. In addition to **Aceh**, which is the only place where the government has legally permitted *syariah* law, other provinces considering its introduction are South **Sulawesi**, Garut, Tasikmalaya in West Java, **Banten** province, West **Sumatra**, and Central **Kalimantan**. In August 2002 the **Majelis Permusyawaratan Rakyat (MPR)** rejected a constitutional amendment put forward by the **Partai Persatuan Pembangunan (PPP)** and other smaller Islamic parties that would have allowed imposition of *syariah* for all Indonesian Muslims. In early 2003, a poll in *Tempo* magazine found that 71 percent of Indonesians now supported the imposition of *syariah* law. *See also KEBATINAN*; PANCASILA. [0693, 1031, 1039, 1329, 1333]

– J –

JAKARTA. Known until 1943 as **Batavia**, Jakarta became Indonesia's capital with the declaration of **independence** in 1945. British forces occupied the city in October 1945, and most Republican offices shifted to **Yogyakarta**, but until July 1947 local administration was shared uneasily by a Republican city hall (Balai Agung) and a **Dutch** municipal administration. With the signing of the **Renville Agreement**, Jakarta ceased formally to be the Republic's capital but was given special status by the Dutch as future capital of the projected federal republic. The special federal territory of Jakarta was abolished along with **federalism**, and in the mid-1950s many proposals were made to shift the capital elsewhere, partly for climatic reasons, partly because of resentment over **corruption** and government expenditure in the city; in a celebrated article, **Takdir Alisyahbana** described the city as a leech on the country's head. In 1957, however, these proposals were abandoned and the expanded city was given a status equivalent to **province** as the Daerah Khusus Ibukota (DKI, Special Capital Territory). A master plan for urban development was accepted in 1967 and from 1977 expanded to encompass the so-called Jabotek (Jakarta–Bogor–Tanggerang–Bekasi) region, extending beyond the boundaries of the DKI.

The city's southward expansion, begun in colonial times, has continued. In 1948 Kebayoran Baru was created in the southwest as an elite residential suburb, and new elite areas have since developed still further south. Ringroads and a freeway to **Bogor**, the so-called Jagorawi highway, have been built. In recent years penetration of seawater into the water table for several kilometers inland has made coastal areas less livable, though it is precisely in these areas that the greatest number of *kampung* are found. All parts of the city are subject to periodic flooding during the rainy season, and in February to March 2002 floods displaced about 380,000 Jakarta residents.

Food shortages reduced Jakarta's **population** during the **Japanese occupation**, but since 1945 the population has increased steadily as people seek work in the growing service and administrative sectors. The city was closed to further immigration in 1970. In 1989 the population was officially estimated at 7 million, and the 2000 **census** recorded a population of 8,389,443. Successive governments have been keen to make the city a showcase of Indonesian development. **Sukarno** installed numerous monuments, especially the National Monument (Monas) in Medan Merdeka. **Ali Sadikin**, who became governor in 1966, promoted the development of the Jalan Sudirman artery while his successors attempted to shift *kampung* residents to the fringes of the city by razing the *kampung,* repossessing **land**, and restricting a number of economic activities followed by the poor such as street selling and ***becak*** riding.

Under the **New Order**, Jakarta was a center of political dissent, erupting into violence in the **Malari** riots of 1974 and the Tanjung Priok affair in 1984 (*see* **WHITE PAPER**), and registering strong votes for the **Partai Persatuan Pembangunan (PPP)**, especially in 1977. **Student** demonstrations in the capital in early 1998 and their occupation of the parliament building were a major factor in **Suharto**'s forced resignation in May of that year. [0585, 0660, 0913]

JAKARTA CHARTER (Piagam Jakarta)**.** *See* ISLAMIC STATE, DEMANDS FOR.

JAMBI. Along with **Srivijaya**, Jambi emerged as a minor trading and raiding state on the Strait of **Melaka** in the fifth century and after (*see* **PIRACY**). It became subordinate to Srivijaya in 683, but after the fall of

Srivijaya in the early 11th century, Jambi briefly rose to replace it as the dominant power on the strait. It was never able to establish the same degree of hegemony and was raided in circa 1275 by King Kertanegara of **Singasari**, thereafter remaining under Javanese suzerainty until it was incorporated into the **Minangkabau** kingdom of Adityavarman, though it was later also subject to **Palembang**.

In the 17th century, an independent sultanate rose once again, based on the **pepper trade**, over which it fought a protracted war with Riau-Johor (*see* **RIAU**). Sultan Muhammad Fahruddin recognized **Dutch** sovereignty in 1834, but the rebellion of a later sultan, Ratu Taha Saifuddin, lasted until 1904. The post of sultan was left empty after 1901. From the late 19th century Jambi became an important area of Dutch **rubber** estates, and it is today Indonesia's largest rubber producer. [0439, 0543, 0546, 0547, 0550, 0840]

JAPAN, HISTORICAL LINKS WITH. Although Austronesian languages may have contributed slightly to the vocabulary of modern Japanese and although some Japanese musical traditions, especially the drum **music** of the south, may owe something to the traditions that led to ***gamelan***, early historical contact between Indonesia and Japan was infrequent. Japanese ships did call at Jayakarta (**Batavia**) Nagasaki was one of the trading posts of the **Dutch East Indies Company (VOC)**, and from 1612 Japanese served as soldiers and occasionally officials of the company in Southeast Asia. After Japan closed its doors in 1640, the small Japanese communities abroad soon assimilated with local populations.

Contact resumed with the opening of Japan in 1854. Japan was first known for providing prostitutes for the region, but its rapid **industrialization** quickly made it a model to which burgeoning Asian **nationalist** movements looked, especially after its victory in the Russo-Japanese War (1904). The assimilation of Japanese to European status (*see* **RACE**) under the "Japannerwet" of 1899 also provided a model. Japanese immigration to the Indies increased markedly in the early 1900s, especially in the **Outer Islands**, and Japanese capital began to flow in, often through Chinese banks. From circa 1914 Japanese **trade** with the archipelago expanded rapidly, Japan providing cheap manufactured articles and **cloth** and receiving **oil** and **sugar** from the Indies. Between 1913 and 1932 Japan's share of Indies imports rose from 1 percent to 32 percent (though it took only 5 percent of Indies exports). In 1933 the so-called Crisis Act provided for discriminatory tariffs against imports from Japan. Several Japanese political leaders had interests in companies trading in the region, and from the 1930s Japanese **shipping** carried a major part of the cargoes in eastern Indonesia. Japanese firms were involved in fishing and **silk** industries in **Minahasa** in the 20th century.

In July 1941, with the consolidation of Japanese power in **China**, the Netherlands Indies followed the **United States** in banning exports of oil, **tin**, **rubber**, and other strategic materials to Japan. Japan had previously tried to pressure the colonial government to guarantee these supplies by threatening to "liberate" the colony. The Netherlands declared war on Japan on 8 December 1941, after Pearl Harbor, and Japanese forces began landing in Borneo in January 1942. The fall of the British naval base in **Singapore** and the Allied defeat in the battle of the **Java Sea** was followed by Japanese landings on **Sumatra** in February 1942 and on **Java** the following month. Dutch forces on Java surrendered on 8 March and on Sumatra on 27 March. *See also* JAPANESE OCCUPATION OF INDONESIA. [0594, 0637, 0638, 0774]

JAPAN, RELATIONS WITH. Japan's attitude to the Indonesian declaration of **independence** on 17 August 1945 was ambiguous. The declaration took place with the active cooperation of a Japanese admiral, Tadashi Maeda, and many in the military were both more sympathetic to Indonesian **nationalism** than to the Allies and afraid of a popular uprising if they suppressed the Republic. They were required, on the other hand, by the terms of the surrender to maintain the political status quo, and they attempted thus a middle way, neither assisting the Republic nor suppressing it, though some local commanders handed over **weapons** to Republican armed units (*see also* **PEMBELA TANAH AIR**).

Formal diplomatic relations between Indonesia and Japan, however, were not established until 1957, following exhaustive discussions over Japan's reparations debt to Indonesia, which was finally agreed at US$223 million, plus $400 million in aid and cancellation of a $177 million trade **debt**. An expansion in Japanese **investment** followed, especially resource exploitation (**oil**, the **Asahan** aluminum project, **rubber**, and later **forestry** and **fisheries**) and textiles. Japan maintained relatively good ties with Indonesia during **Guided Democracy**, providing credits of $49 million in 1963–1965. In return, Japan received 46 percent of Indonesia's total oil exports between 1960 and 1970.

Resentment over Japanese economic power was among the factors leading to the **Malari (Malapetaka 15 Januari)** Affair in 1974. Japan subsequently expanded its foreign aid to Indonesia, especially through the **Inter-Governmental Group on Indonesia (IGGI)**, becoming the largest single donor in 1989, with $1.4 billion. Japan's economic power, however, continued to cause friction. In 1987 Indonesia began a protracted dispute with Japan over the allocation of production from the Asahan aluminum refinery. Nevertheless, in the early 1990s Japan was the destination of more than 50 percent of Indonesia's exports and the single largest foreign investor and most important donor of development assistance to Indonesia. After the financial collapse of the late 1990s, Japan's leadership role in Southeast Asia's economies declined drastically, though it remained the top aid donor to the **Association of Southeast Asian Nations (ASEAN)** and the largest donor to Indonesia in the **Consultative Group on Indonesia (CGI)**. [0446, 0736, 0846, 1131, 1137, 1147]

JAPANESE OCCUPATION OF INDONESIA. Under Japanese rule (1942–1945), Indonesia was divided administratively, **Java** coming under the 16th Army, **Sumatra** and the **Malay Peninsula** initially under the 25th Army, and **Kalimantan** and eastern Indonesia under the 2nd southern squadron of the Japanese navy (Kaigun). In 1943 New Guinea (**Papua**) was separated and placed under the 4th southern squadron, and Malaya was separated from Sumatra and placed under the 29th army.

The Japanese authorities began by restricting the **nationalist** movement to a greater extent than the **Dutch**. All political parties were banned, tertiary educational institutions were closed, and the **Kenpeitai** closely monitored political activity. On Java the military administration (Gunseikanbu) allowed Indonesians to participate only in Japanese-sponsored mass organizations (**Tiga A Movement**, **PUTERA**, and **Jawa Hokokai**), whose main aim was to mobilize support for the war effort. The occupation also dislocated the **economy**. Cut off from their traditional markets in the West, the plantations of Java and Sumatra were forced to close or to change crops; machines, equipment, and wealth were shipped to Japan; and Indonesian laborers (***romusha***) were recruited, often with coercion, for work on defense projects in Indonesia and elsewhere in the Japanese empire, where they were treated harshly and fell victim to disease and malnutrition. In the final year of the war, Allied submarine raids in the South China Sea prevented virtually all import of manufactured goods from Japan, leaving the country desperately short of **cloth**, medicines, and the like.

Japanese rule, however, prepared Indonesia for independence in a number of ways. The Japanese victory shattered the prestige of **Dutch** colonial rule and irreparably damaged the administrative capacity of the colonial state. Indonesians, moreover, were appointed to higher administrative positions during the occupation than they had ever held under the Dutch. The military training of Indonesians in the **Heiho**, **Pembela Tanah Air (Peta)**, and **Giyugun** provided a core of experience valuable in the later war of independence. And the prominence of **Sukarno** and **Mohammad Hatta** within the PUTERA and Jawa Hokokai helped to confirm their political preeminence in the postwar period.

Japan's long-term political intentions for Indonesia were not clear. There is evidence that they intended to incorporate Sumatra and East Indonesia into the Japanese empire, while Java, with less economic and strategic importance, might well ultimately have been granted autonomy. On 7 September 1944, however, with Japan's deteriorating military situation, the Japanese Prime Minister Kuniaki Koiso announced vague plans for granting independence to an Indonesian state embracing the whole of the former Netherlands East Indies. The 25th Army on Sumatra objected to the island being included in these plans until the final weeks of the occupation, when it allowed representatives to be included on a Committee to Prepare for Indonesian Independence (**Panitia Persiapan Kemerdekaan Indonesia, PPKI**), which was established on 7 August 1945, succeeding the **Badan Penyelidik Usaha Persiapan Kemerdekaan (BPUPKI)** set up the previous March. Nothing had been done to implement the independence plans when Japan surrendered on 15 August. *See also* JAPAN, RELATIONS WITH; SUCCESSION. [0644, 0653, 0657, 0659, 0661, 0663, 0667, 0670, 0671. 0675, 0677, 0680, 0846]

JASSIN, HANS BAGUË (1917–2000)**.** Critic, essayist, and editor with the **Balai Pustaka** and *Poedjangga Baru* and of many postwar literary and cultural magazines. He played a major role in placing figures such as **Chairil Anwar** in the canon of national literature, and he established an important documentation center for Indonesian literature. He strongly opposed the **Lembaga Kebudayaan Rakyat (Lekra)**'s emphasis on the social engagement of writers and **artists** and in 1963 signed the **Manifes Kebudayaan**. *See also* GENERATIONS. [0234]

JAVA (Jawa)**.** The most densely populated of the major Indonesian islands, and politically and economically central to the archipelago since the 13th century. For statistical purposes it is generally combined with **Madura**, but historically it is useful to distinguish from the Javanese lands of the central and eastern part of the island, not just Madura but also the Sundanese regions of West Java (*see* **SUNDA**).

The epigraphic evidence is meager, but it appears that **Hindu** and **Buddhist** states began to emerge in Central Java in the eighth century. The earliest of these to achieve any prominence were the Buddhist kingdom of the **Sailendras** and the Hindu kingdom of **Mataram** under King Sanjaya and his successors. The former was responsible for the construction of the **Borobudur** and Mendut temples, the latter for **Prambanan** and Candi Sewu. The precise sequence of and relationship between these kingdoms is unclear. In the 10th century, for reasons also unclear, the center of Javanese power moved to the valley of the Brantas River in East Java, which became the base of a succession of major Hindu kingdoms: Janggala (11th century), **Kediri** (c. 1059–1222), **Singasari** (1222–1292), and **Majapahit** (1294–c. 1527).

Trade with other parts of the archipelago and beyond grew in this period, strengthening the position of the port towns on the north coast (*see* ***PASISIR***), which converted to **Islam** between the 14th and 16th centuries. In circa 1527 Muslim armies led by the sultanate of **Demak** defeated Majapahit, leading to a period of disorder in the interior. A state called **Pajang** briefly emerged but was displaced in the 1570s by a second, Muslim, state of **Mataram** in central Java. The **Dutch East Indies Company (VOC)** established itself in the coastal regions in the early 17th century and began military intervention in Mataram's affairs in the late 17th century, finally breaking the power of the sultanate with the treaty of **Giyanti** in 1755, which partitioned it between the successor courts of **Surakarta** (Solo) and **Yogyakarta**.

Approaching its eventual bankruptcy, the VOC did little to change the social or economic order in Java, but in the early 19th century the Napoleonic-Dutch rule of **Herman Willem Daendels** from 1808 to 1811, a British interregnum under **Thomas Stamford Raffles** from 1811 to 1816, and Dutch rule under the Crown from 1816 saw increasing intervention in the island. The **Java War** of 1825–1830 was the last major attempt by the old aristocracy to assert its power on the island, and under the **Cultivation System** Javanese felt the full force of **Dutch** colonialism, though scholars have still not agreed on its effects. From 1870, with the onset of the **Liberal Policy**, Java ceased to be the main producer of Indies wealth for the Dutch; **population** increased, and the share of the **Outer Islands** in export production expanded. The **Ethical Policy**, introduced in 1901, was in part an attempt to deal with the increasing social problems on the island. **Nationalism** began to emerge on Java first in the form of organizations for cultural preservation and renewal, but soon took a political dimension. Many leaders of the movement came from outside Java, but it was the nationalist influence on the Javanese masses that most worried the colonial authorities. By 1930, 70 percent of the population of the Netherlands Indies lived on Java.

Java-Madura was administratively separated from the rest of the archipelago at the start of the **Japanese occupation** in 1942, and as the war progressed it became increasingly isolated economically. With both exports and imports severely hampered, the people of the island suffered greatly.

During the national **Revolution**, Java formed, with **Sumatra**, the heartland of the Indonesian Republic and although the Dutch had occupied the entire island by the end of 1948, widespread guerrilla resistance made their position untenable. From the 1950s Java became even more the center of politics, and fears of Javanization were among the factors leading to regional rebellions such as the **PRRI/Permesta rebellion**, though part of Outer Island hostility was reserved for the non-Javanese capital, **Jakarta**. Despite efforts by the Dutch and postindependence governments through **transmigration** programs, Java still constituted around 59 percent of Indonesia's total population in 2000. [0345, 0524, 0532, 0557, 0575, 1228, 1239]

JAVA BANK. *See* BANKING.

JAVA MAN. A skull cap and wisdom tooth about 500,000 years old, found in Trinil (East Java) by Eugène Dubois in 1891, has been identified as that of *Pithecanthropus* (now *Homo*) *erectus*. This was the first human fossil find outside Europe, and it led to speculation that **Java** had been the "Garden of Eden." It is now believed, however, that humans (*H. erectus*) arrived a million years ago or earlier, thus predating Peking Man. These early inhabitants appear to have been displaced by later **migrations**. *See also* PREHISTORY.

JAVA SEA, BATTLE OF THE. On 27–28 February 1942, a Japanese fleet under T. Takagi defeated an Allied fleet under Karel Doorman in the Java Sea. Although numerically about equal to the Allies, the Japanese were superior in air power and sank all but a few of the Allied vessels either in the battle or soon after. The defeat left **Java** open to the landing of Japanese land forces. *See also* JAPANESE OCCUPATION; NAVY. [0659]

JAVA WAR (1825–1830)**.** A major uprising against **Dutch** domination of central **Java**, led by Pangeran **Diponegoro** and drawing together several strands of discontent in the central Javanese kingdoms of **Yogyakarta** and **Surakarta**. Increasing **taxation** and harvest failures in the early 1820s had unsettled the peasants, while both Islamic leaders and younger members of the Yogyakarta aristocracy were disturbed by the rise of Dutch power and what was seen as the moral decay of the courts. Javanese messianic expectations focused on Diponegoro as a potential *ratu adil* (just prince) who would establish an era of justice and prosperity. Although the widespread uprising was only loosely coordinated by Diponegoro, it was able to shake Dutch power in the region until Diponegoro's defeat at Gowok near Surakarta in October 1826. Thereafter Dutch counterguerrilla strategies of dividing the Javanese forces and keeping them short of food wore the rebels down. Disunity arose between Diponegoro and his main religious adviser Kyai Maja, and in 1827 Diponegoro's nephew and chief lieutenant Sentot deserted. Diponegoro's capture at Magelang in 1830 ended the war, in which perhaps 250,000 Javanese died. *See also* JOYOBOYO. [0597]

JAVANESE ABROAD. *See* AFRICA, HISTORICAL LINKS WITH; SURINAM, JAVANESE IN.

JAVANESE LANGUAGE. Although numerically spoken by the largest number of Indonesians, Javanese became neither a lingua franca nor the national **language**. This was partly because the grammatical complexity and distinct script of Javanese led the **Dutch** to choose Malay as their language of administration, and it was partly because other ethnic groups (and a good many Javanese) rejected it as feudal in structure. In common with many languages, Javanese speech varies according to the respective ranks of the speaker and the addressee, thus, in the view of many, preserving social inequalities. In 1917 an organization called Djawa Dipa was founded in **Surabaya** with the aim of abolishing high (*kromo*) Javanese and making low (*ngoko*) Javanese standard. *See also* INDONESIAN LANGUAGE; JAVANIZATION; LANGUAGES; TJIPTO MANGOENKOESOEMO. [0272, 0269, 0270, 0283, 0287]

JAWA HOKOKAI (Java Service Association)**.** The association was founded in January 1944 to mobilize the Javanese population (over 14 years of age) for the **Japanese** war effort. **Sukarno** and Hasyim Asyari were senior advisors, **Mohammad Hatta** and Mas Mansur managers. The organization was run at each level by regional Indonesian officials and thus provided a means of government control outside the normal channels. The structure of the Hokokai was repeated to some extent in the PNI-Staatspartij and in **Golkar**. *See also* BARISAN PELOPOR. [0644, 0649, 0661]

JEMAAH ISLAMIYAH (JI, Islamic Community). *See* ISLAMIC STATE; ISLAM IN INDONESIA.

JOURNALISM. *See* NEWSPAPERS.

JOYOBOYO (r. 1137–1157). Ruler of **Kediri**, chiefly remembered for his prophecies of **Java**'s future, which foretold alternating periods of prosperity (*jaman raharja*) and suffering (*jaman edan*). After a period of unprecedented suffering, he foretold, this cycle would be broken by the appearance of a just prince (*Ratu Adil*) who would found a golden age of prosperity and justice. New versions of the prophecies have appeared regularly, often as part of growing peasant discontent with colonial rule. The most celebrated version was that current during the **Japanese occupation**, which asserted that the Javanese would be ruled by white men for three centuries and by yellow dwarves for the lifetime of a maize plant, prior to the achievement of a golden age. *See also* JAVA WAR; *SAMA RASA SAMA RATA*. [0159, 0597]

JOYOHADIKUSUMO, SUMITRO. *See* SUMITRO DJOJOHADIKUSUMO.

JUANDA KARTAWIJAYA (1911–1963). A Sundanese Muslim, Juanda graduated with an engineering degree from the Bandung Technical School in 1933. Though never linked to a political party, he served in many Republican cabinets after 1945 in economic portfolios and in 1957 was appointed by **Sukarno** as nonparty prime minister following the inability of the parties to form a government. In 1959 Sukarno appointed himself prime minister but retained Juanda as first minister with much the same duties as before. Juanda's death in office in 1963 contributed to the absence of an economic policy in the later years of **Guided Democracy**. [0696, 0706]

JUDAISM. In contrast to **India** and **China**, Indonesia never became the home of large, settled, partly acculturated Jewish communities. Jews entered the archipelago as part either of the European colonial elite or of the general Middle Eastern trading diaspora (*see* **ARABS IN INDONE-**

SIA). The Jewish community in **Surabaya** maintains a synagogue. President **Abdurrachman Wahid**, who had visited Israel in 1994, argued in favor of opening diplomatic relations with Israel and attempted to enter into commercial and cultural relations with the Jewish state. The uproar of protest compelled him to postpone and probably cancel the plan. *See also* ARAB WORLD, HISTORICAL LINKS WITH. [1050, 1367]

JUNGHUHN, FRANZ WILHELM (1809–1864)**.** German-born scientist, responsible for the first detailed geographical survey of **Java**'s interior. He measured and climbed most of Java's peaks and studied the pattern of vegetation changes with altitude. He was the first scientist to warn against the ecological consequences of deforestation, and he suggested a ban on forest clearing above 1,500 meters. He also published a major study of the **Bataks** in **Sumatra**. *See also* CINCHONA; ENVIRONMENTAL PROTECTION.

– K –

KAHAR MUZAKKAR (also spelled Qahhar Mudzakkar) (1921–1965)**.** Born in **Luwu**, he was educated in **Muhammadiyah** schools in **Sulawesi** and **Surakarta** (Solo). He returned to Luwu in 1941 to teach in a Muhammadiyah school until banished by the local council in 1943, when he went into business in **Makassar**, then in Surakarta. He led a force of South Sulawesi emigrés in **Java** during the national **Revolution** and returned to South Sulawesi in April 1950. Though strongly opposed to the **Negara Indonesia Timur (NIT)**, he resented its abrupt dismantling by central government forces, which, he said, acted like an army of occupation. In August 1951 he launched a rebellion against the central government and affiliated his movement broadly with **S. M. Kartosuwiryo** and his **Darul Islam (DI)** in August 1952. In 1953 he proclaimed Sulawesi to be part of the Negara Republik Indonesia Islam (NRII, Indonesian Islamic Republic) and attempted to establish Islamic rule in the region, limiting private property, establishing schools and hospitals, and banning titles, lipstick, and jewelry. Kahar controlled much of the hinterland of Makassar until the early 1960s. He was finally shot by government forces in 1965. His defense minister, Sanusi Daris, reappeared in the mid-1980s as a link between South Sulawesi radicals and Abu Bakar Ba'asyir's group in Java. *See* ISLAM IN INDONESIA. [0695, 0699, 1031]

KAHARINGAN. *See* DAYAKS.

KAKAWIN. Classic Javanese poetic form, mostly long and divided into four-line verses with a fixed number of letter groups per line.

KALIMANTAN. Used to denote both the island of Borneo and, as here, its southern, Indonesian portion, approximately 73 percent of its area, with a population of about 11.3 million in 2000. Most Indonesians believe the name signifies Kali Intan, "River of Diamonds," (*kali intan,* i.e., the Barito in southeast Kalimantan), though it probably derives from "land of raw **sago**" (*lamanta)*. Kalimantan has no active volcanoes, and its topography is dominated by a low central mountain spine running roughly northeast-southwest from which a number of rivers—the Kapuas, Sambas, Barito, and Mahakam—flow, often through swampy coastal plains, to the sea. Most of the island is below 200 meters in elevation. The dozens of indigenous ethnic groups, the most numerous of them generally called Iban or **Dayaks**, were pushed from the coastal regions in early times by Malay peoples, who established a series of small states such as **Kutai** at or near the mouths of rivers. These states, most notably **Pontianak** and **Banjarmasin**, provided reprovisioning facilities for interregional **trade**, acted as outlets for produce from the interior (**rattan**, dragon's blood, birds' nests, **gold**, and resins), and generally engaged in **piracy**, as did states on the Strait of Melaka (*see* **SRIVIJAYA**). Usually, however, they remained subordinate to one or the other dominant regional power (Srivijaya, **Kediri**, **Majapahit**, **Melaka**, **Banten**). The coastal states converted to **Islam** around the 16th century. During the 18th century there was extensive settlement by **Bugis** from southern **Sulawesi** in coastal regions.

Through **Banten**, the **Dutch** inherited a nominal interest in western Kalimantan and put trading posts at Sambas and **Sukadana** in the early 17th century. These, however, were soon evacuated. In the late 18th and early 19th century the Dutch established greater control in **Pontianak**, Sambas, and Mempawah to forestall possible British annexation and to restrict what they saw as piracy. From 1790 to 1820 large numbers of **Chinese** came to gold fields between the Kapuas and Sambas Rivers, where some later settled as farmers (*see also* **KONGSI WARS**). Dutch control in Banjarmasin was not established until the 19th century. From 1938 the Dutch portion of the island was ruled as a *gouvernement* (*see* **DECENTRALIZATION**). **Oil**, discovered on the east coast in the late 19th century, transformed that region economically, making it a major target of the **Japanese** invasion in 1942. The Dutch divided Kalimantan into two residencies: (1) South and East Borneo and (2) West Borneo (*Westerafdeeling*). During the national **Revolution**, they briefly toyed with the idea of creating a federal state of Borneo on the island, but eventually declared a number of smaller states (*see* **FEDERALISM**). The island became a single **province** at the time of independence, but in 1957 it was divided again, this time into three provinces: South, East, and Central Kalimantan.

During Indonesia's **Confrontation** with **Malaysia**, Indonesian troops fought British Commonwealth forces along the border with Sarawak. After 1965 the **Partai Komunis Indonesia (PKI)** briefly organized guerrilla resistance in West Kalimantan. Many local Chinese communities, suspected of involvement with the rebels, were expelled by the government. After 1967 East Kalimantan became a major logging region (*see* **FORESTRY**) and the island has been an important **transmigration** settlement site, with immigrants arriving from **Java** and **Madura** during the 1970s and 1980s, while large numbers of Bugis **pepper** farmers came to East Kalimantan from the 1960s on. Widespread deforestation and the **oil palm** plantations that replaced much of the native forests were among the reasons contributing to the enormous fires that destroyed about 3.2 million hectares (ha) of forest areas of East Kalimantan in 1982–1983 and swept through much of the island in 1997. Following the 1997 fires, Dayak tribesmen in West Kalimantan began attacking Madurese settlements, reasserting their claim to their ancestral lands. About 450 Madurese were killed, and thousands fled. Attacks against the Madurese by both Malays and Dayaks followed the fall of **Suharto**, with most of the Madurese migrants fleeing Kalimantan and seeking asylum in **Sulawesi** and Madura. Under the decentralization law of 2001, Kalimantan was divided into four provinces: West, South, Central, and East Kalimantan. [0118, 0264, 0329, 0788, 0795, 0805, 0811, 0812, 1048, 1058, 1158, 1378]

"KAN-T'O-LI." Chinese transcription of the name of an otherwise unknown kingdom on the southeastern coast of **Sumatra**. It sent tribute to **China** from 441 and traded with China, **India**, and other parts of the archipelago. It was superseded by **Srivijaya** in the late seventh century. *See also* "HO-LO-TAN." [0542, 0543]

KARTASURA. *See* MATARAM.

KARTINI, RADEN AJENG (1879–1904). Javanese feminist writer and activist, she was the daughter of a progressive ***bupati***. She received some

Western education but at puberty was secluded in preparation for **marriage**. Nevertheless she opened a school in her father's residence at Japara in 1903 and, after marrying in November of that year, maintained the school in her husband's residence at Rembang. She died in childbirth in 1904. She is known largely for her memorandum to the colonial government, "Educate the Javanese!" (1903), and her letters, published posthumously as *Door duisternis tot licht: gedachten over en voor het Javaanse volk* (From Darkness to Light, Thoughts about and on Behalf of the Javanese People, 1911), edited by J. H. Abendanon and with a foreword by **Louis Couperus**, and in English translation as *Letters of a Javanese Princess* (1964). Her correspondence is important for its assertion of **women**'s right to **education** and freedom from polygamy and child marriage. Royalties from the publication of her letters in the Netherlands helped to found a number of "Kartini schools" giving education to girls. [0876, 0885, 1277, 1287]

KARTOSUWIRYO, SEKARMAJI MARIJAN (1905–1962)**.** Foster son of **Haji Umar Said Tjokroaminoto** (**Cokroaminoto**) and activist in the **Partai Sarekat Islam Indonesia (PSII)** until his expulsion in 1939 over policy differences. In 1940 he established a school, the Suffah Institute, in Garut (West **Java**) to give religious and general **education** to young Muslims; this was closed by the **Japanese** in 1942, but Kartosuwiryo used contacts made then to form a branch of the **Hizbullah** in 1945. He joined **Masjumi** but felt betrayed by the party's agreement to implement the **Renville Agreement** and by the **Siliwangi** Division's abandonment of West Java in early 1948. He established the Islamic Army of Indonesia (Tentara Islam Indonesia, TII) and in May of 1948 an Islamic administration in the Garut region with the name **Darul Islam (DI)** and with himself as *imam,* or religious leader. On 7 August 1949 he officially proclaimed an **Islamic State** of Indonesia (Negara Islam Indonesia, NII), which fought the Republic of Indonesia. He remained the central figure in the West Java DI until he was captured by government forces in April 1962 and executed in September. He is one of the inspirations for Abu Bakar Ba'asyir and others involved in radical Islamic activities in the early 2000s. [0693]

KARYAWAN (from *karya,* task, and *-wan,* person)**.** A term coined in the 1960s to describe all employees of a firm or office, including management. It was used as an alternative to the word *buruh* (worker, laborer) to avoid the implication that workers might have interests separate from those of management. *See also* LABOR; LABOR UNIONS. [0430]

KEBATINAN (also called *kejawen, agama Jawa,* or "Javanism"). Javanese mysticism, incorporating animist, **Hindu-Buddhist**, and Islamic (especially Sufi) mystical elements but often denying adherence to **Islam**. Officially legitimized by Article 29 of the 1945 **Constitution**, which distinguishes and acknowledges both **religion** (*agama*) and belief (*kepercayaan*), it is organized in hundreds of separate associations (e.g., **Paguyuban Ngèsti Tunggal** [**Pangestu**]) and is administered by the Ministry of Education and Culture rather than by Religious Affairs. President **Suharto** was personally associated with *kebatinan,* although during the last decade of his rule he stressed more publicly his Islamic beliefs. *See also ABANGAN*; ISLAMIC STATE, DEMANDS FOR. [1242, 1357, 1368]

KEDIRI. Kingdom in East **Java** created by the decision of **Airlangga** in the mid-11th century to divide his kingdom. Kediri sponsored a major flowering of Javanese culture but was overthrown by **Ken Angrok**, founder of **Singasari** in 1221–1222. *See also* JOYOBOYO.

KEIBODAN. Civil guard formed on **Java** during the **Japanese occupation** to undertake routine security tasks such as evening village patrols. Though Keibodan units were generally armed only with bamboo stakes, the quasi-military experience they provided laid a basis in parts of Java for the formation of **badan perjuangan** during the **Revolution**. [0661, 0663]

KEJAWEN. *See KEBATINAN.*

KEMPEITAI. *See* KENPEITAI.

KEN ANGROK (?–1227). According to both the ***Nagarakrtagama*** and the ***Pararaton,*** the former brigand Ken Angrok first came to prominence when he murdered the regent of Tumapel with a *kris* he had specially commissioned from the master smith Mpu Gandring, whom he also killed. Having implicated the dead regent's bodyguards in the murder, Ken Angrok seized power, married the regent's widow Ken Dedes, and launched a revolt against the king of **Kediri**, whom he defeated at the battle of Genter (1221). He founded the kingdom of **Singasari** at Tumapel in 1222 and reigned as Rangga Rajasa until his death in 1227.

KENPEITAI. Japanese military **police** force, founded in 1881, whose role was extended in occupied Indonesia and elsewhere to surveillance of the civilian population, **censorship**, and the collection of **intelligence**. The Kenpeitai gained a reputation for gratuitous cruelty and of 538 members of staff on **Java** at the end of the war, 199 were later committed for trial on war crimes charges. [0663, 0667, 0680]

KEPERCAYAAN. *See KEBATINAN.*

KERBAU. Water buffalo (*Bubalis bubalis*; not to be confused with the ***banteng***). *Kerbau* were introduced to Indonesia after 1000 B.C., probably from **India** via **Thailand.** They quickly took on great importance as draft animals and sources of milk, becoming a measure of wealth and, by extension, a symbol of power. Buffalo and **tiger** fights were a common entertainment on **Java**, and buffalo fights occasionally replaced battles; according to legend, the **Minangkabau** averted certain defeat in battle with Javanese by proposing a buffalo fight. Against the Javanese buffalo they sent a thirsty calf with knives tied to its head, which gored the Javanese beast while the calf nuzzled for milk. Individual buffalo can be identified by distinctive hair whorls, which are sometimes believed also to reflect individual character. [1154]

KERINCI. Isolated upland valley situated on the border between West **Sumatra** and **Jambi**, taking its name from Mt. Kerinci, the highest mountain (3,806 meters) on Sumatra and an active **volcano**. Culturally and politically, too, Kerinci exists on the fringes of the **Minangkabau** region and the sultanate of Jambi. **Gold** was an important export from the region in the 17th and early 18th centuries, but was gradually overshadowed by **rice** and by **cinnamon** produced for **trade** with the British in **Bengkulu**. [0834, 0840]

KESATUAN AKSI MAHASISWA INDONESIA (KAMI, Indonesian Students' Action Front). Founded on 25 October 1965 to spearhead the suppression of the **Partai Komunis Indonesia (PKI)** and the Left in general following the **Gestapu** coup of 30 September, it staged street marches and launched a campaign of pamphleteering. It was sponsored by and worked closely with the anticommunist Brigadier General Kemal Idris and Colonel Sarwo Edhie. From January 1966 it expressed its demands as the Tritura (Tri-Tuntutan Hatinurani Rakyat, Three Demands from the Bottom of the People's Hearts): abolish the PKI, purge the cabinet, and reduce prices. In much of its action, it cooperated closely with the Komando Aksi Pemuda dan Pelajar Indonesia (KAPPI) representing school children, and the Komando Aksi Sarjana Indonesia (KASI) representing graduates. In the early 1970s KAMI split between those who were absorbed into the government establishment and those who became increasingly critical of **New Order** policies. In 1973 the progovernment group became the core of the new **Komité Nasional Pemuda Indonesia (KNPI)**. *See also* STUDENTS. [0727]

KETERBUKAAN ("openness"). A tentative and ultimately unsuccessful effort in the early 1990s to open up Indonesian society to greater freedom of speech and expression. It began in December 1989 when Army Chief of Staff Edi Sudrajat advocated more open discussion of differences, and **Suharto** followed up in his 1990 independence day speech by calling for greater expression of differences of opinion. However, when Nano Riantiarno in a satirical play, *Suksesi,* accepted the offer, the government closed the play down after only 11 days and again imposed restrictions on such opposition playwrights as **W. S. Rendra**. After he had arranged his reelection to a sixth five-year term in 1993, Suharto made another step toward *keterbukaan,* when he reached a compromise with a few dissidents and released some Islamic radicals from jail. This effort, too, was tentative and short-lived, and in early 1994 the **labor** activist Mochtar Pakpaham and a number of other labor leaders were arrested and the most outspoken news magazines, *Detik, Editor,* and *Tempo,* were closed down. *See also* CENSORSHIP. [0748, 0751, 0940]

KIDUNG SUNDA. Semihistorical Javanese poem. Hayam Wuruk, king of **Majapahit**, obtained the hand of the daughter of the king of **Pajajaran**, but on the arrival of the Sundanese wedding party at Bubat in East **Java**, the Majapahit courtiers insisted that the marriage meant Pajajaran would accept Javanese overlordship and that, in some versions, the princess would be Hayam Wuruk's concubine, not his queen. The Sundanese king refused to accept this insult, fought the Javanese, and was slaughtered along with his men while his daughter committed suicide. [0159]

KOELIEORDONNANTIE. *See* COOLIE ORDINANCE.

KOLUSI, KORUPSI, DAN NEPOTISME (KKN, Collusion, Corruption, and Nepotism). The call to arms of the antigovernment demonstrators in the ***reformasi*** movement characterized the failings of the **Suharto** regime that they were determined to change. It remained a potent charge that was brought against leading politicians in the subsequent **B. J. Habibie**, **Abdurrachman Wahid**, and **Megawati Sukarnoputri** regimes.

KOMANDO JIHAD (Holy War Command)**.** A shadowy Islamic organization probably founded at the instigation of **Ali Murtopo** and his security apparatus in the mid-1970s and said to be fighting for an **Islamic state** in Indonesia, much as the **Darul Islam (DI)** did in earlier years. Former DI leaders reportedly headed the command, but most were arrested in the late 1970s and early 1980s. Actions attributed to or associated with the Komando Jihad include the hijacking of a Garuda DC9 aircraft and an attack on the Cicendo **police** station near **Bandung** in 1981 and a supposedly Islamic rising in **Lampung** in 1989. Imran Muhammad Zein was executed in February 1985 for his part in the 1981 events. It has been reported that the Komando Jihad provided a foundation for the Jemaah Islamiyah (JI, Islamic Community), a shadowy and loose-knit association, allegedly advocating establishment, if necessary by violent means, of an Islamic state embracing not only Indonesia but also **Malaysia** and the **Philippines**. *See also* ISLAM IN INDONESIA. [1031, 1039]

KOMANDO OPERASI PEMULIHAN KEAMANAN DAN KETERTIBAN (Kopkamtib, Operational Command for the Restoration of Security and Order)**.** Extraconstitutional body established on 10 October 1965 under **Suharto**'s command to suppress the so-called **Gestapu** coup. Its tasks soon extended beyond its original mandate of tracking down **Partai Komunis Indonesia (PKI)** supporters. It became the Suharto regime's major instrument of political control with respect to civilian dissidents, such as **student** and Muslim demonstrators, the press, and conduct of the **elections**. Its terms of reference included defense of the **Pancasila** and the 1945 **Constitution**. Operating outside regular legal channels, it had extensive authority to arrest, interrogate, and detain. It was a command within the Indonesian **armed forces**, giving the Kopkamtib commander direct authority over troops independent of the formal military hierarchy, rather than being a distinct institution such as the **Badan Koordinasi Intelijen Negara (Bakin)**, and it was thus a form of permanent martial law command. Its commander was theoretically able to act without reference to the **president**, as Suharto did in 1965–1966. On 22 September 1988 it was replaced by the much less powerful **Badan Koordinasi Bantuan Pemantapan Stabilitas Nasional (Bakorstanas)** as part of a move by Suharto to undermine the power of its head, **Benny Murdani.** For a list of Kopkamtib commanders, *see* APPENDIX E. [0727, 0733, 0972, 1099, 1100]

KOMANDO OPERASI TERTINGGI (Koti, Supreme Operations Command)**.** Military command formed in December 1961 for the liberation of West Irian (*see* **PAPUA**), with **Sukarno**, **A. H. Nasution**, and **A. Yani** as commander, deputy, and chief of staff; actual fighting was under the Mandala Command, headed by **Suharto**. In January 1962 Indonesian forces were defeated and a deputy **navy** commander, Yos Sudarso, was killed, but military pressure was among the factors removing the **Dutch** later that year. The command was reorganized in July 1963 to take charge of **Confrontation**. An operational Komando Siaga (Koga, "Readiness Command") under **air force** commander Omar Dhani was created in May 1964, but in October its authority was limited to **Kalimantan** and **Sumatra** with the title Komando Mandala Siaga (Kolaga). Army units formerly assigned to Koga for a projected invasion of the **Malay Peninsula** were assigned to **Komando Cadangan Strategis Angkatan Darat (Kostrad)** and posted to **Java**. In February 1966 Koti was renamed Komando Ganyang Malaysia (Kogam, Crush Malaysia Command), but it was abolished in July 1967. *See also* DEFENSE POLICY. [0714]

KOMANDO PASUKAN KHUSUS (Kopassus, Special Forces Command). Elite paracommando unit (formerly Komando Pasukan Sandi Yudha [Kopassandha, Secret Warfare Commando Unit], which succeeded **Resimen Para Komando Angkatan Darat [RPKAD]**) employed in 1966 against regions in **Java** and **Bali** that were believed to be procommunist and later in **East Timor** and Irian Jaya (**Papua**). Under command of presidential son-in-law **Prabowo Subianto**, who held the post from 1995 to 1998, the number of men in Kopassus doubled to approximately 7,000. Its forces were blamed for the killing of **students** at Trisakti University in **Jakarta** during the demonstrations prior to **Suharto**'s resignation. Under his successors, there were growing criticisms of the Kopassus, and in January 2001 the **army** announced a decrease in its forces by about 2,000. Seven of its members were accused in the 2001 assassination of moderate Papuan leader "Theys" Eluway. *See also* MASSACRES OF 1965–1966. [0714, 0727]

KOMANDO TERTINGGI OPERASI EKONOMI. *See DWIFUNGSI.*

KOMITÉ NASIONAL INDONESIA (KNI, Indonesian National Committee). Local committees established at every level of government shortly after the proclamation of the Indonesian Republic in 1945. In the absence of direction from the **Komité Nasional Indonesia Pusat (KNIP)**, local KNIs were initially responsible for most areas of government activity, including formation of the **army**. In many cases, the authority of the KNI was exercised mainly through a small Working Committee (Badan Pekerja). Though put together in a very ad hoc manner, KNIs generally represented most political streams in their regions and, depending on the capacity of their members, were often key political decision-making bodies during the first years of the **Revolution** until their role was somewhat taken over by the regional defense councils (Dewan Pertahanan Daerah). *See also* DEWAN PERTAHANAN NASIONAL. [0643, 0661, 0674, 0681]

KOMITÉ NATIONAL INDONESIA PUSAT (KNIP, Central Indonesian National Committee)**.** Representative body that originally grew out of the Japanese-sponsored **Panitia Persiapan Kemerdekaan Indonesia (PPKI)**. Initially the KNIP served merely as an advisory body to the **president** and his cabinet, but at its first session on 16–17 October 1945, it was vested with full legislative power and became the acting parliament of the Republic of Indonesia during the **Revolution**. The Republic's prime minister was responsible to the KNIP, although the **Constitution** prescribed a presidential system of government. KNIP membership, however, was effectively by presidential nomination, and **Sukarno** greatly expanded its size in order to have the 1947 **Linggajati Agreement** ratified. While the full KNIP generally exercised only legislative powers, closer supervision over the government and cabinet was exercised by a Working Committee (Badan Pekerja) that met every 10 days. [0643, 0661, 0674]

KOMODO. With a few neighboring islets, the only habitat of the Komodo "dragon" or monitor, *Varanus komodoensis,* of which approximately 1,600 remain. A nature reserve was declared there in 1966 and a national park in 1980. In 1995 the Komodo National Park, which comprises Komodo and Rinca Islands and the surrounding seas, became a **United Nations** heritage site, but the park fell into disrepair, with the number of visitors declining by two thirds from the 36,000 in 1996. In 2002 the largest environmental group in the **United States**, The Nature Conservancy (TNC), proposed that **Jakarta** cede responsibility for the park for 25 years to a private company, Putri Naga Komodo, owned by TNC and a Malaysian businessman, Feisol Hashim, which would invest about $2 million a year in the park, or about 100 times its current budget. [0078, 1155]

KONFRONTASI. *See* CONFRONTATION.

***KONGSI* WARS.** The term *kongsi* refers commonly to a firm commercial partnership, often of several people, cemented by a sense of loyalty as well as self-interest. It was a characteristic organizational form of **Chinese** in Indonesia. On the goldfields of West Kalimantan, local *kongsi* became so powerful as to resemble ministates, with their own territory, government, justice system, religious centers, **currency**, **taxation**, and schools entirely independent of the sultanates of Sambas and **Pontianak**, and largely responsible for importing miners and exporting **gold** to **China**. Their independence and involvement in trading **salt**, **opium**, and gunpowder led the **Dutch** to suppress them in the so-called *Kongsi* Wars. The term refers to three periods of warfare (1822–1824, 1850–1854, and 1884–1885) separated by periods of uneasy peace and resulting in the dissolution of all the *kongsi* and the imposition of Dutch control. [1048]

KONINKLIJK NEDERLANDSCH INDISCH LEGER (KNIL, Royal Netherlands Indies Army)**.** The three decades following the fall of the **Dutch East Indies Company (VOC)** in 1800 were militarily disastrous for the colonial government in Indonesia. Not only did **Dutch** possessions fall into British hands (*see* **BRITAIN**), but several major uprisings, notably the **Java War**, also took place. In 1830, therefore, Governor-General Johannes van den Bosch founded the KNIL to provide the colonial government with its own reliable military forces. The **governor-general** was commander-in-chief and from 1867 the KNIL was supported by a department of war, whose head was the KNIL commander. Dutch naval forces in the archipelago, operating from a large base in **Surabaya**, remained formally a part of the metropolitan **navy**. An air wing of the KNIL was formed in 1914.

The officer corps of the KNIL was always predominantly Dutch, though toward the end of the colonial period a small number of Indonesians received officer training at the Military Academy in Breda. In addition, the Sunan of **Surakarta** was a titular major-general in the KNIL and many other Javanese aristocrats held courtesy ranks. Troops were diverse in origin. In 1861, 54 percent were "native" and 46 percent "European." The European category included not only a great many Germans but also a number of Africans, the so-called *blanda hitam* (black Dutchmen) from Guinea. Like the British in **India**, the Dutch favored specific indigenous ethnic groups for recruitment. Ambonese and Menadonese were regarded as especially reliable, though Javanese always formed the largest bloc; in 1936 there were 4,000 Ambonese in the KNIL to 13,000 Javanese (*see also* **NATIVE TROOPS**).

The KNIL carried out the conquest of indigenous states in the **Outer Islands** in the 19th and early 20th century, but its primary role was the maintenance of internal security and order (*rust en orde*) (*see* **HEUTSZ, J. B. VAN**). KNIL troops thus were most heavily concentrated on **Java** and in **Aceh** and North **Sumatra**. From 1917 male European residents of the colony were subject to conscription for service in the militia and *landstrom* (home guard) for the defense of the colony, but in the 20th century the authorities relied increasingly on the British naval base in **Singapore** for their defense. The KNIL capitulated to **Japanese** forces at Kalijati in West Java on 9 March 1942, and much of the European component of the **army** spent the rest of the war in prisoner of war camps. KNIL soldiers who had escaped to **Australia** played a small role in the reconquest of eastern Indonesia in 1944–1945.

The postwar KNIL under General S. H. Spoor (1902–1949) recovered rapidly and took part with the Dutch army (Koninklijke Landmacht, KL) in the "**Police Actions**" to crush the Indonesian Republic. In 1948 the KNIL comprised 15,500 Europeans and 50,500 non-Europeans. It was formally abolished on 26 July 1950, its troops being transferred to the KL, transferred to the Indonesian army (APRIS), or demobilized. Troops to be demobilized were entitled to be discharged at a place of their own choosing, and around 4,000 Ambonese requested demobilization in **Ambon**, where they would have been able to join the uprising of the **Republik Maluku Selatan (RMS)** against the Republic. To avoid this, they were unilaterally transferred to the KL and "repatriated" with their families to the Netherlands in 1951 for demobilization. [0479, 0642, 1421]

"KONINKLIJKE" (the "Royal")**.** Common name for a group of companies involved in the extraction and sale of **oil** from Indonesia. The Koninklijke Nederlandsche Maatschappij tot Exploitatie van Petroleumbronnen in Nederlandsch-Indië was formed in 1890 to extract oil from concessions in Langkat in **East Sumatra** and began refining oil at Pangkalan Brandan in 1892. Under J. B. A. Kessler and (from 1901) Henri Deterding, the firm moved into the sale and distribution of oil in Asia. Cooperation with the Nederlandsch-Indische Industrie- and Handel-Maatschappij, a subsidiary of the Shell Transport and Trading Company, led in 1903 to creation of the Asiatic Petroleum Co. In 1907 the parent companies merged their remaining holdings into the Bataafse Petroleum Maatschappij (now Shell Petroleum NV) and the Anglo-Saxon Petroleum Co. (now Shell Petroleum Co.); each owned respectively 60 percent and 40 percent by the **Dutch** and British partners. The Koninklijke sold most of its Indonesian holdings in

1966 after experiencing great difficulties under **Guided Democracy**. In 1970 the group took over the Billiton (**Belitung**) **tin** companies. [0448]

KONINKLIJKE PAKETVAART MAATSCHAPPIJ (KPM, Royal Packetship Company)**.** Formed in 1888 to take over interisland mail routes in the colony, the KPM was able to establish an extensive network and a virtual monopoly of interisland **trade** in the 20th century, as well as a reputation for high-quality, expensive service. The company was a major target for economic **nationalism** after **independence** and from 1952 began to disengage from Indonesia, moving its resources into deep-sea **shipping** and steadily running down its Indonesian operations. On 3 December 1957, its offices in Indonesia were seized by workers, and on the same day the company transferred its management to Amsterdam and ordered all its ships to leave Indonesian territorial waters. Those ships seized in port were later restored to the company after Lloyds insurance agents pressured the Indonesian government to release them. *See also* SHIPPING. [0736, 0741, 0898]

KONSTITUANTE. *See* CONSTITUENT ASSEMBLY.

KORPS PEGAWAI REPUBLIK INDONESIA (Korpri, Corps of Civil Servants of the Indonesian Republic)**.** The compulsory official association of Indonesian government officials, formed in November 1971 by the merger of various Korps Karyawan (Kokar, Employees' Corps) of government departments. It is the sole social organization to which civil servants are ordinarily permitted to belong, ostensibly to prevent civil servants from becoming associated with sectional social interests. Korpri is affiliated with **Golkar** and under **Suharto** played an important role in marshaling civil servant support for the government at **election** time (*see* ***MONOLOYALITAS***). Its hierarchy (like that of the parallel wives' organization, **Dharma Wanita**) closely mirrored that of the departments in which its members worked.

KORTE VERKLARING. *See* NETHERLANDS, CONSTITUTIONAL RELATIONSHIP WITH INDONESIA.

KOSGORO (Koperasi Serba Guna Gotong Royong, All-Purpose Gotong Royong Cooperative)**.** Large cooperative formed on the basis of the East Java **student** army of the revolutionary period, Tentara Republik Indonesia Pelajar (TRIP, Student Army of the Indonesian Republic), and led by Mas Isman (1924–1984), one of the major constituent bodies within **Golkar**.

KOSTRAD (Komando Cadangan Strategis Angkatan Darat, Army Strategic Reserve)**.** Called Cadangan Umum Angkatan Darat, Army General Reserve, until 1963, it was formed in March 1961 as a crack unit under direct control of the General Staff, thus independent of the army's powerful regional commanders. It drew on the existing paracommando unit **Resimen Para Komando Angkatan Darat (RPKAD)** and selected units from the three **Java** commands and formed the military power base of General **Suharto** in his crushing of the **Gestapu** and rise to power. *See also* ARMY. [0714, 0727]

KRAKATAU (Krakatoa, Rakata)**.** Island in the **Sunda** Strait between **Java** and **Sumatra** and the site of major eruptions on 20 May and 26–28 August 1883. Most of the **volcano** collapsed into an immense caldera, causing tsunamis 20 meters high that flooded neighboring coastlines, killing perhaps 36,000 people. Approximately 18 cubic kilometers of ash was thrown into the atmosphere, causing bright red sunsets for two years after. The sound of the explosion was audible over a quarter of the earth's surface. Further eruptions resulted in the appearance of a new island, Anak Krakatau (Child of Krakatau), in January 1928. It was included in the **Ujung Kulon** national park in 1980. [1180, 1181]

KRATON. The palace of an Indonesian, especially Javanese, ruler, typically constructed on a north-south alignment with numerous pavilions (*pendopo*) and enclosed courtyards. Traditionally the *kraton* was regarded as the physical center of the kingdom and the point from which royal power radiated. *See also* ARCHITECTURE. [0518]

KRETEK. The mixing of addictive drugs, such as **betel** and **opium**, with other substances was already widespread in the archipelago before the arrival of **tobacco**, but by the 1930s tobacco and **clove** cigarettes known as *kretek* (perhaps onomatopoeic from the crackling sound they make as they burn) had become especially common. Initially a cottage industry, production of *kretek* came largely into **Chinese** hands in the 1950s and expanded greatly at the expense of conventional cigarettes (*rokok putih*) after 1968, partly with the help of a differential tariff that disadvantaged non-*kretek* brands. The largest firm, Gudang Garam, based in **Kediri** and with 41 percent of national production in 1981, had an annual budget four times that of East **Java** province. In the late 1980s a group headed by **Suharto**'s son, Tommy Suharto, set up a clove monopoly that caused great losses to *kretek* farmers and producers, until the president was forced by the International Monetary Fund (IMF) to end the monopoly. *See also* SUHARTO FAMILY. [0406, 0761]

KRIS. *See* METALWORKING; WEAPONS.

KRISMON. *See* FINANCIAL CRISIS.

KRONCONG. **Music** of the port cities of eastern Indonesia, introduced by the **Portuguese** in the 16th century but rapidly assimilated, especially before the arrival of cassette decks, as the music for *pasar malam* (night markets). It reached **Java** in the late 19th century but is now closely associated with the **Betawi** ethnic group. *Kroncong* typically features a simple melody line, is generally sung by a woman, and has guitar accompaniment and sentimental lyrics. In the 20th century its form was influenced by Hawaiian styles. Far more than ***gamelan***, *kroncong* became a vehicle for nationalist music, typified by the works of Ismail Marzuki (1914–1958). Since the 1970s the popularity of *kroncong* has been somewhat diminished by the rise of ***dangdut***. [0168]

KUBU. Primitive tribe in south **Sumatra**, once thought to be of mixed Veddoid and Negrito origin, and thus probably descendants of pre-Austro-Melanesian inhabitants of the archipelago (*see* **MIGRATIONS**), but now believed to be of mixed Austro-Melanesian and Austronesian origin. They are or were seminomadic forest dwellers, whose main contact with the outside world was by so-called silent barter, in which goods for **trade** were left at an agreed spot, without the Kubu and traders ever meeting.

KUTAI. Region around the lower Mahakam River in east **Kalimantan**. Known only from epigraphic evidence, a **Hindu** or **Buddhist** state perhaps a couple of generations old existed there in the early fifth century, followed by the state of Martapura ruled by King Mulavarman. In circa 1280 refugees from **Singasari** on **Java** settling near the river mouth founded the kingdom of Kertanegara, which converted to **Islam** in 1565 and later conquered the upstream remnants of Martapura. The sultanate was subject to **Banjarmasin** from time to time. The **Dutch** signed a monopoly treaty with the sultan in 1635 and annexed the region in 1699, but warriors from **Wajo'** in **Sulawesi** conquered the area in 1726 and a prolonged period of **Bugis** settlement followed.

The Dutch exerted formal control over Kutai from 1844 when they signed a treaty with the sultan. But their control was primarily aimed at stopping the threat of British expansion. Sultan Mohammad Sulaiman (r. 1845–1899) was able to lease out his lands for **coal** exploitation and plantation purposes to English traders and other merchants. He nevertheless was obliged under terms of the treaty to provide the Dutch with men, gunpowder, and ships to prosecute their wars. The sultan signed a further treaty with the Dutch in 1873, and coal and **oil** extraction began in 1882. His successor, Sultan Alimuddin, was effectively appointed by the Dutch and signed new treaties with them that further restricted his power, transferring much of the governance of the sultanate to an aristocratic bureaucracy. The oil wells in the region were a target of the **Japanese** invasion in 1942 and an **Australian** counterinvasion in July 1945. The sultanate of Kutai was abolished in 1960. By 1958 it had become part of the province of East Kalimantan, which emerged as the leading timber exporter in Indonesia in the late 1960s. *See* FORESTRY. [0812]

KYAI. Javanese title of respect for learned men, now confined to specialists in Islamic learning. *See also* ISLAM. [1336, 1383]

– L –

LABOR. No clear picture of **population** patterns in the archipelago before the 19th century has yet been drawn, but it seems that while **land** was relatively abundant labor was often scarce, and control of labor thus was a major key to political and economic power. The adoption of **Hinduism** and the resulting exaltation of the king seem to have enabled rulers to shift beyond carefully negotiated patron–client relations with a small number of followers to the large-scale raising of corvée labor from the community (*see* **STATE-FORMATION**). The mobilization of labor on this large scale enabled the construction of monuments such as **Borobudur** and **Prambanan** and underpinned the **Dutch** decision to retain the services of traditional elites for the recruitment of labor, especially under the **Cultivation System** (*see also* ***HERENDIENSTEN***). **Slavery** also existed as a means of labor control, mostly at household level.

Immigration of laborers from **China** began on a small scale in the 17th century but continued in waves until the 1930s, successive colonial authorities finding the **Chinese** politically and socially more amenable than Indonesians. In the early 19th century labor was still scarce enough for the colonial authorities to introduce strict regulations on **travel** and residence by Indonesians, and even in 1880 the plantations of **East Sumatra** still needed the state-enforced **Coolie Ordinance** to keep workers in place. In the early 20th century a scarcity of skilled labor enabled the emergence of **labor unions**, especially on **Java**, while after independence unions drew strength from their association with political parties. In 1921 the Dutch established a Kantoor van de Arbeid (Labor Office), which collected information on labor conditions and drafted labor laws. On the whole, however, the steadily growing abundance of labor weakened the bargaining position of workers.

The implications of rising population for **agricultural** labor have been discussed extensively. The **Agricultural Involution** thesis of American anthropologist Clifford Geertz suggested that there was little true employment of labor in the Javanese countryside; rather, a complex system of lease, lease-back, sale, and sharecropping ensured that all had some right to land and that income was based on that right rather than on a strict calculation of wage for service. Fields were thus planted, tended, and harvested in a cooperative way designed to ensure the welfare of all members of the community. More recent research has cast doubt on whether this system was ever as extensive as Geertz seemed to imply, and most observers now see, in any case, a trend away from diffuse land rights and toward a distinct class of wage-earning agricultural laborers, whose bargaining position is severely weakened by the abundance of rural labor.

After independence, the weakness of labor's position was increased by the growing role played by the military in the **economy** and the identification of the strongest labor union during the **Sukarno** period, Sentral Organisasi Buruh Seluruh Indonesia (SOBSI), with the **Partai Komunis Indonesia (PKI)**. The institutional arrangement of state–labor relations in the New Order period has been viewed by some observers as "a legacy of the struggles between the **army** and the Left prior to the mid-1960s."

After the fall of international **oil** prices, the **Suharto** regime adopted a more export-led **industrialization** strategy based in large part on the growth of a low-wage, labor-intensive manufacturing sector, employing large numbers of female workers. Manufacturing zones grew up around major cities, especially in Java, and this was one reason for a change in the status of workers of the period. Although unemployment was officially put at 2.2 percent in 1987, most observers believed the figure to be much higher than this, perhaps 11 million out of a workforce of 67.5 million, though extensive underemployment makes reliable estimates impossible. An industrial working class began to develop during the late 1980s, leading to a growth in militancy among some sectors of the labor force and a notable increase in the number of strikes. (According to government statistics, about 350 strikes occurred in Indonesia in 1996, compared to just 19 in 1989.) Although the government responded in large part through repression, they also implemented a policy in the early 1990s of raising the minimum wage annually, so that by 1997 it was almost three times that in 1990.

Suharto's resignation led to a rise in the number of labor unions and to a further increase in wages so that in November 2001 the minimum wage was raised in **Jakarta** by 38 percent to nearly US$60 a month. Under the **decentralization** law the provincial governments, not the labor ministry, had authority to set local minimum wages, so this rise was not followed throughout the country. (Some provincial governments, however, exceeded Jakarta's rate of increase, East **Kalimantan** declaring a 66 percent increase for 2002.) Economic research groups and companies complained that raising the minimum wage would only result in more unemployment, which stood at the end of 2003 at 42.7 million workers, 10.8 million of them fully unemployed and 31.9 million in the disguised unemployment category. The labor movement, however, which was becoming increasingly assertive after the change from Suharto's authoritarian rule, held out not only for higher wages but also for healthier working conditions and freedom of association for Indonesia's workers. The minimum wage continued to rise, so that in January 2004 it was US$79.3 per month in Jakarta, a 6.3 percent increase over the previous year. [0295, 0320, 0334, 0421–0437, 0595, 0748, 1321]

LABOR UNIONS. Rising demand for skilled and semiskilled **labor** in the growing cities and in the colonial **sugar** industry dramatically strengthened the position of workers in the colony in the early 20th century, leading first to a large number of small-scale strikes in the first decade of the century and then to the formation of labor unions. European government employees were unionized earliest (1905), followed by **railway** workers in the Vereeniging van Spoor-en Tramweg Personeel (VSTP, Union of Rail and Tramway Personnel) in 1908 and the European postal and **pawnshop** workers in 1912 and 1913. Since the program of these unions often included preservation of the favorable treatment of European employees over Indonesians, indigenous workers soon began to form their own unions, especially in the pawnshop service and the railways, where the VSTP had come under Indonesian domination by 1918. There were few unions among ethnic **Chinese** or amongst the employees of smaller private firms. The **Sarekat Islam (SI)** and the **Partai Komunis Indonesia (PKI)** were both active in organizing unions, though their organizers often found themselves torn between promoting the specific interests of the workers and supporting the broader program of the political movement.

By 1920 there was no longer a critical shortage of skilled labor; employers became less tolerant of what they regarded as agitation and they began resisting union claims and, in some cases, dismissing union leaders. Major strikes broke out in the railway service in 1920 and 1923, in the pawnshops in 1921, and in the **ports** in 1925, all of them unsuccessful. Although unions claimed large memberships, union discipline including the payment of membership fees was hard to enforce. By 1932 there were 132 unions registered in the colony with a total of 82,860 members.

Banned during the **Japanese occupation**, labor unions emerged in the hundreds during the **Revolution**, often completely taking over the management of factories and plantations. Many were affiliated through the labor federations Barisan Buruh Indonesia (BBI) and Sentral Organisasi Buruh Seluruh Indonesia (SOBSI) with the PKI, and in 1948 when the Mohammad Hatta government began attempting to reassert managerial control, in order to gain control of agricultural and industrial products, political and class antagonisms coincided. A bitter strike in a state textile factory at Delanggu in Central Java in May, in particular, contributed to the tensions that produced the **Madiun Affair**. During the 1950s and 1960s left-wing control of trade unions diminished with the establishment of more conservative trade union federations, such as Sentral Organisasi Karyawan Seluruh Indonesia (SOKSI). From 1957 severe limits were placed on the right to strike, strikes being prohibited in essential industries (including communications, development projects, the tourist industry, and government corporations) in 1963, and unions in general became vehicles for the mobilization of support for political parties, rather than purely industrial organizations.

Under the **New Order**, the government rejected the idea that unions are institutions for defending worker interests against management and government, and argued instead that they are corporatist bodies for coordinating the workers' role in an essentially cooperative venture with management. The Basic Manpower Law of 1969 acknowledged the right of workers to form unions and to strike, but the principle of **Pancasila** Industrial Relations (Hubungan Industri Pancasila) laid down in 1974 specifically denied that workers may have interests distinct from those of business and industry as a whole. Organizationally, too, unions were brought under close control. On 20 February 1973 all unions except **Korps Pegawai Republik Indonesia (Korpri)** were required to join the Federasi Buruh Seluruh Indonesia (FBSI, All-Indonesian Workers' Federation). Peasant organizations followed on 26 April with the formation of the Himpunan Kerukunan Tani Indonesia (HKTI, Association of Indonesian Peasant Leagues) and the Himpunan Nelayan Seluruh Indonesia (HNSI, All-Indonesia Fishermen's Association) in September 1973. Each of these organizations became in turn a member of **Golkar**. Subsequently, there was a major restructuring of unions into 21 largely industry-based ("vertical") organizations with appointed officials, replacing the former occupation-based ("horizontal") associations. In November 1985 this process was completed with the transformation of the FBSI into the Serikat Pekerja Seluruh Indonesia (SPSI, All-Indonesia Workers' Union), which was even more hierarchical and easily controlled than its predecessor.

Ten years later a further restructuring took place, with the formation of the Federasi Serikat Pekerja Seluruh Indonesia (FSPSI, All-Indonesia Workers' United Federation), an apparent response to the growth of labor unrest and strikes in the early 1990s. It was hoped that this new federation could prevent the growth of independent organizations outside the control of government. A few independent unions had formed in the early 1990s, including the short-lived Serikat Buruh Merdeka Setiakawan (Solidarity Independent Labor Union) and **Muchtar Pakpahan**'s Serikat Buruh Sejahtera Indonesia (SBSI, Indonesian Prosperous Workers' Union). The more radical Pusat Perjuangan Buruh Indonesia (PPBI, Indonesian Workers' Struggle Center) linked to the **Partai Rakyat Demokratik (PRD)** was suppressed after the 27 July 1996 riots in Jakarta. In early 1998 **Ikatan Cendekiawan Muslim Indonesia (ICMI)** established a union called the Persaudaraan Pekerja Muslim Indonesia (PPMI, Indonesian Muslim Workers' Brotherhood).

After the fall of **Suharto** a number of local and national labor groups came into existence, many with strong ties to nongovernmental organizations (NGOs). They were successful in winning better wages and conditions for workers in several industries, but their future influence remained unclear, particularly with the renewed strengthening of the military and security apparatus under **Megawati Sukarnoputri**. *See also* LEGAL AID. [0425, 0430, 0436, 0612]

LADANG. Swidden (slash-and-burn) agriculture, assumed to be the earliest form of farming in the archipelago and still practiced, especially in parts of **Kalimantan**. Typically, swiddeners clear and burn an area of upland rainforest, plant crops for a year or more, and then, as soil fertility diminishes or weed growth becomes insurmountable, move on to a new area, returning perhaps a generation later once the forest has regrown. Over the last century, swidden **agriculture** has aroused strong hostility among ecologists and agricultural scientists, who have argued, among other things, that it irreparably damages the rainforest, causing erosion, disrupting rainfall patterns, and promoting the spread of the grass *alang-alang,* and that it needlessly wastes the precious genetic and timber resources of the forest. More recent research, however, has suggested that swidden agriculture, while contributing some erosion in the short term, seldom leads to *alang-alang* infestation or to permanent damage to the forest, and that much of the ecological change attributed to swidden has been a consequence of commercial exploitation of rainforest areas. Swidden agriculture has been found to be more productive in some respects than intensive wet-**rice** cultivation and certainly than the widespread **oil palm** plantations.

LAMPUNG. Southernmost province of Sumatra, settled according to tradition by three tribes, the Abung, Publian, and Peminggir, probably in the 14th century. The region became an important **pepper**-producing area in the 16th century and came under the rule of **Banten** in circa 1530. The **Dutch East Indies Company (VOC)** founded a fort at Menggala in 1668 and took general control of the region in 1751, **Herman Willem Daendels** formally annexing it in 1808. A long war of resistance led by Muslim communities followed (1817–1856). In 1883, coastal regions were devastated by flooding following the eruption of **Krakatau**.

Lampung was the site of the first attempts at transmigration and in the 1970s became an important area of settlement, but it was closed to further settlement in 1984. Much settlement, however, was already too dense and the clearing of forest for agriculture created major hydrological problems. Lampung became Indonesia's major **coffee**-producing area.

In 1989 a Muslim school in Way Jepara, Lampung, was the site of a bloody confrontation between local Muslims and the **Suharto** government. Members of the school had close ties with former **Darul Islam (DI)** members from West **Java** and **Aceh** and with Jemaah Islamiyah (JI, Islamic Community) students in Central and East Java. In the confrontation the regional military command attacked the school compound, killing close to 100 of the Muslims. *See* ISLAM IN INDONESIA.

LAND. For much of human history, land was relatively abundant in the archipelago. Although the effort involved in clearing it for **agriculture** inevitably gave it value, and religious beliefs may have invested it with spiritual significance, land scarcity was not a major problem and control of **labor** and **trade** seem to have been more important sources of political power. Land may have been held collectively within communities, but individual rights also seem to have been respected. Forest lands and land not in active cultivation seem to have been more freely at the disposal of rulers, and the **Dutch East Indies Company (VOC)** allocated to private individuals large tracts of freehold land on the northern coast of **Java** (*see* **PARTICULIERE LANDERIJEN**). The growth of **population** and the rise of commercial production of crops, however, put an end to this abundance and from at least 1800, control of land was one of the major issues in politics, first on Java and later on other islands.

During the brief British interregnum, **Thomas Stamford Raffles** deemed all land on Java to be government property and on this basis began to charge peasant farmers a **land rent**. Under the **Cultivation System**, however, collective control of land was emphasized, the village receiving the right (*beschikkingsrecht*) to allocate and reallocate land to its members, villagers being required in turn to devote one fifth of their land to crops for the government. Land rights, thus, were something of a burden, and the complicated land tenure arrangements described by, among others, Clifford Geertz as an aspect of "**agricultural involution**" were at least in part an attempt by landowners to shed the **taxation** burden. Correspondingly, Europeans were expected not to have land rights, and even leasehold of land by Europeans was banned from 1836 to 1853; even after a slight liberalization of regulations in 1856, little land came into European hands.

Major changes took place with the introduction of the so-called **Liberal Policy** in 1870. In that year a colonial government Domeinverklaring declared all "waste" land, that is land that was not actively and permanently cultivated, on Java and **Madura** to be government property. Traditional activities such as wood collecting were deemed to represent usufruct rights but not ownership, though the extent to which the state could override traditional use was a topic of continued debate. Also in 1870 the **Agrarian Law** allowed a form of lease called *erfpacht* for up to 75 years, while continuing to ban the sale of land by indigenes to non-indigenes. Regulations on the **sugar** industry specified that no more than one third of village land might be leased out, fixed a minimum rent, and required that land be returned to the village for cultivation at least every three years, though these regulations were often not enforced. In 1885 regulations were introduced to permit so-called *conversierechten* (conversion rights), under which village land might be converted from collective ownership (subject to periodic redistributions) to private ownership, but these were little used, partly because an estimated 75 percent of land was already under individual hereditary title.

Colonial land laws remained in force until 1960, when a new law simplified landholding by distinguishing between *hak milik* (ownership and disposal, restricted to Indonesian citizens) and *hak guna bangunan* (usufruct). A 1963 law on land reform was only weakly implemented.

Under the **New Order**, restrictions on foreign ownership of land were relaxed, and expropriation of land for major public and private development projects led to clashes over competing public and private and national and local land claims. Land conflicts multiplied as the Indonesian **economy** industrialized and farmers were forced off their land to make way for urban and industrial expansion. The increasing value of land, particularly that close to major commercial centers, attracted speculators, and agricultural land was increasingly bought up as an investment by the urban middle class, as well as millions of hectares being part of the holdings of the **Suharto** family and being acquired by companies under their control. In the early 1990s the expropriation of land for huge government projects, such as the Kedung Ombo dam in Central Java, led to increasingly violent disputes with the local people supported by student sympathizers and nongovernmental organizations (NGOs). Land disputes became the largest category of cases handled by the national **human rights** commission in the 1990s.

After the fall of the Suharto regime, there were huge demonstrations demanding the return of land in **Sumatra** and Java, and displaced farmers occupied the Suharto ranch near **Bogor** and the resort areas and golf courses that had been forcibly acquired over the previous decade. The government issued new regulations requiring that all land with cultivation or other long-term rights attached to it be worked productively, and new measures were passed aimed at reforming legislation with respect to land ownership.

The registration of land ownership, however, still presents major problems in densely populated rural areas, where complicated tenure relationships cannot easily be summed up in a title deed; in urban areas where large numbers of people have been resident for years on what is technically government or private land and are thus subject to expulsion at short notice and with meager compensation; and in outlying regions where indigenous rights over land for purposes such as **hunting** and gathering have been disregarded in the acquisition of land for **transmigration** sites. *See also* LEGAL AID. [0335, 0337, 0338, 0372, 0595]

LAND REFORM. While many government measures have attempted to modify the pattern of landholding in Indonesia, the term "land reform" frequently refers to measures for the redistribution of **land** provided for by the 1960 Basic Law on Agriculture (Undang-Undang Pokok Agraria), which applied mainly to **Java**. The law, passed at the urging of the **Partai Komunis Indonesia (PKI)**, provided for the breaking up of larger concentrations of land in the Javanese countryside. Although there was no class of large landholders in Java, there were clear social differences in access to land as well as a general trend toward concentration of landholdings. The land reform law did not so much envisage the arbitrary distribution of land to the poor—there was clearly nowhere near enough land to go around—but rather aimed to assist those smallholders who had recently lost or were in danger of losing their land as a result of indebtedness. The PKI turned the issue into one of popular concern by linking it to the attempts of landlords to restrict participation of the population in production, especially at harvest time (*see* ***GOTONG ROYONG***).

Only in rare instances was the land reform law implemented. Landowners commonly reduced the size of their holdings by distributing them among relatives or by donating them to religious institutions, especially mosques and ***pesantren***, or they relied on delaying tactics by the land reform committees. In late 1963 the PKI announced *aksi sepihak* (unilateral or direct action) to implement land reform measures, accompanied by a campaign against the so-called seven village devils. In several areas land was seized and commonly restored to former owners, but the party was accused of choosing its victims more for their hostility to the PKI than for their class, and most of the landlords targeted were ***santri*** Muslim supporters of the **Nahdlatul Ulama (NU)**. The actions aroused enormous tensions in the countryside of Java and contributed to the motives for the **massacres of 1965–1966**.

Although under the **New Order** the Basic Agrarian Law of 1960 was never rescinded, few efforts were made to implement its provisions. After 1971 the state also discontinued its annual financial support of the land reform program, further weakening the hand of the small landholders via-à-vis the government. Land was expropriated for large-scale development often after bloody clashes with landholders, who received little if any compensation. In 1978 a Joint Ministerial Interim Report on agrarian reform tried to reaffirm the importance of the law and urged a redistribution of land and more equitable rural relations, but none of these recommendations were carried out. In the final years of the **Suharto** regime, land reform courts were abolished and legal limitations on landholding gave way to commercial interests.

After the fall of Suharto, there were moves to implement comprehensive land reform measures. The National Land Agency and the post of minister of agrarian affairs were abolished, and in October 1999 a draft regulation was accepted in the **Majelis Permusyawaratan Rakyat (MPR)** asserting that agrarian reform had to be based on recognition of cultural diversity and associated resource rights, including the control, exploitation, and management of land through a pluralist tenure system taking into account local ***adat*** law. [0337, 0338, 0954]

LAND RENT (*landrente*)**.** From the late 18th century a number of reformers, such as **Dirk van Hogendorp** and H. W. Muntinghe, sought ways of streamlining Dutch rule of **Java** by bypassing the entrenched position of the ***bupati*** as prime agents of the colonial government and bringing peasants into the money **economy** as a market for European manufactured goods. They proposed to achieve this by creating, among other things, a direct **taxation** relationship with the peasantry, and to do so they suggested recognizing peasants' land rights, which could then be taxed. **Thomas Stamford Raffles** first introduced land rent in Kedu and **Banten** in 1812 and it was gradually extended, but, because of the need to obtain surveys of landholding, the whole of Java (excluding the Vorstenlanden and particuliere landerijen) was not covered until 1872, while a unified system of assessment based on fairly accurate surveys was established only between 1907 and 1921. Land rent was also levied in **Bali**, **Lombok**, and South **Sulawesi**. Land rent provided nearly half the revenue of the colonial government in 1867, but this proportion had sunk to 10 percent by 1928. After **independence**, land rent was formally abolished, though it seems still to have been collected in many regions. In 1959 it was replaced with an agricultural produce tax (*pajak hasil bumi*), and the proceeds were allotted to local (*kabupaten*) authorities. In 1965 it was renamed Iuran Pembangunan Daerah (Ipeda, Regional Development Tax). [0392, 0588]

LANGE, MADS JOHANSEN (1806–1856)**.** Danish trader and adventurer, one of a number of Europeans who were able to prosper as intermediaries between the indigenous courts and Western traders. After operating in the Balinese court on **Lombok** from 1834, Lange settled at **Kuta** on the south coast of **Bali** in 1839, where he worked closely with the raja of Badung, who was also the chief trader of his kingdom. Both became immensely wealthy from the **trade** in slaves and other goods, but war and an outbreak of smallpox in Bali in midcentury undermined their position. After the sultan's death, Lange was unable to find a suitable new patron and died, probably of poison, in 1856. *See also* WHITE RAJAS. [0825]

LANGKAT. Sultanate in East **Sumatra**, acquired by the Dutch from **Siak** in 1858. Like the rest of East Sumatra it became a major area of Dutch **tobacco** plantations and in 1892 was the site of the colony's first commercial **oil** well at Telaga. The sultan was deposed in the social revolution of 1946. [0818, 0673]

LANGUAGES. Though it is often difficult to distinguish languages and dialects, it is commonly said that around 200 indigenous languages are spoken in the Indonesian archipelago. Most of the languages of western and central Indonesia are of the Western Austronesian division, formerly known as the Indonesian branch of the Malayo-Polynesian family, which includes also Malagasy (*see* **MADAGASCAR, HISTORICAL LINKS WITH**) and the indigenous languages of Taiwan. Languages of the Pacific islands belong to the Eastern Austronesian division. Linguistic and archeological evidence suggests that the Austronesian languages first reached the eastern archipelago and had begun to disperse by at least 3000 B.C. (*see* **MIGRATIONS**). Features of these languages are a relatively simple morphology for nouns and verbs, use of roots that can become nouns or verbs, reduplication of words, and distinct forms for the second person including and excluding the listener. Within the Western Austronesian division, the Sumatran languages Malay, **Minangkabau**, Acehnese, Rejang, and **Kerinci**, together with Madurese, form one subgroup, with **Gayo** and **Batak** somewhat more distant relatives. Malay expanded from a relatively small base in east and south **Sumatra** and the **Malay Peninsula** in the 13th century to become a major lingua franca in the archipelago by the 16th century, and it was the basis of modern Indonesian (*see* **INDONESIAN LANGUAGE**). Javanese and Sundanese, numerically the largest and second largest language groups (excluding

Indonesian), form a distinct subgroup strongly influenced by Sanskrit. A large number of indigenous languages exist in **Kalimantan**, but Ngaju, a language of the southeast, acts as a lingua franca for much of the southern part of the island. In eastern Indonesia, approximately 100 Austronesian languages are spoken, but these are usually classified into Bima-Sumba, Ambon-Timor, Sula-Bacan, south **Halmahera**–western Irian, and several **Sulawesi** groups. Buginese is the most widely spoken of the Sulawesi languages. A number of Eastern Austronesian languages are spoken in the province of **Papua**, mainly along the north coast. All Western Austronesian languages show successive vocabulary influences from Sanskrit, Arabic, and/or European languages, depending on the history of their speakers.

Entirely distinct from the Austronesian family is the Papuan, or Indo-Pacific, group of languages, whose speakers occupy three quarters of the island of New Guinea, with communities on **Halmahera**, **Timor**, and **Alor**. Insufficient research has been done to say that all languages classified as Papuan are related, but it seems probable that this is the case. Most are spoken by relatively few people and are highly complex grammatically. Verbs, for instance, vary enormously depending on the number and other characteristics of both subject and objects. Many are tonal; that is, changes in the pitch of a vowel or syllable change its meaning.

Of the European languages, Portuguese was an important lingua franca in the archipelago in the 16th and 17th centuries, and Portuguese-speaking communities survived in some regions until the late 19th century. The Dutch generally did not promote the use of their own language by Indonesians, developing Malay instead as the principal language of administration.

A number of Malay words have entered English: amok (from ***amuk***), compound (from *kampung*), kapok, mandarin (via Portuguese from *menteri*, itself derived from a Sanskrit word), paddy, and sarong. Gong derives from Javanese. *See also* ETYMOLOGY. [0262, 0264–0272, 0275–0287]

LASKAR JIHAD. This group was founded in early 2000 in central **Java** and headed by Ja'far Umar Thalib, a religious leader of Yemenese ancestry who fought against the **Soviet Union** in Afghanistan in the 1980s. Its stated agenda was to wipe out Christians in **Maluku** and central **Sulawesi**, and establish an **Islamic state**. Although Thalib reportedly met with Osama bin Laden, there was no concrete evidence of links between al Qaeda and the Laskar Jihad.

The Laskar Jihad forces arrived in Poso (Sulawesi) in August 2001, long after other Muslim militias were well established, but they were believed to be responsible for much of the violence both there and on **Ambon**. The Laskar Jihad was a suspect in a massacre of 14 Ambon villagers on 28 April 2002, and the following month the government ordered the arrest of Ja'far Umar Thalib, who was taken into custody in **Surabaya**, for allegedly inciting new violence on Ambon and making threats against the family of former President **Sukarno**. Two weeks earlier Alex Manuputty, a leader of the Maluku Sovereignty front, a mainly Christian separatist group, had been arrested. The Laskar Jihad was then reported to have shifted its major operations to **Papua**. In mid-October 2002 in the wake of the **Bali** bombings, about 1,000 of its members returned to Java from Ambon and Ja'far Umar Thalib announced that the militia had been disbanded. [1021, 1028]

LASYKAR. Originally denoting a **militia** or home guard, this term referred in the **Revolution** to well-organized irregular armed units that supported the Republic but resisted incorporation into the **army**. Most *lasykar* opposed negotiation with the Dutch, preferring a policy of armed struggle. *See also* BADAN PERJUANGAN. [0674]

LATAH. Sociopsychological condition occurring among Javanese, which leads them to utter obscene words or phrases or to imitate the words or actions of others. *See also AMUK.*

LAW. The early legal systems of Indonesia are difficult to reconstruct since these were amongst the first institutions affected by the successive waves of Indian, Muslim, and European juridical thinking. Codified ***adat*** law represents an attempt by Dutch scholars to record the traditional legal thinking of the archipelago, but this attempt was affected inevitably by Dutch political conceptions. The idea of civil actions between private individuals was not well developed. Punishment commonly included monetary fines, enslavement, torture, and death (reserved for treason, lèse-majesté, murder, and theft) but rarely imprisonment or beating. Islamic law (*syariah*; *see* **LAW, ISLAMIC**), introduced in some regions from the 13th century, greatly clarified commercial and personal law and added whipping and amputation to the catalog of acceptable punishments.

When the **Dutch East Indies Company (VOC)** arrived in Indonesia in the 17th century, it had little interest in territorial jurisdiction except as far as was necessary for its commercial purposes, and it therefore left non-Europeans as far as possible under the authority of their traditional rulers. Within VOC territories, European law applied to all. Law for VOC possessions was codified first under **Governor-General Anthony van Diemen** in 1650, when Joan Maetsuyker compiled the Bataviaasche Statuten; these remained the basis of European law in the colony until 1848 (*see also* **DUTCH IN INDONESIA; NETHERLANDS, CONSTITUTIONAL RELATIONSHIP WITH INDONESIA**). Courts to administer Dutch law were established in **Batavia** in 1629 and **Maluku** in 1651. In 1747, however, as it acquired more territory (*see* **MATARAM**), the company decided to retain native law for its indigenous subjects outside the **cities** and established *inlandsche rechtsbanken* or landraden to apply native law on the northern coast of Java. **Chinese** and other nonindigenous minorities were subject to the same courts, though legal issues within each community were often left to Dutch-appointed community chiefs.

In the 19th century, with the introduction of direct Dutch rule, this pluralistic system was formalized with the specification of legal racial categories for Dutch subjects in the Indies (*see* **RACE**). In 1824 *adat* law was declared applicable to all natives (including those in the cities). In 1848, with the adoption of a new Dutch **constitution**, the Bataviaasche Statuten were abolished and a large part of metropolitan Dutch law was declared applicable to Europeans in the colony. From 1919 sections of this law (excluding family law) were also applied to foreign orientals, though they continued to be administered through native courts. Not until the late 19th century, however, was a major program to codify *adat* carried out. At the close of the colonial period, the legal system was divided into native ("*inheemse*") and government jurisdictions, which coincided generally though not always with the distinction between directly ruled territories and ***zelfbesturen***. Native rulers, aristocrats, and their families were not subject to civil legal action except with permission of the governor-general. In 1918 the various branches of criminal law in the colony were united in a new criminal code, the Wetboek van Strafwet (now Kitab Undang-undang Hukum Pidana, KUHP), but this was never actually implemented for Indonesians and in 1941 it was supplemented by a separate criminal code for natives, the Herzien Inlandsch Reglement (HIR, Revised Native Regulations). Islamic courts (priesterraden) were established on **Java** and Madura in 1882 to administer Muslim marriage and family law.

The 1945, 1949, and 1950 Constitutions of the Indonesian Republic all validated Dutch colonial law insofar as it did not conflict with other provisions of the constitution. Especially during **Guided Democracy**, this created some legal uncertainty, as many laws of the colonial era could be regarded as in conflict with principles of social justice. Law came to be administered in a three-tier system, cases passing from the Pengadilan Negeri through the Pengadilan Tinggi (appeal court) to the Mahkamah Agung (**Supreme Court**).

Under the **New Order** the judiciary lost virtually all of its independence as the government, through the Department of Justice, used the system of dual court administration to bring the judicial apparatus under its political control. A new procedural code for criminal law, the Kitab Undang-undang Hukum Acara Pidana (KUHAP), was adopted on 31 December 1981, but many practical aspects of these regulations remain to be determined. A network of over 300 religious courts continues to adjudicate on marriage, inheritance, and other domestic disputes. *See also* LEGAL AID; SUBVERSION; YAP THIAM HIEN. [0027, 0479, 0576, 1075–1078, 1082–1084, 1087, 1090, 1095, 1099, 1100]

LAW, ISLAMIC (*syariah*)**.** Prior to the coming of the Dutch, **Islam**ic justice was administered in the archipelago in a variety of ways. By the early 17th century there were Islamic courts in **Aceh** and **Banten** and probably in other of the Islamic states. Among the Javanese, the *penghulu* was responsible for administering Islamic justice. Under a Dutch **law** of the 1830s, any decisions by the Islamic courts had to be ratified by the civil courts. This changed in 1882 when a Royal Decree formally chartered a system of Islamic tribunals called "Priests' Councils" (*priesterraden*) operating alongside regular courts in **Java** and **Madura**. In 1937 a series of regulations was passed setting up Islamic appeals courts in Java, Madura, and **Kalimantan** and transferring authority over inheritance from Islamic to civil courts.

After independence, the 1951 law on judicial organization and procedure provided the foundation for the establishment of a nationwide system of Islamic courts, and in 1957 a regulation was passed authorizing establishment of Islamic courts everywhere in the **Outer Islands** where they did not already exist, with their competence including inheritance as well as marriage and divorce cases. Under the **New Order**, in the early 1970s the government attempted to transfer laws governing **marriage** to the civil courts, thus weakening the Islamic courts and marginalizing Islamic doctrine, but these efforts failed and the 1974 Marriage Act retained the role of the Islamic courts. The 1989 Religious Judicature Act provided a uniform designation for Islamic courts throughout the country, placing their organization under the minister of religion and defining their powers over marriage, inheritance, and charitable foundations. *See also* ISLAMIC STATE; SUPREME COURT. [1080, 1081, 1085, 1089, 1094, 1097]

LEGAL AID SERVICES. These began in Indonesia with the formation of informal consultation bureaus run by law students in **Jakarta** in 1967. A full Legal Aid Bureau, the Lembaga Bantuan Hukum (LBH), was formed in 1971 by the legal association Persatuan Advokat Indonesia (Peradin, Indonesian Advocates' Union) with financial assistance from the Jakarta governor **Ali Sadikin**. Since then over 100 legal aid organizations have sprung up, with varying degrees of affiliation to the government and other organizations. They have taken an especially active role in siding with the poor in **land** and **labor** disputes. *See also* LAW. [1090]

LEIMENA, JOHANNES (1905–1977)**.** Medical doctor and one of the founders of the **Partai Kristen Indonesia (Parkindo)** in 1945. As minister of health in several early cabinets, he usefully represented the Protestant minority in government and became a deputy prime minister in **Sukarno**'s first nonparliamentary *Kabinet Kerja* in 1957. He resigned from Parkindo in 1959 but remained deputy prime minister along with **Chaerul Saleh** and **Subandrio** in 1963 after the death of **Juanda Kartawijaya**. He had, however, little influence on policy under **Guided Democracy** and was permitted to retire in peace after 1966. [0695]

LEMBAGA KEBUDAYAAN RAKYAT (Lekra, Institute of People's Culture)**.** Lekra was founded in August 1950 in opposition to the "Gelanggang [Arena]" group, a literary renewal movement that saw itself as heir to **Chairil Anwar** (who had died in 1949) and whose members included **H. B. Jassin**, Rivai Apin, Asrul Sani, and initially **Pramoedya Ananta Toer**. In early 1950 the "Gelanggang" group, which was loosely associated with the **Partai Sosialis Indonesia (PSI)** and also the **Partai Nasional Indonesia (PNI)**, had published a "Surat Kepertjajaan" (Letter of Belief) glorifying their views of the **Revolution**. In response, a group of younger intellectuals founded the Lekra and published its manifesto, "Mukadimah" (Introduction), expressing the disillusionment of the young people at the perceived failure of the older political leaders to achieve the Revolution's aim of establishing a People's Democratic Republic. The Lekra manifesto called on **artists** to help realize this goal. Young people affiliated with the **Partai Komunis Indonesia (PKI)**, such as Dipa Nusantara Aidit (1923–1965) and Njoto (1925–1965), were closely tied to its foundation, as was the essayist and poet A. S. Dharta, who became the organization's first secretary-general.

In 1956 Lekra published a new "Mukadimah" and adopted the doctrine of socialist realism, arguing that art should reflect social realities and promote social progress rather than simply explore the human personality. In particular, it promoted the idea of "People-ness" (*kerakyatan*) in art and urged artists to move downward (*turun ke bawah*) to draw inspiration from the mass of the people. Lekra was rather more successful in recruiting in the visual arts than in literature; well-known painters such as **Affandi**, Henk Ngantung, and **Hendra Gunawan** applied Lekra ideas to their work with success, whereas works produced by Lekra writers were generally less successful. (Pramoedya Ananta Toer, who became increasingly associated with Lekra during the 1950s, and Rivai Apin, who now edited its journal *Zaman Baru,* were notable exceptions.) The prose of the Lekra writers tended to be realistic but their poetry became increasingly propagandistic, and most of their writings were in the form of short stories and poetry rather than novels.

Lekra associated itself with **Sukarno**'s "concept" (*konsepsi*) of an Indonesian form of democracy, and the president was present at its first National Congress held in Solo in 1959. It consistently argued that artists should receive state support and became itself a major patron of the arts during **Guided Democracy**. In 1963 it claimed 200 branches and 100,000 members. After 1962 it began a series of sharp attacks on those it regarded as opponents of *kerakyatan,* notably **Hamka** (Haji Abdul Malik bin Abdulkarim Amrullah) and H. B. Jassin, to which Jassin and his colleagues responded with a Manifes Kebudajaan (Manikebu, "Cultural Manifesto") in 1963 defending the independence of art. Lekra organized a campaign against the Manikebu, which Sukarno banned the following year. During this period, however, work by Lekra writers also faced increasing restriction and censorship by the military. The bitterness engendered by these exchanges created lasting animosities in the literary world. Along with other PKI affiliates, Lekra was banned after the installation of the **New Order**. *See also* CULTURE, DEBATE ON THE ROLE OF. [0221, 0225, 0994]

LESSER SUNDAS (Nusatenggara)**.** *See* BALI; FLORES; KOMODO; LOMBOK; ROTI; SAVU; SOLOR ARCHIPELAGO; SUMBA; SUMBAWA; TIMOR.

LIBERAL POLICY. Term generally applied to the colonial policy in force from 1870 to 1900, though signs of economic liberalism emerged as early as 1853 when some renting of **land** to Europeans was permitted. In 1870 the **Cultivation System** was formally abolished (though many of its features remained in force), and private Western businesses were admitted to the colony. In contrast with the state-directed exploitation of the Cultivation System, the Liberal Policy was a time of extensive investment by large companies, especially in the **rubber** and **tobacco** plantations of East **Sumatra**, the **sugar** and **tea** plantations of **Java**, and the **oil** wells of **Kalimantan**. *See also* AGRARIAN LAW OF 1870. [0601]

LIEM SIOE LIONG (Sudono Salim) (1916–)**.** Born in Fujian in southern China, he arrived in **Java** in 1936. He established a business supplying **cloves** to *kretek* factories in Kudus before the war and during the **Revolution** was apparently an important supplier to the Republican **army** in Central Java. In the 1950s he was involved in various business dealings with **Suharto**, then commander of the Diponegoro Division, and began to diversify into manufacturing and banking. When the **PRRI/Permesta rebellion** cut off clove supplies from **Minahasa**, he pioneered imports from **Madagascar** and Zanzibar.

Under the **New Order**, Liem Sioe Liong emerged as a major business partner of members of the **Suharto family** and was allocated monopolies and licenses that enabled his group to expand into **trade**, manufacture, property, finance, and logging. He founded the **Salim Group** in 1968, which by the 1990s was reputed to be the largest conglomerate in Southeast Asia. Liem was granted a monopoly over clove imports in 1968, and his capital base derived especially from that and later from **automobile** distributorships. In the late Suharto period, through the Salim group he was heavily represented in manufacture (especially cement and flour) and banking, with extensive offshore interests (*see also* **CENDANA GROUP**). Liem was also involved in many joint ventures with foreign investors as well as partnerships with local state and private enterprises.

LIGA DEMOKRASI (Democratic League)**.** Coalition formed by the **Partai Sosialis Indonesia (PSI)**, **Masjumi**, **Ikatan Pendukung Kemerdekaan Indonesia (IPKI)**, and others in 1960 to oppose **Sukarno**'s dissolution of the **Dewan Perwakilan Rakyat (DPR)** in March. It was hampered by the complicity of members of the Masjumi and PSI in the **PRRI/Permesta** uprising, and it disappeared when both parties were banned in August 1960.

LIMBURG STIRUM, J. P. GRAAF VAN (1873–1948). **Governor-general** (1916–1921), closely associated with the **Ethical Policy**. In November 1918, with political upheavals in the Netherlands suggesting an imminent socialist revolution there, van Limburg Stirum promised constitutional revisions to give greater say to Indonesians in the running of the colony. These "November promises" (*November beloften*) were not fulfilled and came to be seen by nationalists as a sign of Dutch unreliability, though a government inquiry completed in 1920 did lead to constitutional changes in 1922. *See also* NETHERLANDS, CONSTITUTIONAL RELATIONSHIP WITH INDONESIA. [0620]

LINGGAJATI AGREEMENT. Initialed by the Netherlands and the Republic of Indonesia on 12 November 1946 and signed on 25 May 1947 as a settlement to the Indonesian-Dutch dispute. Its principal provisions were that the Dutch government recognized the Republic as the de facto authority in **Java** and **Sumatra**, and that both sides would work toward establishment of "a sovereign, democratic, federal state" consisting of the Republic of Indonesia (Java and Sumatra), Borneo (**Kalimantan**), and the Great East (**Sulawesi**, the Lesser Sundas, **Maluku**, and West New Guinea [**Papua**]) (*see* **FEDERALISM**). The federal state would then join with the Netherlands in a Netherlands-Indonesian Union. Negotiations were conducted under strong British pressure (*see* **BRITAIN**), and the agreement was the result of a personal rapprochement between the leaders of the two delegations, **Sutan Sjahrir** and the former Dutch Prime Minister Willem Schermerhorn (1894–1977). It was immensely unpopular in both countries. **Sukarno** and **Mohammad Hatta** were only able to have it ratified by the Republican parliament (**Komité Nasional Indonesia Pusat [KNIP]**) by stacking the membership and making the issue one of confidence in their leadership, and the Dutch parliament ratified it only after adding unilaterally a number of additional interpretations and conditions. The agreement broke down formally over the Dutch refusal to allow Republican participation in decision making for the Dutch-controlled territories and over continued breaches of the cease-fire by both sides. *See also* POLICE ACTIONS; RENVILLE AGREEMENT. [0661, 0674, 0682, 1146]

LINSCHOTEN, JAN HUYGEN VAN (1563–1611). As secretary to the archbishop of **Portuguese** Goa (1583–1589), he traveled much in the Indian Ocean region, later publishing two books describing what he had seen. His 1596 *Itinerario naer Oost ofte Portugaels Indien* (Itinerary to the East or Portuguese Indies) was read widely in western Europe and stimulated formation of both the **Dutch East Indies Company (VOC)** and the **English East India Company**. He argued especially that poor Portuguese relations with Asian peoples gave other European countries an opportunity to compete in the markets there, and he identified **Java** as a suitable base for Dutch operations. [0081]

LITERACY. *See* EDUCATION; WOMEN; WRITING SYSTEMS.

LOMBOK. The indigenous Sasak people of Lombok came under Muslim Javanese influence in the 16th century, but from the early 17th century Muslim **Makassar** and **Bima** fought the Hindu Balinese kingdom of Karangasem for control of the island. Balinese power grew from 1677, and by 1740 Karangasem controlled the whole island. Many Balinese settled in the west, and by the early 19th century four independent Balinese kingdoms had emerged there, based partly on **rice** exports to **China**, **Singapore**, and **Australia**. The kingdom of **Mataram** emerged as the dominant power in 1838 but faced continual resistance and occasional rebellion from the Sasaks in the east. The raja accepted Dutch sovereignty in 1843, but in the late 19th century the Dutch sought closer control to suppress **opium** trading and **slavery**. A major Sasak rebellion in 1891 was supported by the Dutch in 1894. After heavy fighting, Mataram was destroyed, and the defeated court committed ritual suicide (*puputan*). *See also* BALI; NAGARAKRTAGAMA. [0100, 0529, 0810]

LONTAR (*Borassus flabellifer,* Arecaceae)**.** From Sanskrit ron tal, leaf of the tala tree, it was probably introduced from India but is now well established especially in eastern Indonesia. Palm leaves were used for writing on **Bali** from the seventh century, though earliest use was probably of Corypha leaves rather than lontar. The fragile nature of palm leaves, especially in the tropics, is a major reason for the tiny proportion of traditional literature preserved in the archipelago. Lontar was gradually displaced by paper from about the 17th century. *See also* ROTI. [0576, 1220]

LUBIS, MOCHTAR (1922–)**.** Journalist and novelist, founder of the newspaper *Indonesia Raya* (1949–1974) and author of various novels, including *Road with No End* (Jalan tak ada ujung, 1952) and *Senja di Jakarta* (Twilight in Jakarta, 1957). He was a prominent part of the liberal opposition to various aspects of both **Guided Democracy** and the **New Order** and was jailed by both governments. [0247, 0926]

LUBIS, ZULKIFLI (1923–1994?). A Mandailing Batak born in **Aceh**, Lubis was a cousin of **A. H. Nasution**. Trained as an intelligence officer by the Japanese, he was responsible for setting up the Republic's **intelligence services** in 1945. During the **Revolution** he headed successive Republican intelligence organizations, notably the Polisi Militer Khusus (Special Military Police) and the Field Preparation. In October 1952, he opposed **army** officers (including Nasution) who organized demonstrations urging **Sukarno** to dissolve parliament. As acting army chief of staff, Lubis led a boycott of the installation ceremony of his successor, Bambang Sugeng (1913–1977) in 1955 and attempted a coup against Nasution in 1956. He was accused of responsibility for the assassination attempt against Sukarno in November 1957 and fled to **Sumatra**, where he emerged as a military commander of the **PRRI/Permesta rebellion**. Jailed in 1961 after the rebellion failed, he was released in 1966. [0695, 0708, 0714, 1121]

LUWU. The earliest **Bugis** state in southern **Sulawesi**, which emerged in the ninth century at the head of the gulf of **Bone**. Little is known of its early history, but it may have been based partly on **trade** in **nickel** from the interior. From the 15th century it began to lose influence to states such as **Wajo'** and Bone. It was converted to **Islam** in the 17th century. [0549]

– M –

MADAGASCAR, HISTORICAL LINKS WITH. Extensive Austronesian migration to Madagascar took place from the fifth century, continuing in sporadic waves until the 12th or even 15th century. The specific ethnicity of the migrants, who were probably pirates or traders or both and who probably traveled via Ceylon or South India, is uncertain. Ninety-four percent of the basic vocabulary in modern Malagasy is of Indonesian origin and is closest to the languages of the Batak and the Manyaan **Dayak**. The Austronesians brought with them a number of Asian plants, including probably **rice**, **yam**, and banana, and created on Madagascar a hybrid Indonesian-African culture. Cultural and technological influences include rice cultivation in irrigated terraces, outrigger canoes, double funerals, and the use of megaliths in ancestor worship. **Hindu**istic cultural influence from Indonesia, including an established aristocracy, is strongest among the Imerina in central Madagascar. Approximately one third of the genetic composition of contemporary Madagascar population is Austronesian. *See also* AFRICA, HISTORICAL LINKS WITH; MIGRATIONS. [0537]

MADIUN AFFAIR. Uprising by sections of the **Partai Komunis Indonesia (PKI)** in **Java** in September and October 1948. After the first Dutch **"Police Action,"** the Republican enclave in east and central Java faced an economic crisis that forced the government of **Mohammad Hatta** to dismiss large numbers of government employees and to demobilize significant parts of the **armed forces**. Prime targets for demobilization were those associated with the leftist former prime minister, **Amir Sjarifuddin**, and politics in the Republic polarized increasingly between left and right as the austerity program bit deeper. PKI leaders probably did not intend to stage a rebellion at this time, but when tensions reached the point of armed clashes and the Hatta government treated the left as rebels, PKI leaders in Madiun declared a communist government. Party leaders including **Musso** and Amir then sided with the rebels, accusing the Hatta government of having betrayed the ideals of the **Revolution**. Full-scale civil war followed, in which Muslim-communist antagonisms led to a number of massacres on both sides. Within a month, the rising was suppressed, especially by the West Javanese troops of the Siliwangi Division. Musso was killed, while Amir was arrested, only to be killed by government forces during the second Dutch "Police Action." The affair made a lasting impression on Indonesian politics: the PKI was accused not only of gratuitous brutality in its massacres of Muslims but also of stabbing the Republic in the back as it defended national independence against the Dutch; the party in turn accused Hatta of cynically provoking the affair so as to have an excuse to remove the proponents of armed revolution and to come to a compromise with the Dutch. [0645, 0683, 0684, 1128]

MADJID, NURCHOLISH (1939-). A leading Muslim intellectual who was born in Jombang, East **Java**, into a **Nahdlatul Ulama (NU)** family, but whose father remained with the **Masjumi** when the NU split off in 1953. Schooled first in ***pesantren*** in East Java, including the Gontor school in Ponorogo, he continued his studies at the State Institute of **Islam** in **Jakarta**. In the late 1950s and early 1960s, he was active in the Muslim student organization, **Himpunan Mahasiswa Indonesia (HMI)**, becoming its chairman. Later, as director of the student action committee **Kesatuan Aksi Mahasiswa Indonesia (KAMI)**, he cooperated with the military in the demonstrations leading to the overthrow of **Sukarno**. In the debates over the government's banning of the Masjumi party, he argued for the secularization of the political arena and against an **Islamic state**. In the late 1970s Nurcholish attended the University of Chicago, gaining his Ph.D. in 1984 with a thesis on the thinking of Ibnu Taimiyah. Two years later he established Paramadina, an association aimed at urban proselytization, and he became rector of Paramadina Mulya University in **Jakarta**. He was an influential member of **Ikatan Cendekiawan Muslimin Indonesia (ICMI)**, and has been a constant voice for moderation in the Muslim intellectual community, arguing for pluralism and democratic values. In May 2003 he announced that he would be a candidate in the 2004 presidential election. [1029, 1034, 1355, 1356]

MADRASAH*.** Nonresidential private Islamic schools offering a mixed religious and secular curriculum. Although tracing their roots back to 11th-century Sunni educational institutions, *madrasah* became widespread in Egypt in the late 19th century where development of their curricula was tied to educational reforms of the modernist movement. Many founded in **Java** in the early 20th century by the **Muhammadiyah** competed with the traditionalist ***pesantren and took their method of instruction from European models. The **Sumatra** Thawalib, an extensive network of modernist schools offering both religious and secular education, developed out of the traditionalist *surau* in Padang Panjang, West Sumatra, from the early 20th century, and in 1915 an even more modern Diniyah school was established by Zainuddin Labai (1890–1924), also in Padang Panjang. *See also* EDUCATION, PRIVATE AND ISLAMIC. [0045, 0807, 1039, 1273]

MADURA. Island off the northeast coast of **Java**, generally united with it for statistical purposes. Dry, relatively infertile, and suffering regularly from famine, it was ruled by **Majapahit** until 1466, when a revolt under Kyai Demung founded Sumenep (Bangkalan) as an independent state. **Islam** was established in the early 16th century (c. 1528) and the three sultanates of Sumenep, Pamekasan, and Madura became trading powers, though the island was best known for **salt** production and military forces. **Sultan Agung** of **Mataram** conquered Madura in 1623, installing the Cakraningrat dynasty as his vassals. In 1671, however, the Madurese prince **Trunojoyo** rebelled, conquered the island, captured the court of Amangkurat I of Mataram, and was only beaten back from the mainland after the intervention of **Dutch East Indies Company (VOC)** troops.

During this time, many Madurese settled in eastern Java. The company was able to conquer the eastern part of Madura in 1705, and the Mataram ruler ceded the remainder in 1740, though not until 1745 was Dutch control firmly in place, the company placing restrictions on the rulers' foreign relations and demanding tribute in the form of cash, **cotton**, **coconut** oil, and troops. Madurese barisan (formed 1831) were an important element in the colonial armed forces until the early 20th century (*see* **NATIVE TROOPS**). In the 19th century, although the Cakraningrats remained the dominant family, their status was steadily eroded as they lost **taxation** rights; in 1813 **Thomas Stamford Raffles** introduced a government salt monopoly, which was largely farmed out to wealthy **Chinese** entrepreneurs (*see* ***PACHT***). In 1885 the Dutch introduced direct rule, the sultans being demoted to the rank of ***bupati***. A later member of the family was employed by the Dutch to head the *Negara Madura,* formed on 21 January 1948, as part of the proposed postwar Indonesian federation (*see* **FEDERALISM**). [0008, 1265]

MAHABHARATA**.** Epic poem originally from **India**, the earliest known Old Javanese text dating from the late 10th century. Episodes (*lakon*) are widely performed in ***wayang*** *kulit, golek,* and *wong,* and are often presented as allegories of contemporary events. The story tells of the prolonged struggle between the five Pandawas (sons of Pandu) and 100 Kurawas (sons of Dhrarashta), which culminated in the destruction of almost all the characters in a final cataclysmic battle, the Bharatayudha. *See also RAMAYANA.* [0132, 0159]

MAHKAMAH MILITER LUAR BIASA (Mahmillub, Extraordinary Military Tribunal)**.** First established by President **Sukarno** on 24 December 1963 to try those deemed by the president to be a threat to the security of the Indonesian state and people, but used primarily after 1965 to try those accused of involvement in the **Gestapu** coup of 1965. Trials began on 13 February 1966 with the surviving **Partai Komunis Indonesia (PKI)** leader Nyono and went on to include **Subandrio**, the air force chief Omar Dhani, and the coup leader Untung. Sukarno was not brought to trial, but evidence presented, especially at the trial of Jusuf Muda Dalam, appeared to implicate his regime in **corruption** and abuse of power. A total of 894 people were tried until March 1978, most being sentenced to death or to prison terms of 20 or more years. Many of the accused were defended by **Yap Thiam Hien**. *See also TAHANAN POLITIK*. [0727, 0741]

MAJAPAHIT. Kingdom in East **Java**, generally regarded as the high point of **Hindu**-Javanese culture, though relatively little is known of it. After the overthrow of King Kertanegara of **Singasari** by rebels from **Kediri**, Java was abruptly invaded in 1292–1293 by a Mongol army seeking revenge for Kertanegara's expulsion of Mongol envoys in 1289. Unaware of the details of Javanese politics, they were persuaded by Kertanegara's son Wijaya (?–1309) to help him overthrow the Kediri prince Jayakatwang. With Kediri defeated, Wijaya then turned on the Mongols and drove them out. He moved his capital to Trowulan, established the kingdom of Majapahit, and took the name Kertarajasa Jayavardhana.

Majapahit experienced a golden age under the rule of Hayam Wuruk (Rajasanagara, r. 1350–1389) and his prime minister, Gajah Mada. Agricultural production was the basis of the state, but Majapahit also seems to have traded food, especially to **Maluku**, and the king was probably a major trader in his own right. State religion was Sivaitic Hinduism in which the Buddha was also worshipped. Majapahit society was extensively described by the court poet Prapanca in the *Nagarakrtagama,* which also includes a list of supposed dependencies covering the whole archipelago, including parts of New Guinea as well as the **Malay Peninsula**, the southern Philippines, and perhaps northern **Australia**. This list has sometimes been used to give the idea of an archipelago-wide state a respectable, noncolonial antiquity (*see* **NATIONALISM**; **SUCCESSION**), and even to imply vague Indonesian claims on surrounding territories, but most scholars now believe that Majapahit's influence outside East and Central Java was limited to coastal areas of **Kalimantan** and **Sumatra** and parts of Maluku and **Nusatenggara**, though a military expedition to **Bali** in 1343 is said to have established Old Javanese culture there. Majapahit apparently declined after Hayam Wuruk's death and was wracked by civil war and rebellion through much of the 15th century. Either it or a Hindu successor state was conquered by the coastal Muslim state of **Demak** in circa 1527. [0528, 0535, 0573]

MAJELIS ISLAM A'LAA INDONESIA (MIAI, Supreme Islamic Council of Indonesia). Federation of Muslim organizations, founded in September 1937 by K. Mansur, Ahmad Dahlan, and Abdul Wahab for the discussion of religious matters. At the 1938 All **Islam** Congress, delegates from the **Partai Sarekat Islam Indonesia (PSII)** and the **Partai Islam Indonesia (PII)** pushed the organization to take a stand on political issues, and in 1942 a conference of Muslim leaders under Japanese auspices agreed to recognize it as a central coordinating body for Muslim affairs. The Japanese in the event declined to deal with the MIAI, instead creating on Java the **Masjumi**. [0648]

MAJELIS PERMUSYAWARATAN RAKYAT (MPR, People's Deliberative Assembly)**.** Indonesia's supreme representative body, which meets once every five years following the national elections and has had the major functions of electing the **president** and **vice president**; determining the Broad Outlines of State Policy (Garis Besar Haluan Negara, GBHN), which state the broad aims and principles of government policy for the next five years; and amending the **Constitution**, though in 1966 it declared that the preamble to the constitution, containing the **Pancasila**, was inalterable. It also has the power to impeach the president. The 1945 Constitution provided for the MPR, but it was not assembled until 1959, when **Sukarno** added presidential nominees (94 from the **provinces** and 200 from the functional groups) to the existing 281-member house of representatives to create a 575-member MPR-Sementara (MPRS, Provisional MPR). This MPRS met in 1959, 1963, and 1965 under Sukarno; in 1966 to ratify the transfer of power to Suharto; in 1967 to appoint **Suharto** acting president; and in 1968 to elect him full president.

Under regulations passed in November 1969, a full MPR (no longer provisional) was constituted with 920 members, comprising all 460 members of the largely elected **Dewan Perwakilan Rakyat (DPR)** together with 207 presidential nominees, 121 nominees from elected parties, 130 provincial representatives, and two nominees from parties unsuccessful in the DPR elections. In 1987 membership was increased to 1,000, about half of whom wre not DPR members.

A turning point leading to the fall of Suharto occurred when the head of the MPR, Harmoko, who was a Suharto loyalist, called on the president to resign in an MPR session on 18 May 1998. The MPR also came into conflict with Suharto's successors, especially **Abdurrachman Wahid**. It urged him in August 2000 to take stronger measures against separatist movements, and it refused to endorse his decision to change Irian Jaya's name to **Papua**. In June 2001 it removed him from office through impeachment, naming as his successor his vice president, **Megawati Sukarnoputri**. In August 2002 the MPR voted to introduce direct presidential elections in 2004, under which if no single candidate receives more than 50 percent of the vote, there will be a second round of balloting. In the same session it also voted to abolish in 2004 the 38 parliamentary seats reserved for the military, and it rejected calls from the **Partai Persatuan Pembangunan (PPP)** and other smaller parties to introduce **Islamic law**. Starting in 2002 a series of constitutional amendments stripped the MPR of much of its power. Under Article 11 of Law No. 22/2003 its functions were limited to amending the constitution, making the final decision on the impeachment of the **president** or **vice president**, formally installing the president and vice president and selecting a new president and vice president in emergency situations. A constitutional amendment in August 2002 provided for MPR membership to be drawn entirely from elected members of the DPR and the new Regional Representative Council (DPD). *See also* KOMITÉ NASIONAL INDONESIA PUSAT. [1100]

MAKASSAR (Gowa, Goa)**.** Kingdom in South **Sulawesi**, which grew after circa 1530 from the **ports** of Gowa and Tallo. Reorganized from a loose federation to a centrally governed state by Karaëng (King) Tumapa'risi in the early 16th century, partly with the assistance of Malay refugees from the fall of **Melaka**, it dominated the west coast of southern Sulawesi by the end of the century. With the decline of the **rice** trade from **Java**, Karaeng Matoaya, ruler of Tallo and prime minister of Makassar, expanded local rice production for **trade** to **Maluku** in exchange for **nutmeg** and **cloves**. In 1605 Makassar converted to **Islam** and began a series of campaigns to control the region, conquering its main rival, **Bone**, in a campaign from 1608 to 1611. Overseas expansion followed, with operations against **Sumbawa** (1617), **Buru**, Seram, **Banten**, and eastern **Kalimantan**, though in all cases it ruled through vassals rather than directly. It may have been these campaigns that dispersed the Bajau from the region. From early in the 17th century, Makassar became a major base for **Portuguese**, British, Danish, and Asian traders attempting to thwart the Dutch spice monopoly in Maluku, and it came under corresponding pressure from the Dutch to grant them a monopoly. In 1666 Cornelis Speelman launched a major expedition against Sultan Hasanuddin (1653–1669), who was defeated in 1667 by the Dutch and **Bugis** (*see* **ARUNG PALAKKA**) forces. Under the treaty of Bungaya (1667), Makassar was reduced to little more than the port of Gowa. A rebellion by Hasanuddin in 1668–1669 was suppressed.

After a period of decline in the 18th century, the city emerged in the 19th century as a major trade center in eastern Indonesia and the capital city respectively of the gouvernement of the Grote Oost (*see* **PROVINCES**), the Japanese naval administration in eastern Indonesia, and the **Negara Indonesia Timur (NIT)**. Local support for the Indonesian Republic was suppressed first by Australian troops and then, in a brutal fashion, by Dutch forces under **R. P. P. Westerling**. In 1971 the city's name was changed to Ujung Pandang, but it was changed back to Makassar after **Suharto**'s fall. [0508, 0549, 0574, 0660, 0786, 0787, 0831, 1246]

MALACCA. *See* MELAKA.

MALARI (Malapetaka 15 Januari, Disaster of 15 January). **Student** demonstrations in **Jakarta** on 15–16 January 1974, which were seen as the first major political challenge to the **New Order**. Occurring at a time when **oil** prices were skyrocketing, a visit by Japanese Prime Minister Kakuei Tanaka became the occasion for widespread demonstrations not only by students but also by large numbers of Jakarta's poor people. Japanese cars were among the targets of the demonstrators, but the growing strength of foreign companies in general, the increasing wealth of military bureaucrats and their **Chinese** business partners (***cukong***), and the general **corruption** and extravagance of the government were the principal complaints. Student demands, like those of the 1966 **Kesatuan Aksi Mahasiswa Indonesia (KAMI)**, were summarized as Tri Tuntutan Rakyat (Tritura, Three Demands of the People), namely the dissolution of the presidential staff or ASPRI (Asisten Presiden Republik Indonesia), lower prices, and an end to corruption. The play *The Struggle of the Naga Tribe* by **W. S. Rendra** and the song "Tante Sun" by Bimbo played some role in focusing discontent, but the demonstrations were also a vehicle for intraregime rivalries between General Soemitro, head of **Komando Operasi Pemulihan Keamanan dan Ketertiban (Kopkamtib)**, and General **Ali Murtopo** of the **Operasi Khusus**. A student, Hariman Siregar, and a lecturer, Syahrir, both of Universitas Indonesia, were later tried and sentenced under the Anti-Subversion Law for inciting the riots. (*See also* **SUBVERSION**.)

Malari led to important changes in New Order policy that calmed the opposition. Soemitro was dismissed, six newspapers (*Abadi, Harian KAMI, Indonesia Raya, Mahasiswa Indonesia, Nusantara,* and *Pedoman*) were closed, and Daud Yusuf was appointed **education** minister with the task of depoliticizing the universities. At the same time **Suharto** introduced a number of regulations encouraging greater participation by indigenous entrepreneurs in the economy by stipulating that all new foreign **investment** would have to be in the form of joint ventures with ***pribumi*** partners rather than with Chinese and that foreign investors would have to present plans for the local businessmen to achieve eventual majority ownership of the joint business ventures. [0399, 0733, 0736, 0742]

MALARIA. A fever disease caused by the protozoan parasite *Plasmodium* that has been one of the blights of life in Indonesia since early times and may have been one of the factors limiting state formation and the growth of complex societies in the region. **Cinchona** bark was recognized from the late 18th century as offering relief and sometimes cure, and its extensive cultivation on Java helped to make the tropics habitable. The connection between the disease and the bites of various species of the mosquito *Anopheles* was discovered only in 1898, and from 1924 a Central Malaria Bureau of the colonial government began eradication programs, both by water management and by use of insecticides. Extensive spraying with DDT began in 1951. *See also* HEALTH. [1204]

MALAY PENINSULA, HISTORICAL LINKS WITH. Although attached to the Southeast Asian mainland by the isthmus of Kra, the Malay Peninsula belonged historically to the island world of the Indonesian archipelago almost as much as neighboring **Sumatra**. The indigenous Malay population of the peninsula was ethnically identical to the Malays of the eastern coast of Sumatra and the **Riau** archipelago, and states along the Strait of **Melaka** traditionally sought control of both sides of the waterway, regardless of which shore they happened to be on (*see* **ACEH**; **JAMBI**; **SRIVIJAYA**). **Buddhism** and later **Islam** reached both sides of the strait at about the same time, and with comparable impact, though the peninsula was much later in developing major kingdoms than was Sumatra. The cultural and political influence of **Siam**, on the other hand, was not significantly felt beyond the northern and eastern parts of the peninsula.

The **Anglo-Dutch Treaty** of 1824 separated the peninsula from the archipelago politically, but economic ties remained strong. Penang, founded in 1786, became the major port for produce from East Sumatra, first **pepper** and later **rubber**, and **Singapore** became a major entrepôt for much of the western archipelago. During the 19th and 20th centuries, there was extensive migration from Sumatra and **Java** to the peninsula; **Minangkabau** communities are especially strong in Negeri Sembilan. Sumatra and the peninsula were both under the Japanese 25th army from 1942 to 1943, and in the period immediately after the Japanese surrender, an organization called Kesatuan Raayat Indonesia Semenanjung (KRIS, Union of Indonesian People of the Peninsula) under Ibrahim Yaakob briefly campaigned for the inclusion of Malaya in the new Indonesian Republic. During the **Revolution**, Singapore and Penang were major centers for the smuggling of weapons to the nationalists and for the legal and clandestine sale of Indonesian produce. In the 1950s, the Federation of Malaya provided support and encouragement to the

PRRI/Permesta rebellion in Sumatra. *See also* MALAYSIA, RELATIONS WITH. [1068, 1110, 1121, 1363]

MALAYSIA (term). *See* INDONESIA; MALESIA.

MALAYSIA, RELATIONS WITH. After World War II, the British in Malaya began to move gradually to grant greater autonomy to their Southeast Asian possessions (the **Malay Peninsula** and **Singapore**, Sarawak, Brunei, and North Borneo [Sabah]). In 1961 these moves crystallized in plans to create a federal state of Malaysia incorporating all British territories. Indonesia was unhappy about this proposal for several reasons: Britain was to retain its naval base in Singapore, the Malay sultans were to retain a powerful political role, people in northern Borneo seemed hostile to the federation, and Indonesia, although the largest power in the region, had not been consulted on the plan. **Sukarno** announced in January 1963 that the Malaysia proposal was unacceptable, a position that was also adopted by the Philippine president, Diosdado Macapagal. At Macapagal's instigation, leaders of the three countries met first in Tokyo and then in Manila (*see* **MAPHILINDO**), where they agreed that the federation would be formed after a **United Nations**' ascertainment of attitudes toward it in North Borneo and Sarawak (Brunei had by this time pulled out of the proposal). But in late August **Britain** announced the federation would form regardless of opinion in the Borneo states. Indonesia then announced a **Confrontation** against Malaysia, which ended only on 11 August 1966 after the overthrow of the Sukarno regime.

In 1970 a "Friendship Treaty" regulated the complex marine border between the two counties, dividing the **Melaka** Strait along a median line while acknowledging Malaysian traditional fishing rights and a general right of free passage in the South China Sea between East and West Malaysia, though this left unresolved a dispute over the ownership of two islands off the eastern coast of Borneo near the Sabah–Kalimantan border. Since the 1970s the Malaysian government has informally permitted the migration of significant numbers of Indonesian Muslims to Malaysia to increase the "indigenous" ("*bumiputera*") proportion of the **population**. Malaysia became the first country to recognize Indonesia's archipelagic concept in February 1982. In December 1987 Indonesia and Malaysia signed an agreement to cooperate in the marketing of **oil palm**, **rubber**, and other agricultural products. Both countries are members of the **Association of Southeast Asian Nations (ASEAN)**.

On 1 August 2002 a new Malaysian law went into effect calling for the imprisonment and caning of all illegal workers, which led to the deportation and exodus of thousands of Indonesian migrant workers (some estimates as high as 400,000). [0478, 1027, 1120, 1319]

MALESIA. Latin-Italian term for the Malay world, first popularized by Odo Beccari (1843–1920) in his three-volume natural history work *Malesia* (1877). Up until 1962 the term "Malaysia" was more common, but the imminent creation of the state of Malaysia (1963) demanded a change in usage, and the term *Malesia* was adopted for the botanical region encompassing insular Southeast Asia, peninsular Malaysia, and New Guinea, including the Bismarck Archipelago. *See also* INDONESIA; WALLACE'S LINE.

MALIK, ADAM (1917–1984). Journalist and nationalist politician, one of the early leaders of the **Antara** news agency before the war and an employee of the Japanese news agency Domei during the occupation. During the **Revolution**, Malik was close to **Tan Malaka** and in 1948 joined the **Murba** party. Although a strong supporter of the general structure of **Guided Democracy**, he opposed the rising strength of the **Partai Komunis Indonesia (PKI)**, helping to form the anticommunist **Badan Pendukung Sukarnoisme (BPS)** in 1964. After the **Gestapu** coup, he became minister of foreign affairs (1966–1977) in a symbolic **New Order** triumvirate with **Suharto** and **Hamengkubuwono IX**. His greatest achievement in this position was probably his success in 1970 in keeping Indonesia out of the **Cambodia** conflict. He served as **vice president** from 1977 to 1982. [0741, 0862]

MALUKU. The large archipelago lying between **Sulawesi**, **Papua**, and **Timor**, consisting especially of the islands of **Ambon**, **Aru**, **Banda**, **Buru**, **Halmahera**, Seram, Tanimbar, **Ternate**, **Tidore**, Sula, Kai, and Wetar. The area around Ambon formerly known as the South Moluccas is now known as central Maluku. The region is ethnically and culturally diverse, showing both Malay and Papuan influences (*see also* **MIGRATIONS**; **WALLACE'S LINE**). It has been economically significant since early times for its spices (e.g., **cloves** and **nutmeg**). In the 14th century it seems to have been dominated by the Javanese kingdom of **Majapahit**, while in the 16th century the sultanates of Ternate and Tidore ruled many of the islands. The **Portuguese** signed an alliance with Ternate in 1511 and for much of the following century and a half, the Portuguese, Spanish, and Dutch competed with each other and with local powers for control (*see also* **DUTCH EAST INDIES COMPANY**; ***HONGI* RAIDS**). Extensive Christianization took place in the region. It was the center of the strongest opposition to the Republic's imposition of authority after the transfer of sovereignty from the Dutch (*see* **REPUBLIK MALUKU SELATAN**).

After **Suharto**'s resignation in 1998, Maluku became a center of interethnic and interreligious violence. From January 1999 there was fighting in Ambon and southern areas of Maluku, and after the establishment in October 1999 of a new province in North Maluku (which encompasses Halmahera and the surrounding islands, including Ternate and Tidore [*see* map 12] and also the Sula archipelago to the southeast), fighting spread to that area. The North Maluku provincial government estimated that over 2,000 people died over the next five months, and in Maluku as a whole more than 5,000 people were killed between 1999 and 2002. Internal displacement was estimated at between 123,000 and 370,000. Many refugees began returning in mid-2001, but a large proportion of the Christians decided not to go back, the largest group (approximately 30,000—mostly from Ternate, Tidore, and southern Halmahera) being in refugee camps in northern Sulawesi. In February 2002 Christian and Muslim leaders from the Moluccan Islands signed a peace accord in Makassar (Malino II) agreeing to surrender their weapons, but two months later violence again broke out with at least 12 people killed. On 29 April the military asked for martial law to be imposed on Maluku. [0079, 0650, 0781, 0967, 1221]

MANADO. See MINAHASA.

MANDAR. Region on the western coast of South **Sulawesi**, traditionally divided into several small communities that sometimes coalesced, especially for warfare, into one or two confederations. In the early 17th century, it came under the domination of **Makassar**. [0549]

MANGKUBUMI (?–1792)**.** Prince of **Mataram** who rebelled against Pakubuwono II in 1742 and again in 1745, especially as a result of Pakubuwono's 1743 decision to lease the north coast of **Java** to the **Dutch East Indies Company (VOC)**. He had himself declared king on Pakubuwono's death in 1749, taking the title sultan and the name Hamengkubuwono (I) in 1755. After a protracted war with the VOC and its protégés in Mataram, he agreed in the Treaty of **Giyanti** to accept half the kingdom together with 10,000 *reals* as his share of proceeds from the VOC lease on the north coast. He established his court in **Yogyakarta** and was founder of the present dynasty. *See also* HAMENGKUBUWONO IX.

MANGKUNEGARAN. Minor court in **Surakarta**, established in 1757 by the partition of the Sunanate. The court's armed forces, the Legiun Mangkunegaran, were reorganized by **Herman Willem Daendels**, making them one of the few significant indigenous military forces on **Java** in the late colonial period (*see* **NATIVE TROOPS**). Mangkunegoro II (1796–1835) and IV (r. 1853–1881) established an extensive **sugar** and **tobacco** plantation sector in the Mangkunegaran lands. In 1946 the Mangkunegaran was formally abolished, along with the Surakarta court, after it failed to support the Republic unequivocally, but its informal position improved during the **Suharto** presidency due to its family connection with his wife, Siti Hartinah ("Tien").

MANIFES KEBUDAYAAN (Manikebu, Cultural Manifesto). Issued in October 1963 by a group of writers, intellectuals, and artists, including **H. B. Jassin**, Gunawan Muhamad, and Wiratmo Sukito, as an affirmation of the values of "universal humanism" and a rejection of the idea, promoted by **Lembaga Kebudayaan Rakyat (Lekra)**, that artistic quality was better judged by social criteria than by self-referencing aesthetic notions. After extensive debate, the manifesto was banned by **Sukarno** on 8 May 1964. *See also* CULTURE, DEBATE ON THE ROLE OF. [0159, 0225]

MANIFESTO POLITIK. 1. Statement issued by Republican leaders on 1 November 1945, promising inter alia that the Indonesian Republic would respect the property rights of foreign investors. The government hoped in this way to win international approval, but the policy aroused strong domestic opposition. [0643, 0913]

2. (Also called MANIPOL.) The ideology of **Guided Democracy** as set out in **Sukarno**'s independence day speech on 17 August 1959 and adopted by the Dewan Pertimbangan Agung (DPA) as the Broad Outlines of State Policy (Garis Besar Haluan Negara, GBHN) in September 1959. In it Sukarno called for social justice, a return to the spirit of the **Revolution**, and a "retooling" of state organs. In 1960 MANIPOL was elaborated with the addition of the acronym USDEK (Undang-undang '45, 1945 Constitution; Sosialisme à la Indonesia,

Indonesian socialism; Demokrasi Terpimpin, Guided Democracy; Ekonomi Terpimpin, Guided Economy; and Kepribadian Indonesia, Indonesian Identity). The precise meaning of each of these terms remained vague, but MANIPOL soon became associated as a slogan with the Left in Indonesian politics, and it was formally repudiated by the Majelis Permusyawaratan Rakyat—Sementara (MPR-S) in 1967. [0859]

MAPHILINDO. Rubric for the proposed confederation of Malaya, the Philippines, and Indonesia, proposed by President Diosdado Macapagal of the Philippines and discussed by leaders of the three states in a series of meetings and conferences held in May–August 1963. Both Indonesia and the Philippines, however, had already announced their reservations regarding the formation of **Malaysia**, and the Maphilindo idea disappeared with the full launching of Indonesia's **Confrontation** against the new federation in September 1963, though it provided some basis for the later formation of **Association of Southeast Asian Nations (ASEAN)**. [0478, 1123, 1144]

MARDIJKERS. Portuguese-speaking descendants of freed slaves, who formed a separate, large social category in 17th-century **Batavia**. *See also* DEPOK. [0584, 0585]

MARÉCHAUSSÉE. The failure of conventional military tactics in the war in **Aceh** led the colonial authorities in 1890 to form small military units of mixed race to operate as counterguerrilla or commando forces largely independent of the tactical command of **Koninklijk Nederlands-Indisch Leger (KNIL)** officers. These units, familiar with the countryside and each other, and small enough to move unobtrusively, were a qualified success and in the early 20th century were used in other areas as a kind of militarized **police** force.

MARHAEN. The term adopted by **Sukarno** (probably from a Sundanese word for a small farmer) to denote the large numbers of Indonesians, especially peasants, who, although poverty-stricken and oppressed by colonial capitalism, were nonetheless owners of some of the means of production (e.g., a small plot of **land** or a few tools) and were thus not proletarians. In Sukarno's early usage, the term encompassed most Indonesians; later it was restricted to poorer sections of society. *See also* CLASS ANALYSIS; MARXISM. [0859, 0918]

MARIJUANA. *See* CANNABIS.

MARRIAGE, POLITICAL SIGNIFICANCE OF. Among aristocracies in early Indonesia, marriage seems to have been, as it was in Europe, a tool for allying families and kingdoms. On the one hand, rulers typically had many wives, drawn from the families of vassals and allies, and the status of those wives was often a measure of the vassals' and allies' status (*see* ***KIDUNG SUNDA***). On the other hand, **women** were in some respects at least the locus of power, and rulers gained their legitimacy in part by virtue of the women they married. Thus, **Ken Angrok** married his predecessor's widow and the sultans of **Yogyakarta** symbolically marry the Queen of the South Seas, Nyai Loro Kidul, when they ascend the throne. The queens of **Aceh** were more or less prevented from marrying in order to prevent them from allying formally with any of the internal forces in the state. In a later time, **Sukarno**'s marriage to a Japanese former nightclub hostess, Nemoto Naoko (Ratna Dewi Sari), led to suggestions that he was too close to **Japan**. The political value of marriage tended to mean that both sons and daughters were married at or soon after puberty, but in the rest of society, later marriages (between the ages of 15 and 21) seem to have been more common and monogamy was the general rule, though divorce by either side was easy and frequent. A bride price was commonly paid, but it went to the bride herself rather than to her family.

The arrival of **Islam** transformed the character of marriage, though the extent to which Islamic marriage law was followed varied widely. Where Muslim influence was strongest, daughters in particular married earlier, arranged marriages became more common, and women lost the right to initiate divorce. In European society, formal marriage between Europeans and Indonesians was always strongly discouraged and sometimes prohibited, but concubinage was common. A nyai or concubine was sometimes little more than a sexual slave, but many became powerful partners of their European husbands and some were strong traders and managers in their own right. The status of children from these unions varied: if the father formally acknowledged them they had European status, if not they took that of the mother. When interracial marriages were permitted, the wife took the legal status of her husband (*see* **RACE**). Jean Taylor has shown that in 17th- and 18th-century **Batavia**, political alliances between senior and junior **Dutch East Indies Company (VOC)** officials were often cemented by marriages between junior officials and the Eurasian daughters of their seniors.

In the 20th century the Dutch allowed Muslim marriages to be conducted and registered by Muslim officials of the Department of Religious Affairs. This system was retained by the Republic. Protests against early marriage for girls began in the early 20th century, with, for example, **R. A. Kartini** writing against it and letters also appearing in the West Sumatran women's paper *Soenting Melajoe* arguing against parental pressure for girls to marry early. The women's branch of the **Sarekat Islam** embraced policies to combat child marriage.

The Republic retained the practice of marriages being conducted by Muslim officials of the Religious Affairs Department. A series of unsuccessful efforts was made to enact legislative reforms of Islamic marriage law, but none was successful. In 1973, however, the government prepared a draft marriage law that would have enforced monogamy, required state registration of all marriages, and permitted cross-religion marriages, which are anathema to Islam. The draft law led to fierce opposition by the **Partai Persatuan Pembangunan (PPP)** and other Muslim groups, and to heated debate in parliament. The amended law, which was eventually passed in 1974, permitted polygamy but put greater restrictions on husbands' rights to divorce and take multiple wives. It also set guidelines for all marriages, set minimum ages for marriage, and introduced greater security and equity for Indonesian wives, making it easier for Muslim women to achieve divorce. It contained a provision that Muslim couples settle their differences in the religious courts. *See also* LAW, ISLAMIC; PROSTITUTION. [0552, 0584, 1036, 1400, 1421]

MARXISM. Although the **Partai Komunis Indonesia (PKI)** adhered in general to Marxism-Leninism, it developed Marxist theory in a number of distinctive ways. Pointing to the enormous social and cultural diversity in Indonesia, it argued that the historical stages identified by Marx were telescoped in Indonesia into a single, comprehensive struggle against capitalist imperialism of which most Indonesians were victims. The party accordingly downplayed open class struggle (though this was less the case after 1963), arguing that the primary enemies of the Indonesian people were foreign. The clear influence of elements from Marxism on nationalist leaders such as **Sukarno** and **Mohammad Hatta** assisted this analysis. From this followed the theory of the Dual Nature of the State, which asserted that although Indonesian society was "semicolonial" and "semifeudal," the independent Indonesian state after 1949 was at least partly "pro-people" and the party's struggle should thus be to maximize the pro-people element and not to overthrow the state as such. The party, accordingly, never had a well-formulated program for armed rebellion. Party philosophy instead emphasized the promotion of socialist ways of thinking and put a high priority on establishing the hegemony of Marxist ideas in philosophy and the **arts**. *See also* CLASS ANALYSIS; LEMBAGA KEBUDAYAAN RAKYAT. [0621, 0912, 0917, 0919, 0922, 0931]

MASJUMI (Madjelis Sjuro Muslimin Indonesia, Consultative Council of Indonesian Muslims)**.** The Masjumi was established on **Java** on 7 November 1945. It was a new Muslim political organization and should not be confused with its predecessor on Java, which had been established under the Japanese as an amalgamation primarily of the **Muhammadiyah** and **Nahdlatul Ulama (NU)**. The postindependence Masjumi subsumed also prewar Islamic political organizations. On **Sumatra** the Masjumi was established in February 1946 as a fusion of the Muhammadiyah and the Majelis Islam Tinggi (MIT, High Council of **Islam**), a major Islamic federation that had existed on the island during the **Japanese occupation**. The military organizations **Hizbullah** and Sabilillah had been formed previously, and they acted as the Masjumi's armed militias during the early Revolution when the party strongly opposed the government's negotiations with the Dutch. However, many Hizbullah units cut their ties with Masjumi in 1948 when the party backed the negotiating policy of the **Mohammad Hatta** government, some joining S. M. Kartosuwiryo in the **Darul Islam (DI)** movement.

The **Partai Sarekat Islam Indonesia (PSII)** declared its independence of Masjumi in 1947, and the NU left the organization in 1952, despite the efforts of the Masjumi's Javanese chairman, **Sukiman Wiryosanjoyo**, to bridge the differences between the religious socialists—among whom **Mohammad Natsir** and **Sjafruddin Prawiranegara** were most influential—and the more traditionally oriented rural Javanese leaders of the NU. After the departure of the NU, the subsequent major division in the Masjumi was between modernist elements, including the religious socialists, and the Islamic purists, especially Isa Anshary, who advocated early realization of an **Islamic state**. The NU's secession was largely responsible for Masjumi's disappointing showing in the 1955 **elections** when it received only 20.9 percent of the vote (with the NU gaining 18.4 percent).

These elections showed that Masjumi's strength lay mainly in the Sundanese regions of West Java and in the **Outer Islands**. The party sympathized with the democratic and anticommunist goals of the

PRRI/Permesta rebellion of the late 1950s. Under harassment in **Jakarta**, three of its prime leaders (Mohammad Natsir, Sjafruddin Prawiranegara, and **Burhannudin Harahap**) joined the rebels at the end of 1957. When the party's central leadership refused to expel these men, splits developed in the Masjumi leadership in **Jakarta**, which led to a decline in its influence and provided an excuse for **Sukarno** to move to replace party government with **Guided Democracy**. Excluded from the councils that Sukarno then established, the Masjumi became a major leader of the ineffective Liga Demokrasi protesting against the dissolution of parliamentary democracy. On 14 April 1961 Sukarno outlawed the Masjumi, arresting several of its leaders, including some who had not participated in the rebellion.

After the installation of the **New Order**, former Masjumi leaders hoped that the party might be allowed to re-form, and the Partai Muslimin Indonesia (Parmusi) was initially intended as a direct successor to Masjumi. The military authorities, however, banned former Masjumi leaders from executive positions in the new party and also forbade them from engaging in politics. The influence of the Masjumi, however, did not completely disappear, and in the 1999 elections, at least two political parties made use of its name—the Partai Politik Islam Indonesia Masyumi (PPIM) and the Partai Masyumi Baru—though they gained few votes and only one seat in the parliament. [0648, 0695, 0706, 0983, 1036, 1329]

MASS ORGANIZATIONS (organisasi massa, ormas)**.** Term referring to organizations with mass memberships, generally organized around social categories such as **students**, **women**, workers (*see* **LABOR UNIONS**), and the like, and commonly associated with political parties, though parties themselves are formally also ormas. Ormas emerged on a massive scale during the Indonesian **Revolution**, and parties typically recruited much of their support through affiliated ormas rather than by appealing directly to the public. Thus the peasant organization **Barisan Tani Indonesia (BTI)** with a claimed membership of 12 million was a major pillar of the **Partai Komunis Indonesia (PKI)**, and one of the main strategies of the **army** in resisting the rise of the Left was the coordination of mass organizations, first in the *badan kerja sama* and later in **Golkar**. Under the **New Order**, the government sought to deprive potential opposition groups of access to the political base represented by the ormas, both by direct intervention in individual ormas and in 1985 by passing a Law on Mass Organizations, which required them to accept the **Pancasila** as their sole basic principle (*see* **AZAS TUNGGAL**), restricted their access to foreign funds, and gave legal grounds for closer government control. After the passing of this law, a clearer distinction emerged between ormas and orsos (organisasi sosial, social organizations), which were constructed as foundations without public membership and were thus free of some of the formal restrictions placed on ormas.

MASSACRES OF 1965–1966. The suppression of the ostensibly left-wing **Gestapu** coup of 30 September 1965 was followed not only by the banning of the **Partai Komunis Indonesia (PKI)** and affiliated organizations but also by an extensive massacre of people associated with the Left. The killings, which began in October 1965 and continued for six months, were most extensive in East and Central **Java**, **Bali**, and North **Sumatra**, but few regions were left untouched. No reliable figures exist on the number of people killed. The first official figure was 78,000 and other estimates seldom exceed 1 million; most scholars today accept a figure of at least 500,000.

In part the killings were a planned operation by the **army** to remove the PKI as a political force. In Central Java in particular, units of the **Resimen Para Komando Angkatan Darat (RPKAD)** engaged in the systematic slaughter of communists in several areas. In some other areas, the initiative seems to have come from local people: longstanding social tensions aligned with political antagonisms created deep hatreds between groups so that the killings, when they came, were not directed simply at destroying communist leaders but at extirpating whole communities. In East Java, where such antagonism was strongest, ***santri*** communities, represented by the **Nahdlatul Ulama (NU)** youth group Ansor, waged a sustained campaign of destruction against their *abangan* neighbors; in Bali, (where it is estimated that about 80,000 people died, roughly 5 percent of the **population**) as on Java, military authorities encouraged rival political parties, particularly the **Partai Nasional Indonesia (PNI)**, to destroy the PKI. On Sumatra the most extensive killings occurred in **Aceh** and on the plantation estates of East Sumatra, where an estimated 27,000–40,000 people died. Another important stimulus to the killing was the fact that many people who had made accommodation with the left-wing trends of **Guided Democracy** felt a need to demonstrate their anticommunist credentials clearly by promoting the destruction of the Left. Some observers initially described the killings as a kind of massive running amuck (*see* ***AMUK***), but this seems an inadequate explanation for the systematic character of the murders.

Until the fall of **Suharto**, Indonesians remained reluctant to talk about the massacres. The general memory of this time continued to play an important role in the political legitimacy of the **New Order**, which stressed the extent to which the killings were conducted by ordinary citizens and attributed them to the tensions created by the free operation of political parties under Guided Democracy and earlier periods. Since 1998 the atmosphere has been more open, but the deep divisions engendered by the killings remain. **Abdurrachman Wahid** failed in his efforts to heal the wounds by apologizing for the killings and admitting that many NU members had participated. Most Muslim leaders rejected his suggestion that the 1966 **Majelis Permusyawaratan Rakyat (MPR)** decision outlawing the PKI should be revoked. [0691, 0702, 0711, 0763, 0783, 0807, 0830]

MATARAM. Name of two states on **Java** and one on **Lombok**. The early state on Java was brought to prominence by the Hindu ruler Pu Sanjaya (732–c. 760), who is generally credited with establishing Hindu notions of god-kingship on the island (*see* **HINDUISM; INDIA, HISTORICAL LINKS WITH**). He erected a lingga (phallic monument) on the Dieng plateau, the Javanese center for the worship of Siva, and claimed a special personal relationship with Hindu gods and with his ancestors. His successors built the temple of **Prambanan** and struggled for power in central Java with the **Sailendras**. In the early 10th century, King Sindok shifted his capital to East Java for reasons still unclear.

The Javanese sultanate of **Mataram** emerged in the 1570s under Kyai Gede Pamanahan (? –c. 1584) in the vicinity of modern **Surakarta**. It began major expansion under his son and heir Panembahan Senapati Inalaga (r. 1584–1601), who defeated Pajang and pushed his control to the northern coast and into the Madiun valley. Senapati fought **Surabaya** and established his *kraton* at Kuta Gede, near modern **Yogyakarta**. His successor Panembahan Seda-ing Krapyak (r. ca 1601–1613) allowed the **Dutch East Indies Company (VOC)** a trading post at Japara on the north coast. **Sultan Agung**, the greatest of Mataram's rulers, defeated **Madura** (1624) and Surabaya (1625), thus establishing hegemony over most of central and eastern Java. In 1628 and 1629 he tried unsuccessfully to drive the Dutch from **Batavia**. The latter part of his reign was occupied with campaigns against rebellious vassals in Giri (1636) and Balambangan (1636–1640).

Agung's son and successor Sunan Amangkurat (Mangkurat) I (r. 1646–1677) lost control of the north coast and faced a major uprising by the Madurese **Trunojoyo**. After Amangkurat was driven from his own court by Trunojoyo, the VOC intervened on Mataram's behalf to defeat Trunojoyo (1678–1679) and establish Amangkurat's son Amangkurat II (r. 1677–1703) on the throne, with his court at Kartasura. The following decades were a time of cultural flowering but political disorder. In the First War of Javanese Succession (1704–1705), Amangkurat II was deposed by his uncle Pakubuwono I, who ceded **Cirebon**, **Priangan**, and half of Madura to the VOC. A Second War of Succession broke out on Pakubuwono's death in 1719, lasting until 1723, when Amangkurat IV was installed on the throne with VOC help. In 1740 the revolt of the **Chinese** in Batavia spread along Java's north coast and was joined by Pakubuwono II. In a series of complicated maneuvers, however, he attempted to deal with the Dutch, was deposed by his followers, and was restored to power by the Dutch in 1743, establishing his court at Surakarta (Solo) and ceding the entire north coast of Java and all territories east of Pasuruan to the VOC. A Third War of Succession broke out in 1746, when the king's brother Mangkubumi revolted. Pakubuwono II meanwhile ceded the remains of his kingdom to the VOC and promptly died in 1749. Mangkubumi was declared sultan by his followers in 1749, taking the name Hamengkubuwono, while the Dutch installed Pakubuwono's son as Pakubuwono III. The rebellion ended with the partition of Mataram into distinct kingdoms of Yogyakarta and Surakarta under the treaty of **Giyanti**. For a list of rulers of Mataram, *see* APPENDIX C. *See also* MAP 3. [0572, 0578, 0581]

MATOAYA, KARAENG (c. 1573–1636)**.** A prince of the royal family of Tallo in South **Sulawesi**, he became chief minister under King Tunipasulu and headed a coup by the nobility that overthrew the king after he had tried to reduce noble privileges. He continued as chief minister and was architect of the alliance with **Bugis** states, which became the basis of the powerful **Makassar** state. As the campaigns of **Sultan Agung** devastated the north coast of **Java**, Matoaya turned Makassar into a major free port for **trade** from **Maluku**, which the Dutch were then trying to monopolize. He also presided over the peaceful conversion of Makassar to **Islam**. To defend Makassar against the expected Dutch attack, Matoaya also sponsored the development of firearms manufacture. *See also* PATTINGALLOANG.

MAX HAVELAAR**.** Semiautobiographical novel by **Eduard Douwes Dekker**, writing under the pseudonym Multatuli ("I have suffered much") and describing his experiences as assistant-resident in Lebak in **Banten** in the mid-19th century. The central character, an idealistic young colonial official, attempts to redress wrongs inflicted on local people by the indigenous aristocracy but discovers that the colonial authorities have no interest in the welfare of their Indonesian subjects and is himself eventually dismissed for his pains. The novel, often compared in spirit to *Uncle Tom's Cabin,* played some role in mobilizing Dutch public opinion against the **Cultivation System** and is considered a classic of Dutch colonial literature. It was filmed in a joint Dutch-Indonesian venture in 1976, but the result was banned in Indonesia from 1977 to 1988 on the grounds that it showed that people "were exploited not by the Dutch but by the local aristocracy." [0248, 0624]

MEDAN. *See* DELI; EAST SUMATRA.

MEDIA. Prior to the **New Order**, all newspapers had to be affiliated with a political party or **mass organization**. This regulation was annulled in 1966, leading to a depoliticization of the media, with its emphasis shifting to popular culture and economic development. Economic growth and concomitant social changes in the 1970s shaped the development of **films**, magazines, and pop music. A publishing boom developed in the 1970s and 1980s when new **newspapers** and popular novels flourished, together with glossy magazines directed to specific social groups and interests. Popular music found a wide market among young people. In the film industry, a levy was introduced on foreign films in 1967 with the money used to finance Indonesian productions, which thus increased in number. **Radio** had long been a popular medium in Indonesia, and a state **television** service had been established in 1962, which expanded greatly in the late 1970s after the launching of Indonesia's Palapa satellite. State-owned Televisi Republik Indonesia (TVRI) was a monopoly until 1989 when the government licensed five private television channels to compete with it. In the later years of the **Suharto** regime, members and associates of the **Suharto family** acquired control of several of the growing media conglomerates, especially in the commercial television sector but also in the print media. Through these ties and through the government's control of licensing and its selective closure of outlets that aired dissenting views, the regime was able to maintain control over the range of public discourse. *See also* CENSORSHIP. [0730, 0761, 0763]

MEDICINE. *See* HEALTH.

MEGALITHS. Prehistorians once identified a "megalithic" stage in the development of Indonesian culture, based on widespread signs of reverence for large stones (megaliths). Prehistorians today, however, are increasingly skeptical of this view, arguing that there is insufficient knowledge of the ancient use of megaliths, little evidence that their use had a common origin, and no certainty that they were a central feature of the cultures involved; it may be that they survived other more important cultural features simply because they were stone. Megalithic traditions survive today in **Nias**, **Sumba**, and parts of **Kalimantan**, and some observers have attributed the easy acceptance of **Hinduism** and **Buddhism** to a blending of megalith worship with reverence for the lingga of Siva and the stupa of Buddhism. [0487, 0533]

MEGAWATI SUKARNOPUTRI (1948–). **Sukarno**'s second child and oldest daughter, Megawati was a 39-year-old housewife with no political experience in 1987 when she and her husband agreed to run for parliament on the **Partai Demokrasi Indonesia (PDI)** ticket after her elder brother Guntur had refused the PDI's invitation. In part because of the enthusiastic public response to her campaign, the PDI's percentage of the vote increased from 7.9 to 11 percent in the 1987 **elections**. She was a largely passive member of the PDI delegation in the **Dewan Perwakilan Rakyat (DPR)** over the next six years. Nevertheless, the party's **Jakarta** branch nominated her to chair the PDI in 1993 after the government refused to recognize the reelection of chairman Soerjadi (1939–) at the PDI conference in Medan in July of that year. (The authorities had been angered by Soerjadi's parliamentary motion after the previous election that the number of presidential terms should be restricted.) Though the government initially attempted to sabotage Megawati's nomination, it eventually acquiesced when a special PDI convention elected her to its leadership. But two years later, in June 1996, the PDI held a special congress in Medan under government auspices and protection that deposed her and unanimously reinstated Soerjadi as party head. Megawati stated her determination to contest this action in the courts, and her supporters refused to give up PDI headquarters in **Jakarta**, where they held a daily "free speech forum" (*mimbar bebas*) demanding democratization. In response, **army** and government-backed militias took over the building and forcibly ejected 150 PDI adherents, sparking widespread riots in Jakarta. From then on, Megawati became the major figure around whom opposition to **Suharto** coalesced.

Megawati submitted a slate of candidates for the 1997 elections that the government rejected, resulting in widespread demonstrations and continuous protests when the Soerjadi slate was allowed to compete. She did not direct her supporters to boycott the elections, but did ask them not to vote for PDI and said she herself would not vote. She played no direct role in the events leading up to the overthrow of Suharto, but in the first free post-Suharto elections in 1999 the new party that she had formed (the **Partai Demokrasi Indonesia—Perjuangan [PDI-P]**) outvoted all the other parties, gaining 153 seats in the parliament. Nevertheless, Megawati lacked the political skills of her rivals and was outmaneuvered by **Abdurrachman Wahid** in the parliament, so that he was elected president. To placate the outrage of her followers, he nominated her as **vice president**. Initially the position was largely ceremonial, except that she was charged with responsibility for the eastern half of Indonesia, a task in which she did not excel.

As dissatisfaction with Wahid's presidency grew, he was compelled to grant Megawati greater powers, and after his impeachment she was unanimously elected to replace him as **president** on 23 July 2001. She does not seem to have acquired an interest in politics but holds to a few strong beliefs, largely mirroring those of her father—particularly maintenance of a unitary state and moving harshly against any secessionist movements. Like him, she appears to mistrust the political force of **Islam**, but nevertheless chose Hamzah Haz, the leader of the **Partai Persatuan Pembangunan (PPP)**, as her vice president in an attempt to appeal to Muslim opinion. She also follows Sukarno in her desire to pursue a neutral **foreign policy**, and at least until the **Bali** bombing of October 2002, she tried to resist pressures particularly from the **United States** to pursue an aggressive policy against suspected Islamic terrorists. Subsequently she did cooperate in the "war on terrorism," searching out and arresting a number of suspects in the Bali bombing, but she opposed any war on Iraq without United Nations sanction. She differs from Sukarno in her closeness to the military and her willingness to grant them stronger powers than they enjoyed under either **B. J. Habibie** or Abdurrachman Wahid, as she shares with army leaders an overriding concern for Indonesian unity. In the economic field after coming to office in July 2001, Megawati cut fuel subsidies and passed a budget keeping spending in check. As her tenure lengthened, she displayed an increasingly conservative bent, expanding the powers of the military to crack down on protest demonstrations, initially opposing the **Majelis Permusyawaratan Rakyat (MPR)**'s proposal for direct election of the president, and choosing to pursue a military solution to the rebellion in **Aceh**. [0725, 0867, 0882, 0964]

MELAKA (Malacca)**.** Port city on the peninsular coast of the Melaka Strait, founded in circa 1400 by Parameswara, a prince of **Palembang**. In the tradition of **Srivijaya**, with which it claimed a dynastic connection, and **Jambi**, Melaka attracted traders by virtue of its strategic position, its servicing facilities, and its regularized **taxation**, becoming the most powerful state on the strait in the 15th century. It competed with **Siam** for control of the **Malay Peninsula** and established outposts in **Sumatra**, especially in **Siak**. From 1400 to 1430 it received several visits from the **Chinese** admiral **Zheng He** and worked closely with the Ming rulers of China to suppress piracy and to keep **trade** flowing smoothly. Its commercial orientation later turned westward, and it became a major entrepôt for the flow of goods from the archipelago to **India** and the West. It also moved into **pepper** production and trade for the Indian market and in 1436 adopted **Islam**.

Melaka's wealth, described in glowing terms by **Tomé Pires**, continued to come principally from its entrepôt role and made it in many respects a model for later sultanates in the region. Wealth also made it a prime target for the **Portuguese**, who captured it in 1511 with a force of 1,200 men and 18 ships (*see also* **UPAS**). Much of Melaka's trade then went to **Aceh** and **Banten**, and the city was attacked repeatedly by Aceh and by **Riau**, where descendants of the Melaka sultans had reestablished their kingdom. Melaka fell to a combined Dutch-Riau force in 1641, but under Dutch rule the city declined further as the **Dutch East Indies Company (VOC)** directed trade as much as possible to **Batavia**. British forces seized Melaka in 1795 during the Napoleonic Wars, but it was restored to the Dutch in 1818. The **Anglo-Dutch Treaty** of 1824 placed it definitively under Britain's rule as part of a general tidying up of colonial borders in the region. [0543, 0556, 0571]

MELAYU. *See* JAMBI.

MENTAWAI. Archipelago off the west coast of **Sumatra**. The indigenous inhabitants cultivate taro, **yams**, and **sago** and raise **pigs** and fowl. Their society shows many supposedly primitive features, such as little social differentiation between men and **women**, an absence of political leaders (though a category of traditional healers, or *kerei,* exists), and a belief that all things have a soul. The main island of the group, Siberut, is also the habitat of four endemic primate species.

MERANTAU (from *rantau,* regions around)**.** Temporary migration by males to other regions to earn money, especially in **trade**, is a common feature of many Indonesian societies (*see* **ACEH**; **BAWEAN**; **GAYO**; **MINANGKABAU**). It generally reflects and reinforces a social structure in which the domestic influence of **women** is strong. [1237]

MERAUKE. *See* PAPUA; SABANG TO MERAUKE, FROM; SUCCESSION.

"MERDEKA!" ("Freedom!"). Common greeting during the **Revolution**.

MESTIZO CULTURES. *See* DEPOK; INDO-EUROPEANS; MARDIJKERS; *PERANAKAN*.

METALWORKING. Indonesia's neolithic societies first gained access to metal in the form of bronze objects introduced from mainland Southeast Asia in the third to second centuries B.C. (*see* **GAMELAN**). The casting of bronze by the lost wax method, however, was quickly developed for both **weapons** and musical instruments. The working of bronze is known from mainland Southeast Asia from 2000 B.C., and most bronze used in the archipelago was probably imported, since the local deposits of **tin** in **Bangka** and **Belitung** were not known before 1709. **Iron** working is known from the 10th century. The Javanese *kris* was traditionally made using alternating fine layers of dark nickelous meteoric iron and lighter colored terrestrial iron, the result symbolizing a fusion of heaven and earth and forming a distinctive striated pattern on the blade. Master smiths (*mpu*) were said to forge *kris* on their knees using the heat of their fists. The fiery transformation of ore into metal and of metal into fine shapes was seen widely, perhaps under the influence of Tantrism, as analogous to the transformation of the soul after death. *See also* COPPER; GOLD. [0143, 0576, 1272, 1360]

"MIDDLE WAY" FOR THE ARMED FORCES. Doctrine articulated in November 1958 by **A. H. Nasution** in response to the declaration of martial law in 1957 (though the term "middle way" was coined by the lawyer Jokosutono). Nasution argued that the armed forces should not be a "dead tool" of the government of the day, nor should they seize power from it. Rather they should follow a "middle way" of responsible involvement in political decision making. This doctrine was the basis of the **army**'s partnership with **Sukarno** in **Guided Democracy** but was subsequently superseded by the doctrine of ***dwifungsi***. [0714, 0727, 0733, 0872]

MIGRATIONS. Prehistorians once identified successive waves of so-called proto- and deutero-Malays said to have entered the archipelago from mainland Southeast Asia via the **Malay Peninsula**, but it now seems that the inhabitants of western Indonesia are descended from Austronesians who emerged first in what is now Taiwan and who moved southward from 4000 B.C. through the **Philippines** and into **Sulawesi** before turning west and east to establish themselves in much of the archipelago by 3000 to 2000 B.C., partly displacing and partly absorbing the established Austromelanesian peoples. Others went on to reach **Madagascar**, Easter Island, and Hawaii by 1000 A.D. They brought with them the bow and arrow, canoes with outriggers, pottery, and timber and thatched houses, as well as **pigs**, fowl, **rice**, and millet. The Austronesian migration was followed by a series of smaller migrations of Mongoloid peoples from the Asian mainland, especially and most recently **Chinese**, who assimilated into and contributed culturally to Austronesian societies rather than displacing them. The distinction formerly made between proto- and deutero-Malays is now believed to reflect differing degrees of Austromelanesian and Mongoloid influence. *See also* LANGUAGES; PREHISTORY.

MILITARY BUSINESS OPERATIONS. During the Indonesian **Revolution**, most armed units established so-called *badan ekonomi* (economic organizations) to help fund military operations, and such outfits have remained in place under various names. Initially most were involved in taking plantation produce to markets outside Indonesia, notably **Singapore**, to be exchanged for **weapons** and other necessities. After the **Revolution** the military moved into a wide range of commercial, construction, and other fields. This was especially the case after the nationalization of Dutch businesses in 1957, most of which were handed over to the **army** to run.

In the **New Order** years, the military was forced to rely on its own resources for half of its annual spending and until the financial crisis most of this came from its business enterprises. Komando Cadangan Strategis Angkatan Darat (**Kostrad**) owned Mandala airline and **Komando Pasukan Khusus (Kopassus)** owned a shopping mall near its headquarters. Army-owned companies numbered in the hundreds and included PT Tri Usaha Bakti, formerly headed by Sujono Humardani (1919–1986); the Yayasan Dharma Putra, associated with Kostrad; and the Propelat group, associated with the former Siliwangi Division.

A second avenue of military involvement in business has been through **state enterprises**, both those seized from the Dutch in 1957 and those set up since then. Prior to the economic downturn of 1997, the most important of these were **Pertamina** and **Badan Urusan Logistik (Bulog)**. In 1974 active duty officers were forbidden to engage directly in business, but this regulation was enforced only sporadically. The army's holding company Yayasan Kartika Eka Paksi (YKEP) had 11 subsidiaries and 22 affiliated companies, including logging and plywood operations, a bank, a pharmaceutical company, and a small airline. These enterprises were severely hurt by the Asian financial crisis, and in 2001 an outside audit revealed that only two of the 38 enterprises then under YKEP were generating profits. Although the government increased the military budget from Rp 7.7 trillion in 2001 to Rp 13 trillion in 2002, this amount still fell far short of its needs. Most of its budgetary shortfalls were met by payoffs from provincial governments and increasing military involvement in drug smuggling (it was reportedly disagreements over shares in this that led to the September 2002 clash near Medan with the **police**), protection rackets, illegal **mining** and logging, fuel smuggling, **gambling**, and **prostitution**. *See also CUKONG*. [0313, 0373, 0727, 0731]

MILITIAS. Irregular armed units formed during the **Revolution** by political parties and other interest groups (*see **LASYKAR***). In the late **Guided Democracy** period, militias tied to the **Pemuda Pancasila** offered to go to fight in support of the West Irian (*see* **PAPUA**) campaign. Under **Suharto**, both the military and security forces made use of militias or gangs that were believed responsible for inciting riots and extorting money from businesses. After riots were carried out against "Tien" Suharto's Mini Indonesia project at the end of 1971, the **Komando Operasi Pemulihan Keamanan dan Ketertiban (Kopkamtib)** outlawed all independent gangs of youths, but by instituting training programs for their leaders, the Kopkamtib incorporated many of them into the state's security apparatus. After Suharto's fall, militias became responsible for much of the violence in dissident regions. From the time that President **B. J. Habibie** proposed a referendum in **East Timor**, armed forces set about organizing militias in each of its 13 districts. Chief operative was former military intelligence chief Major General Zacky Anwar Makarim, and before the vote on 30 August 1999 some 10,000 militia members, including 2,000 heavily armed irregulars, "had flooded East Timor." Other militias, particularly the **Laskar Jihad**, were suspected of inciting violence in **Maluku** and subsequently in Papua. After the invasion of **Aceh** in May 2003, it was announced that the **army** would be setting up militias in that province. [0743, 0754, 0959, 1021, 1028]

MINAHASA. Region at the end of **Sulawesi**'s northern peninsula, often including the neighboring Sangir and Talaud islands. The early inhabitants of the region have left little trace but for impressive sandstone sarcophagi (waruga), but they seem to have been culturally similar to the inland tribes of the southern **Philippines**. The major political unit was the *walak*, a territorially based clan or clan-group, and the name Minahasa is said to refer to an alliance of such groups against the neighboring kingdom of Bolaäng-Mongondouw. They cultivated **rice** in labor cooperatives (*mapalus*) and raised **pigs** and fowl; from the 17th century maize became a major crop. The Spanish established settlements at Kema and Manado (Menado) circa 1560, and Catholic missionaries were active during the next century. The Spanish, **Portuguese**, and Dutch competed for control of the coastal regions in the 17th century, the Dutch becoming dominant from 1679, when they signed an alliance with Minahasa chiefs. Catholic converts in the region were then unilaterally declared to be Calvinist. The region came under British rule from 1801 to 1816, and a major uprising took place in Tondano in 1807–1809. Missionary activity by the Nederlandsch Zendelingsgenootschap (*see* **PROTESTANTISM**) began in 1824, and the region was largely converted by the late 19th century. An independent regional church, the Gereja Masehi Injil Minahasa, was formed in 1934.

Under the treaty of 1679, the Minahasa chiefs agreed to supply a number of products (e.g., **gold** and fibers) to the **Dutch East Indies Company (VOC)**. **Coffee** was introduced in 1797 and became a government monopoly in 1822, **labor** being obtained by corvée. Forced cultivation of cacao, **nutmeg**, and manila hemp followed. Labor conscription ended in 1893, but coffee remained a government monopoly until 1899. Under Dutch rule, the *walak* were initially preserved as the units of administration, though their number was steadily diminished from 27 in 1824 to six in 1940. In 1877, following the **Agrarian Law of 1870** on **Java**, the colonial government declared all "waste" land to be its property. This caused great debate over the status of the region, whether allied or subject to the Netherlands Indies. In 1881 the *majoor*, or *walak* heads, became salaried government officials. In the early 20th century, **coconut** cultivation for copra became a major industry largely conducted by smallholder producers, who frequently, however, became seriously indebted to **Chinese** middlemen. A Copra Contracten Ordonnantie in 1939 attempted to regulate copra contracts in favor of producers, but had no time to have effect.

From early times, a militia had been necessary in the colony for protection against pirates from the southern Philippines, and from the early

19th century Minahasa became a major recruitment area for the **Koninklijk Nederlands-Indisch Leger (KNIL)**. The presence of missionary schools led to a relatively high level of **education** and of fluency in Dutch in the region. Government education also expanded in the 1880s, and many people left the region to find employment elsewhere, especially as teachers and in other government services, so that along with the Ambonese, Menadonese (the colonial-era term for Minahasa Christians) gained a reputation as indigenous agents of Dutch rule. A Perserikatan Minahassa (Minahasa Association) was established in 1910 by G. S. S. J. Ratulangi (1890–1949), but it argued for promotion of **trade** and industry in the region rather than for independence.

The **Revolution** brought deep divisions to Minahasa, with Ratulangi espousing the unitarian doctrine and being appointed as the Republic's governor for **Sulawesi** (Celebes), while another party formed in March 1946 campaigned for the integration of Minahasa into the Dutch state as the 12th province. One of the most effective Republican military organizations was the Minahasan militia Kebaktian Rakjat Indonesia Sulawesi (KRIS, Loyalty of the Indonesian People from Sulawesi), which inducted Minahasans of all political shades into the Republican struggle. In the latter part of the revolutionary period, a Minahasa organization, the Komité Ketatanegaraan Minahasa (Minahasa Constitutional Committee), was formed that opposed the increasingly pro-Republican **Negara Indonesia Timor (NIT)** and argued against the region's inclusion in independent Indonesia.

In the 1950s, in opposition to the central government's attempts to impose a monopoly over copra purchase and marketing, the region became a major center of smuggling. An unsuccessful attempt by the central government in 1956 to close the port of Manado was among the causes of the Permesta revolt, which became part of the **PRRI/Permesta rebellion**. From 1958 the Minahasans were the only group offering serious resistance to the central government. [0028, 0100, 0450, 0802, 0823]

MINANGKABAU. Making up approximately 90 percent of the population of the province of West **Sumatra**, the Minangkabau are one of the largest matrilineal societies in the world and at the same time devoutly Islamic. The Minangkabau region is traditionally known as Alam Minangkabau (the Minangkabau world) rather than by a state name. Their original settlements were in three upland valleys of the region, particularly around the Merapi volcano: Agam, Tanah Datar, and Limapuluh Kota. Two broad customary law traditions existed: the rather autocratic Kota Piliang, which was most prevalent in Tanah Datar, and the more democratic Bodi Caniago tradition, which was followed mostly in Agam and Limapuluh Kota. The first historical record of the Minangkabau appears in 1347 when inscriptions indicate that Adityavarman, a prince of mixed Javanese-Sumatran parentage, threw off allegiance to **Majapahit** and ruled the gold-rich regions of Tanah Datar until at least 1375. The Minangkabau were traditionally organized not in kingdoms but into largely autonomous villages (*nagari*), themselves federations of kinship groups. **Gold** mines in the Tanah Datar area were the principal economic base of Minangkabau communities and up to the 17th century the area was the main gold producer on the archipelago. A **Dutch East Indies Company (VOC)** post was established on the coast under the treaty of Painan (1663).

Islam reached the region in the 16th century, spreading first through Islamic schools (***surau***). Christine Dobbin argues that economic change in the late 18th century stimulated the dramatic growth of Islam. Gold production declined; production of cinnamon, **coffee**, gambier, and **salt** expanded; and Minangkabau men became increasingly involved in long-distance **trade** with the outside world. Islam offered not only a means for creating a trading diaspora, whose members helped each other with credit and commercial information, but also gave a platform for a political challenge to the old order. This challenge took the form of the so-called Paderis, a modernist Muslim movement following Wahhabi principles, which sought to purify Islam in West Sumatra from accretions deriving from ***adat*** practices. Many Paderi opponents fled the highlands and sought assistance from the Dutch, whose presence hitherto had been largely confined to the coastal trading **ports**. The Dutch began military actions against the Paderi in 1821 and sporadic warfare continued until they defeated the Paderi forces and exiled their leader, **Imam Bonjol**, in 1837.

The Dutch directed much of their administration to controlling and monopolizing coffee production through the **cultivation system**, and the Minangkabau region became a major coffee producing and exporting area. With the relaxation of the monopoly and forced cultivation in the early 20th century, the Minangkabau moved extensively into private production of coffee, copra, and **rubber**. Anticolonial uprisings took place in 1908 and 1927 (*see also* **PARTAI KOMUNIS INDONESIA**), and many Minangkabau leaders (e.g., **Mohammad Hatta**, **Sutan Sjahrir**, Muhammad **Yamin**, and **Tan Malaka**) assumed prominent leadership roles in the nationalist movement. Strongly loyal to the Indonesian Republic during the **Revolution**, West Sumatra was the seat of the **Pemer-**

intah Darurat Republik Indonesia (PDRI) after the second Dutch **"Police Action"** of December 1948.

In the 1950s dissatisfaction with the centralist policies of the **Sukarno** government led the Minangkabau region to become the major locus of the 1958 **PRRI/Permesta rebellion**. The government's repression of the region after defeating the rebellion demoralized the local people and accelerated traditional Minangkabau migration (*merantau*), causing large-scale **population** movements to the major urban centers of Sumatra and **Java**, especially **Jakarta**. The centralizing policies of the **Suharto** regime and the stringent control it exercised over political and religious expression undermined particular characteristics of the region, but after his fall many Minangkabau embraced the new decentralization policies, and there were signs that local forces were reasserting their regional identity. [0776, 0791, 0797, 0798, 0807, 0838, 1077, 1207, 1235–1237, 1263]

MINING. Indonesia has fabulously rich mineral resources, many of which have only recently been opened up for exploitation. Principal among mining operations, other than those for **oil** and **gas**, are **bauxite** (Bintan Island, **Riau**), **coal (Sumatra**, **Kalimantan)**, **copper (Papua)**, **gold** (Sumatra, **Java**, **Kalimantan**, **Sulawesi**, Papua), **nickel** (Sulawesi, Kalimantan, **Halmahera**, Papua), and **tin** (Riau archipelago). The **Sukarno** government nationalized Dutch mining companies for bauxite, tin, and coal in 1957, which resulted in falling output because of lack of investment to replace and repair equipment. Under the **Suharto** government, the mines were again opened to foreign investment. The 1967 Mining Law, together with the 1967 Foreign **Investment** Law, allowed foreign companies to act as contractors for the exploitation of Indonesia's natural resources. In the 1970s and 1980s there were growing worries about the effects of mining on the environment, but generally government regulations continued to favor industry needs over those of the environment. With the financial crisis of 1997 and the fall of Suharto, mining became a much less attractive proposition for foreign investors. Spending on exploration in Indonesia dropped from $160 million in 1996 to an estimated $22 million in 2001. Total investment in the mining industry fell from $915 million in 2000 to $413 million in 2001, with revenue dropping to $738 million (from $888 million in 1999). **Decentralization** has also affected mining operations, as after January 2001 district governments were empowered to pass their own legislation regarding mining in their regions. *See also* ENVIRONMENTAL PROTECTION. [0407, 0411, 0413, 0416, 1379]

MINISTRY OF COLONIES. *See* COLONIES, MINISTRY OF; NETHERLANDS, CONSTITUTIONAL RELATIONSHIP WITH INDONESIA.

MISSIONARY ACTIVITY. *See* CATHOLICISM; PROTESTANTISM.

MOESO. *See* MUSSO.

MOLUCCAS. *See* MALUKU.

MONEY. *See* CURRENCY.

MONGOL INVASION. *See* CHINA, HISTORICAL LINKS WITH; MAJAPAHIT.

MONOLOYALITAS (monoloyalty)**.** Exclusive loyalty to the state and government demanded by the **Suharto** government of all state employees, especially in **elections**. First articulated in 1970, *monoloyalitas* was intended to prevent the bureaucracy from being an arena for competing interests and to guarantee the bureaucratic base of the **New Order**. *See* CENTRE FOR STRATEGIC AND INTERNATIONAL STUDIES; FLOATING MASS; KORPS PEGAWAI REPUBLIK INDONESIA. [0736]

MOOK, HUBERTUS JOHANNES VAN (1894–1965)**.** Indies-born colonial official and politician, van Mook studied Indology at Leiden University where he was strongly influenced by the "Ethical" ideas of **Cornelis van Vollenhoven** and others. He returned to the Indies, where he held the increasingly senior administrative posts of director of economic affairs in 1937–1941, lieutenant governor-general in 1941–1942 and 1944–1948, and minister of colonies in 1941–1945. Unusually for colonial civil servants, he was also involved in politics, as leader of the **Stuw** group and from 1931 member of the **Volksraad**. He was an advocate of increased autonomy for the Indies and the gradual elimination of racial distinctions.

Van Mook headed the colonial government-in-exile in **Australia** during World War II and returned to Indonesia in October 1945 as head of the **Netherlands Indies Civil Administration (NICA)** and later of the restored colonial government, though he was never promoted to **governor-general**. His hope that the Indonesian-Dutch conflict could be resolved by dealing reasonably with "moderate" nationalists such as **Sutan Sjahrir** was frustrated by the metropolitan Dutch insistence on restoring Dutch authority and on limiting concessions to **nationalism**, but his own insistence that the Dutch retain a tutelary role during an extended transition to independence was unacceptable to a great many Indonesian nationalists. By 1948 his unpopular role in the development of **federalism** and in the launching of the first **"Police Action"** had made him a liability in Dutch negotiations with the Republic, and he was dismissed on 25 October 1948. *See* also SUCCESSION. [0478, 1146]

MUFAKAT. *See* MUSYAWARAH.

MUHAMMADIYAH ("followers of Muhammad")**.** Muslim organization founded in 1912 by Kyai Haji Ahmad Dahlan (1868–1933), a mosque official in **Yogyakarta** to promote the modernist Islamic thought developed by Muhammad Abduh and Rashid Rida in Cairo. Modernists believed that the condition of Muslims under colonial rule and other despotism was in part a consequence of their own straying from the basic principles of the religion, and their aim was thus, as they saw it, to cleanse and revitalize **Islam** by discarding tradition and ritual and returning to the central texts, that is, the Qur'an and the Hadiths. These views brought them into direct conflict with Islamic traditionalists who stressed the importance of studying the full body of Islamic texts in order to understand the Qur'an correctly (*see* **NAHDLATUL ULAMA [NU]**). The modernists stressed the strict observance of the five pillars of Islam (the confession of faith, prayer five times a day, fasting during Ramadan, paying the religious tax or *zakat*, and making the ***haj*** if possible). They also advocated the use of head-covering by women and the segregation of the sexes in public.

Muhammadiyah's main aims were to spread adherence to Islam and to promote the religious understanding of believers. It emphasized social welfare, including **education**, and under the Dutch advocated noninvolvement in politics, though individual branches of the organization, such as that in West **Sumatra**, defied such directives. In 1945 it advocated an **Islamic state** for Indonesia and joined **Masjumi**, which soon came to be dominated by modernist ideas. It survived the banning of Masjumi in 1960 and continued to be a major Muslim cultural and educational institution, claiming a membership of over 20 million.

Throughout much of the **Suharto** regime it maintained its apolitical stance, concentrating on social and religious activities promoted through its schools, health clinics, mosques, and welfare institutions. This changed when **Amien Rais** became chair of the organization and used it as a podium for stringent criticisms of the **corruption** and malfeasance of the president and his family and cronies. Though much of the Muhammadiyah distanced itself from these criticisms, emphasizing that it favored a gradual and peaceful approach to reform, younger members enthusiastically embraced the oppositional stance of its chairman. [0627, 0648, 1016, 1358, 1361]

MUIS, ABDUL (1890–1959)**.** Journalist and politician, educated as a protégé of J. H. Abendanon (1852–1925) under the Association Principle, but best known for his novel *Salah Asuhan* (A Wrong Upbringing, 1928), which describes the difficulties faced by European-educated Indonesians in fitting into their own society. [0224]

MULTATULI. *See* DOUWES DEKKER, EDUARD; *MAX HAVELAAR*.

MURBA (Partai Murba, Proletarian Party)**.** Founded in October 1948 by followers of the radical nationalist communist **Tan Malaka**, after the government of **Mohammad Hatta** crushed the **Partai Komunis Indonesia (PKI)** in the **Madiun Affair**. The party strongly opposed negotiations with the Dutch, and Hatta banned it shortly before the second Dutch **"Police Action"** of December 1948. It revived in the early 1950s as a bitter competitor of the PKI but though several of its leaders (notably **Adam Malik** and **Chaerul Saleh**) played influential political roles, the party only won 0.5 percent of the vote in the 1955 **elections**, gaining two seats. It strongly supported **Guided Democracy** and moved closer to the Soviet Union when the PKI was adopting a more pro-**China** stance. In 1964, in a move to combat the growing influence of the PKI, Adam Malik and others associated with the Murba formed an organization under the name of Body to Support Sukarno (BPS), portraying it as an alternative to **Marxism**. The PKI persuaded **Sukarno** that this was in fact a move to undermine him and persuaded the president to ban both the BPS (in December 1964) and Murba (in January 1965). Murba reemerged under the **New Order**, but won no seats in the 1971 elections and was absorbed in 1973 with other secular parties into the **Partai Demokrasi Indonesia (PDI)**. *See also* BADAN PENDUKUNG SUKARNOISME; PERSATUAN PERJUANGAN. [0695]

MURDANI, L. BENNY (1932-)**.** A Javanese Catholic, born in Cepu, Murdani joined the revolutionary struggle at the age of 16 in December 1948.

He was trained in the **Resimen Para Komando Angkatan Darat (RPKAD)** after the **Revolution** and became a company commander. As a paratroop officer in the Cakrabirawa regiment, he took part in the commando raid on West **Sumatra** in 1958 to quell the **PRRI/Permesta rebellion**. He was associated with **Suharto** in 1964 when Suharto headed the Mandala Command for the Liberation of West Irian (**Papua**), and Murdani won acclaim for leading a successful parachute attack in Merauke. Suharto appointed him to the General Staff, and he began his **intelligence** career in Komando Cadangan Strategic Angkatan Darat (**Kostrad**).

Murdani acted as liaison for **Ali Murtopo** in the negotiations to end **Confrontation**, and in August 1966 he was sent to head the new Indonesian liaison office in Kuala Lumpur. After a tour as consul general in Seoul, South Korea, in the early 1970s, he was recalled to Indonesia at the time of the **Malari** Affair and resumed his intelligence career as assistant for intelligence in the Defense Ministry from August 1974. From August 1977 he was also concurrently head of the Center for Strategic Intelligence (Pusintelstrat) in the Defense Ministry, and from early 1978 deputy head of **Badan Koordinasi Intelijen Negara (Bakin)**. By the early 1980s he had become one of the most powerful men in Indonesia, holding key intelligence positions in the (Departemen) Pertahanan dan Keamanan (Hankam, Department of Defense and Security), **Komando Operasi Pemulihan Keamanan dan Ketertiban (Kopkamtib)**, and Bakin and having been entrusted by Suharto with sensitive clandestine tasks in foreign affairs, such as negotiating purchase of jet fighters from Israel, planning and directing the invasion of **East Timor**, acting as liaison with the Vietnamese government in Hanoi, and supervising the storming of a highjacked **Garuda** jetliner in Bangkok in 1981.

Murdani became commander in chief of the **armed forces** in 1983, while continuing to head Pusintelstrat (now reorganized into Badan Intelijen Strategis [Bais]), holding the post until 1988. During his tenure he increasingly centralized power over the military in his own hands, a situation that raised the suspicions of the president, who abruptly removed him from the post of commander in chief in February 1988, appointing him instead as minister of defense. During the following five years, Murdani unsuccessfully attempted to regain his powers, but Suharto dismissed him from the Defense Ministry in 1993, shortly afterward replacing Bais by a new intelligence body (BIA), thus further undermining Murdani's personal ties in the intelligence community. Thereafter Murdani's influence drastically declined, though several officers retained feelings of loyalty to him and even after **B. J. Habibie** became president there were indications that his advice was still heeded. [0031, 0680, 0733, 0972]

MURTOPO, ALI (1924–1984). Murtopo was born in Blora in 1924 the son of a **batik** trader in an impoverished *priyayi* family. Toward the end of the **Japanese occupation**, he joined the **Hizbullah**, becoming a company commander when it was absorbed into the Indonesian **army**. He served in Ahmad Yani's Banteng Raiders unit of the Diponegoro division in 1952, becoming deputy chief of the Diponegoro's territorial and political affairs branch in 1957. He followed **Suharto** into army **intelligence** headquarters and from there into the West Irian (**Papua**) campaign and Komando Cadangan Strategis Angkatan Darat (**Kostrad**). During the West Irian campaign in the early 1960s, Murtopo developed a new combat intelligence unit that became **Operasi Khusus (Opsus)**. As head of Opsus he opened secret contacts with Malaysian officials in August–September 1964, and in November he went to Bangkok for secret negotiations aimed at limiting and eventually ending **Confrontation**. He also established contacts with former **PRRI/Permesta** rebels and with them organized massive regional smuggling in **rubber** and other commodities. He spent much of this period outside Indonesia arranging emergency funding for Suharto from **Chinese** business sources in **Singapore**, Hong Kong, and Taiwan. In 1969, as head of Opsus, he was deeply involved in persuading (largely through arrests and bribes) leaders in West Irian to opt for Indonesia. He became one of Suharto's closest advisors (SPRI) and deputy head of **Badan Koordinasi Intelijen Negara (Bakin)**.

Murtopo was closely tied with a group of Catholic intellectuals of Chinese descent who cooperated with him in the early postcoup period, and he sponsored and headed their think tank, the **Centre for Strategic and International Studies (CSIS)**. He was closely involved in directing the success achieved by **Golkar** in the first **New Order elections** in 1971, and in the amalgamation of the political parties immediately afterward. In October 1974 Suharto put him in charge of negotiations with Portugal over **East Timor**, and he took control of the Operasi Komodo (Komodo Operation), which was closely involved in fomenting the civil war in the region that eventually led to Indonesia's invasion of East Timor in December 1975. Murtopo remained until his death one of Suharto's closest advisers. [0031, 0736, 0845]

MUSIC. The long tradition of cultural hybridization, especially in Indonesian port cities, was also reflected in musical history. Although traditional ***gamelan*** music on **Java** has been relatively resistant to Western influence, a form of creole music called ***kroncong*** developed in the 16th and 17th centuries and gradually spread throughout the archipelago. In the 20th century something of an independent jazz tradition began to develop in the clubs of **Batavia**, and records were produced locally from the 1920s. Music was at first relatively free of the debate over the role of culture and even Indonesia's national anthem, "Indonesia Raya," composed in 1928, shows no distinctly Indonesian motifs. In the 1950s, however, Muslim and nationalist groups increasingly opposed the spread of Western pop and rock music, arguing that it was corrupting and inconsistent with Indonesian identity. Although the suppression of Western music was never entirely successful, later decades saw the growth of strong national (pop Indonesia) and regional (pop daerah) traditions, often bearing a loose resemblance in style and content to country and western music (*see also* ***DANGDUT***). A thriving domestic cassette market exists for all these forms of music. *See also* COPYRIGHT. [0159, 0174–0176, 0179, 0183, 0204]

MUSSO (or Moeso) (1897–1948)**.** One of the major leaders of the **Partai Komunis Indonesia (PKI)** until killed by Republican forces after the **Madiun Affair**. He was born in the residency of **Kediri** and attended teacher training school in **Batavia**. Musso lived for a while in **Surabaya** at the boarding house run by the wife of Umar Said **Tjokroaminoto**, with whom he became close and where he met **Sukarno**. A leading figure in the PKI when it broke off from the **Sarekat Islam (SI)**, Musso was arrested by the Dutch over the Afdeling B affair. After his release he became active especially in the PKI's relations with **labor**. He was probably present at the Prambanan meetings where the party decided to mount the 1926–1927 uprising, but was in Moscow seeking Comintern support for the revolt during the planning period. He was in **Singapore** when the revolt broke out and was briefly arrested by the British authorities, but then released and allowed to return to the **Soviet Union**. Musso returned briefly to Indonesia in 1935, where he established the so-called Illegal PKI. He finally returned to **Yogyakarta** in August 1948, where he headed a new coalition of communist and leftist forces under the PKI and posed a direct challenge to the Sukarno-Hatta leadership. When the Madiun rebellion broke out in September 1948, he was on a tour of central **Java** with other leaders, including **Amir Sjarifuddin**, but he came out in support of the rebellion and publicly challenged the people to choose between him and Sukarno. The rebellion was soon put down and Musso fled to the countryside, where he was captured and killed at the end of October 1948. [0478, 0661, 0683, 0684]

MUSYAWARAH. Discussion of issues, often at exhaustive length, by all involved in order to reach a consensus (*mufakat*). Many nationalists, especially **Sukarno**, argued that *musyawarah* was the basis of traditional village democracy in Indonesia and that it should be used in place of a Western-style system of decision making by majority vote. *See also GOTONG ROYONG.*

MYSTICISM. *See KEBATINAN.*

– N –

NAGARAKRTAGAMA. Also known in many other spellings, including *Negarakertagama*, this lengthy panegyric poem in Old Javanese was composed by Prapanca, poet to the 14th-century court of Hayam Wuruk, king of **Majapahit**. The poem praises the king while providing a detailed description of the life and social structure of Majapahit. A **lontar** leaf manuscript of the Nagarakrtagama was captured by **Dutch** troops on **Lombok** in 1894; further copies were found on **Bali** in 1978. [0528]

NAHDLATUL ULAMA (NU, Revival of the Religious Scholars)**.** Founded in **Surabaya** in 1926 by K. H. Hasyim Asyari (1871–1947) to resist the rise of modernism in Indonesian **Islam** that, in emphasizing direct recourse to the Qur'an and Hadiths, largely dispensed with the learning of religious scholars or *ulama*. The organization quickly developed a strong following in East **Java** and South **Kalimantan** and was also active in founding schools and **cooperatives**. It joined **Muhammadiyah,** however, in the **Majelis Islam A'laa Indonesia (MIAI)** in 1937 to promote Islamic unity, and in 1943 it was given a prominent role by the **Japanese** in the Japanese-sponsored **Masjumi** organization on **Java**.

NU joined the Masjumi, formed in 1945, but there was friction between the traditionalist leaders of NU and the modernists who dominated the Masjumi leadership and in 1952 under Wahid Hasyim NU seceded from the party. Led by K. H. Idham Khalid (1917–?) after Wahid Hasyim's death, NU's political priorities were always strictly religious and it was willing to trade its support on what it saw as peripheral issues for other parties' support on religious matters. NU was represented in all cabinets from 1955 to 1971 (generally holding the Ministry of Religion), and Idham Khalid became a deputy prime minister in **Sukarno**'s first *kabinet karya* in 1957. Its constituency was based largely in the ***santri*** communities of East and also Central Java and especially in the ***pesantren***. It ferociously opposed government policy on matters of public morality, such as state-sponsored **gambling**, and in 1973 the **marriage** law. Under its supervision, the Ministry of Religion grew into the largest government department. NU surprised most observers by coming in third in the 1955 **elections**, but it shared little of Masjumi's unhappiness at the end of parliamentary rule in the 1950s. It was a willing partner in Sukarno's **Guided Democracy**, representing the "A" (for *agama*, or religion) in **Nasakom**, but its rural landowning supporters were strongly opposed to the **Partai Komunis Indonesia (PKI)**'s **land reform** activities in the countryside, and it called for and spearheaded attacks on communists and their sympathizers in the killings that followed the 1965 coup.

NU subsequently became one of the pillars of the so-called **New Order** coalition, but it soon grew unhappy with the regime's failure to favor Islam. It did, however, largely preserve its vote in the 1971 elections and formed a major electoral component of the **Partai Persatuan Pembangunan (PPP)** from 1973. Its influence within the PPP was always far less than its numerical following warranted, and in 1984 it formally left the party in order to return to its original charter and concentrate on its social, educational, and religious goals. In fact, however, the NU leadership soon began to criticize the PPP and draw closer to **Golkar**. At this time, the government was insisting that all political parties and organizations adopt the **Pancasila** as their *azas tunggal* (sole foundation). Under the leadership of Achmad Siddiq and **Abdurrachman Wahid**, NU was the first Islamic **mass organization** to accept this directive. In the NU's national congresses of 1989 and 1994, there were strong moves to remove Wahid as chairman because of his reformist stands, but he weathered both efforts, in part because in the 1994 election many NU members resented government interference in the electoral process. Opposition continued, however, within NU to Wahid's tolerant stands and his closeness with **Megawati Sukarnoputri**, opposition that was nurtured particularly by adherents of **Ikatan Cendekiawan Muslim Indonesia (ICMI)**.

In the political maneuvering following the fall of **Suharto**, NU support was divided among several political parties, the two strongest being the **Partai Kebangkitan Bangsa (PKB)** and the Partai Nahdlatul Ulama

(PNU), which received 51 and five seats respectively in the postelection parliament. [0695, 0765, 1026, 1029, 1343, 1351]

NAMES, PERSONAL. Reference to Indonesian personal names often causes considerable difficulty to Westerners, the classic gaffe being the "Achmad" sometimes (but now rarely) added to **Sukarno**'s name to give it an impression of completeness. Many Indonesians, particularly on **Java**, have only one name, though there is an increasing tendency for people to follow the ***priyayi*** custom of giving their children multiple names, which now show some tendency to become fixed surnames. When an individual possesses two or more names, there is not necessarily any firm rule as to which should be used. **Ali Sastroamijoyo** was generally "Ali," whereas **Ahmad Yani** was always "Yani." Although the 1973 government regulation on spelling is generally applied to historical figures (**Tjokroaminoto**, for instance, being spelled *Cokroaminoto*), many contemporary Indonesians retain or have adopted Dutch-style spelling for sentimental, idiosyncratic, or prestige reasons. Nor is the division between names firmly fixed: the former **vice president Adam Malik** was once commonly known as *Adammalik*, while a name such as *Suriakartalegawa* may also be given as *Suria Karta Legawa*. A further complication is the use of **titles** as proper names. Among the **Bataks** and the people of the **Minahasa**, surnames in the Western sense are common, while some **Chinese** Indonesians used traditional Chinese surnames. Changes of name, however, are not uncommon when an individual wishes to mark some important change in his or her life: **Suwardi Suryaningrat** changed his name to *Ki Hajar Dewantoro* as he became more deeply involved in **Taman Siswa**, while the Indo-European E. F. E. Douwes Dekker became *Setiabudi* to symbolize his political allegiance to Indonesia. Under pressure from the **New Order** government, many Chinese Indonesians adopted quasi-Indonesian names that they use as surnames, *Liem*, for example, becoming *Salim*. Among other ethnic groups, however, the appropriate name for address or reference is often not clear, and one must be guided by common usage rather than firm rules. A fairly common practice, especially on **Sumatra**, is for a son to take his father's first name as his second name. On the spelling of names in this volume, *see* READER'S NOTE.

NASAKOM (*NASionalisme*, *Agama* [religion], *KOMunisme*)**.** Political doctrine formulated by **Sukarno** as a counter to the ideological and religious diversity of the nationalist movement before World War II, though he did not coin the term *Nasakom* until the late 1950s. Sukarno argued that religious belief, **communism**, and **nationalism** were not fundamentally incompatible ideologies but aspects of a concern for spirituality, social justice, and national self-respect that all Indonesians shared. His refusal to accept the division between these ideologies contributed to his success as a uniting national leader.

In installing **Guided Democracy** in 1957–1959, Sukarno renewed his stress on the fundamental unity of the various ideological streams within Indonesia, and *Nasakom* became the grounds for including the **Partai Komunis Indonesia (PKI)** in a broad range of government institutions from 1960 and including a few far left members in the cabinet from 1962. Opinions differ on whether "Nasakomization" meant the "domestication" of the PKI within the state or whether it was a step in the direction of a communist takeover, but in the latter years of Guided Democracy, *Nasakom* was closely associated with the Left in general; the Right appealed rather to the principle of **Pancasila**, which emphasized belief in God and made no reference to communism. After the victory of the Right and the banning of the PKI in 1965, Sukarno tried briefly to revive Nasakom as *Nasasos*, with *sosialisme* in place of communism. *See also* MARXISM. [0859, 0934]

NASUTION, ABDUL HARIS (1918–2001)**.** Born in North **Sumatra**, Nasution was one of Indonesia's leading military commanders and principal theoreticians. Trained before World War II at the Dutch military academy at Bandung, he was serving in the **Koninklijk Nederlands-Indisch Leger (KNIL)** at the time of the **Japanese** invasion. During the Indonesian **Revolution**, he soon emerged as one of the Republic's most capable military commanders, heading the West Java **Siliwangi** Division from 1946 and the Java Command from 1948. After initially favoring a Western-style frontal strategy, he developed a range of guerrilla tactics whose success contributed to the **Dutch** withdrawal in 1949.

As **army** chief of staff in 1949–1952 and 1955–1962 and minister of defense in 1956–1966, Nasution played a major role in strengthening internal military discipline. On 17 October 1952, after politicians associated with regional military leaders attempted to end his reforms, he backed public demonstrations in **Jakarta** calling for the dismissal of parliament and was suspended from his post for indiscipline, but he was reinstated in 1955. He made energetic but largely unsuccessful attempts to combat **corruption** in the army. In 1957 he proposed declaring martial law in order to defuse military rebellions in the **Outer Islands**, and his alliance with **Sukarno** was instrumental in establishing **Guided Democracy**. He formulated a theory of limited military involvement in politics, known as the **"Middle Way"** thesis, but in practice he intervened heavily in politics, restricting opposition political activity and sponsoring the **Badan Kerja Sama**. In June 1962 Sukarno maneuvered him into the relatively powerless post of **armed forces** chief of staff, but he remained powerful as defense minister.

In 1965 Nasution narrowly escaped being killed in the **Gestapu** coup attempt of 30 September but, apparently for personal reasons (he was injured and his daughter was killed in the attempt), took a back seat to General **Suharto** in suppressing the affair. He played a relatively small role in the construction of a political format for the **New Order** and was relegated to the post of speaker of the **Majelis Permusyawaratan Rakyat (MPR)**. After the 1970s he became increasingly critical of what he described as corruption and maladministration under the New Order and was a signatory of the **Petition of Fifty** in 1980. He also began to question the role that Suharto and his allies had played in the Gestapu. [0668, 0669, 0709, 0714, 0733, 0872]

NATIONALISM. Although a number of early opponents of **Dutch** rule in the archipelago, such as **Diponegoro** in Central **Java** and **Imam Bonjol** in West **Sumatra**, have been mythographically promoted as national heroes, many historians hold that the emergence of modern Indonesian nationalism coincided with what nationalist historians themselves call the *kebangkitan nasional*, or the national awakening of the early 20th century. The distinctive feature of this "awakening" was that it drew on Western thinking and took account of the socioeconomic changes brought about by colonialism to argue for an end to colonialism without a simple return to the precolonial order. Indonesian nationalism was never united by a single ideology or by a single organization, but its members shared a strong sense of participation in a movement (*pergerakan*), which was historically bound to win.

In comparison with the **Philippines** and British **India**, where fully fledged movements were campaigning for independence before the turn of the century, nationalism was rather late to develop in Indonesia. This was probably a result of the limited range of educational facilities available in the Netherlands Indies until the 20th century, which meant that Indonesians had little access to the formerly European ideas that initially inspired movements elsewhere (*see* **EDUCATION**). The emergence of modern nationalism indeed generally coincided with the rise of a technical elite, trained for employment in company and government offices under the **Liberal** and **Ethical Policies** or as professionals (physicians, lawyers, engineers, and the like). The fact that this nationalism was *Indonesian* and not more regionally based owed much to colonial administrative and education policies. It was also probably indebted to the Islamic religious ties and trading connections among many groups in the archipelago. Although the Netherlands Indies was in some senses a patchwork of distinct administrations and legal systems (*see* **LAW**; **NETHERLANDS, CONSTITUTIONAL RELATIONSHIP WITH INDONESIA**; ***ZELFBESTUREN***), the palace of the **governor-general** in **Batavia** remained the unequivocal seat of power in the colony and the principal focus of nationalist action.

The *pergerakan* included some hundreds of organizations, but it has been customary to identify the following main lines of development. **Budi Utomo** (founded 1908), with its emphasis on progress, represented a first awakening of protonationalist consciousness, though the focus of the organization was Javanese and elitist rather than Indonesian and popular. The **Indische Partij**, dominated by Indo-Europeans, was the first to demand full independence for the Indies, but it aimed otherwise to preserve many of the structures of colonial society. **Sarekat Islam (SI)** (established in 1912) was the first Indonesia-wide mass party but faced insuperable problems of working out both a common political program and a plan of action. By the early 1920s it had split, with its strongest faction organizing the **Partai Komunis Indonesia (PKI)**. The PKI, however, was suppressed by the **Dutch** after its unsuccessful rebellions in 1926–1927, and the center of the nationalist stage was then taken by the so-called secular or radical nationalists, who emphasized a common Indonesian identity irrespective of religion, race, or class. **Partai Nasional Indonesia (PNI)**, **Pendidikan Nasional Indonesia (PNI Baru)**, and **Partai Indonesia (Partindo)** and leaders such as **Sukarno**, **Mohammad Hatta**, and **Sutan Sjahrir** were only briefly able to operate before a final decade of Dutch repression restricted political freedom to relatively moderate cooperative parties, notably **Partai Indonesia Raya (Parindra)** and **Gerakan Rakyat Indonesia (Gerindo)**. Only during the **Japanese occupation** were the radical nationalists able to resume leadership of the *pergerakan*.

Some scholars have argued that this general view is misleading because it gives the eventual victors (the radical nationalists) a more central role than they in fact played, and that more "moderate" and regional organizations such as the **Pakempalan Kawula Ngayogyakarta** and

Paguyuban Pasundan and conservative figures such as **Ahmad Djajadiningrat** and Noto Suroto need to be given more emphasis. Another argument, however, states that both views overestimate the roles of both radical and conservative nationalists. It instead emphasizes the Islamic character of much of the nationalist movement and points to the fact that Muslim organizations were the most effective in keeping nationalism alive during periods of Dutch repression and that these organizations were the basis of the strongest **militias** that opposed the reassertion of Dutch rule.

From the start, all nationalist groups acknowledged that they faced an enormous obstacle in the form of the colonial state, especially the political police (**Politiek Inlichtingen Dienst**), and strategy for overcoming this was a major topic of debate. The PKI unsuccessfully ventured armed rebellion in 1926–1927, but for most nationalists the issue was how much to cooperate with the colonial government in quasi-representative institutions such as the **Volksraad**. Those favoring cooperation ("Co") hoped that this would ameliorate the conditions of Indonesians under colonialism and would lead eventually to responsible government. Those rejecting it ("Non-Co") argued that the Volksraad was no more than window-dressing and that progress could only be made by withdrawing cooperation from the colonial government so that it would eventually cease to operate. The nationalists were also divided on whether to expect support from abroad. Members of the PKI looked to the Comintern for aid. Some Muslims hoped for assistance from the Muslim world, while others looked to **Japan**, especially after the Russo-Japanese War. In the late 1930s, on the other hand, the Left was keen to cooperate with the colonial authorities against Japanese fascism, and toward the close of the **Japanese occupation** younger nationalists were anxious that Japanese plans for a puppet state in Indonesia should not lead to independence being achieved as a "gift" of any other country. This view developed during the **Revolution** into a preference for military action to defeat the Dutch rather than negotiation toward a compromise settlement.

During the Revolution, the Dutch endeavored to promote and recognize regional identities in a federal system (*see* **FEDERALISM**), but only in **Ambon** did a serious separatist movement emerge at this time. After the transfer of sovereignty, the Dutch retained control of West New Guinea (**Papua**) and encouraged hopes for independence among the Papuans that survived the territory's transfer to Indonesian rule in 1963. These hopes, together with insensitive and at times brutal actions by Indonesian forces, form the ideological underpinning of the **Organisasi**

Papua Merdeka (OPM) or Free Papua Movement. [0502, 0586, 0593, 0613, 0621, 0626, 0627, 0651, 0661, 0807, 0844, 0907, 0925]

NATIONALIZATION. Under the **Liberal Policy**, the colonial government promoted foreign **investment** and resorted to nationalization only of German and Italian firms after the occupation of the Netherlands in 1940. During the **Japanese occupation**, firms belonging to Allied subjects were appropriated, and handed in some cases to government bodies as a source of finance, in other cases to existing Japanese firms (*see* **SUGAR**). At the start of the **Revolution**, most such firms came into the hands of their workers, though the Republican government was publicly committed to handing all but a small number of essential industries, such as the **railways** and public utilities, back to their foreign owners.

In December 1957, workers and **labor unions** throughout Indonesia took over the offices of Dutch firms in the name of worker control. Within a few weeks, control was put in the hands of the **armed forces** (*see* **MILITARY BUSINESS OPERATIONS**) and the seizures were ratified by parliament. Some 246 enterprises were taken over, accounting for 90 percent of the country's plantation output and 60 percent of foreign **trade**. British and American property was nationalized in 1963–1965, but much of it was returned after 1966. Strong guarantees were also given at this time against further nationalization. *See also* INDONESIANIZATION; STATE ENTERPRISES. [0315]

NATIVE STATES. *See ZELFBESTUREN.*

NATIVE TROOPS. Alongside the colonial army (*see* **KONINKLIJK NEDERLANDSCH INDISCH LEGER**), the **Dutch** retained a number of auxiliary units more or less descended from the armies of defeated or subordinated indigenous rulers. Some of these, such as the Legiun **Mangkunegaran**, remained under the command of the ***zelfbesturen***, while others such as the *prajurits* of **Java** and the *barisans* on **Madura** operated as a kind of auxiliary **police** force under the command of the Dutch civilian government, though the *barisans* also took part in military expeditions to other islands. During World War I many Indonesians agitated for the establishment of a native **militia** to aid in the defense of the colony. The Dutch, however, rejected this for security reasons. In the latter part of the Indonesian **Revolution**, the Dutch established several quasi-auxiliary units. *Hare Majesteits Ongeregelde Troepen* (Her Majesty's Irregular Troops) consisted of former ***lasykar***

recruited to the Dutch cause. In West **Java** especially, *ondernemingswachten* (plantation guards) recruited many Indonesians, while *Veiligheidsbataljons* in North **Sumatra** and West Java and the *Barisan Cakra* in **Madura** were intended partly to maintain law and order, partly as military backing for the federal states (*see* **FEDERALISM**). *See also* MARÉCHAUSSÉE.

NATSIR, MOHAMMAD (1908–1993). One of the outstanding modernist Islamic leaders in independent Indonesia, Natsir was born in Alahan Panjang, West **Sumatra**, and received scholarships to continue his **education**, graduating from the Algemene Middelbare School (AMS, General Secondary School) in **Bandung** in 1930. He became a member of the Jong Islamieten Bond, but was associated most closely before the war with the **Persatuan Islam (Persis)** and with an Islamic education organization that he organized and led until it was closed by the **Japanese** in 1945. He also became known through his exchange in the late 1930s with **Sukarno** (then in **exile** in **Bengkulu**), in which he argued against what he viewed as Sukarno's overemphasis on rationalism as the key to understanding **Islam**. In November 1945 Natsir was one of the leaders of the "progressive" wing of the **Masjumi** party (often termed the "religious socialists") and in September 1950 headed the first cabinet of the unitary Indonesian Republic. His pro-Western government emphasized national reconstruction and enjoyed the benefits of the Korean War boom, but fell in April 1951, partly over the financial austerity program it pursued under Finance Minister **Sjafruddin Prawiranegara**. Natsir remained a strong proponent of democratic government and differed with Sukarno over this and over the president's Irian (*see* **PAPUA**) policy.

At the end of 1957, after he was harassed, with other Masjumi leaders, over an assassination attempt against Sukarno in which members of the party's youth branch had been involved, Natsir fled to **Sumatra** to join the **PRRI/Permesta rebellion**. He was one of the last rebels to surrender in September 1961, and he was subsequently jailed until after the fall of Sukarno in 1966. He and his Masjumi colleagues were forbidden to play any political role under the **New Order**, and he turned his major attention to education and social work, especially the missionary work of the Dewan Dakwah Islamiyah Indonesia (DDII, Indonesian Islamic Preaching Council), which he helped found in 1967. He remained an influential critic of the **corruption** of Indonesian society under the **Suharto** regime, and in 1980 was one of the signers of the **Petition of**

Fifty, as well as joining 10 years later with **A. H. Nasution** and a senior leader of the former **Partai Nasional Indonesia (PNI)** in a public appeal deploring the **Suharto** government's departure from the social and political goals of the **Revolution** and Indonesian **Constitution**. [0627, 0695, 0844, 0929, 1121]

NAVY. Whereas the colonial army (**Koninklijk Nederlands-Indisch Leger [KNIL]**) was institutionally distinct from the metropolitan army, the naval forces in colonial Indonesia were formally part of the Dutch navy placed at the operational disposal of the **governor-general**, an arrangement that led to continued disputes over the appropriate division of costs between the two governments. Colonial security policy placed more emphasis on the maintenance of order within the colony than on defense from external attack, and especially after the construction of the **Singapore** naval base in 1921–1938 the colonial government tended to rely on **Britain** for naval protection. The Dutch fleet in the east was largely destroyed in 1942 in the battle of the **Java Sea**.

In 1945, former members of the Kaigun **Heiho** (naval auxiliaries) formed by the **Japanese occupation** forces founded the Angkatan Laut Republik Indonesia (ALRI, Navy of the Indonesian Republic), which was, however, mainly a commercial operation, trading plantation produce to Singapore and elsewhere; after 1949, the high capital costs of maintaining a navy and the demands of internal security kept the navy small, though it received some equipment from the **Soviet Union** after 1960, and from **Germany** in the 1980s. [0714]

NEDERLANDSCHE HANDEL MAATSCHAPPIJ (NHM, Netherlands Trading Company, also known as the Factorij). Founded on 29 March 1825 by King Willem I on the advice of H. W. Muntinghe as a quasi-official trading corporation, the NHM acted initially as agent for the sale of government produce acquired under the **Cultivation System**, earning enormous profits. Multatuli's novel ***Max Havelaar*** was subtitled "The **Coffee** Auctions of the Netherlands Trading Company." The NHM was also responsible for supplying produce, especially textiles, to Dutch industry, and from 1827 to 1833 it had a monopoly of **opium** sales in Dutch territory. After losing government preference in 1872, the firm moved increasingly into the financing of plantations and thence into general **banking**, which became its major activity in the 20th century. In 1964 the NHM merged with the Twentse Bank to form the Algemene Bank Nederland.

NEGARA INDONESIA TIMUR (NIT, State of East Indonesia). Federal state formed on 24 December 1946 after the Malino conference of July that year, encompassing **Sulawesi**, **Maluku**, and **Nusatenggara** as a model of **Dutch** postcolonial plans for Indonesia. **Makassar** was its capital. From March 1947 semiautonomous regions (*daerah*) were formed within the NIT itself. Although conservative, its leaders were sufficiently aware of nationalist strength to seek good relations with the Republic, and it was NIT's insistence after the second Dutch **"Police Action"** that the Republic be included in negotiations on the country's future, which ended Dutch hopes of using **federalism** to destroy the Republic. In April 1950 the **Minahasa** *daerah* seceded from NIT and merged with the Indonesian Republic, and it was followed by the remaining *daerah* except South **Sulawesi**. In May 1950, the NIT *walinegara* (head of state), Cokorde Gde Rake Sukawati, agreed to dissolve the state on 17 August 1950. The arbitrary actions by Republican troops sent from **Java** to take control, however, aroused resentment that contributed to the revolt of **Kahar Muzakkar**. *See also* REPUBLIK MALUKU SELATAN. [0660, 0661, 0674, 0784]

NEGARA KALIMANTAN TIMUR. *See* PONTIANAK.

NEGARA SUMATERA SELATAN. *See* PALEMBANG.

NEGARA SUMATERA TIMUR. *See* EAST SUMATRA.

NEKOLIM (neocolonialism, colonialism, and imperialism). Term coined by **Ahmad Yani** but popularized by **Sukarno** to describe what he saw as the major international enemies of the Indonesian people and reflecting his understanding that formal independence did not necessarily mean an end to imperialist control. Sukarno amplified the concept in 1960 by contrasting the progressive NEFO (new emerging forces) with the reactionary OLDEFO (old established forces), and he sought to make this idea a rallying point for progressive countries, holding a Games of the New Emerging Forces (GANEFO) in November 1963 and attempting to convene a Conference of the New Emerging Forces (CONEFO) in 1965. *See also* FOREIGN POLICY. [0859]

NETHERLANDS, CONSTITUTIONAL RELATIONSHIP WITH INDONESIA. From shortly after the first **Dutch** trading expeditions to the archipelago, Dutch power in the region was represented almost exclusively by the **Dutch East Indies Company (VOC)** under a charter from the Netherlands States General. On rare occasions, the Dutch government itself dispatched one or more **commissioners-general** to the East to act on its behalf, but for the most part it left the company with untrammeled freedom of action in the region. The company's possessions, however, were not thought of as strictly sovereign, since they derived neither from older ideas of divine appointment nor from newer ideas of popular assent. In practice, moreover, under the racially based legal order (*see* **RACE**) in VOC territories, the company exercised much less than full sovereign power. Even in 1795, when the **Batavian Republic** took over the assets of the VOC, it seems to have regarded them as primarily commercial rather than territorial and sovereign, though by that time the company was already the dominant power on **Java**.

From 1795 to 1815, the constitutional relationship remained confused and often vague. Until 1800, States General ruled formally through the VOC. When the company's charter lapsed in 1800, the colony came under direct rule, but the Napoleonic Wars and later British occupation of Java made this of little significance. A **Ministry of Colonies** was formed in 1806, though it was often united with other departments, especially that of the **navy**, until 1842. From 1815 to 1848 the Ministry of Colonies, and thus the colony itself, was directly under the authority of the Dutch king, who used his position and shareholding in the **Nederlandsche Handel Maatschappij (NHM)** to make a considerable personal fortune. In the late 1820s the post of commissioner-general, as representative of the Dutch government, was first united with that of **governor-general**, as agent of the Ministry of Colonies, and then abandoned.

In the 20th century the Netherlands Indies gradually developed as a state distinct from the Netherlands. In 1903 the colonial treasury was separated from that of the Netherlands, and in 1913 the colonial government received the right to contract public loans. The colonial government established quasi-diplomatic representation in Arabia (in connection with Muslim pilgrimage, *see* ***HAJ***). Governors-General J. B. van Heutsz (1904–1909), A. W. F. Idenburg (1909–1916), and J. P. G. van Limburg Stirum (1916–1921) increasingly defended what they saw as Indies interests (which were not necessarily the interests of the indigenous population) against those of the metropolis. The establishment of the **Volksraad** in 1918 gave a quasi-democratic weight to those Indies government actions that it supported. In 1922 the colony became formally a *rijksdeel* on a notionally equal footing with the Netherlands in the Dutch **Constitution**, though remaining under the Ministry of

Colonies. On 27 November 1949 the Netherlands government transferred sovereignty over the Netherlands Indies, excluding West New Guinea (**Papua**), to the **Republik Indonesia Serikat (RIS)**, which was linked to the Kingdom of the Netherlands in a Netherlands-Indonesian Union under the Dutch Crown. *See also* NETHERLANDS INDIES, EXPANSION OF; NETHERLANDS, RELATIONS WITH; SUCCESSION. [0006, 0638, 0674]

NETHERLANDS, RELATIONS WITH. Indonesian-**Dutch** relations began in 1949 with a legacy of mistrust stemming from the experience of colonialism and the **Revolution**, from the unpopular Netherlands-Indonesian Union (*see also* **DEBT, INTERNATIONAL**), and from what was seen as Dutch support for the **Republik Maluku Selatan (RMS)** and other dissidents. Dutch unwillingness to contemplate a transfer of West Irian (**Papua**) to the Republic at or after the transfer of sovereignty in 1949, however, became the major stumbling block in relations during the following years, especially after the Netherlands categorically refused to transfer the territory in 1952 and began plans to bring it to separate independence. Indonesia attempted to pressure the Netherlands on the issue by cooling relations: negotiations on the dissolution of the Union began in 1954, though the two sides were unable to agree on how to achieve this and the Union was finally dissolved unilaterally by Indonesia in 13 February 1956. The inherited debt was repudiated on 4 August of the same year, though practically all of it had by then been repaid. In October 1957, after the **United Nations** again refused to discuss the Irian issue, the government coordinated an anti-Dutch boycott that was followed by the **nationalization** of Dutch firms in December. Indonesia finally cut all links on 17 August 1960, but relations were restored in March 1963, after the Dutch finally surrendered West Irian.

Cordiality returned to the relationship only after the **New Order** came to power in 1965–1966. Indonesia asked the Netherlands to chair the **Inter-Governmental Group on Indonesia (IGGI)**, while the Netherlands became Indonesia's largest **trading** partner in Europe. Indonesia saw the Netherlands as a useful counterweight to the **United States** and **Japan** in international affairs, but became irritated by Dutch complaints over **human rights** abuses in Indonesia. Tension over this issue reached a head in 1991 when the Dutch suspended aid to Indonesia after the Dili massacre in **East Timor**, and **Suharto** responded by disbanding the IGGI, which was replaced by the **Consultative Group on Indonesia (CGI)** from which the Netherlands was excluded. Relations between the two countries warmed slightly over succeeding years, and Queen Beatrice became the first Dutch monarch to visit Indonesia in September 1995, the 50th anniversary of the country's independence. [0695, 1138, 1143, 1146]

NETHERLANDS INDIES CIVIL ADMINISTRATION (NICA). Militarized Dutch colonial administrative corps attached to the advancing Allied forces during World War II to take over the government of areas liberated from the **Japanese** prior to the formal restoration of civil government. The prospect of a return to colonial rule aroused such hostility among Indonesians that the term was soon dropped officially, but NICA remained a derogatory shorthand word for the postwar Dutch administration until the end of the **Revolution**. *See also* MOOK, H. J. VAN. [1146]

NETHERLANDS INDIES, EXPANSION OF. Although Indonesian nationalists and Western historians alike were inclined to speak of "350 years of Dutch colonial rule," the growth of **Dutch** power in the archipelago was gradual and uneven. The **Dutch East Indies Company (VOC)** established influence first by means of treaties with indigenous rulers. The earliest of these treaties typically gave the VOC a monopoly of **trading** rights in certain commodities (e.g., **cloves** and **nutmeg**) and the right to build trading posts. Coming from a Europe that had only recently emerged from the complex hierarchy of medieval feudal relationships, the VOC did not see its activities as formally diminishing the sovereignty of indigenous states. In successive years, however, both the character of new treaties and the interpretation of old ones changed to give the Dutch what increasingly amounted to sovereign powers. After 1825, at the end of the disruption caused by the abolition of the VOC and the Napoleonic Wars (*see* **BATAVIAN REPUBLIC**), Dutch authority extended over **Java**, parts of West **Sumatra** (**Minangkabau**), **Palembang**, **Bangka**, **Belitung**, **Banjarmasin**, **Pontianak**, **Makassar**, the **Minahasa**, and much of **Maluku**; in addition, the Dutch held nominal authority over **Lampung**, **Siak**, and **Riau**. The independent regions thus still included **Aceh**, **East Sumatra** (including the **Batak** regions of the interior), **Siak**, **Kutai** and the interior of **Kalimantan**, the remainder of **Sulawesi**, **Bali**, **Lombok**, West Irian (**Papua**) and many regions of Maluku, and **Nusatenggara**.

The situation, however, was rather confused, with the Netherlands asserting a general sphere of influence over the entire archipelago yet formally acknowledging the independence of "native states in amity with the Netherlands government," a term that only disappeared in 1915 (*see* ***ZELFBESTUREN***). From the mid-19th century and especially after 1870, the colonial state began to fill out the territorial boundaries of modern Indonesia by conquering or incorporating these independent states. Increasingly, the colonial government preferred to demand *verklaringen* (declarations) of submission from indigenous rulers, rather than signing formal treaties with them. The sultan of **Deli** made such a declaration in 1862, a model formula for declarations was prepared in 1875, and in 1898 the so-called *Korte Verklaring* was adopted as a relatively standardized acknowledgment by indigenous rulers that they accepted the general suzerainty of the Netherlands Indies, agreed to follow instructions from the **governor-general**, and agreed to have no relations with foreign powers. Dutch sovereignty was effectively established over the entire archipelago (with the possible exception of the interior of Papua) by 1911. *See also* NETHERLANDS, CONSTITUTIONAL RELATIONSHIP WITH INDONESIA. [0006, 0491, 0553, 0583, 0629, 0818]

NEW EMERGING FORCES. *See* NEKOLIM.

NEW GUINEA: WEST, *see* PAPUA; *see* PAPUA NEW GUINEA.

NEW ORDER (*Orde Baru*, *Orba*)**.** General term for the political system in force after the accession of **Suharto** to power in 1966 (*see* **SUPERSEMAR**) until his fall in May 1998. It was first used to refer to the so-called New Order coalition of **army**, **students**, intellectuals, and Muslims opposed to **Sukarno** and the **Partai Komunis Indonesia (PKI)**. The term soon came to imply a sharp contrast with the so-called Old Order (*Orde Lama*, *Orla*) of Sukarno, especially in government policies. The New Order abandoned Indonesia's **Confrontation** with **Malaysia** as well as the Jakarta–Peking axis (*see* **FOREIGN POLICY**), opened the country to foreign **investment**, suppressed the PKI, purged both state and society of left-wing influence (*see* **MASSACRES OF 1965–1966**), and abandoned the rhetoric of popular democracy. Indonesia became strongly anticommunist (especially anti-**Chinese**) in its foreign policy, promoted economic stabilization based on political stability, and emphasized the suppression of allegedly particularist interests in the cause of **development**.

Many authors have suggested, however, that the contrast between the Old and New Orders may not be as sharp as first appeared. They point in particular to the continuing and expanding role of the military, to continued political repression, and to the patrimonial, neomonarchical styles of both Sukarno and Suharto. *See also* POLITICAL CULTURE. [0716–0752]

NEWS AGENCIES. The Algemene Nieuws en Telegraaf Agentschap (ANETA, General News and Telegraph Agency), founded by D. W. Berretty (1890–1934), was the first news agency in the Indies, but it was followed quickly by a number of small **Dutch** and Indonesian firms, including the Borneo Pers en Nieuws Agentschap (1926) and the Indonesische Pers Agentschap (Inpera) in 1936. Complaints that ANETA was neglecting local news led to the establishment of **Antara** in 1937. Many journalists tied to Antara worked in the Domei agency during the **Japanese occupation**. ANETA closed in 1940–1946 and changed its name in 1954 to Persbiro Indonesia. In 1963 it was merged into Antara. *See also* NEWSPAPERS. [1293, 1304]

NEWSPAPERS. From 1615, Governor-general **J. P. Coen** sent news from the Indies to Europe in a handwritten circular later called *Memorie der Nouvelles*, but the first true newspaper produced for sale to the public, the *Bataviase Nouvelles*, appeared only in 1745 and was banned in 1746 on order of the **Dutch East Indies Company (VOC)**. From 1810 the colonial government published the *Bataviasche Koloniale Courant*, which became the *Java Government Gazette* during the British interregnum, and resumed publication as the *Bataviasche Courant* in 1816 and the *Javasche Courant* in 1828. Independent newspapers (apart from advertisement bulletins) began publishing after 1848, the *Java-Bode* (**Batavia**) appearing in 1852 and *De Locomotief* (**Semarang**) in 1863. The earliest indigenous newspapers were the Javanese-language *Bromartani* (1855) and the Malay *Soerat Chabar Melajoe*, and from the 1870s the number of newspapers in most regions grew dramatically. The nationalist press began with Abdul Rivai's *Bintang Hindia* in West **Sumatra** (1902) and with the *Medan Prijaji* of Tirtoadisuryo appearing in **Bandung** in 1906. There was also a lively **Chinese**-language press, including *Sin Po* (1910). The Persatuan Jurnalis Indonesia (Indonesian Journalists' Association) was formed in 1933 under Moh. Tabrani. It was replaced in February 1946 by the Persatuan Wartawan Indonesia (PWI, Indonesian Reporters' Association).

During the **Japanese occupation**, publication was restricted to government papers, notably *Jawa Shinbun*, but press publishing blossomed again during the **Revolution** and the early 1950s; a national survey in 1954 recorded 105 dailies, though many of these were closer in style to political pamphlets than to conventional newspapers. During the 1950s and early 1960s the **Partai Komunis Indonesia (PKI)** newspaper *Harian Rakjat* had the largest circulation, followed by *Pedoman* (**Partai Sosialis Indonesia [PSI]**), *Suluh Indonesia* (**Partai Nasional Indonesia [PNI]**), and *Abadi* (**Masjumi**), with *Indonesia Raya* under **Mochtar Lubis** a major investigatory paper. From the mid-1950s, however, and especially after the declaration of martial law in 1957, increasing restrictions were placed on the press, causing circulation and numbers to drop.

When **Suharto** came to power, his government closed about a quarter of Indonesia's 160 or so newspapers because of their alleged communist links. Thereafter the remaining newspapers enjoyed a period of relative freedom, though any questioning of the official version of the events in September–October 1965 was forbidden. In 1974, however, in the aftermath of the **Malari** incident, 12 newspapers were closed down, including Mochtar Lubis's *Indonesia Raya*, and he and several other leading journalists were arrested; as a result, the press became more cautious. Any challenge to the Suharto government usually resulted in printing bans; for example, after the **student** protests of 1977–1978 seven Jakarta papers were temporarily banned, and after they published criticisms from the members of the **Petition of Fifty**, newspapers were forbidden from printing the members' pictures or their comments. From July 1978 the government began a program known as *koran masuk desa* (newspapers enter the village), under which free copies of the **armed forces** newspapers *Angkatan Bersenjata* and *Berita Yudha* were distributed to villages throughout the country, but these were replaced in December 1979 by a new series of 27 weekly newspapers and magazines published by the government especially for distribution to the villages. In 1980 all newspapers were restricted to 12 pages in length.

Newspaper publication flourished during the 1980s, dominated in **Jakarta** by the dailies *Kompas* and *Suara Pembaruan*, and the weekly *Tempo*, joined in 1985 by the financial daily *Bisnis Indonesia*, financed by **Liem Sioe Liong**'s business interests. These groups in the capital competed also in publishing regional newspapers, alongside the *Jawa Pos* group in **Surabaya** and the Jakarta daily *Media Indonesia.* For example, the *Kompas* group collaborated with such regional newspapers as *Sriwijaya Pos* in **Palembang**, *Serambi Indonesia* in **Aceh**, *Berita Nasional* in **Yogyakarta**, and *Mandala* in Bandung. The Suharto government maintained control over the press, however, by various forms of

censorship and by having various members of the president's family (*see* **SUHARTO FAMILY**) and close associates buy into the **media** industry. In 1993 **Ikatan Cendekiawan Muslim Indonesia (ICMI)** launched the daily newspaper *Republika*, which became a major outlet for **B. J. Habibie**'s policies.

The fall of Suharto led to an immediate burgeoning of newspapers when the information minister canceled the need for press publication permits and issued more than 1,200 licenses, and parliament in September 1999 enacted a new Press Law guaranteeing freedom of the press. *See also* NEWS AGENCIES; *KETERBUKAAN*. [0756, 1290, 1293, 1295, 1304, 1307, 1309]

NGANTUNG, HENK (1921–)**.** Painter especially noted for his landscapes and portraits of *becak* drivers and other people. He was elected to parliament on the **Partai Komunis Indonesia (PKI)** ticket in 1955 and was appointed by **Sukarno** to represent **artists** on the **Dewan Nasional** in 1957. In 1961 he became vice mayor of **Jakarta** and was city governor in 1964–1965. He was chairperson of the Central Committee of **Lembaga Kebudayaan Rakyat (Lekra)**. [0159]

NIAS. Island off the west coast of **Sumatra**, known especially for what was once seen as its surviving **megalithic culture**, associated with ancestor worship, though this receded greatly when missionary activity began in the late 19th century. Precolonial society was strictly divided into three classes: aristocrats, farmers, and **slaves**.

NICKEL. Formerly obtained both from meteorites and from mines in central **Sulawesi** (*see* **LUWU**). A large mine was opened at Soroako in southeast Sulawesi by the Canadian firm International Nickel in 1978. The state mining firm Aneka Tambang has been **mining** nickel on Pulau Gebe off **Halmahera** since 1978. *See also* METALWORKING. [0413, 0416]

NUSANTARA. Used in the ***Nagarakrtagama*** for the **Outer Islands** as distinct from **Java**, but revived in the early 20th century as a poetic name for the Indonesian archipelago. *See* ARCHIPELAGIC CONCEPT; INDONESIA.

NUSATENGGARA (Lesser Sundas)**.** The chain of islands stretching east from **Java**: **Bali**, **Lombok**, **Sumbawa**, **Komodo**, **Sumba**, **Savu**, **Flores**, **Roti**, **Timor**, and the **Solor** archipelago.

NUTMEG (*pala*). Nut of *Myristica fragrans* (Myristicaceae), native of **Maluku** and far western New Guinea (**Papua**), and cultivated from early times on **Banda**. Highly prized as a spice, the nuts were traded to **China**, **India**, and Europe from the sixth century. Like **cloves**, they were a major target of **Portuguese** expansion in the region. After the Dutch seized Maluku in the early 17th century, they extirpated wild and cultivated trees from all places they could find them except Banda in order to keep a close control of the **trade** and to drive up prices (*see* **DUTCH EAST INDIES COMPANY**; ***HONGI*** **RAIDS**). In 1769 the French successfully smuggled plants to Mauritius, from where they spread to **Singapore**, Penang, and Grenada (West Indies), breaking the Dutch monopoly. Extensive cultivation began in **Minahasa** in 1840, but declined after plantations were struck by disease in 1873. [0527]

– O –

OEI TIONG HAM (1886–1924). The biggest **Chinese** businessman in prewar Indonesia. He began as the holder of an **opium** farm or ***pacht*** from the colonial government, but after the Opiumregie was founded he diversified into **sugar**, **banking**, real estate, and general trading. His empire was managed after his death by his sons, but was nationalized in 1961. [0373]

OIL. Seeping naturally from the ground in northern **Sumatra** in early times, oil was collected for use as medicine, for fuel, for caulking boats, and as an incendiary, especially in naval warfare. The commercial search for oil began in 1866, after the development of drilling techniques in the **United States**, and the first sales of oil, extracted by the Dortsche Petroleum Maatschappij from wells near **Surabaya**, took place in 1889. Exploratory drilling began in Sumatra in 1883 in **Langkat**, where oil was found at 100 meters in depth. From 1890 the wells at Langkat and from 1892 the refinery at Pangkalan Brandan became the center of the oil interests of the Koninklijke Nederlandsche Maatschappij tot Exploitatie van Petroleumbronnen in Nederlandsch-Indië (generally known as the **"Koninklijke"**). Another company, later called Shell Oil, began drilling in **Kutai** in East **Kalimantan** in 1891. After an oil boom in the last decade of the 19th century, which saw dozens of companies rise and fall, the Koninklijke and Shell merged in 1907 to form the Bataafse Petroleum Maatschappij (BPM). Although the BPM dominated the Indonesian oil industry from that time and launched a number of joint ventures with the colonial government (*see also* **STATE ENTERPRISES**), a significant part of the production was in the hands of the Nederlandsche Koloniale Petroleum Maatschappij, a subsidiary of the American Standard Oil Company.

Although production began on **Java**, fields there were soon overshadowed by those of Sumatra, which produced a light grade of oil, and, even more important, those of East Kalimantan, which produced a heavy grade suitable in some cases for direct use as ship's fuel. The Netherlands Indies fields were especially important to **Japan**, and it was an embargo on oil supplies from the colony to Japan that, among other things, prompted the Japanese to invade the region in 1941–1942. The wells of East Kalimantan were a major target, though considerable damage was done to them by Dutch scorched-earth tactics before the Japanese arrival. They were also among the first areas seized by the Allies on their return to the archipelago in 1945.

Oil from Cepu in Java was an important source of fuel for the Indonesian Republic during the **Revolution**, and the south Sumatra fields were contested by the Republic and the **Dutch**. The American companies Stanvac and Caltex as well as Japanese firms took important shares of postwar production, but all foreign companies were under pressure to distribute a larger share of the profits to Indonesia. Indonesia joined the Organization of Petroleum Exporting Countries (OPEC) in 1962, and foreign companies increasingly operated as production-sharing agents of the three state oil firms, all under **army** control: Permina, headed by Ibnu Sutowo and based in the south Sumatra fields; Permigan (formerly Nglobo Oil Mining) in Central Java and eastern Indonesia, controlled by the army's Diponegoro Division; and Pertamin (formerly Permindo), formerly a BPM-government joint venture. Oil was a major, though insufficient, source of state income under the **Guided Economy**.

Production-sharing agreements continued and expanded under the **New Order**. The state companies merged in 1968 to form **Pertamina**, which rode a wave of enormous profits, with new oil discoveries and a dramatic increase in oil prices, until its debt crisis in 1975. In 1977 the **United States** replaced Japan as Indonesia's largest customer. The decline of oil prices in 1982 and 1986 imposed severe **budget** restrictions. The government responded by attempting to diversify Indonesia's exports, so that oil and liquefied natural **gas** fell from 73 percent of Indonesia's exports in 1984 to 51.7 percent in 1987.

In the late 1990s oil companies increased their exploration activities, pumping $4.8 billion into exploration in 1997, compared with $3.6 billion the previous year. In 2002 ExxonMobil discovered possibly the largest oilfield on Java (at Cepu), perhaps containing 1 billion barrels of oil, and offered Pertamina a 10 percent stake in the field. Pertamina, however, was holding out for a 50 percent share of the profits together with a $400 million signing fee. The **decentralization** law drawn up in 1999 planned to allow the regions to keep 15 percent of all their oil revenues (except for Aceh, which was to be allowed 70 percent of the province's net oil income), and the Oil and Gas Act of 2001 attempted to force Pertamina to cede its control over production-sharing contracts with foreign and domestic oil companies to a separate regulatory agency by November 2002. Violence continued to plague the operations of ExxonMobil in Aceh, which was forced to close down production for four months in 2001 and thereafter employ 3,000 Indonesian troops to guard its facilities. In 2002 Acehnese villagers brought a suit against the company in U.S. courts for tolerating the brutality and **human rights** abuses of the troops guarding its facilities. *See also* MAP 11. [0294, 0371, 0375, 0400, 0405, 0448]

OIL PALM (*Elaeis guineensis*, Arecaceae)**.** Originally from **Africa**, the oil palm first appeared in Indonesia as an ornamental tree in 1848. The first commercial plantation was established on **Java** in 1859, but oil palm did not become a major crop until the laying out of extensive estates in **East Sumatra** from 1911. Not until the **Suharto** regime, however, did oil palm plantations begin to replace the forests in many parts of **Sumatra** and **Kalimantan**. Suharto sanctioned the conversion of large areas of Kalimantan and coastal Sumatra from native vegetation to oil palm plantations, aiming to make Indonesia the world's largest palm oil producer. According to some estimates, the land affected could be measured in millions of hectares. Land clearing was carried out during severe drought conditions, and this was one of the major causes of the fires that swept through both islands in 1997. Many of the plantations were developed on a sensitive peat soil base that, when burned, loosed large carbon emissions into the air. By 2001 Indonesia and **Malaysia** accounted for more than 80 percent of global palm oil output, and in that year Indonesia lowered its export **tax** from 5 percent to 3 percent. *See also* FORESTRY. [0316, 0331, 0332, 0765]

OLD ORDER. *See* NEW ORDER.

ONTVOOGDING. *See* DECENTRALIZATION; *ZELFBESTUREN*.

OPERASI KHUSUS (OPSUS, Special Operations)**.** Organization established within **Komando Cadangan Strategis Angkatan Darat (Kostrad)** in circa 1963 by **Ali Murtopo**, an intelligence officer and member of **Suharto**'s inner circle, and Sujono Humardani (1919–1986). It was used initially to establish covert contacts with the **Malaysian** government during **Confrontation**. Opsus later helped to ensure progovernment votes in the 1969 "Act of Free Choice" in West Irian (**Papua**) and in the general **elections** in 1971 and after. It played an important role in the restructuring of political parties after 1971 and was officially disbanded in 1974, partly in response to the **Malari** Affair. *See also* INTELLIGENCE SERVICES.

OPIUM (*Papaver somniferum* Papaveraceae)**.** Widely cultivated in **India** from the 15th century, extensive exports of opium to Indonesia began soon after. Opium had some use in Tantric religious rituals, but its main use was recreational. From about 1670 the **Dutch East Indies Company (VOC)** dominated the **trade** to Indonesia, and sale on **Java** was subject to a loosely enforced company monopoly, for the sake of which production in the archipelago was banned.

Various methods were used to market opium. Initially it was sold directly by the VOC, but company rights were transferred in 1745 to an Opium Society consisting of private traders; this society was replaced in 1794 by a state Opium Directorate, which **Herman Willem Daendels** replaced in turn with a system of farms or ***pachten***. **Thomas Stamford Raffles** attempted to restrict sales, partly for humanitarian reasons, partly because of extensive smuggling, but he was overruled by the British authorities in Bengal. Control of opium sales was given to the **Nederlandsche Handel Maatschappij (NHM)** from 1827 to 1833, when the farms were restored. In 1894, after a prolonged humanitarian campaign in the Netherlands, the farm system was replaced once more by a state monopoly, the Opiumregie, which imported raw opium, refined it in **Batavia**, and sold it to registered addicts through a network of government shops. Sales continued on a smaller scale during the **Japanese occupation**, and the Indonesian Republic earned important foreign exchange during the national **Revolution** by selling the remaining Opiumregie stocks within Indonesia and abroad. The Regie was abolished in 1950.

Proceeds, direct or indirect, from opium sales were a significant part of state revenues, especially during the 19th century, and were most commonly associated with forced **labor**. Opium addiction helped to keep laborers pliant and subservient through both clinical dependence and debt. Opium farms were generally in the hands of **Chinese** entrepreneurs who maintained private security forces to enforce their regional monopolies. During the 19th century the vast majority of addicts were Javanese, but in the 20th century a strong campaign by both nationalists and **Ethical Policy**–minded colonial officials, combined with the effects of the **Depression of the 1930s**, dramatically reduced consumption, and by 1942 most users were Chinese. [0599, 0630, 1061]

ORANGUTAN (*Pongo pygmaeus*, formerly known as *Simia satyrus*)**.** Large ape occurring widely in **Kalimantan** and less commonly in **Sumatra**. It first drew attention as a possible "missing link" in the Darwinian evolution of humankind. **Hunting** on behalf of wildlife collectors became a serious threat to its existence. These depredations were minor, however, compared to the extensive logging and destruction of the forests during the late **New Order** period and the resulting extensive forest fires of 1997 and thereafter (*see* **FORESTRY**). There is a preserve that is attempting to save them from extinction in Sabah, Malaysia. *See also* CONSERVATION, NATURE. [1158]

ORGANISASI MASSA. *See* MASS ORGANIZATIONS.

ORGANISASI PAPUA MERDEKA (OPM, Free Papua Movement)**.** Founded in 1965 in the Central Highlands of West Irian (**Papua**) to oppose Indonesian rule, the OPM drew its support initially from members of the Dutch-sponsored former Papuan Volunteer Corps and from the coastal Arfak people. Under the influence of Indonesian policies in the interior such as **transmigration**, however, it gained wide though uneven support throughout the province by the early 1990s. Its support was especially strong in the Baliem Valley, along the border with **Papua New Guinea**, and in the Carstensz Mountains. Its armed forces, the Pasukan Pembebasan Nasional, were regularly augmented by the desertion of Papuan troops from the Indonesian **army**, but they remained poorly armed and trained. In 1971 Seth Rumkorem declared a Republic of West Papua, and the movement claimed to control about one quarter of Papua. The OPM was racked by factionalism, partly tribal, partly ideological, and many of its leaders went into **exile**.

After the fall of **Suharto**, the OPM cooperated with other groups in Papua and gained some success in persuading the administrations of presidents **B. J. Habibie** and **Abdurrachman Wahid** to grant greater autonomy to the province. Several exiled leaders returned to participate in discussions and in the national congress held in May–June 2000, but many mistrusted the new leadership under Theys Eluay and others, who were seen as too close to the Indonesian political and military leadership. On 29 November 2000 the **police** arrested Theys Eluay and other leaders, refusing to release them at the request of President Wahid. Theys Eluay's murder a year later, allegedly at the hands of Indonesia's Special Forces (**Kopassus**), contributed to further alienation of both the OPM and of the Papuan people in general. Other **militias** arose during this period, and the OPM seems to have been affiliated with the National Liberation Army (Tentera Pembebasan Nasional, TPN), which trained opposition forces to the Indonesian government. *See also* MELANESIAN BROTHERHOOD. [0754, 0755, 0809, 0815, 0816]

OTTOMAN EMPIRE. *See* TURKEY, HISTORICAL LINKS WITH.

OUDHEIDKUNDIGE DIENST. *See* ARCHEOLOGY.

OUTER ISLANDS. Term equivalent to the Dutch *buitengewesten*, outer regions, and sometimes considered slightly pejorative, for the Indonesian islands other than **Java**, **Madura**, and occasionally **Bali**. In general, these "outer" regions are less densely populated, lack extensive wet-**rice** fields, and are in some cases rich in natural resources. Shifts in the focus of economic activity can be seen in the fact that the Outer Islands accounted for only 10 percent of Indonesian exports in 1890, but 70 percent in 1940. The term also contains a sense of political distance from the center. The term is a convenient one but carries little analytical weight. *See also* NUSANTARA. [0323]

– P –

PACHT (revenue farm, pl. *pachten*)**.** One of the most common sources of state revenue before the 20th century. The state typically sold or granted rights over a particular sector of the **economy** to a private entrepreneur, who was then at liberty to extract what he could from it and to enforce his rights with his own private **police** force. *Pachten* were commonly granted for the running of toll houses, **pawnshops**, and **gambling** dens; the sale of **opium** and **salt**; the collection of **land**, market, and poll tax;

the management of forests; and the harvesting of produce such as birds' nests, **pearls**, trepang, and sponges. In the late 19th and early 20th centuries, the colonial government replaced many of these farms with state monopolies. *See also* TAXATION.

PADANG. Capital of the province of West **Sumatra**, Padang was a fishing and **salt**-making village, until under Acehnese control in the 17th century it became a major entrepôt for the **pepper trade**. It was seized by the **Dutch East India Company (VOC)** in 1664, and then by the British in 1793, who restored it in 1819 to the **Dutch**. It became a major center for the export of **coffee** in the late 19th century. The Dutch built a railway line to connect it with the interior and with a new port (Emmahaven, now Teluk Bayur), which was established approximately 10 km south of the town. From there **coal** was shipped from the Ombilin coalfields, as well as cement from Indarung (PT Semen Padang), and it is the main port for West Sumatra's other major exports of **rubber**, copra, **cloves**, coffee, cinnamon, and **rattan**. *See also* MINANGKABAU. [1380]

PADERI WAR. *See* MINANGKABAU.

PAGUYUBAN PASUNDAN. Sundanese cultural association founded in 1914 initially to promote Sundanese cultural identity, though it later founded schools and took part in local councils. Under Oto Iskandardinata (1897–1946?), it became the largest **mass organization** in West **Java**, but it never promoted Sundanese separatism. Like the **Pakempalan Kawula Ngayogyakarta (PKN)**, it was part of a movement for the support of regional culture within the broader nationalist *pergerakan*. The prewar popularity of the Paguyuban Pasundan, however, was a factor encouraging the **Dutch** to create the federal state of **Pasundan** in 1948. *See also* NATIONALISM; SUNDA.

PAJAJARAN. The last **Hindu** kingdom in West **Java**, founded in 1344 at Pakuan (near modern **Bogor**). Although primarily an agrarian kingdom, it traded **pepper** and other produce through Sunda Kalapa, near modern **Jakarta**, until that was lost to **Banten** in 1527. Banten captured the capital and slaughtered the royal family in the 1570s.

PAJANG. Central Javanese successor state to **Majapahit**, based probably near modern **Surakarta**. It was defeated by **Mataram** in 1587–1588.

PAK **("father").** Term of affectionate but deferential address. *See BAPAK*.

PAKEMPALAN KAWULA NGAYOGYAKARTA (PKN, Yogyakarta People's Party)**.** Founded in June 1930 by Pangeran Sosrodiningrat, whom many of his followers saw as a new *ratu adil*, or just prince (*see* **JOYOBOYO**). With 250,000 members, it was the largest political organization in 1930s Indonesia, but it worked mainly on local issues, especially forming **cooperatives** and preserving the powers of **Yogyakarta**'s traditional rulers. *See also* NATIONALISM.

PAKPAHAN, MUCHTAR (1953–). Muchtar Pakpahan established the Serikat Buruh Sejahtera Indonesia (SMSI, Indonesian Prosperous Workers' Union), the first independent **labor** organization under **Suharto**, in 1992 (*see* **LABOR UNIONS**). He was arrested in 1996 and the SMSI banned in 1997. After Suharto's fall he was one of the first political prisoners to whom President **B. J. Habibie** granted amnesty, and he was invited to register his SMSI again and to join the Indonesian contingent at the annual meeting of the International Labor Organization (ILO) in Geneva. He used the SMSI as a springboard to launch a National Labor Party (Partai Buruh Nasional, PBN) to contest the 1999 elections, but it only gained about 111,000 votes and no seats. [0424, 0760, 1010]

PAKUALAMAN. Minor court established in **Yogyakarta** in 1812 under the sponsorship of **Thomas Stamford Raffles**, with separate apanage rights from the **Yogyakarta** sultanate.

PALAPA. Indonesia's domestic satellite communications system, named for a vow by **Gajah Mada**, prime minister of **Majapahit**, to abstain from *palapa* (perhaps a fruit, a spice, or possibly sex) until the kingdom was united. Initially planned in Repelita II, it was finally commissioned in August 1976. *See also* MEDIA; TELEGRAPH.

PALEMBANG. City and state on the Musi River in south **Sumatra**. Probably the capital of the kingdom of **Srivijaya**, Palembang lost its importance after the Chola raids of 1025 and fell into the hands of the **Chinese** pirate Liang Danming (*see* **PIRACY**; **ZHENG HE**). A new sultanate of Palembang became a major exporter of **pepper** in the 16th century, but it declined and fell subject to **Riau** in 1659. Palembang reemerged in the 18th century after the discovery of **tin** on **Bangka** and **Belitung** in 1709, and from 1722 monopoly contracts for tin **mining** provided the sultanate's most important source of income. In 1812–1816, however, **Thomas Stamford Raffles** forced Sultan Ahmad Najamuddin to cede the tin-rich islands. In a series of military and political maneuvers, the **Dutch** gradually tightened their control, annexing the sultanate in 1823. Sultan Taha launched an unsuccessful revolt in 1858, and the Dutch did not subdue the upland Rejang and Pasamah areas until the 1860s. They remained unable to control the smallholder producers of **coffee** and **rubber**, who succeeded in building up an international network of **trade** in both these products. The Palembang region also had extensive reserves of **coal** and particularly **oil**, becoming the largest source of oil exports for the Netherlands East Indies in the late colonial period. During the early **Revolution**, trade in rubber to **Singapore** was a major source of Republican finance. Much of the area was occupied in the first **"Police Action"** in 1947, and on 18 December 1948 the Dutch established a Negara Sumatra Selatan (NSS) under Abdul Malik based in Palembang (*see* **FEDERALISM**). The NSS was abolished on 9 March 1950. South Sumatra was the economic base of two of the early **New Order**'s most important "financial generals," Ibnu Sutowo and Ratu Alamsyah Perwiranegara. [0569, 0837, 0839]

PAMONG PRAJA ("guardians of the realm"). Formerly *pangreh praja* ("rulers of the realm"), the civil service on **Java** conceived as an institution dating from precolonial times. *See BUPATI; INLANDSCH BESTUUR*.

PALM OIL. *See* OIL PALM.

PAMUNGKAS, SRI BINTANG. Educated at the **Bandung** Institute of Technology (ITB) and then at Iowa State University, Sri Bintang Pamungkas became a lecturer in the Department of Economics at the University of Indonesia and in the late 1980s gained a reputation as a courageous critic of government policies and **corruption**. He refused to join **Golkar** and was elected to parliament in 1992 as a member of the **Partai Persatuan Pembangunan (PPP)**. His speeches in Bandung and **Germany** demanding higher teacher salaries, questioning aspects of the **Pancasila**, and outlining future challenges to the Indonesian **economy** sparked a **police** investigation into his activities in April 1995. In 1996 Pamungkas founded and led the **Partai Uni Demokrasi Indonesia (PUDI)**. He was blamed for anti-**Suharto** demonstrations in Germany during the president's state visit there and was arrested and sentenced in May 1996 to 34 months in prison. After his appeal, he was rearrested in March 1997 on a charge of subversion. He was released when **B. J. Habibie** became president in 1998. [0760]

PANCASILA. The five principles of state ideology, as follows: *Ketuhanan yang maha esa*, belief in the one supreme God; *Kemanusiaan yang adil dan beradab*, just and civilized humanitarianism; *Persatuan Indonesia*, Indonesian unity; *Kerakyatan yang dipimpin oleh hikmat kebijaksanaan dalam permusyawaratan/perwakilan*, popular sovereignty governed by wise policies arrived at through deliberation and consensus; and *Keadilan sosial bagi seluruh rakyat Indonesia*, social justice for the entire Indonesian people.

The Pancasila was formulated by **Sukarno** on 1 June 1945 in a speech to the committee drafting Indonesia's 1945 **Constitution** and was incorporated into the preamble of that constitution and its 1949 and 1950 successors. The general character of the *silas* allows widely varying interpretations of the Pancasila's content. Early Western observers saw it as a promising synthesis of Western democracy, **Islam**, **Marxism**, and indigenous village democratic ideas, while it was initially embraced most enthusiastically in Indonesia by those wishing to avert the creation of an **Islamic state**; during the 1950s, and especially in the sessions of the **Constituent Assembly**, secularists and members of other religions put forward the notion of a state based on the Pancasila as a preferable alternative to a state based on a single **religion**. Under **Guided Democracy**, on the other hand, conservative groups stressed the religious content of the Pancasila, in the form of the first principle, in order to distinguish it from ideas of the **Partai Komunis Indonesia (PKI)** and from leftist concepts of Sukarno, such as **Nasakom**. After 1965, with the PKI vanquished, the Pancasila became once more a tool used by the government to resist pressures for an Islamic state.

From the start, the **New Order** government frequently referred to its political system as "Pancasila Democracy," but it was not until 1978 that it attempted to appropriate the Pancasila by formulating the Pedoman Penghayatan dan Pengalaman Pancasila (P4, Guide to Realizing and Experiencing the Pancasila), promoting the values of "hierarchy, harmony, and order." These became a compulsory part of **education** curricula at all levels and part of the indoctrination process for civil servants and all sectors of society. In 1985 all noncommercial, nongovernment organizations were required by **law** to adopt the Pancasila as their sole guiding principle (*azas tunggal*) as a presumed guarantee of future political orthodoxy and harmony (*see* **PETITION OF FIFTY**; **WHITE PAPER**).

The Pancasila was used to underpin a corporatist, authoritarian state system; in particular, while interpreting *silas* 2–5 as precluding politics based on **class** or other adversarial social divisions, the **Suharto** regime ignored their prescriptions of popular sovereignty and social justice. *See also* GARUDA; *KEPERCAYAAN*. [0480, 0661, 0844, 0859, 0911, 0920, 0924, 1040]

PANGESTU (Paguyuban Ngèsti Tunggal, Association for Striving toward Harmony with God). Javanese mystical organization, founded in 1949 by R. Sunarto Mertowardoyo (1899–1965). With over 20,000 members, it is one of the largest of the ***kebatinan*** groups. [0714]

PANGLIMA**.** Military commander, originally referring to senior *uleëbalang* (regional chiefs) in **Aceh** but adopted by the Republican **army** in 1945 as its senior appointment. Initially used for any division or military region (Kodam) commander, it is now restricted to the **Tentara Nasional Indonesia (TNI)** commander.

PANGREH PRAJA**.** *See PAMONG PRAJA*.

PANITIA PERSIAPAN KEMERDEKAAN INDONESIA (PPKI, Committee for the Preparation of Indonesian Independence). Formed on 7 August 1945 to replace the **Badan Penyelidik Usaha Persiapan Kemerdekaan Indonesia (BPUPKI)**, it acted as a kind of protoparliament for the impending state. It consisted entirely of Indonesians with **Sukarno** and **Mohammad Hatta** as chairman and vice chairman respectively. After the **declaration of independence**, it met to enact the new Republic's **constitution**, adopting the draft previously prepared by the BPUPKI, and elected Sukarno and Hatta as **president** and **vice president**; and on 29 August, it transformed itself into the **Komité Nasional Indonesia Pusat (KNIP)**. [0647, 0661, 0674]

PANJI **STORIES.** Cycle of stories derived from East **Java** and based on the adventures of Prince Panji in search of his bride, a princess of Daha (**Kediri**), who disappeared mysteriously on their wedding night. [0159]

PANTUN**.** Malay verse form in four lines rhyming a-b-a-b. Typically the first couplet contains a cryptic allusion to the second, which may take the form of a proverb or message.

PAPER. Produced on **Java** from at least 1200, using the inner bark of the paper mulberry *Broussonetia papyrifera* (Moraceae). It was probably a development from earlier felted **cloth** under the influence of **Chinese** paper technology and was used mainly for painting and wrapping, ***lontar*** leaves being the preferred writing surface. *Lontar*, however, was not suited to the writing of Arabic curves and dots, and the use of paper grew from the 14th century with the spread of **Islam**. In the 17th century, paper was an important item of **trade** for the European companies, and the **Dutch East Indies Company (VOC)** established a paper mill in **Batavia**. *See also* WRITING SYSTEMS.

PAPUA. The territory of West New Guinea under the **Dutch**, and thereafter called Irian Barat (West Irian), a term that was abandoned in 1972 as implying possibly territorial claims on the eastern part of the island and replaced with the official name Irian Jaya. Indigenous separatists on the island preferred the term Papua, or West Papua, derived from the Portuguese *papuas*, said to be from a local word meaning "curly hair," and in 2001 the Indonesian government under President **Abdurrachman Wahid** named the province Papua. The indigenous **population** in 2000 numbered 2.2 million, speaking 200 distinct **languages**.

The island was settled by Melanesians around perhaps 20,000 B.C. Archeological evidence of increased erosion and charcoal deposits suggests that extensive **agriculture** began in 7000 B.C. Domestic **pigs**, which are not native to the island, were present from 6000 B.C., and by 4000 B.C. a strong **economy** based on tropical tubers such as taro was in place, enabling the Melanesians to resist the later Austronesians, though some Papuan tribes came to speak Austronesian languages (*see* **MIGRATIONS**). Bronze tools were in use by 1000 B.C., and irrigation ditches in the highlands date from at least the first century A.D.

The island had little contact with western Indonesia until the 20th century, though there is evidence of **trade** with **Majapahit**. In the early 17th century the **Portuguese** Luis Vaez de Torres discovered accidentally that the island was separate from **Australia**. Offshore islands and some coastal regions were claimed by the sultan of **Tidore**, and the Dutch claim rested on their conquest of Tidore. During the 19th century, repeated European expeditions mapped the coastline and investigated the natural history of the island, but a Dutch settlement at Lobo in 1828 was abandoned in 1836 because of cost overruns and debilitating disease, and permanent occupation was not restored until 1896 when the Netherlands feared expansionism by Australia on the island. The border between Dutch, Australian, and German holdings was fixed at 141°E in 1875. Much of the coastal region was "explored" in the 1920s, and a penal settlement for Indonesian nationalists and those involved in the uprising of the **Partai Komunis Indonesia (PKI)** was established at **Boven Digul** in the southeast in 1926. The densely populated Baliem Valley of the interior was "discovered" only in 1938. Merauke, in the far southeastern corner, remained under Dutch rule throughout World War II, and the rest of the island was reconquered by Allied troops (those of the **United States** and Australia) in 1944, before the **Japanese** surrender.

When the **Netherlands** transferred sovereignty to the Indonesian Republic in 1949, it retained provisional control over Papua, arguing that the indigenous inhabitants were ethnically and culturally dissimilar to other Indonesians and would become victims of "Javanese imperialism." Wishing to provide a place of settlement for displaced **Indo-Europeans**, some Dutch also saw retention of the region as a way of maintaining their status as a world power and were impressed by the **mining** potential of the province. Since, however, it had never been constitutionally distinguished from the rest of Indonesia in the colonial era, Indonesians regarded this separation as an attack on national sovereignty and an attempt to preserve colonialism in the region. The status of the territory was left unresolved by the **Round Table Conference** in 1949, and when the Dutch refused to negotiate the issue it quickly became a running sore in relations between Indonesia and the Netherlands. Dutch actions to bring the Papuans to a separate independence included the establishment of a semirepresentative Nieuw-Guinea Raad (New Guinea Council) and the official raising of the "Morning Star" flag next to that of the Dutch on 1 December 1961.

Under **Guided Democracy**, **Sukarno** stepped up pressure on the Dutch, announcing a military campaign (Trikora [Tri Komando Rakyat], People's Triple Command) for its recapture on 19 December 1961. Military infiltration began in early 1962. After protracted negotiations and heavy pressure from the United States, the Dutch administration handed over the territory to the **United Nations** on 15 August 1962; the United Nations in turn handed it to Indonesia on 1 May 1963, establishing a UN Temporary Executive Authority (UNTEA) to oversee the transfer and assist in preparation for an "Act of Free Choice" to be held in five years to determine the wishes of the people of the territory. No details of this Act were specified, and **Ali Murtopo**'s **Operasi Khusus** led the campaign for integration and carried out the Act of Free Choice in July–August 1969 by inviting the opinions of 1,025 selected tribal leaders, assembled especially for the occasion, who agreed without a vote to confirm integration with the Republic.

Under the **Suharto** regime, the **economy** of the province was transformed by the expansion of **forest** exploitation, by a massive **Freeport gold** and **copper** mine, by the arrival of Javanese settlers under the **transmigration** program, and by the immigration of **Bugis** smallholders. Christian and, to a lesser extent, Muslim missionary activities were extensive, and Indonesian officials encouraged tribespeople to abandon their traditional dress and customs.

Resentment over government cultural and economic policies and over the domination of government posts by non-Papuans had led in 1965 to the founding of the **Organisasi Papua Merdeka (OPM)**, which conducted sporadic guerrilla war against government forces. Indonesian military operations along the border with **Papua New Guinea (PNG)** were a source of friction between the two countries, especially as Papuan refugees from Irian crossed the border into PNG.

With the fall of Suharto, hopes for independence were reignited and the "morning star" flag was raised throughout the region in July 1998. The military quickly responded, killing or wounding hundreds of Papuans. President **B. J. Habibie**, however, was more conciliatory, meeting with a hundred Papuans on 26 February 1999 and listening to their grievances. On 1 December, thousands raised the Papuan flag and leading members of the community called on the provincial parliament to convey their demand for independence to the central government. Habibie's successor as president, **Abdurrachman Wahid**, held public talks with Papuan leaders, agreeing to their flying the "morning star" flag alongside, but below, that of Indonesia, and using the name Papua instead of Irian Jaya. At a National Congress held in Jayapura at the end of May 2000, representatives from throughout Papua outlined plans for achieving independence.

Since 1999, a number of **militia** groups have arisen in the region, the two main ones being the Papua Taskforce (Satuan Tugas Papua/Satgas Papua), led until his death by Theys Eluay, which supports independence; and the Red and White Taskforce (Satgas Merah Putih, SMP), which supports continuation of Indonesian rule. A third group, the National Liberation Army (Tentera Pembebasan Nasional, TPN), was believed to be affiliated with the armed opposition group, the OPM. Tensions rose between those advocating independence and their opponents after Wahid gave **Megawati Sukarnoputri**, then **vice president**, responsibility for government relations with eastern Indonesia. Following the example of her father, Sukarno, Megawati strongly opposed Papuan independence and allowed the military to conduct a much more aggressive campaign to maintain control of the territory. She recommended that Wahid rescind his promise to open the Papuans' National Congress and urged him to act forcefully against Papuan separatism. In October 2000, when the police cut down the "morning star" flag in Jayapura, riots broke out with dozens of non-Papuans being killed and many fleeing the area.

When Megawati succeeded Wahid as president in July 2001, she cooperated with the army leadership in inaugurating a stricter policy of military repression against the possibility of Papuan separatism. The largest operation took place from April to October 2001 after an armed group of Papuans attacked logging companies in the Wasior district, killing nine. In response units of the Police Mobile Brigade detained over a hundred people, imprisoning and torturing many of them and allegedly executing seven of the detainees. The moderate Papuan independence leader Theys Eluay was assassinated in November 2001, further strengthening Papuan distrust of the Jakarta government and military. Three special forces (**Komando Pasukan Khusus [Kopassus]**) officers were initially charged with his murder, and in early May 2002 a national investigation commission also named three other soldiers as suspects. A total of seven Kopassus members faced trial in **Surabaya** for his murder in April 2003. On 31 August 2002 an ambush near the Freeport mine left two Americans and an Indonesian dead, an incident that was later discovered to have been the work of the Indonesian **army**. On 4 April 2003 OPM forces attacked a weapons warehouse in Wamena and killed two soldiers, Army chief of staff Ryamizard Ryacuda blaming this upsurge in violence on the earlier withdrawal of the Kopassus troops. Despite widespread opposition in Papua, in August 2003 the government divided the province into three: Papua, Irian Jaya Barat, and Irian Jaya Tengah (*see* **MAP 12**). *See also* ASMAT; DANI. [0744, 0754, 0755, 0809, 0813, 0815, 0816, 0821, 0946, 1105, 1124, 1252]

PAPUA NEW GUINEA (PNG)**, RELATIONS WITH.** Since PNG became independent in 1975, relations have been dominated by Indonesian fears that PNG may be a base for **Operasi Papua Merdeka (OPM)** separatists, and by PNG fears that Indonesia may at some time attempt to take it over. PNG formally denies sanctuary to the OPM, though controlling the 750-km, poorly marked border is difficult and there is much popular sympathy for the OPM in PNG. Indonesian policies aimed at diluting the Melanesian character of **Papua** and heavy-handed operations against the OPM sent a flood of refugees across the border from Indonesia to PNG in the early 1980s, with a peak in 1984, and PNG confidence in Indonesian intentions diminished when Indonesian **armed forces**

crossed the border without permission on a number of occasions. It was also discovered in 1983 that the Indonesian-built Trans-Irian Highway was being built on PNG territory for part of its length. In October 1986 the two countries signed a Treaty of Mutual Respect, Friendship, and Cooperation that provided, among other things, that neither side would allow its territory to be used for purposes hostile to the other.

PARARATON **(**"Book of Kings"**).** Javanese text dated 1613, telling stories of **Ken Angrok** and Raden Wijaya (*see* **MAJAPAHIT**). The manuscript was discovered on **Bali** in the late 19th century. [0170]

PARLIAMENTS. *See* CHUO SANGI-IN; DEWAN PERWAKILAN RAKYAT; KOMITÉ NASIONAL INDONESIA PUSAT; MAJELIS PERMUSYAWARATAN RAKYAT; VOLKSRAAD.

PARTAI AMANAT NASIONAL (PAN, National Mandate Party)**.** A political party established 23 August 1998 on the basis of the Majelis Amanat Rakyat (MARA), an organization founded in the last days of the **Suharto** regime by 50 opposition figures, notable among them **Amien Rais**, Gunawan Mohammad, Adnan Buyung Nasution, and Emil Salim. It was headed by Amien Rais and came in fifth in the 1999 **elections**, with 7,528,956 votes (7 percent), gaining 34 seats in the parliament. [0763, 1010]

PARTAI BULAN BINTANG (PBB, Crescent Moon and Star Party)**.** An Islamic party established in July 1998 as the heir of the former **Masjumi**, it described its basis as "Islamic modernism" and advocated an **Islamic state** for Indonesia. In the 1999 general **elections**, it received 2,049,708 votes and gained 13 parliamentary seats. It qualified to contest the 2004 elections under leadership of Yusril Ihza Mahendra.

PARTAI BURUH INDONESIA (PBI, Indonesian Labor Party)**.** A Marxist party established in **Kediri** in November 1945 by S. K. Trimurti, Setiajit, and Sakirman. It was a member of the **Sayap Kiri** and merged with the **Partai Komunis Indonesia (PKI)** in September 1948. The party reappeared after the **Madiun** Affair but rejoined the PKI in February 1951. A short-lived splinter Partai Buruh was formed in December 1949 by members opposed to the Madiun uprising. [0674, 1128]

PARTAI DEMOKRASI INDONESIA (PDI, Indonesian Democratic Party)**.** Formed in January 1973 by a government-enforced merger of the

Partai Nasional Indonesia (PNI), **Partai Katolik**, **Partai Kristen Indonesia (Parkindo)**, **Murba**, and **Ikatan Pendukung Kemerdekaan Indonesia (IPKI)**. As its largest component, the PNI formed the new party's core, but with the new government policy of ***monoloyalitas*** the party lost much of the bureaucratic vote to the **Golkar** and was reduced to a narrow "natural" constituency, especially among the Christian community. Government intervention in support of the conservative faction of Mohammad Isnaeni and Sunawar Sukowati against that of the more progressive Usep Ranuwijaya and Sanusi Harjadinata weakened the party's internal organization.

The party's poor performance in the 1977 and 1982 **elections** raised the prospect that it might disappear entirely, leaving the Muslim **Partai Persatuan Pembangunan (PPP)** as the only opposition party. After the late 1970s, therefore, the government gave the PDI discreet assistance in the form of direct financial grants and aid in the preparation of election materials and the conduct of campaigns. Sections of the party always sought to present it as the heir to the ideas of **Sukarno** and his portrait was prominent at PDI rallies, but the government restricted the extent to which the former **president**'s name could be used. In large part as a result of the candidacy of **Megawati Sukarnoputri**, daughter of the former president, the party registered a substantial recovery in 1987, overtaking the PPP as second party in the **Jakarta** region.

In the 1992 election campaign, Soerjadi, general chairman of PDI, attacked some of the business ventures of the **Suharto family** and also proposed limitations on presidential terms. This challenge lost him the president's support, and the government refused to recognize his reelection in July 1993. The PDI then elected Megawati to replace him. But in 1996 the government reversed itself and supported Soerjadi, pushing through his election at a special congress of the PDI in Medan in June of that year. When Megawati's supporters continued to occupy the PDI headquarters in Jakarta, government-backed mobs forcibly ejected them, sparking widespread riots. Megawati commanded wide popular support, and when in September 1996 the government rejected a slate of candidates submitted by her group, further antigovernment demonstrations erupted. These continued for months, and on 15 April 1997 thousands of Megawati's supporters protested in front of the parliament building in Jakarta demanding that her slate and not that of Soerjadi be accepted in the forthcoming elections as representing the PDI. Shortly before the elections, Megawati announced that she would not be casting a vote and, though she did not ask her supporters to follow her lead in boycotting the elections, she requested that they not vote for the PDI. Soerjadi and his supporters in the PDI ran a lackluster campaign, facing demonstrations from Megawati's supporters at all their rallies. In the May elections, the party received only 3.5 million votes and was allotted only 11 seats in the parliament. At the PDI party congress in 1997, Budi Hardjono replaced Soerjadi as party chairman.

Megawati's split from the party and formation of her **Partai Demokrasi Indonesia—Perjuangan (PDI-P)** gutted the PDI's support. In the post-Suharto general election of 1999, the PDI only succeeded in gaining 655,049 votes and 2 seats in parliament. [0736, 0760, 1010]

PARTAI DEMOKRASI INDONESIA—PERJUANGAN (PDI-P, Indonesian Democratic Party of Struggle). The PDI-P developed out of **Megawati Sukarnoputri**'s faction of the **Partai Demokrasi Indonesia (PDI)**. After the PDI congress in August 1998 in Palu, **Sulawesi**, when the new chairman, Budi Hardjono, refused to disband the party, Megawati's faction held a congress in **Bali** from 8–10 October. In her speech there, she referred to the congress as a gathering of the Partai Demokrasi Indonesia Perjuangan (PDI-P). Most of the PDI's base and many of its former leaders moved to Megawati's party, which in the 1999 **elections** gained 35 percent of the vote (35,689,073) and the largest number of parliamentary seats (153) [0760, 1010]

PARTAI INDONESIA (Partindo). 1. Party founded in 1931 by Mr. R. M. Sartono to replace the recently dissolved **Partai Nasional Indonesia (PNI)**. After failing to bridge the differences between Partindo and the **Pendidikan Nasional Indonesia** of **Mohammad Hatta** and **Sutan Sjahrir**, **Sukarno** joined Partindo in 1932. The party pressed for independence by means of mass action, and its membership soon swelled to a claimed 20,000. Its mass rallies soon attracted **Dutch** repression; its leaders were arrested and exiled, its 1934 party congress was forbidden, and the party decided to dissolve in November 1936. [0613, 0661]

2. A small left-wing party that seceded from the **Partai Nasional Indonesia (PNI)** in July 1958, partly to back the policies of Sukarno. Its existence was used to justify the appointment of more left-wingers to official posts alongside the **Partai Komunis Indonesia (PKI)**, to which it became increasingly close. It was banned in 1966. [0475]

PARTAI INDONESIA RAYA (Parindra, Greater Indonesia Party). Formed as a merger of **Budi Utomo** and the **Persatuan Bangsa Indonesia** in December 1935 it was led by **Sutomo**, M. H. Thamrin, Susanto Tirtoprojo, and Sukarjo Wiryopranoto. More conservative than **Gerakan Rakyat Indonesia (Gerindo)**, it was willing to cooperate with the **Dutch** and was instrumental in forming the moderate nationalist coalition **Gabungan Politik Indonesia (Gapi)**. It claimed 10,000 members in 1940. In 1938 it founded a commercial company, the Pertanian Bumi Putera, to initiate party-controlled agricultural and industrial enterprises. Parindra was hopeful that Japanese pressure on the Indies would lead to reforms, and the Dutch detained Thamrin in February 1941 on suspicion of "treasonous" dealing with **Japan**. The party was banned, like all others, during the **Japanese occupation**, but it reemerged in November 1949 under R. P. Suroso, who sat in several cabinets until the party disappeared in the 1955 **elections**. [0586, 0888]

PARTAI KATOLIK (Catholic Party)**.** The earliest political association of Indonesian Catholics was the Pakempalan Politik Katolik Jawi (Political Association of Javanese Catholics), founded in February 1923 and headed from 1925 by Ignatius Joseph Kasimo (1900–1987?). The PPKJ was represented in the **Volksraad** from 1924 and in the nationalist federations **Permufakatan Perhimpunan Politik Kebangsaan Indonesia (PPPKI**) and **Gabungan Politik Indonesia (Gapi)**. It changed its name several times, becoming the Persatuan Politik Katolik Indonesia (PPKI, Political Union of Indonesian Catholics) in 1930, the Persatuan Katolik Republik Indonesia (PKRI) in December 1945, and the Partai Katolik in August 1950, still led by Kasimo. With a small but solid constituency in **Flores** and Central **Java**, it was present in all parliaments from 1945 until it was merged into the **Partai Demokrasi Indonesia (PDI)** in 1973. [0695, 1003]

PARTAI KEADILAN (PK, Justice Party)**.** A modernist Muslim party, established in July 1998 after **Suharto**'s fall and led by Nur Mahmudi Ismail. More progressive than the **Partai Bulan Bintang (PBB)**, the other major heir to **Masjumi**, it had ties with anti-Suharto **student** activist organizations and had support among university graduates hoping to see Indonesia become a modern Islamic society. It received 1,436,565 votes in the 1999 general **elections**, gaining seven parliamentary seats. Several of its leaders are graduates of Saudi Arabian universities, and the party espouses the introduction of Islamic law (*syariah*) in Indonesia. After failing to qualify for the 2004 elections, the Partai Keadilan joined with another Islamic party to form the new Partai Keadilan Sejahtera (PKS, Justice and Welfare Party), which was expected to support Amien Rais as presidential candidate. [1010, 0765]

PARTAI KEBANGKITAN BANGSA (PKB, Rise of the People Party). Founded in July 1998 with close ties to the **Nahdlatul Ulama (NU)** and the electoral vehicle of **Abdurrachman Wahid**, it was chaired by H. Matori Abdul Djalil. In the 1999 **elections** its platform was pluralistic and nationalistic, advocating **Pancasila** and asserting that it served all Indonesians irrespective of race, religion, or profession. At least four other parties competed with it for the NU's following (the Partai Solidaritas Uni Nasional Indonesia [SUNI, Indonesian National Solidarity Party], the Partai Nahdlatul Ulama [Partai NU], the Partai Kebangkitan Ummat [PKU, Awakening of the Muslim Nation Party], and the **Partai Persatuan Pembangunan [PPP]**), each of them representing different factions within the organization. The PKB came in fourth in the 1999 elections, with its 13,336,982 votes concentrated mostly in the NU strongholds of East and Central **Java**. This meant that it gained fewer seats in the parliament (51) than its proportion of the votes would seem to justify. It cooperated with other Islamic parties in parliament to ensure Wahid's victory over **Megawati Sukarnoputri** in the struggle for the presidency in September 1999. After his impeachment, Wahid remained as advisory chairman of the PKB (its chairman was now Alwi Shihab, former minister of foreign affairs), and he dismissed two PKB leaders from their positions in the party because of their support for his impeachment two years earlier. In April 2003 the **Jakarta** High Court upheld this action and prohibited the two from using the party's flag, symbols, and anthem for the new splinter party they formed after their ouster. The PKB is likely to name Wahid as its presidential candidate for the 2004 election, although the names of NU head Hasyim Muzadi and former general Susilo Bambang Yudhoyono have been mentioned as possible alternatives. [0765, 1010]

PARTAI KOMUNIS INDONESIA (PKI, Indonesian Communist Party). Founded on 23 May 1920 as successor to the **Indische Sociaal-Democratische Vereeniging (ISDV)** and initially named Perserikatan Komunis di Hindia (Communist Association of the Indies). The PKI was the first communist party in Asia outside the borders of former tsarist Russia and joined the Comintern in December 1920. Its leaders initially followed a "bloc within" strategy, joining the **Sarekat Islam (SI)** and attempting to shift it to the Left, but this led to bitter disputes within SI and in October 1921 PKI members were effectively expelled. The party then campaigned vigorously in its own right among Indonesia's small proletariat and via so-called Sarekat Merah (Red Unions) in the countryside. Encouraged by the party's popularity and alarmed by the effectiveness of the colonial security forces in dismantling the party apparatus (including the **exile** of **Tan Malaka** in 1922 and Semaun in 1923), the leaders **Musso** and Alimin (1889–1964) planned an uprising but were strongly opposed by Tan Malaka. Intended as an Indonesia-wide rebellion, the rising fizzled out in revolts in **Banten** in November 1926 and West **Sumatra** (*see* **MINANGKABAU**) in January 1927. The party was banned, and alleged leaders of the rebellions were exiled to **Boven Digul**. Thereafter **Dutch** repression kept the party small and underground, though it developed a remarkable resilience that enabled it to survive, recruit, and campaign despite Dutch, and later **Japanese**, repression.

The party reemerged in November 1945, though it continued to work also through such parties as the **Partai Buruh Indonesia (PBI)** and the **Partai Sosialis (PS)**, with which in 1948 it made up the **Sayap Kiri**. The party argued initially that the national **Revolution** should be safeguarded by making concessions to Western economic interests, but in early 1948 after the fall of the government of **Amir Sjarifuddin** the party took a radical turn, arguing in *A New Road for the Indonesian Republic* for socioeconomic reform as a condition for achieving independence. After the return of Musso from protracted exile in the **Soviet Union** in August 1948, the Sayap Kiri parties federated first into the **Front Demokrasi Rakyat (FDR)** and then into an expanded PKI. After the party's suppression for its part in the abortive **Madiun** Affair, it resumed the strategy of divided parties under leadership of Tan Ling Djie (1904 to 1965–1966), but in 1951 strategy changed dramatically under a new party leadership of Dipa Nusantara Aidit (1923–1965), M. H. Lukman (1920–1965), Nyoto (1925–1965), and Sudisman (1920–1968).

The new leaders emphasized the party's commitment to the legal political process and marked out a strong nationalist position, rejecting the continuing ties with the **Netherlands** and the privileges given to Western business. The lack of a large proletariat and of a clear poor peasant **class** was a strategic difficulty, but the party emphasized attitude rather than class origin and it pursued a mass **education** program through party schools, training courses, and a university, the Aliarkham Academy, using recruits to build up an organization second only to the **army** in purpose and discipline, though its strength was heavily concentrated among ***abangan*** Javanese. This effort was rewarded when the party came fourth, with 16.4 percent of the vote, in the 1955 **elections**. The growth of PKI support and influence was among the reasons for the **PRRI/Permesta rebellion**, and army commanders in many regions, remembering the party's role in the Madiun Affair, put restrictions on its activities. Certain of increasing its vote at future elections, the party was at first unhappy with **Sukarno**'s proposals for a **Guided Democracy**. Facing full-scale suppression by the army, however, if it did not accede, the PKI became an enthusiastic supporter of the **president**, offering him the popular backing that he needed to balance the growing power of the army. In return the party received considerable freedom to operate on **Java**, building its membership to perhaps 3 million by 1965; affiliated organizations such as the **Barisan Tani Indonesia (BTI)** accounted for many millions more. Through its cultural affiliate, **Lembaga Kebudayaan Rakyat (Lekra)**, it attempted to establish **Marxist** discourse as orthodoxy in cultural affairs. And under the principles of **Nasakom**, it was given an increasing say in legislative and other official bodies. It was never, however, given important executive functions, and Donald Hindley has argued that the party, for all its apparent strength, was in fact "domesticated"—implicated in a regime that failed to implement social reforms and that was losing control of the **economy**, but denied access to the levers of power.

When the party attempted, moreover, a program of direct action (*aksi sepihak*) in rural Java to implement **land reform** laws in late 1963, it was swiftly curbed. The party remained generally aloof from the Sino-Soviet split, but in the mid-1960s swung somewhat to **China**, following Indonesian **foreign policy**. Opinions are still deeply divided on whether and to what extent the party was involved in the **Gestapu** coup of 1965, but the outcome of the affair was fatal to it. Within weeks, the army had begun to detain PKI cadres and to oversee the killing of party members and supporters (*see* **MASSACRES OF 1965–1966**). The party was formally banned on 12 March 1966. Surviving members attempted to begin guerrilla resistance in Blitar (East Java) and in West **Kalimantan** (*see* **PONTIANAK**), and a PKI analysis of its mistakes, called *Otokritik*, was prepared, but these movements were crushed by 1968, leaving the party represented primarily by scattered exile communities, the most prominent being the so-called PKI Delegation in China led by Jusuf Ajitorop.

In the closing years of the **Suharto** regime, the Indonesian government showed continuing concern over the alleged existence of PKI elements in Indonesian society, and a number of acts of sabotage were attributed unconvincingly to the party. After the fall of Suharto, President **Abdurrachman Wahid** sought to loosen restrictions on the party, but these attempts were combated by the army and Islamic political figures, and the party remained an outcast in Indonesian society. [0621, 0667, 0674, 0683, 0695, 0798, 0836, 0858, 0904, 0917, 0921, 0931, 0991, 0992, 0994, 0997]

PARTAI KRISTEN INDONESIA (Parkindo, Indonesian Christian Party). **Protestant** party based in **Minahasa**, **Ambon**, and the **Batak** regions of **Sumatra**, formed in November 1945. From the 1950s it was led by **Johannes Leimena**, who enjoyed a close relationship with **Sukarno** and became a long-term deputy prime minister under **Guided Democracy**. In 1973 the party was merged into the **Partai Demokrasi Indonesia (PDI)**. *See also* PROTESTANTISM. [0695, 1003]

PARTAI MURBA. *See* MURBA.

PARTAI MUSLIMIN INDONESIA (Parmusi, Indonesian Muslims' Party). The banning of **Masjumi** in 1960 left the modernist Muslim stream largely unrepresented in Indonesian party politics, though some former Masjumi members were active in the so-called **New Order** coalition that helped to bring down **Sukarno**. Parmusi was created on 20 February 1968 as a legal successor to Masjumi, but the military government, wary of Muslim power, excluded former Masjumi members from leadership positions. Jaelani (Johnny) Naro, an associate of **Ali Murtopo**, emerged as a major pro-government powerbroker and with party leaders Jarnawi Hadikusumah and Mintareja removed the **Jakarta Charter** from the party's platform. After a poor **election** performance in 1971, Parmusi was merged into the **Partai Persatuan Pembangunan (PPP)** in 1973. [1002]

PARTAI NASIONAL INDONESIA (PNI, Indonesian Nationalist Party). 1. Nationalist party founded by **Sukarno** and members of the **Algemene Studieclub** on 4 July 1927 with the name Perserikatan Nasional Indonesia (Indonesian Nationalist Union) and becoming Partai Nasional Indonesia in May 1928. It aimed from the start at full independence and sought to represent Indonesians of all religious, ethnic, and **class** groups, though its support was strongest among the middle class and the ***abangan*** peasantry. It refused to seek membership of the **Volksraad** and instead aimed to build a mass following, claiming 10,000 members by 1929. Though smaller than **Sarekat Islam (SI)** had been, it alarmed the colonial government, which arrested and jailed Sukarno and his colleagues in December 1929. The remnants of the party formally dissolved in April 1931. [0613, 0661, 0844]

2. The name PNI-Baru (New PNI) was given to the nationalist organization **Pendidikan Nasional Indonesia**.

3. On 21 August 1945, immediately after the declaration of **independence**, Sukarno and **Mohammad Hatta** announced the formation of a

single state party, generally called PNI-Staatspartij (State Party). It was based on the cadre of the **Jawa Hokokai** and was intended to mobilize popular support for the **Revolution**. Internal divisions and hostility to its **Japanese** origins, however, made it unworkable, and it was dissolved on 31 August 1945, though some branches survived to join the PNI (definition 4). [0661, 0643]

4. Formed in 1945 after the collapse of the PNI-Staatspartij, the PNI inherited the name of Sukarno's prewar party but not Sukarno's leadership. During the Revolution it became a broadly based party drawing support especially from the administrative elite and from the *abangan* peasantry on **Java** and containing a wide range of ideological viewpoints. Its leaders included conservative exponents of peace, order, and good administration; populist nationalists distrustful of the outside world and committed to improving welfare without promoting social conflict; and left-wing reformers willing to bring about radical social change. It summed up these views as **Marhaen**ism or "proletarian nationalism." The party took a radical, often anti-Western view on international affairs and opposed liberalism and individualism domestically. Under the prime ministership of **Ali Sastroamijoyo**, it became even more strongly entrenched in the state bureaucracy and by a narrow margin won the largest vote in the 1955 **elections**. Already, however, the party had begun to lose peasant support as activity by the **Partai Komunis Indonesia (PKI)** in rural areas developed, and some leaders approved of Sukarno's **Guided Democracy** as a means to stop communist growth. During the early 1960s, with Ali as chairman and Surakhman (?–1968) as secretary, the party increasingly shifted to the Left, and in 1964 it adopted the *Deklarasi Marhaenis*, which maintained that Marhaenism was **Marxism** adapted to Indonesian conditions.

After the **Gestapu** coup of 1965, the PNI was heavily purged of its left wing and in April 1970 the **Semarang** party boss, Hadisubeno Sosrowerdoyo (1912–1971), formerly associated with the business activities of president **Suharto**, was imposed as party chairman. More than other surviving parties, the PNI suffered from the establishment of **Golkar** as a state party, for it was precisely the PNI's bureaucratic base that Golkar seized. After a poor performance in the 1971 election, PNI was merged into the **Partai Demokrasi Indonesia (PDI)** in 1973. [0643, 0661, 0695, 1000]

PARTAI PERSATUAN PEMBANGUNAN (PPP, Unity Development Party)**.** Formed on 5 January 1973 as a forced merger of the four legal Muslim parties, **Partai Muslimin Indonesia (Parmusi)**, **Persatuan**

Tarbiyah Islamiyah (Perti), **Nahdlatul Ulama (NU)**, and **Partai Sarekat Islam Indonesia (PSII)**, together with the nonparty **Himpunan Mahasiswa Islam (HMI)**, though all the constituent elements continued to retain their separate identities. The party was not permitted to have an Islamic name but until 1986 was allowed to use the Ka'abah as its party symbol. It was also not permitted to advocate an **Islamic state**, but was generally pro-Muslim in international affairs, opposed to foreign cultural influences in Indonesia, and in favor of extending religious **education**. In 1973 it was instrumental in having a **Marriage** Bill significantly amended to bring it closer to Islamic law (*syariah*). In 1977 PPP members of the **Majelis Permusyawaraten Rakyat (MPR)** walked out over government plans to give official recognition to belief (*kepercayaan*) alongside **religion**. The party suffered a major blow in 1984, when the NU, which had been its most successful component in maintaining electoral support, left in order to concentrate its efforts on religious renewal. The PPP did, however, continue to receive electoral support from most of the NU members during the **Suharto** era.

After Suharto's fall, the PPP competed with at least four other parties for the vote of the traditionalist Muslim base of the NU, most notably with the **Partai Kebangkitan Bangsa (PKB)** associated with **Adurrachman Wahid**'s leadership. It did so by sharpening its Islamic identity, basing the party on **Islam**, and again adopting the Ka'abah as its symbol. It was better organized than the PKB and had a network of supporters in provincial and local assemblies, which gave it an advantage over its competitor. Although it won fewer votes than the PKB in the 1999 **elections** (11,329,905), its broader support in the **Outer Islands** as well as on **Java** enabled it to gain a larger number of parliamentary seats (58). When **Megawati Sukarnoputri** succeeded Abdurrachman Wahid as **president**, she chose Hamzah Haz, PPP's leader, as her **vice president**. Shortly afterward, a number of retired generals entered the party.

On 20 January 2002 some members of the party broke off to create a new party, PPP Reformasi, in part as a protest against Haz's postponement of the party's leadership election and in part, too, to register the opposition among younger members to its stance in favor of the introduction of Islamic law (*syariah*). The party was one of five Islamic parties to oppose the Megawati government's antiterrorism law in September 2002. *See also KEBATINAN*. [0736, 0765, 1010]

PARTAI RAKYAT DEMOKRATIK (PRD, Democratic People's Party). A pioneer of the new parties that only formed after **Suharto**'s fall, the

PRD had its origins in the **student** committees of **Yogyakarta** in 1994, which spread to **Bogor** and other universities. Budiman Sudjatmiko established it as a political party in July 1996 with the goal of expanding democratic structures in the fields of politics, **economy**, and culture. This was at a time when it was illegal to form **political parties**. When on 27 July the nearby headquarters of the **Partai Demokrasi Indonesia (PDI)** was attacked, the government accused the PRD of being a subversive organization and behind antigovernment unrest. Thirteen of its leaders were arrested, with its head Budiman Sudjatmiko sentenced to 13 years in jail, Garda Sembiring to 12 years, and Indah Sari to six years. Many of its leaders were kidnapped and some were killed, and the party was thus unable to consolidate. Its top leaders were not released from jail until March 1999. Several went on hunger strike to protest the treatment of their colleagues, and as a result, some of them, including Sudjatmiko, were hospitalized. They only received 78,730 votes in the 1999 **elections** and no parliamentary seats. [0760, 1010]

PARTAI REPUBLIK INDONESIA (Pari, Indonesian Republican Party)**.** A nationalist communist party established in Bangkok in 1927 by **Tan Malaka**, Soebakat, and Djamaloedin Tamin, three nationalist communists who had broken with the **Partai Komunis Indonesia (PKI)** over the launching of the 1926–1927 uprising. [0635, 0807, 0873]

PARTAI SAREKAT ISLAM INDONESIA (PSII, Party of the Indonesian Islamic Union)**.** Formed in 1923 by **H. U. S. Tjokroaminoto** and Haji Agus Salim (1884–1954) to formalize the political status of the **Sarekat Islam (SI)**. Shorn of SI's left-wing components, it soon shrank further with the secession of the **Nahdlatul Ulama (NU)**. The party on **Java** was conservative and pan-Islamic, though some of its branches, notably in West **Sumatra**, maintained a political and anticolonial stance until their leaders were arrested and exiled by the **Dutch** in 1933. After the death of Tjokroaminoto, the party came into the hands of Abikusno Cokrosuyoso and **S. M. Kartosuwiryo**. Salim and Mohamad Roem (1908–1983) were expelled, and the party took a hard-line, noncooperative attitude to the colonial government at a time when other parties had begun to soften under pressure of Dutch repression. Kartosuwiryo himself was expelled in 1940 and formed a "PSII Kedua" (Second PSII) in Malangbong, which later became part of the political base of the **Darul Islam (DI)**. PSII activity was banned by the Dutch in 1940 under State of War and Siege regulations, but it reemerged in 1947 under Aruji Kartawinata and the brothers

Anwar and Harsono Tjokroaminoto, refusing to join the **Masjumi** coalition. Never large, it campaigned incessantly for an **Islamic state**, but was a supporter of **Sukarno**'s **Guided Democracy**. In 1973 it was forced to join the **Partai Persatuan Pembangunan (PPP)**. [0695, 1329]

PARTAI SOSIALIS (PS, Socialist Party)**.** The PS was formed in December 1945 as a merger of the Partai Rakyat Sosialis (Paras, Socialist People's Party) of **Amir Sjarifuddin** and the Partai Sosialis Indonesia (Parsi, Indonesian Socialist Party) of **Sutan Sjahrir**. It formed the basis of the successive governments of Sjahrir and Amir, but from early 1947 became increasingly factionalized between the two leaders and effectively split when Amir deposed Sjahrir in June 1947, though a formal division did not take place until February 1948, when Sjahrir established the **Partai Sosialis Indonesia (PSI)**. *See also* SAYAP KIRI. [0661, 0674, 0865, 0916]

PARTAI SOSIALIS INDONESIA (PSI, Indonesian Socialist Party)**.** In November 1945 **Sutan Sjahrir** formed a political party of this name (but abbreviated Parsi) that soon merged with Amir Sjarifuddin's Partai Rakyat Sosialis (Paras, Socialist People's Party) to form the **Partai Sosialis (PS)**. A second party called PSI emerged from the Partai Sosialis in February 1948, again associated with Sjahrir. It had a generally Fabian socialist program, emphasizing economic planning, modernization, and social welfare, but it accepted the need for continued foreign capital **investment** in Indonesia and the political consequences of that. **Sumitro Djojohadikusumo** was a prominent member of the party in the 1950s and influenced its emphasis on regional development programs, small-scale industry, and **cooperatives**. Popular among intellectuals, in some sections of the officer corps and among some minorities, the PSI never developed a significant mass base and won only five seats in the 1955 **elections**. After Sumitro's participation in the **PRRI/Permesta rebellion**, the party was banned in 1960. Under the **New Order**, however, Sumitro and a number of other PSI figures regained important policy influence to the extent of being viewed at times as a malign secretive influence, being accused for instance of involvement in the **Malari** Affair. [0661, 0695, 0865, 0916]

PARTAI UNI DEMOKRASI INDONESIA (PUDI, Indonesian Democracy Union Party)**.** **Sri Bintang Pamungkas**, previously a member of the **Partai Persatuan Pembangunan (PPP)**, founded the PUDI in May

1996 because he believed that the existing **political parties** had no ideals. This was at a time when the establishment of independent political parties was forbidden. The following year, Sri Bintang summarized PUDI'S political position as a rejection of the 1997 general **elections** and of the nomination of **Suharto** for president and calling for setting up a new political structure in the post-Suharto era. The party suffered from the fact that it was a "one-man show" and received only 140,980 votes in the 1999 elections and no seats in parliament. [0760, 1010]

PARTICULIERE LANDERIJEN. Private estates, especially on the northern coastal plain of West **Java**, given or sold by the **Dutch East Indies Company (VOC)** from 1630 to its servants and supporters. Owners held not only freehold title to the **land** but also quasi-feudal rights over its inhabitants, including compulsory **labor** services (*herendiensten*), a portion of all crops, and a wide range of incidental **taxes**. In some texts these rights are described as "sovereign" and the landlords likened to the semiautonomous native rulers or ***zelfbesturen***. It was on these estates that commercial **sugar** cultivation was first introduced, but by the 19th century **rice** for **Batavia** was the main crop. By the 20th century some of the estates, such as the British-owned Pamanukan- & Tjiasemlanden (P & T Lands), had developed into efficient commercial operations with well-trained staffs; other estates remained depressed backwaters. Such estates remained outside the colonial government's provision of **education**, **health**, and other social services under the **Ethical Policy**, and became a byword for agricultural misery. Literacy rates were very low, morbidity was high, and **bandit** gangs were powerful. From 1912 the colonial government began the repurchase of estates, which were then incorporated into the administrative structure of the rest of Java. Repurchases stopped during the **Depression**, but in 1935 the government established a semiofficial company, the Javasche Particuliere Landerijen Maatschappij, to acquire and administer estates, using the proceeds both for further purchases and to bring social services and infrastructure to a level where the estates could be turned over to the government without placing extra strain on the treasury. Under the **Japanese** the remaining estates were nationalized, but the landlords were generally retained as administrators. Estate workers and bandits took control of the estates during the **Revolution**, but former owners were restored with freehold title, but without feudal rights, after the Dutch seized West Java in 1947. The last of the foreign-owned estates was nationalized in 1954. [0585]

PARTIES, POLITICAL. The formation of political parties in the Netherlands Indies was first permitted in 1918, though several parties had existed effectively earlier as nominally cultural, social, or commercial associations. In 1912, the **Indische Partij** had been banned, and throughout the 1920s and 1930s the colonial government frequently banned or restricted the activities of individual parties (*see* **NATIONALISM**). The **Japanese** dissolved all party organizations for the duration of their occupation, and the independent Republic of Indonesia briefly considered permitting only a single all-encompassing national party, the **Partai Nasional Indonesia** (**PNI**-Staatspartij). Parties, however, quickly emerged after the declaration of **independence**, and the multiparty system was officially authorized by Decree "X" of 16 October 1945. Twenty-seven parties won seats in the 1955 parliamentary **elections**.

From 1956 feeling arose increasingly that the parties were too strong in defending their sectional interests and too weak in considering the national interest. In 1956 **Sukarno** urged the parties to "bury themselves," and **Guided Democracy** was in part a system designed to diminish the access of parties to state power. Presidential Edict no. 7 of 1959 required all parties to adhere to the 1945 **Constitution**, **Pancasila**, and **MANIPOL-USDEK** and sought to eliminate smaller parties by requiring all parties to have 150,000 members spread over 65 electoral districts. In 1960 Sukarno issued a decree banning parties that had taken part in rebellions against the state; this was used to ban **Masjumi** and the **Partai Sosialis Indonesia (PSI)** but not the **Partai Komunis Indonesia (PKI)**. Further bans followed, leaving only 11 legal parties at the close of Guided Democracy. The PKI and **Partai Indonesia (Partindo)** were banned in 1966.

At the outset of the **New Order**, the **army** was determined that the open multiparty system of the 1950s should not be restored and a considerable debate opened over just what role parties should play. The parties themselves were given little opportunity to influence this debate: leading figures from before 1965 were often removed from party positions under government pressure and compliant supporters of the government were put in their places. Some army groups favored an entrenched two-party system; others suggested a "simplification" into five groups: Islamic, Christian, nationalist, socialist-Pancasila, and functional. The 1969 Law on Political Parties banned independent candidates and denied legal status to any party with fewer than 1.2 million members, 100 branches, and 2 percent of the vote in the coming election. Nine parties were elected to parliament in 1971, but the government forced their representatives in parliament to form two blocs (and allowed each bloc only one formal spokesperson). In 1973 these semiformal parliamentary groupings were formalized under government pressure by a fusion of the party organizations into the **Partai Persatuan Pembangunan (PPP)**, comprising the four Muslim parties, and the **Partai Demokrasi Indonesia (PDI)**, comprising the rest. The 1975 Law on Political Parties and **Golkar** banned parties from maintaining permanent branches below *kabupaten* level, as well as removing their right to challenge Pancasila. The government electoral organization, Golkar, was not regarded officially as a party and was exempt from these restrictions, although it increasingly assumed the character of a party. There were persistent suggestions during the latter years of **Suharto**'s rule that it should become the basis of a *partai tunggal*, or sole party.

The fall of Suharto in 1998 opened up the political process and political parties proliferated. Initially 234 parties were established. However, a Team of Eleven was assigned to verify which political parties were eligible to compete in the forthcoming elections, and eventually only 48 met the guidelines imposed. Under these, the party had to demonstrate among other things that it had branches in nine provinces with offices in at least half the districts in each of these provinces. In the 1999 elections, 21 of these parties received enough votes for them to be allotted at least one seat in parliament, but the top five (**Partai Demokrasi Indonesia—Perjuangan [PDI-P]**, Golkar, **Partai Kebangkitan Bangsa [PKB]**, PPP, and **Partai Amanat Nasional [PAN]**) received 86.7 percent of the vote. The other parties gaining more than one seat were the **Partai Bulan Bintang** (13 seats), **Partai Keadilan** (7 seats), Partai Keadilan dan Kesatuan (PKK, Justice and Unity Party, 4 seats), Partai Nahdlatul Ulama (PNU, Party of the Revival of Religious Scholars, 5 seats), Partai Demokrasi Kasih Bangsa (PDKB, People's Love for Democracy Party, 5 seats), and the PDI (2 seats). Twenty-seven of the 48 contending parties rejected the election results, so they were never approved by the General Elections Commission.

In 2001–2002 splits occurred in many of the major parties, which had been plagued by widespread dissatisfaction with their ineffectiveness and corruption. Only six of the 1999 parties (PDIP, Golkar, PPP, PKB, PAN, and PBB) qualified to run in the 2004 elections, along with 18 new parties (*see* APPENDIX F). Although the Partai Keadilan failed to qualify, it joined with another Islamic party to form the new Partai Keadilan Sejahtera (PKS, Justice and Welfare Party). In order to nominate a presidential candidate in 2004 a party has to win 16 seats (3 percent) or 4 percent of the votes in the April election. Two new parties, the Partai Karya Peduli Bangsa (PKPB), headed by former army chief of staff General R. Hartono, and the Partai Demokrat (PD, Democratic Party) were hoping to nominate General Susilo Bambang Yudhoyono, and Siti Hardijanti

Rumnana (Suharto's daughter, usually known as *Mbak Tutut*) respectively as their presidential candidates. *See also* ELECTIONS. [0695, 1001, 1012]

PASAI (Samudra)**.** This state in northern **Sumatra** was based near modern Lhokseumawe. After converting to **Islam** at the end of the 13th century, Pasai became the major port of the Strait of **Melaka**, maintaining diplomatic contacts with **China**, **India**, and **Siam**. It exported **pepper**, **oil** (from seeps close to the surface), and perhaps **silk**. It was visited by **Marco Polo** in 1292 and Ibn Battuta in 1355 and was raided by **Majapahit** in the 1360s. In the late 15th century it was increasingly eclipsed by Melaka and by **Aceh**, which conquered it in 1524.

PASISIR (Javanese, "coast")**.** The northern coast of **Java** (and by extension coastal regions of **Sumatra** and elsewhere), especially as distinguished from the kingdoms and courts of the interior. Opportunities for **trade** to and from Java gave rise from at least the 13th century to a succession of prosperous city states along this coast—**Banten**, **Demak**, **Cirebon**, and **Surabaya**—which were incorporated only with difficulty, if at all, into the agrarian kingdoms of the interior. With the conversion of these **cities** to **Islam** from the 15th century, political tension between the two regions grew. The inland kingdom of **Majapahit** was defeated by a coalition of coastal states led by Demak, and Majapahit's successor **Mataram** only briefly controlled the *Pasisir* rulers, who increasingly recruited assistance from the **Dutch East Indies Company (VOC)** to resist the court, giving the VOC a foothold in Javanese politics.

The term *pasisir* has also been applied particularly to the culture of this coastal region, suggesting an alternative Javanese cultural tradition to that of the courts of the interior. This culture is identified as internationally minded (many rulers of *pasisir* states were not Javanese), commercially oriented, and culturally eclectic. The **batik** of this region, for instance, shows considerable **Chinese** and European influence. [1371]

PASTEUR INSTITUTE. Established in 1895 for the treatment of rabies victims and attached to the already existing Parc Vaccinogène (*see* **SMALLPOX**). The institute began research on cholera in 1910, on **bubonic plague** in 1911, and later on typhus, staphylococcus, and other diseases. [1194]

PASUNDAN. Official prewar name for the colonial province of West **Java** and the name commonly used for the political party **Paguyuban Pasun-**

dan. On 24 April 1948 the **Dutch** sponsored a federal state called Pasundan in the territories they controlled in West Java, led by the former ***bupati*** of Bandung, R. A. A. M. Wiranatakusumah, in an attempt to exploit Sundanese fears of Javanese domination (*see* **FEDERALISM**). After the second Dutch **"Police Action,"** however, the West Java state largely disintegrated, under pressure not only of the forces of the Republic's returning **Siliwangi** division but also of the **Darul Islam (DI)**. In late 1949, leaders of the state toyed briefly with the idea of seeking full independence as an **Islamic state** on the model of Pakistan, perhaps with backing of the DI, and also negotiated with the Dutch adventurer **R. P. P. Westerling** for armed backing. After Westerling's abortive putsch in **Bandung** and **Jakarta** in January 1950, Pasundan was discredited, and it was dissolved on 9 February 1950. [0661, 0674, 1146]

PATRIMONIALISM. Term coined by Max Weber to describe states in which a single ruler disposes of state wealth and power by virtue of traditional authority, rather than charisma or a regularized legal and administrative system. As an ideal type, it has some application to traditional Indonesia and fits closely with the Indian-derived ideology of the *dharma-raja* or all-powerful king (*see* **INDIA, HISTORICAL LINKS WITH**). Some authorities have questioned, however, whether traditional states were truly patrimonial, pointing both to elements of collegiality among powerful men within each kingdom (especially regional authorities such as the ***bupati***) and to supposedly democratic elements in the relationship between ruler and subject. The term "neopatrimonialism" has been used to describe the concentration of state authority in the hands of leaders of independent Indonesia. *See also* WHITE RAJAS. [0521, 0796]

PATTINGALLOANG (c. 1600–1654)**.** Son of Matoaya, chief minister of **Makassar**, and from 1639 also chief minister. Fluent in several European languages, he was a keen follower of the latest developments in geography and astronomy, and also had European works on gunnery translated into Makassarese. He maintained his father's policy of keeping Makassar an open port for all traders, but fractured the previous alliance between **Bugis** and Makassarese by conquering **Bone** in 1646, laying the basis for the later rebellion of **Arung Palakka**.

PAWNSHOPS. The right to run pawnshops was farmed, like other state revenue sources (*see* ***PACHT***), until 1903 when a government pawnshop service was created for **Java** and **Madura**. The service operated to some extent in the **Outer Islands**, but most of the 457 government pawnshops in the Netherlands Indies in 1931 were on Java and Madura. Annual profits were *f*6 to *f*11 million.

PEARLING. This was widespread in the archipelago in early times, and pearls were among exports to **China** from the 10th century. The coasts of **Java** were once known for seed pearls, used in medicine, but with the gradual exhaustion of shell beds fishing retreated to eastern Indonesia. Western companies began to move into the industry from the 1860s after the invention of the diving suit. Since the early 20th century, the **Aru** islands have been the industry's main center. Culturing of pearls has been done by the Marine Fisheries Research Institute in Aru and **Sulawesi** since 1960.

PEDIR (Pidië)**.** Muslim state in northern **Sumatra** in the 15th century. Like **Pasai**, it was an important entrepôt for **pepper**. It was conquered by **Aceh** in 1524.

PEMBANGUNAN ("development")**.** *See* DEVELOPMENT IDEOLOGY.

PEMBELA TANAH AIR (Peta, Defenders of the Fatherland)**.** Military force formed by the **Japanese** in October 1943 on **Java** (equivalent to the **Giyugun** on **Sumatra**) to involve Indonesians in defending the archipelago against the Allies. The Peta consisted of 65 battalions by August 1945, with 37,000 men. Battalion commanders were generally locally prominent Indonesian civilians—teachers, officials, and the like—whose role was to recruit and to maintain morale rather than to command. Military leadership was mainly in the hands of company commanders and Japanese instructors. Training included use of **weapons** and elementary tactics, but it emphasized spirit (*semangat*) and intense discipline. In February 1945 a Peta unit at Blitar revolted under command of Supriyadi (?–1945) but was crushed by Japanese forces. Between 18 and 25 August, after the surrender and before Indonesia's declaration of **independence** was widely known, the Japanese disarmed and disbanded most Peta units. Many, however, soon reassembled to form part of the basis of the Republic's **army**. *See also* HEIHO. [0663, 0664]

PEMERINTAH DARURAT REPUBLIK INDONESIA (PDRI, Emergency Government of the Republic of Indonesia)**.** In November 1948 Vice President **Mohammad Hatta** sent **Sjafruddin Prawiranegara** to **Sumatra** to establish a government presence there should the **Dutch** succeed in overrunning Java. After the Dutch in their second **"Police Action"** of 19 December 1948 arrested **Sukarno**, Hatta, and most of their cabinet, Sjafruddin Prawiranegara proclaimed an Emergency Government on 22 December. The PDRI was headquartered in the interior of West Sumatra and viewed itself as a legal successor to the Republican government. Headed by Sjafruddin, it had Sumatra governor Tengku Mohammad Hassan as his deputy, and the Republic's representative in **India**, Mr. Maramis, as minister of foreign affairs. The PDRI was recognized by the Republic's guerrilla forces on Sumatra and Java (under General **Sudirman**), but it was ignored by the Dutch and by the jailed Republic leadership when in April 1949 they entered into the talks that led to the **Roem–van Roijen Agreement** of the following month. Both the PDRI and General Sudirman opposed the concessions made in these agreements but were ultimately persuaded to go along. Sjafruddin returned his mandate to Sukarno in **Yogyakarta** on 13 July 1949. [0660, 0686]

PEMUDA (youth)**.** The notion of youth was a strong element in the national awakening of Indonesia in the early 20th century, especially through their role in promulgation of the "**youth pledge**" of 1928. The term *pemuda* came into common political use, however, only during the national **Revolution** of 1945–1949, when young Indonesians spearheaded the declaration of **independence** and flocked in tens of thousands to the armed units that endeavored to defend that independence against the **Dutch**. *Pemuda* in that time came to denote a spirit of daring and refusal to compromise. *Pemuda* were later important instruments in **Sukarno**'s ouster when they acted in close cooperation with the **army** in establishing the **New Order** government. *See also* GENERATIONS; STUDENTS. [0643, 0652]

PEMUDA PANCASILA. Founded as a subordinate wing of **A. H. Nasution**'s **Ikatan Pendukung Kemerdekaan Indonesia (IPKI)** party on 28 October 1959, Pemuda Pancasila was formally inaugurated at IPKI's 1961 congress. It became prominent in the closing years of **Sukarno**'s rule when it offered to send troops in support of the West Irian (*see* **PAPUA**) campaign (Trikora). Pemuda Pancasila had centers in **Jakarta** and Medan, where it was largely an extortion agency, operating primarily against **Chinese** businesses. It was active in both areas after the 1965 coup (*see* **GESTAPU**), taking a leading role in killing suspected communists particularly in North **Sumatra**. Under **Suharto** it became one of the foremost organizations of gangs, carrying out "thug" politics (*politik premanisme*). These gangs formed part of the security apparatus and were closely tied to the military in organizing riots and extracting money from businesses. Pemuda Pancasila groups reemerged in the early 1980s in the aftermath of the **Petrus (Pembunuhan Misterius)** killings, when they were reportedly the major instrument used by Suharto and **Benny Murdani** in wiping out **Ali Murtopo**'s gangster organization. Their ties to the military became closer in the late 1980s when their regional branches were matched with the **army**'s Komando Daerah Militer (Kodam) structure, and their **militias** were used by the army in maintaining local control. Pemuda Pancasila was suspected of providing many of the gangs that attacked **Megawati Sukarnoputri**'s **Partai Demokrasi Indonesia (PDI)** headquarters in July 1996, and the organization's leaders were some of Suharto's last outspoken supporters in May 1998, again being suspected of responsibility for much of the destruction of businesses on 13–14 May. Their influence apparently declined after Suharto's fall. [0743]

PEMUDA RAKYAT (People's Youth)**.** Youth organization affiliated with the **Partai Komunis Indonesia (PKI)**, formed in 1950 to replace the **Pemuda Sosialis Indonesia (Pesindo)**. It used educational and social activities to draw the interest of young people, especially in the urban and rural *kampung*, but was banned along with the PKI in 1966. [0994]

PEMUDA SOSIALIS INDONESIA (Pesindo, Indonesian Socialist Youth)**.** Armed youth wing of the ruling **Partai Sosialis (PS)**, founded in November 1945. Pesindo fought the Dutch and also provided quasi-military backing to the government when its policies aroused the hostility of the **army** and other sections of society. It became increasingly trusted and favored under **Amir Sjarifuddin**, who made it the core of the so-called TNI Masyarakat (People's Indonesian National Army), created to balance the power of the more conservative conventional **army**. In 1948 it joined the left-wing **Front Demokrasi Rakyat (FDR)** and was heavily involved in fighting during the **Madiun** Affair. In 1950 it became firmly affiliated with the **Partai Komunis Indonesia (PKI)** and changed its name to **Pemuda Rakyat**. [0661, 0674]

PENDIDIKAN NASIONAL INDONESIA (PNI, Indonesian National Education; also called PNI-Baru, New PNI)**.** A nationalist party founded by **Mohammad Hatta** and **Sutan Sjahrir** in December 1931. Both were concerned by the relative ease with which the **Dutch** had been able to destroy the first **Partai Nasional Indonesia (PNI)** by arresting its leadership, and they proposed instead to build a strong, less obtrusive party of nationalist caders that would have the strength to resist Dutch repression.

They were given, however, relatively little time to put these ideas into practice since both were arrested and **exiled** in February 1934 to **Boven Digul** and then to **Banda**. [0613, 0661, 0865, 0875, 0915]

PENGHULU. The title of a **Minangkabau** clan head, but also used in colonial times for religious officials in state employment. *See* RELIGION AND POLITICS. [0648]

PEPPER (*Piper nigrum* Piperaceae)**.** Properly not the fleshy hollow fruit of various *Capsicum* species (chili peppers) but the small hard berries of a woody vine. Whereas the *sirih*, *P. betle*, leaves of which are used in the chewing of **betel**, is probably native to the archipelago, true pepper was introduced from **India**, probably as early as 100 B.C. Commercial production was well established on **Sumatra**, **Kalimantan**, and **Java** by the 14th century. **Pedir** and **Pasai** in northern Sumatra were the earliest states to depend heavily on the pepper **trade**, followed in the 16th century by **Aceh** and **Banten**. Indiscriminate clearing of forest for pepper production in this era created large areas of ***alang-alang*** in Sumatra and Kalimantan. At the end of the 16th century, Banten produced 25,000 bags of pepper a year and all male inhabitants were obliged to maintain 500 pepper plants and to deliver the produce to the sultan at a fixed price. Pepper was traded especially to the West, becoming a major target of **Portuguese** and, from the late 16th century, Dutch commercial expansion in the archipelago. The **Dutch East Indies Company (VOC)** attempted to enforce monopoly contracts in pepper ports as they had done in **Maluku** with **cloves** and **nutmeg** but were relatively unsuccessful due to the wide distribution of the plant and the relative ease with which it can be cultivated. From the18th century, **China**'s market for pepper grew while Europe's declined. Production on Java had largely ceased by the end of the 18th century. Although pepper production in North Sumatra increased in the 19th century and **Chinese** immigrants became important growers, the center of the trade shifted to Penang and **Singapore**. [0331]

PERANAKAN ("native born")**.** Term applied to those of non-Indonesian ethnic origin born in Indonesia, and generally implying some degree of cultural adaptation to local conditions. *See* CHINESE IN INDONESIA.

***PERDIKAN* VILLAGES.** The traditional rulers of **Java** occasionally freed a village of the obligation to pay **land tax** or provide corvée **labor**, either as a reward for service or in exchange for the village's acceptance of the obligation to carry out some task, such as the maintenance of a school or holy place. Such villages, called *perdikan desa*, were found most commonly on **Madura** and in Central **Java** and were preserved under **Dutch** rule. They were commonly major centers of handicrafts, including **batik**. The tax exemption of *perdikan* villages was abolished by the Indonesian Republic in 1946.

PERGERAKAN. *See* NATIONALISM.

PERHIMPUNAN INDONESIA (PI, Indonesian Association)**.** Organization of Indonesian **students** in the Netherlands founded in 1922, based on the Indische Vereeniging (Indies Association), founded in 1908. The PI was small, with only 38 members at it peak, but its members included such later national leaders as **Mohammad Hatta**, **Sutan Sjahrir**, **Ali Sastroamijoyo**, and **Sukiman Wiryosanjoyo**. Its major aim was to prepare Indonesian students to provide political leadership on their return, but it also sought to inform the **Dutch** public on conditions in the colony. Its ideology was strongly influenced by **Marxism** and especially by Lenin's theory of imperialism, but many of its members, including Hatta, despaired of communism after the Comintern decision in 1927 to abandon cooperation with noncommunist nationalists, and the organization gradually split between a **Partai Komunis Indonesia (PKI)** wing led by Rustam Effendi and the radical nationalists led by Hatta and Sjahrir, who were finally expelled in 1931.

PERIODIZATION OF INDONESIAN HISTORY. The conventional historiography of Indonesia commonly divides the country's history into three broad periods, precolonial, colonial, and independent, normally subdivided as follows: traditional societies, **Hindu-Buddhist** kingdoms, the arrival of **Islam** and the emergence of Muslim sultanates, European commercial penetration and company rule, British interregnum, **Cultivation System**, **Liberal Policy**, **Ethical Policy**, the rise of **nationalism**, **Japanese occupation**, **Revolution**, parliamentary democracy, **Guided Democracy**, **New Order**, and now the post-**Suharto** or ***reformasi*** era. This sequence can be criticized on a number of grounds. First, the earlier of these periods are visible clearly only on **Java**, though it is possible to apply them to other regions by, for instance, omitting the Muslim period, setting the date of colonial penetration later, and so forth. More important, as a system of periodization based on government policy and organization, it ignores deeper structures, patterns, and continuities. J. C.

van Leur and John Smail, in particular, have criticized it for the prominence it gives to the European role in Indonesian history and have argued for an "autonomous" (Smail's term) approach concentrating on the experiences of Indonesians rather than of their European rulers. Indonesian historians have often used the notion of successive **generations** in periodizing. [0502, 0504, 0505, 0521]

PERMUFAKATAN PERHIMPUNAN POLITIK KEBANGSAAN INDONESIA (PPPKI, Confederation of Indonesian Political Organizations)**.** Conference of nationalist groups, especially the **Partai Nasional Indonesia (PNI)**, **Partai Sarekat Islam Indonesia (PSII)**, **Budi Utomo**, and **Paguyuban Pasundan**, formed in **Bandung** in December 1927 to give a relatively united voice to the nationalist movement. Decisions were taken by exhaustive deliberation (***musyawarah***), intended to avoid the imposition of majority views on minorities. In April 1929 the PPPKI recognized the **Perhimpunan Indonesia (PI)** as its representative in the Netherlands. The term *Permufakatan* in its title changed in 1930 to *Persatuan* (Unity, Association) and the word *Kebangsaan* (Nationality) to *Kemerdekaan* (Freedom) in 1933. The PPPKI strongly opposed the restrictive **labor** regulations of the time (*see* **COOLIE ORDINANCE**) and promoted nationalist **education**, but its internal diversity prevented it from acting decisively. In 1933 the colonial government refused to permit its annual conference, and the PPPKI withered. *See also* GABUNGAN POLITIK INDONESIA. [0613, 0661]

PERSATUAN BANGSA INDONESIA (PBI, Association of the Indonesian People)**.** Successor to one of the study clubs of **Sutomo**, formed in 1930 to promote self-help among Indonesians. It was involved in the promotion of **cooperatives**, **education**, and village banks and credit unions. In 1935 it merged with **Budi Utomo** to form the **Partai Indonesia Raya**. [0661, 0888]

PERSATUAN INDONESIA RAYA (PIR, Greater Indonesian Association)**.** Conservative party of civil servants and aristocrats founded in 1948. In 1953 it split over the issue of participation in the government of **Ali Sastroamijoyo**, and two PIRs, under respectively Hazairin and Wongsonegoro, competed in the 1955 **elections**, losing heavily. [0695]

PERSATUAN ISLAM (Persis, Islamic Union)**.** Modernist Muslim organization founded in **Bandung** in 1923. It opposed **nationalism** on the grounds that it divided **Islam** and because it was Western and humanist in origin. It was active in establishing Muslim schools and was strongest in West **Java**. Its leaders included **Mohammad Natsir**. In 1939 it joined the **Majelis Islam A'laa Indonesia (MIAI)**. [1023]

PERSATUAN PERJUANGAN (PP, Struggle Union)**.** Coalition of radical nationalist organizations formed on 4–5 January 1946 to oppose the Republican government's negotiations with the **Dutch** and **Mohammad Hatta**'s attempts to create a multiparty state rather than uniting Indonesian forces into a national front. **Tan Malaka**'s ideas of total struggle inspired the PP and the organization was supported at first by the **army** commander, **Sudirman**. The movement brought down the first cabinet of **Sutan Sjahrir** in February 1946, but was unable to agree on a coalition to replace him, partly because **Sukarno** moved deftly to break its fragile consensus on what should be done. On 17 March 1946 the government arrested Tan Malaka and some of his most prominent supporters. The PP then disintegrated, though some of its members were involved later in 1946 in an ambiguous confrontation with Sukarno known as the 4 July Affair, and eventually formed the core of the Gerakan Rakyat Revolusi (GRR, Revolutionary People's Movement) and the **Murba**. [0643, 0674, 0807]

PERSATUAN TARBYIAH ISLAMIYAH (Perti, Islamic Education Association)**.** Founded in West **Sumatra** in 1930 to combat the influence of modernist Islamic associations, Perti was an organization of **Minangkabau** and Acehnese Islamic traditionalists, based in religious centers and ***pesantren***. Similar in style to the **Nahdlatul Ulama (NU)**, it was willing to trade its support on general political issues for specific concessions to **Islam**. It retained its major strength in West Sumatra, where it ran second to **Masjumi** in the 1955 **elections**. In the regional unrest of 1957, it sided first with the dissidents, then when the **PRRI/Permesta** was proclaimed in 1958 it shifted to the government side. Under **Guided Democracy**, it strongly supported the president and was sometimes considered pro-**Partai Komunis Indonesia (PKI)**; its leader H. Sirajuddin Abbas frequently visited communist countries and was briefly detained because of alleged involvement in the **Gestapu** coup. After his release he returned to a leading position in the Perti, which was heavily purged after 1966. In 1973 it was merged into the **Partai Persatuan Pembangunan (PPP)**. [0695, 0807]

PERTAMINA (Perusahaan Tambang Minyak Negara, State Oil Mining Company)**.** Created in 1969 as a state-owned monopoly with the task of managing the country's **oil** and **gas** development, Pertamina was Indonesia's sole state oil company, responsible for managing concessions and production-sharing agreements but little involved in production itself. Oil was already an important source of discretionary funds for **Suharto**'s government early in the **New Order**, but the sudden increase in oil prices in 1973 gave Pertamina under its president-director Ibnu Sutowo (1914–2001) enormous wealth that was funneled, along with borrowed funds, into a wide range of development projects and economic ventures, including an air service, Pelita, telecommunications, real estate, and the P. T. Krakatau Steel works in Cilegon, West **Java**. Sutowo was close to the **Centre for Strategic and International Studies (CSIS)** think tank, which promoted import substitution **industrialization** rather than comparative advantage trading, and his freewheeling style attracted admiration from economic nationalists and condemnation from the so-called technocrats of **Badan Perencanaan Pembangunan Nasional (Bappenas)**. An investigation in 1970 criticized Pertamina sharply for loose auditing, for failure to pass on profits to the government, and for the luxurious lifestyle of its senior executives.

In March 1975 Pertamina was unable to meet payment on some short-term debts and a Bappenas investigation under J. B. Sumarlin revealed a huge debt problem (US$10.5 billion), brought about by **corruption**, optimism, incompetence, and waste. Sutowo was dismissed from his post in 1976 and replaced by General Piet Haryono. Pertamina's activities outside the oil business were curtailed and an austerity policy was introduced, so that the firm was solvent once more by 1978. In 1980 the Indonesian government took legal action in **Singapore** to try to recover allegedly corrupt income from the estate of the former Pertamina employee H. Tahir. But Pertamina retained its power because it was a critical source of capital for **Suharto**'s **family** and cronies, giving some of the president's children their start in business through lucrative deals that included exclusive distribution contracts. It was estimated that in two years in the mid-1990s, Pertamina lost nearly $5 billion due to inefficiency and **corruption**.

After Suharto's fall, the government made an effort to break up Pertamina's oil monopoly, with the **B. J. Habibie** administration failing in an attempt in 1999 to place major foreign oil firms directly under the Ministry of Mines and Energy. In June 2000 the ministry tried again, drawing up legislation to break Pertamina's monopoly by handing the control of production-sharing contracts to an agency created under the office of the **president**. In October 2001 the legislature passed an Oil and Gas Act, giving Pertamina two years to transform itself into a state-owned commercial enterprise, relinquishing control over foreign and local oil companies and surrendering its downstream role to a separate regulatory agency (while maintaining control over its LNG contracts). But it was unclear whether the **Megawati Sukarnoputri** administration would have any more success than previous administrations in curbing the powerful company. In October 2002 the company signed an $8.5 billion deal to supply **China** with LNG from the Tanggung field in **Papua**. [0375, 0400, 0405, 0736, 0951]

PESANTREN. Called *surau* in **Minangkabau** and *dajah* in **Aceh**, these are traditional rural Islamic schools, headed by a *kyai* (religious teacher). Formerly, influenced by the style of **Hindu-Buddhist** *asrama*, *pesantren* instructed resident pupils in religious knowledge and mystical practice, emphasizing absolute submission to both Allah and the *kyai*. In the 19th century, influenced by returning pilgrims from Mecca (*see* ***HAJ***), they took on the role of more formal religious instruction, though without discarding their primarily religious orientation. In the 1920s classroom teaching and a partly secular curriculum were introduced. The first *pesantren* for female students was opened at Jombang (East **Java**) in 1924.

In the early 20th century, the place of *pesantren* as the main providers of Muslim religious **education** on Java was challenged by ***madrasah***, many of which were sponsored by the modernist **Muhammadiyah**, which disliked the traditionalist teaching in the *pesantren*.

Although reliable enrollment figures are not available for many of the *pesantren* and *madrasah* in the postwar period, they have continued to provide a significant part of the education of Indonesian children since 1945. *Pesantren* were valued both because of the moral values they taught and because they contributed to local social cohesion. Enrollments in Islamic schools apparently declined under the **New Order** but have had growing influence in the post-**Suharto** years. [0045, 1273, 1283, 1352]

PETITION OF FIFTY (*Petisi Lima Puluh*)**.** In March and April 1980 President **Suharto** made speeches implying that he was the embodiment of **Pancasila**, describing it as under threat from **nationalism**, religion, and other ideologies, and calling on the **armed forces** to defend it against these challenges. The speeches aroused special alarm in two dissident groups whose members were generally associated with the establishment of the **New Order** in 1965–1966, namely, the Forum Studi dan Komunikasi (FOSKO), including **H. R. Dharsono**, and Lembaga Kesadaran Berkonstitusi (LKB, Institute for Constitutional Awareness), including **A. H. Nasution** and **Ali Sadikin**. In response, a group of 50 former generals, politicians, academics, **students**, and others, including Nasution, Sadikin, **Mohammad Natsir**, and **Sjafruddin Prawiranegara**, signed a petition dated 5 May 1980 expressing concern about the speeches and inviting the **Majelis Permusyawaratan Rakyat (MPR)** to "review" them. The government reacted strongly to this criticism, banning news coverage of the petitioners, preventing them from traveling, and depriving firms associated with them of their government contracts. [0733]

PETRUS (Pembunuhan Misterius, mysterious killings, or Penembakan Misterius mysterious shootings). An acronym given to a paramilitary operation lasting for two years from March 1983 to curb the incidence of violent crime, in which at least 5,000 and perhaps more than 10,000 people labeled criminals were murdered in a number of Indonesia's main cities, beginning in **Yogyakarta**. The operation was probably planned and organized by **Benny Murdani** and the **Komando Operasi Pemulihan Keamanan dan Ketertiban (Kopkamtib)**, which he then headed. [0721, 0734, 0969]

PHILIPPINES. The Austronesian people reached Indonesia through the Philippines (*see* **MIGRATIONS**), and contacts between the southern islands and eastern Indonesia remained strong, especially in **trade**. In the 17th century the **Dutch** and **Spanish** fought for influence in Mindanao, and the Dutch alliance with the Mindanao sultanate was partly responsible for its emergence as paramount power in the region. After the **United States** conquered the Philippines in 1898, the Americans initially saw the Netherlands Indies as offering many lessons in the management of a tropical colony, and American welfare expenditure in the Philippines found echoes in the **Ethical Policy**. As the Philippines progressed toward self-government, however, the Dutch grew increasingly uneasy, fearing both encouragement for Indonesian **nationalism** and possible southward expansion by **Japan**. These fears were heightened by the visit of Manuel Quezon to Indonesia in 1934 and the later founding of a (short-lived) Pan-Malayan People's Union under Philippine leadership. During the Indonesian **Revolution**, Manila was an important source of supplies for the beleaguered Republic.

Since 1950, Indonesia and the Philippines have combined to limit commerce and other traffic across their borders, so as to discourage links between the Muslim Moro rebels in Mindanao and Sulu and radical Muslims in Indonesia, and between Christian communities in **Minahasa** and the northern Philippines. But during the **PRRI/Permesta rebellion**, American and rebel pilots made use of bases in the Philippines to bomb sites in eastern Indonesia, raising tensions between the two countries. The two did, however, cooperate in 1963 in initial opposition to the establishment of **Malaysia** and in attempting to realize Philippine President Diosdado Macapagal's concept of **Maphilindo**, an effort that failed though it contributed to the later formation of the **Association of Southeast Asian Nations (ASEAN)**. As another archipelagic nation, the Philippines has strongly supported Indonesia's **archipelagic concept**, but has been in dispute with Indonesia over jurisdiction over seas around the Indonesian island of Miangas, off Mindanao, known by the Filipinos as Las Palmas. [0833, 1106]

PIAGAM JAKARTA (Jakarta Charter). *See* ISLAMIC STATE, DEMANDS FOR.

PIG (*Sus scrofa*). Until the 20th century, it is difficult to distinguish accounts of the introduced domestic pig from those of indigenous warty pigs (*S. verrucosus* of **Java**, *S. barbatus* on **Kalimantan** and **Sumatra**, and *S. celebensis* on **Sulawesi**). It seems likely, however, that *S. celebensis* was the first species to be domesticated and was taken by people to **Timor** and that the pigs of **Papua** are a stable hybrid of *S. celebensis* and *S. scrofa* developed between 8000 and 4000 B.C. Wild pigs were an important food source for most peoples until the arrival of **Islam**, and Douglas Miles has shown that the adoption of Islam among **Dayaks** has had significant nutritional effects. Feral and warty pigs are widespread in the archipelago and seem to do best where human cultivation provides abundant accessible food. Since the early 1970s, the introduction of the pig tapeworm *Taenia solium* into Papua has had serious health consequences. *See also* TIGER. [1154]

PIRACY. A distinction between the regular depredations of the state and the irregular depredations of criminals was slower to emerge on the sea than on land in traditional Indonesia (*see* **BANDITRY**). "Piracy," in the form of waterborne raids against neighboring communities and the plundering of passing vessels, formed an important part of the political order in maritime societies in Indonesia (*see also* ***HONGI*** **RAIDS**). It provided an important source of income in the form of products and slaves (*see* **SLAVERY**), and within communities it established the social basis for rule by pirate chiefs. It also gave successful chiefs the means to subjugate rivals and to regularize their plunder by guaranteeing safe passage through their sphere of influence in exchange for a fixed payment. The suppression of piracy and the subjugation of rivals were thus often two sides of the same coin. Conversely, when **trade** declined or departed, kingdoms often returned to piracy. Although this approached a system of customs collection, war vessels were often still needed to force passing merchant vessels to call at the required **port**. This system was adopted by the **Portuguese** on their arrival in the East.

From the early 19th century **Dutch** and **British** colonial authorities, in the name of free trade, worked not just to suppress slavery and unambiguous piratical activities but also to prevent local rulers from collecting customs dues. For much of the 19th century, Dutch efforts to crush piracy were impeded by the fact that people moved freely between piracy and other occupations, and were thus often easily able to evade attempts at capture. By the early 20th century, however, piracy was in retreat, in part because Europeans were able to hunt down the pirates' ships with steam-powered vessels that were able to sail against the wind and also because the colonial state had spread its control to many of the peripheral areas that harbored the pirates. Occasional incidents of piracy continue to occur in the Strait of Melaka. It was reported that more than a quarter of the world's 445 major piracy incidents in 2003 occurred in Indonesian waters, including the Melaka Strait. [0637, 0833]

PIRES, TOMÉ (1468-1539?)**. Portuguese** apothecary and author of the *Suma Oriental,* which describes his residence in **Melaka** from 1512 to 1515. Rediscovered in 1937, this work is a major account of daily life and political and economic conditions in Southeast Asia in this period. [0082]

PLAGUE. *See* BUBONIC PLAGUE.

PLANNING, ECONOMIC. *See* ECONOMY; GUIDED ECONOMY; RENCANA PEMBANGUNAN LIMA TAHUN.

PLURAL SOCIETY. Term coined by J. S. Furnivall to characterize a society in which "two or more elements or social orders . . . live side by side . . . without mingling in one political unit," by which he was referring to the legal and social separation of ethnic groups in the Netherlands Indies. *See* DUALISM; LAW. [0606]

POENALE SANCTIE. *See* COOLIE ORDINANCE.

POLICE. Until the 20th century, police tasks in the Netherlands Indies were primarily the responsibility of local authorities. Indonesian officials commanded their own local police squads under a variety of names, the officers of **Chinese** communities were in charge of policing their own people, and policing functions in the European community lay largely with the civil bureaucracy itself, while all policing forces were backed ultimately by the colonial **army** (*see* **KONINKLIJK NEDERLANDSCH INDISCH LEGER**; **LAW**; **MARÉCHAUSSÉE; NATIVE TROOPS**). Some centralization of policing was achieved with the creation of mobile "armed police" (*gewapende politie*) in 1897, but it was only after the establishment of the Office of the Attorney-General (Procureur-Generaal) that central control of the police emerged. The police force nonetheless remained divided into distinct rural police (*veldpolitie*, who absorbed the *gewapende politie* in 1920), urban police (*stadspolitie*), and political (**Politiek Inlichtingen Dienst**) sections.

The **Japanese** (1942–1945) dismissed some senior staff from the Dutch period and handed political surveillance to the **Kenpeitai**, but otherwise preserved and strengthened the police force. During the **Revolution** (1945–1949), the police were at first formally under the control of the Internal Affairs ministry but shifted in July 1946 to the Prime Minister's Office. Much of the police force, however, was dispersed by social revolutions, and a multitude of local police forces emerged, generally attached to regional **armed forces**, regular and irregular. Dual control by Internal Affairs and the prime minister was established in 1950, but in 1962 the police were formally militarized and placed under the authority of the armed forces commander.

After the fall of **Suharto**, tensions rose between the police and armed forces particularly over the violence in **Maluku** and other regions, and moves began in 1999 to separate the police from the **army** and place them under civilian control, a division that formally went into effect in April 1999 but was not completed until early 2001. The effectiveness of the 190,000-strong police force was hindered by its insufficient numbers and lack of training, and there was dissatisfaction among younger officers with police chief Surojo Bimantoro. However, when President **Abdurrachman Wahid** attempted to dismiss Bimantoro in June 2001 and ordered the deputy chief to assume command, 100 top police officers defied him and were instrumental in Wahid's downfall the following month. The police were expected to have a better relationship with President **Megawati Sukarnoputri**, but it was unclear whether they would be any more effective in their peacekeeping functions. Tension continued between the police and the army, particularly over internal security responsibilities, with the most violent clash breaking out in North **Sumatra** on 30 September 2002, allegedly over control of the marijuana **trade**, when a five-hour gun battle between them resulted in eight people dead and more than 20 wounded.

Mocked for their ineptitude in the pursuit of Tommy Suharto (*see* **SUHARTO FAMILY**), the police gained more respect in their investigation of the **Bali** bombings and other terrorist actions when, working in conjunction with investigators sent from the **United States** and **Australia**, they succeeded in capturing and bringing to trial a number of suspected leaders of the terrorist network. *See also* BAKIN. [0635, 0653]

"POLICE ACTIONS" (*Politionele acties*). Military operations launched by the Netherlands Indies against the Indonesian Republic in **Java** and **Sumatra** on 21 July 1947 and 19 December 1948. They were called police actions to stress their allegedly internal character and to avoid giving the Indonesian Republic the formal recognition as belligerent implied by an act of war. The first, called Operation Product, was aimed primarily at seizing plantation areas to improve the parlous financial situation of the colonial government. The resulting demarcation line was known as the van Mook line and left the Republic on Java crowded into heavily populated parts of the island's center and east and **Banten**. On Sumatra, the **Dutch** did no more than significantly expand their coastal enclaves in east, west, and south Sumatra. The second Police Action was intended to destroy the Republic, and Dutch troops entered all regions except **Aceh**. Guerrilla warfare (*see* **GERILYA**), however, kept Dutch forces too thinly spread to consolidate their initial advances, and international pressure brought the Dutch to negotiate once more with the Republic, leading to the **Round Table Conference**. Indonesian texts generally refer to the "police actions" as *Agresi* or Clash I and II. [0660, 0661]

POLITICAL CULTURE. The proposition that shared cultural values can lead to a shared attitude toward politics is a plausible one and has led many analysts, Indonesian and foreign, to argue for the existence of a distinctive Indonesian political culture. A major objection to this has traditionally been the ethnic and cultural diversity of the archipelago. The

Dutch in particular saw pronounced cultural dissimilarities among the peoples of the colony and at times claimed on this basis that only their rule would preserve Indonesian unity. The argument, however, is generally not that particular values are universally held, but that they are dominant values that to a greater or lesser extent establish the terms on which people must operate politically. Hildred Geertz identified a "metropolitan super-culture" as providing such dominant values.

Indonesian political leaders have often argued that the collectivist village culture of traditional Indonesia leads to a preference for consensual politics with especial attention being given to the wisdom of the elders in society (*see* ***DESA***; ***MUSYAWARAH***; **SUKARNO**), making Indonesia unsuited to the supposedly adversarial style of Western party politics. Under the **New Order**, this has led to the labeling of criticism of President **Suharto** and his family as un-Indonesian (*see* **SUBVERSION**). Other observers, such as **Mochtar Lubis**, have argued that Indonesian political culture is characterized by a feudal deference to constituted authority, while still others have seen this deferential submissiveness (*nrimo*) as typical only of Javanese society and as contrasting with more dynamic and independent styles in the other islands.

Western observers have been intrigued by apparent parallels in style between both Sukarno and **Suharto** on the one hand and traditional Javanese kings on the other. Most of the parallels refer to elements of individual style: Sukarno's monument building (especially the *lingga*-like National Monument in Jakarta; *see* SEX, POLITICAL SIGNIFICANCE OF), his unification of seeming irreconcilables, and his sexual encounters; Suharto's reluctance to exercise his power visibly; both leaders' emphasis on unity, the centralization of authority, and the use of powerful words; and both leaders' avoidance of naming a successor. The principal objection to this line of argument is that it provides at best only a partial explanation of those leaders' actions and that much of the behavior involved can be explained in terms of *realpolitik* calculations. [0132, 0891, 0896, 0897, 0906, 0926]

POLITICAL PARTIES. *See* PARTIES, POLITICAL.

POLITICAL POLICE. *See* BAKIN; INTELLIGENCE SERVICES; KENPEITAI; POLITIEK INLICHTINGEN DIENST.

POLITICAL PRISONERS. *See* BOVEN DIGUL; EXILE; *TAHANAN POLITIK*.

POLITIEK INLICHTINGEN DIENST (PID, Political Intelligence Service). A clear distinction between political and conventional policing developed in the Netherlands Indies only after the rise of Indonesian **nationalism** in the early 20th century and led to the formation of the PID in 1916. The PID was formally abolished in 1919, but its place was taken in 1920 by the Algemene Recherche (Criminal Investigation Division) and the term PID remained in common use until the end of **Dutch** rule. The political police worked both by the collection of intelligence on political organizations and by directly intervening in their activities, for instance, by breaking up meetings. It was largely due to prior arrests and other preventive measures that the 1926–1927 **Partai Komunis Indonesia (PKI)** uprisings in **Banten** and West **Sumatra** were not more widespread. The Algemene Recherche's monthly *Politiek-Politionele Overzichten* (Police Political Surveys), appearing first in 1927, became the colonial government's principal source of information on the **nationalist** movement. After World War II the political intelligence functions of the Algemene Recherche were partly taken over by the Netherlands Forces Intelligence Service (Nefis). *See also* BAKIN; INTELLIGENCE SERVICES; KENPEITAI; POLICE. [0628, 0635, 0652]

POLO, MARCO (1254?–1324?). Venetian traveler. On his return from **China** to Europe in 1292–1295, Polo traversed the Strait of Melaka, visiting **Pedir** and **Pasai**. His account is most often mentioned for his statement that some of the states of northern **Sumatra** were already Muslim at that time, but his description is vague. [0085]

POLOWIJO. Subsidiary crops grown on wet-**rice** land (*sawah*) after the rice harvest, including chili, **soya beans**, eggplant, maize, onions, and **sugar cane**.

PONTIANAK. City and state on the Kapuas River in West **Kalimantan**, founded in 1772 by a part-Arab pirate Syarif Abdurrahman (*see* **PIRACY**), who in 1778 accepted **Dutch** suzerainty in exchange for recognition as sultan and Dutch aid in establishing control of the Kapuas basin. Pontianak's history has been dominated by three major ethnic groups—**Dayak**, Malay, and **Chinese**—with Dayaks and Malays each about 40 percent of the population and Chinese well over 10 percent. The kingdom's source of wealth was its control of **trade** down the Kapuas in **gold**, **diamonds**, and forest products. The **Dutch East Indies Company**

(VOC) withdrew its presence in 1791 but the Dutch returned in 1818, installing a resident to ensure closer control of affairs.

Several thousand, a majority of them Chinese but also including the sultan and most of his family, were killed by the **Japanese** between 1943 and 1945, leaving a younger son, Hamid Algadrie, to reign as Hamid II. He was persuaded by the Dutch to head a federal state of West Borneo (Kalimantan Barat), founded on 11 May 1947 (*see* **FEDERALISM**), and became a major figure in Dutch attempts to influence the constitutional and political shape of postwar Indonesia. He was implicated in a failed coup d'état on 22 January 1950 by **R. P. P. Westerling** and was jailed. The Negara Kalimantan Barat was dissolved on 4 April 1950. During **Confrontation**, West Kalimantan was an important base for Indonesian infiltration into the Malaysian state of Sarawak, partly conducted by the ethnic Chinese Pasukan Gerilya Rakyat Serawak (PGRS, Sarawak People's Guerrilla Movement). After the change of regime, the **New Order** forces used the issue in 1967 to encourage anti-Chinese actions especially by the Dayak community, with the local military commander alleging that all Chinese were supporters of Communist **China** and the **Partai Komunis Indonesia (PKI)**. Most of the Chinese (a reported 50,000–80,000) fled the interior, together with many immigrants from **Madura** and **Java**.

During the 1970s and 1980s large numbers especially of Madurese arrived in the Pontianak region under the **transmigration** program, and by the late 1990s they were estimated to constitute between 2 and 3 percent of West Kalimantan's population. During the downturn in the **economy** in 1997, Madurese became the major target of Dayak violence. Tribesmen attacked their settlements northwest of the town, killing about 450 and forcing about 20,000 to flee, attacks that were renewed in 1999 in other regions of West Kalimantan. *See also* KONGSI WARS. [0002, 0607, 1048]

POPULATION. Indonesia's first full **census** was taken in 1930 and gave the country a population of 60.7 million. Population figures before this date are based on partial surveys and guesswork with varying degrees of inspiration; consequently, they yield often widely varying results.

Demographers have given greatest attention to **Java** because of the island's greater density of population. Early scholars, extrapolating backward from the 19th-century estimates, assumed that Java's population in early times was between 1 and 3 million. The scope of irrigation works, monument construction, and political organization on the island, however, suggests perhaps a fairly steady population of around 10 million from about the 10th century. **Thomas Stamford Raffles** surveyed Java's population in 1815 at 4.6 million, but this is certainly an underestimate: those responsible for reporting population were already long accustomed to underreporting population in order to minimize **taxation**. From 1815 to 1865, Java's population probably grew at around 1 percent per year, and then at around 1.2 percent until the end of the 19th century, reaching 30 million in 1900. Although **Dutch** authorities and many later researchers attributed this growth to Malthusian factors such as increased **health** care and the absence of war, economic changes seem also to have been important, specifically the expansion of **rice** cultivation and the improvement of rice technology, together with the opening of employment opportunities on commercial estates. Paul Alexander has argued that the heavy **labor** demands made on **women** under the **Cultivation System** reduced the period of breastfeeding and thus also the period of postpartum infertility. From 1900 population grew at an average of 1.4 percent per year (though there was probably little growth in the 1940s). From 1961 to 1971, the rate was about 2 percent. Until 1900 most of the other islands, except **Bali**, were relatively sparsely populated, but population has grown dramatically in North **Sumatra**, **Lampung**, South **Sulawesi**, and **Minahasa**, especially as a result of immigration, **transmigration**, and the shift to intensive **agriculture**.

Until about the end of the 18th century, population was a valuable political resource for rulers and there was no question of population control as policy, though women were able to space children by prolonging breastfeeding to 2–3 years and abortion by massage and herbs was apparently common. In the early 19th century, however, Raffles raised the prospect of overpopulation on Java, and since then the topic has seldom been off the political agenda. Transmigration was the first solution proposed, but from the 1970s more emphasis was put on **family planning**. Fertility rates declined in the period 1967–1985 from an average of 5.5 births per woman to an average of 3.3, due to the increased availability of contraceptives, awareness of the costs of educating children, and the availability of other consumption options. The total population of Indonesia grew from 147.5 million in 1980 to 206.3 million in 2000, but the rate of population increase declined from 1.97 percent in the 1980–1990 decade to 1.49 percent in the decade between 1990 and 2000. [0069, 0075, 0295, 0479, 1311–1324]

PORTS. Lying mostly outside the cyclonic zone, many Indonesian ports were traditionally little more than roadsteads, ships anchoring offshore to be loaded and unloaded by lighter vessels. Geographical location, the provision of naval protection, and the availability of supplies rather than the technical characteristics of the harbor itself were most important. The development of steam shipping and of larger draft vessels, however, led to the building of more elaborate facilities. A modern port for **Batavia** was constructed at Tanjung Priok in 1886–1887; Teluk Bayur, the port for **Padang**, was constructed at the end of the 19th century under the name Emmahaven to make **coal** embarkation from the Ombilin mine more efficient; **Surabaya** was turned from a roadstead into a port in 1917–1920; new wharves were installed in **Makassar** in 1918; and Belawan, the port for **Deli**, was opened in 1922. In 1954 port service facilities were transferred to Indonesian firms (*see* **NATIONALIZATION**). A major element in Indonesian port policy has been the desire to establish direct "gateways" to the rest of the world, bypassing **Singapore**. From early times, ports also formed the nuclei for the growth of **cities** and were much more important centers of urbanization than the inland settlements around the courts of Javanese rulers. *See also* BATAM; CORRUPTION; *PASISIR*; SHIPPING. [0460, 0464]

PORTUGUESE IN INDONESIA. The commercial reputation of **Melaka** led the Portuguese to establish a post there in 1509, as part of their Asia-wide string of **ports** and offices. Expelled by the sultan, they returned in 1511 under Alfonso de Albuquerque (c. 1459–1515) and after a prolonged struggle captured the city, going on to found settlements in **Ternate**, **Ambon**, **Timor**, and **Tidore**. Except for guns and clocks, Portuguese goods had little demand in Asia, and they concentrated on using their naval supremacy to tax intra-Asian **trade** (*see* **PIRACY**). Portuguese became a lingua franca in much of the archipelago, leaving many words in the local **languages**. High tariffs in Melaka, however, drove traders to **Aceh**, **Riau**, and ports on **Java**, diminishing Portuguese revenue and leading them into a series of military and diplomatic adventures especially on the eastern coast of **Sumatra**, where they fought and negotiated intermittently with Aceh, **Pedir**, and **Pasai**. Illegal trade by Portuguese officials, a lack of manpower, a lack of tact in dealing with local powers (which contributed to the rapid spread of **Islam**), and the growth of the power of the **Dutch** and **English East Indies Companies** contributed to their decline. After losing Melaka in 1641, they ceased to be a major power in the region, though they retained possessions in **Nusatenggara**. *See also* CATHOLICISM; EAST TIMOR. [0554–0555]

POSTAL SERVICE. Letters are, of course, a phenomenon nearly as ancient in the archipelago as **writing** and, as a means of communication between people, were not always encouraged by rulers. From 1636 to 1701, for instance, the **Dutch East Indies Company (VOC)** banned all private correspondence to protect its **trade** secrets. The first official post office was established by Governor-General G. W. van Imhoff, 12.5 cents being charged to send a letter to the Netherlands and 25 cents to receive one, though the "poor" were exempt from these charges. Postal services were initially the responsibility of **police** officials, but from 1789 they were farmed out to private contractors (*see* ***PACHT***), rates being fixed by the company. Postmarks were used to indicate the amount to be paid by the addressee. **Herman Willem Daendels** restored state control of the system and recruited forced **labor** to construct a 1,000-km post **road** along the northern coast of **Java** from Anyer to Panarukan. Lodgings and horse stations were provided every 15 km, and the road was maintained by compulsory labor services from the local population. A commission for roads and posts was installed in 1808 to ensure regular services. Regulations in 1862 provided for the first postage stamps for prepayment (issued 1864) and formally made the postal service a government monopoly, though the mail contract to the **Outer Islands** was always let out to private tender. *See also* SHIPPING; TELEGRAPH. [0462]

PRABOWO SUBIANTO (1952–). Son of **Sumitro Djojohadikusumo**, Prabowo spent his early years in England and Switzerland during his father's **exile**. When his family returned from Europe in 1967, he entered the military academy. He joined the special forces (**Komando Pasukan Khusus [Kopassus]**) in 1974 and spent 10 years in **East Timor** and was believed to have been in charge of the campaign of intimidation against **students** and demonstrators there in 1991. He attended training courses in the **United States** and in 1995 was appointed commander of Kopassus, a post he held until March 1998, during which time he doubled the number of its troops. A favorite with Americans because of his English and smooth manners, he married one of **Suharto**'s daughters, Siti Hediyati Harijadi. In May 1998 at the age of 46 he was the army's youngest three-star general and the head of Army Strategic Reserves (**Kostrad**). He was in charge of the security forces that fired on the students at Trisakti University on 12 May, killing several of them. Prabowo had developed a reputation for treating his troops brutally and was known for his outspoken anti-**Chinese** and anti-Semitic rhetoric. In the closing days of Suharto's rule, he was suspected of trying to engineer a takeover, inciting rioting so that his forces had the excuse for a crackdown. Removed by **Wiranto** on 21 May 1998 and assigned to the Staff College in **Bandung**, he was brought before a military tribunal charged with involvement in kidnappings and torture of political activists. He was dismissed from the military, and the tribunal recommended further investigation into his role in the mid-May riots. Prabowo left the country for extended travel abroad, spending most of his time in Jordan, ostensibly looking after his family's business interests. Apparently he also visited Kupang, meeting with West Timor **militia** leaders, including Enrico Guterres, shortly before the murder of **United Nations** representatives there.

PRAMBANAN. Ninth-century **Hindu** temple in Central **Java**, dedicated to Durga, the consort of Siva. [0115]

PRAMOEDYA ANANTA TOER (1925–)**.** The son of a schoolteacher in Blora, in central **Java**, Pramoedya is Indonesia's greatest, best-known, and most controversial prose writer. During the **Japanese occupation** he worked in the *Domei* **news agency**, and after 1950 he became an editor at **Balai Pustaka**, the government publishing house, and editor of *Indonesia*, a leading cultural journal. His early writings, many of which were written while in a Dutch jail from 1947 to 1949, show a terse, personal style. A nationalist and humanist, he was harshly critical of the **Partai Komunis Indonesia (PKI)** because of its role in the **Madiun** Affair, but his viewpoint changed during the 1950s with disillusionment at the **corruption** and ineffectiveness of the postrevolutionary political situation. After being a member of the Gelanggang group in 1950 he became a major figure in the **Lembaga Kebudayaan Rakyat** (**Lekra**), arguing for popular commitment in literature and helping to formulate the doctrine of socialist realism as it applied to Indonesia in the 1960s. In 1965 he was detained and later sent to the penal island of **Buru**, where he wrote his major quartet of historical novels based on the emergence of Indonesian national consciousness in the early 20th century. These have all been translated and published in English as *This Earth of Mankind*, *Child of All Nations*, *Footsteps,* and *House of Glass*.

Pramoedya was not released until late 1979 and was kept under city arrest, barred from traveling outside **Jakarta**, until 1998. The awarding of the Ramon Magsaysay Award to Pramoedya in 1995 raised a storm of protest among his ideological enemies from the 1960s, notably **Mochtar Lubis**, and the government forbade him from going to Manila to receive the prize. His books were banned throughout the **Suharto** era, and remained technically so even after Suharto's fall. Still controversial, Pramoedya himself remained bitter, refusing to accept an apology offered by President **Abudurrachman Wahid** in 2000. *See also* CULTURE, DEBATE ON THE ROLE OF. [0221, 0227, 0234, 0250–0257]

PREHISTORY. The prehistory of the archipelago is relatively little known. Remains of the hominids *Pithecanthropus modjokertoensis* and *Meganthropus palaeojavanicus* have been found in volcanic deposits on **Java** dated to 1.9 million years ago, while **Java Man** (*Homo [Pithecanthropus] erectus* and *Pithecanthropus soloensis*) lived in Central Java 1 million or more years ago. The earliest known *Homo sapiens* is Wajak Man, who lived in East Java about 40,000 years ago (though similar remains in Sarawak date from 50,000 years ago), while other *H. sapiens* remains from eastern Indonesia seem to date from about 30,000 years before present. Wajak Man was probably an Austromelanesian (Australoid) close to the ancestors of today's Australian Aborigines, but whether *H. erectus* and the rest were the ancestors of Wajak Man is uncertain—some authorities believe the Austromelanesians migrated from the Asian mainland between 50,000 and 100,000 years ago. They appear to have occupied most of what is now Indonesia and **Australia**, but were divided 15,000 to 8,000 years ago by a 130-meter rise in sea level, which created the Indonesian archipelago and made contact with Australia vastly more difficult. It was not until 4000–2000 B.C. that the Austronesian ancestors of the modern inhabitants of western Indonesia reached the archipelago. *See also* CONTINENTAL DRIFT; MIGRATIONS; SUNDA SHELF.

PRESIDENT, OFFICE OF THE. Under Indonesia's 1945 **Constitution**, the president is the head of state and of executive government and is the-supreme commander of the **armed forces**. She or he must be ***asli*** Indonesian, more than 40 years old, believe in God, and not have been involved in subversive activities. She or he is officially mandatory of the **Majelis Permusyawaratan Rakyat (MPR)** for the execution of government policy during a five-year term, though the MPR-S conferred on **Sukarno** the title president-for-life in 1963 and revoked it in 1966. Presidents report to the newly elected MPR at the end of their term in office, and there is commonly no procedure to hold them accountable to the MPR. For the first nearly 60 years of independence, the MPR elected the president, but in 2002 it passed a measure that, beginning in 2004, the president would be directly elected by the people. The successful candidate would need to win more than 50 percent of the votes cast, and if this were not achieved on the first ballot, there would be a second round. The president can be dismissed by the MPR at any time, as happened to Sukarno, and can also be impeached, as was **Abdurrachman Wahid** in 2001. The president appoints and dismisses ministers and cooperates with the **Dewan Perwakilan Rakyat (DPR)** in the passing of legislation and the state budget, though she or he can also make extensive use of presidential decrees (Keputusan Presiden, Keppres) and government regulations (Peraturan Pemerintah, PP), which do not require legislative ratification. *See also* VICE PRESIDENT. [1100]

PRIANGAN (Dutch, Preanger)**.** A mountainous region in southern and central West **Java**, extending roughly from Sukabumi to Tasikmalaya. The heartland of the **Sundanese**, it was the first extensive region on **Java** to fall under **Dutch** rule (in 1677) and was governed through local rulers (*regenten*) in a form of indirect rule. Under the "Preanger-Stelsel" (Priangan system), the Dutch obliged these rulers to supervise the forced cultivation of **coffee**, **pepper**, and **tea**. [0358, 0561]

PRIBUMI ("indigene")**.** Often abbreviated to "Pri" and distinguished from "Nonpri," it is ostensibly a racial distinction between broadly Malay and Melanesian ethnic groups long settled in the archipelago and more recently arrived minorities (e.g., **Chinese** and **Arabs**), but is most commonly used to distinguish unassimilated Chinese (nonpri) from others. *See also* ALI-BABA FIRMS.

PRIYAYI*.** The traditional, largely hereditary, bureaucratic aristocracy of **Java**. Although access to the *priyayi* might be by descent, political position, or both, the defining feature of the class was its culture, which stressed the often pre-Islamic courtly arts of literature, **music**, drama, and philosophy, as well as justice and integrity in government (*see* **GAMELAN**; ***KEBATINAN; ***WAYANG***). A (male) *priyayi* was expected to possess, it is said, a wife, a house, a **horse**, a **kris**, and a singing bird, representing social stability, military prowess, and aesthetic sensibility. A wide range of aphorisms, many still in use, urged these values on the *priyayi*. *Tut wuri handayani*, for instance, the motto of the Department of Education and Culture, means "helping unobtrusively from behind."

Although these values were ostensibly traditional, they were encouraged among the *priyayi* by the **Dutch**, especially during the 19th century, as a means of increasing the dignity and prestige of the traditional authorities and so facilitating the system of indirect rule (*see* ***BUPATI***; ***INLANDSCH BESTUUR***). This tended to widen the apparent gap between Javanese village culture (*see* ***ABANGAN***; ***DESA***) and that of the courts. Especially after 1966, the **New Order** government has encouraged traditional *priyayi* values as a way of bolstering corporatism in the bureaucracy (*see* **KORPS PEGAWAI REPUBLIK INDONESIA**). *Priyayi* cultural forms, expressed especially in weddings, are now commonplace among village elites. *See also ALIRAN*; *PAMONG PRAJA*. [0485, 0572, 0636, 1244]

PROCLAMATION OF INDEPENDENCE (*Proklamasi*). *See* INDEPENDENCE, DECLARATION OF.

PROSTITUTION. Not easy to define or trace in precolonial Indonesia, prostitution must certainly have existed, especially in the **port** cities. Sexual relations seem to have been relatively easy, divorce was common, and quasi-contractual liaisons seem to have been frequent, especially between foreign traders and indigenous women (continued today as *kawin kontrak*) or by the purchase of **slave** women for sexual purposes. Prostitution began to grow in the 16th century, perhaps because Muslims disapproved of temporary marriage, but large-scale prostitution emerged only in the 19th century with the decline of concubinage among soldiers of the **Koninklijk Nederlands-Indisch Leger (KNIL)** and among European officials and with the increase in **labor** mobility, which saw large numbers of indigenous men leaving their families temporarily to seek employment in the **cities** and on plantations. During the 19th century, government concern over the spread of **syphilis** led to supervision of prostitution, without, however, any attempt to improve working conditions in the industry. From 1912 the **Sarekat Islam (SI)** campaigned against prostitution, and in the 1970s Islamic groups strongly objected when the **Jakarta** governor, **Ali Sadikin**, legalized prostitution in order both to improve conditions and to generate **tax** revenue. *See also* MARRIAGE, POLITICAL SIGNIFICANCE OF; WOMEN AND MEN. [0576, 1411, 1421]

PROTESTANTISM. Protestant missionary activity began in Indonesia in the 17th century, soon after the arrival of the **Dutch East Indies Company (VOC)**. From 1623 to 1633 a seminary existed in Leiden under company sponsorship for the training of missionaries, and by 1795 the indigenous Christian population of the archipelago was estimated at 70,000, much of it on **Java** and in **Maluku**. In 1820 the various Protestant churches were brought under government supervision through the Commissie tot de Zaken der Protestantse Kerken in Nederlandsch Oost- en West-Indië (Commission on the Affairs of the Protestant Churches in the Dutch East and West Indies), also known as the Haagse Commissie, which acted as a kind of embassy from the Dutch churches to the colonial government. In the mid-19th century, however, an independent Javanese Protestant community was founded in Central **Java** by Kiai Sadrach (1841–?). All official Protestant churches in the colony were united into a single, state-sponsored church, the "Indische Kerk," which was disestablished only on 1 August 1935.

English methodism and German pietism prompted another wave of European missionary activity from the late 18th century, especially by the Nederlandsch Zendelingsgenootschap (estabished 1797). By 1906, 30 missionary societies, including many of **German** origin, were members of the so-called Zendingsconsulaat (Mission consulate), which coordinated mission relations with the colonial government. Most missions were given their own area for proselytization, and all missions were excluded from certain areas (**Bali**, **Lombok**, **Sumbawa**, **Flores**, and large areas of **Sumatra** and **Kalimantan**). German Protestant missions were active in the Toba area of North Sumatra from 1861 and later on **Nias** and in southern Kalimantan. The indigenous Protestant churches conduct services in local languages and are thus administratively divided according to ethnic group, though most churches are represented in the Dewan Gereja Indonesia (DGI, Indonesian Council of Churches). Protestantism is strongest in the **Batak** area of Sumatra and in **Maluku** and **Minahasa**. *See also* CATHOLICISM. [0835, 1003, 1341, 1365]

PROTO-MALAYS. *See* MIGRATIONS.

PROVINCES. Although some steps toward **decentralization** were taken under Dutch rule, the establishment of a full set of provincial governments in Indonesia was not carried out until the abolition of the last federal states (*see* **FEDERALISM**) in 1950. Provinces have been the major subnational administrative division in modern Indonesia and provincial governors, as important agents of central rule, have always been appointed by the central government, except for a brief period from 1957 to 1959 when they were elected. Under the 1974 law on regional government, however, governors were appointed from a panel of candidates chosen by a partly elected provincial assembly, the Dewan Perwakilan Rakyat Daerah Tingkat I (Level I Regional People's Representative Council), with which they co-legislate on provincial matters. The formal title of governors is thus Gubernur/Kepala Daerah (governor/regional head).

On 18 August 1945 the Indonesian Republic divided the country into eight provinces: **Sumatra**, Borneo [*sic*], West **Java**, Central Java, East Java, **Sulawesi**, **Maluku**, and Sunda Kecil (Lesser Sundas or **Nusatenggara**). This structure was overtaken by the **Revolution** and the formation of the federal **Republik Indonesia Serikat (RIS)**, but was partly re-created in 1950 with the dissolution of the RIS and the establishment of provinces in West, Central, and East Java and North, Central, and South Sumatra; the division of Sumatra had been announced by the Republic in 1948 but never implemented. **Aceh** had been briefly separated from North Sumatra as a distinct province in 1949 but was reincorporated into it under the **Mohammad Natsir** government the following year. In 1950, too, **Yogyakarta** and the Pakualaman were separated from Central Java as the Daerah Istimewa Yogyakarta (DIY, Yogyakarta Special Territory). **Kalimantan**, which regained provincial status in 1953, was divided into West, South, and East provinces in 1957. As part of a settlement with the rebels there, Aceh became a province once more in 1956 and a *daerah istimewa* in 1959. In 1957 Maluku was restored as a province, while Central Sumatra was split into **Jambi**, **Riau**, and West Sumatra, with Jambi initially including Indrapura on the west coast. **Jakarta** was also declared a capital territory (Daerah Khusus Ibukota, DKI) in 1957. In 1958 the provinces of Bali, Nusatenggara Barat, and Nusatenggara Timor were established in the lesser Sundas, while Central Kalimantan was removed from South Kalimantan. (*See* **MAP 8**.) In 1960 provinces of North and South Sulawesi were formed; Central Sulawesi and Southeast Sulawesi separated from North and South respectively in 1964. **Lampung** separated from South Sumatra in 1964, and **Bengkulu** followed in 1967. Irian formally became a province with the "Act of Free Choice" in 1969. Timor Timur (**East Timor**) was annexed and constituted Indonesia's 27th province from 1976 until 1999, when it voted to break its ties with Jakarta. In 2002 East Timor completed the process of its independence from Indonesia.

The introduction of the decentralization laws in 1999 resulted in more regions wishing to establish themselves as provinces. That same year North Maluku split from Maluku; in 2000 Banten split from West Java, Bangka-Belitung split from South Sumatra, and Gorontalo split from North Sulawesi. Thus in 2002 there were 27 provinces:

Bali
Bangka-Belitung

Banten
Bengkulu
Gorontalo
Jambi
West, Central, and East Java (3)
West, South, Central, and East Kalimantan (4)
Lampung
Maluku and North Maluku (2)
West and East Nusatenggara (2)
Papua (whose name had been changed from Irian Jaya)
Riau
South, Central, Southeast, and North Sulawesi (4)
West, South, and North Sumatra (3)

There were also two special regions (Aceh and Yogyakarta) and one special district (Greater Jakarta). Proposals for further divisions included splitting the Riau Islands from the mainland of Riau province (which was enacted in 2003) and separating Flores, together with the nearby island of Lembata, from the province of East Nusatenggara. The government proposal to split Papua into three provinces was strongly condemned by the Papuan people but was formally enacted in August 2003 with the establishment of the provinces of Central and West Irian Jaya. *See* MAP 12. [0359, 0661, 0944, 0948, 0950]

PRRI/PERMESTA REBELLION (PRRI = Pemerintah Revolusioner Republik Indonesia, Revolutionary Government of the Republic of Indonesia; PERMESTA = Piagam Perjuangan Semesta Alam, Universal Struggle Charter). A regional, but not separatist, rebellion based primarily in the **Minangkabau** region of central **Sumatra** and the **Minahasa** region of northern **Sulawesi**, though it had adherents in other parts of Sumatra and Sulawesi and throughout Indonesia. Generally anticommunist, it was intended to establish a conservative national government in the face of Indonesia's swing toward **Guided Democracy**. The rebellion had three distinct roots: the political polarization of national politics in the late 1950s, in which a coalition of **Sukarno**, **Partai Nasional Indonesia (PNI)**, **Nahdlatul Ulama (NU)**, and **Partai Komunis Indonesia (PKI)**, all based on **Java**, grew increasingly powerful at the expense of **Masjumi** and the **Outer Islands**; the economic discrimination, whereby the regions outside Java saw most of their wealth and resources channeled to Java, particularly **Jakarta**; and the discontent of regional military commanders with attempts (especially by **A. H. Nasution**) to centralize the **army** and strengthen military discipline by transferring officers from their home bases.

The revolt began on 20 December 1956, when Ahmad Husein (1925–1998?), the local commander in West Sumatra, took over civil government, appointing a Banteng Council (Dewan Banteng) to administer the region. Other units followed suit in North and South Sumatra and later in **Kalimantan**, Sulawesi, and **Maluku**. On 2 March 1957, Lieutenant Colonel H. N. V. Sumual (1923–) unilaterally issued a document (Permesta) announcing martial law in eastern Indonesia (**Nusatenggara**, Sulawesi, and Maluku). Army councils (particularly on Sumatra) moved against **corruption**, arrested PKI members, and began to repair **roads** in an effort to win support, while demanding that a new government headed by **Mohammad Hatta** replace the crumbling **Ali Sastroamijoyo** cabinet. On 14 March 1957, however, Sukarno announced a "working cabinet" under **Juanda Kartawijaya**, and Nasution declared martial law throughout the country in an effort to undercut the local armies' support. Juanda moved to compromise with the rebels, but the situation became polarized after an assassination attempt against Sukarno in November 1957, which was blamed on **Zulkifli Lubis** and youths tied to the **Masjumi** party. Intimidation by Sukarno supporters led Masjumi leaders **Mohammad Natsir**, **Sjafruddin Prawiranegara**, and **Burhannudin Harahap** to flee to Sumatra. They were joined there, too, by **Sumitro Djojohadikusumo**, Zulkifli Lubis, and others. Many PRRI supporters hoped they could achieve their goals by reaching a compromise with the central government and without resort to rebellion, but on 10 February 1958 their leaders on both Sumatra and Sulawesi issued an ultimatum that Sukarno withdraw to a figurehead presidency, that Hatta form a cabinet, and that Nasution be dismissed. When this was rejected, they declared a new national government, the PRRI, on 15 February, with Sjafruddin as prime minister. Two days later, the Permesta rebels allied with the declaration.

The rebels received clandestine support from the **United States** principally in the form of arms and training. Malaya, **Singapore**, and the **Philippines** also provided them with bases and sanctuary. The government's military response was harsh, and after landings in March and April 1958 it occupied the major rebel strongholds on Sumatra. After subsequent attacks in Sulawesi, the major towns in both regions were largely under government control by August, and the PRRI/ Permesta soon found its power base limited to the rural areas of central Sumatra and the rich Minahasa region of North Sulawesi. Guerrilla warfare on a gradually decreasing scale continued for about three more years before the rebels finally conceded defeat in 1961. The rebellion enabled a far-reaching purge of the **armed forces** to take place and provided the Sukarno government with a basis for banning Masjumi and the **Partai Sosialis Indonesia (PSI)** in 1960 on the grounds that members of the parties had participated in the rebellion and their leadership had not condemned it. [0697, 0699, 0708, 0828, 1111, 1121]

PURBAKALA, DINAS. *See* ARCHEOLOGY.

PUSAT TENAGA RAKYAT (PUTERA, Center of the People's Power)**.** Japanese-sponsored mass organization on **Java** that succeeded the **Tiga A Movement** in March 1943, under the leadership of **Sukarno**, **Mohammad Hatta**, Ki Hajar Dewantoro (*see* **SUWARDI SURYANINGRAT**), and Mas Mansur (1896–1946). Its principal task was to increase public enthusiasm for the war effort and to drive out remnants of Western cultural and political influence, and its activity was limited to little more than **radio** broadcasts and other propaganda. It operated under strict Japanese control and was given only limited access to the countryside. It nonetheless gave massive public exposure to Sukarno and Hatta and reinforced their standing as national leaders. It was replaced in January 1944 by the Jawa **Hokokai**. *See also* JAPANESE OCCUPATION OF INDONESIA. [0644, 0657, 0661, 0663]

– R –

RAAD VAN INDIË (Council of the Indies)**.** Senior council for Indies affairs, generally with the task of advising the **governor-general** on matters of state. [0032, 0045, 0638]

RACE. In traditional societies, where the notion of genetic characteristics is absent, it is difficult to judge the extent of "racial" consciousness as opposed to a simple distinction between locals and outsiders. Evidence suggests, however, that just as the traditional societies of the archipelago were rather open to cultural influences from abroad, so they were relatively accepting of those who assimilated culturally to Indonesian ways of life, the most important "ethnic" marker being **religion**. In the trading **cities** of the coastal regions, in particular, there seems to be a long tradition of settlement and acculturation by other Asians, to the extent that it is difficult or impossible from available records to identify those who might by today's norms be called "Chinese," "Arab," or "Indian." On the other hand, expatriate communities in these **ports** have a long tradition of maintaining their distinct cultural identities.

The **Dutch East Indies Company (VOC)** also used religion at first as its main criterion of ethnicity, regarding Christian Indonesians, in some respects at least, as Europeans for legal purposes (*see* **LAW**). Although separate native courts were established in 1747, a formal legal distinction between Europeans and others did not come into effect until 1848, when the new commercial and civil codes and codes of civil and criminal procedure were declared applicable to Europeans only. Article 109 of the 1854 Regeeringsreglement (**constitution**) formally distinguished between *Europeanen*, who were thereby equalized to Dutch citizens in the Netherlands, and *Inlanders* (natives). While this distinction enabled some special protection to be given to Indonesians, for example, in the **Agrarian Law of 1870**, it generally permitted discrimination against indigenes in conditions of employment and the provision of services. The exact criteria for racial classification were not specified, but in general legitimate children followed the race of their father, illegitimate children that of their mother. Groups that did not fall clearly into either category were allocated to one or the other: Armenians, for instance, as Europeans; wives of Europeans (from 1896) as Europeans; and **Arabs** as natives. In 1885 **Chinese** were made subject to European commercial law in order to simplify their dealings with European business houses and a third category, foreign orientals (*vreemde oosterlingen*), gradually emerged, though it was not legally defined until the revised constitution of 1925 (Article 163). From 1899 Japanese were classified as Europeans, and they were joined by Turks in 1926 on the grounds that Turkey had adopted a European style of legal system.

Movement between legal categories was also possible by means of *gelijkstelling* ("alike-making"), under which a person of native or foreign oriental status could gain full legal European status if he could demonstrate that he was culturally assimilated to the European community or had special legal need for European status. In the late 19th century a campaign began in Dutch circles for the abolition of racial classification as a hindrance to social development, but this was blocked by a coalition of colonial conservatives and ***adat*** law specialists, who argued for the sanctity of traditional, ethnically based law; steps toward legal unification were abandoned in 1928. From 1910, with the introduction of limited

elections, a further legal distinction was made between Dutch citizens and Dutch subjects (*Nederlands onderdaan, niet Nederlander*). All formal racial distinctions were abolished by the Indonesian constitution of 1945 (but *see* ***ASLI***), though discimination against Indonesian citizens of foreign descent (*warganegara Indonesia keturunan asing*), especially Chinese, continues in a number of respects. *See also* INDO-EUROPEANS.

RADICALE CONCENTRATIE (Radical Concentration)**.** Coalition of progressive parties, Indonesian and non-Indonesian, formed in the **Volksraad** in November 1918 to press for movement toward responsible government in the colony, especially after the colonial government had rejected the recommendations of the Carpentier Alting Commission on constitutional reform. The coalition fell apart as the demands of Indonesian **nationalism** for full independence became stronger. [0661]

RADIO. The first radio station in the Netherlands Indies was established in Sabang in 1911 for naval communications; amateur broadcasts began soon after and the first commercial station, the Bataviase Radio Vereeniging, started broadcasting in 1925. The official Nederlandsch-Indische Radio Omroep Maatschappij (NIROM) began in 1934. The first indigenous radio station, Perikatan Perkumpulan Radio Ketimuran (Federation of Asian Radio Associations), was permitted in 1937 but could only broadcast on cultural and social affairs. During the **Japanese occupation**, radios were used widely for propaganda in the villages, and figures such as **Sukarno** received unprecedented national coverage as a result. A national station, Radio Republik Indonesia (RRI), was founded in August 1945. Like **television** and cassettes, broadcasts from this national station have provided the government with a powerful tool for projecting its message and spreading a national culture. Local stations have also proliferated and been active in promoting regional **music**, **languages**, and culture, but throughout the **Suharto** regime none of the hundreds of private radio stations were allowed to carry their own news broadcasts. After the fall of Suharto, requirements on broadcasters were eased and radio journalists were free to report critically. *See also* CENSORSHIP; MEDIA. [0154, 0622, 0761, 1300, 1301]

RAFFLES, THOMAS STAMFORD (1781–1826)**.** An official of the **English East India Company**, Raffles was appointed lieutenant-governor of **Java** in 1811 after **Britain**'s seizure of the island during the Napoleonic Wars (*see* **BATAVIAN REPUBLIC**). Hoping to persuade his superiors to retain control of the island, he attempted to restructure the Javanese **economy** to create a market for British manufactured goods, especially **cotton**, and attempted to break open the subsistence economy of the rural interior by abolishing the system of forced **labor** (except in **Priangan**) and requiring peasants to pay a **land rent** that would require them to earn money by bringing cash crops onto the market. He reduced the role of the traditional aristocracy on Java (*see* ***INLANDSCH BESTUUR***), abolished the sultanates of **Banten** and **Cirebon**, and captured the city of **Yogyakarta** in 1812, installing a new ruler there. Many of his reforms were based on ideas already in circulation among Dutch opponents of **Dutch East Indies Company (VOC)** policy, such as **Dirk van Hogendorp**. He made extensive studies of the natural history and culture of the island, publishing a *History of Java* (2 vols., 1817). In March 1816 he was removed from his post after accusations of **corruption**. In 1817, after Java was returned to the Dutch, Raffles was appointed British lieutenant-governor of **Bengkulu**. He founded **Singapore** in 1819. [0291, 0588, 0843]

RAILWAYS AND TRAMWAYS. Railways were constructed, mainly on **Java**, from 1873 by both the state railways (Staatsspoorwegen) and 11 private companies, of which the largest was the **Semarang-**based Nederlandsch-Indische Spoorwegen Maatschappij. Separate small systems also existed in South, West, and North **Sumatra** and in **Aceh**. State railways accounted for 1,870 miles of track in 1942, private lines for 531 miles. There were also many Decauville lines, which were usually two-foot gauge, serving mines, plantations, and industrial installations. Most traffic was short-haul: freight traveled an average of 62 miles, passengers under 19 miles. The rail system fell into decline after 1931, when little new investment was made and much rolling stock and some rails were removed by the **Japanese** during the occupation. Under the **New Order**, however, the **World Bank** provided aid for a national program of rehabilitation. *See also* ROADS; SHIPPING. [0060, 0465, 0622, 0977]

RAIS, AMIEN (1944–)**.** Born in Surakarta, Amien Rais studied at Gadjah Mada University and the Institut Agama Islam Negeri (IAIN, State Islamic Religious Institute) in **Yogyakarta**, before going to the **United States** in 1968 to continue his studies, gaining a Ph.D. from the University of Chicago in 1981, writing a thesis entitled "The Muslim Brotherhood in Egypt: Its Rise, Demise and Resurgence." He became a lecturer in political science at Gadjah Mada and general chairman of the **Muhammadiyah**. During the 1980s he developed a reputation for responding quickly to threats to **Islam** and was a strong critic of the "Christianization" of Indonesian society. Rais joined the **Ikatan Cendekiawan Muslim Indonesia (ICMI)** and became chairman of its Council of Experts. In 1997, however, he was publicly critical of the **Suharto** government, of the "nepotism" in that year's **elections**, and of the government's "collusion" with foreign investors in exploiting Indonesia's natural resources (*see* ***KOLUSI, KORUPSI, DAN NEPOTISME***). As a result, **B. J. Habibie** forced him from his position in ICMI. Nevertheless, he retained widespread support in Muhammadiyah, and after the installation of the People's Congress in October 1997 he expressed his willingness to stand as a presidential candidate against Suharto, proposing that a poll be conducted to determine the people's choice. In December, he publicly spoke out against Suharto's reelection.

Amien Rais was a prominent leader of the ***reformasi*** movement against Suharto in 1998, being sidelined, however, at the last moment when he canceled a scheduled May demonstration because of his fear of it sparking widespread violence. After Suharto's resignation, Rais left his post in Muhammadiyah to form a new **Partai Amanat Nasional (PAN)**, which he tried to make into a grouping that would appeal to Indonesians of different faiths and backgrounds. It gained only 7 percent of the vote and 13 parliamentary seats. Recognized, however, as second only to **Abdurrachman Wahid** as an Islamic leader, Rais was elected chairman of the **Majelis Permusyawaratan Rakyat (MPR)** in October 1999 with the backing of Wahid and **Golkar**, as well as some other Islamic factions. [0760, 1029, 1362]

RAMAYANA. Epic story derived from **India** and set down in Old Javanese as the *Ramayana Kakawin* by Yogaswari, probably in the 10th century. Reliefs depicting the story decorate the **Hindu** temples of **Prambanan** and Panataran in **Java** and many temples in **Bali**. The story is presented in ***wayang*** *kulit*, *wayang golek*, and *wayang wong*, though the celebrated moonlight performances at Prambanan are a recent innovation. As with the ***Mahabharata***, episodes from the *Ramayana* are often used as allegories of contemporary events.

In the story, Prince Rama, his wife Sita, and his brother Laksamana are exiled from their father's kingdom of Ayodhya. As they wander in the forest, Sita is kidnapped by the demon king, Rawana, who takes her to his palace in Alengka (Sri Lanka). With the help of a white monkey,

Hanuman, Rama discovers Sita's whereabouts and leads a monkey army to rescue her. Reunited, they return to Ayodhya and live, according to some versions, happily ever after. In other versions, however, Rama rejects Sita on suspicion that she may have been unfaithful to him during her captivity. *See also MAHABHARATA*. [0132, 0159]

RAMI (*Boehmeria nivea* Urticaceae)**.** Fiber plant, perhaps native to **Sulawesi**, it can be used to produce tough cord and extremely hard-wearing, coarse **cloth**. Attempts at commercial cultivation began in the early 19th century but were always hampered by the difficulty of separating the fiber from the other plant materials. When this is done by hand it is a labor-intensive process, but 454 rami processes and machines patented between 1873 and 1900 were unable to make the crop commercial. During World War II both Japan and the United States developed effective processing techniques, and the **Japanese** planted it extensively on **Java** as a substitute for jute from **India**. [0331, 0332]

RANIRI, NURUDDIN AL- (?–1666)**.** Gujerati Muslim scholar who arrived in **Aceh** in 1637 and was appalled by what he saw as the mystical heresies being followed at the court of Sultan Iskandar Thani, especially in the writings of **Hamzah Fansuri** and Syamsuddin of **Pasai**. After winning over Iskandar Thani, he began to persecute the followers of Hamzah and Syamsuddin and ordered their books to be burned. He himself, however, composed one of the classics of Malay literature, the *Bustan as-Salatin* (Garden of Kings), which covered the history of **Islam** as well as recent scientific knowledge. He lost favor under the rule of Iskandar Thani's widow and successor Taj al-Alam and returned to **India** in 1644.

RATTAN (Arecaceae, *rotan*)**.** Climbing rainforest palms of several genera harvested extensively for their strong pliant stems, and preferred to bamboo for pliability, durability, and appearance. Overcollection and the clearing of jungle have steadily reduced supplies and increased prices, but Indonesia still produces around 80 percent of the world's supply. In October 1986 export of unprocessed rattan was banned in order to encourage local processing; semiprocessed rattan was included in the ban in July 1988. [0342]

RATU ADIL. *See* JAVA WAR; JOYOBOYO.

REFORMASI. Reform movement spearheaded by **students** that began in late 1997 demanding a reform of Indonesia's political and economic structures. It escalated in 1998 to calls for President **Suharto**'s resignation and for an open and democratic **election** to select his successor. After Suharto's fall, the term came to denote the struggle for a more democratic and inclusive Indonesia wherein ideals of accountability and transparency would replace the **corruption** and cronyism of the Suharto era. *See also KOLUSI, KORUPSI, DAN NEPOTISME (KKN).*

REGENTS. *See BUPATI.*

RELIGION AND POLITICS. The division between religion and state now common in the West is of relatively recent origin and has little meaning for most of Indonesian history. While it is true to say that rulers and religious leaders have used religion for political ends and have used politics for religious ends, the distinction is not really valid in societies where every aspect of social organization and behavior was in some respect a matter for religious concern. Religions were inevitably closely associated with the political order and with challenges to it. All the major religions of Indonesia, however, recognize at least some division of responsibility between religious and secular authorities, and the sharpening or blurring of this distinction was often driven by political motives. Traditional rulers found that successively **Hinduism**, **Buddhism**, **Islam**, and **Christianity** could be used as buttresses to their rule, either as a means of acquiring allies or to reinforce the loyalty of their subjects. Under the **Dutch East Indies Company (VOC)**, Dutch Reformed **Protestantism** was the established religion and in **Minahasa**, for instance, people previously converted to **Catholicism** were arbitrarily declared to be Protestant when the region came under **Dutch** rule. Freedom of religion was granted in 1818, after the fall of the company, except where it disturbed public order.

Islam, strongly offended by *kafir* (infidel) rule and with its strong emphasis on the community of Muslims, became an important focus for revolt both against traditional rulers (*see* **ACEH**; **MINANGKABAU**) and against the Dutch (*see* **JAVA WAR**). In the late 19th century, after failing to suppress Islamic radicalism, the colonial authorities adopted suggestions of Christian **Snouck Hurgronje** to "domesticate" Islam and undermine much of its political thrust by supporting religious practice, particularly in the area of **law**. A network of government religious officials (*penghulu*) was established to administer Islamic family and property law. In the early years of the nationalist movement, Islam became a vehicle for opposition to the commercial position of the **Chinese** (*see* **SAREKAT ISLAM**).

Independent Indonesia did not become an **Islamic state**. Nor, however, is it wholly secular: not only does the state ideology, **Pancasila**, set down "belief in God" as a basic principle of the state but religious affairs are also administered by a Department of Religion, founded on 3 January 1946, which was for many years the largest government department. The department was at first entirely Muslim and its primary goal was the promotion of Islam but, especially after January 1965 when the official definition of religion was broadened to recognize Hinduism, Buddhism, and **Confucianism** as well as Islam and Christianity as official religions, its political agenda became the promotion of religion (*agama*) in general (though Islam still took a major part of its budget and energies). After 1966, under the **New Order** regime, the promotion of religion had the added purpose of "immunizing" people against communism, and only a tiny proportion of the population was classed as *belum beragama* (not yet having a religion), though this was achieved partly by allowing animist peoples such as the **Dayak** and **Toraja** to have their beliefs classified as Hindu. In 1969 President **Suharto** confirmed the legal right of people to change religions, and in the 1960s and early 1970s there was substantial conversion from Islam to Christianity and Hinduism in parts of **Java**. In 1978, however, the Department of Religion issued regulations forbidding proselytization among followers of recognized religions and limiting the extent to which local religious organizations could receive support from abroad.

Through his policies regarding **political parties**, Suharto attempted to depoliticize religion, culminating in 1982 with his emasculation of the religious parties through his decree that the Pancasila was to be the sole foundation of all parties and organizations. Removal of religion from the country's political life was reinforced by **SARA**, whereby religion, as well as other potentially contentious issues, was excluded from public debate. But after repressing Islam, particularly its political expression, up to the mid-1980s, Suharto then began to encourage its freedom of action as evidenced in such measures as his promotion of **Ikatan Cendekiawan Muslim Indonesia (ICMI)** in 1990, his expansion of the authority of Muslim courts, his support of an Islamic bank, and his personal demonstration of piety by undertaking the ***haj*** pilgrimage in 1991.

In the aftermath of Suharto's fall, around 20 new political parties based on Islam qualified to contest the 1999 elections and they garnered just about 38 percent of the vote. At the same time religious tensions, particularly in Eastern Indonesia, led to widespread violence between Muslims and Christians. The government, whether under former **Nahdlatul Ulama (NU)** head **Abdurrachman Wahid** or his successor **Megawati Sukarnoputri**, still committed itself to the principle of a Pancasila state, though **Aceh** and some other majority Muslim provinces introduced measures to institute **Islamic law** (*syariah*) on a regional basis.

There are no current reliable numbers of the breakdown of religious groups in Indonesia, but in 1982 the official percentages of religious adherence were

Muslim	88.0 percent
Protestant	5.8 percent
Catholic	2.9 percent
Hindu	2.0 percent
Buddhist	0.9 percent

However, an alternative unofficial estimate gave the figures Muslim 77 percent, Protestant 11 percent, Catholicism 4 percent, Hinduism 3 percent, Buddhism and Confucianism 0.4 percent, and ***Kebatinan*** 17 percent (*Kebatinan* had some overlap with other categories). [0983, 1016–1040, 1274]

RENCANA PEMBANGUNAN LIMA TAHUN (Repelita, Five-Year Development Plan). Official title of successive economic plans under the **New Order**. Repelita I ran from 1969 to 1974 and stressed rehabilitation of the **economy** after the **Guided Economy** of **Sukarno** and increased **rice** production and the improvement of infrastructure; Repelita II (1974–1978) stressed raising living standards by increasing availability of food, clothing, housing, and so on; Repelita III (1978–1984) aimed to expand employment by extensive public sector investment and to promote more equitable distribution of income (though it was vague on the latter point) and its aims, dependent on heavy capital inflow, had to be curtailed sharply after the fall in **oil** prices; Repelita IV (1984–1989) stressed **agriculture** and **industry**; Repelita V (1989–1994) shifted its educational emphasis from primary to secondary **education**; and Repelita VI (1994–1999) established a target of universal education for children up to the lower secondary school level (i.e., nine years of schooling) and also aimed to reduce the numbers of people below the poverty line to 6 percent by 1999 and to zero by 2004. Although the initial inclinations of the New Order's economic policy makers in the **Badan Perencanaan Pembangunan Nasional (Bappenas)** were for economic liberalism, the unrestricted operation of market forces was neither politically acceptable nor economically desirable, and successive economic plans aimed especially at import-substitution industrialization, particularly in fertilizer, cement, and textiles, as well as at the improvement of infrastructure. [0295, 0313, 0718]

RENDRA, WILLIBRORDUS S. (1935–). Poet and dramatist. Admired initially for his lucid, straightforward use of language in poetry, Rendra became increasingly known for his drama, in which he attempted to adapt the techniques of Western experimental drama to Indonesian conditions and styles. His best known work is *The Struggle of the Naga Tribe* (1975). Throughout the late **New Order** period, he used his plays to give voice to the people's needs and to criticize the regime's attempts to silence their depiction and artistic expression in general. From the late 1970s, his plays were therefore frequently banned. *See also* CENSORSHIP; MALARI. [0258, 0761]

RENVILLE AGREEMENT. The agreement signed on 17–19 January 1948 aboard the USS *Renville*, anchored in **Jakarta** Bay, between representatives of the Indonesian Republic and the Netherlands Indies and providing, like the **Linggajati Agreement**, for a peaceful end to the Indonesian-**Dutch** conflict by merger of the Republican and Dutch territories into a federal republic. Whereas the Linggajati Agreement had limited the number of component states of this federation to three, *Renville* opened the possibility for people in Dutch-occupied territories to opt by plebiscite for separate *negara* (federal state) status (*see* **FEDERALISM**) or for inclusion into the Republic. On the basis of these states, but excluding the Republic of Indonesia, the Dutch proceeded to establish a Provisional Federal Government (Voorlopige Federale Regeering) in 1948. One key provision of Renville that was never implemented was the Dutch agreement to hold plebiscites to determine the people's preference between the Republic and the Dutch-sponsored state in areas their troops had occupied in the first **"Police Action."** In December 1948, Dutch forces launched a second "Police Action" to incorporate all Republican territory into the federation. [0478, 0661, 0674, 1117]

REPUBLIK INDONESIA SERIKAT (RIS, Republic of the United States of Indonesia, also RUSI). Formed on 27 December 1949 as a consequence of the **Round Table Conference**. The RIS was a member of the Netherlands Indonesian Union (*Unie*), along with the Kingdom of the **Netherlands**, and was guaranteed to consult the Netherlands on matters of common interest such as international **debt** and foreign **investment**. It was governed under a prime ministerial system with a bicameral legislature consisting of a popular assembly (**Dewan Perwakilan Rakyat**) and a Senate, with two representatives from each of the states (*negara*) and territories (*daerah*) making up the federation. The figurehead president of the federation, elected 16 December 1949, was **Sukarno**. In its fullest form, the federation consisted of seven *negara*—the Republik Indonesia, founded 17 August 1945; **Negara Indonesia Timur**, formed 24 December 1946, dissolved 17 August 1950; **Madura** (21 January 1948–9 March 1950); **Pasundan** (24 April 1948–9 February 1950); **Sumatra** Timur (25 December 1947/16 February 1948–17 August 1950, *see* **EAST SUMATRA**); Sumatra Selatan (18 December 1948–9 March 1950, *see* **PALEMBANG**); Jawa Timur (East Java; 26 November 1948–9 March 1950)—and nine other territories of varying statuses: Banjar, **Bangka**, Billiton (**Belitung**), **Riau**, and **Dayak** Besar, all called *neo-landschappen*, denoting that they had formerly been directly ruled territories; **Kalimantan** Barat, Kalimantan Timur, and Kalimantan Tenggara, all of the preceding federations of *landschappen*, or formerly *zelfbesturen*; and Jawa Tengah, **Padang** in West Sumatra, and Pulau Weh (Sabang) off **Aceh**, whose status was indefinite. All these entities were represented in the RIS Senate, but the RIS also included the capital territory of **Jakarta** and several other smaller unaffiliated territories. The Republik Indonesia, with borders as at the signing of the **Renville Agreement**, held one third of the seats in the federal parliament but in fact dominated the federation from the start, the remaining *negara* having, with two or three exceptions, little popular support or administrative strength. With the exception of the Republik Indonesia, the federal states were dissolved in the course of 1950, and the RIS was dissolved into the Republik Indonesia on 17 August 1950. *See also* FEDERALISM; SUCCESSION. [0661, 0674, 0679, 0695]

REPUBLIK MALUKU SELATAN (RMS, Republic of the South Moluccas)**.** Proclaimed on 25 April 1950 by Christian Ambonese, led by **Negara Indonesia Timur (NIT)** justice minister C. R. S. Soumokil, who were dissatisfied with the incorporation of the NIT into the **Republik Indonesia Serikat (RIS)**. Fighting took place on **Ambon** and **Buru** from July to November 1950 and continued on **Seram** until 1956, though Soumokil was not captured until 1963. Moluccan **exiles** in the **Netherlands** continued to campaign for the RMS, but their energy was diminished in the late 1980s by agreements permitting the exiles to return to

Indonesia without risk. During the violence in Ambon that followed the fall of **Suharto**, the remnant RMS organization in the Netherlands was allegedly sending financial aid to **Protestant** relatives in Maluku. Despite **army** claims that they had unearthed RMS weapons caches and training camps, however, it was unlikely that the RMS organization in Ambon had revived and was again seeking a separation from Indonesia. Nevertheless, there was growing disillusionment with **Jakarta** and some support for the earlier aims of the RMS. As many as 129 separatist supporters were arrested in April 2003 for actions connected with celebrating the 53rd anniversary of the declaration of the RMS. *See also* KONINKLIJK NEDERLANDSCH INDISCH LEGER. [0782, 0967]

RESIMEN PARA KOMANDO ANGKATAN DARAT (RPKAD, Army Para-Commando Regiment)**.** Formed in 1956 as part of the **army** command's effort to reduce the power of regional commanders by creating a mobile strike force under the direct authority of the center. Under Colonel Sarwo Edhie (1927–1989), the RPKAD played a major role in the **massacres of 1965–1966** in Central **Java**. Under the names Kopassandha (Komando Pasukan Sandi Yudha, Secret Warfare Unit Command) and **Kopassus (Komando Pasukan Khusus**, Special Unit Command), it later played a major role in the suppression of dissent in **Papua** and **East Timor** and in the so-called mysterious killings (*see* **PETRUS**) of 1982–1983. *See also* ARMY; PRABOWO SUBIANTO. [0714, 0727]

RETOOLING. *See* MANIFESTO POLITIK.

REVENUE FARMS. *See PACHT*.

REVOLUTION. The years 1945–1949 are commonly referred to as the "Revolution" (*Revolusi*), reflecting both the usage of the time and the perception that the violent change from colonial rule to independence was indeed revolutionary. Especially during **Guided Democracy**, **Sukarno** maintained that the Revolution had not been completed in 1949 with the formal transfer of sovereignty by the **Dutch** and that not only did the province of West Irian (*see* **PAPUA**) have to be recovered but Indonesia's social, political, and economic order also had to be transformed. Under the **New Order**, the rhetoric of continuing revolution was soon dropped and the period 1945–1949 came increasingly to be referred to as the war of independence (*perang kemerdekaan*), partly to emphasize the role of the **army** in securing independence, partly to avoid the suggestion that revolutions might be desirable events. [0643, 0661, 0674]

RHINOCEROS. Both the one-horned Javan rhinoceros (*Rhinoceros sondaicus*) and the two-horned Sumatran rhinoceros (*Dicerorhinus sumatrensis*), once common, have been hunted close to extinction. The Javan rhino is now restricted to **Ujung Kulon**, the Sumatran to small pockets in southern **Sumatra** and Burma. By 1998 it was believed that the number of Sumatran rhinoceros had declined to only about 250, and several zoos in **Britain** and the **United States** were returning rhinoceros to the island in the hopes of increasing the population. Most parts of the animal were used medicinally, bezoar stones being most highly prized. Poachers today usually take only the horn. Many **roads** on **Java** are said to follow ancient rhino tracks through dense jungle. [1154]

RIAU (Rhio)**.** Sultanate established on Bintan Island, south of **Singapore**, by Sultan Mahmud I of **Melaka** after the fall of his capital to the **Portuguese** in 1511. It controlled a fluctuating territory in the Riau archipelago, on the coast of **Sumatra** and on the **Malay Peninsula**, and derived its income as an entrepôt. The capital shifted frequently between the Riau archipelago and Johor on the peninsular mainland, and in 1641 the kingdom joined the **Dutch** in expelling the Portuguese from **Melaka**. After the assassination of Sultan Mahmud II (r. 1685–1699), Riau was riven by a prolonged civil war. The *bendahara* (chief minister) of the kingdom, Abdul Jalil Riayat Syah (?–1721), seized the throne and with the help of his able younger brother, Tun Mahmud, attempted to concentrate **trade** at Riau. He quickly faced rebellions in **Palembang** and Perak and among the **Bajau**, and he was eventually deposed in 1718 and later murdered (*see* **SIAK**). **Bugis** mercenaries then gained control of the hereditary office of *Yang di Pertuan Muda*, and they effectively dominated the state until it was occupied by the Dutch in 1784. The last independent ruler, Mahmud Riayat Syah III (r. 1761–1812), attempted to play off Bugis, Malay, Dutch, and British interests but was unable to end the internal chaos.

In 1819, **Britain** obtained the island of **Singapore** in the heart of the kingdom, and the **Anglo-Dutch Treaty** of 1824 definitively divided the former territory of Riau between the two colonial powers, depriving Raja Ali Haji Ibn Ahmad (1809?–1870?) of office. An accomplished writer, Raja Ali is best known for his *Tuhfat al-Nafis* (Gift of the Prophet), which he expanded from a shorter draft by his father, Raja Ahmad.

After independence Riau was incorporated into the **province** of Central Sumatra, but in 1957 it became a separate province embracing the contrasting ecological regions of mainland Riau (*Riau daratan*) and island Riau (*Riau kepulauan*). The majority of its inhabitants were classified as Malay, though there were large minorities of **Minangkabau**, Mandailing, Buginese, and Javanese. Under the centralizing policies of late **Guided Democracy** and the **New Order**, the people of Riau did not enjoy the fruits of their province's vast wealth, which provided more than half of Indonesia's **oil** production and possessed significant **gas** reserves as well as large tracts of **oil palm** and forest. Not only did almost all of the wealth from these resources flow to Jakarta, but the low **education** standards in the province also meant that the oil companies recruited their employees largely from **Java** and West Sumatra and not from the local people. It was estimated that at the turn of the 21st century, only 3 percent of Riau natives were college graduates.

Under the 1999 **decentralization** law the situation drastically changed, for the provincial and district governments were now to receive 15 percent of the oil revenues, 30 percent of the gas, and 80 percent of the **forestry** revenues. In 2001 their budgets multiplied sixfold and were expected to increase further with the expansion of oil production. In 2003 Riau was divided into two provinces, Mainland Riau and Island Riau. *See* MAP 12. [0502, 0550, 0774, 0785, 1386]

RICE (*Oryza sativa* Poaceae)**.** Wild rice occurs naturally in mainland Southeast Asia, and it was cultivated there perhaps as early as 6000 B.C. It appears, however, to have entered the archipelago much later, the earliest known cultivation being at Ulu Leang in **Sulawesi** around 3500 B.C., probably because the early varieties were highly sensitive to climatic change (*see* **MIGRATIONS**). It was probably a staple food of **Srivijaya** but does not appear on the reliefs of **Borobudur**, suggesting that other staples, perhaps including millet, were in use. Rice was certainly well established by the mid-13th century, but even as late as the 19th century it had not reached its current status of preferred food for most of the people of the archipelago. In the late 18th and early 19th century, the colonial government sponsored a major expansion of wet-rice **agriculture**, with the expansion of irrigation and the clearing of **land**, and in 1905 it began a sustained program to breed improved varieties. Increasing rice production was also a major aim of the **Japanese occupation** government in World War II.

It was initially hoped that production would increase with independence, and Java actually exported rice to **India** in 1946, but in the 1950s and 1960s production failed to keep pace with **population** growth and imports increased, despite the introduction of new varieties developed in the Philippines by the International Rice Research Institute. Promotion of rice production became a major program of the **New Order**, and self-sufficiency by 1973 was an aim of the first five-year plan (*see* **RENCANA PEMBANGUNAN LIMA TAHUN**). But outbreaks of **wereng** (brown plant hopper) pest appeared in the 1974–1975 season, devastating the rice crop, and by the late 1970s Indonesia was importing up to one third of the world's traded rice. Nevertheless, the introduction of high-yielding varieties, with their attendant shorter growing cycles and heavy application of fertilizers, herbicides, and pesticides, helped achieve a rapid increase in rice production after 1978. In November 1985 President **Suharto** announced that rice self-sufficiency had been achieved. Subsequently, however, rice production markedly slowed, with its output growing by only 2.5 percent per year between 1986 and 1995. The drought of 1991 led the government to suspend its prohibition on rice imports, and a further serious drought in 1997 forced it to begin again importing rice. After the fall of Suharto, rice production continued to decline, with figures for 2001 4.45 percent less than those for 2000, due mainly to a decline both in the area harvested and in productivity. The government estimated that production in 2002 would be 48.65 million tons, or a further decline of 1.89 percent. *See also* AGRICULTURAL INVOLUTION. [0055, 0295, 0296, 0319, 0331, 0332, 0333, 0341, 0345, 0346, 0353, 0730]

ROADS. These have naturally played a relatively small role in long-distance communication in the archipelago; even within islands, geographical barriers such as forests, mountains, and swamps tended to make waterborne communication far more important than overland links. The first road to run the length of **Java** was laid by **Herman Willem Daendels** in the early 19th century, and the colonial authorities began a trans-**Sumatra** road in the 20th century. Responsibility for roads was one of the tasks devolved to the **provinces** in 1931 (*see* **DECENTRALIZATION**), but by the end of the colonial era Indonesia was still relatively underprovided with asphalted roads.

Between 1939 and 1959 the length of asphalted roads decreased by about 20 percent due to lack of investment, while the number of vehicles on those roads doubled. Plans for the Trans-Sumatra Highway were revived in the early 1960s, but extensive road building did not resume until after 1966, when the **World Bank** assisted in a number of highway rehabilitation projects. The Trans-Sumatra and Trans-**Sulawesi** Highways were completed in the 1980s (though some sections need major upgrading), and highways across **Kalimantan** and **Papua** were constructed in the late **Suharto** period. The fact that Indonesia drives on the left-hand side of the road (unlike the **Dutch**) is attributed (perhaps apocryphally) to the English colonial official **Thomas Stamford Raffles**. *See also* RAILWAYS. [0060, 0357, 0367, 0372, 0977]

ROEM–VAN ROIJEN AGREEMENT. The result of negotiations begun on 14 April 1949 between J. H. van Roijen, chief of the Netherlands delegation, and Mohamad Roem, representing the imprisoned Republican government of **Sukarno** and **Mohammad Hatta**. The agreement, which was formally accepted by both sides on 7 May, provided for the Dutch to release political prisoners and for the Republican leaders to return to their capital in **Yogyakarta**. It was also agreed that a **Round Table Conference** would be held in which Republican representatives together with those of the Dutch-supported Federal Consultative Assembly (BFO) would negotiate with the Dutch for the transfer of sovereignty from the Netherlands to Indonesia. *See also* PEMERINTAH DARURAT REPUBLIK INDONESIA (PDRI); SUDIRMAN. [0661, 0674, 0686, 0807]

ROMUSHA (Japanese, "laborer"). Forced laborers drafted from October 1943 by the **Japanese occupation** authorities especially on **Java** for work on defense and other projects not only on Java and **Sumatra** but also in many parts of Southeast Asia. Perhaps 200,000–500,000 were taken to work in appalling conditions with high death rates. Only 70,000 are known to have survived, and many were left stranded in various parts of the region by the end of World War II. The social dislocation caused by the removal of *romusha* from Javanese society contributed both to the hatred of officials involved in recruiting and to the sense of crisis at the end of the war. Some regarded **Sukarno**'s role in recruiting as constituting a war crime. *See also* LABOR. [0646, 0649, 0653, 0663]

RONGGOWARSITO, RADEN NGABEI (1802–1873). Court poet of **Surakarta** and author of the *Paramayoga* and the *Pustakaraja Purwa*, which describe a mythical history of **Java** from the time of Adam to the year 730 A.J. (*see* **CALENDARS**). He is generally regarded as the last of the great Javanese court poets. [0217, 0578]

ROTI. Island near **Timor** whose people are noted especially for their extensive use of the **lontar** palm for food and manufacture. The **Dutch**

East Indies Company (VOC) signed a treaty with local rulers in 1662 in order to obtain a supply base and a possible refuge in its operations in the region. Extensive conversion to **Christianity** took place in the 18th century, and during the 19th century the **Dutch** encouraged Christian Rotinese to settle around Kupang on Timor to create a buffer zone against the Timorese. Rotinese also moved extensively into administrative posts. [0029, 1220]

ROUND TABLE CONFERENCE. Following the **Roem–van Roijen Agreement** of 7 May 1949 in which the **Dutch** and the Indonesian Republic agreed to work toward a settlement on the basis of the **Renville Agreement**, a Round Table Conference took place in The Hague from 23 August to 2 November 1949 to prepare a formal transfer of sovereignty to a fully independent Indonesia, draft a **constitution** for the new state, and prepare an agreement of Union between the new state and the **Netherlands**. The conference was attended by delegates of the Republik Indonesia; of the Bijeenkomst voor Federale Overleg (Federal Consultative Meeting), consisting of representatives of the various *negara* and *daerah* (*see* **FEDERALISM**); and of the Dutch, with a number of minority representatives attending as "advisors" to the Dutch delegation. In part because of pressure from the **United States**, the Indonesian delegation to the conference agreed to assume the entire internal **debt** of the colonial government (approximately US$1.3 billion) as well as $589 million of its external debt. The conference deferred agreement on the status of West New Guinea (West Irian, **Papua**), which remained temporarily under Dutch control. Sovereignty over the remainder of the archipelago was transferred from the Netherlands to the **Republik Indonesia Serikat** as a result of the conference. [0661, 0674, 1117]

RUBBER (*Hevea brasiliensis* Euphorbiaceae)**.** Of Brazilian origin, rubber was not cultivated in Indonesia until the 1880s, when plantation production began in **East Sumatra**. Production began to expand dramatically in the 20th century, and the plantations were joined by numerous smallholders, especially in central and southern **Sumatra**. Oversupply during the **Depression** led to an international production agreement that the colonial government implemented very much at the expense of smallholders, but the industry survived to become a major economic pillar for the Republic in Sumatra during the national **Revolution**. The cutting off of rubber by the **Japanese occupation** had led to the development of synthetic rubber in the **United States**, but this did not have a serious impact on rubber markets until 1960. In 1980 Indonesia signed a further international rubber agreement intended to stabilize prices. After the outbreak of **AIDS**, the rubber industry benefited considerably from the increased demand for rubber gloves and condoms. On 1 January 1989, Indonesia banned the export of some categories of raw rubber to promote domestic processing. Falling rubber prices at the turn of the century led **Thailand**, **Malaysia**, and Indonesia to form a Tripartite Rubber Corporation in 2002 in an effort to limit supply and so raise prices. Almost immediately, however, rubber prices began to rise, climbing in 2003 to a seven-year high, with the annual average price of 85¢ per lb on the Singapore commodity exchange in 2003, up from 47¢ in 2001. [0316, 0317, 0324, 0331, 0332, 0817, 1118, 1170]

RUKUN TETANGGA (lit., neighborhood basis or foundation)**.** Administrative division below the village level, formed initially during the **Japanese occupation** as *tonari-gumi* and reestablished in 1954, they are especially important for social control and the marshaling of popular participation in government projects. [0663]

RUMPHIUS (Georg Everhard Rumpf) (1628?–1702)**.** Born in **Germany**, he was recruited by the **Dutch East Indies Company (VOC)** and in 1653 posted to **Ambon**. He pioneered botanical investigation of the archipelago with his posthumously published *Herbarium Amboinense* (6 vols., 1741–1750), much of which he completed after he fell blind in 1670. He also devised for the Ambonese an improved method of processing **sago**. *See also* UPAS. [1189]

RUSSIAN FEDERATION, RELATIONS WITH. Over the 13 years following the visit of **Suharto** to the **Soviet Union** in September 1989, there were few direct ties between Indonesia and the new Russian Federation, and total **trade** between the two countries amounted only to approximately US$203 million. On 25 September 2002, however, the Indonesian foreign minister on an official visit to Moscow attended the first session of the Joint Commission of the Republic of Indonesia–Russian Federation, where efforts were initiated to strengthen bilateral ties between the two countries, particularly in the fields of **economy** and trade but also with respect to technology, agriculture, and security measures. The commission held a second session in Indonesia the following February, President **Megawati Sukarnoputri** paid a visit to Russia in April, and that same month a much-criticized deal was made for Indonesia to buy six Russian-made combat aircraft.

– S –

SABANG TO MERAUKE, FROM. The symbolic dimensions of the Indonesian Republic. Sabang is a port town on Pulo Weh off the northwestern tip of **Sumatra**, and Merauke is in the far southeastern corner of **Papua**. Used during the **Revolution** as a simple affirmation of national unity, the phrase later became an assertion especially of Indonesia's rejection of **Dutch** control of West New Guinea (Papua).

SABILILLAH ("Way of God"). Auxiliary wing of the **Hizbullah** during the **Revolution** but often forming frontline units in its own right. Many units joined the **Darul Islam** in 1948. [0648, 0663, 0693]

SADIKIN, ALI (1927–). Marine commander appointed by **Sukarno** as governor of **Jakarta** in April 1966. Sadikin's energetic rule transformed the face of the **city**: infrastructure such as highways was built, and commercial construction was encouraged. His ruthlessness toward those who stood in the way of a showcase city (***becak*** drivers, *kampung* dwellers, and the like) was somewhat balanced by his efforts to provide services such as public transport, electricity, and recreation of benefit to much of the **population**. His legalization of **prostitution** and use of lotteries as a source of city revenues—29 percent of total city revenue in 1968 (*see* **GAMBLING**)—aroused hostility in Islamic circles, but he retired in 1977, one of the most popular figures in the **New Order**. His association with the dissident groups who produced the **Petition of Fifty** was a major source of political concern to the **Suharto** government. *See also* LEGAL AID. [0585, 0733]

SAGO (*Metroxylon rumphii* and *M. sagu* and other palms, Arecaceae). Palm trees found widely in swamps, especially in eastern Indonesia, where flour prepared from the pith of the trunk is a staple food. Wild and domestic varieties are indistinguishable and sago was seldom an object of **trade**, being mainly consumed by its producers. Only in the early 19th century was sago briefly in commercial demand for use in sizing **cotton**, until it was displaced by maize starch. [0344]

SAILENDRA. A powerful family of **Buddhist** rulers who arose in Central **Java** in the mid-eighth century and adopted the title *maharaja* (*see* **INDIA, HISTORICAL LINKS WITH**). Their court became a major center of Buddhist scholarship, and they were responsible for the construction of **Borobudur**. Although they almost certainly ruled through a diffuse system of alliances and vassalages, they promoted a largely Indian doctrine of divine kingship. Through intermarriage, Sailendras also came to rule **Srivijaya** in the late ninth century after they had been displaced on Java.

SALEH, CHAERUL. *See* CHAERUL SALEH.

SALEH, RADEN (Raden Saleh Bustaman) (1814–1880). After showing interest in Western culture, especially painting, Raden Saleh was sponsored by Governor-General van der Capellan to study art in the Netherlands. He came under the influence of Delacroix and lived in Europe for 20 years, becoming royal painter at the **Dutch** court. On his return to **Java**, he was in some demand as a painter of landscapes and portraits. He is recognized as the first modern native painter in the Indies, and he influenced the "Beautiful Indies" school whose naturalistic landscapes and portraiture dominated modern Indonesian **art** in the first decades of the 20th century. [0159, 0202]

SALIM GROUP. Incorporated in 1968, the Salim group was successor to PT Waringin, a trading company that had been granted lucrative official licenses to export primary products. It was headed by **Liem Sioe Liong**, Djuhar Sutanto (Liem Oen Kian), **Suharto**'s cousin Sudwikatmono, and Ibrahim Risyad. Its major foreign partners were Datsun and Mazda. The crown jewel of the Salim group was Bank Central Asia, but this was taken over by the government after a multibillion-dollar bailout in 1998. In early 2002, when Indonesia was preparing to seize a majority stake in the bank, the Salim group tried to buy it back. Of growing importance in the Salim group's holdings was Indofood, the world's largest manufacturer of instant noodles, which became one of Indonesian's leading companies in 2002. *See also* BANKING. (0314, 0761)

SALT. As an essential for life, salt was manufactured from seawater from very early times along the coasts of Indonesia and from mineral sources in a few inland regions; in Grobogan in Central **Java**, salty mud **volcanoes** are tapped, while the **Dani** in **Papua** extract it by soaking palm and banana leaves in saltwater seeps, drying and burning them. The southern coastal regions of **Madura** and north coast of East Java, however, have long been the main areas of salt production, local rulers traditionally farming out ***pachten*** to **Chinese** businessmen. In 1813 **Thomas Stamford Raffles** established a government monopoly on salt production and sale, though the operation was still run through *pachten*. In 1904 the **trade** in salt was placed under a government production and selling agency, the Zout-Regie, whose operations were combined with those of the state **opium** monopoly. The salt monopoly was abolished in 1957, the state salt works becoming a formal **state enterprise** in 1960.

SAMA RASA SAMA RATA (lit., "same feeling, same level")**.** Term coined by Mas Marco Kartodikromo (?–1932) in 1918 to express the egalitarian element in nationalist thought. It was modern socialist in its inspiration but reflected traditional ideas of a "golden age" of justice and prosperity. *See also* JOYOBOYO. [0632]

SAMIN MOVEMENT. Peasant movement founded around 1890 by Surontiko Samin (?–1914) in the Blora area of Central **Java**. Saminists attracted **Dutch** attention by refusing to pay **taxes**, but their beliefs were broader, encompassing egalitarianism, individual ownership of **land**, and a "religion of Adam" that apparently predated **Hindu** and Muslim influence on Java (*see* ***ASLI***). Samin was exiled in 1907 but the movement survived until at least the 1960s. [0472, 0486]

SANDALWOOD (*Santalum album*, Santalaceae, *cendana*)**.** Small, parasitic evergreen tree, probably native to Indonesia, cultivated for its aromatic heartwood and root, which are most fragrant in trees growing in dry, rocky soils. Sandalwood occurs extensively from East **Java** to **Timor** and was exported to **China** and **India** for incense, medicines, perfumery, and cosmetics. [0339, 0527]

SANGIË (or Sangir) **ISLANDS.** *See* MINAHASA.

SANTRI. Term originally referring to a student of any religion (hence ***pesantren***) but now commonly used, after Clifford Geertz, for one of the broad sociocultural groupings or ***aliran*** of modern **Java**, that is, the so-called pious or orthodox Muslims, also called *putihan* or white ones, whose religion contains relatively fewer or no influences from the pre-Muslim traditions of Java. Like the expression "**Outer Islands**," the term is immensely useful for general discussion but has serious flaws when used for detailed analysis, largely because the term has been taken from Geertz's East Java context and applied to many different cases where Muslims of different degrees of orthodoxy face each other. *See also* ISLAM. [1340]

SARA (*Suku, Agama, Ras, Antar-golongan*, or ethnicity, religion, race, and intergroup relations)**.** Areas that under the **New Order** were to be avoided as topics of public discussion, especially in the field of politics, in order to limit the possibility of conflict among contending groups.

SAREKAT ISLAM (SI, Islamic Association)**.** Founded in 1909 as Sarekat Dagang Islam (SDI, Islamic Traders' Association) by Kyai Samanhudi (1868–?), a **batik** manufacturer and merchant from **Surakarta**, along with R. M. Tirtoadisuryo and Haji **Umar Said Tjokroaminoto**, both ***priyayi*** involved in the batik **trade**. The initial aim of the association was to combat **Chinese** penetration of the batik industry, and SDI sponsored **cooperatives** among indigenous traders and organized boycotts of the Chinese. On 10 September 1912 the SDI took the name Sarekat Islam and adopted a broader political program challenging the colonial government while continuing its promotion of cooperatives and publishing the nationalist **newspaper** *Oetoesan Hindia* (Indies Courier).

SI's expression of discontent with the colonial order won it wide popular support, and in 1919 it claimed a membership of 2,000,000, though its practical following was always far smaller. Its program, however, was confused. It aimed at the promotion of **Islam** and of commercial spirit among Indonesians, but it was also influenced by the anticapitalism of the **Indische Sociaal-Democratische Vereeniging (ISDV)**, many of whose members, including Semaun, also joined SI. At its first national congress in June 1916, SI promised cooperation with the colonial government for the good of the country, and in 1918 SI leaders accepted seats in the **Volksraad**, but already in 1917 the party had condemned "sinful" (i.e., exploitative and foreign) capitalism and in 1919 a secret branch within the SI, called the Afdeling B (Section B), was implicated in subversive activities in West **Java**. Arrests and surveillance by the colonial authorities followed, and much of SI's following fell away.

Although relatively conservative urban traders initially dominated SI, more radical Muslim *kyai* from the villages, together with members of the ISDV and later the **Partai Komunis Indonesia (PKI)**, had gradually gained more influence, sharpening the contrast between SI's Islamic and **Marxist** wings. At the **Surabaya** congress in October 1921, **Abdul Muis** and Haji Agus Salim (1884–1954) forced a break with the PKI by insisting that SI members could belong to no other party. PKI leaders left the central SI in 1922 and local branches divided into "Red" and "White" SI according to their allegiances, the Red branches later calling themselves Sarekat Rakyat (People's Unions) and affiliating with the PKI.

This infighting further damaged SI's support and by 1923, when Tjokroaminoto transformed the SI rump into the **Partai Sarekat Islam Indonesia**, it was only a minor political force. [0632, 0661]

SAREKAT RAKYAT. *See* SAREKAT ISLAM.

SASAKS. *See* LOMBOK.

SAVU (Sawu)**.** Small island in **Nusatenggara**. As on **Roti**, the **economy** was based on tapping **lontar** palms. The **Dutch** signed a treaty with local rulers in 1756. Savunese were extensively recruited by the **Dutch East Indies Company (VOC)** as soldiers, and Savunese **Christian** migrants formed much of the elite in **Sumba** and Dutch Timor in the 19th and 20th centuries. The island was devastated by **smallpox** in 1869. [1220]

SAWITO KARTOWIBOWO (1932–)**.** In 1976 Sawito prepared a series of documents, some of which were signed by such eminent figures as **Mohammad Hatta**, **Haji Abdul Malik bin Abdulkarim Amrullah (Hamka)**, Cardinal Darmojuwono, and T. B. Simatupang (1920–1990), criticizing alleged failures in national development under the **New Order** and calling on **Suharto** to resign and hand over power to Hatta. Though Sawito had no institutional base and no prospect of success, his challenge was unexpected and unwelcome. The affair was described as a "constitutional coup" by government spokesmen, and in 1978 Sawito was convicted of **subversion** and sentenced to eight years in jail. [0722]

SAYAP KIRI (Left Wing)**.** Semiformal coalition of left-wing parties, the **Partai Sosialis (PS)**, the **Partai Buruh Indonesia (PBI)**, and the **Partai Komunis Indonesia (PKI)**, formed in December 1946. The *Sayap Kiri* formed the basis of the **Sjahrir** and **Amir Sjarifuddin** cabinets and pursued a policy of negotiating with the **Dutch** while building up the Republic's **armed forces**. Under Sjarifuddin, special favor was given to semiregular forces such as the **Pemuda Sosialis Indonesia (Pesindo)**. In opposition from January 1948, the parties turned sharply against all negotiations and coalesced in February into the **Front Demokrasi Rakyat (FDR)**. [0661, 0674, 0865]

SCANDINAVIA, HISTORICAL LINKS WITH. The Danish East India Company traded to **Java** in the 17th century, maintaining posts at

Japara and **Banten**, and in the same period a great many Scandinavians served as officials and soldiers with the **Dutch East Indies Company (VOC)**. The great Swedish botanist Carl Linné (Linnaeus, 1701–1778) worked with Indies plants in Leiden in 1735–1737 and was the first to cultivate a banana tree to fruit in northern Europe. A number of his students, notably Pehr Osbeck (1725–1805), Carl Peter Thunberg (1743–1832), and Clas Fredrick Hornstedt, made important botanical collections on Java, in some cases with the cooperation of the Swedish East India Company. *See also* LANGE, M. J.

SCOUTING. The Nederlandsch-Indische Padvinders Vereeniging (Netherlands Indies Scouting Association) was formed in 1917 as a multiracial nonpolitical organization along the lines of Robert Baden-Powell's organization. Later, however, exclusively Indonesian scouting organizations, the Kepanduan Bangsa Indonesia and Persatuan Pandu **Islam**, were formed, especially on **Sumatra**, as an adjunct to the nationalist movement. Many political organizations had affiliated scouting groups, which numbered 76 by 1960. In 1961, **Sukarno** forced all scouting groups to merge into the Pramuka (Praja Muda Karana). In 1978 Pramuka had a membership of 7 million.

SEINENDAN. Semimilitary youth corps established by the **Japanese occupation** authorities on **Java** on 29 April 1943 to mobilize young men aged 14–25 for the war effort, especially in urban areas. Its duties included patrol and guard duties, and many Seinendan units later became the basis for ***badan perjuangan***. *See also* KEIBODAN. [0663, 0674]

SEMAR. One of the clowns (*punakawan*) of traditional Javanese ***wayang***. Foolish and ugly, he is also immensely wise and powerful, representing in some views the strength of the common people. Though he appears in the Indian-origin ***Mahabharata***, Semar appears to be an indigenous tradition and during the **New Order** was sometimes identified with President **Suharto**. *See also* SUPERSEMAR. [0132, 0159, 0736]

SEMARANG. Town and entrepôt in north-central **Java**, ceded by Susuhunan Amangkurat II (r. 1677–1703) to the **Dutch East Indies Company (VOC)** in 1678, an agreement confirmed in 1705. During their 1740 uprising, the **Chinese** besieged the VOC's headquarters at Semarang, supported by forces of Pakubuwana II. The VOC retook the town the following year, massacring the Chinese. During the second half of the 18th century and the first half of the 19th century, Semarang was the seat of the governor of Java's Northeast Coast, becoming economically the most important town in central Java and its major center for **trade**. In 1870 the Dutch dug a canal connecting it to the sea so that large trading ships could carry their goods directly to the town. In the late colonial period, as the headquarters of the **railway** and tram workers' union, it became an important center of the left wing of the **Sarekat Islam (SI)** under Semaun, with 20,000 members in 1917.

At the end of the **Japanese occupation** in October 1945, it was the site of bitter conflict between Japanese, Republicans, and **British** for control of the town, which left perhaps more than 2,000 Japanese and Indonesians dead. The Dutch occupied Semarang during their first **"Police Action"** of July 1947. [0484, 0632, 0643]

SENTRAL ORGANISASI BURUH SELURUH INDONESIA (SOBSI, All-Indonesia Federation of Labor Organizations). Founded in November 1946, it was for much of the **Revolution** the only such coordinating body for **labor unions**. Though never formally affiliated with the **Partai Komunis Indonesia (PKI)**, it was influenced by the party from its foundation and was a part of the broad communist front from 1950, when Nyono Prawiro became president. Although a federation of unions that included Sarbupri (plantation workers), SBG (sugar industry workers) and Sarbuksi (forest workers), it regarded members of its constituent unions as direct SOBSI members. It was estimated to control 50 to 60 percent of organized **labor**, but was shadowed in every field by noncommunist unions such as those affiliated with the **Sentral Organisasi Karyawan Seluruh Indonesia (SOKSI)**, which made the organization of strike activity difficult. SOBSI was banned in 1966. [0436, 0994]

SENTRAL ORGANISASI KARYAWAN SELURUH INDONESIA (SOKSI, All-Indonesia Federation of Employee Organizations). **Labor union** federation that grew out of the **Badan Kerja Sama** and worked as a rival to **Sentral Organisasi Buruh Seluruh Indonesia (SOBSI)**, especially on **army**-controlled plantations. By 1963 it had 146 member organizations, claimed 7.5 million members, and was one of the core organizations of **Golkar**. In 1973 it was absorbed into the **Federasi Buruh Seluruh Indonesia (FBSI)**. *See also* KARYAWAN. [0436, 0741]

SERAM (Ceram). Island in central **Maluku**. The original inhabitants, generally called Alfurs, were slash-and-burn agriculturalists, **sago** being a major source of food, but from the 17th century were drawn into limited **trade** with the **Dutch** and other Europeans. Coastal communities began to convert to **Christianity** and **Islam** in this period. The island was drawn into the Dutch sphere of influence by its proximity to **Ambon**, but until the 19th century Dutch involvement was limited to periodic **hongi** patrols. After independence, the jungles of Seram became a last refuge for guerrillas of the **Republik Maluku Selatan (RMS)**. [0025, 0607]

SERDANG. Sultanate in **East Sumatra**, purchased by the Dutch from **Siak** in 1884. [0818]

SETIABUDI. *See* INDISCHE PARTIJ.

SEX, POLITICAL SIGNIFICANCE OF. Until the arrival of **Islam**, sexual prowess was commonly an attribute of political power, both because rulers could seize or otherwise acquire sexual partners (*see* MARRIAGE, POLITICAL SIGNIFICANCE OF) and because local understanding of Tantric doctrines intimately linked intercourse with the release of energy. The *lingga,* or phallic monument, was an important token of rulership. Prolific sexual activity could be both a sign of abundant power and a wasteful dissipation of power, and the downfall of kingdoms was held to be associated with a rise in licentiousness. Islam and **Christianity** regarded sexual promiscuity as morally wrong, rather than a waste of energy, though the burden of chastity was placed more heavily on **women** than on men, encouraging the rise of professional **prostitution** on the one hand and varying degrees of seclusion of "respectable" women on the other.

Only in the 20th century, however, did sexual scandal in the contemporary sense emerge. Colonial society in **Batavia** was shaken by revelations of homosexuality in the 1930s, and during **Guided Democracy Sukarno**'s sexual activity was widely deplored by strict Christians and Muslims. Some Western observers argued that Sukarno was simply behaving as a pre-Muslim ruler and described the tall national monument (Monas) in central **Jakarta** as a *lingga*. False accusations of gross licentiousness among members of the left-wing women's organization **Gerakan Wanita Indonesia (Gerwani)** were used in 1965–1966 to help discredit the **Partai Komunis Indonesia (PKI)**, while under the **New Order** rumors of marital infidelity among members of the ruling elite were taken by some as a sign of moral exhaustion. *See also* PALAPA. [0576, 1427, 1430]

SHAHBANDAR. Senior official, often of foreign descent, in charge of **port** and **trade** affairs in traditional states of the archipelago. [0550]

"SHARED POVERTY." Term coined by American anthropologist Clifford Geertz to describe what he saw as social arrangements that discouraged the formation of capital and the development of commercial elites in Javanese villages by having the wealthy provide income-earning opportunities to the poor. According to Geertz (1963),

> Under the pressure of increasing numbers and limited resources, Javanese village society did not bifurcate, as did that of so many other "underdeveloped" nations, into a group of large landlords and a group of oppressed near serfs. Rather it maintained a comparatively high degree of social and economic homogeneity by dividing the economic pie into a steadily increasing number of minute pieces, a process to which I have referred elsewhere as "shared poverty." (p. 97)

A characteristic institution of shared poverty is the open harvest, in which all can participate and receive a part of what they gather.

Debate on shared poverty, which forms an integral part of Geertz's idea of **agricultural involution**, has focused on the extent and significance of social differentiation in rural **Java**. Extensive landholdings are absent, but there is a sharp contrast between landed peasants (especially village officials) and others (*see* **LAND**). The practices Geertz identifies as promoting shared poverty, moreover, seem to be under constant challenge by wealthier farmers attempting to increase their share of village wealth. *See also* CLASS ANALYSIS; *DESA*. [0328]

SHELL, ROYAL DUTCH. *See* "KONINKLIJKE"; OIL.

SHIPPING. From early times until the 17th century, there was a large indigenous shipping industry in the Indonesian archipelago. Vessels of up to 500 metric tons were built of **teak** and sailed the **trade** routes of the region. The term "junk," later used for **Chinese** vessels, derives from the Javanese *jong*. After the 17th century the size of locally built vessels, generally called *prau* (*perahu*), declined to 100 metric tons or less.

In 1825 a steam ship called the *van der Capellan* was built in **Surabaya** to provide a regular government-funded **postal service** from **Java** to other islands, but in 1864–1865 the mail contract was awarded to a private British-owned firm, the Netherlands Indies Steam Navigation Co. The NISN had a virtual monopoly of interisland shipping until

1890, when it lost the mail contract to the **Dutch**-owned **Koninklijk Paketvaart Maatschappij (KPM)**. With the opening of the Suez Canal in 1869, regular steamship services to the Netherlands were provided by the Stoomvaart Maatschappij Nederland from 1870.

In the 20th century, interisland shipping was dominated by the KPM, though there was some scope for small operators (the so-called mosquito fleet), to run feeder services to the major KPM lines. In 1935 the KPM founded the Celebes Kustvaart Maatschappij to meet competition from these feeder services. Under the 1936 Shipping Law, only **East Sumatra** was opened to foreign carriers and was serviced primarily by firms from **Singapore** and Penang.

Interisland shipping declined dramatically during World War II with **Japanese** requisition of ships and destruction of vessels by Allied submarines. From early 1947, the Dutch **navy** blockaded Republican regions to prevent the export of produce allegedly originating from Dutch-owned plantations. At independence, control of interisland shipping was a major item on the Republic's economic agenda, and plans were laid for a state shipping enterprise that would exclude the KPM. The Central Shipowning Authority (Pemilikan Pusat Kapal-Kapal, Pepuska) was formed on 6 September 1950 to take over government-owned feeder services and to purchase vessels for lease to indigenous competitors of the KPM (*see* **INDONESIANIZATION**). On 28 April 1952, Pelayaran Nasional Indonesia (Pelni, Indonesian National Shipping) took over the assets of Pepuska and soon began to run vessels in direct competition with the KPM. By 1956, Pelni carried about 25 percent of total interisland tonnage, though an important part of this was government cargoes.

The seizure of KPM assets on 3 December 1957, officially ratified on 10 December, removed important competition for Pelni, but commercial shipping declined on the whole during **Guided Democracy** as plantation production diminished, infrastructure deteriorated, and trading operations came increasingly into the hands of **military business operations**. By March 1963, one third of the commercial interisland fleet was said to be in the hands of the **armed forces**, both for military purposes and for the military trading operations. Rehabilitation of interisland shipping, especially of **ports**, was a priority in the **New Order**'s first Five-Year Development Plan (*see* **RENCANA PEMBANGUNAN LIMA TAHUN**). In 1984 the government banned ship purchases from abroad in order to encourage local shipbuilding; the local industry, however, was unable to meet the demand and the ban was partially lifted in 1988. In 1996 the government allowed 1,000 boats to be imported over four years, but the terms for buying or leasing these boats were so onerous (including the need to be already operating three other vessels) that few people were able to take advantage of the import relaxation. [0076, 0463, 0464, 0615]

SIAK (Siak Sri Indrapura)**.** Not to be confused with **Indrapura**, this dynasty in **Sumatra** was founded in 1718 by Raja Kecil (or Kecik), a **Minangkabau** who revolted against Sultan Abdul Jalil Riayat Syah of **Riau** and established a polity on Sumatra's east coast, independent of Johor. In the 18th century Siak became a powerful regional state, controlling the sultanates of **Deli**, **Langkat**, and **Serdang**. Control over timber allowed the Siak elite to gain benefits from their trading partners in **Melaka** or Penang and to persuade the Dutch to allow them direct access to the **rice** and **salt trade** from **Java** without compensating the **Dutch East Indies Company (VOC)**. The Dutch signed a political contract with the sultan in 1858, on the strength of which they seized control of these northern dependencies. The last sultan, Ismail, was forced to abdicate in 1864. [0441, 0778]

SIAM, HISTORICAL LINKS WITH. Extensive trading contact between Siam and Indonesia began in the 13th century with the export of Thai ceramics, and for the next four centuries Siam was part of the general trading world of the archipelago, exporting **rice**, **tin**, **iron**, **sugar**, and **cloth**. In the 17th century, the kingdom of Ayudhya extended its influence far down the **Malay Peninsula** and onto the east coast of **Sumatra**, establishing a tributary relationship with some local kingdoms that was expressed in the sending of a *bunga mas*, or golden flower, to the Thai ruler. *See also* SOUTH EAST ASIA LEAGUE; THAILAND.

SILIWANGI. Reputed first king of **Pajajaran**, his name was later applied to the West **Java** division of the Indonesian **army**, formed in May 1946. Shaped by its first commander, **A. H. Nasution**, the Siliwangi was the most Westernized and conventional division of the army during the **Revolution**. It was unable to prevent the Dutch from overrunning much of West Java in the first **"Police Action"** in 1947, and after the signing of the **Renville Agreement** 22,000 Siliwangi troops were ordered to retreat from guerrilla strongholds in West Java to Republican Central Java. There, they became a major pillar of the **Mohammad Hatta** government and took part in the suppression of the **Madiun** Affair, with many of their officers being sent to head units in other parts of Republican territory.

SILK. Produced in **Wajo'** in South **Sulawesi** and northern **Sumatra** (*see* **PASAI**) from perhaps the 13th century, silk was for a time exported to **India**. Production declined, however, in the 17th century with the growing export of fine silk from **China**. The **Dutch** attempted to establish the cultivation of silk on **Java** after 1700, but without success. In 1934, **Japanese** entrepreneurs established a small industry in **Minahasa**, exporting cocoons to **Japan** for processing. After the 1960s, production was revived in Soppeng (South **Sulawesi**). [0045]

SINGAPORE. Port city on an island at the southern tip of the **Malay Peninsula**, part of the kingdom of **Riau** until the 19th century. In 1819 **Thomas Stamford Raffles** founded a British settlement there. Exempt from customs duties (state revenues came largely from a lucrative **opium** monopoly) and protected from **piracy** by the British navy, Singapore grew rapidly as a major **trade** center for the archipelago, facing little competition from the **Dutch**, whose attentions were focused on **Java** and the **Cultivation System**. From the 1880s the Dutch, concerned over the concentration of trade on Singapore, introduced a variety of measures (e.g., preferential tariffs) to encourage direct shipments to Europe. Singapore's influence was reduced, though it remained, along with Penang, the principal port for **Sumatra**.

From 1921, the British naval base in Singapore became a central element in Dutch **defense policy** in the Indies, and the fall of Singapore to **Japanese** forces in February 1942 made the loss of the Netherlands Indies inevitable. During the Indonesian **Revolution**, trade in plantation products and opium to Singapore was a major source of finance for the Republic, especially on Sumatra. From 1950, however, Indonesian governments sought once more to direct trade away from Singapore.

From 1989 Singapore began to promote economic relationships with regions of Indonesia, particularly **Batam** and Bintan Islands, but also parts of Sumatra and **Sulawesi**. Through these so-called **growth triangles**, local governments in Indonesia provided manpower and facilities while private companies in Singapore put up capital for establishing labor-intensive industries in these regions. Batam and Bintan provided Singapore with cheap **land** and **labor** and the opportunity to develop a manufacturing hinterland. Singapore also invested widely in Indonesia's telecommunications industry, purchasing shares in the phone company Indosat (Indonesia satellite) in December 2002. *See also* SHIPPING.

SINGASARI. Kingdom in eastern **Java** founded in 1222 by **Ken Angrok**. It marked the end of the division of Java that followed the rule of **Airlangga** and the start of a period of rich cultural development on Java, especially the closer blending of **Hindu-Buddhism** and local folk religion. The last ruler of Singasari, Kertanegara (r. 1268–1292), annexed **Bali** and **Madura** and sought to expand his rule to parts of **Kalimantan** and **Sumatra** (*see* **JAMBI**). After envoys from Kublai Khan demanded that Singasari accept closer **Chinese** suzerainty, Kertanegara expelled them from the kingdom in 1289. In 1292, while the Singasari army was on its way to Sumatra on a military expedition, Kertanegara was deposed and killed by prince Jayakatwang of **Kediri**. *See also* CHINA, HISTORICAL LINKS WITH; MAJAPAHIT.

SISINGAMANGARAJA. A line of **Batak** holy kings originating probably in the 16th century. The first of these was revered as a reincarnation of Batara Guru, the Batak high god. Usually defined as priest kings, their special importance lay in maintaining stable relations between the Batak and outside worlds, expressed in terms of symbolic vassalship to **Aceh**. In 1825, however, Muslim **Minangkabau** overran southern Tapanuli, and Sisingamangaraja X emerged as a leader of the armed resistance, though he was killed in the struggle. As **Dutch** power in the region grew, along with Christian missionary activity, Sisingamangaraja XI and XII became foci of anticolonial resistance. Sisingamangaraja XII led a revolt against the Europeans in 1878 but was defeated and killed in 1883.

SJAFRUDDIN PRAWIRANEGARA (1911–1989)**.** After studying law in **Jakarta**, Sjafruddin worked in the colonial, **Japanese**, and Republican departments of finance and for a time as Republican finance minister. He was a prominent member of the modernist wing of the **Masjumi** and in December 1948, after the Second **"Police Action,"** he became prime minister of the Emergency Government of the Indonesian Republic (**Pemerintah Darurat Republik Indonesia**, **PDRI**) in **Sumatra**. He was finance minister again in the **Mohammad Hatta** and **Mohammad Natsir** governments, and he introduced a system of multiple exchange rates for the rupiah (*see* **CURRENCY**). As governor of the Bank of Indonesia from 1951 to 1958, he was a strong opponent of the **Benteng** Policy on the grounds that most Indonesians were in the agricultural sector and were not ready for accelerated **industrialization**.

In December 1957, Sjafruddin fled to Sumatra and joined the regional rebellion, becoming prime minister of the **PRRI/Permesta** government; he returned to Jakarta under an amnesty in 1961 but was jailed until **Suharto** came to power. Initially a supporter of the **New Order**, he grew unhappy with its policies toward **Islam**, particularly its attempts to control the ***haj***, and also with the extent of **corruption** in the government. In 1980 he signed the **Petition of Fifty** and in 1983 he published an open letter to Suharto protesting the government order that all organizations accept the **Pancasila** as their sole foundation. [0661, 0686, 0695, 1040]

SJAHRIR, SUTAN (1909–1966)**.** Born in West **Sumatra**, he studied in the Netherlands where he became a member of the **Perhimpunan Indonesia (PI)**. He returned to Indonesia in December 1931, preceding **Mohammad Hatta**, and acting as his agent he founded the **Pendidikan Nasional Indonesia** or PNI-Baru, which aimed at building up a nationalist cadre in preparation for a prolonged independence struggle. Arrested in 1934, he was exiled first to **Boven Digul** and then in 1936 to **Banda**. He was returned to **Java** in January 1942 at the time of the **Japanese** invasion.

Sjahrir refused to cooperate with the Japanese, building instead a network of young intellectuals who became the basis for the later **Partai Sosialis Indonesia (PSI)**. After the declaration of **independence** in 1945, he campaigned strongly against the preservation of occupation-era institutions, such as the **Pembela Tanah Air (Peta)** and the **Partai Nasional Indonesia—Staatspartij**, within the Republic. Operating through the Working Committee of the **Komité Nasional Indonesia Pusat (KNIP)**, he was able to convert the Republic's nascent political system to the principle of parliamentary accountability and on 14 November 1945 became its first prime minister, with **Amir Sjarifuddin** as his deputy. His strong espousal of diplomatic means for dealing with the **Dutch**, however, soon made Sjahrir unpopular, and he was strongly opposed by **Tan Malaka** and the **Persatuan Perjuangan (PP)**. His cabinets fell three times over the issue, and on 27 June 1946 he was briefly arrested by opposition troops. Displaced by Amir in June 1947, Sjahrir went abroad to argue the Republic's case at the **United Nations** but returned to be an advisor to **Sukarno** and was captured by the Dutch in the second **"Police Action."** He led the PSI throughout the 1950s, presiding over its disastrous performance in the 1955 elections. Sukarno had Sjahrir arrested in 1962 but permitted him to leave for medical treatment in Switzerland in 1965, where he died the following year. [0661, 0674, 0865, 0916, 0932, 0933]

SLAVERY. Although definitions are contentious, most societies of the archipelago recognized slavery in the form of hereditary transferable ownership of human beings. **Labor** was a scarce commodity and slaves were both a means to and a store of wealth, though they were used mainly in domestic and commercial service, other forms of bondage such as corvée being more important for **agriculture** and the construction of monuments (*see* ***HERENDIENSTEN***). "Free" labor, in the sense of independent manual workers available for hire for a day or longer, seems to have been virtually unknown; casual labor was obtained by renting slaves from their owners. People entered the status of slavery generally as a result either of indebtedness or of capture in **warfare**, though servitude could also be inherited. Tribal people such as those of **Nias**, **Sumba**, **Maluku**, **Papua**, and upland **Sumatra** were most commonly victims of slave trading, though **Java** was a major slave exporter in 1500 and **Bali** was an important source to the 19th century. Slavery incurred certain advantages, such as exemption from corveé duties for rulers, and it was not unknown for people to sell themselves into bondage, though slaves employed in small-scale manufacture and **mining** often lived in appalling conditions. Movement out of slavery was sometimes possible by redemption, manumission, or simply gradual assimilation to the status of free servant.

The **Dutch East Indies Company (VOC)** was a major trader in slaves, which it employed for general laboring tasks and in agriculture. In 1673 half the population of **Batavia** was said to be slave, and an elaborate set of rules formally governed their working conditions. The colonial government banned **trade** in slaves on Java in 1818, but did not announce until 1854 that slavery would be abolished in the directly ruled territories by 1860, and did not issue an ordinance to this effect until 1 July 1863. A continuing obstacle to effective abolition, however, was the existence, especially in South **Sulawesi**, of debt slavery, a blurred form of servitude difficult to regulate, and full-scale slave trading continued in parts of eastern Indonesia until at least 1910. *See also* BUTON; COOLIE ORDINANCE. [0407, 0413, 0434, 0452, 0576, 0833]

SMALLPOX. A major disease in Indonesia, repeatedly introduced through the centuries by trading contacts with the Eurasian land mass. Severe epidemics swept **Ternate** in 1558, **Ambon** in 1564, **Sumatra** in 1780–1783, **Savu** in 1869, and **Java**, **Kalimantan**, and Sumatra in 1918–1924. In 1815, shortly after the development of vaccination, the Netherlands Indies government sent a surgeon to Martinique in the West

Indies with a number of slave children. One of these children was inoculated there with the vaccine and the surgeon carried out successive inoculations of the other children during the voyage, so that the vaccine reached Java live. A similar technique was initially used to spread the vaccine through the colony, until the development of air-dried vaccine. Colonial officials estimated that 25 percent of the **population** of Java was vaccinated by 1835. Production of vaccine from **cattle** began in 1884 at a Parc Vaccinogène, which merged in 1895 with the **Pasteur Institute**. Although never compulsory, vaccination was a condition of entry to lower schools. In 1968, the World **Health** Organization launched a mass vaccination program in Indonesia. The last recorded case of the disease in the archipelago was in 1972. [0576]

SNOUCK HURGRONJE, CHRISTIAAN (1857–1936)**.** From 1891 he was advisor to the colonial government on **Aceh** and from 1889 advisor on Islamic and indigenous affairs. He brought lasting change to colonial policy on **Islam**, arguing that the religion was not inherently opposed to colonial rule and that the bitter opposition of many Muslims to the **Dutch** could be assuaged if, instead of opposing all manifestations of Islam, the colonial government protected and promoted religious observance while suppressing only Islamic political movements. His advice led to the establishment of an extended network of state-employed religious officials. Snouck believed that support for Islam should be paired with a vigorous introduction of Western secular culture to the Indonesian elite (the **Association Principle**) in order to create a modern elite that would share with the Dutch the task of ruling the colony. He also advocated abolition of the separate European and native hierarchies within the ***Binnenlandsch Bestuur***. His advice that the colonial authorities should cultivate the traditional aristocracy (*uleëbalang*) in the war in **Aceh** also contributed to the eventual Dutch victory there. After his departure from Indonesia, Snouck continued to influence colonial policy as professor of Indology at Leiden University (1907–1927), where he played a major role in training colonial civil servants. *See also* ETHICAL POLICY; RELIGION AND POLITICS. [0590, 1018, 1261]

SOEDJATMOKO MANGOENDININGRAT (1922–1989)**.** One of independent Indonesia's most respected intellectuals, Soedjatmoko was the eldest son of a Javanese physician. He entered medical school in Jakarta during the **Japanese occupation**, but was expelled in 1943 possibly because of his contacts with noncooperating political leaders, including **Sutan Sjahrir**. After independence he became a member of the **Partai Sosialis (PS)**, and in British-occupied **Jakarta** in 1946 he published a Dutch-language weekly, *Het Inzicht.* From 1947 to 1950, he served on the Republic's observer delegation to the **United Nations.** He remained close to Sjahrir and was the **Partai Sosialis Indonesia (PSI)**'s major intellectual and historian, founding its daily *Pedoman* in 1952 and representing the party in the **Constituent Assembly** (1956–1959).

After Sjahrir's death and the crises of 1965–1966, Soedjatmoko's interest shifted to foreign affairs, and **Suharto** appointed him ambassador to the **United States** in 1968. In 1980 he was appointed rector of the United Nations University in Tokyo, where he served until 1987.

SOLO. *See* SURAKARTA.

SOLOR ARCHIPELAGO. Consists of the islands of Solor, Adonara, and Lomblen, at the eastern end of **Nusatenggara**. They were listed in the ***Nagarakrtagama*** as a dependency of **Majapahit** but by the 16th century were under the influence of **Ternate**. The archipelago became a shelter for European ships en route to **Timor** for beeswax and **sandalwood**, and the **Portuguese** established a fortress on Solor in 1566. A strong political division developed between the Catholic Demonara (Demong) communities, who generally supported the Portuguese, and the Muslim Puji, who supported the **Dutch**, though neither group ever formed a single state in its own right. The Portuguese largely abandoned the islands in 1653 but only in 1859 were they handed definitively to the Dutch as part of a general tidying of colonial boundaries in the region. Effective Dutch rule through the rajas of Adonara and Larantuka was established only in the late 19th century. [0491]

SOUTH EAST ASIA LEAGUE. The first initiative for regional cooperation between the independent states of Southeast Asia, the league was founded in Bangkok in 1947 and brought together representatives of Burma, Indonesia, **Siam (Thailand)**, and **Vietnam**. Its aim was to promote the decolonization of Southeast Asia (and, in Thailand's case, to resist British encroachment on its sovereignty). It seems to have been an initiative especially of the Thai Prime Minister Pridi Panomyong and disappeared after his fall and that of **Amir Sjarifuddin**. *See also* FOREIGN POLICY.

SOVIET UNION, RELATIONS WITH. Suspicious of Republican leaders' cooperation with the **Japanese** and more interested in European affairs, the Soviet Union paid little attention to the Indonesian Republic in its first years. Only after **Amir Sjarifuddin** became prime minister did relations become closer and in January 1948 an Indonesian envoy, Suripno, negotiated a consular treaty with the USSR that was, however, repudiated by the incoming **Mohammad Hatta** government, anxious not to appear aligned with communists. Relations cooled more sharply when the USSR endorsed the **Partai Komunis Indonesia (PKI)** in the **Madiun** Affair, and diplomatic relations were not established until 1953. The USSR backed Indonesia over the West Irian (**Papua**) dispute and became a major arms supplier from 1956; after 1960, Indonesia was the largest noncommunist recipient of Soviet bloc military aid. Relations cooled again, however, with the Soviet–**United States** detente and as Indonesia's **Nekolim** doctrine drew it closer to **China**.

The PKI's swing toward China and the fact that Indonesia owed circa US$1 billion (later rescheduled) muted Soviet criticism of the **Suharto** government's suppression of the Left after 1965, while Indonesia cultivated ties to preserve the appearance of nonalignment in its **foreign policy**. After the establishment of a Soviet naval base in Cam Ranh Bay in **Vietnam** in 1975, however, Indonesia criticized the Soviet Union for bringing great power rivalries into the region, and it was also hostile to the Soviet invasion of Afghanistan.

From the early 1980s, Indonesia shared with the Soviet Union a desire not to see the Chinese-backed Khmer Rouge displace the Vietnamese-backed Hun Sen government in **Cambodia**. Steadily improving relations culminated in an economic protocol between the two countries signed on 29 October 1985, a visit by President Suharto to Moscow in September 1989, and a relaxation of Indonesian restrictions on Soviet **trade** and visits. On 11 January 1990, a Soviet state enterprise signed an agreement with **Liem Sioe Liong** to establish a **palm oil** processing plant near Moscow. *See also* DEBT, INTERNATIONAL; MURBA; RUSSIA. [1113, 1128]

SOYA BEAN (*Glycine max* Fabaceae, *kedele*). Seed crop probably from northeast Asia, which reached Indonesia via **India**. It is a major **polowijo** crop and is used to prepare a number of important foods. *Tahu* (tofu, bean curd) is made by grinding the beans and heating them in water to precipitate casein, which is then pressed into cakes; *tempe* is made by inoculating parboiled beans with the fungus *Aspergillus oryzae*; and *kecap* (soy sauce) is made by inoculating boiled beans with *Aspergillus*, submerging the fermented mass in brine, exposing it to sunlight, and adding flavors such as aren sugar, anise, and ginger. Contamination of soya beans with aflatoxins (from *A. flavus*) is a major cause of stomach cancer in Indonesia.

SPAIN, HISTORICAL LINKS WITH. Although Magellan's fleet sailed through the Indonesian archipelago in 1521, it was not until after the union of the Spanish and **Portuguese** crowns in 1580 that the Spanish began to move south seriously from their base in the **Philippines**. Between 1582 and 1603 they sent a series of largely unsuccessful expeditions against **Ternate**, but in the 17th century Spanish attention soon shifted back north to the Philippines. Many useful plants of American origin reached Indonesia on Spanish ships. *See* AMERICAS, HISTORICAL LINKS WITH.

SPELLING. *See* INDONESIAN LANGUAGE.

SRIVIJAYA. Buddhist kingdom centered on the modern city of **Palembang** in southern **Sumatra** and dominating the Strait of **Melaka** from the seventh to early 11th centuries. In its day the most powerful state in the archipelago, Srivijaya's position was derived from its role as an entrepôt for **gold** and forest products such as benzoin from the region, as a staging post in **trade** between **China** and eastern Indonesia on the one hand and **India** and the West on the other, as well as from its naval control of the Strait. It transformed the haphazard **piracy** of earlier eras into more regular **taxation** of trade, which greatly smoothed commerce in the region. Relatively little is known of Srivijaya's internal political structure; the grandiloquent assertions of divine authority made by its rulers are not plausible as reflections of reality (*see* **SAILENDRAS**). Srivijaya seems likely to have been a carefully managed system of alliances with coastal chiefs and upland tribes rather than a centralized bureaucratic state. Although fabulously wealthy by accounts of the time, Srivijaya has left few material remains: in the absence of easily obtainable building stone, most of its construction seems to have been in wood and has not survived.

The precise nature of Srivijaya's relationship with China is also unclear. The Chinese regarded it as tributary and its prosperity was closely tied to that of the **ports** of southern China, but whether Srivijaya acknowledged the relationship as tributary is unknown. Srivijaya maintained important cultural links with India, especially with the Buddhist monastery at Nalanda in Bihar, and was itself a major center of Buddhist learning (*see* **BUDDHISM**). Srivijaya's power was abruptly smashed in 1027 by a raid from the South Indian Chola dynasty. The empire's capital moved to **Jambi**, but it was overshadowed by the rise of independent kingdoms in northern Sumatra and on the **Malay Peninsula** (*see* **PASAI**). The inability of any state to revive Srivijaya's hegemony may relate to the rise of Chinese "private" as opposed to tributary trade. *See also* STATE-FORMATION. [0023, 0514, 0522, 0531, 0542–0545]

STAATSPARTIJ. *See* PARTAI NASIONAL INDONESIA.

STATE ENTERPRISES. Since the arrival of the **Dutch East Indies Company (VOC)** in the archipelago, there has been an intimate connection between the state and business enterprise. The company itself was an enterprise with an attached state, rather than the reverse, while the early years of Crown rule, especially the **Cultivation System**, were largely an example of the direct commercial activity of the colonial state. Private firms such as the **Nederlandsche Handel Maatschappij (NHM)** benefited greatly from close cooperation with the colonial government but were not true state enterprises.

Distinct state enterprises first emerged in the 20th century. In 1921, the colonial government launched the Nederlandsch-Indische Aardolie Maatschappij, a joint venture with the BPM to drill for **oil** in **Jambi**. The idea that some separation should be made between the state and its commercial ventures was only given legal expression in 1927 with the Indische Bedrijvenwet (Indies Enterprises Law), which allowed the government to separate commercial enterprises from the state **budget**. This was then applied to the **opium** factory; the **pawnshops**; the government quinine and **tea** industries; the **ports** of Belawan, **Makassar**, and Emmahaven (Teluk Bayur); the posts and telegraph service (*see* **POSTAL SERVICE**; **TELEGRAPH**); the **Bangka tin** industry; the military grasslands; and the reproduction section of the topographical service.

Under the **Japanese occupation**, some existing enterprises were handed over to Japanese commercial interests (*see* **SUGAR CANE**), but many were placed under government departments as a source of direct finance. This system remained in place in practice during the Indonesian **Revolution**, when plantations in particular came under the control of local armed units. The Republican government set up a number of centralized state corporations, including the Badan Textiel Negara and the Badan Industri Negara, but these suffered from a critical shortage of capital and were often unable to take charge of the factories they nominally controlled as these were in the hands of the workers or of ***lasykar*** or **army** groups. More successful was the semigovernmental Banking and Trading Corporation (BTC) of **Sumitro Djojohadikusumo**, which traded produce to **Singapore** and the **United States**.

After 1950, successive governments were determined to establish a significant publicly owned sector in the **economy**. **Railways** and the Java Bank were nationalized, and the Bank Industri Negara helped finance new state corporations in the fields of **shipping**, air services (*see* **GARUDA**), textiles, cement, glass, **automobile**, and hardboard manufacture. In 1956, a state trading corporation, USINDO, was formed to handle the export of goods from these factories. With the **nationalization** of Dutch enterprises in December 1957, the state sector expanded dramatically. In April 1958, nationalized Dutch trading firms were reorganized into six new state trading corporations with a joint monopoly on the import of many commodities, including **rice** and textiles. Fifty-five percent of profits from these firms were owed to the state, but proceeds were generally disappointing due to **corruption** and deterioration of infrastructure. A central authority, the Badan Pimpinan Umum, was placed in charge of state enterprises in 1960.

Under the **New Order**, this extensive state presence in the economy was preserved, despite **Inter-Governmental Group on Indonesia (IGGI)** preferences for private ownership, partly because of a lack of domestic capital to take them over, partly because they were an important source of income and a useful tool for state intervention in the economy. The largest state enterprises in the 1980s were **Pertamina**; the tin firm PN Timah; PN Aneka Tambang, which conducts general **mining** operations; and Perhutani (formerly Inhutani), the state **forestry** corporation. Public utilities, of course, are also state enterprises, as are the largest banks and two major manufacturing firms, PT Krakatau Steel and the fertilizer producer PT Pusri.

In 1986, influenced by analyses reporting that 92 of the 189 state enterprises were economically unsound, President **Suharto** announced plans for privatization. From 1989, state enterprises were permitted to sell 20 percent of their shares to the public, but progress was slow and by 1994 only the cement manufacturer P. T. Semen Gresik was listed on the Jakarta **Stock Exchange**. *See also* INDONESIANIZATION. [0311, 0351, 0695]

STATE-FORMATION. The boundary between tribal and other "primitive" political formations on the one hand and states on the other is an arbitrary one, but most scholars regard true states as having emerged in the archipelago only as part of the adoption and transformation of Indian, and later Islamic and Western, political ideas. Thus the earliest states in the western archipelago (**"Ho-lo-tan," "Kan-t'o-li,"** and **Kutai**) were culturally Indian in at least some respects and were probably stimulated at least in part by the emergence of **trade** between Indonesia and **India** around the fifth century.

Information on these early states allows us to say that they consisted of court bureaucracies that rested on carefully constructed networks of alliances with regional power holders (*see* ***BUPATI***), but the relative strength of court and "feudal" lords is hard to judge, even apart from the fact that it must have varied significantly over time. The longevity of a state such as **Srivijaya** and the internal organization required by the Javanese states that constructed **Borobudur** and **Prambanan** suggest a significant degree of institutionalization, but other evidence suggests highly personalized rule and the distinction between king, vassal, and bandit leader seems to have been a fluid one (*see* **BANDITRY**; **PIRACY**). In contrast, the strong bureaucratic structure of the **Dutch East Indies Company (VOC)** gave it an organizational coherence and resilience that enabled it ultimately to subdue the entire archipelago. *See also* SUCCESSION. [0529, 0716]

STATISTICS. The Centraal Kantoor voor de Statistiek was established in 1924, and its work was continued after independence by the Biro Pusat Statistik (BPS, Central Bureau of Statistics). In 1997 a nondepartmental Indonesian government institution, the Badan Pusat Statistiek (BPS, Central Statistical Body), was established, directly responsible to the **president**, to provide statistical data to the government and the public. *See also* CENSUSES.

STOCK EXCHANGE. The Jakarta Stock Exchange was established in 1977 but for its first 10 years of operation was largely used by the government to promote **Indonesianization.** In late 1988 only 24 companies were listed on the exchange. This changed dramatically in 1990 when **Suharto** approved proposals from the technocrats to let foreigners purchase up to 49 percent of the listed shares of an Indonesian-owned company. By 1995, the number of firms listed on the stock exchange had increased to 238 while the number of listed shares had risen from 60 million to 46 billion. In early 1996 the exchange was capitalized at $67 billion at the current exchange rate.

The 1997 **financial crisis** sparked a drastic downturn in the stock market as investors sold their stock to buy foreign currencies, a move that accelerated after the government floated the rupiah on 14 August. In the subsequent five months, stock market prices shrank at one point to half their previous value. [0353, 0385]

STRIKES. *See* LABOR UNIONS.

STUDENTS. Students played a major role in Indonesia's 20th century history, alongside other ***pemuda*** groups, most notably in the anti-Dutch independence struggle and in the demonstrations that helped drive **Sukarno** from power, the latter in alliance with the **army**. In 1965–1966 they formed the **Kesatuan Aksi Mahasiswa Indonesia (KAMI)**, which encompassed both Islamic student organizations, such as **Himpunan Mahasiswa Islam (HMI)**, and a few secular student organizations that had severed any former ties with the **Partai Komunis Indonesia (PKI)**.

Students were early outspoken supporters of the **Suharto** regime, which appointed several of the KAMI leaders to government posts. But by the early 1970s, student dissatisfaction with the **New Order** led them to spearhead protests against its growing authoritarianism and the rampant **corruption** that was beginning to characterize it. The government attempted to co-opt the students by establishing in 1973 the Komite Nasional Pemuda Indonesia (KNPI, Indonesian Youth National Committee), led by a former KAMI leader David Napitupulu. Affiliated with **Golkar** and close to the **Centre for Strategic and International Studies (CSIS)** and **Ali Murtopo**, the KNPI was intended as a youth **labor union**, with the sole right to represent Indonesian youth in political and social affairs so that their energies might be directed exclusively to the benefit of the New Order. Its success was very limited, and students were prime movers in the **Malari** protests in January 1974 calling for price reductions and an end to corruption. Although several of their leaders were then arrested in the ensuing crackdown, further student protests developed in 1977–1978, especially in **Bandung** and **Jakarta**, against Suharto's reelection (*see* **WHITE BOOK**). In response, the government further curbed student activity through the 1978 Campus Normalization Law, under which university deans were charged with keeping the universities free from politics. Thus during the 1980s student activity had to be largely restricted to internal campus issues. In the later 1980s students began to turn their attention to issues of social justice, particularly with respect to **land** and its expropriation, and poverty exacerbated by government policies.

In 1993 students cooperated with Muslim groups in successfully opposing a state-sponsored lottery, and this success led them to expand their activity again into protests against the regime and the corruption of the **Suharto family**. Thereafter the students' profile was raised once more as they formed or allied with activist movements including the **Persatuan Rakyat Demokratik (PRD)**.

Students were in the forefront of the demonstrations that ultimately forced Suharto's resignation in May 1998. Their organized protests began in **Jakarta** in the second half of February when they demanded a return to democracy and initiated a free forum (*mimbar bebas*) to express their dissatisfaction with the corruption of the Suharto regime. These protests were echoed on campuses throughout the country, as a network of student activists in the universities coordinated their activities through e-mail and cell phone communication among the campuses. Thus on 15 April students were able to organize nationwide coordinated protests that escalated again in early May in opposition to a rise in fuel and electricity prices. By this time, the student demands included calls for Suharto to step down. The trigger for the final showdown came on 12 May when **Komando Pasukan Khusus (Kopassus)** and **police** forces shot at students demonstrating at Trisakti University in Jakarta, killing six of them. In the huge protest demonstrations that followed, students occupied the parliament building and were a key element in ultimately forcing Suharto's resignation. The student movement splintered immediately after Suharto's fall over whether or not to support the new government, headed by **B. J. Habibie**, and though still active in the ***reformasi*** period, students were unable to regain their earlier influence. [0748, 0760]

STUW, DE (The Push)**.** Political journal published from 1930 by the Association for the Furtherance of the Social and Political Development of the Netherlands Indies, usually called the *Stuw*-group. Most of its members were government officials or academics, and most had been influenced by **Christiaan Snouck Hurgronje** at Leiden University. Their association was primarily a study and discussion group, though it argued generally for the creation of an Indies commonwealth (*see* **SUCCESSION**). The group was largely disbanded by 1933, partly because it appeared to be damaging the careers of its younger members in the conservative political climate of the day. Several of its members, however, gained influential positions in the postwar colonial administration, notably **H. J. van Mook** as lieutenant governor-general and J. H. A. Logemann and J. A. Jonkman as minister for **colonies**. They had little success, however, in pushing the Dutch government toward greater concessions to Indonesian **nationalism**, and their often paternalistic ideas on cultural and economic development antagonized Indonesian nationalists. [0620, 1146]

SUBANDRIO (1915–). As a young intellectual with medical training, Subandrio was posted abroad to promote the Republic during the Indonesian **Revolution**. After serving in London (1947–1954) and Moscow (1954–1956), he returned to Indonesia where he joined the **Partai Nasional Indonesia (PNI)** in 1957 and in the same year became foreign minister in **Sukarno**'s first *kabinet karya*. He held the post until 1966 and was one of the architects of the **foreign policy** of **Guided Democracy**, including **Confrontation** with **Malaysia**. On becoming deputy prime minister in 1959, he resigned from the PNI to project a more national image. A skilled political manipulator, he was seen by many as typifying the byzantine politics of Guided Democracy and was among the first government figures targeted by conservative forces after 1965. Subandrio was arrested in March 1966, tried by the **Mahmillub** in October, and convicted of participation in the **Gestapu** coup. Although sentenced to death, he remained in detention in **Jakarta** for nearly 30 years, until 1995 when **Suharto** decided to release some prominent political prisoners, including Subandrio and Omar Dhani (a former **air force** commander), under pressure from **human rights** advocates. In 2000 Subandrio published his version of events surrounding the Gestapu. [0712, 1144]

SUBVERSION. Both colonial and independent governments in Indonesia have been deeply and constantly concerned about alleged problems of subversion. The **Dutch East Indies Company (VOC)** feared collusion between inhabitants of **Batavia** and enemies outside, and periodically executed those suspected of treason. In 1916 the colonial government founded the **Politiek Inlichtingen Dienst (PID)** or Political Intelligence Service, whose place was taken under the **Japanese** by the **Kenpeitai** and in the **Suharto** period by the **Badan Koordinasi Intelijen (Bakin)** (*see also* **INTELLIGENCE SERVICES**).

These police organs have been backed by a series of laws on subversion, beginning with the so-called *haatzaai-artikelen* of 1914, based on the penal code of British India, which banned the "sowing of hatred" of the government or of any group of Indonesian inhabitants; by irony, one of the first prosecutions under these articles was of the editor of a colonial military journal that published an article critical of the quality of Javanese soldiers. These *haatzaai-artikelen* were used in 1984 to convict the dissident **H. R. Dharsono.** Lèse-majesté regulations of the colonial era have also been retained by independent Indonesia (with substitution of **president** and **vice president** for queen and **governor-general**) and were used against the authors of the 1978 **White Book**. Finally, the 1963 **Law** on Subversion, which bans both the arousing of "hostility, disturbances or anxiety among the population or broad sections of society" and the undermining of **Pancasila** or the **Garis Besar Haluan Negara (GBHN)**, was used against **Sawito Kartowibowo** and against the alleged plotters behind the **Malari** riots. *See also* MAHKAMAH MILITER LUAR BIASA. [0635, 0923]

SUCCESSION. The idea that the colony of the Netherlands Indies should be succeeded by some sort of independent state emerged in the early 20th century. Proponents initially envisaged gradual decolonization, perhaps via an increase in the powers of the **Volksraad**, toward a commonwealth arrangement along British lines, with Indonesia being essentially self-governing but deferring to the Netherlands on matters of common interest (*see* ***STUW, DE***). The idea of full independence became a part of the platform of the nationalist movement in the 1920s, though the exact mechanism of succession was not spelled out. Nationalists did not agree at first on whether the colony should gain independence as a whole or in a number of ethnically based states (*see* **NATIONALISM**). By the 1920s, there was general agreement that the successor state should encompass the entire Netherlands Indies.

Succession by **Japanese** military rule was sanctioned in international **law** by the formal surrender of Dutch forces on 8 March 1942, but was called into question by the establishment of a Netherlands Indies government-in-exile in **Australia** under **H. J. van Mook** and the fact that the Dutch still held the town of Merauke in the southeastern corner of West New Guinea (*see* **PAPUA**).

Japan surrendered on 14 August 1945, and the Indonesian Republic was declared on 17 August. The Republic based its claim to succession on the right of national self-determination, on the argument that Dutch sovereignty had ceased with the Dutch loss of the colony in 1942 and on the initially slender international recognition it received from other countries. The **Linggajati Agreement** of November 1946 and the **Renville Agreement** of January 1948 gave the Republic vague "de facto" recognition by the Dutch, but this was withdrawn in the **"Police Actions"** of

July 1947 and December 1948. The Republic received full recognition from Egypt and Syria in 1947.

Under van Mook, the postwar Netherlands Indies government recognized the inevitable end of colonialism but sought to push the colony's successor state in the direction of a multiracial paternalistic meritocracy. In the latter part of the **Revolution**, this took the form of a federation (*see* **FEDERALISM**). On 9 March 1948, the colonial government was renamed the Provisional Federal Government (Voorlopige Federale Regeering) and the term Netherlands Indies was replaced in the Dutch **Constitution** by Indonesië. On 3 November the post of **governor-general** was replaced with that of high commissioner of the Crown. On 27 December 1949 sovereignty over the Netherlands Indies was transferred to the **Republik Indonesia Serikat** (Federal Republic of Indonesia, usually translated as Republic of the United States of Indonesia). West New Guinea, however, was retained by the Dutch, partly on grounds of the ethnic dissimilarity between the Papuans and other Indonesians, partly on the grounds that Dutch sovereignty over the territory was stronger by virtue of the permanent Dutch presence in Merauke. West New Guinea (West Irian, Papua) was handed by the Dutch in 1962 to **United Nations** administration, which in turn handed it to Indonesia in 1963. The incorporation of the territory into Indonesia was ratified by an "Act of Free Choice" in 1968.

The issue of succession dominated the last years of both the **Sukarno** and **Suharto** regimes, as neither president was willing to institute an orderly method for the transfer of power after his resignation or death. Although under the Constitution the **Majelis Permusyawaratan Rakyat (MPR)** was responsible for electing the **president**, under neither the Old nor the **New Order** was it believed that the parliament could act independently of the will of the president himself. The bloody initiation of the Suharto presidency had led to questions as to its legitimacy, and Suharto was always eager to stress the legality of the handover of power from Sukarno through the **Supersemar**. Suharto's unwillingness to indicate a possible successor led to great uncertainty during the early 1990s and contributed to the chaos that followed his May 1998 resignation. In the post-Suharto period, the issue of succession has been clarified through the measures passed by the MPR whereby a president can only serve two five-year terms and is now elected by the population as a whole and not by maneuvering within the parliament. [0751,0940,0970]

SUDHARMONO (1927–). After serving in the **army** from 1945, Sudharmono attended the military law academy in the late 1950s and, at the beginning of the **New Order**, **Suharto** appointed him as his private secretary for general affairs. He then became state secretary in 1973 and chairman of **Golkar** in 1983. Sudharmono attempted to make Golkar into a real political party by lessening its dependence on the executive. Both as state secretary and head of Golkar, he also weakened the military's influence by helping a group of indigenous businessmen gain greater access to government projects and state funding, undermining the **army**'s financial strength. The army leadership responded by placing military representatives in some two thirds of Golkar's provincial chairmanships and spreading rumors that Sudharmono had communist links. The army's campaign against him ensured that he was replaced as leader of Golkar, but it was unable to prevent **Suharto** from appointing him as his **vice president** in March 1988, where he served until 1993. [0748, 0751]

SUDIRMAN (1915?–1950)**.** Former schoolteacher and **Pembela Tanah Air (Peta)** battalion commander, he was elected **army** commander in **Yogyakarta** on 12 November 1945. Sudirman emphasized the valued of martial and national spirit over hierarchy and formal organization in defeating the Dutch, and he was initially sympathetic to the radical nationalism of **Tan Malaka**, though he stopped short of supporting him against the **Sjahrir** government. Although his charisma made him a focal point of army loyalty, he was gradually edged out of direct command by a group of Western-trained officers including **A. H. Nasution**. In December 1948, however, after the Republican cabinet was captured in the second Dutch **"Police Action,"** Sudirman, dying of tuberculosis, led Republican forces in a guerrilla struggle against the Dutch in the Javanese countryside. Along with the **Pemerintah Darurat Republik Indonesia (PDRI)** he opposed the **Roem–van Roijen** Agreement, but in July 1949 he reluctantly submitted to the Republican government that had been restored to Yogyakarta. He died in January of the following year. [0886]

SUGAR CANE (*Saccharum officinarum* Poaceae)**.** Probably native to Indonesia and first domesticated there, but improved techniques for cultivating and processing it were developed in **India**. **Chinese** visitors reported it from **Java** in 400 A.D., but other sources of sugar (e.g., aren, honey, and **lontar**) were more important. Under sponsorship of the **Dutch East Indies Company (VOC)**, Chinese settlers on Java produced the first commercial sugar cane in the countryside around **Batavia** in the 17th century for export to Europe and **Japan**. Of 150 mills on the island in 1710, all but four were Chinese-owned, though production declined later in the18th century because of the loss of external markets, political disturbances on Java, and lack of firewood.

Sugar production was an important part of the **Cultivation System**. Sugar grown under government monopoly was delivered to private sugar mills, often owned by European entrepreneurs who, though they had to deliver the processed sugar at fixed prices to the **Nederlandsche Handel Maatschappij (NHM)**, made enormous profits. In the first half of the 19th century, sugar was by far the dominant export of the colony, accounting for 77.4 percent of the total value of exports in 1840. Private companies established sugar plantations in the **Vorstenlanden** in this period.

In 1870, the government decided to hand over sugar production to private enterprise, though the government monopoly was not formally abolished until 1891. Sugar cane requires much the same kind of agricultural conditions as **rice** (and three times the volume of water) as well as a seasonal **labor** force, and most sugar plantations were therefore established in areas already under indigenous rice cultivation. Under a variety of exploitative relationships, the sugar growers generally gained access to their choice of land and to abundant water while leaving a portion of the rice economy intact to tide their labor force over seasonal dips in labor demand. A world crisis in 1883 drove many smaller companies out of production but set the stage for massive capital investment, especially by the NHM, which turned the Java sugar industry into the world's most efficient. The industry fared badly in the **Depression** of the 1930s, and its share of the value of exports sank to around 7 percent by 1938.

During the **Japanese occupation**, the sugar plantations and mills of Java were handed over to Japanese sugar firms in proportion to their share of Japanese production. Since the combined production of Java, the **Philippines**, and Taiwan was far more than the needs of the Japanese empire, production on Java was steadily reduced. During the Indonesian **Revolution**, the preferential laws that had given sugar plantations access to village lands were abolished, and the industry was never able to recover the access to cheap **land** and labor that had previously underpinned its success. Postwar policies of keeping sugar prices low contributed to underinvestment and generally low yields, exacerbated by primitive technology and use of low-yielding plant varieties. In 1971 the **Badan Urusan Logistik Nasional (Bulog)** took over distribution and price support, and in 1972 the government launched an intensified smallholder cane program, which included reductions in **tax** and an improved marketing system. In 1975 plans were announced to phase out the renting of land for large sugar plantations, but despite some progress, the industry remained inefficient, absorbing 20 percent of total agricultural credits for only 3 percent of the total value of agricultural output.

In order to boost rice production it was proposed that sugar cane cultivation should be moved from Java, which in 1988 produced 83 percent of the country's sugar. No basic change was made in the government's policies, however, although there was some expansion outside Java, particularly to **Lampung**. [0552, 0603, 0617, 0730, 1249]

SUHARTO (1921–). Second president of Indonesia. Born 8 June 1921, in a village near **Yogyakarta** to a peasant family, Suharto joined the **Koninklijk Nederlands-Indisch Leger (KNIL)** in 1940 and rose to the rank of sergeant before the **Japanese** invasion. After demobilization, he joined first the **police** and then the **Pembela Tanah Air (Peta)** in 1943 and the Republican **army** in Central Java in 1945. During the **Dutch** occupation of Yogyakarta (1948–1949), he commanded a "general attack" (*serangan umum*) in which Indonesian forces briefly occupied the city before being driven back by the Dutch. In 1956 he became commander of the army's Diponegoro division but was dismissed in October 1959 for putting illegal levies on commercial activities in Central **Java**. Posted to the Sekolah Staf dan Komando Angkatan Darat (Seskoad) in **Bandung**, he was involved peripherally in the development of the army's doctrine of ***dwifungsi*** before being appointed in 1961 as commander of the army's strategic reserve Komando Cadangan Strategis Angkatan Darat (**Kostrad**). In 1962 Suharto was placed in command of the Mandala campaign to recover West Irian (**Papua**) but was Kostrad commander in **Jakarta** at the time of the **Gestapu** coup in 1965 when his troops were instrumental in suppressing the coup. With his appointment as commander of Komando Operasi Pemulihan Keamanan dan Ketertiban (**Kopkamtib**) on 10 October 1965, he set about dismantling **Guided Democracy** and installing the regime that soon became known as the **New Order**.

The **Supersemar** order of 11 March 1966 enabled him to suppress the **Partai Komunis Indonesia (PKI)** and to purge the government bureaucracy. Suharto was sworn in as acting president in March 1967, and in March 1968 he was selected by the **Majelis Permusyawaratan Rakyat (Sementara) (MPRS)** as **president**. He called general **elections** for 1971 and was reelected by the new MPR in 1972. Usually with no opposition, he was reelected every five years from then until 1998.

Suharto initially appeared to many observers to be a quiet and efficient military manager, using a consensual style and drawing heavily on the economic skills of the **Badan Perencanaan Pembangunan Nasional (Bappenas)** staff (*see* **WIDJOJO NITISASTRO**) and on political managers such as **Ali Murtopo** of the **Centre for Strategic and International Studies (CSIS)**. In the mid- and late 1970s, his presence retreated somewhat from the national stage as rivalry between competing generals in Suharto's inner circle not only broke into public view but also was expressed obliquely in the **Malari** Affair. An attitude of *mumpungisme* ("get what you can while you can") seemed to be the order of the day, and observers began to refer to the leadership as a junta and to speculate that Suharto was no more than a figurehead for concealed and more powerful figures. With the drop in **oil** revenues and a more austere economic regime in the 1980s, however, he seemed much more clearly in control, removing apparently powerful subordinates, directly determining much government policy, and promoting **Pancasila** as the state ideology. By the late 1980s he had begun to court Islamic groups (*see* **IKATAN CENDEKIAWAN MUSLIM INDONESIA [ICMI]**) and made a tentative but short-lived effort to allow for some dissent within Indonesian society (*see* ***KETERBUKAAN***). Several members of his immediate family (*see* **CENDANA GROUP**; **SUHARTO FAMILY**) began to prosper enormously.

During his last decade in power, Suharto seemed to lose his political touch. This became clear as the ***Korupsi, Kolusi, dan Nepotisme*** **(KKN)** within the system intensified, with the first family personifying how far these excesses had corroded Indonesian society. After a sudden heart attack killed his wife in April 1996, Suharto seemed even less willing to curb the greed of his children and close associates. He increasingly leaned on them, rather than the technocrats, for economic advice. When the Asian **financial crisis** began to affect Indonesia in mid-1997, there was a wave of domestic and international criticism that led to the rapid collapse of his regime.

Suharto was initially defiant, appointing the erratic technocrat, **B. J. Habibie**, as his **vice president** after the March 1998 elections, and his daughter Tutut (Siti Hardijant Rukmana) and the notorious timber baron **Muhammad "Bob" Hasan** to his cabinet. But the public responded with wide-scale rioting and looting in Jakarta and other major **cities**. **Student** demonstrations calling for ***reformasi*** and for Suharto's resignation spread throughout the archipelago, intensifying after the military shot to death several university students at Trisakti University on 12 May. Suharto returned from a meeting in Cairo on 15 May still determined to serve out his term of office, but the escalating demonstrations and the defection of both his vice president and General **Wiranto**, chief of the **armed forces**, left him with no alternative. He resigned on 21 May, handing over power to Vice President Habibie. *See also* CULTURE; INTELLIGENCE SERVICES; POLITICAL SUBVERSION; SUMITRO DJOJOHADIKUSUMO. [0719, 0729, 0845, 0878, 0976]

SUHARTO FAMILY (sometimes referred to by the acronym, PPP [*putra, putri presiden*]). Suharto and his wife, Siti Hartinah (Tien) Suharto, had six children. They had three sons, Sigit Harjojudanto, Bambang Trihatmodjo (Bamban Tri or simply BT), and Hutomo Mandala Putra (Tommy); and three daughters, Siti Hardijanti Hastuti Rukmana (Mbak Tutut), Siti Hediati Harijadi Prabowo (Titiek), and Siti Hutami Endang Adiningsih (Mamiek). Most of them, together with other of his relatives, including his brother-in-law Probosutejo and son-in-law **Prabowo Subianto**, were deeply involved in exploiting Indonesia's **economy**, often in competition with one another.

Mbak Tutut and Tommy were the best known economically and politically. Tutut, "the toll-road queen," headed firms participating in the building and management of toll **roads** in Indonesia, **Malaysia**, the **Philippines**, and **China**, and also the Citra Flour Mills and Citra Transport Nusantara. After 1994 she was sole agent in Indonesia for Malaysia's Proton national car. In the mid-1990s she was a chairperson of the **Golkar** and member of the **Ikatan Cendekiawan Muslim Indonesa (ICMI)** advisory council, and she was mentioned in 1997 as a potential **vice president**. Suharto appointed her minister of social affairs in his last cabinet (March–May 1998).

Equally well known was Tommy, who headed the Humpuss (Hutomo Mandala Putra Soeharto Sumahardjuno) Group and was director of the Timor national car (*see* **AUTOMOBILE INDUSTRY**). **Megawati Sukarnoputri**'s government finally arrested him in March 2002 for his alleged involvement in the murder of a **Supreme Court** judge (who had sentenced him to 18 months in jail for **corruption**), and he was convicted in July and sentenced to 15 years in jail. *See also* CENDANA GROUP.

SUKADANA. Kingdom in southwest **Kalimantan**, reportedly founded by exiles from **Majapahit**. Its **economy** was based on the export of Kalimantan diamonds and of **iron** from Karimata. It was conquered by **Mataram** in 1622.

SUKARNO (1901–1970)**.** Often affectionately called **Bung** (Brother) Karno, he was a nationalist leader and Indonesia's first **president**. Born 6 June 1901, Sukarno became involved in the nationalist movement early as a protégé of **H. U. S. Tjokroaminoto**, and after studying engineering at the Bandung Institute of Technology (ITB) he helped to found an Algemene Studieclub (General Study Club) in **Bandung** in 1926. In 1927 he founded the **Partai Nasional Indonesia (PNI)**, which expanded dramatically under the influence of his oratory. He was jailed in December 1929, and on his release he joined the **Partai Indonesia (Partindo)**, to which he also drew an enthusiastic mass following. Arrested again in 1933, he apparently offered to abstain from politics if he were pardoned, but he was **exiled** nonetheless to **Flores** and then to **Bengkulu**.

Sukarno returned to **Jakarta** shortly after the **Japanese** invasion and agreed to cooperate with the occupation authorities. In exchange for exhorting the Indonesian people to support the war effort, he received extensive public exposure and an opportunity to broadcast lightly concealed nationalist messages to the public. He was later criticized for his role in recruiting ***romusha*** laborers for the Japanese. His speech formulating the **Pancasila** was made to a meeting of the independence preparatory body **Badan Penyelidik Usaha Persiapan Kemerdekaan Indonesia (BPUPKI)** in June 1945. On 17 August 1945, two days after the Japanese surrender, he and **Mohammad Hatta** proclaimed Indonesia's independence, and the following day the Japanese-sponsored **Panitia Persiapan Kemerdekaan Indonesia (PPKI)** elected them president and **vice president**.

During the **Revolution** Sukarno played a key role in keeping the revolutionary movement relatively united, although he wielded less actual governmental power than Hatta. He consistently backed the socialist governments of **Sutan Sjahrir** and **Amir Sjarifuddin**, and after the fall of Amir's government following the **Renville Agreement** Sukarno appointed Hatta to head a presidential cabinet. He had planned to flee the Republican capital of **Yogyakarta** to head a government in exile, but the Dutch launched their second **"Police Action"** on 19 December 1948 before the evacuation plane arrived, and he was captured, together with Hatta and his cabinet. He was exiled to the island of **Bangka** until allowed to return to Yogya in July 1949 after the **Roem–van Roijen Agreement.**

In the early 1950s Sukarno became increasing dissatisfied with party politics, and in 1957 he called for a system of **Guided Democracy** to replace what he saw as the tyranny of the majority in a conventional parliamentary system. He took an active hand in forming governments after the fall of the second **Ali Sastroamijoyo** cabinet in 1957 and in 1959, with **army** backing; took over the prime ministership; and instituted his system of Guided Democracy. Once in power, however, Sukarno proved to be less than competent at day-to-day administration, concentrating on symbolic projects such as the recovery of West Irian (**Papua**), **Confrontation** with **Malaysia**, and the formulation of a national ideology called **Nasakom** to reconcile the conflicting nationalist (*NASionalis*), religious (*Agama*), and communist (*KOMunis*) **political parties**.

His self-assurance seemed to increase, and in 1963 Sukarno had himself declared president-for-life. Politically, however, he was increasingly forced to balance the army and the **Partai Komunis Indonesia (PKI)** in an uneasy triangular relationship. His role in the **Gestapu** coup of September 1965 remains unclear, though it seems improbable that he had any direct hand in plotting it. In its aftermath, he did his best to protect the PKI from the subsequent **massacres of 1965–1966**. **Suharto**'s crushing of the Gestapu overthrew the balance of power of late Guided Democracy, enabling Suharto gradually to push Sukarno aside until he obtained full executive authority under the **Supersemar** order of March 1966. Sukarno was stripped of his presidency on 12 March 1967 and was confined under house arrest until he died on 21 June 1970. (*See also* **MAHMILLUB**; **NEKOLIM**.)

Scholars continue to argue over the nature of Sukarno's ideology. He was strongly influenced by **Marxism**, and especially the Leninist theory of imperialism; one of his theoretical coinages was the notion of the **Marhaen**, a category of poor Indonesians who were oppressed by capitalism and imperialism but were not proletarians since they owned, in the form of a little **land** and a few tools, some of the means of production. But he was also a pious ***abangan*** Muslim and a strong nationalist. He argued that there was no contradiction between these three beliefs, and the core of his thinking was an attempt to synthesize them for Indonesian use. Though under the Suharto regime Pancasila and Nasakom came to have opposing political connotations, they were both attempts at ideological syncretism. This blending of ideologies makes it difficult to judge how much social change Sukarno wished to introduce; his rhetoric was always that of radical change, but his practice was often less so.

Sukarno was buried in the East Java town of Blitar, initially in a humble grave that has since been made a substantial mausoleum. After his death the Suharto regime and its apologists made various attempts to downplay Sukarno's role in national development; in 1980–1981, in particular, it was alleged that Sukarno was not the author of the Pancasila, while in 1987 detractors circulated false rumors of vast sums he had corruptly secured that were held in foreign bank accounts. But he remained one of the most potent symbols in Indonesian politics. His memory was used especially by the **Partai Demokrasi Indonesia (PDI)** that claimed to be his heir in its concern for the less well off, and the continued widespread loyalty to him was largely responsible for the rise of his daughter, **Megawati Sukarnoputri**, to lead the PDI and ultimately become president. [0643, 0725, 0844, 0850, 0851, 0859, 0881, 0934–0936]

SUKARNOPUTRI, MEGAWATI. *See* MEGAWATI SUKARNOPUTRI.

SUKIMAN WIRYOSANJOYO (1896–?)**.** Member of the **Perhimpunan Indonesia (PI)** and later leader of the **Partai Sarekat Islam Indonesia (PSII)** until he left in 1933 to form the Partai Islam Indonesia (PII). He was one of the modernist leaders who took control of **Masjumi** in 1945, and he served as prime minister from April 1951 to February 1952. His term in office was marked by hostility to the **army**: pro-army leaders were excluded, and ***lasykar*** captured by the army after the **Revolution** were released. Sukiman also attempted to suppress the **Partai Komunis Indonesia (PKI)**, arresting perhaps 15,000 party members in August 1951. Pro-Western in its foreign **policy**, his cabinet fell after it signed a secret aid agreement with the **United States** committing Indonesia to help defend the "free world." [0695]

SULAWESI (Celebes)**.** Island in the Greater Sundas. The origin of the name is uncertain: Sulawesi may derive from *sula besi*, "island of **iron**," while Celebes may come from the **Portuguese** Punta des Celebres, Cape of the Infamous. The island's distinctive shape with four arms separated by broad gulfs has led it to be compared variously to a spider, an orchid, a giraffe, a starfish, and a drunken letter K. Only the southern arm around **Makassar** and the northern arm around **Minahasa** are volcanic, and these fertile areas are the most heavily populated parts of the island, which in the 2000 census had a population of just under 15 million.

Bronze Buddha images dating from the fourth to fifth century have been found in southern Sulawesi, suggesting first Hindu influences at about the same time as on **Java**, **Sumatra**, and **Kalimantan**, but no major early kingdoms developed there. Four ethnic groups dominate this region: the Makassarese in the far south, the **Bugis** farther north, the Luwunese still farther north, and the Mandar to the northwest. The kingdom of **Luwu** or La Galigo emerged on the southern peninsula in the ninth century, and the Bugis kingdoms of **Bone**, **Wajo'**, and Soppeng and the Makassarese kingdom of Gowa (Goa) arose in the 13th century among a scattering of perhaps 50 small states, variously Hindu and animist. Gowa and its sister port Tallo accepted **Islam** in 1605 and, now commonly known as Makassar, soon became influential beyond the peninsula in **Kalimantan** and **Sumbawa**. In 1660, however, Makassar was captured by the Dutch in alliance with **Arung Palakka** of Bone.

The rest of the island meanwhile remained largely under small tribes, most notably the **Toraja** of the central mountains, though the kingdom of Bolaäng Mongondouw on the northern peninsula flourished briefly until it was subjected by the **Maluku** kingdom of **Ternate**, which also dominated the gulf of Tomini (*see* **GORONTALO**). The entire island was claimed by the **Dutch** in 1846 and was ruled loosely by the governor of *Celebes en Onderhoorigheden* (Sulawesi and dependencies), but Dutch control in the interior was not felt until the late 19th century.

After the **Japanese occupation**, the island was reoccupied by Australian troops, who were instrumental in suppressing the initial attempt by local nationalists to join the Indonesian republic. Thereafter, Sulawesi was a linchpin in Dutch plans for **federalism** in Indonesia and Makassar was the capital of the short-lived **Negara Indonesia Timur (NIT)**. After the dissolution of the NIT in 1950, Sulawesi was the site of rebellions against the central authorities by both the **Darul Islam (DI)** and the Permesta (Piagam Perjuangan Semesta Alam). (*See* **PRRI/PERMESTA REBELLION**.) Under the **New Order**, **nickel mining** expanded on the southeastern peninsula, and parts of the island were an important destination for Balinese **transmigration** settlements.

After **Suharto**'s fall, interreligious violence first broke out in Poso, Central Sulawesi, on 24 December 1998, and flared and subsided over the subsequent years. Although Christians and Muslims reached a peace deal in December 2001, surrendering hundreds of weapons to the **police**, violence soon resumed. It was estimated that in the district of Poso at least 500 people were killed, about 80,000 forced to flee, and 10,000 buildings destroyed. The Muslim side was reinforced by about 500 members of **Laskar Jihad** from Java. Christian refugees fled mostly to the nearby town of Tentena and Muslims fled to Palu, the provincial capital. A respite in the sporadic violence occurred between December 2002 and May 2003, but during the last three months of the year shootings and bombings upsurged, especially in the Poso area. [0161, 0549, 0786, 0787, 0831, 1227, 1254, 1327, 1376, 1396]

SUMATRA (Sumatera, from Samudra, former name of the kingdom of **Pasai**). The westernmost and third largest of Indonesia's main islands, it is divided geographically into a mountainous spine, the Bukit Barisan, in the west and an area of flat lowland, often swampy, in the east. The rugged terrain of the Bukit Barisan has made overland travel difficult, and a number of distinct peoples—the **Gayo**, **Batak**, **Minangkabau**, Rejang, and Lebang—developed in the relatively isolated valleys of the interior. The coastal regions of the east and south were dominated by **Malays** and were tied politically, culturally, and economically to the **Malay Peninsula** until the hardening of colonial and national borders. In the north, the Acehnese came under Muslim influence in early times.

The earliest major kingdoms on Sumatra (**Srivijaya** and **Jambi**) arose initially as river-based controllers of the Strait of **Melaka** (*see also* **PIRACY**) that were vital to the **India–China** trade, but they also depended on alliance with peoples and rulers in the interior who supplied forest and **mining** products such as **camphor**, **pepper**, and **gold** for **trade**. Later kingdoms (Pasai, **Pedir**, and **Aceh**), for the most part Muslim, depended more on this entrepôt role, and Aceh was probably the most successful in bringing regions of the interior under its control.

European domination of the trade routes from the 18th century left new coastal states (**Palembang**, **Deli**, and **Riau**) relatively weak, but European powers did not attempt to extend significant control over territory until the early 19th century. After the return of **Java** to the **Dutch** in 1816, **Thomas Stamford Raffles** attempted to build the British colony in **Bengkulu** into a major base, and the Dutch became involved soon after in the politics of Minangkabau through the Paderi War. The British ceded Bengkulu and other possessions in Sumatra to the Dutch in the Treaty of London of 1824 (*see* **ANGLO-DUTCH TREATY**). Aceh was not fully conquered until 1903. The introduction of plantation crops to **East Sumatra** by private Dutch companies—**tobacco** in 1864, **rubber** and **oil palms** in the early 20th century—together with the discovery of **oil** dramatically changed the **economy** of the island, making it the richest export area of the Netherlands Indies and later of Indonesia. The social character of East Sumatra changed drastically with the introduction of many Javanese and **Chinese** indentured laborers.

Sumatrans—**Mohammad Hatta**, **Sutan Sjahrir**, **Tan Malaka**, **Muhammad Yamin**, **Amir Sjarifuddin**, and others—took a major part in the rise of Indonesian **nationalism** in the 20th century and although the island was administratively united with Malaya under the 25th army during part of the **Japanese occupation**, local nationalists enthusiastically declared for the Republic in 1945. Fierce social revolutions broke out against aristocratic associates of the Dutch in Aceh and **East Suma-**

tra. In the latter part of the **Revolution**, the Dutch attempted to establish federal states in East and South Sumatra, but these were abolished in 1950.

After the transfer of sovereignty, Sumatra was divided into three **provinces**: North, Central, and South Sumatra. Resentment in much of the island grew during the 1950s. A revolt broke out in Aceh from 1953 to 1957, southern Sumatra had become a major destination for settlers under the **transmigration** program, while in North Sumatra the government insisted on removing squatters from foreign-controlled plantation lands occupied during the Revolution. Sumatrans also felt that their island was generating most of Indonesia's wealth while getting little in return. Dissatisfaction over **Jakarta**'s allocation of income earned by Sumatra's exports was among the reasons for regional movements led by local military commanders emerging in **Padang**, Medan, and **Palembang**. These developed into the **PRRI/Permesta rebellion** in February 1958, when military and civilian leaders proclaimed a revolutionary government with its center in West Sumatra.

After the rebellion was suppressed in 1961, military forces on the island were largely under Javanese leadership until the closing years of the **New Order**. The **Suharto** government accelerated the transmigration policy, particularly to the **Lampung** area of South Sumatra. Also, large areas of the island were converted from native vegetation to **oil palm** plantations, with huge tracts of **forest** being destroyed. **Land** clearing was carried out, often during severe drought conditions, and this was one of the major causes of the fires that swept across the region in 1997–1978 and during subsequent years. [0077, 0124, 0284, 0291, 0569, 0775,1179, 1187, 1240]

SUMBA. An island in **Nusatenggara** whose abundant **sandalwood** trees attracted European attention in the 17th century; the area was repeatedly raided for **slaves**. The **Dutch** obtained treaty rights in 1756 and instituted direct rule in 1866, but the island was relatively neglected and few of its inhabitants converted to **Christianity**. The raising of horses for export began in the 1840s, and the island is also known for its production of ikat **cloth**. *See also* SAVU. [0147, 1220, 1395]

SUMBAWA. Mountainous island in **Nusatenggara**, commonly divided into two kingdoms, **Bima** in the east and Sumbawa in the west. The island was a major exporter of **sandalwood** and later horses but was devastated in 1815 by the eruption of Mt. **Tambora**, in which 50,000 people were reportedly killed. After independence it became part of the province of Nusatenggara and in 1958 of West Nusatenggara.

SUMITRO DJOJOHADIKUSUMO (1917–2001). Son of the founder of the Bank Negara Indonesia, Margono Djojohadikusumo (1894–1978), Sumitro was born in Central **Java** and earned his doctorate in economics at the Rotterdam School of Commerce. On graduating, he remained in the Netherlands and participated in the underground struggle during World War II. He returned to Indonesia in 1946, and during the **Revolution** he negotiated a number of trading agreements in the **United States** intended to draw American business interests to the side of the Republic. He was a leading member of the **Partai Sosialis Indonesia (PSI)** and an assistant to **Sutan Sjahrir** (once unsuccessfully challenging Sjahrir for the party's leadership). In 1949 he played an important role in defending the economic position of the Republic against Dutch demands during the **Round Table Conference** in The Hague. He was appointed minister of **trade** and industry in the **Mohammad Natsir** cabinet and was responsible for launching the **Benteng Program**, also arguing in favor of foreign **investment** as a key to development. Dean of the Economics Faculty at the University of Indonesia, he cooperated with the Ford Foundation in training a cadre of economists who became known as the Berkeley Mafia.

Accused by the **army** of financial manipulations, Sumitro fled to **Sumatra** at the end of 1957 and joined with the **PRRI/Permesta rebellion**, serving as its foreign minister. After the rebellion was suppressed he remained in **exile** in **Malaysia** until the advent of the **New Order**, when he returned to Indonesia and was appointed minister for trade and commerce in 1968, but he retreated to the portfolio of state research in 1973 after widespread accusations that PSI figures were too influential in the regime. He remained an important advisor to his former pupils in **Badan Perencanaan Pembangunan Nasional (Bappenas)**. His son, **Prabowo Subianto**, married one of **Suharto**'s daughters (Siti Hediati Harijadi). [1121]

SUNDA. Though its boundaries are hard to define precisely, Sunda refers generally to the western third of the island of **Java**, dominated by the Sundanese people, though much of the northern coast is now not Sundanese. One of the earliest historical states in the archipelago, **Tarumanegara**, had its center near modern **Bogor**, and the region was apparently dominated by **Srivijaya** in the late seventh century, but little else is known of it until the emergence of Hindu **Pajajaran** in the 14th century. **Islam** reached **Banten** and **Cirebon** in the 16th century, and the conversion of the interior began soon after the fall of Pajajaran in 1579. Less influenced by Hindu-Buddhist traditions than the rest of Java, the Sundanese became increasingly strongly Muslim, and the region was one of the centers of the **Darul Islam (DI)** rebellion. *See also* PASUNDAN; PRIANGAN. [0358]

SUNDA KELAPA. *See* BANTEN; PAJAJARAN.

SUNDA SHELF. A large southern extension of the Asian continental land mass carrying the islands of **Sumatra**, **Kalimantan**, and **Java**. During 20 successive periods of glaciation over the last 2 million years, and most recently circa 50,000–15,000 years ago, the entire shelf has been exposed. **East Sumatra** and West Kalimantan were then drained by the great Sunda River, flowing into the South China Sea north of Sarawak, while Java and South Kalimantan were drained by another major river flowing into what is now the **Flores** Sea. There were glaciers on Mt. Leuser in Sumatra at this time, and the climate seems to have been drier, but it is difficult to reconstruct the region's **prehistory** since most areas of possible human habitation have been flooded. *See also* CONTINENTAL DRIFT.

SUPERSEMAR (Surat Perintah Sebelas Maret, Executive Order of 11 March 1966). Signed reluctantly by **Sukarno**, it ordered General **Suharto** "to take all necessary steps to guarantee security and calm and the stability of the running of the government and the course of the Revolution," thus transferring full executive authority to Suharto. *See also* SEMAR. [0727]

SUPREME COURT (Mahkamah Agung). At independence Indonesia inherited from the Netherlands East Indies a Supreme Court (now renamed the Mahkamah Agung) operating in a constitutional system calling for a separation of government powers. Rejecting a proposal from **Muhammad Yamin** that the newly independent country adopt a balance of powers doctrine, the meetings of the **Badan Penyelidik Usaha Persiapan Kemerdekaan Indonesia (BPUPKI)** retained the colonial system of separation of powers, thus leaving the Court within a system favoring executive rather than judicial power. This meant that the Court had no right of judicial review of the constitutionality of Acts of Parliament. The government strengthened its grip over the judiciary during **Guided Democracy**, by reducing the judiciary's salaries and defining its powers more narrowly.

Under the **New Order**, the judiciary strove to retain its autonomy, but the government successfully ensured its institutional loyalty through the political appointments of Supreme Court leaders and strengthening the powers of these leaders within the Court. The struggle to change the Supreme Court and the judiciary continued to focus on the separation of powers doctrine, with the government increasingly after 1970 replacing the Supreme Court in controlling judiciary personnel management. Also after 1970, constitutional review was seen as requiring a special constitutional authority, so the possibilities of judicial review were restricted. In 1985 Law no. 14 categorized the Supreme Court's tasks into four functions: judicial, advisory, regulatory, and administrative, the principal one being the judicial function, which refers to dispute settlement (cassation). These functions are primarily directed toward ensuring a uniform application of the **law** in the lower courts. At the same time the workload of the Court increased, and by the early 1990s it faced a backlog of more than 20,000 undecided cases. The burden of this caseload meant that the Court was unable to supervise the lower courts effectively, and the lack of control led to a larger number of irregularities and indirectly to a lowering of professional standards among the judges.

After the fall of **Suharto**, President **Abdurrachman Wahid** attempted to reform the Supreme Court by replacing 17 of its judges with new figures not touched by **corruption**. Without a more widespread reform of the institution and a correction of the abuses in the legal system, however, this move seemed unlikely to have a major effect on the Supreme Court's effective operation. This was recognized in the amendments to the 1945 **Constitution** passed in August 2002, when parliament approved the establishment of a Constitutional Court to be set up by August 2003 separate from the Supreme Court to decide a range of disputes with the authority to try cases at the first and final level, as well as review laws against the Constitution. A Commission of Judiciary was also established to propose candidates for appointments to the Supreme Court. [0989, 1095, 1096, 1098]

SURABAYA. Port city at a mouth of the Brantas River in East **Java** founded, according to official accounts, in 1293, when Raden Wijaya drove out the Mongols to become ruler of **Majapahit**. It became an important port in the 15th century under Raden Rahmat or Sunan Ngampel, but was first subject to **Demak**, then briefly independent, and finally in 1625 conquered by **Mataram**. It was seized by the **Dutch East Indies Company (VOC)** in 1743. **Herman Willem Daendels** established a naval base there. Under Dutch rule it became the major city of East Java, the principal commercial center for eastern Indonesia, and headquarters of the Dutch **navy** in the east. It was heavily bombed by the Allies during World War II and was the scene of fierce fighting between Indonesian nationalist forces and British Indian troops in November 1945. 11 November is celebrated as Heroes' Day in its honor. [0652, 0789]

SURAKARTA (Solo)**.** Javanese court city founded in 1743 by Sunan Pakubuwono II (r. 1726–1749) of **Mataram**. After the treaty of **Giyanti** (1755), which divided Mataram, the rump of the old kingdom became the Sunanate (*Kasunanan*) of Surakarta, remaining a relatively prosperous center of **trade**, **agriculture**, and **batik** manufacture. As in **Yogyakarta**, political impotence generated a cultural florescence, Solo producing a style said to be gentler and less martial than Yogyakarta's. The Sunanate was abolished by the Indonesian Republic in 1946, after the sunan had failed to join it unequivocally against the Dutch. *See also* MANGKUNEGARAN. [0577, 0632, 1248, 1392]

SURAPATI (?–1706)**.** Former Balinese slave in **Batavia** who escaped to the surrounding countryside to lead a bandit gang. In 1683 he surrendered to the Dutch and joined the **Dutch East Indies Company (VOC)** forces, but in 1684 he attacked the company again and fled to Kartasura, capital of **Mataram**, where he successfully ambushed a VOC unit sent to capture him. He then fled to Pasuruan in East **Java** and established an independent kingdom, defeating a Mataram army in 1690 and pushing his domains east to Madiun in 1694. Surapati was finally killed in joint campaigns by the VOC, Mataram, and **Madura** in 1706, but his descendants continued to rule the region until the mid-18th century. *See also* BALAMBANGAN. [0567]

SURAU. *See MADRASAH; PESANTREN.*

SURINAM, JAVANESE IN. Toward the end of the 19th century, **Dutch** concern over the growth of **population** in **Java** and a desire to limit the number of contract laborers from British **India** on plantations in the Dutch South American colony of Surinam led to the recruitment of Javanese for work there. Between 1891 and 1939, 32,976 Javanese entered the colony, usually on five-year contracts. Some 7,684 of these were repatriated before World War II and about 1,000 in 1954, the remainder settling in the colony. In 1962 the Javanese population was 43,000.

SUTARJO PETITION. Presented to the **Volksraad** in July 1936 by Sutarjo Kartohadikusumo, a career bureaucrat, rather than a member of the nationalist movement, the petition asked for a conference to prepare dominion status for Indonesia after 10 years, along the Philippine Commonwealth model. Many nationalists believed the petition asked for too little, but the colonial authorities' failure to act on its proposals after it had been passed by the Volksraad became a symbol of Dutch political intransigence. [0587]

SUTOMO, DR. (1888–1938)**.** Physician, founder of several "study clubs" intended to spread nationalist awareness among young intellectuals, cofounder of the protonationalist **Budi Utomo**, and later head of **Partai Indonesia Raya (Parindra)**, he argued especially that adherence to **Islam** was incompatible with **nationalism**. *See also* ALGEMENE STUDIECLUB. [0502, 0888]

SUTRISNO, TRY (1935–)**.** Born in **Surabaya**, Sutrisno graduated from the **Army** Technical Academy (Aktedkad) in 1959. He was **Suharto**'s adjutant (1974–1978) and served as chief of staff in **East Timor** and commander of Kodam IV in South **Sumatra** before being appointed to head the **Jakarta** command (Kodam X) in 1982. He became army chief of staff in 1986 and replaced **Benny Murdani** as **armed forces** commander in February 1988. He had a reputation for being charming but weak, established good ties with the Muslim community, and was a personal favorite of Suharto. Sutrisno did not display great ability or good judgment in his military career, heading the Jakarta command during the Tanjung Priok riots (*see* **WHITE PAPER**) and a period of great lawlessness in the city, and then being commander of the armed forces during the **Lampung** Affair and the 1991 massacre in **East Timor**, where he defended his officers' performance in the face of the evidence of widespread abuse. Nevertheless, with military backing he was appointed **vice president** in March 1993, serving in the post until 1998. [0751]

SUWARDI SURYANINGRAT, R. M. (1889–1959)**.** Early nationalist and leader of the **Indische Partij**. His article "If I were to be a Dutchman"

("Als ik eens Nederlander was," 1913) was a classic turning of the arguments of European liberalism against colonialism. Exiled to Holland 1913–1919, he became interested in **educational** philosophy and in 1922, taking the name Ki Hajar Dewantoro, founded the **Taman Siswa** school system. In 1943 he briefly joined the leadership of the **Japanese**-sponsored mass organization Putera, but soon withdrew to concentrate on educational matters. He remained close to **Sukarno**, and his ideas on the governance of Taman Siswa schools were one of the elements contributing to the philosophy of **Guided Democracy**. *See also* NATIONALISM.

SWEET POTATO (*Ipomoea batatas* Convolvulaceae)**.** Introduced from South America by the 17th century, it gradually replaced the **yam** in much cultivation, especially in **Papua**, since it is quicker to grow and prepare, though it stores much less well.

SYPHILIS. Though this was probably restricted to the **Americas** until 1492, there is evidence for some sort of venereal disease in Indonesia early in the 14th century. The fact that syphilis apparently did not cause an immediate epidemic when it arrived in the 16th century suggests the earlier presence of some related disease, perhaps yaws. Nonetheless, the disease was widespread by the early 19th century, and **Thomas Stamford Raffles** established a hospital for sufferers in **Yogyakarta** in 1811. From 1852 regular medical checks for syphilis were required of prostitutes in all parts of **Java**, but since this proved costly and the connection with **prostitution** was unclear, the tests were abandoned in 1911. *See also* HEALTH. [0576]

– T –

TAHANAN POLITIK (*TAPOL*, political prisoners)**.** Term generally applied to the approximately 700,000 persons detained after October 1965 on suspicion of complicity in the **Gestapu** coup attempt of 1965, though the criterion was association with the **Partai Komunis Indonesia (PKI)** rather than activities on the evening in question. "A" category prisoners, often major figures, were brought to trial; "B" category, generally lesser figures, were detained without trial, about 10,000 being shipped after 1969 to **Buru**; and "C" category, about 550,000 persons, were detained only briefly. Most "B" *tapol* were released by late 1979. All former *tapol*, however, were noted as such on their identity cards and were barred from a number of political and social activities. *See also* MAHKAMAH MILITER LUAR BIASA.

TAMAN SISWA (Garden of Pupils)**.** School system founded in Yogyakarta in 1922 by Ki Hajar Dewantoro (**Suwardi Suryaningrat**), under the influence of the ideas of Rabindranath Tagore and Maria Montessori. Though receiving no government subsidy, the system rapidly expanded to 166 schools in 1932, teaching from primary to teachers' training level. Taman Siswa schools aimed at sound development of personality and freedom of the individual within a broad national, rather than international, colonial, or Islamic, culture. Although explicitly nonpolitical in curriculum, the schools played a major role in developing self-confidence and skills among young Indonesians. *See also* EDUCATION; NATIONALISM. [1279, 1288]

TAMBORA. Volcano on the island of **Sumbawa** that erupted in April 1815 in the most massive explosion in recent human history, substantially exceeding that of **Krakatau**. Perhaps 12,000 people were killed on Sumbawa, and a total of 117,000 died from the effects of the eruption. The kingdoms of Tambora and Papegat on Sumbawa were destroyed; the rain of ash caused crop failure and famine on **Bali**, **Lombok**, and neighboring islands; and ash in the atmosphere made 1816 a "year without summer" in Europe. [1176]

TAN MALAKA (Sutan Ibrahim gelar Datuk Tan Malaka) (1897–1949)**.** An Indonesian revolutionary and Marxist theorist, he was born in West **Sumatra** and educated there and in the Netherlands (1913–1919). On his return to Indonesia, he was involved in **labor union** and later **Partai Komunis Indonesia (PKI)** activity, becoming party chairman in December 1921. After backing a **pawnshop** workers' strike, he was exiled in March 1922 to Holland, where he stood for parliament on the Dutch Communist Party ticket before going to Moscow to join the staff of the Comintern. He argued strongly for an alliance of **communism** with **nationalism** and Pan-Islam, and in 1923 he was appointed Comintern agent for Southeast Asia, with headquarters in Canton. From **exile**, he opposed the PKI's decision to abandon its alliance with **Sarekat Islam** and to launch a premature revolution. After the uprisings of 1926–1927 failed, the party accused him of sabotage. The inaccurate description of him as "Trotskyist" dates from this time.

On 1 June 1927 Tan Malaka founded the **Partai Republik Indonesia (PARI)** in Bangkok, a secretive underground party that spread over many parts of Indonesia (particularly Sumatra and **Java**) during the next decade, though he himself remained abroad in southern **China** until 1937 and thereafter mostly in **Singapore**. In 1942, after the **Japanese** takeover, he returned secretly to Indonesia, traveling via Sumatra to **Banten**, where he worked mostly as a clerk in a coalmine in southern Banten.

On the outbreak of the **Revolution** in 1945, Tan Malaka opposed the more cautious policies of the **Sukarno/Mohammad Hatta** leadership and favored mass mobilization on a platform of revolutionary change. He became the central figure in the radical **Persatuan Perjuangan** demanding 100 percent independence. Accused of trying to overthrow the state, he was jailed from March 1946 until September 1948, when the Hatta government released him in order to strengthen the anti-PKI forces. He remained, however, an implacable critic of negotiation with the Dutch and in November 1948 became "promoter" of the new **Murba** party. He continued campaigning against the Republican government after the second **"Police Action"** and was captured and shot by Republican troops in February 1949. [0643, 0853, 0866, 0871, 0873]

TANAH BENGKOK (*ambtsvelden*)**. Land** allocated to officials in lieu of salary. The allocation of *bengkok* lands was abolished by Fransen van de Putte in 1867 except at the village level, where it remained common in Central and East **Java**. The strong hold of officials on these lands became a recurrent source of social tension, especially during the late 1940s and early 1960s. *See also* LAND REFORM.

TANAH MERAH. *See* BOVEN DIGUL.

TANIMBAR (Timor Laut) **ISLANDS.** An archipelago of about 70, mostly low, limestone and coral islands with coastal villages engaged in fishing and warfare. In 1646 the **Dutch East Indies Company (VOC)** signed a monopoly treaty with some village chiefs for the **trade** in **slaves**, turtleshell, shark fins, ambergris, beeswax, and sapanwood and briefly established forts in the archipelago that they had abandoned by the end of the century. The **Dutch** showed little interest in the islands in the 18th or 19th centuries, but in 1912 a military expedition was sent to subdue them. Extensive conversions to **Catholicism** and **Protestantism** then took place.

TANJUNG PRIOK. *See* JAKARTA; PORTS; WHITE PAPER.

TAPANULI. *See* BATAKS.

TARUMANEGARA. Early state in West **Java**, based in the vicinity of modern **Bogor**. Its existence is known only from four Sanskrit inscriptions from around 450 A.D., which record King Purnavarman as presiding over canal construction, one of the earliest records of water management in Southeast Asia. *See also* "HO-LO-TAN"; KUTAI; SUNDA.

TAXATION. An important measure of state power throughout Indonesian history. Early rulers in the archipelago obtained significant income through personal **trade**, plunder (*see* **PIRACY**), and direct control of production by means of control of **labor** and **land**, but the development of a state apparatus for regularized revenue collection was a gradual phenomenon. There appear to have been two key elements in this process. One was the emergence of an appanage system, under which rulers allocated particular regions or blocks of **population** to "vassals" in exchange for a guarantee of military and political support, a broadly feudal system. The other was the emergence of tax farms (*see* ***PACHT***). The forced delivery system of the **Dutch East Indies Company (VOC)** in West Java (*see* **PRIANGAN**) was an attempt at the direct taxation of peasants with indigenous rulers as collection agents. This system was intensified with the institution of **land rent** and the **Cultivation System**. Export and import duties were an important part of state revenue after the abolition of the VOC, while property tax was introduced in 1890. Company tax was first levied in 1907 and income tax in 1908 (it was made uniform for all races in 1920). In 1908 a poll tax (*hoofdgeld*, capitation) was levied in North and West **Sumatra** as substitute for land rent. The poll tax levied on **Java** and **Madura** as a substitute for ***herendiensten*** was abolished in 1927.

After independence, export and company taxes remained the central pillar of state revenues and, in 1980–1981, 60 percent of all government revenue came from tax on **oil** companies. Less than 1 percent of the population was subject to income tax. After 1983 a number of tax reform measures were introduced, aimed in part at making Indonesia a more attractive country for foreign **investment** and broadening the state's tax base. These included lowering the maximum tax rate from 45 to 35 percent, introducing in April 1985 a 10 percent VAT (on many items such as petroleum and **tobacco** as well as a number of farm inputs, particularly fertilizers, but not on farmers' products), and reforming the income tax laws. As a result of these reforms, nonoil income tax revenue increased markedly, with 59 percent of government expenditures being funded by this revenue in 1996 compared with only 24.7 percent prior to the reforms. Government revenue from income tax rose from Rp 12.5 billion in 1992–1993 to Rp 55 billion in 1999–2000, with revenue from VAT rising from Rp 10.7 billion to Rp 33 billion in the same period. (This rise, however, would have been more than offset by the fall in the exchange rate of the rupiah during the **financial crisis**.) In effect from 1 January 2001, the finance ministry imposed a new tax structure for individual and corporate taxpayers, with five different rates, ranging from 5 to 35 percent, the highest rate being applied to those with an annual income of more than Rp 200 million (US$22,700). *See also* GAMBLING; PERDIKAN VILLAGES; TOBACCO. [0053, 0376, 0380, 0386, 0399]

TEA (*Camellia sinensis* Theaceae)**.** Chinese in origin, tea was first grown in Indonesia at the instigation of Governor-General Joannes Camphuys in 1690. Extensive cultivation began in 1825 and was continued under the **Cultivation System**, though never with much profit, and the government monopoly on production was lifted in 1865. After 1870 there was a massive expansion of private tea plantations in mountainous areas of West **Java** and later in North **Sumatra**. The industry suffered badly in the **Depression**, especially because of the British Imperial Preference scheme, but by 1940 a total of 213,000 hectares (ha) was under tea production, about one third of it by smallholders, and tea was the Indies' second export earner after **rubber**. Extensive clearing of plantations during the **Japanese occupation** greatly reduced the planted areas (now 125,000 ha), and the industry was further hampered by the **Darul Islam (DI)** rebellion in West Java. Dutch plantations were nationalized in 1957, and a combination of disease, lack of investment and replanting, and poor agricultural practices has meant that Indonesian tea tends to be of lesser quality than fine teas from **India** and Sri Lanka, though it has high production volume and commands about 8 percent of the world market. In the 1970s, commercially bottled sweet tea (*teh botol*) gained an important share of the soft drink market. [0316, 0331, 0332]

TEAK (*Tectona grandis* Verbenaceae)**.** Introduced from **India**, probably about the 10th century, teak forests along the northern coast of **Java** became a major source of income for the **Dutch East Indies Company (VOC)**. Prized for its hard wood and resistant to worms and ants, teak was used for the construction of ships in precolonial times and was extensively grown by the Netherlands Indies **forestry** service in Central and East Java. Under the **Suharto** regime, these major teak plantations (in Cepu, Kebonhardjo, Kendal, Lawu, and Madiun) were managed by the state-owned Perum Perhutani (State Forestry Corporation). They received certification from the Forest Stewardship Council (FSC) in 1998, a certification that was withdrawn in October 2001 for four of the five plantations because long-term sustainability of the plantation resources was at serious risk and Perhutani had failed to crack down on illegal logging. [1148]

TELEGRAPH. The first telegraph lines in Indonesia were laid in 1857 between **Batavia** and Buitenzorg (**Bogor**) and were briefly restricted to government use. An undersea cable between Batavia and **Singapore** was laid in 1859 and the first lines on **Sumatra** in 1866. A link with **Australia** was established via Banyuwangi in 1871. In 1905 the German-Dutch Telegraph Co. of Cologne completed a cable link to Yap in the German Pacific territories, linking the colony with Europe via Siberia and the **United States**, a line independent of British colonies and British firms. In 1905 the colonial government purchased a cable ship to establish undersea connections throughout the archipelago. *See also* PALAPA.

TELEVISION. The national broadcaster Televisi Republik Indonesia (TVRI) began operations in 1964. During the 1980s, under an Information Ministry program called *televisi masuk desa* (television enters the village), sets were provided to virtually all villages throughout the country, creating a major information conduit from the central government. Commercial advertisements were banned from television in 1981. In 1987 there were an estimated 6 million television sets throughout the country. The state-owned TVRI was a monopoly until 1989 when the government licensed five private television channels to compete with it, allowing them to make a profit by advertising but requiring that a portion of their revenues go to the state network. Licenses for four of these new channels went to **Suharto**'s friends and family. In 1999 President **B. J. Habibie** doubled the number of commercial TV licenses. *See also* MEDIA; PALAPA; RADIO. [0154, 1294, 1299, 1302]

TENGGER. *See ASLI*; HINDUISM.

TERNATE. Kingdom in northern **Maluku** that rose in the 13th century on the basis of **trade** in **cloves**. It converted to **Islam** in the 15th century and under the warlike Sultan Baabullah (r. 1570–1583) dominated much of the surrounding region, including northern and eastern **Sulawesi**, **Banda**, and the coasts of **Papua**. The **Portuguese**, who established a fort there in 1522, were expelled in 1574, but the island was conquered by **Spanish** forces in 1606. The **Dutch East Indies Company (VOC)** competed with Ternate for control of the clove trade, fighting a fierce war (1652–1658) before Ternate finally accepted VOC suzerainty in 1667. *See also* TIDORE. [0026]

THAILAND, RELATIONS WITH. After the tentative efforts toward regional cooperation promoted by Thai leaders in the period immediately following World War II (*see* **SOUTH EAST ASIA LEAGUE**), there were few ties between the two countries until the establishment of the **Association of Southeast Asian Nations (ASEAN)** in the late 1960s. During the **Sukarno** era, Indonesian foreign policy leaders tended to view Thailand as a feudal military regime, and during the **Vietnam** war, its membership in the Southeast Asia Treaty Organization (SEATO) and the presence of American bases on its territory led Indonesians to see Thailand as a satellite of the **United States**. Despite economic and some military cooperation between the two countries within ASEAN during the 1970s and 1980s, they differed in their approach to **China** and Vietnam, with Thailand regarding Vietnam as the most immediate threat and Indonesia instead viewing China as more minatory. As a result they favored competing strategies in resolving the conflicts in Indochina, though ASEAN formally adopted the Thai position. Indonesia's closest economic ties have been with the other members of ASEAN, but southern Thailand participates in a **growth triangle** encompassing parts of **Sumatra** and **Malaysia**. *See also* CAMBODIA; SIAM, HISTORICAL LINKS WITH. [1103, 1144]

TIDORE. A kingdom in northern **Maluku**, geographically close and rival to **Ternate**, and like it based on the **clove trade**. It had major trading and raiding links with **Halmahera** and **Papua** (and for this reason was chosen in 1956 as provisional capital of the province of Irian Barat, then still held by the **Dutch**). The **Portuguese** established a fort there in 1578, and the **Spanish**, then united with the Portuguese, made it a center of their operations in the region in the early 17th century. The island was captured by the Dutch in 1654. [0026, 1251]

TIGA A (Triple A) **MOVEMENT.** Initially a slogan "Japan the Light of Asia, Japan the Leader of Asia, Japan the Protector of Asia" sponsored by the **Japanese** on their arrival in **Java** in March 1942 and drawing on widespread enthusiasm for Japan's role in ending **Dutch** colonialism. By April 1942 the slogan had ostensibly become an organization, apparently for the mobilization of Indonesians in the war effort. It appears, however, that the organization had little substance and certainly little participation from senior Indonesian or Japanese figures. It was superseded by **Putera** in March 1943 but had long been of no significance. [0663]

TIGA DAERAH (Three Regions) **AFFAIR.** From October to December 1945, a social revolution broke out in Brebes, Tegal, and Pemalang, the so-called three regions of Pekalongan residency, in which the local elite were killed or driven out and a coalition of local **Partai Komunis Indonesia (PKI)** members, radical Muslims, and gangsters (*lenggaong*) established a revolutionary government. The revolutionaries were nominally loyal to the Indonesian Republic, but the Republic's leaders saw them as dangerous and embarrassing, and the **army** suppressed the movement in December 1945. [0660, 0665]

TIGER (*Panthera tigris*)**.** The largest predatory animal in western Indonesia, preying mainly on **pig** and deer. As pig numbers increased with the spread of cultivation, so apparently did those of the tiger, becoming a major danger to human and animal life until the 19th century when forest clearing began to remove its habitat. A bounty was offered on carcasses in many regions until 1897. Separate subspecies occurred on **Sumatra**, **Java**, and **Bali**, the latter two of which are now extinct. The Balinese subspecies probably disappeared before World War II; the Javanese was reduced to perhaps four individuals in 1989 and has since become extinct. Leopards (sometimes called panthers), also found on Java, appear to account for many reported tiger sightings. Only about 500 wild Sumatran tigers remain, 75 percent of them inhabiting the island's six national parks. *See also* WALLACE'S LINE. [1149, 1154, 1179, 1187]

TIMOR. Island at the eastern end of **Nusatenggara**, mountainous, arid, and now seriously deforested. The indigenous population was of mixed Austronesian-Melanesian ancestry and included the Atoni in the west and the Belu in the center. Traders visited the island for **sandalwood** from the seventh century, and **Portuguese** arrived for the same reason in 1520. Portugal's regional center was on **Solor**, but coastal Timor came to be dominated by the Topasses, or "black Portuguese," mestizo descendants of **Dutch** and Portuguese settlers and Solorese who also dominated eastern **Flores**. In the 17th century, Makassarese influence led to the conversion of some regions to **Islam**. A Dutch settlement was founded at Kupang in 1653 and a Portuguese post at Dili in 1769, but it was not until 1839 that negotiations began to sort out a colonial division of territory on the island. A treaty was signed in 1859, but only in 1914 was the border finally fixed and colonial rule firmly established in the interior on either side of the border. *See also* EAST TIMOR; ROTI. [0029, 0953, 1220, 1255, 1266]

TIMOR GAP. *See* ARCHIPELAGIC CONCEPT.

TIMOR LAUT. *See* TANIMBAR.

TIN. Rich alluvial tin (cassiterite) deposits are found in Indonesia on the islands of **Bangka** and **Belitung**, geologically an extension of the **Malay Peninsula**, which was a major early source of tin for the production of bronze (*see* **COPPER**). Small amounts of tin were exported to **China** from the 13th century. Large-scale extraction was begun on Bangka in 1710 by the Sultan of **Palembang**. **Mining** was undertaken by **Chinese**, organized in ***kongsi***, who contracted with the sultan to pay for the right to extract tin from defined areas. This system was taken over by the **Dutch** in 1823, the government supplying advances of **rice**, **oil**, and money and contracting to buy tin at a price fixed in advance according to the expected productivity of the soil.

Mechanization of the mining began in the early 20th century, and in 1927 the so-called Bangka Tinwinning was established as a **state enterprise** of the colonial government; after World War II, operations were taken over by a private firm, the Gemeenschappelijke Mijnbouw Billiton, which was nationalized in 1953. Mining began on Belitung in 1850 and by 1860 was in the hands of a private company, the Billiton-Maatschappij. Actual extraction of the tin, however, was done by Chinese *kongsi*. Large-scale offshore mining using dredges began in 1966. In the early 1990s many of the mines began to be closed, and mining phased out as world prices made it unprofitable to mine the tin reserves. The state-owned company PT Tambang Timah began producing low-lead tin in 1992 to meet the more stringent import requirements of the **United States** and Europe. [0411, 0801]

TITLES. A wide variety of titles, hereditary and conferred, were used by the traditional aristocracies of the archipelago, and many of these were preserved by the **Dutch** as part of their policy of retaining native rulers as agents of colonial rule. During and immediately after the **Revolution**, many titles fell out of use, but they seem now to be being revived. The Javanese lower aristocratic title *Raden* (abbreviated R.) and its female equivalent *Raden Ajeng* (R.A.) are commonly used today as are the Minangkabau *Sutan* (St.), the Malay *Datuk* and *Pangeran*, and the Bugis *Karaëng* and *Arung*.

Many elite Indonesians have academic titles obtained from the Dutch or Netherlands Indies **education** system. Mr. (*meester in de rechten*) was the primary **law** degree but has now been replaced by SH (*sarjana hukum*), placed after the holder's name. Drs. (*doctorandus*, now SS or *sarjana sastra*) is sometimes misleadingly described as denoting completion of all requirements for a doctorate but the dissertation. It was in fact the standard undergraduate course in arts and economics, but since it included a short thesis (*scriptie*) it is perhaps most closely equivalent to a master's degree. Ir. (*ingenieur*) was the primary degree for graduates in engineering, **agriculture**, and similar technical fields. Dr. was the standard title of the holder of a medical degree, but was commonly spelled *dokter* or dr. to distinguish it from the thesis-based higher doctorates. *See also* NAMES.

TJIK DI TIRO, TEUNGKU (1836–1891). An Acehnese *ulama* (religious teacher), he joined guerrilla resistance to the Dutch in **Aceh** in 1878 and soon emerged as principal leader of the *ulama*, touring the countryside to preach holy war. His example helped to establish the *ulama* firmly as the symbols of opposition to colonialism, unlike secular war leaders (*uleëbalang*) such as **Teuku Umar**. [0818]

TJIPTO MANGOENKOESOEMO (1886–1943). Physician and one of the founders of **Budi Utomo** in May 1908. Unlike his colleagues, he was strongly critical of the feudalism and conservatism of traditional Javanese culture, and he tried to move Budi Utomo away from exclusively focusing on **Java** and on the ***priyayi***. He advocated especially the elimination of the Javanese **language** whose levels of address, he argued, preserved social inequalities. Dissatisfied with Budi Utomo, he left in October 1909 and in 1911 helped to found the radical multiracial **Indische Partij**. He was expelled from the Indies 1913–1914 but on his return was appointed to the first **Volksraad** as a representative of **Insulinde**. He was exiled to **Banda** in 1928–1941, accused of complicity in the 1926–1927 **Partai Komunis Indonesia (PKI)** uprisings.

TJOKROAMINOTO, HAJI UMAR SAID (1882–1934)**.** Although trained as a government official, he left to work in various jobs before becoming **Surabaya** leader of the Sarekat Dagang Islam. A charismatic figure, he soon emerged as a national leader and was chosen to head **Sarekat Islam (SI)** when it took its new shortened name in September 1912. Many peasants believed him to be the ***ratu adil***, or just prince, of Javanese mythology, and he was reputed (incorrectly) to have been born as **Krakatau** erupted. Under his leadership, SI won a huge following, claiming about 2 million members, but it became increasingly divided between Marxists of the **Indische Sociaal-Democratische Vereeniging (ISDV)** and radical Muslim scholars, whom Tjokroaminoto tried to balance in an uneasy compromise. He also sought to avoid provoking Dutch repression and accepted appointment to the first **Volksraad**. He became less sympathetic to the Marxists after they criticized him in 1920, but was in jail for alleged perjury over the Afdeling B Affair when they were expelled. In February 1923 he formed the remains of SI into the **Partai Sarekat Islam Indonesia (PSII)**, but this too lost much support with the founding of the **Nahdlatul Ulama (NU)** in 1926.

TOBACCO (*Nicotiana tabacum* Solanaceae)**.** One of the first New World plants to reach the archipelago, being reported from the court of **Mataram** on **Java** in 1601. The chewing of **betel** and the smoking of **opium** and probably **cannabis** were then already known in the archipelago, and tobacco spread only gradually as a drug of addiction, often being used in conjunction with betel, opium, or both. From 1830 to 1864 tobacco was grown widely on Java under the **Cultivation System**. Later in the century, the **Vorstenlanden** and West **Kalimantan** became major areas of Western-owned plantation tobacco, while there was extensive smallholder cultivation on Java, especially in Kedu and Banyumas. The main area of production, however, was **East Sumatra**, where J. Nienhuys established the first plantation in 1863–1864. Indonesian cigarette consumption today is dominated by ***kretek***, cigarettes in which the tobacco is mixed with **cloves**. The importance of tobacco excise to state income and of cigarettes as *penghibur rakyat* (comforters of the people) led the government to discourage the emergence of an antismoking campaign.

TONARIGUMI. *See* RUKUN TETANGGA.

TORAJA. Ethnic group in the mountains of central **Sulawesi**. The region was divided into numerous small communities subject to periodic slaving and plundering raids by coastal kingdoms such as **Luwu**, though in the 17th century most joined a temporary alliance against **Bugis** invasion. **Coffee** was introduced as a major crop in the 1870s, and increased revenue from coffee exports seems to have enabled a few chiefs, such as Pong Tiku of Pangala, to establish themselves as regional warlords in the final decades of the 19th century. The **Dutch** conquered the region in 1905–1906 as part of their general consolidation of power in the archipelago, but their administrative reorganization and demands for taxes and corvée **labor** sparked a major rebellion in 1917. **Christianity** has since spread to 80 percent of the **population**, Islam to 10 percent. In the 1980s traditional Toraja religion was recognized, under the name Aluk, as a sect of **Hinduism**. [0130, 1269, 1270, 1272]

TOTOK. Colonial-era term for anyone recently arrived in the Indies or, more generally and in contrast to ***peranakan***, to unacculturated immigrant communities. *See also* CHINESE IN INDONESIA.

TOURISM. Organized tourism, with fixed timetables and itineraries and prepayment for services, began only after **travel** permit requirements were abolished for Europeans on **Java** and **Madura** in 1902, detailed tourist guides being published soon after and ever since. In general, prewar tourism showed visitors natural phenomena (including landscapes), antiquities, and colonial **architecture**; postwar tourism emphasized indigenous culture and food. In 1987, 1.05 million foreign tourists visited Indonesia, **Bali** being the favored destination.

Despite the unrest plaguing Indonesia in the post-**Suharto** years, more than 5 million foreigners visited the country in 2001, bringing in more than $5 billion in foreign exchange. Tourism was the biggest foreign exchange earner after **oil** and **gas**. The number of tourists visiting Indonesia, however, plummeted after the rise in terrorism, especially after the 12 October 2002 bombing of the nightclub in Bali. [0088–0090, 0093, 0095, 0130]

TOWNS. *See* CITIES.

TRADE. The exchange of goods between individuals and groups is as old in the Indonesian archipelago as anywhere in the world, but it was not until improvements in **shipping** technology around the beginning of the Christian era that the region became part of the great maritime trade route that extended from southern **China** to the eastern Mediterranean.

The route was in fact a complex of trade routes in which most commodities traveled only part of the total distance and typically passed repeatedly from one trader to another at the entrepôt **ports** that dotted the coastline. Until the 10th century, commerce in Indonesian waters was primarily in Indonesian hands, and Southeast Asians controlled most of the shipping north to China. Indian merchants, on the other hand, dominated trade in the Bay of Bengal, though the absence of Indian vocabulary derived from trade in Indonesian **languages** suggests that they did not penetrate far. The rhythm of this trade was seasonal, following the changing pattern of the monsoons.

The principal goods of this trade are fairly well known. **Cotton** cloth from **India** and **silk** and porcelain from China were major imports, while the archipelago exported a more varied range of spices, minerals, and forest products. The organization of the trade is less well understood. It has commonly been suggested that most traders were "peddlers" operating as individuals with small capital and carrying small quantities of relatively high-value goods between entrepôts. There is a good deal of evidence, however, that local rulers were involved not only in taxing and plundering trade (*see* **PIRACY**) but also in large-scale commercial enterprises.

It is fairly clear that the arrival of the **Portuguese** in Indonesia in the 16th century brought little change to the pattern of trade. The Portuguese strength lay primarily in their naval power and their consequent ability to seize ports such as **Melaka** and to extract customs duties from passing merchants. The European trading companies, however, have generally been seen as a major organizational innovation, partly because their capital reserves enabled them to outlast local competitors in difficult markets, partly because their bureaucratic structures made them less dependent on the will and ability of single individuals. The **Dutch East Indies Company (VOC)**, however, also relied to a considerable extent on armed force to hold its dominant position in the trade of the archipelago. The rise of the European trading companies changed the balance of political power in the archipelago, impoverishing the former merchant princes of the coastal states and strengthening the hand of the feudal elites of the interior.

In the early years of independence, the Republic attempted to counter Dutch domination of the import-export trade by establishing the Central Trading Company in 1948 to export agricultural products, and in 1956 it established the USINDO to export factory products and import raw materials. Until the 1960s Indonesia's primary exports were **rubber**, **oil**, **tin**,

copra, **coffee**, **sugar**, **tobacco**, and **coffee** (in that order), with rubber providing nearly 50 percent of export earnings in the early 1950s. Oil increasingly assumed the primary role, and in 1965 oil and rubber contributed almost 70 percent of Indonesia's export earnings. During the early years of the **New Order**, the volume of exports grew rapidly with oil and associated products making up more than 80 percent of Indonesia's export earnings at the peak of the oil boom. This changed with the collapse of oil prices in the mid-1980s, after which the government attempted to diversify Indonesia's exports (*see* **ECONOMY**). Oil and liquefied natural gas, which had constituted 73 percent of the total value of Indonesian exports in 1984, formed only 51.7 percent in January–September 1987, with agricultural, industrial, and **mining** exports making up the remaining 48.3 percent. By 1993 nonenergy exports—notably plywood, textiles, garments, and shoes—had risen to 76 percent of total export earnings. Between 1987 and 1996, there was a surge in low-skill, labor-intensive manufactured exports.

The late 1960s was a time of economic liberalism in the field of trade policy, but import bans began to appear again in the early 1970s accelerating after the **Malari** demonstrations of 1974. Trade restrictions were expanded in the late 1970s and further tightened through the early 1980s, when increasing numbers of nontariff barriers were imposed in the form of restrictive import licensing bans and quotas. Under pressure from the technocrats and international lending institutions, however, in 1986 import liberalization measures were instituted, including an across-the-board tariff reduction, and in October of that year the first reform package was introduced, followed by others in 1988, 1990, and 1991 that transformed Indonesian industry, making it internationally competitive. The government initiated further tariff reductions in 1995, and this series of trade liberalization measures culminated in June 1996 when it was announced that tariffs would be cut on 1,497 items, simplifying trade procedures and offering more flexibility for foreign manufacturers. This brought the average tariffs in Indonesia down to around 15 percent. But the growing cronyism of the regime meant that many businesses owned by those close to **Suharto** were unaffected by these reforms. Between 1970 and 1997, Indonesia's trade as a percentage of gross domestic product (GDP) rose from 28 percent to 56 percent.

Between 1966 and the 1990s, there was a major shift in Indonesia's trading relationships from North America and Europe toward Japan and other East Asian nations, with a growing volume of trade among the **Association of Southeast Asian Nations (ASEAN)**. At the peak of the oil boom, Japan/East Asia absorbed about 70 percent of Indonesia's exports, with the **United States** receiving around 15–30 percent.

In the 2–3 months immediately following Suharto's resignation, exports continued to increase because the collapse in the value of the rupiah meant that Indonesian products were competitively priced, but in the closing months of 1998 exports plunged as oil prices declined and East Asian economies failed to recover from the **financial crisis**. The decline continued in subsequent years, with total exports falling from US$62.1 billion in 2000 to US$57 billion in 2002. [0290, 0301, 0303, 0313, 0438–0459, 0516, 0521, 0540, 0542, 0558, 0571, 0769]

TRADE UNIONS. *See* LABOR UNIONS.

TRANSMIGRATION. The government policy of shifting people from the heavily populated Inner Islands of Indonesia (**Java**, **Madura**, **Bali**, and **Lombok**) to the ostensibly underpopulated **Outer Islands** began in 1902 as part of the **Ethical Policy**. By 1931, 36,000 people were living in the first transmigration settlement in **Lampung**. After independence, transmigration was often seen as a panacea for the problems of rural Java, and extravagant plans were drafted in 1952 for using it to reduce the **population** of Java (then over 50 million) to 31 million by 1987. **Sukarno** announced an annual resettlement target of 1.5 million in 1964, and **Suharto** raised this to 2 million in 1966. In fact, however, no more than 340,000 people were shifted from Java to **Sumatra** in the years 1950 to 1965. Between 1969 and 1982 about 1 million people were moved, during which time the population of Java-Madura rose by about 17 million.

The program became a major undertaking of the **New Order** and was given legislative basis in the 1972 Law on Transmigration. It received financial and technical support from the **World Bank** but has proven very expensive, at its peak in the mid-1980s costing $7,000 per family moved and consuming 6 percent of the national **budget**. Officially people are not compelled to take part, but those displaced by development projects or natural disasters are often heavily pressured to join. Until 1985 former political prisoners (*see* ***TAHANAN POLITIK***) were encouraged to take part, but they have since been banned.

The initial rationale for transmigration was the relief of population pressure on Java, but government statements later emphasized that the benefits of transmigration would fall to those who took part rather than those who stayed behind. A further goal, less publicly stated, was the transmission of Javanese agricultural techniques and culture to other regions both for economic development and for national integration. The Suharto regime saw settlements of Javanese and Balinese in outer regions as a useful obstacle to potential local secessionist movements. Transmigration, however, in some cases increased local tensions, especially where transmigrants were settled on **land** that local people believed to be theirs; the national government was generally unwilling, for instance, to recognize the land rights of shifting cultivators and **hunting** communities. There was some killing of transmigrants in **Sulawesi** during the **PRRI/Permesta** rebellion and later of transmigrants in **Papua**. In the 1980s, criticism of the **environmental** consequences of transmigration also increased. After the fall of Suharto, the transmigration policies of his regime were frequently blamed for the interethnic violence that broke out in **Kalimantan**, **Maluku**, and Papua. *See also* JAVANIZATION; POPULATION. [0955, 0977, 1322, 1378]

TRAVEL. To protect its trading monopoly, the **Dutch East Indies Company (VOC)** banned from its possessions all Europeans not in its service. After the fall of the company, various more liberal regulations were introduced, but under the **Cultivation System** the old restrictions were largely restored before being lifted in stages between 1861 and 1911 (on **Java** and **Madura**; 1916 in the **Outer Islands**) when Europeans became free to **trade** and reside anywhere in the archipelago, subject only to the *exorbitante rechten* of the **governors-general**. Formal restrictions on the travel of Indonesians began only in 1816, with the introduction of a pass system intended to keep the **labor** force in place. Passes were abolished in 1863 and liberalization of travel regulations continued, a pace or two behind that for Europeans, until 1914 (on Java; 1918 in the Outer Islands), when travel and residence throughout the archipelago was virtually unrestricted. **Chinese** and other "foreign orientals" (*see* **RACE**) were regulated separately but in a similar way to Indonesians, being subject to pass laws from 1816 to 1863 and being required from 1835 to 1919 to live in so-called *wijken* (districts) or Chinatowns. Current regulations require Indonesians to obtain a *surat jalan* for long or interprovincial journeys. In November 1982, a so-called fiscal fee was introduced to discourage overseas travel by Indonesians. In 1989 Indonesia announced it would abolish the requirement that citizens leaving the country obtain exit permits. *See also* LINSCHOTEN, J. H. VAN; MARCO POLO; PIRES, TOMÉ; ROADS; SHIPPING; TOURISM. [1078, 1100]

TREKKERS. Dutch residents of the Indies intending to return to the Netherlands at the end of their term of service, in contrast to the *blijvers* who intended to remain in the colony on retirement. *See also* DUTCH IN INDONESIA

TRIBUTE SYSTEM. *See* CHINA, HISTORICAL LINKS WITH.

TRUNOJOYO, RADEN (c. 1649–1680). A prince of **Madura** who conspired with the crown prince of **Mataram** against King **Amangkurat I**, who had had Trunojoyo's father killed. After seizing Madura in 1671 he attacked **Java**, declaring himself king in 1675. He defeated Mataram in 1677, capturing the court and sending the king into **exile**. His former co-conspirator the crown prince, however, as Amangkurat II, obtained help from the **Dutch East Indies Company (VOC)** and defeated the rebels in 1679. Trunojoyo was executed in 1680. [0484, 0560]

TURKEY, HISTORICAL LINKS WITH. After the capture of Constantinople in 1453, the Ottoman Turkish Empire was the preeminent military power and cultural center in the Islamic world and a natural focus of attention among the newly Islamizing peoples in the Indonesian archipelago, especially as a potential ally against the **Portuguese**. A Turkish diplomat, Seh Ibrahim, helped to mediate the Treaty of **Giyanti** in 1755. **Aceh** is said to have accepted Ottoman suzerainty in the 16th century, and Sultan Ibrahim renewed the submission in 1850; his successors appealed to the Ottomans for help in 1869, just prior to the Aceh War. Turkey's abolition of the Caliphate in 1924 helped to crystallize division within the **Sarekat Islam (SI)** over the place of **Islam**: many modernists saw the reforms of Kemal Atatürk as a model for what might be achieved in an independent Indonesia, but traditionalists saw them as an example of dangerous secularism, and this concern contributed to the founding of the **Nahdlatul Ulama (NU)** in 1926. [1363]

TURMERIC. Spice prepared from the ends of the root fibers of *Curcuma domestica* (Zingiberaceae), valued both for its bright yellow color and its flavor. Originally exported from Southeast Asia to **China** and **India**, it soon came to be cultivated in both places. [0527]

TURTLE. The shell of the hawksbill turtle (*Eretmochelys imbricata*) has been exported from Indonesia to **China** for at least two millennia. Turtle eggs are a source of food for some communities in eastern Indonesia. [1154]

– U –

UJUNG KULON. Peninsula on the southwestern corner of **Java**, the sole remaining habitat of Javan **rhinoceros**. A nature reserve was declared in 1921, a game reserve in 1937, and a national park, including the volcanic island of **Krakatau**, in 1980. *See also* CONSERVATION. [1154]

UJUNG PANDANG. *See* MAKASSAR.

***ULAMA*.** Muslim teachers and religious leaders. *See* ISLAM; NAHDLATUL ULAMA.

UMAR, TEUKU (1854–1899)**.** Acehnese war leader (*uleëbalang*) and opportunist. In the prolonged **Aceh** War, he sided alternately with the **Dutch** (1883–1884 and 1893–1896) and the Acehnese (1873–1883, 1884–1893, and 1896–1899). While Umar's own motives seem to have been mainly personal ambition, his career typified the ambivalence of the *uleëbalang* toward the colonial authorities on the one hand and the *ulama* (religious teachers) on the other, and was a forerunner of the *uleëbalang*-Dutch coalition that uneasily ruled Aceh in the first part of the 20th century. [0818]

UNIÃO DEMOCRÁTICA TIMORENSE (UDT, Timorese Democratic Union)**.** Founded on 11 May 1974 as the party of the **East Timor** establishment and the first party after the Lisbon coup. It was dominated by mixed-race **Portuguese**-Timorese from the small commercial, administrative, and agricultural elites, as well as traditional chiefs (*liurai*), and it more or less inherited the membership of the **Acção Nacional Populár**. Its program called for general political liberalization and movement to self-government under Portuguese tutelage. From January to May 1975 it was in coalition with **Fretilin**, but after staging an unsuccessful coup on 11 August it joined **Associação Popular Democrática Timorese (Apodeti)** in seeking integration with Indonesia. After incorporation, the UDT leader Francisco Lopez da Cruz became deputy governor, but the party ceased to exist in early 1976. [0806]

UNIÃO NACIONAL. *See* ACÇÃO NACIONAL POPULÁR.

UNITED KINGDOM, RELATIONS WITH. *See* BRITAIN, RELATIONS WITH.

UNITED NATIONS (UN). From its inception in 1945, the United Nations took an active interest in decolonization and was drawn into the Indonesian-**Dutch** dispute in July 1947, when **India** and **Australia** raised the Dutch first **"Police Action"** in the Security Council. The UN responded in October 1947 by appointing a so-called Good Offices Commission, consisting of Australia, Belgium, and the **United States**, to facilitate a settlement. This commission presided over the **Renville Agreement** of January 1948. At the beginning of 1949, after the second "Police Action," the Security Council demanded the full transfer of sovereignty to Indonesia by mid-1950.

Indonesia joined the UN on 26–29 September 1950 and was able to use UN good offices again in the early 1960s in the transfer of West Irian (**Papua**) from Dutch rule, when the UN acted as intermediary in receiving the territory from the Dutch in 1962 and handing it to Indonesia on 1 May 1963. Although thereafter a UN Temporary Executive Authority (UNTEA) was still acting as the overseer for the Act of Free Choice that was to be held in five years' time to determine the wishes of the Papuan people, on 2 January 1965 **Sukarno** indignantly pulled Indonesia out of the international body. This was when **Malaysia** became a temporary member of the Security Council (*see* **CONFRONTATION**). Indonesia then tried to organize an alternative UN in the form of a Conference of the New Emerging Forces (Conefo), but this had made little headway by the time Sukarno lost power. Indonesia rejoined the UN in September 1966.

In November 1975, Portugal formally requested UN help in solving its **East Timor** problem, and on 12 December the General Assembly passed a motion calling on Indonesia to withdraw. On 22 December 1975 and 22 April 1976, the Security Council condemned the Indonesian invasion of East Timor and again instructed it to withdraw; Indonesia ignored this instruction, as well as annual motions of condemnation passed by the General Assembly from 1975 to 1982.

After **Suharto**'s resignation, **Jakarta** finally proposed granting a special status to East Timor, and UN-brokered talks began in late 1998 between **Portuguese** and Indonesian representatives, focusing on a plan for "autonomy with special status" for East Timor. The UN supervised a referendum on independence on 31 August 1999, but it left security in the hands of the Indonesians rather than introducing a UN peacekeeping force. When it became clear that a vast majority of the voters had opted for independence, Indonesia-supported **militias** went on a rampage, killing hundreds of civilians (including UN staff members). Indonesia declared martial law and tried to retain control, but finally yielded to threats from the international community and financial institutions, and permitted a 7,500-soldier UN-backed International Force for East Timor headed by Australia to land on 20 September to restore order.

The UN set up a transitional government in the territory, but an estimated 120,000 East Timorese remained in refugee camps in West Timor and the continuing tension broke into open violence with the murder of three UN workers on 6 September 2000 on the West Timor side of the border. After general **elections** through which **Jose Alexandre "Xanana" Gusmão** was elected president, the UN secretary-general ceded governing authority on 20 May 2002 to the newly independent Democratic Republic of East Timor. [0661, 0744, 0855, 0959, 1123, 1141]

UNITED STATES, HISTORICAL LINKS WITH. Traders from **Britain**'s American colonies were present in Indonesian **ports** well before the Revolution of 1776, and the American scientist Thomas Horsfield (1773–1859) conducted important research on **Java** in the early 19th century, but U.S. interest in Indonesia did not become substantial until the middle of the 19th century, when U.S. missionary groups began conversion in **Sumatra** and growing U.S. industrialization stimulated **trade**. In the 1860s, the United States exported **oil** to Indonesia, but from 1871 American companies, especially Socony, took an important role in oil exploration in the archipelago. U.S. **investment** in **East Sumatra**'s **rubber** was important, and the United States became a major market for Indies spices, **coffee**, **tobacco**, and, after 1905, oil. The Acehnese unsuccessfully requested U.S. help against the Dutch in 1873. [1118]

UNITED STATES, RELATIONS WITH. Indonesian nationalists were aware from at least 1944 that the United States was a major power in the Western Pacific, and the first actions of the Indonesian Republic were designed in part to win U.S. support for the independence struggle. Republican leaders explicitly compared their **declaration of independence** to that of the United States and further guaranteed the position of U.S. commercial interests in the archipelago. During the **Revolution**, **Sumitro Djojohadikusumo** on behalf of the Indonesian government made extensive efforts to involve the United States on the side of Indonesia by making commercial agreements with U.S. firms more generous than the Dutch were ever likely to concede. The United States, however, remained generally lukewarm toward the Republic, particularly since it needed to keep the Netherlands amenable to participation in the North

Atlantic Treaty Organization (NATO), and it aimed primarily but unsuccessfully at a settlement acceptable to both sides. After the suppression of the **Partai Komunis Indonesia (PKI)** at **Madiun** in 1948, however, U.S. official opinion swung strongly behind the **Mohammad Hatta** government as a likely bastion against communism in Southeast Asia, and after the Second **"Police Action,"** U.S. pressure was one of the factors forcing the Dutch to make a rapid transfer of sovereignty to the Republic (*see also* **UNITED NATIONS**).

The United States cultivated Indonesian governments in the 1950s as potential noncommunist allies in Asia, but the idea of direct alliance with the United States was unpopular in Indonesia and in 1952 the **Sukiman** government fell over its acceptance of U.S. military aid. The United States' unease with Indonesia's leftward swing under **Ali Sastroamijoyo** and then under **Guided Democracy** led it to give clandestine military support to the **PRRI/Permesta** rebellion in 1958, which was exposed with the shooting down of an American B-25 pilot, Alan Pope, over **Ambon** on 18 May. Relations improved in the early 1960s, when the United States pressed the Netherlands to abandon its claim to West Irian (*see* **Papua**), but they deteriorated rapidly from 1962. An economic stabilization program offered by the United States under International Monetary Fund (IMF) supervision was rejected by **Sukarno** because of **Confrontation** with **Malaysia**. But the United States maintained continuing contact with the Indonesian **army** via training and supplies (by 1965, half the officers corps had received some U.S. training).

The United States was delighted with the accession to power of General **Suharto** in 1965–1966, though the extent to which it played a role in his success is unclear; Suharto certainly knew that the United States would support the removal of Sukarno and the banning of the PKI, and the Central Intelligence Agency (CIA) clearly played a propaganda role in ensuring that the ambiguous **Gestapu** coup of 30 September 1965 was seen unequivocally by the general public in Indonesia as a communist plot. After the consolidation of the **New Order**, relations between the United States and the Suharto regime were stable. Indonesia remained officially nonaligned and committed to the removal of great power influence from the region, but in practice it aligned itself fairly closely with the United States. Indonesia's invasion of **East Timor** in December 1975 was carried out only after it was clear that the action had been approved by President Gerald Ford. The subsequent U.S. unwillingness to accept Indonesia's annexation of the territory without demur strained relations, and from this time U.S. concern over Indonesia's **human rights** record and the question of

copyright protection caused further difficulties. President Suharto annoyed Washington in 1988 with calls for a nuclear weapons–free zone in Southeast Asia. In May 1989 a visit by Vice President Dan Quayle was greeted with demonstrations against the role of U.S.-based transnational corporations in **environmental** destruction, especially in Papua.

In 1991 the U.S. Congress suspended Indonesia's participation in the International Military Education and Training program (IMET) because of the Dili massacre in East Timor, and in 1999 after the army was implicated in the killing and destruction surrounding the plebiscite there, Congress banned all military sales to Indonesia. Military ties began to be resumed after Indonesia agreed to East Timor's independence, and, in the aftermath of the terrorist attacks on New York City and Washington on 11 September 2001, Congress set aside $21 million for regional counterterrorism training programs in Indonesia, signifying U.S. hopes for stronger ties with the Indonesian military.

President **Megawati Sukarnoputri** was one of the first foreign leaders to visit the United States after 11 September, and she pledged that she would participate in the global fight on terrorism. But her government refused to endorse military strikes against the Taliban in Afghanistan and declined to grant the U.S. military permission to fly through Indonesian air space. In addition, in the U.S. Congress the Leahy amendment still retained the condition that human rights abusers had to be brought to justice. Resumption of military ties was thus impeded in Congress by the Indonesian military's refusal both to accept responsibility for bloodshed in East Timor and to extradite those indicted, as well as by its reluctance to move against Islamic radicals allegedly linked to Jemaah Islamiah (*see* **ISLAM IN INDONESIA**).

Nevertheless, the U.S. State Department sought approval from Congress for $16 million in aid to Jakarta for peacekeeping and counterterrorism, and the Pentagon pushed ahead with plans to give Indonesia $8 million for training and equipping a domestic peacekeeping force to combat communal, sectarian, and ethnic violence. Another $8 million was earmarked for training civilian-led Indonesian counterterrorism units. Despite the Indonesian government's foot-dragging on human rights, in mid-2002 the U.S. administration pressured Congress to provide financing for a new "command and control" unit for the Indonesian army to carry out peacekeeping tasks in places like **Maluku** and to allow Indonesian officers to receive training in the United States. At the beginning of August 2002, the secretary of state announced that the United States would resume direct military training aid to Indonesia, and in late September the first three officers arrived in the United States to participate in an antiterrorism program. The State Department also urged a U.S. federal court to dismiss a lawsuit brought by human rights groups against ExxonMobil in behalf of Acehnese villagers complaining of the **oil** companies' complicity in the human rights violations by Indonesian soldiers.

When the foreign aid bill was passed in mid-February 2003, the Senate made the aid conditional on certification that military officers were being prosecuted for alleged involvement in "gross violations of human rights," which included not only the massacre in East Timor but also the killings in Papua and **Aceh**. Unaffected was the money provided for counterterrorism programs, most of which went to civilian and **police** training, and $400,000 allocated for officer training.

After the **Bali** bombings of 12 October 2002, the Indonesian government became more cooperative in hunting for terrorists and soon arrested and brought to trial several suspects in the Bali bombing and other violence. But the U.S. refusal to share intelligence information obtained from Riduan Isamuddin (Hambali), the alleged head of Jemaah Islamiyah, after his arrest in Thailand in August 2003 angered the Indonesians. U.S.–Indonesian relations were also strained over measures passed in early 2003 ordering all Indonesian men in the United States to show that they had valid documents, a measure that applied to people of no other Southeast Asian country. Tension further increased after an FBI investigation found that Indonesian soldiers, not members of the **Organisasi Papua Merdeka (OPM)**, were responsible for the August 2002 killings of two Americans near the **Freeport** mine in Papua. Nevertheless, leaders in the Pentagon continued to press Congress for increased aid to the Indonesian army and support for Indonesia in the fight against terrorism, pressure that gained strength with Jakarta's hiring of former senate majority leader Robert Dole as a lobbyist to represent Indonesia's interests in Washington. *See also* ISLAMIC STATE. [0973, 1109, 1117, 1121, 1126, 1127, 1144]

UPAS (*Antiaris toxicaria* Urticaceae, *ipoh*)**.** Tree that produces a highly poisonous sap, formerly smeared, sometimes in conjunction with locally produced strychnine, on **darts** and arrows for **hunting** and on swords and daggers for **warfare**. It was extensively used in the defense of **Melaka** against the **Portuguese** in 1511. The tree became the subject of a widespread scientific myth initiated by **Rumphius**, which held that its fumes would rapidly kill any living thing, plant or animal, within a radius of several meters or more. The legend probably derived originally from efforts by producers of the poison to discourage closer investigation of its origins. [1148, 1189]

URBANIZATION. *See* CITIES.

– V –

VADERLANDSE CLUB. Conservative association of Europeans in the Netherlands Indies founded in 1929 to promote **Dutch** interests in the colony and to resist Indonesian **nationalism** and the expansion of indigenous **education**. It had 9,000 members in 1930. Though sometimes vocal, it had little influence on government policy. [0602]

VEREENIGDE OOST-INDISCHE COMPAGNIE. *See* DUTCH EAST INDIES COMPANY (VOC).

VICE PRESIDENT. The post of vice president has no formal responsibilities except to support and, if necessary, to replace the **president**. **Mohammad Hatta**, elected vice president in 1945 under the first **constitution**, was prime minister 1948–1950 by virtue of his national standing rather than his vice presidency. He was reappointed vice president by **Sukarno** in October 1950 under the provisional constitution, but resigned in 1956, after which the post remained vacant until 1973. In the **New Order**, **Hamengkubuwono IX** was vice president from 1973 to 1978; **Adam Malik** (1917–1984) from 1978 to 1983; **Umar Wirahadikusumah** from 1983 to 1988; **Sudharmono** from 1988 to 1993; **Try Sutrisno** from 1993 to 1998; and **B. J. Habibie** from March to May 1998. After the first post-Suharto **elections**, **Megawati Sukarnoputri** became **Abdurrachman Wahid**'s vice president from 1999 to 2001; and Hamzah Haz, chairman of the **Partai Persatuan Pembangunan (PPP)**, was appointed vice president when Megawati became president in 2001. As vice president Megawati was given major responsibility for the problems of eastern Indonesia, and when she replaced Wahid as president, she chose Hamzah Haz as her vice president largely to provide a balance between her nationalist-oriented **Partai Demokrasi Indonesia—Perjuangan (PDI-P)** and Muslim groups. [0970, 1100]

VIETNAM HISTORICAL LINKS AND RELATIONS WITH. Strong **Chinese** influence in Vietnam tended to limit its role in Southeast Asia in early times, though it was a major exporter of ceramics to Indonesia in the 15th century. Thereafter the rise of European power in the region strengthened the mutual isolation. In 1947 Vietnam and Indonesia cooperated briefly in the **South East Asia League** but made little attempt otherwise to coordinate their national struggles. **Sukarno** recognized the Democratic Republic of Vietnam (DRV) and accepted a National Liberation

Front (NLF) mission in **Jakarta**. At the request of the **United States**, Indonesian troops were posted in South Vietnam as part of the International Commission of Control and Supervision under the Paris Accord of 1972.

Following Vietnam's reunification in 1975, refugees from Vietnam began to arrive in large numbers in Indonesia's Natuna archipelago, and between 1977 and 1981 the Indonesian camp on Pulau Galang received over 65,000 refugees for processing and transit to third countries. There was domestic concern over the high proportion of Vietnamese Chinese among the refugees, and none were accepted for permanent settlement. Indonesia joined the **Association of Southeast Asian Nations (ASEAN)** condemnation of Vietnam's 1979 invasion of **Cambodia**, upholding the "Democratic Kampuchea" seat in the **United Nations**, but it consistently sought compromise over the issue. It believed that Vietnam had no hegemonic ambitions beyond Indochina and that its isolation dangerously increased the scope for great power (especially Chinese) intervention in the region. ASEAN appointed Jakarta to act as mediator in Vietnam's conflict with Cambodia, and Indonesia played a major role in reaching an acceptable solution. In March 1989 an Indonesian private bank, Summa Bank, announced plans to join the Saigon Industrial and Commercial Bank in the Indochina Bank, Vietnam's first **banking** joint venture. After Vietnam became the seventh member of ASEAN in July 1995 political relations further eased, but Vietnam remained a major economic competitor to Indonesia in the low-income segment of the export market. *See also* SOVIET UNION, RELATIONS WITH. [1125, 1144]

VILLAGES. *See DESA*.

VOLCANOES. Located at the junction of three tectonic plates (*see* **CONTINENTAL DRIFT**), Indonesia is volcanically active, 829 active volcanoes being found widely scattered in eastern Indonesia and along the spines of **Sumatra** and **Java**. Ejecta of low pH are responsible in Java, **Bali**, and other places for exceptionally fertile soil; ejecta of high pH in Sumatra and elsewhere are less productive. An eruption 75,000 years ago in North Sumatra created the valley now partly filled by Lake Toba, when an estimated 1,500–2,000 km of material was ejected, leaving a caldera 100 km long. The greatest eruption in recent history was that of **Tambora** on **Sumbawa** in 1815, which claimed at least 117,000 lives and destroyed the vegetation of entire regions, leading to widespread famine in Sumbawa, **Lombok**, and Bali. The eruption of **Krakatau** in the Sunda Strait in 1883 is better known and recorded, though a much smaller quantity of volcanic material was released than in Tambora and fewer people were killed (approximately 36,000). Kelud in East Java has also been particularly destructive, less because of the force of its periodic eruptions (1752, 1771, 1811, 1848, 1864, 1901, 1919) than because water trapped in its crater is flung out to create dangerous mud avalanches. In 1963 Gunung Agung on Bali erupted with much devastation and loss of life. Sulphur collection has been an important local industry on several volcanoes, and a number of volcanoes have been harnessed for steam power (Kamojan, near Garut, since 1926, Salak more recently). A Vulkanologisch Dienst (Vulcanological Service) was established by the colonial government in 1920. [1165, 1174, 1176, 1178]

VOLKSLECTUUR, COMITE OR KANTOOR VOOR DE. *See* BALAI PUSTAKA.

VOLKSRAAD (People's Council)**.** Representative body of the Netherlands Indies, established in 1918 with 39 members, approximately half elected and half appointed. Membership was on an ethnic basis, with initially 15 indigenes and 23 Europeans and "foreign orientals" (*see* **RACE**). In 1931 membership was expanded to 60, with 30 indigenes, of whom 20 were elected, 25 Europeans (15 elected), and five others (three elected). Elected indigenous representatives were chosen for a four-year term by indigenous members of the local and *kabupaten* councils as a single electorate. Initially the Volksraad had only advisory power, though as its members had parliamentary immunity it provided a platform for those nationalists who accepted election (*see* **NATIONALISM**). From 1931 the Volksraad approved the annual **budget** of the Netherlands Indies and appointed a College van Gedelegeerden (Chamber of Delegates) to examine and approve ordinances of the colonial government. While all government ordinances required its approval, rejected ordinances could come into force in any case as general government regulations (*algemene maatregelen van bestuur*). *See also* CHUO SANGI-IN. [0638, 0661]

VOLLENHOVEN, CORNELIS VAN (1874–1933)**.** Professor of **law** at Leiden University from 1901 to 1933 and foremost proponent of ***adat*** or traditional Indonesian law. He strongly resisted moves for a single set of legal codes for the colony and was mainly responsible for the codification of *adat* in successive *Adatrechtbundels*. [1083]

VOORLOPIGE FEDERALE REGEERING. *See* SUCCESSION.

VORSTENLANDEN. The princely states of Central **Java**, that is, the Sultanate of **Yogyakarta**, the Kasunanan (Sunanate) of **Surakarta**, and the lesser **Pakualaman** and **Mangkunegaran**. Descendants of the divided kingdom of **Mataram**, these were the only indirectly ruled part of the island in the latter colonial period and were thus exempt from many of the colonial regulations applied to other areas. The **Cultivation System**, for instance, was not introduced in the Vorstenlanden, and large privately owned plantations developed there rather earlier than elsewhere. The authority of the Vorstenland rulers was limited to Javanese within their domains. Europeans and others were the administrative and legal responsibility of **Dutch** residents.

VREEMDE OOSTERLINGEN. *See* RACE.

– W –

WAHID, ABDURRACHMAN (GUS DUR)**.** *See* ABDURRACHMAN WAHID.

WAJO'. Bugis state in southwestern **Sulawesi**, founded in 1471 by exiles from **Luwu**. Its ruler, called the Arung Mataa, was elected by a council of 40 princes. In 1737 under Arung Singkang (La Ma'dukelleng, 1700?–1765) Wajo' attacked **Bone**, and in 1739 it headed a federation of southern Sulawesi states in a series of unsuccessful attacks on the **Dutch** in **Makassar**. A Dutch protectorate was established in 1860–1861.

WALI SONGO (Nine Saints)**.** Said to have converted **Java** to **Islam** in the 16th century, their individual careers, which were not especially connected, are shrouded in legend, but several appear to have been non-Javanese and to have studied in **Melaka**. The first Muslim state on Java, **Demak**, is said to have been founded by Sunan Gunungjati (?–1570).

WALLACE'S LINE. This was named for Alfred Russell Wallace (1823–1913), a British scientist who collaborated with Charles Darwin, author of the theory of evolution. Previous scientific opinion had held that animal and plant forms were a direct response to **environmental** conditions, such as climate. During research in Indonesia from 1854 to 1862, however, Wallace noted that, although the Indonesian islands were climatically similar and geographically close, there was a dramatic difference in fauna and flora between the west, where typical Eurasiatic species such as **tigers, rhinoceros**, monkeys, and oaks were found, and the east of the archipelago, where marsupials, megapodes (mound-building birds), and eucalypts were common. It is now known that the former were characteristic of the old northern supercontinent of Laurasia, while the latter derive from the southern supercontinent of Gondwana, though present biological distribution does not exactly reflect the geological origin of the islands (*see* **CONTINENTAL DRIFT**). The line that Wallace drew between **Bali** and **Lombok** and between **Sulawesi** and **Kalimantan** separating these two zones has been called Wallace's line. Wallace himself, however, recognized the existence of a transition zone, and it is now more common to refer to this distinct zone, covering roughly Sulawesi, **Maluku**, and **Nusatenggara**, as Wallacea. *See also* PREHISTORY; SUNDA SHELF. [0100, 1186, 1192]

WARFARE. The ferocity of traditional battle in the archipelago seems to have been limited by a number of factors. First, warfare was largely aimed at capturing people, who represented a valuable **labor** resource, and obtaining allegiance of their rulers rather than winning territory, which was relatively abundant, and so combatants tended to be somewhat sparing of life. Second, prolonged defense of **cities** in a tropical climate was difficult and so retreat, which avoided confrontation, seems to have been a common strategy. Third, trickery, deception, and bluff on the part of commanders seem to have been prized, and surrogate battle by champions in single combat was a common strategy (*see* ***KERBAU***). When conflict actually came to battle, running ***amuk*** seems to have played a major role, though the main reason for this furious charge into enemy ranks in disregard for one's own safety seems to have been to cause terror rather than destruction. And fourth, combatants seem to have attributed the outcome of warfare at least in part to supernatural factors, keeping for instance *jimat* or charms for their own personal protection and taking account of portents of the final result.

Against this somewhat optimistic picture must be set the accounts of warfare described by Europeans in the 16th century and after, in which massacres and other military brutality are common. Some authors have indeed suggested that the Europeans brought an increased ruthlessness to warfare, but this is hard to specify or document. It does seem clear, however, that the initial military advantage of Europeans was slender and that it derived from their use of a standing **army** of professional soldiers rather than from technological superiority of **weapons**. Mercenary troops became common in the archipelago from the 17th century, but whether they were an older phenomenon is hard to tell. A major consequence of the **Dutch** presence was the gradual disarming of the indigenous population, so that **Java**, for instance, once known as a land of warriors, gained a reputation for exceptional peace.

During the **Revolution** there was relatively little battlefield combat between Republican and Dutch forces in view of the overwhelming Dutch superiority in weaponry. The Republic's greatest successes were in guerrilla warfare (*see* ***GERILYA***) carried out by both regular and irregular troops. After independence this pattern continued. Government troops could overwhelm any dissident forces through their superior weaponry, and rebel opposition (whether by forces of the **PRRI/Permesta** rebellion, **Darul Islam**, or antigovernment movements in **Aceh**, **East Timor**, or **Papua**) was generally conducted only through small-scale guerrilla operations. *See also* DEFENSE POLICY; KONINKLIJK NEDERLANDSCH INDISCH LEGER; WEAPONS. [0576]

WATER. The first public purification of water took place in **Batavia** in 1923. Since the 1980s, bottled water has become a common drink. *See also* TEA.

WAWASAN NUSANTARA. *See* ARCHIPELAGIC CONCEPT.

WAYANG. Literally "shadow," this term is now applied to a wide range of Javanese dramatic forms: *wayang kulit* (shadow puppets), *wayang golek* (solid wooden puppets), *wayang beber* (painted screens), *wayang klitik* (flat wooden or rod puppets), *wayang topeng* (masks), and *wayang wong* (dance dramas). Although now named as if variants of a single art, these forms probably have different origins, *wayang beber* deriving perhaps from traditional storytelling and *wayang wong* from traditional dance, though it took its present form only in **Yogyakarta** in the 19th century. *Wayang golek* is said to have been invented by one of the ***Wali Songo***, Sunan Kalijaga, near Yogyakarta in 1586, but it was reported by **Tomé Pires** in 1515. *Wayang kulit* may be derived ultimately from South Indian shadow puppetry, though authorities are not in agreement on this.

Wayang kulit employs flat leather shadow puppets manipulated by a *dalang* (puppeteer), who simultaneously provides all voices and cues the ***gamelan***. Its earliest recorded use was in the ninth century. In former times, the audience watched the shadows of the puppets cast on a white cloth screen by an oil lamp above the *dalang*'s head; more recently, audiences have tended also to shift around behind the *dalang* and *gamelan* to watch the finely painted puppets themselves.

Wayang golek is also performed by a *dalang* with a *gamelan* orchestra, and there are currently three major variants: *Wayang golek papak* (flat *wayang golek*), which recount local legends of West **Java** and are usually performed in the central plains of West Java; *wayang golek purwa*, whose stories are usually derived from those of *wayang kulit* and are usually performed in the Sundanese highlands; and *wayang golek Menak*, now rarely performed, which are connected with the Kebumen area and recount Islamic history and legend.

Wayang kulit generally presents episodes from the ***Mahabharata*** and ***Ramayana***, but within this framework the *dalang* has enormous scope for improvisation. The so-called Nine Walis used *wayang kulit* to spread **Islam** on Java (it is said that the distorted shape of the characters was adopted to satisfy the Islamic prohibition on the representation of humans), and prewar nationalists, communists, and postindependence governments have all seen it as a tool for spreading information and ideas rapidly to the rural **population** of Java. **Suharto** used it in legitimizing his rule and popularizing its objectives, but especially in the closing years of his regime his opponents also chose to express their opposition through *wayang* plays. [0008, 0017, 0132, 0140, 0153, 0163, 0169, 0170, 0181, 0182]

WEAPONS. A number of traditional weapons have been in use in the archipelago, namely, the *kris* on **Java**, **Bali**, and **Lombok**; the *klewang*, a long, generally straight-bladed knife (**Aceh**); and **darts** among the **Dayaks** and **Bataks**. Bows and arrows have also been common. Cannons were introduced by the **Chinese**, Gujeratis, and Turks in the 15th century. [0143, 0576]

WERENG. General name for various flying insects of the families Cicadelidae and Delphacidae (Order Hemiptera) occurring in plague proportions in **Java** since 1969 and transmitting major viral diseases of **rice**. Their spread is closely related to the **Green Revolution**, under which more susceptible rice varieties were introduced, overuse of pesticides diminished the bird and other predator populations, and the number of crops per year was increased so that the life cycle of the wereng was never disrupted by lack of food. The plague was checked briefly after 1976 by the introduction of new resistant rice varieties, but within a decade the wereng had adapted and by 1986 wereng were said to be responsible for an annual loss of 200,000–300,000 potential tons of agricultural produce. In November 1986, however, with dramatic success Indonesia introduced a program of integrated pest management for rice, involving bans on the use of many pesticides and a start with rotation of crops between different rice varieties.

WEST NEW GUINEA, WEST IRIAN. *See* PAPUA.

WESTERLING, RAYMOND PAUL PIERRE (1919–1987). A Dutch commando and counterguerrilla specialist, Westerling was born in Istanbul and thus known as "The Turk" though he was reportedly of mixed Turkish, Dutch, and Greek descent. After being parachuted into **Sumatra** in late 1945, he was posted with his Korps Speciale Troepen to South **Sulawesi** in 1946 and used particularly brutal techniques in suppressing local Indonesian nationalists. The official Indonesian figure of 40,000 dead is probably inflated, but his victims certainly numbered several thousands. After resigning from the **Koninklijk Nederlandsch Indisch Leger (KNIL)** in July 1949, he mobilized appoximately 8,000 troops and launched an unsuccessful coup in **Bandung** and **Jakarta** in an effort to topple **Mohammad Hatta**'s government. In doing so he brought about the fall of the **Pasundan** government, further discredited **federalism**, and hastened the movement toward a unitary state. [0674]

WHALES AND WHALING. Both the blue whale (*Balaenoptera musculus*) and Rudolphi's whale (*B. borealis*) occur in Indonesian waters, the former very sporadically. *B. borealis* is hunted using traditional means by the villagers of Lamakera (**Solor**) and Lamararap (Lomblen). [1387]

WHITE BOOK (*Buku Putih*). 1. A systematic critique of **New Order** policies issued on 14 January 1978 by **students** at the **Bandung** Institute of Technology (ITB) opposed to President **Suharto**'s reelection. The book was banned and about 30 student leaders arrested and tried, including Heri Akhmadi, who was convicted on charges of insulting the head of state.

2. Prepared in 1978 by Nugroho Notosusanto, head of the **army**'s Military History division, this White Book is the government's account of the events surrounding the 1965 **Gestapu** coup. It was never published but was distributed among a limited circle of government officials.

3. Written by a government team headed by Moerdiono (minister of the State Secretaritat, Mensecneg) in 1994, this book was entitled

G-30-S: Pembrontakan Partai Komunis Indonesia—Latar Belakang, Aksi dan Penumpasannya (The 30th of September Movement: The Rebellion of the Communist Party of Indonesia, Its Background, Action and Annihilation). It unsuccessfully aimed at ending the controversy surrounding the events of 1965. *See also* SUBVERSION. [0725, 0923]

WHITE PAPER (*Lembaran Putih*). On 12 September 1984, **army** units in the **Jakarta port** of Tanjung Priok shot dead between nine and several hundred members of a crowd that, after having heard speeches from Muslim preachers, had marched on an army post to demand release of two men detained for allegedly assaulting two security officers who had reportedly defiled a prayer house. The White Paper, drafted by **Ali Sadikin**, retired **Siliwangi** division commander **H. R. Dharsono**, and others, was one of several pamphlets that questioned the official version of the event. Following bomb explosions in Jakarta banks on 4 October, Dharsono was arrested and later tried under the colonial era *haatzaai-artikelen* and on charges of undermining government authority (*see* **SUBVERSION**). He was sentenced to 10 years in jail (later reduced to seven).

WHITE RAJAS. The flexibility of allegiances and alliances that enabled the rapid rise and fall of petty states in many coastal regions of the archipelago, especially on **Kalimantan**, also allowed a number of European adventurers to establish themselves as local rulers with local and traditional power bases. The Brookes of Sarawak were the best known of these, but others included Raja Wilson of Bengkalis, Baron van Overbeek of Sabah, Clunies Ross of Cocos, and Joseph Torry, Raja of **Ambon**. *Lord Jim* by **Joseph Conrad** is a fictionalized account of one such ruler. **Governors-general** of the Netherlands Indies took the indigenous title Sri Paduka yang Dipertuan Besar. *See also* KUTAI. [0243, 0629]

WIDJOJO NITISASTRO (1927–). Educated at the University of Indonesia's Department of Economics and at the University of California, Berkeley, Widjojo became head of President **Suharto**'s team of economic advisors in 1966. He is credited with fashioning the successful economic policies of the early years of the **New Order** and with enjoying the complete trust of Suharto, whom he tutored and guided in economic matters. He left the government in the 1980s, and Suharto's cronies and family largely replaced the so-called Berkeley Mafia in shaping Indonesia's economic priorities. When **B. J. Habibie** became president, he gave Widjojo an enhanced advisory role in the government in an effort to reassure the International Monetary Fund (IMF) and Indonesia's business community.

"WILD SCHOOLS." *See* EDUCATION, PRIVATE AND ISLAMIC.

WILOPO (1909–1981)**.** A leader of the **Partai Nasional Indonesia (PNI)** and prime minister from April 1952 to June 1953 after the fall of **Sukiman**. His cabinet fell over the use of **police** to remove peasant squatters from foreign-owned plantations in **East Sumatra**. [0695]

WIRANTO (1947–)**.** Born in **Yogyakarta**, Wiranto graduated from the Military Academy in 1968. After serving from 1989 to 1993 as **Suharto**'s military adjutant and from 1993 to 1996 as military commander of **Jakarta**, he was appointed **army** chief of staff in 1997 and **armed forces** commander in February 1998. After Suharto's fall, **B. J. Habibie** also appointed him minister of defense, and in his strengthened position Wiranto was able to remove his major military rival, Suharto's son-in-law **Prabowo Subianto**, from his position as head of **Komando Pasukan Khusus (Kopassus)**. Wiranto was also largely responsible for separating the **police** from control of the armed forces in April 1999, and for steps to lessen military involvement in civilian affairs under ***dwifungsi***.

Although disappointed in his hope to become **vice president**, Wiranto was appointed coordinating minister for defense and security in **Abdurrachman Wahid**'s cabinet on 27 October 1999. But his tenure was short-lived, especially because after the widespread massacres carried out by military-supported **militias** following the referendum in **East Timor**, the national **Human Rights** Commission recommended that the Attorney General's office investigate Wiranto's responsibility for the military's actions there. The president suspended him as coordinating minister in February 2000, and he formally resigned three months later on 16 May. In February 2003 the **United Nations** indicted him for crimes against humanity for his responsibility in the massacres during the vote for East Timor's independence in 1999, an indictment that the Indonesian government ignored. In October 2003 Wiranto emerged as a strong contender for **Golkar**'s nomination for the presidency in 2004. [0731, 0972]

WOMEN AND MEN. As elsewhere in the world, a social division of **labor** between men and women has been the rule throughout most of the archipelago, derived partly from religious notions of a distinction between active and productive energy. Thus, men were traditionally responsible for tasks such as **metalworking**, raising animals, plowing fields, felling trees, **hunting**, and building, while women were assigned transplanting, harvesting, pottery, weaving, food preparation, and marketing. There seems also to have been a widespread tradition of bilateral and matrilineal kinship, seen most strongly today in **Minangkabau** society, where ownership of land passes exclusively through the female line and men are frequently absent from the community on ***merantau***. This combination of conceptual dualism and female economic power seems to have led to societies in which the access of women to power, position, and **education** was not dramatically less than that of men, or at least was considerably greater than in **Chinese**, Indian, or Islamic societies. Thus, female literacy was high (*see* **WRITING SYSTEMS**), there were many important women traders and diplomats (women were traditionally regarded as more adept in financial matters and in negotiation than men, partly because they were not bound by rigid male codes of honor), and the courts of **Aceh** and **Mataram** had a tradition of women bodyguards. Women took part in the **Java War** as generals. South **Sulawesi** in the 14th to 19th centuries and **Aceh** in the 17th century were ruled by a succession of queens.

Hindu, Muslim, and perhaps Chinese influences all helped to diminish the access of women to education and to positions of power and influence. All accepted polygamy and preferred some degree of seclusion of women, though their influence was felt at first most strongly in elite circles. In rural areas in particular, the role of women in market **trade** and in harvesting assured their continuing social significance, though changes in both areas in recent years have damaged their position (*see* **GREEN REVOLUTION**). In other sectors of the **economy**, women are most numerous as unskilled and semiskilled factory workers and as domestic help, and they face the common problems of low wages and sexual harassment.

Participation by women in modern politics was unknown until the late 19th century, when the growing presence of educated European women as wives of government officials increased the social pressure on the wives of indigenous elite men to be conversant with public affairs. This consideration led, for instance, to the Western education given to **R. A. Kartini**. Indonesian women first graduated in **law** in 1921 and in medicine in 1922, and a number of women were prominent in the nationalist movement. While often members and leaders of women's groups, the most prominent of these worked alongside men in nationalist organizations. One of the most outstanding was Rasuna Said (1910–1965), who taught in the Diniyah Putri school in Padang Panjang, West **Sumatra**, and then was a leader of the Persatuan Muslimin Indonesia (Permi) and subsequently close to **Sukarno** in the **Partai Nasional Indonesia (PNI)**. Another was Maria Ulfah Santoso (1911–1988), who was the first Indonesian woman to receive a law degree in the Netherlands (Leiden 1933), and the first woman cabinet minister when she served as minister of social affairs in **Sutan Sjahrir**'s second cabinet (1946–1947).

The 1945 **Constitution** specified legal equality for men and women, but most **political parties** maintained affiliated women's organizations rather than integrating women fully into their structures (*see*, e.g., **GERAKAN WANITA INDONESIA**). Official policy in the late **Suharto** period stressed the role of women as wives and mothers, but women continued to hold a number of senior administrative posts. While Suharto's wife held no official position, with her influence dependent largely on her relationship with her husband and her commercial activities, his eldest daughter, Siti Hardijanti Hastuti Rukmana (Tutut), was prominent not only in the commercial field but also as a leader of **Golkar**. **Megawati Sukarnoputri** was elected to lead the **Partai Demokrasi Indonesia (PDI)** in 1993 and ultimately became Indonesia's first woman president in 2001. *See also* DHARMA WANITA; MARRIAGE, POLITICAL SIGNIFICANCE OF; RACE. [0552, 0566, 0576, 0584, 1400, 1409, 1412, 1416, 1417, 1419, 1421, 1424, 1425, 1427, 1430, 1432]

WOMEN'S MOVEMENT. R. A. Kartini is generally credited with founding the women's movement in Indonesia by identifying and promoting the specific interests of **women**. The earliest women's organizations were concerned mainly with the spreading of information on matters of interest to women. The first women's journal, *Poetri Hindia*, began publication in **Bogor** in 1908. In 1912 *Soenting Melajoe* published its first issue in West **Sumatra**. One of its founders was Rohana Kudus (1884–1974), often viewed as the **Minangkabau** Kartini. The early movements stressed women's **education**, both Islamic and western. One of the most successful and influential of the women's schools was the Diniyah Putri founded in Padang Panjang in 1923 by Rahmah El Yunusiyah (1900–1969), which had as many as 500 female students drawn from throughout the archipelago and Malaya. From 1914 the journal *Poetri Merdeka* began to argue that women's problems had a political solution, and four Indonesian women's conferences were held 1928–1932, at the first of which a number of generally nationalist women's associations federated to form an organization that in 1932 took the name Perikatan Perhimpunan Istri Indonesia (PPII, Federation of Indonesian Women's Associations). The federation established scholarships for girls; opposed polygamy, **prostitution**, and child marriage; and promoted **scouting** and hygiene. The organization Istri Sedar (The Conscious Woman), founded in **Bandung** in 1930, was particularly active in these areas and came frequently into conflict with the Muslim Aisyiyah. In 1932 Istri Sedar merged with other women's groups to become Isteri Indonesia (Indonesian Women).

During the **Revolution** women's organizations regrouped to form the Badan Kongres Wanita Indonesia (Kowani, Congressional Body of Indonesian Women) committed to an independent Indonesia, which dissolved in 1950 and was replaced by an organization of the same name (Kowani), which, however, played only a coordinating role among its many affiliates. *See also* DUTCH IN INDONESIA; GERAKAN WANITA INDONESIA (GEKWANI). [0627, 1282, 1287, 1422, 1428, 1430, 1432]

WORLD BANK (International Bank for Reconstruction and Development, IBRD)**.** Indonesia joined the World Bank in April 1954, left on 17 August 1965 without having contracted loans with it, and rejoined in April 1967. Experts from the bank, as well as from the International Monetary Fund (IMF), helped devise the **Suharto** regime's new economic stabilization policies. The first IBRD credit to Indonesia, in September 1968, was for US$5 million. Credits have continued to be primarily in the area of **agriculture** and communications. The IBRD is a member of the **Inter-Governmental Group on Indonesia (IGGI)**. The bank has been a major funder of Indonesia's **transmigration** program, but in October 1986 it issued a report strongly critical of aspects of the program's management, including lack of provision of facilities for transmigrants and lack of attention to the program's **environmental** consequences. Subsequently, as **Suharto** increasingly began to ignore the advice of the technocrats in favor of the personal circle surrounding him (*see* **CENDANA GROUP**; **SUHARTO FAMILY**), the bank became more critical of the government's policies and by mid-1997 was pressing for policy changes, including measures against **corruption**. It also warned against the growth in external **debt** and the decline in the growth of non**oil** exports. Following the 1997 Asian **financial crisis**, the World Bank cut its lending to Indonesia to an average of $400 million per year from about $1.5 billion annually before. In late 2002 it stated that it would consider raising this to $1 billion if Jakarta continued to reform its **economy**, reduce the **budget** deficit, and restore economic stability. [0378, 0395]

WRITING SYSTEMS. The fifth-century inscriptions of **Kutai** and **Tarumanegara**, which are the earliest written documents from the archipelago, are in southern Indian Grantha script, but by the eighth century an indigenous adaptation of that script, usually called Kawi, was in use on Java for writing both Sanskrit and old Javanese. Writings, from left to right, were commonly etched onto **lontar** leaves. Kawi was the basis for several other scripts in the archipelago, notably Balinese, Sundanese, Rejang, **Batak**, **Lampung**, and Madurese. Of the indigenous scripts in the archipelago, only that of **Bugis** is not based on Javanese but developed directly from Sanskrit. From the 14th century, Malay commonly used Jawi script, an adaptation of Arabic script for Persian.

Evidence is sparse on the level of literacy in precolonial times; Rijklof van Goens in 1648–1654 believed that a majority of Javanese were literate, and the same was said to be true of **Bali** in the 19th century. The 1920 **census** showed a literacy rate of 6.83 percent among Javanese men and 0.26 percent among women, and many observers have suggested that precolonial levels could not have been much higher. Anthony Reid, however, suggests that this reflects a decline in literacy from earlier times, pointing out that literacy in the otherwise neglected region of Lampung was recorded at 45 percent and 34 percent for men and women respectively in the 1930 census as a result of the survival of the Lampung script for use in *manjau*, "a courting game whereby young men and women would gather in the evenings and the youths would fling suggestive quatrains (***pantun***) written in the old script to the young women they fancied." The Lampung script had about 14 characters and a few vowel markers and would have been easy to learn. Such literacy would have had immensely strong social incentive and was probably taught at home rather than in school. *See also* EDUCATION; PAPER; WOMEN AND MEN. [0576]

– Y –

YAM (*Dioscorea* spp. Dioscoreaceae). A food plant with large starchy roots, it can grow to two meters in length. An important food crop of slash-and-burn peoples in **Kalimantan** and **Papua**, it is now being displaced by the **sweet potato**, which is much easier to prepare.

YAMIN, MUHAMMAD (1903–1962). Writer and politician from West **Sumatra**. He helped to formulate the **Youth Oath** in 1928, and in the late 1920s he wrote some of the first patriotic poems in Indonesian, especially the collection *Indonesia tumpah darahku* (Indonesia, land of my birth, 1929). He later prepared a biography of **Gajah Mada**, prime minister of **Majapahit**, which marks the start of a nationalist historiography. He graduated in **law** in **Batavia** in 1932, joined the Sukarnoist **Partai Indonesia (Partindo)** in the same year, and in 1937 became one of the founders of the antifascist **Gerakan Rakyat Indonesia (Gerindo)**. He left the party in 1939, when he entered the **Volksraad** as representative of West Sumatra, participating in it until 1942. As a member of the independence preparation investigation committee (**Badan Penyelidik Usaha Persiapan Kemerdekaan Indonesia [BPUPKI]**), in 1945 Yamin argued for the inclusion of the **Malay Peninsula**, northern Borneo, and **East Timor** in a Greater Indonesia. During the **Revolution** he supported **Tan Malaka**'s ideas of a vigorous program of struggle and was arrested in June 1946, being released finally in August 1948. He was close to the **Murba** but did not join it and served in several cabinets in the 1950s. In 1959 **Sukarno** chose him as head of the National Planning Council (Dewan Perancang Nasional), and he became one of the leading ideologists of **Guided Democracy**. [0502]

YANI, AHMAD (1922–1965). Career **army** officer. He commanded government troops in the suppression of the **PRRI/Permesta** rebellion on **Sumatra** in 1958 and was chief of staff of **Komando Operasi Tertinggi (Koti)**, the command for the liberation of West Irian (*see* **PAPUA**) in 1961. In 1962 **Sukarno** appointed him army chief of staff in a move to limit the influence of **A. H. Nasution**; both officers were anticommunist, but Yani was less puritanical and closer in outlook to Sukarno, coining, for instance, the term **Nekolim (Neo-Kolonialis, Kolonialis, dan Imperialis)**. Yani strongly opposed plans to arm workers and peasants as a **"Fifth Force"** and in 1965 was accused of joining a Council of Generals planning a coup to forestall a **Partai Komunis Indonesia (PKI)** takeover. He was killed in the **Gestapu** coup attempt of September–October 1965. [0714, 0889]

YAP THIAM HIEN (1913–1989). A lawyer and **human rights** activist, Yap was born in **Aceh** and educated first in **Java**, then in the **law** school in Leiden. A founding member of the **Badan Permusyawaratan Kewarga-Negaraan Indonesia (Baperki)**, he was a major proponent of the strengthening of the rule of law in Indonesia. By the time of the 1965 coup, Yap was a notable defender of the rights of all Indonesia's citizens. He defended **Subandrio** in the **Mahmillub** trials. His own arrest in 1968 was turned into a test of the **New Order**'s commitment to due legal process, and he was released after five days. He was a firm advocate of the full legal equality of **Chinese** Indonesians and fiercely opposed the adoption of ethnic Indonesian names, seeing this as essentially coercive and prejudicial. He remained closely involved with the Lembaga Bantuan Hukum (Legal Aid Institute), founded by Buyung Nasution in 1971, and was involved in nearly every major national project of legal reform or defense of human rights. [0860]

YOGYAKARTA (Ngayogyakarta Hadiningrat)**.** City and sultanate in Central **Java**, founded after the splitting of **Mataram** in 1755. Formed after **Dutch** supremacy on Java was well established, Yogyakarta was never militarily powerful and was weakened by the creation of a minor court, the **Pakualaman**, within its territory in 1812; by territorial losses following the **Java War** of 1825–1830; and by economic decline in the 19th century. Perhaps in compensation for this weakness, successive sultans (all called Hamengkubuwono) became patrons of Javanese culture, encouraging tradition and innovation to varying degrees.

As a princely territory (***Vorstenland***), Yogyakarta, like **Surakarta,** was administratively distinct from the rest of Dutch Java. Nonetheless, its people participated generally in the emergence of Indonesian **nationalism** in the 20th century. **Sultan Hamengkubuwono IX** was a strong adherent of the Republic, and Yogyakarta became the seat of its government from shortly after the declaration of **independence** until the end of the **Revolution** in 1949, with a brief period of Dutch occupation from 18 December 1948 to 6 July 1949. Since 1946 Yogyakarta (including the Pakualaman) has been a special territory (*daerah istimewa*) of the Republic, with the Yogyakarta sultan as governor and the Pakualam as his deputy. [1390]

YOUTH. *See* KOMITÉ NASIONAL PEMUDA INDONESIA; *PEMUDA*; STUDENTS.

YOUTH PLEDGE (*Sumpah Pemuda*)**.** At the second national Youth Congress, held in **Batavia** in 1928, delegates formally adopted Indonesia as the framework for the struggle against the **Dutch**, affirming that they were one people (*bangsa Indonesia*), with one language, Indonesian, and one homeland, Indonesia. *See also* "INDONESIA RAYA"; NATIONALISM.

– Z –

ZELFBESTUREN **(**“self-governing regions”**).** Official name for the native states within the Netherlands Indies, which numbered 282 in 1942. All were originally independent or semi-independent states with which the **Dutch** had concluded political contracts, either the so-called *lange politieke contracten*, long political contracts that set out in detail an allied or subordinate relationship, or the **Korte Verklaring**, or short declaration, which simply acknowledged Dutch suzerainty (*see* **NETHERLANDS INDIES, EXPANSION OF**). Within all states, the colonial government had extensive powers to intervene, including the free use of **land**, control of **mining**, and the right to appoint a ruler’s successor. Until the 20th century the general trend had been for the Dutch to abolish such states as it became convenient. The *Zelfbestuursregelen* (Self-governing territories regulations) of 1919 and 1927, however, set the notionally “indirect” form of rule on a legal basis within the colonial administrative structure; and under the *ontvoogding* (detutelization) measures of 1929, a number of states that had been abolished, such as the kingdoms on **Bali**, were restored. The Republic’s Law no. 22 of 1948 and the **Negara Indonesia Timor (NIT)** Law no. 44 of 1950 retained the *zelfbesturen* as a level of government under the name *swapraja* or *daerah swatantra*, but in 1960 these were abolished. *See also* DECENTRALIZATION. [0472, 0591, 0948]

ZEVEN PROVINCIËN, **MUTINY ON THE.** On 5 February 1933, Indonesian and **Dutch** sailors on the Dutch naval vessel *De Zeven Provinciën* mutinied off **Aceh** over a 17 percent wage cut introduced by the government to reduce expenditure during the **Depression**. Dutch aircraft bombed the ship to suppress the mutiny. Though the mutineers protested their political loyalty, the colonial government saw the rising as a product of nationalist agitation and used it to justify greater political restrictions soon after.

ZHENG HE (Cheng Ho) (1371–1435)**.** Chinese eunuch raised as a Muslim. In 1405, after a successful military career in northern **China**, he was sent by the Yongle Emperor of the Ming dynasty as leader of a major maritime expedition to Southeast Asia. The expedition consisted of 27,000 crew in over 300 vessels; its purposes remain unclear, but they probably included a desire to suppress **piracy** and to establish Chinese hegemony in the region. Zheng He successfully destroyed the fleet of a Chinese pirate based on the **Sumatra** coast of the Melaka Strait, near **Palembang**; seems to have developed close relations with **Melaka**; and followed the 1405 expedition with six others, but the expeditions seem to have had no long-term significance.

Appendix A
Governors-General of the Netherlands Indies

GOVERNORS-GENERAL

1609–1614	Pieter Both (?–1615)
1614–1615	Gerard Reynst (?–1615)
1616–1619	Laurens Reael (1583–1637)
1619–1623	Jan Pieterszoon Coen (1587–1629)
1623–1627	Pieter de Carpentier (1588–1659)
1627–1629	Jan Pieterszoon Coen (1587–1630)
1629–1632	Jacques Specx (1588–?)
1632–1636	Hendrik Brouwer (1581–1643)
1636–1645	Anthony van Diemen (1593–1645)
1645–1650	Cornelis van der Lijn (1608?–?)
1650–1653	Carel Reyniersz (1604–1653)
1653–1678	Joan Maetsuycker (1606–1678)
1678–1681	Rijkloff van Goens (1619–1682)
1681–1684	Cornelis Janszoon Speelman (1628–1684)
1684–1691	Joannes Camphuys (1634–1695)
1691–1704	Willem van Outhoorn (1635–1720)
1704–1709	Joan van Hoorn (1653–1713)
1709–1713	Abraham van Riebeeck (1653–1713)
1713–1718	Christoffel van Swoll (1663–1718)
1718–1725	Hendrick Zwaardecroon (1667–1728)
1725–1729	Mattheus de Haan (1663–1729)
1729–1732	Diederik Durven (1676–1740)
1732–1735	Dirck van Cloon (1684–1735)
1735–1737	Abraham Patras (1671–1737)
1737–1741	Adriaen Valckenier (1695–1751)
1741–1743	Johannes Thedens (1680–1748)
1743–1750	Gustaaf Willem, baron van Imhoff (1705–1750)

1750–1761	Jacob Mossel (1704–1761)
1761–1775	Petrus Albertus van der Parra (1714–1775)
1775–1777	Jeremias van Riemsdijk (1712–1777)
1777–1780	Reynier de Klerk (1710–1780)
1780–1796	Willem Arnold Alting (1724–1800)
1796–1801	Petrus Gerardus van Overstraten (1755–1801)
1801–1805	Johannes Siberg (1740–1817)
1805–1808	Albertus Henricus Wiese (1761–1810)
1808–1811	Herman Willem Daendels (1762–1818)
1811	Jan Willem Janssens (1762–1838)

ENGLISH INTERREGNUM

1811–1816	Thomas Stamford Raffles (1781–1826)
1816	John Fendall (1762–1825)

COMMISSIONERS-GENERAL

1814–1816	C. Th. Elout (1767–1841) and A. A. Buyskes (1771–?)

GOVERNORS-GENERAL

1816–1826	Godert Alexander Gerard Philip, baron van der Capellen (1778–1848)
1826–1830	Leonard Pierre Joseph, Burggraaf du Bus de Gisignies (1780–1849)
1830–1834	Johannes van den Bosch (1780–1839)
1834–1836	Jean Chretien Baud (1789–1859)
1836–1840	Dominique Jacques (de) Eerens (1781–1840)
1841–1844	Pieter Merkus (1787–1844)
1845–1851	Jan Jacob Rochussen (1797–1871)
1851–1856	Albertus Jacobus Duymaer van Twist (1809–1887)
1856–1861	Charles Ferdinand Pahud (1803–1873)
1861–1866	Ludolf Anne Jan Wilt, baron Sloet van de Beele (1806–1890)
1866–1872	Pieter Mijer (1812–1881)
1872–1875	James Loudon (1824–1884)

1875–1881	Johan Wilhelm van Lansberge (1830–1905)
1881–1884	Frederik s'Jacob (1822–1901)
1884–1888	Otto van Rees (1823–1892)
1888–1893	Cornelis Pijnacker Hordijk (1847–1908)
1893–1899	Jhr Carel Herman Aart van der Wijck (1840–1914)
1899–1905	Willem Rooseboom (1843–1920)
1905–1909	Joannes Benedictus van Heutsz (1851–1924)
1909–1916	Alexander Willem Frederik Idenburg (1861–1935)
1916–1921	Jean Paul, Graaf van Limburg Stirum (1873–1948)
1921–1926	Dirk Fock (1858–1941)
1926–1931	Jhr Andries Cornelis Dirk de Graeff (1872–1957)
1931–1936	Jhr Bonifacius Cornelis de Jonge (1875–1958)
1936–1945	Alidius Warmoldus Lambertus Tjarda van Starkenborgh Stachouwer (in Japanese detention, 1942–1945) (1888–1978)

LIEUTENANT GOVERNORS-GENERAL

1941–1942	Hubertus Johannes van Mook (1894–1965)
1944–1948	Hubertus Johannes van Mook (1894–1965)

JAPANESE MILITARY GOVERNORS OF JAVA

March–November 1942	Imamura Hitoshi
November 1942–November 1944	Harada Kumakichi
November 1944–August 1945	Yamamoto Moichiro

HOGE VERTEGENWOORDIGER VAN DE KROON

1948–1949	Louis Joseph Maria Beel (1902–1977)
1949	Antonius Hermanus Johannes Lovink (1902–1995)

GOVERNORS OF WEST NEW GUINEA

1950–1953	Simon L. van Waardenburg
1953–1958	Jan van Baal
1958–1962	Pieter J. Plateel (1911–1978)

Appendix B
Netherlands Ministers of the Colonies

(*Note:* Keys to abbreviations follow.)

ZAKEN VAN INDIË EN VAN DEN KOOPHANDEL (THE INDIES AND TRADE)

Paulus van der Helm (dir. gen.)	29 July 1806–10 December 1807
Jacob Jan Cambier	10 December 1807–8 January 1808

MARINE EN KOLONIËN (NAVY AND COLONIES)

Paulus van der Helm	8 January 1808–1811

FRENCH OCCUPATION OF THE NETHERLANDS

No minister

ZAKEN VAN KOOPHANDEL EN KOLONIËN (TRADE AND COLONIES)

G. A. G. Ph. baron van der Capellen (sec. v. staat)	6 April 1814–29 July 1814
J. C. van der Hoop (sec. v. staat, w.)	29 July 1814–14 September 1814
Jhr J. Goldberg (w.)	14 September 1814–16 September 1815
Jhr J. Goldberg (dir. gen.)	16 September 1815–19 September 1818

PUBLIEK ONDERWIJS, DE NATIONALE NIJVERHEID EN DE KOLONIËN (PUBLIC EDUCATION, NATIONAL INDUSTRY, AND THE COLONIES)

A. R. Falck	19 March 1818–30 March 1824

NATIONALE NIJVERHEID EN KOLONIËN (NATIONAL INDUSTRY AND COLONIES)

C. Th. Elout	30 March 1824–5 April 1825

MARINE EN KOLONIËN (NAVY AND COLONIES)

C. Th. Elout	5 April 1825–6 September 1829
J. J. Quarles van Ufford (sec. gen., w.)	6 September 1829–29 December 1829

WATERSTAAT, DE NATIONALE NIJVERHEID EN KOLONIËN (WATER CONTROL, NATIONAL INDUSTRY, AND COLONIES)

P. L. J. Servais van Gobbelschroij	29 December 1829–4 October 1830
G. G. Clufford (a.i.)	4 October 1830–1 January 1832

NATIONALE NIJVERHEID EN KOLONIËN (NATIONAL INDUSTRY AND COLONIES)

G. G. Clufford (a.i.)	1 January 1832–1 January 1834

KOLONIËN (COLONIES)

A. Brocx (sec. gen., w.)	1 January 1834–30 May 1834
J. G. van den Bosch	30 May 1834–25 December 1839
J. Chr. Baud (a.i.)	25 December 1839–21 July 1840

MARINE EN KOLONIËN (NAVY AND COLONIES)

J. Chr. Baud	21 July 1840–15 March 1848

KOLONIËN (COLONIES)

J. Chr. Baud	1 January 1842–15 March 1848
J. C. Rijk (a.i.)	25 March 1848–21 November 1848
G. L. Baud	21 November 1848–18 June 1849
E. B. van den Bosch	18 June 1849–1 November 1849
C. F. Pahud	1 November 1849–19 April 1853
C. F. Pahud	19 April 1853–31 December 1855
P. Mijer	1 January 1856–1 July 1856
P. Mijer	1 July 1856–18 March 1858
J. J. Rochussen	18 March 1858–23 February 1860
J. J. Rochussen	23 February 1860–31 December 1860
J. S. Lotsy	1 January 1861–9 January 1861
J. P. Cornets de Groot van Kraaijenburg	9 January 1861–14 March 1861
J. Loudon	14 March 1861–31 January 1862
G. H. Uhlenbeck	31 January 1862–3 January 1863
G. H. Betz (a.i.)	3 January 1863–2 February 1863
I. D. Fransen van de Putte	2 February 1863–10 February 1866
I. D. Fransen van de Putte	10 February 1866–30 May 1866
P. Mijer	30 May 1866–15 September 1866
N. Trakranen	15 September 1866–20 July 1867
J. J. Hasselman	20 July 1867–4 June 1868
E. de Waal	4 June 1868–16 November 1870
L. G. Brocx (a.i.)	16 November 1870–4 January 1871
P. P. van Bosse	4 January 1871–6 July 1872
I. D. Fransen van de Putte	6 July 1872–27 August 1874
Willem baron van Goltstein	27 August 1874–11 September 1876
F. A. Mees	11 September 1876–3 November 1877
P. P. van Bosse	3 November 1877–21 February 1879
H. O. Wichers (a.i.)	21 February 1879–12 March 1879
O. van Rees	12 March 1879–20 August 1879
Willem baron van Goltstein	20 August 1879–1 September 1882
W. M. de Brauw	1 September 1882–23 February 1883

W. F. van Erp Taalman Kip (a.i.)	23 February 1883–23 April 1883
F. G. van Bloemen Waanders	23 April 1883–25 November 1883
A. W. Ph. Weitzel (a.i.)	25 November 1883–27 February 1884
J. P. Sprenger van Eijk	27 February 1884–21 April 1888
L. W. C. Keuchenius	21 April 1888–24 February 1890
Aeneas baron Mackay	24 February 1890–21 August 1891
W. K. baron van Dedem	21 August 1891–9 May 1894
J. H. Bergsma	9 May 1894–27 July 1897
J. Th. Cremer	27 July 1897–1 August 1901
T. A J. van Asch van Wijck	1 August 1901–9 September 1902
J. W. Bergansius (a.i.)	9 September 1902–25 September 1902
A.W.F. Idenburg	25 September 1902–17 August 1905
D. Fock	17 August 1905–12 February 1908
Th. Heemskerk	12 February 1908–20 May 1908
A. W. F. Idenburg	20 May 1908–16 August 1909
J. H. de Waal Malefijt	16 August 1909–29 August 1913
Th. B. Pleijte	29 August 1913–8 December 1915
J. J. Rambonnet (w.)	8 December 1915–9 September 1918
A. W.F. Idenburg (ARP)	9 September 1918–13 November 1919
Ch. J. M. Ruys de Beerenbrouck (w.) (RKSP)	13 August 1919–13 November 1919
S. de Graaf (ARP)	13 November 1919–18 September 1922
S. de Graaf (ARP)	18 September 1922–4 August 1925
H. Colijn (a.i.) (ARP)	4 August 1925–26 September 1925
Ch. J. I. M. Welter (RKSP)	26 September 1925–8 March 1926
J. C. Koningsberger (Lib.)	8 March 1926–10 August 1929
S. de Graaf (ARP)	10 August 1929–26 May 1933
H. Colijn (ARP)	25 May 1933–31 July 1935
H. Colijn (ARP)	31 July 1935–24 June 1937
Ch. J. I. M. Welter (RKSP)	24 June 1937–25 July 1939
C. van den Bussche (Lib.)	25 July 1939–10 August 1939
Ch. J. I. M. Welter (RKSP)	10 August 1939–3 September 1940
Ch. J. I. M. Welter (RKSP)	3 September 1940–27 July 1941
Ch. J. I. M. Welter (RKSP)	27 July 1941–17 November 1941
P. S. Gerbrandy (a.i.) (ARP)	17 November 1941–21 February 1942
P. S. Gerbrandy (ARP)	21 February 1942–21 May 1942
H. J. van Mook	21 May 1942–23 February 1945

OVERZEESE GEBIEDSDELEN (OVERSEAS TERRITORIES; CREATED 23 FEBRUARY 1945)

J. I. J. M. Schmutzer (RKSP)	23 February 1945–24 June 1945
J. H. A. Logemann (became PvdA)	24 June 1945–3 July 1946
J. A. Jonkman (PvdA)	3 July 1946–7 August 1948
E. M. J. A. Sassen (KVP)	7 August 1948–14 February 1949
J. H. van Maarseveen (a.i.), (KVP)	14 February 1949–15 June 1949
J. H. van Maarseveen (KVP)	15 June 1949–24 December 1949

UNIEZAKEN EN OVERZEESE RIJKSDELEN (UNION AFFAIRS AND OVERSEAS TERRITORIES; CREATED 24 DECEMBER 1949)

J. H. van Maarseveen (KVP)	24 December 1949–15 March 1951
W. Drees (a.i.) (PvdA)	15 March 1951–30 March 1951
L. A. H. Peters (KVP)	30 March 1951–2 September 1952

OVERZEESE RIJKSDELEN (OVERSEAS TERRITORIES; CREATED 7 NOVEMBER 1952)

W. J. A. Kernkamp (CHU)	2 September 1952–18 July 1956
C. Staf (a.i.) (CHU)	18 July 1956–13 October 1956

ZAKEN OVERZEE (AFFAIRS OVERSEAS; CREATED 14 FEBRUARY 1957, ABOLISHED 19 AUGUST 1959)

C. Staf (a.i.) (CHU)	13 October 1956–16 February 1957
G. Ph. Helders (CHU)	16 February 1957–22 December 1958
G. Ph. Helders (CHU)	22 December 1958–19 May 1959
H. A. Korthals (VVD)	19 May 1959–18 August 1959

KEY TO PARTIES

ARP	Anti-Revolutionaire Partij (Antirevolutionary Party)
CHU	Christelijk-Historische Unie (Christian Historical Union)
KVP	Katholieke Volkspartij (Catholic People's Party)
Lib.	Liberalen (Liberals)
PvdA	Partij van de Arbeid (Labor Party)
RKSP	Rooms-Katholieke Staatspartij (Roman Catholic State Party)
VVD	Volkspartij voor Vrijheid en Democracy (People's Party for Freedom and Democracy)

KEY TO ABBREVIATIONS

a.i.	ad interim (provisional)
dir. gen.	director-general
sec. v. staat	secretaris van staat (secretary of state)
w.	waarnemend (acting)

NOTE

Based on G. F. E. Gonggryp, *Geillustreerde encyclopedie van Nederlandsch-Indie* (Leiden: Leidsche Uitgeversmaatschappij, 1934); and H. Daalder and C. J. M. Schuyt, eds., *Compendium voor politiek en samenleving in Nederland* (Alphen aan den Rijn, The Netherlands: Samsom, 1986; fifth supplement, 1988), section A 0500.

Appendix C
Rulers of the Early States

ACEH

1496	Ali Mughayat Syah
1528	Salah ud-din ibn Ali
1537	Ala'ad-din al Kahar ibn Ali
1568	Husain
1575	Sultan Muda (a few days)
1575	Sultan Sri Alam
1576	Zainil Abidin
1577	Ala'ad-din of Perak (Mansur Syah)
1589?	Sultan Boyong
1596	Ala'ad-din Riayat Syah
1604	Ali Riayat Syah
1607	Iskandar Muda
1636	Iskandar Thani
1641	Safiyat ud-din Taj al-Alam bint Iskandar Muda (widow of Iskandar Thani)
1675	Naqiyat ud-din Nur al-Alam
1678	Zaqiyat ud-din Inayat Syah
1688	Kamalat Syah Zinat ud-din
1699	Badr al-Alam Syarif Hasyim Jamal ud-din
1702	Perkara Alam Syarif Lamtui
1703	Jamal al Alam Badr al-Munir
1726	Jamal al-Alam Amin ud-din (a few days)
1726	Shams al-Alam (a few days)

Bugis Dynasty

1727	Ala'ad-din Ahmad Syah
1735	Ala'ad-din Johan Syah
1764	Badr ad-din Johan Syah
1765	Mahmud Syah (restored)
1769	Mahmud Syah
1773	Sulaiman Syah (Udahna Lela)
1773	Mahmud Syah (restored)
1781	Ala'ad-din Jauhar al-Alam
1795	Ala'ad-din Jauhar al-Alam
1823	Muhammad Syah
1838	Sulaiman
1857	Ali Ala'ad-din Mansur Syah (Ibrahim)
1870	Mahmud Syah
1874	Muhammad Daud Syah

SINGASARI AND MAJAPAHIT

1. 1222	Rajasa (Ken Angrok)
2. 1227	Anusapati, stepson of 1
3. 1248	Tohjaya, son of 1
4. 1248	Wisnuwardhana, son of 2
5. 1268	Kertanegara, son of 4
6. 1292	Jayakatwang of Kediri (usurper)
7. 1293	Kertarajasa Jayawardhana (Wijaya), nephew and son-in-law of 5
8. 1309	Jayanegara, son of 7
9. 1329	Tribuwana, daughter of 7
10. 1350	Rajasanegara (Hayam Wuruk), son of 9
11. 1389	Wikramawardhana, nephew and son-in-law of 10
12. 1429	Suhita, daughter of 11
13. 1447–1441	Kertawijaya, son of 11

MATARAM

1582	Sutawijaya Senopati
1601	Mas Jolang

1613	Cakrakusuma Ngabdurrahman, Sultan Agung
1645	Prabu Amangkurat I, Sunan Tegalwangi
1677	Amangkurat II
1703	Amangkurat III, Sunan Mas
1705	Pakubuwono Sunan Puger
1719	Amangkurat IV
1725	Pakubuwono II
1749	Pakubuwono III

SURAKARTA

?	Pakubuwono III (of Mataram)
1788	Pakubuwono IV
1820	Pakubuwono V
1823	Pakubuwono VI
1830	Pakubuwono VII
1858	Pakubuwono VIII
1861	Pakubuwono IX
1893	Pakubuwono X
1939	Pakubuwono XI
1944–1946	Pakubuwono XII

YOGYAKARTA

1749	Hamengkubuwono I, Mangkubumi
1792	Hamengkubuwono II, Sultan Sepuh
1810	Hamengkubuwono III, Raja
1814	Hamengkubuwono IV, Seda Pesijar
1822	Hamengkubuwono V, Menol
1855	Hamengkubuwono VI, Mangkubumi
1877	Hamengkubuwono VII
1921	Hamengkubuwono VIII
1939	Hamengkubuwono IX
1989–present	Hamengkubuwono X

Appendix D
Cabinets of the Republic of Indonesia

Presidential Cabinet	31 August 1945–14 November 1945
Sjahrir I	14 November 1945–12 March 1946
Sjahrir II	12 March 1946–2 October 1946
Sjahrir III	2 October 1946–27 June 1947
Amir Sjarifuddin I	3 July 1947–11 November 1947
Amir Sjarifuddin II	11 November 1947–29 January 1948
Mohammad Hatta I (presidential cabinet)	29 January 1948–4 August 1949
Emergency Cabinet	19 December 1948–13 July 1949
Mohammad Hatta II (presidential cabinet)	4 August 1949–20 December 1949
Susanto Tirtoprojo (Republic of Indonesia, Yogyakarta)	20 December 1949–21 January 1950
Abdul Halim (Republic of Indonesia, Yogyakarta)	21 January 1950–6 September 1950
Mohammad Hatta III (RIS[i])	20 December 1949–6 September 1950
Mohammad Natsir	6 September 1950–27 April 1951
Sukiman Wiryosanjoyo	27 April 1951–3 April 1952
Wilopo	3 April 1952–1 August 1953
Ali Sastroamijoyo I	1 August 1953–12 August 1955
Burhanuddin Harahap	12 August 1955–26 March 1956
Ali Sastroamijoyo II	26 March 1956–9 April 1957
Juanda I (*Kabinet Karya*)	9 April 1957–25 June 1958
Juanda II	25 June 1958–9 July 1959
Kabinet Kerja I (Sukarno)	9 July 1959–18 February 1960
Kabinet Kerja II (Sukarno)	18 February 1960–6 March 1962
Kabinet Kerja III (Sukarno)	6 March 1962–13 November 1963

Kabinet Kerja IV (Sukarno)	13 November 1963–2 September 1964
Kabinet Dwikora I (Sukarno)	2 September 1964–24 February 1966
Kabinet Dwikora II "Cabinet of 100 Ministers"	24 February 1966–30 March 1966
Kabinet Dwikora III	30 March 1966–28 July 1966
Kabinet Ampera	28 July 1966–10 June 1968
Kabinet Pembangunan I (Suharto) (Development Cabinet)	10 June 1968–27 March 1973
Kabinet Pembangunan II	27 March 1973–29 March 1978
Kabinet Pembangunan III	29 March 1978–19 March 1983
Kabinet Pembangunan IV	19 March 1983–22 March 1988
Kabinet Pembangunan V	21 March 1988–17 March 1993
Kabinet Pembangunan VI	17 March 1993–14 March 1998
Kabinet Pembangunan VII	14 March 1998–23 May 1998
Kabinet Reformasi Pembangunan (Habibie)	23 May 1998–26 October 1999
Kabinet Kesatuan Nasional (Abdurrachman Wahid)	26 October 1999–23 August 2000
2nd Abdurrachman Cabinet	23 August 2000–1 June 2001
3rd Abdurrachman Cabinet	1 June 2001–9 August 2001
Kabinet Gotong Royong (Megawati)	9 August 2001–present

NOTE

Sukarnoerg cabinets based principally on Susan Finch and Daniel S. Lev, comps., *Republic of Indonesia Cabinets 1945–1965* (Ithaca, NY: Cornell University Modern Indonesia Project, 1965).

1. Republik Indonesia Serikat (Republic of the United States of Indonesia).

Appendix E
Republic of Indonesia Officeholders

PRESIDENTS

Sukarno	18 August 1945–12 March 1967
Suharto (acting)	12 March 1967–27 March 1968
Suharto	27 March 1968–19 May 1998
B. J. Habibie	19 May 1998–26 October 1999
Abdurrachman Wahid	26 October 1999–23 July 2001
Megawati Sukarnoputri	23 July 2001–present

Vice Presidents

Mohammad Hatta	18 August 1945–1 December 1956
Hamengkubuwono IX	27 March 1968–23 March 1978
Adam Malik	23 March 1978–12 March 1983
Umar Wirahadikusumah	12 March 1983–11 March 1988
Sudharmono	11 March 1988–17 March 1993
Try Sutrisno	17 March 1993–14 March 1998
B. J. Habibie	14 March 1998–19 May 1998
Megawati Sukarnoputri	26 October 1999–23 July 2001
Hamzah Haz	23 July 2001–present

PRIME MINISTERS

Republik Indonesia (Republic of Indonesia, declared independent 17 August 1945)

Sutan Sjahrir (PS)	14 November 1945–13 March 1946
Sutan Sjahrir (PS)	13 March 1946–2 October 1946

Sutan Sjahrir (PS)	2 October 1946–27 June 1947
Amir Sjarifuddin (PS)	3 July 1947–11 November 1947
Amir Sjarifuddin (PS)	11 November 1947–29 January 1948
Mohammad Hatta	29 January 1948–4 August 1949
Mohammad Hatta	4 August 1949–20 December 1949

Pemerintah Darurat Republik Indonesia (Emergency Government of the Republic of Indonesia on Sumatra)

Sjafruddin Prawiranegara (Masjumi)	19 December 1948–13 July 1949

Republik Indonesia (Republic of Indonesia, Constituent State of the Republik Indonesia Serikat)

Susanto Tirtoprojo (PNI)	20 December 1949–21 January 1950
Abdul Halim	21 January 1950–6 September 1950

Republik Indonesia Serikat (Federal Republic of Indonesia)

Mohammad Hatta	20 December 1949–6 September 1950

Republik Indonesia

Mohammad Natsir (Masjumi)	6 September 1950–27 April 1951
Sukiman Wiryosanjoyo (Masjumi)	27 April 1951–3 April 1952
Wilopo (PNI)	3 April 1952–1 August 1953
Ali Sastroamijoyo (PNI)	1 August 1953–12 August 1955
Burhanuddin Harahap (Masjumi)	12 August 1955–26 March 1956
Ali Sastroamijoyo (PNI)	26 March 1956–9 April 1957
Juanda Kartawijaya	9 April 1957–9 July 1959
Juanda Kartawijaya[1]	9 July 1959–7 November 1963
Sukarno	9 July 1959–12 March 1967
Subandrio (1st deputy prime minister)	13 November 1963–18 March 1966
Johannes Leimena (2nd deputy PM)	13 November 1963–30 March 1966

Khaerul Saleh) (3rd deputy PM)	13 November 1963–18 March 1966
K. H. Idham Khalid (4th deputy PM)	24 February 1966–30 March 1966
Johannes Leimena (1st deputy PM)	30 March 1966–28 July 1966
K. H. Idham Khalid (2nd deputy PM)	30 March 1966–28 July 1966
Ruslan Abdulgani (3rd deputy PM)	30 March 1966–28 July 1966
Hamengkubuwono IX (4th deputy PM)	30 March 1966–28 July 1966
Suharto (5th deputy PM)	30 March 1966–28 July 1966
Adam Malik (6th deputy PM)	30 March 1966–28 July 1966

FOREIGN MINISTERS

Republik Indonesia (Republic of Indonesia, 17 August 1945–20 December 1949)

Ahmad Subarjo	31 August 1945–14 November 1945
Sutan Sjahrir (PS)	14 November 1945–27 June 1947
Haji Agus Salim (Masjumi)	3 July 1947–20 December 1949

Pemerintah Darurat Republik Indonesia (Emergency Government of the Republic of Indonesia on Sumatra)

A. A. Maramis (PNI)	19 December 1948–13 July 1949

Republik Indonesia Serikat (Federal Republic of Indonesia)

Mohammad Hatta	20 December 1949–6 September 1950

Republik Indonesia

Mohammad Roem (Masjumi)	6 September 1950–27 April 1951
Ahmad Subarjo (Masjumi)	27 April 1951–3 April 1952
Wilopo (PNI, ad interim)	3 April 1952–29 April 1952

Mukarto Notowidagdo (PNI)	29 April 1952–1 August 1953
Sunario (PNI)	1 August 1955–26 March 1956
Ruslan Abdulgani (PNI)	26 March 1956–9 April 1957
(nonactive)	28 January 1957–14 March 1957
Subandrio	9 April 1957–30 March 1966
Adam Malik (ad interim)	30 March 1966–28 July 1966
Adam Malik	28 July 1966–29 March 1978
Mochtar Kusumaatmaja	28 March 1983–21 March 1988
Ali Alatas	21 March 1988–26 October 1999
Alwi Shihab	26 October 1999–9 August 2001
Hassan Wirayuda	9 August 2001–present

MINISTERS OF INTERNAL AFFAIRS

Republik Indonesia (Republic of Indonesia, 17 August 1945–20 December 1949)

R. A. A. Wiranatakusumah	31 August 1945–14 November 1945
Sutan Sjahrir (PS)	14 November 1945–12 March 1946
Sudarsono (PS)	12 March 1946–2 October 1946
Mohammad Roem (Masjumi)	2 October 1946–27 June 1947
Wondoamiseno (PSII)	3 July 1947–11 November 1947
Mohamad Roem (Masjumi)	11 November 1947–22 January 1948
Sukiman Wiryosanjoyo (Masjumi, ad interim)	29 January 1948–4 August 1949
Wongsonegoro (PIR)	4 August 1949–20 December 1949

Pemerintah Darurat Republik Indonesia (Emergency Government of the Republic of Indonesia on Sumatra)

Teuku Mohammad Hasan	19 December 1948–13 July 1949

Republik Indonesia (Republic of Indonesia, Constituent State of the Republik Indonesia Serikat)

Susanto Tirtoprojo (PNI)	20 December 1949–21 January 1950
Susanto Tirtoprojo (PNI)	21 January 1950–6 September 1950

Republik Indonesia Serikat (Federal Republic of Indonesia)

Anak Agung Gde Agung	20 December 1949–6 September 1950

Republik Indonesia

Assaat	6 September 1950–27 April 1951
Iskaq Cokroadisuryo (PNI)	27 April 1951–3 April 1952
Mohamad Roem (Masjumi)	3 April 1952–1 August 1953
Hazairin (PIR)	1 August 1953–23 October 1954
Haji Zainul Arifin (NU)	23 October 1954–19 November 1954
Sunaryo (NU)	19 November 1954–12 August 1955
Sunaryo (NU)	12 August 1955–19 January 1956
R. P. Suroso (Parindra)	19 January 1956–26 March 1956
Sunaryo (NU)	26 March 1956–9 April 1957
Sanusi Harjadinata (PNI)	9 April 1957–9 July 1959
Ipik Gandamana	9 July 1959–6 March 1962
Saharjo	6 March 1962–13 November 1963
Ipik Gandamana	13 November 1963–2 September 1964
Sumarno	2 September 1964–18 March 1966
Basuki Rahmat	30 March 1966–9 January 1969
Amir Machmud	23 January 1969–28 March 1973
Suparjo Rustam	28 March 1973–21 March 1988
Rudini	21 March 1988–17 March 1993
M. Yogie Memet	17 March 1993–22 May 1998
Syarwan Hamid	22 May 1998–26 October 1999
Surjadi Soedirdja	29 October 1999–9 August 2001
Hari Sabarno	9 August 2001–present

MINISTERS OF DEFENSE

Republik Indonesia (Republic of Indonesia, 17 August 1945–20 December 1949)

Supriyadi (deceased)	6 October 1945–14 November 1945
Sulyoadikusumo (ad interim)	20 October 1945–14 November 1945
Mustopo (self-appointed)	November 1945

Hamengku Buwono IX	(chosen by army but never took office)
Amir Sjarifuddin (PS)	14 November 1945–29 January 1948
Mohammad Hatta (ad interim)	29 January 1948–15 July 1948
Hamengku Buwono IX	15 July 1948–20 December 1949

Pemerintah Darurat Republik Indonesia (Emergency Government of the Republic of Indonesia on Sumatra)

Sjafruddin Prawiranegara (Masjumi)	19 December 1948–13 July 1949

Republik Indonesia Serikat (Federal Republic of Indonesia)

Hamengku Buwono IX	20 December 1949–6 September 1950

Republik Indonesia

Abdul Halim (ad interim)	6 September 1950–17 August 1950
Mohammad Natsir (Masjumi, ad interim)	17 December 1950–27 April 1951
Sewaka (PIR)	9 May 1951–3 April 1952
Hamengku Buwono IX	3 April 1952–2 June 1953
Wilopo (PNI)	2 June 1953–1 August 1953
Iwa Kusumasumantri (Persatuan Progresif)	1 August 1953–13 July 1955
Burhanuddin Harahap (Masjumi)	12 August 1955–26 March 1956
Ali Sastroamijoyo (PNI, ad interim)	26 March 1956–9 April 1957
Juanda Kartawijaya	9 April 1957–9 July 1959
Abdul Haris Nasution	9 July 1959–24 February 1966
M. Sarbini	24 February 1966–29 March 1973
Maraden Panggabean	28 March 1973–17 April 1978
Andi Mohammad Yusuf	17 April 1978–28 March 1983
S. Poniman	28 March 1983–21 March 1988
L. B. (Benny) Murdani	21 March 1988–21 March 1993
Edi Sudrajat	21 March 1993–14 March 1998
Wiranto	22 March 1998–26 October 1999

Juwono Sudarsono	26 October 1999–23 August 2000
Mohammad Mahfud	23 August 2000–9 August 2001
Matori Abdul Djalil	9 August 2001–present

COMMANDERS OF THE ARMY

The formal title of the army's most senior commanding officer was *panglima* (1945–1949), *Kepala staf* (chief of staff, 1949–1960), *menteri/Kepala staf* (minister/chief of staff, 1960–1963), *menteripanglima* (1963–1967), *panglima* (1967–1969), and *Kepala staf* (1969–present).

Supriyadi (deceased)	6 October 1945–14 November 1945
Urip Sumoharjo (acting chief of HQ)	6 October 1945–18 December 1945
Sudirman (elected)	12 December 1945–18 December 1945
Sudirman (appointed)	18 December 1945–19 January 1950
A. H. Nasution	19 January 1950–15 December 1952
Bambang Sugeng	16 December 1952–2 May 1955
Zulkifi Lubis (acting)	12 May 1955–27 June 1955
Bambang Utoyo	10 June 1955–24 July 1955
Zulkifli Lubis (acting)	24 July 1955–7 November 1955
A. H. Nasution	7 November 1955–25 June 1962
Ahmad Yani	25 June 1962–1 October 1965
Pranoto (acting)	1 October 1965–16 October 1965
Suharto	16 October 1965–29 May 1967
Maraden Panggabean (acting)	29 May 1967–17 May 1968
Maraden Panggabean	17 May 1968–4 December 1969
Umar Wirahadikusumah	4 December 1969–2 April 1973
Surono Reksodimejo	2 April 1973–10 April 1974
Makmun Murod	10 April 1974–26 January 1978
Widodo	26 January 1978–15 April 1980
S. Poniman	15 April 1980–7 March 1983
Rudini	7 March 1983–24 June 1986
Try Sutrisno	24 June 1986–27 February 1988
Edi Sudrajat	27 February 1988–6 April 1993
Wismoyo Arismunandar	6 April 1993–11 February 1995
R. Hartono	11 February 1995–13 June 1997

Wiranto	13 June 1997–23 February 1998
Subagyo Hadi Siswoyo	23 February 1998–? December 1999
Tyasno Sudarto	7 December 1999–9 October 2000
Endriartono Sutarto	9 October 2000–3 June 2002
Ryamizard Ryacudu	3 June 2002–present

COMMANDERS OF THE ARMED FORCES

T. B. Simatupang (chief of staff) (post abolished)	19 January 1950–c. August 1953
Abdul Haris Nasution	25 June 1962–12 March 1967
Suharto	12 March 1967–28 March 1973?
Maraden Panggabean	28 March 1967–17 April 1978
Andi Muhammad Yusuf	17 April 1978–28 March 1983
L. B. (Benny) Murdani	28 March 1983–27 February 1988
Try Sutrisno	27 February 1988–19 February 1993
Edi Sudrajat	19 February 1993–21 May 1993
Feisal Etno Tanjung	21 May 1993–20 February 1998
Wiranto	20 February 1998–5 November 1999
Widodo Adi Sucipto	5 November 1999–7 June 2002
Edriartono Sutarto	7 June 2002–present

KOPKAMTIB COMMANDERS

Suharto	10 October 1965–19 November 1969
Maraden Panggabean	19 November 1969–27 March 1973
Sumitro	27 March 1973–28 January 1974
Suharto	28 January 1974–17 April 1978

(Day-to-day command exercised by KOPKAMTIB Chief of Staff Sudomo.)

Sudomo	17 April 1974–29 March 1983
L. B. (Benny) Murdani	29 March 1983–22 September 1988

KOPKAMTIB was abolished in September 1988 and replaced by BAKORSTANAS, which was abolished in March 2000.

KEY TO ABBREVIATIONS

Masjumi	Madjelis Sjuro Muslimin Indonesia (Consultative Council of Indonesian Muslims)
NU	Nahdlatul Ulama (Revival of the Religious Scholars)
Parindra	Partia Indonesia Raya (Greater Indonesia Party)
PIR	Persatuan Indonesia Raya (Greater Indonesian Association)
PNI	Partai Nasional Indonesia (Indonesian Nationalist Party)
PS	Partai Sosialis (Socialist Party)
PSI	Partai Sosialis Indonesia (Indonesian Socialist Party)
PSII	Partai Sarekat Islam Indonesia (Party of the Indonesian Islamic Union)

NOTE

1. Although Juanda's formal position from 9 July 1959 was that of first minister (Menteri Pertama), rather than prime minister (Perdana Menteri), with Sukarno holding the posts of president and prime minister concurrently, he was effectively prime minister, that is, head of the cabinet, until his death on 7 November 1963.

Appendix F
Parliamentary Strengths and Electoral Performance of the Parties, 1945–1999

KOMITÉ NASIONAL INDONESIA PUSAT, FOUNDED 16–17 OCTOBER 1945 (200 SEATS)[1]

Party	Seats	(%)
PNI	45	(22.5%)
Masjumi	35	(17.5%)
Partai Sosialis	35	(17.5%)
Partai Buruh	6	(3.0%)
PKI	2	(1.0%)
PARKINDO	4	(2.0%)
Partai Katolik	2	(1.0%)
Sumatra	1	(0.5%)
Borneo	4	(2.0%)
Sulawesi	5	(2.5%)
Maluku	2	(1.0%)
Sunda Kecil	2	(1.0%)
Chinese	5	(2.5%)
Arabs	2	(1.0%)
Europeans	1	(0.5%)

KOMITÉ NASIONAL INDONESIA PUSAT, EXPANDED 2 MARCH 1947 (514 SEATS)[2]

Party	Seats
PNI	45
Masjumi	60
Partai Sosialis	35

Partai Buruh	35
PKI	35
PARKINDO	8
Partai Katolik	4
Workers*	40
Peasants*	40
Sumatra	50
Borneo	8
Sulawesi	10
Maluku	5
Sunda Kecil	5
Chinese	7
Arabs	3
Europeans	3

DEWAN PERWAKILAN RAKYAT OF THE UNITARY REPUBLIC OF INDONESIA (FORMED 17 AUGUST 1950, 236 SEATS)[3]

Origins

1. Members of RIS Dewan Perwakilan Rakyat	
A. Representing the Republic of Indonesia	50
B. Representing states and territories of the RIS other than the Republic of Indonesia and Pasundan	79
C. Representatives for Pasundan appointed by the Republic of Indonesia	19
2. Members of the RIS Senate	29
3. Members of the Working Committee of the Republic of Indonesia KNIP	46
4. Members of the Dewan Pertimbangan Agung of the Republic of Indonesia	13

Affiliation

Party	Seats	(% of DPR, total 232)
Masjumi	49	(21%)
PNI	36	(16%)

PSI	17	(7.3%)
PIR	17	
PKI	13	(5.6%)
Fraksi Demokrasi	13	
PRN	10	
Partai Katolik	9	(3.9%)
PARINDRA	8	
Partai Buruh	7	
PARKINDO	5	(2.2%)
PSII	5	
Murba	4	(1.7%)
Front Buruh	4	
Fraksi Kedaulatan Rakyat	4	
Serikat Kerakyatan Indonesia	3	
Golongan Tani (peasants)	2	
No formal affiliation	26	

DEWAN PERWAKILAN RAKYAT, ELECTED 29 SEPTEMBER 1955[4]

Party	No. of Valid Votes	% of vote	Seats
PNI	8,434,653	22.3	57
Masjumi	7,902,886	20.9	57
Nahdatul Ulama	6,955,141	18.4	45
PKI	6,176,914	16.4	39
PSII	1,019,160	2.9	8
PARKINDO	1,003,325	2.6	8
Partai Katolik	770,740	2.0	6
PSI	753,191	2.0	5
IPKI	541,306	1.4	4
Perti	483,014	1.3	4
PRN	242,125	0.6	2
Partai Buruh	224,167	0.6	2
GPPS (Gerakan Pembela Pancasila)	219,985	0.6	2
PRI	206,261	0.5	2
PPPRI	200,419	0.5	2

Murba	199,588	0.5	2
Baperki	178,887	0.5	1
PIR-Wongsonegoro	178,481	0.5	1
Gerinda (Gerakan Indonesia)	154,792	0.4	1
Permai	149,287	0.4	1
Partai Persatuan Daya	146,054	0.4	1
PIR-Hazairin	114,644	0.3	1
PPTI	85,131	0.2	1
AKUI	81,454	0.2	1
PRD	77,919	0.2	1
PRIM (Partai Rakyat Indonesia Merdeka)	72,523	0.2	1
Acoma (Angkatan Comunis Muda)	64,514	0.2	1
R. Soejono Prawirosudarso & Associates	53,305	0.1	1
Others	1,022,433	2.7	—
Total	37,785,299	100.0	257

CONSTITUENT ASSEMBLY ELECTIONS, 15 DECEMBER 1955[5]

PNI	9,070,218
Masjumi	7,789,619
NU	6,989,333
PKI	6,232,512
PSII	1,059,922
PARKINDO	988,810
Partai Katolik	748,591
PSI	695,932
IPKI	544,803
PERTI	465,359
PRN	220,652
Partai Buruh	332,047
Murba	248,633

PIR (Wongsonegoro)	162,420
PIR (Hazairin)	101,509
Permai	164,386
Baperki	160,456
Gerinda	157,976
Partai Persatuan Daya	169,222
PRIM	143,907
AKUI	84,862
Acoma	55,844
PPTI	74,913
PRD	39,278
R. Soedjono	38,356
Prawirosoedarso & Associates	

JAVA PROVINCIAL ELECTIONS, JUNE-AUGUST 1957 (RESULTS IN 1955 ELECTIONS IN SAME REGIONS IN BRACKETS)[6]

	Jakarta	West Java	Central Java	East Java
Masjumi	153,709	1,841,030	833,707	977,443
	(200,460)	(1,844,442)	(902,387)	(1,109,742)
PNI	124,955	1,055,801	2,400,282	1,899,782
	(152,031)	(1,541,927)	(3,019,568)	(2,257,069)
NU	104,892	597,356	1,865,568	2,999,785
	(120,667)	(673,552)	(1,772,306)	(3,370,554)
PKI	137,305	1,087,269	3,005,150)	2,704,523
	96,363)	(755,634)	(2,326,108)	(2,299,785)

DEWAN PERWAKILAN RAKYAT—GOTONG ROYONG (DPR-GR), JULY 1960[7]

PNI	44
PKI	30
Partai Katolik	5
PSII	5
PARKINDO	6

Murba	1
NU	36
PERTI	2
Army (functional group)	15
Navy	7
Air force	7
Police	5
Workers	26
Peasants	25
Islamic teachers	24
Youth	9
Women	8
Intellectuals and teachers	5
Total	283

SECOND GENERAL ELECTIONS, 3 JULY 1971

Party	Votes	(%)	Seats in DPR
Golkar	34,348,673	(62.80)	227
Nahdatul Ulama	10,213,650	(18.67)	58
PNI	3,793,266	(6.94)	20
PARMUSI	2,930,746	(5.36)	24
PSII	1,308,237	(2.39)	10
PARKINDO	733,359	(1.34)	7
Partai Katolik	603,740	(1.10)	3
PERTI	381,309	(0.70)	2
IPKI	338,403	(0.62)	—
Murba	48,126	(0.09)	—
Total	54,699,509		351

THIRD GENERAL ELECTIONS, 2 MAY 1977[8]

Party	Votes	%	Seats
PPP	18,743,491	27.78	99
Golkar	34,348,673	64.33	232
PDI	5,516,894	7.87	29

FOURTH GENERAL ELECTIONS, 1982[9]

Party	Votes	%	Seats
PPP	20,871,880	27.78	94
Golkar	48,334,724	64.34	246
PDI	5,919,702	7.88	24

FIFTH GENERAL ELECTIONS, 23 APRIL 1987[10]

Party	Votes	%	Seats
PPP	13,730,456	16.04	61
Golkar	62,433,161	72.94	299
PDI	9,434,667	11.02	40

SIXTH GENERAL ELECTIONS, 9 JUNE 1992[11]

Party	Votes	%	Seats
PPP	16,624,647	17	62
Golkar	66,559,331	68	282
PDI	14,565,556	16	56

SEVENTH GENERAL ELECTIONS, 29 MAY 1997[12]

Party	Votes	%	Seats
PPP	25,340,028	22.4	89
Golkar	684,187,907	74.5	325
PDI	3,565,556	2.6	11

EIGHTH GENERAL ELECTIONS, 1999[13]

Party	Votes	%	Seats
PDI-P	35,689,073	33.76	153
Golkar	23.741,749	22.46	120
PKB	13,336,982	12.62	51

Party	Votes	%	Seats
PPP	11,329,905	10.72	58
PAN	7,528,956	7.12	34
PBB	2,049,708	1.94	13
PK	1,436,565	1.36	7
PKP	1,065,686	1.01	4
PNU	679,179	0.64	5
PDKB	550,846	0.52	5
PP	551,028	0.52	1
PPIIM	56,718	0.43	1
PDR	427,854	0.40	1
PSII	152,820[14]	0.14	1
PNI-FM	365,176	0.35	1
PBI	364,290	0.34	1
PNI-MM	345,720	0.33	1
IPKI	328,564	0.31	1
PKU	300,064	0.28	1
PKD	216,675	0.20	1

None of the other 27 parties that contested the elections received a seat in parliament.

NINTH GENERAL ELECTIONS, 5 APRIL 2004[15]

A total of 24 political parties qualified to contest the 2004 elections, including only six that had participated in the 1999 general elections.[16] These six were: Partai Demokrasi Indonesia-Perjuangan (PDIP); Golkar; Partai Persatuan Pembangunan (PPP); Partai Kebangkitan Bangsa (PKB); Partai Amanat Nasional (PAN); and Partai Bulan Bintang (PBB).

The other qualifying parties were: Partai Nasional Indonesia Marhaenisme (PNIM), Partai Buruh Sosial Demokrat (PBSD), Partai Merdeka (PM), Partai Persatuan Demokrasi Kebangsaan (PPDK), Partai Perhimpunan Indonesia Baru (PIB), Partai Nasional Banteng Kemerdekaan (PNKB), Partai Demokrat (PD), Partai Keadilan dan Persatuan Indonesia (PKPI), Partai Penegak Demokrasi Indonesia (PPDI), Partai Persatuan Nahdlatul Ummah Indonesia (PPNUI), Partai Karya Peduli Bangsa (PKPB), Partai Keadilan Sejahtera (PKS), Partai Bintang Reformasi (PBR), Partai Damai Sejahtera (PDS), Partai Patriot Pancasila (PPPan), Partai Serikat Indonesia (PSI), Partai Persatuan Daerah (PPD), and Partai Pelopor (PP).[17]

NOTES

1. George McTurnan Kahin, *Nationalism and Revolution in Indonesia* (Ithaca, N.Y.: Cornell University Press, 1952), 201.

2. Kahin, *Nationalism and Revolution,* 201.

3. Herbert Feith, *The Decline of Constitutional Democracy in Indonesia* (Ithaca, N.Y.: Cornell University Press, 1962), 94–95.

4. Feith, *The Decline,* 434–35.

5. Herbert Feith, *The Indonesian Elections of 1955* (Ithaca, N.Y.: Cornell University Modern Indonesia Project, 1957), 65.

6. Daniel S. Lev, *The Transition to Guided Democracy* (Ithaca, N.Y.: Cornell University Modern Indonesia Project, 1966), 93–96.

7. Herbert Feith, "The Dynamics of Guided Democracy," in *Indonesia,* ed. Ruth T. McVey (New Haven, Conn.: HRAF, 1963), 345.

8. Kees van Dijk, "The Indonesian Elections," *RIMA* 11, no. 2 (1977): 42–43.

9. Leo Suryadinata, "Indonesia's Political System: Continuity and Change," *Comtemporary Southeast Asia* 9, no. 4 (March 1988): 272.

10. *Jakarta Post,* 27 April 1987.

11. Aloysius Arena Ariwibowo et al., *Pemilu* 1997 (Jakarta: Penakencana, 1997): 327.

12. Ariwibowo et al, *Pemilu*, 327.

13. *Kompas online*, 27 July 1999; Pompe, Sebastiaan, De *Indonesische Algemene Verkiezingen* 1999 (Leiden, KITLV, 1999), pp. 39–40.

14. According to Pompe, PSII received 375,920 votes.

15. *Indonesia Backgrounder: A Guide to the 2004 Elections* (Jakarta/Brussels: International Crisis Group Asia Report No. 71, 18 December 2003) and *Forum Keadilan*, 4 January 2004

16. The 1999 election law had provided that only parties that won 2 percent of the seats in the DPR (or 3 percent in the local representative councils in half the provinces and half the districts) could participate in the 2004 election. If they did not qualify, they could reform or merge to meet the criteria in the new election law.

17. *Forum Keadilan*, 8. In order to qualify parties needed to demonstrate "full leadership" in at least two thirds of the provinces and two thirds of the districts within those provinces. *Indonesia Backgrounder*, 5.

Bibliography

This bibliography is a classified collection of articles, monographs, and books on Indonesia up to the present day selected from a very much larger body of writings. Works have been included for various reasons. Some are classics in their fields, perhaps out-of-date now but nonetheless influential and worthy of continuing attention. Others are substantial monographs that are important, reliable, and likely to withstand the test of time. Many of the more recent items are less substantial but offer the most up-to-date analysis or statement of a problem and are included because they usefully summarize the state of the art in their field, provide an introduction to other works, or offer current information. A few works have been included because they are the only available source on a particular topic, even if they are out-of-date. And some have been included because they are favorites of the compilers or because they round out the picture of writing on Indonesia. Because of the rapid flow of events in Indonesia over the past decade, and especially since the resignation of Suharto, the bibliography now contains a number of articles and a few collections detailing the political and economic events of these years and the different personalities and political forces that have emerged in the new era.

As this dictionary is targeted at a mainly English-speaking readership, priority has been given to works in English and to English translations of works in other languages. But recognizing that the vast majority of scholarship on the Netherlands Indies prior to World War II was written by Dutch scholars and administrators, much of which has never been surpassed, it includes a considerable number of entries in Dutch especially for the colonial period and in the fields of anthropology, language, and science. It also includes many recent monographs and articles in both English and Dutch that have appeared in publications of the Koninklijk Instituut voor Taal-, Land- en Volkenkunde (KITLV) as well as other Dutch institutions that have been in the forefront of more recent scholarship on

Indonesia. There is also a selection from the growing body of scholarship on Indonesia in French (especially from the journal *Archipel*), Japanese, and Indonesian, although the Japanese works are all in English translation.

The general section that opens the bibliography provides a good guide to the main categories of scholarship on Indonesia, and it includes some useful recent bibliographies of archival collections on Java [0005, 0009, 0010]. The Royal Tropical Institute in Amsterdam has completed its series on the *Changing Economy in Indonesia* [0052–0068], which is an invaluable guide to the colonial economy. In the subsequent section on culture, Astri Wright's treament of contemporary Indonesian painters, *Soul, Spirit, and Mountain* [0202], joins Claire Holt's classic *Art in Indonesia* [0159] to provide an excellent introductory overview of Indonesian art up to the present day.

Many works in the economic section overlap different categories, and for this reason the reader would probably find it useful to check the bibliographical references in the relevant dictionary entries.

Subdivisions in the history section differ somewhat from those in the first edition. In particular, there is a single section covering the Dutch colonial period (History, 1800–1942) rather than the previous two. Similarly, the Japanese and revolutionary periods have been fused into a single section (History, 1942–1949). Indonesia's postindependence history has been divided into the Sukarno, Suharto, and post-Suharto periods. (These subdivisions correspond to the breakdowns now followed in the chronology.) A new section has been added on regional history, which should help those wishing to trace the roots of the recent ethnic and religious unrest in the histories of the regions where it occurred.

The remaining sections—Politics, Science, and Society—follow the lines of the original dictionary, with a subsection on media and the press now added to the society section.

Following current Indonesian developments from outside the country has never been easy. But in the past decade, the Internet has provided an invaluable means of gaining a wide perspective of viewpoints regarding events of the day. For a listing of useful websites on general issues, the environment, and human rights, see the Internet resources section at the end of this bibliography.

All the major Jakarta newspapers and some provincial ones have web pages, and the easiest way of accessing these is through a search engine—Google.com seems to have the widest and most accessible database. In addition, a number of Indonesian newspapers and journals, notably *Tempo* and *Kompas,* now have both Indonesian and English-language editions, in print and online. The weekly *Far Eastern Economic Review* carries brief mentions of most major events in Indonesia, but it increasingly emphasizes economic news over that in the political sphere and emphasizes East over Southeast Asia. The *Asian Wall Street Journal, International Herald Tribune, New York Times, Washington Post, Sydney Morning Herald,* and the Dutch-language *NRC Handelsblad* occasionally publish accounts of Indonesian developments when they affect the interests of the United States, Australia, or the Netherlands.

At the end of the bibliography, there is a list of journals that frequently carry articles concerning recent developments in Indonesia as well as the most recent scholarship on all fields of study. On economic matters, the *Bulletin of Indoensian Economic Studies* (*BIES*) is the most useful and it also publishes a quarterly economic survey. The journal *Indonesia* publishes frequent updates on officeholders in the military, *Inside Indonesia* focuses on contemporary issues, and *Asian Survey* publishes an annual roundup of political events in its January or February issue.

Both *Excerpta Indonesica* (*EI*) and the *Bibliography of Asian Studies* (*BAS*) are essential tools for keeping in touch with recent academic research. *EI* appears twice a year and provides abstracts of recent articles on Indonesia in the social sciences and humanities. Its e-mail address is kitlvpress@kitlv.nl. *BAS* now appears online. Details for accessing the database (which covers 1971–present) for organizations subscribing to *BAS Online* can be obtained from www.hti.umich.edu/b/bas/. Inquiries for individual subscriptions can be sent to abeard@aasianst.org.

As already indicated in the reader's note, all bibliographical entries are numbered, and these numbers appear at the end of entries in the dictionary to guide readers to the relevant sources.

ABBREVIATIONS

ANU, Australian National University
BCAS, Bulletin of Concerned Asian Scholars (now *Critical Asian Studies*)
BEFEO, Bulletin de l'Ecole Française d'Extrême Orient
BIES, Bulletin tot de Taal-, Land- en Volkenkunde
BPS, Biro Pusat Statistik
ISEAS, Institute of Southeast Asian Studies
JAS, Journal of Asian Studies
JMBRAS, Journal of the Malaysian Branch of the Royal Asiatic Society
JSEAH, Journal of Southeast Asian History

JSEAS, Journal of Southeast Asian Studies
KITLV, Koninklijk Instituut voor Taal-, Land- en Volkenkunde
MAS, Modern Asian Studies
OUP, Oxford University Press
RIMA, Review of Indonesian and Malaysian Affairs

CONTENTS

GENERAL

Bibliographies

[0001] *ASEAN: A Bibliography.* Singapore: ISEAS, 1984.

[0002] Avé, Jan B., Victor T. King, and Joke G. W. de Wit. *West-Kalimantan: A Bibliography.* Leiden, The Netherlands: KITLV, 1983.

[0003] Baal, J. van, K. W. Galis, and R. M. Koentjaraningrat. *West-Irian: A Bibliography.* Dordrecht, The Netherlands: Foris, 1984.

[0004] Boland, B. J., and I. Farjon. *Islam in Indonesia: A Bibliographic Survey.* Dordrecht, The Netherlands: Foris, 1983.

[0005] Carey, Peter, and Mason C. Hoadley. *The Archive of Yogyakarta, Vol. II: Documents Relating to Economic and Agrarian Affairs.* New York: OUP, 2000.

[0006] Char Lan Hiang. *Southeast Asian Research Tools: Indonesia.* Honolulu: University of Hawai'i Southeast Asian Studies Program, 1979.

[0007] Coolhaas, W. Ph. *A Critical Survey of Studies on Dutch Colonial History,* 2nd. ed. The Hague: Nijhoff, 1980.

[0008] Farjon, I. *Madura and Surrounding Islands: An Annotated Bibliography 1860–1942.* Leiden, The Netherlands: KITLV, 1980.

[0009] Florida, Nancy. *Javanese Literature in Surakarta Manuscripts, Volume 1: Introduction and Manuscripts of the Karaton Surakarta.* Ithaca, N.Y.: Cornell Southeast Asia Program, 1993.

[0010] ——. *Javanese Literature in Surakarta Manuscripts, Volume 2: Manuscripts of the Mangkunagaran Palace.* Ithaca, N.Y.: Cornell Southeast Asia Program, 2000.

[0011] Groenendael, Victoria M. Clara van. *Wayang Theatre in Indonesia: An Annotated bibliography.* Leiden, the Netherlands: KITLV, 1987.

[0012] Hicks, George L., and Geoffrey McNicoll. *The Indonesian Economy 1950–1965: A Bibliography.* New Haven, Conn.: Yale University Southeast Asian Studies, 1967.

[0013] Jacobs, M., and T. J. J. de Boo. *Conservation Literature on Indonesia: Selected Annotated Bibliography.* Leiden, the Netherlands: Rijksherbarium, 1982.

[0014] Jaquet, F. G. P. *Sources for the History of Asian and Oceania in the Netherlands,* 2 vols. Munich: K. G. Saur, 1982–1983.

[0015] Johnson, Donald Clay. *Index to Southeast Asian Journals: A Guide to Articles, Book Reviews and Composite Works,* 2 vols. Boston: Hall, 1977–1982.

[0016] Kemp, H. C. *Annotated Bibliography of Bibliographies on Indonesia.* Leiden, The Netherlands: KITLV, 1990.

[0017] Kennedy, Raymond. *Bibliography of Indonesian Peoples and Cultures,* 2nd ed. New Haven Conn: Yale University Southeast Asia Studies, 1962.

[0018] Klooster, H. A. J. *Bibliography of the Indonesian Revolution: Publications from 1942 to 1994.* Leiden, The Netherlands: KITLV, 1997.

[0019] Koentjaraningrat. *Anthropology in Indonesia: A Bibliographical Review.* Leiden, The Netherlands: KITLV, 1975.

[0020] Kratz, Ernst Ulrich. *A Bibliography of Indonesian Literature in Journals.* Yogyakarta, Indonesia: Gadjah Mada Press, 1988.

[0021] Lan Hiang Char. *Southeast Asian Research Tools: Indonesia.* Honolulu: University of Hawai'i, 1979.

[0022] Langenberg, Michael van, ed. *Bibliography of Indonesian Politics and the Economy since 1965.* Sydney: Research Institute for Asia and the Pacific, 1988.

[0023] Manguin, Pierre-Yves. *A Bibliography for Sriwijayan Studies.* Jakarta: l'Etude Française d'Extreme-Orient, 1989.

[0024] Nagelkerke, Gerard A. *The Chinese in Indonesia: A Bibliography, 18th century—1981.* Leiden, The Netherlands: KITLV, 1982.

[0025] Polman, Katrien. *The Central Moluccas: An Annotated Bibliography.* Leiden, The Netherlands: KITLV, 1983.

[0026] ———. *The North Moluccas: An Annotated Bibliography.* Leiden, The Netherlands: KITLV, 1981.

[0027] Pompe, Sebastiaan. *Indonesian Law 1949–1989: A Bibliography of Foreign-Language Materials with Brief Commentaries on the Law.* Dordrecht, The Netherlands: Martinus Nijhoff, 1992.

[0028] Schouten, Mieke. *Minahasa and Bolaangmongondouw: An Annotated Bibliography, 1800–1942.* Leiden, The Netherlands: KITLV, 1981.

[0029] Sherlock, Kevin. *A Bibliography of the Island of Timor, Including East (Formerly Portuguese) Timor, West (formerly Dutch) Timor and the Island of Roti.* Canberra: Australian National University, 1980.

[0030] Volkman, Toby Alice. *Film on Indonesia.* New Haven, Conn.: Yale University Southeast Asia Studies, 1985.

Reference Works

[0031] *Apa dan Siapa: sejumlah orang Indonesia, 1981–1982; 1983–1984; 1985–1986.* Jakarta: Grafiti, 1981, 1983, 1986.

[0032] *Encyclopaedie van Nederlandsch-Indië,* 4 vols. and 4 suppls. The Hague: Martinus Nijhoff, 1917–1939.

[0033] *Ensiklopedi Indonesia,* 7 vols. Jakarta: Ichtiar Baru-van Hoeve, 1980–1984.

[0034] *Ensiklopedi Indonesia supplemen,* vols. 1 and 2. Jakarta: Ichtiar Baru-van Hoeve, 1986–1990.

[0035] *Orang Indonesia jang terkemoeka di Djawa.* [Jakarta]: Gunseikanbu, 2604 (i.e., 1944).

[0036] *The Indonesian Military Leaders: Biographical and Other Background Data,* 2nd ed. Jakarta: Sritua Arief, 1978.

[0037] *Who's Who in the Indonesian Military.* Jakarta: Sritua Arief, 1977.

[0038] Boomgard, P., ed. *The Colonial Past: Dutch Sources on Indonesian History.* Amsterdam: Royal Tropical Institute, 1991.

[0039] Bruinessen, Martin van. *Kitab kuning, pesantren dan tarekat: tradisi-tradisi Islam di Indonesia.* Bandung, Indonesia: Mizan, 1995.

[0040] Crawfurd, John. *A Descriptive Dictionary of the Indian Islands and Adjacent Countries.* Kuala Lumpur, Malaysia: OUP, 1971.

[0041] Cribb, Robert. *Historical Atlas of Indonesia.* Honolulu: University of Hawai'i Press, 2000.

[0042] Day, Tony, and Will Derks, eds. *Encompassing Knowledge: Indigenous Encyclopedias from Ninth-Century Java to Twentieth-Century Riau. BKI,* special issue, 155, no. 3 (1999).

[0043] Drooglever, P. J., M. J. B. Schouten, and Mona Lohanda. *Guide to the Archives on Relations between the Netherlands and Indonesia, 1945–1963.* The Hague: Institute of Netherlands History, 1999.

[0044] Gibb, H. A. R., and J. H. Kramers. *Shorter Encyclopaedia of Islam.* Ithaca, N.Y.: Cornell University Press, 1953

[0045] Gonggryp, G. F. E. *Geillustreerde encyclopedie van Nederlandsch-Indie.* Leiden, The Netherlands: Leidsche Uitgeversmaatschappij, 1934.

[0046] Ikhwan, Abdul Halim, et al. *Ensiklopedi Haji and umrah.* Jakarta: PT Raja Grafindo Persada, 2002.

[0047] Parsidi, Agata. *Kamus akronim, inisialisme dan singkatan.* Jakarta: Grafiti Pers, 1992.

[0048] Pompe, S. "A Short Review of Doctoral Theses on the Netherlands-Indies Accepted at the Faculty of Law of Leiden University in the Period 1850–1940." *Indonesia* 56 (October 1993): 67–98.

[0049] Roeder, O. G. *Who's Who in Indonesia,* 2nd ed. Jakarta: Gunung Agung, 1971, 1980.

[0050] Suryadinata, Leo. *Eminent Indonesian Chinese: Biographical Sketches.* Singapore: ISEAS, 1978.

[0051] The Liang Gie, and Andrian The. *Ensiklopedi ilmu-ilmu.* Yogyakarta, Indonesia: Gadjah Mada University Press, 2001.

Statistical Abstracts

Changing Economy in Indonesia, published by the Royal Tropical Institute, Amsterdam

[0052] 1. Creutzberg, Piet. *Indonesia's Export Crops, 1816–1940.* 1975.

[0053] 2. ——. *Public Finance, 1816–1939.* 1976.

[0054] 3. ——. *Expenditure on Fixed Assets.* 1977.

[0055] 4. ——. *Rice Prices.* 1978.

[0056] 5. ——. *National Income.* 1979.

[0057] 6. Van Laanen, J. Th. M. *Money and Banking, 1816–1940.* 1980.

[0058] 7. Altes, W. Korthals. *Balance of Payments, 1822–1939.* 1987.

[0059] 8. Segers, W. I. A. M. *Manufacturing Industry, 1870–1942.* 1987.

[0060] 9. Knaap, Gerrit J. *Transport, 1819–1940.* 1989.

[0061] 10. Boomgaard, P., and J. L.van Zanden. *Food Crops and Arable Lands, Java 1815–1942.* 1990.

[0062] 11. Boomgaard, P. *Population Trends, 1795–1942.* 1991.

[0063] 12a. Korthals, W. L. *General Trade Statistics 1822–1940.* 1991.

[0064] 12b. Clemens, Adrian, J. Thomas Lindblad, and Jereon Touwen. *Regional Patterns in Foreign Trade 1911–1940.* 1992.

[0065] 13. Dros, Nico. *Wages 1820–1940.* 1992.

[0066] 14. Van Baardewijk, Frans. *The Cultivation System, Java 1834–1880.* 1993.

[0067] 15. Altes, W. L. Korthals. *Prices (Non-Rice), 1814–1940.* 1994.

[0068] 16. Boomgaard, P. *Forests and Forestry, 1823–1941.* [1996].

[0069] Berita Resmi Statistik. "Hasil sensus penduduk 2000." *Berita Resmi Statistik* 26, no. 5 (3 June 2002).

[0070] *Indisch Verslag 1939, II: Statistisch jaaroverzicht van Nederlandsch-Indiê over het jaar 1938.* Batavia (Jakarta): Landsdrukkerij, 1939.

[0071] *Penduduk Indonesia: hasil sensus penduduk 1990.* Jakarta: BPS, 1992.

[0072] *Penduduk Indonesia: hasil survei penduduk antar sensus 1995.* Jakarta: BPS, 1996.

[0073] *Statistik Indonesia 1996.* Jakarta: BPS, 1996.

[0074] *Statistik Indonesia.* Jakarta: BPS, 2000.

[0075] Netherlands Indies Departement van Economische Zaken. *Volkstelling 1930,* 8 vols. Batavia (Jakarta): Landsdrukkerij, 1933–1936.

[0076] Touwen, Jeroen. *Shipping and Trade in the Java Sea Region 1870–1940: A Collection of Statistics on the Major Java Sea Ports.* Leiden, The Netherlands: KITL, 2001.

Travel and Tourism

[0077] Anderson, John. *Mission to the East Coast of Sumatra in 1823.* Edinburgh: Blackwood, 1826. Reprint, Kuala Lumpur, Malaysia: OUP, 1971.

[0078] Attenborough, David. *Zoo Quest for a Dragon [Komodo].* London: Lutterworth, 1957.

[0079] Bickmore, Albert S. *Travels in the East Indian Archipelago.* London: Murray, 1868.

[0080] Bonneff, Marcel. *Pérégrinations javanaises: les voyages de R.M.A. Purwa Lelana: une visie de Java au XIXe siècle (c. 1860–1875).* Paris: Editions de la Maison des Recherche Scientifique, 1986.

[0081] Burnell, A. C., and P. A. Tiek, eds. *The Voyage of J. H. van Linschoten to the East Indies,* 2 vols. London: Hakluyt Society, 1885.

[0082] Cortesåo, Armando, trans. and ed. *The Suma Oriental of Tomé Pires,* 2 vols. London: Hakluyt Society, 1944.

[0083] Foster, Sir William, ed. *The Voyage of Sir Henry Middleton to the Moluccas, 1604–1606.* London: Hakluyt Society, 1943.

[0084] Gibb, H. A. R., ed. and trans. *Ibn Battuta: Travels in Asia and Africa, 1325–54.* London: Routledge, 1953.

[0085] Jack-Hinton, Colin. "Marco Polo in South-East Asia." *JSEAH* 5, no. 2 (1964): 43–103.

[0086] Kayam, Umar, and Harri Peccinottiq. *The Soul of Indonesia: A Cultural Journey*. Baton Rouge: Louisiana State University Press, 1985.

[0087] Kenji, Tsuchiya, and James Siegel. "Invincible Kitsch or as Tourists in the Age of Des Alwi." *Indonesia* 50 (October 1990): 61–76.

[0088] Macnaught, T. J. "Mass Tourism and the Dilemmas of Modernization in Pacific Island Communities." *Annals of Tourism Research* 9, no. 3 (1982).

[0089] Maurer, Jean-Luc. *Tourism and Development in a Socio-Cultural Perspective: Indonesia as a Case Study.* Geneva: Institut universitaire d'études du développement, 1979.

[0090] McCarthy, John. *Are Sweet Dreams Made of This? Tourism in Bali and Eastern Indonesia.* Northcote, Australia: Indonesian Resources and Information Program, 1994.

[0091] McPhee, Colin. *A House in Bali.* New York: John Day, 1944.

[0092] Milton, Giles. *Nathaniel's Nutmeg: Or, The True and Incredible Adventures of the Spice Trader Who Changed the Course of History.* New York: Farrar, Straus and Giroux, 1999.

[0093] Noronha, R. "Paradise Reviewed: Tourism in Bali." In *Tourism: Passport to Development?* edited by E. de Kadt. New York: OUP, 1979.

[0094] Picard, Michel. *Bali: Cultural Tourism and Touristic Culture.* Singapore: Archipelago Press, 1996.

[0095] ——. "'Cultural Tourism' in Bali: Cultural Performances as Tourist Attraction." *Indonesia* 49 (April 1990): 37–74.

[0096] Pollmann, Tessel, Juan Seleky, and Bert Nienhuis. *Terug op de Molukken.* Amsterdam: De arbeiderspers, 1982.

[0097] Powell, Hickman. *The Last Paradise.* Oxford: OUP, 1982 [orig.1930].

[0098] Severin, Tim. *The Spice Islands Voyage: In Search of Wallace.* London: Little, Brown, 1998.

[0099] Valentijn, François. *Oud en nieuw Oost-Indiên*, 5 vols. Dordrecht, The Netherlands: Van Braam, 1724–1726.

[0100] Wallace, Alfred. *The Malay Archipelago,* 2 vols. London: Macmillan, 1869.

[0101] Wright, Arnold, and Oliver T. Breakspear, eds. *Twentieth Century Impressions of Netherlands India: Its History, People, Commerce, Industries, and Resources.* London: Lloyd's Greater Britain Publishing, 1909.

[0102] Yoety, Oka A. *Perencanaan dan pengembangan pariwisata.* Jakarta: Pradyna Paramita, 1997.

Guidebooks

[0103] Cochrane, Janet. *The National Parks and Other Wild Places of Indonesia.* London: New Holland, 2000.

[0104] Cockell, Charles. *The Expeditions to Indonesia Handbook.* Hailsham, East Sussex, UK: CSC Expeditionary Publications, 1994.

[0105] Dalton, Bill. *Indonesia.* New York: Odyssey Publications, 1999.
[0106] *Destination Indonesia.* Jakarta: Directorate General of Tourism, 1992–1993.
[0107] Eliot, Joshua, Jane Bickersteth, and Liz Capaldi. *Indonesia Handbook.* Bath, UK: Footprint Handbooks, 1998.
[0108] Henley, David E. F., et al. *Indonesia: Sumatra, Java, Bali, Lombok, Sulawesi: An Up-to-Date Travel Guide.* Edison, N.J.: Hunter, 2000.
[0109] *Indonesia: Travel Atlas.* Singapore: Periplus, 1998.
[0110] Jepson, Paul. *Fielding's In-Depth Guide to Birding on the World's Largest Archipelago.* Hong Kong: Periplus, [1997].
[0111] Smith, Holly S. *Adventuring in Indonesia: Exploring the Natural Areas of the Pacific's Ring of Fire.* San Francisco: Sierra Club Books, [1997].

CULTURE

Archeology

[0112] Dumarçay, Jacques. "Le Candi Badut." *Archipel* 63 (2002): 7–14.
[0113] Gomez, Luis O., and Hiram W. Woodward. *Barabudur: History and Significance of a Buddhist Monument.* Berkeley, Calif.: Asian Humanities Press, 1981.
[0114] Harkantiningsih, Naniek. "Le site de Léran à Gresik, Java-Est: étude archéologique préliminaire." *Archipel* 63 (2002): 17–26.
[0115] Kalus, Ludvik, and Claude Guillot. "La Jérusalem javanaise et sa mosqué al-Aqsâ: texte de fondation de la mosquée de Kudus datée 956/1549." *Archipel* 63 (2002): 27–56.
[0116] Krom, N. J. *Barabadur: Archaeological Description,* 2 vols. The Hague: Nijhoff, 1927.
[0117] Manguin, Pierre-Yves. "Etude Sumatranaises 1. Palembang et Sriwijaya: anciennes hypotheses, recherches nouvelles (Palembang ouest)." *BEFEO* 76 (1987).
[0118] McKinnon, E. Edwards. "Buddhism and the pre-Islamic archaeology of Kutei in the Mahakam Valley of East Kalimantan." In *Studies in Southeast Asian Art: Essays in Honor of Stanley J. O'Connor*, edited by Nora Taylor, 217–40. [0196]
[0119] ——. "Ceramic Recoveries (Surface Finds) at Lambara, Aceh." *Journal of East-West Maritime Relations* 2 (1992).
[0120] ——. "The Sambas Hoard: Bronze Drums and Gold Ornaments Found in Kalimantan in 1991." *JMBRAS* 67, no. 1 (1994): 9–28.
[0121] Miksic, John N. "Evolving Archaeological Perspectives on Southeast Asia, 1970–95." *JSEAS* 26, no. 1 (March 1995): 46–62.
[0122] Simangjuntak, Truman. "New Light on the Prehistory of the Southern Mountains of Java." In *Indo-Pacific Prehistory,* ed. Peter Bellwood et al. Canberra: Indo-Pacific Prehistory Association, ANU, 2001.
[0123] Stutterheim, W. F. *Studies in Indonesian Archaeology.* The Hague: Nijhoff, 1956.

[0124] Suleiman, Satyawati, *Sculptures of Ancient Sumatra.* Jakarta: Proyek Penelitian Purbakala, 1981.

Architecture

[0125] Dumarçay, Jacques. *The House in South-East Asia.* Singapore: OUP, 1987.
[0126] Keeler, Ward. *Symbolic Dimensions of the Javanese House.* Clayton, Victoria, Australia: Monash University Centre of Southeast Asian Studies, 1983.
[0127] Kusno, Abidin. *Behind the Postcolonial: Architecture, Urban Space, and Political Cultures in Indonesia.* London: Routledge, 2000.
[0128] Macrae, Graeme, and Samuel Parker. "Would the Real Undagi Please Stand Up? On the Social Location of Balinese Architectural Knowledge." *BKI* 158, no. 2 (2002): 253–81.
[0129] Prijotomo, Josef. *Ideas and Forms of Javanese Architecture.* Yogyakarta, Indonesia: Gadjah Mada University Press, 1984.
[0130] Volkman, Toby Alice, and Charles Zerner. "Tourism and Architectural Design in the Toraja Highlands." *Mimar* 25 (September 1987): 20–25.
[0131] Wijaya, Made. *Architecture of Bali: A Source Book of Traditional and Modern Forms.* Honolulu: University of Hawai'i Press, 2002.

Arts

[0132] Anderson, Benedict R. O'G. *Mythology and the Tolerance of the Javanese.* Ithaca, N.Y.: Cornell Modern Indonesia Project, 1965.
[0133] Barbier, Jean Paul. *Indonesian Primitive Art: Indonesia, Malaysia, the Philippines.* Dallas, Tex.: Dallas Museum of Art, 1984.
[0134] Barendregt, Bart. "The Sound of 'Longing for Home': Redefining a Sense of Community through Minang Popular Music." *BKI* 158, no. 3 (2002): 411–50.
[0135] Becker, Judith. *Traditional Music in Modern Java: Gamelan in a Changing Society.* Honolulu: University of Hawai'i Press, 1980.
[0136] Bernet Kempers. *Ancient Indonesian Art.* Amsterdam: van der Peet, 1959.
[0137] Bodrogi, Tibor. *Art of Indonesia.* London: Academy Editions, 1973.
[0138] Brakel-Papenhuyzen. "Javanese Talèdhèk and Chinese Tayuban." *BKI* 151, no. 4 (1995): 545–69.
[0139] Brakel-Papenhuyzen, and Wim van Zan, eds. "Performing Arts in Southeast Asia." *BKI,* special issue, 151, no. 4 (1995).
[0140] Brandon, James R. *On Thrones of Gold: Three Javanese Shadow Plays.* Cambridge, Mass.: Harvard University. Press, 1970.
[0141] Causey, Andrew. "The Folder in the Drawer of the Sky Blue Lemari: A Toba Batak Carver's Secrets." *Crossroads* 14, no. 1 (2000): 1–34.
[0142] Coomaraswamy, Ananda K. *History of Indian and Indonesian Art.* New York: Dover, 1965.

[0143] Draeger, Donn. *Weapons and Fighting Arts of the Indonesian Archipelago.* Rutland, Vt.: Tuttle, 1972.

[0144] Elliott, Inger McCabe. *Batik: Fabled Cloth of Java.* Harmondsworth, UK: Viking, 1985.

[0145] Feinstein, Alan. "Modern Javanese Theatre and the Politics of Culture: A Case Study of Teater Gapit." *BKI* 151, no. 4 (1995): 617–38.

[0146] Fontein, Jan. *The Sculpture of Indonesia.* Washington, D.C.: National Gallery of Art, 1990.

[0147] Forshee, Jill. *Between the Folds: Stories of Cloth, Lives and Travels from Sumba.* Honolulu: University of Hawai'i Press, 2001.

[0148] Foulcher, Keith. "Rivai Apin and the Modernist Aesthetic in Indonesian Poetry." *BKI* 157, no. 4 (2001): 771–97.

[0149] Frederick, William H. "Rhoma Irama and the Dangdut Style: Aspects of Contemporary Indonesian Popular Culture." *Indonesia* 34 (October 1982): 102–30.

[0150] George, Kenneth M., and Mamannoor. *AD Pirous, Vision, Faith, and a Journey in Indonesian Art, 1955–2002.* Bandung, Indonesia: Yayasan Serambi Pirous, 2002.

[0151] Gittinger, Mattiebelle. *Splendid Symbols: Textiles and Tradition in Indonesia,* rev. ed. Singapore: OUP, 1990.

[0152] ——, ed. *To Speak with Cloth: Studies in Indonesian Textiles.* Los Angeles: Museum of Cultural History, University of California, 1989.

[0153] Groenendael, Victoria M. Clara van. *The Dalang behind the Wayang: The Role of the Surakarta and Yogyakarta Dalang in Indonesian-Javanese Society.* Leiden: KITLV, 1985.

[0154] Hatley, Barbara. "Cultural Expression." In *Indonesia's New Order: The Dynamics of Socio-Economic Transformation,* edited by Hal Hill, 216–66. [0730]

[0155] Heins, E. *Bibliography of Javanese Gamelan 1923–1990.* Basel, Switzerland: Amadeus Verlag, 1990.

[0156] Hellman, Jôrgen. "The Double Edge of Cultural Politics: Revitalizing Longser Theater in West Java, Indonesia." *Crossroads* 14, no. 2(2000): 79–99.

[0157] Herbst, Edward. *Voices in Bali: Energies and Perceptions in Vocal Music and Dance Theater.* Hanover, N.H.: University Press of New England, 1997.

[0158] Hobart, Angela. "The Enlightened Prince Sutasoma: Transformations of a Buddhist Story." *Indonesia* 49 (April 1990): 75–102.

[0159] Holt, Claire. *Art in Indonesia: Continuities and Change.* Ithaca, N.Y.: Cornell University Press, 1967.

[0160] ——. *Dance Quest in Celebes.* Paris: Archives Internationales de la Dance, 1939.

[0161] Hood, Mantle. "Bronze Drum" and (with others) "Indonesia." In *The New Grove Dictionary of Music and Musicians,* edited by Stanley Sadie. London: Macmillan, 1980.

[0162] Hooker, Virginia Matheson. "Expression: Creativity Despite Constraint." In *Indonesia beyond Suharto: Polity, Economy, Society, Transition,* edited by Donald K. Emmerson, 262–91. [0761]

[0163] Irvine, David. *Leather Gods and Wooden Heroes: Java's Classical Wayang.* Singapore: Times Editions, 1996.

[0164] Jessup, Helen I. *Court Arts of Indonesia: Continuities and Change.* New York: Asia Society Galleries, 1990.

[0165] Jones, A. M. *Africa and Indonesia: The Evidence of the Xylophone and Other Musical and Cultural Factors,* 2nd ed. Leiden: E. J. Brill, 1971.

[0166] Kartomi, Margaret J. "Change in Manggarai Music and Ritual in the Twentieth Century."*RIMA* 35, no. 2 (summer 2001): 61–98.

[0167] ——. "Is Maluku Still Musicological Terra Incognita? An Overview of the Music-Cultures of the Province of Maluku." *JSEAS* 25, no. 1 (March 1994): 141–71.

[0168] ——, ed. *Studies in Indonesian Music*. Clayton, Victoria, Australia: Monash University Centre of Southeast Asian Studies, 1978.

[0169] Kats, J. *De wajang poerwa: een vorm van Javaans toneel,* 2nd ed. Leiden, the Netherlands: KITLV, 1984.

[0170] Keeler, Ward. *Javanese Shadow Plays, Javanese Selves*. Princeton, N.J.: Princeton University. Press, 1987.

[0171] ——. "Release from Kala's Grip: Ritual Use of Shadow Plays in Java and Bali." *Indonesia* 54 (Octoher 1992): 1–26.

[0172] Kévonian, Kéram. "Raden Saleh, peintre de Mariam Haroutunian." *Archipel* 62 (2001): 91–126.

[0173] Kitley, Philip. "Ornamentation and Originality: Involution in Javanese Batik." *Indonesia* 53 (April 1992): 1–20.

[0174] Kunst, Jaap. *Hindu-Javanese Musical Instruments,* 2nd ed. The Hague: Nijhoff, 1968.

[0175] ——. *Music in Java: Its History, Its Theory, and Its Technique.* The Hague: Nijhoff, 1973.

[0176] ——. *Music in New Guinea: Three Studies.* Leiden, the Netherlands: KITLV, 1967.

[0177] Lindsay, Jennifer. *Javanese Gamelan.* Kuala Lumpur, Malaysia: OUP, 1979.

[0178] McGowan, Kaja. "Maritime Travelers and Tillers of the Soil: Reading the Landscape(s) of Batur." In *Studies in Southeast Asian Art*, edited by Nora A. Taylor, 32–48. [0196]

[0179] McPhee, Colin. *Music in Bali.* New Haven, Conn.: Yale University Press, 1966.

[0180] Morgan, Stephanie, and Laurie Jo Sears, eds. *Aesthetic Tradition and Cultural Transition in Java and Bali.* Madison: University of Wisconsin Center for Southeast Asian Studies, 1984.

[0181] Mrázek, Jan. "Javanese Wayang Kulit in the Times of Comedy: Clown Scenes, Innovation, and the Performance's Being in the Present World." Parts 1 and 2. *Indonesia* 68 (October 1999): 38–128; 69 (April 2000): 107–72.

[0182] ——. "More than a Picture: The Instrumental Quality of the Shadow Puppet" In *Studies in Southeast Asian Art,* edited by Nora A. Taylor, 49–73. [0196]

[0183] ——. "A Musical Picture of Indonesia." *Indonesia* 71 (April 2001): 187–210.

[0184] Pemberton, John. "Musical Politics in Central Java, or How Not to Listen to a Javanese Gamelan." *Indonesia* 44 (April 1987): 16–29.

[0185] Rodgers, Susan. *Power and Gold: Jewelry from Indonesia, Malaysia and the Philippines.* Geneva: Asia Society, 1985.

[0186] Rubinstein, Raechelle. *Beyond the Realm of the Senses: The Balinese Ritual of Kakawin Composition.* Leiden, The Netherlands: KITLV, 2000.

[0187] Schumacher, Rüdiger. "Musical Concepts in Oral Performance of Kakawin in Bali." *BKI* 151, no. 4 (1995): 485–515.

[0188] Sen, Krishna. *Indonesian Cinema: Framing the New Order.* London: Zed Books, 1994.

[0189] ——, ed. *Histories and Stories: Cinema in New Order Indonesia.* Clayton, Victoria, Australia: Monash University, 1988.

[0190] Soemantri, Hilda. "Modern Indonesian Ceramic Art." In *Studies in Southeast Asian Art,* ed. Nora A. Taylor, 74–85. [0196]

[0191] Spanjaard, Helena. *Widayat: The Magical Mysticism of a Modern Indonesian Artist.* Magelang, Indonesia: Museum H. Widayat, 1998.

[0192] Suhartono. *Rahardjo, ragam hulu keris sejak zaman kerajaan.* Yogyakarta, Indonesia: Kreasi Wacana, 2003.

[0193] Sumarsam. *Gamelan: Cultural Interaction and Musical Development in Central Java.* Chicago: University of Chicago Press, 1995.

[0194] Susanto, Budi. *Ketoprak: politik masa lalu untuk masyarakat Jawa masa kini.* Yogyakarta, Indonesia: Lembaga Studi, 1997.

[0195] Sutton, R. Anderson. *Traditions of Gamelan Music in Java: Musical Pluralism and Regional Identity.* Cambridge, UK: Cambridge University. Press, 1991.

[0196] Taylor, Nora A., ed. *Studies in Southeast Asian Art: Essays in Honor of Stanley J. O'Connor.* Ithaca, N.Y.: Cornell Southeast Asia Program, 2000.

[0197] Taylor, Paul Michael. *Fragile Traditions: Indonesian Art in Jeopardy.* Honolulu: University of Hawai'i Press, 1994.

[0198] Taylor, Paul Michael, and Lorraine V. Aragon. *Beyond the Java Sea: Art of Indonesia's Outer Islands.* Washington, D.C.: Smithsonian Institution, 1991.

[0199] Tenzer, Michel. *Gamelan Gong Kebyar: The Art of Twentieth-Century Balinese Music.* Chicago: University of Chicago Press, 2000.

[0200] Wright, Astri. "Javanese Mysticism and Art: A Case of Iconography and Healing." *Indonesia* 52 (October 1991): 85–104.

[0201] ——. "Lucia Hartini, Javanese Painter: Against the Grain, towards Herself." In *Studies in Southeast Asian Art*, edited by Nora A. Taylor, 93–121. [0196]

[0202] ——. *Soul, Spirit, and Mountain: Preoccupations of Contemporary Indonesian Painters.* Kuala Lumpur, Malaysia: OUP, 1994.

[0203] Yampolsky, Philip. "Forces of Change in the Regional Performing Arts of Indonesia." *BKI* 151, no. 4 (1995): 700–725.

[0204] ——. *Music of Indonesia,* 20 vols. Washington, D.C.: Smithsonian Folkways and Indonesian Society for the Performing Arts, 1991–1999.

[0205] Zoete, B. de, and W. Spies. *Dance and Drama in Bali.* New York: Harper, 1982.

Literary Studies

[0206] Ajidarma, Seno Gumira. "Fiction, Journalism, History: A Process of Self-Correction." Translated by Michael H. Bodden. *Indonesia* 68 (October 1999): 164–71.

[0207] Arps, Bernard, Sirtjo Koolhof, and Henk Maier. *Traditionele en moderne poëzie van Indonesië.* Leiden: Instituut Indonesische Cursussen, 1994.

[0208] Aveling, Harry, ed. *Secrets Need Words: Indonesian Poetry, 1966–1998.* Athens: Ohio University Center for International Studies, 2001.

[0209] Beekman, E. M. "The Passatist: Louis Couperus's Interpretation of Dutch Colonialism." *Indonesia* 37 (April 1984): 59–76.

[0210] ——. *Troubled Pleasures: Dutch Colonial Literature from the East Indies, 1600–1950.* Oxford: Clarendon Press, 1996.

[0211] Bodden, Michael H. "Seno Gumira Ajidarma and Fictional Resistance of an Authoritarian State in Indonesia." *Indonesia* 68 (October 1999): 153–56.

[0212] ——. "Utopia and the Shadow of Nationalism: The Plays of Sanusi Pane 1928–1940." *BKI* 153, no. 3 (1997): 332–55.

[0213] ——. "Woman as Nation in Mangunwijaya's Durga Umayi." *Indonesia* 62 (October 1996): 54–82.

[0214] Clark, Marshall. "Shadow Boxing: Indonesian Writers and the Ramayana in the New Order." *Indonesia* 72 (October 2001): 159–87.

[0215] Clerkx, Lily E., and Wim F. Wertheim. *Living in Deli: Its Society as Imaged in Colonial Fiction.* Amsterdam: VU University Press, 1991.

[0216] Florida, Nancy K. "Reading the Unread in Traditional Javanese Literature." *Indonesia* 44 (October 1987): 1–16.

[0217] ——. *Writing the Past, Inscribing the Future.* Durham, N.C.: Duke University Press, 1995.

[0218] Foulcher, Keith. "Perceptions of Modernity and the Sense of the Past: Indonesian Poetry in the 1920s." *Indonesia* 23 (April 1977): 39–58.

[0219] ——. *Pujangga Baru: Literature and Nationalism in Indonesia, 1933–1942.* Bedford Park, South Australia: Flinders University Asian Studies Monograph no. 2, 1980.

[0220] Foulcher, Keith, and Tony Day, eds. *Clearing a Space: Postcolonial Readings of Modern Indonesian Literature.* Leiden, The Netherlands: KITLV, 2002.

[0221] Heinschke, Martina. "Between Gelanggang and Lekra: Pramoedya's Developing Literary Concepts." *Indonesia* 61 (April 1996): 145–69.

[0222] Hellwig, Tineke. *In the Shadow of Change: Images of Women in Indonesian Literature.* Berkeley, Calif.: Center for Southeast Asian Studies, Monograph no. 35, 1994.

[0223] ——. "Scandals, Homicide in Batavia and Indo Identity: Literary Representations of Indies Society." *Archipel* 63 (2002): 153–72.

[0224] Kato, Tsuyoshi. "Images of Colonial Cities in Early Indonesian Novels." In *Southeast Asia over Three Generations: Essays Presented to B. R. O'G. Anderson,* edited by James T. Siegel and Audrey R. Kahin. Ithaca, N.Y.: Cornell Southeast Asia Program, 2003.

[0225] Maier, Henk M. J. "Chairil Anwar's Heritage: The Fear of Stultification: Another Side of Modern Indonesian Literature." *Indonesia* 43 (April 1987): 1–29.

[0226] Marrison, Geoffrey E. "Modern Balinese: A Regional Literature of Indonesia." *BKI* 143, no. 4 (1987): 468–98.

[0227] *Pramoedya Ananta Toer and His Work. Indonesia,* special issue, 61 (April 1996).

[0228] Raffel, Burton. *The Development of Modern Indonesian Poetry*. Albany: State University of New York Press, 1967.

[0229] Rafferty, Ellen. "The New Tradition of Putu Wijaya." *Indonesia* 49 (April 1990): 103–16.

[0230] Richardson, Vanessa. "An Analysis of Culture, Gender and Power in the Films *Niji Ronggeng* and *Roro Mendut*." *RIMA* 28, no. 2 (1994): 37–52.

[0231] Rosidi, Ajip. *Sejarah sastra Indonesia*. Jakarta: Bina Aksara, 1988.

[0232] Sears, Laurie J. *Shadows of Empire: Colonial Discourse and Javanese Tales.* Durham, N.C.: Duke University Press, 1996.

[0233] Soedarsono. *Wayang Wong: The State Ritual Dance Drama in the Court of Yogyakarta.* Yogyakarta, Indonesia: Gadjah Mada University. Press, 1990.

[0234] Teeuw, A. *Modern Indonesian Literature,* 2 vols., 2nd and 3rd eds. The Hague: Nijhoff, 1979–1986.

[0235] ——. *Pramoedya Ananta Toer: De verbeelding van Indonesië.* Breda, The Netherlands: De Geus, 1993.

[0236] Tiwon, Sylvia. *Breaking the Spell: Colonialism and Literary Renaissance in Indonesia.* Leiden, The Netherlands: Department of Languages and Cultures of Southeast Asia and Oceania, University of Leiden, 1999.

[0237] Weix, G. G. "Gapit Theater: New Javanese Plays on Tradition." *Indonesia* 60 (October 1995): 17–41.

[0238] Zoetmulder, P. J. *Kalangwan: A Survey of Old Javanese Literature.* The Hague: Nijhoff, 1974.

Works of Literature

[0239] Achdiat K. Mihardja. *Atheis.* St. Lucia, Queensland, Australia: University of Queensland Press, 1972.

[0240] Ajidarma, Seno Gumira. *Jazz, Parfum dan insiden.* Yogyakarta, Indonesia: Yayasan Bentang Budaya, 1996.

[0241] ——. *Eyewitness.* Sidney: ETT Imprint, 1995. Originally published as *Saksi Mata* (Yogyakarta, Indonesia: Yayasan Bentang Budaya, 1994).

[0242] Aveling, Harry, ed. *From Surabaya to Armageddon* [short stories]. Singapore: Heinemann, 1976.

[0243] Conrad, Joseph. *Lord Jim.* Edinburgh: Blackwood, 1900. Reprint, Boston: Allen and Unwin, 1988.

[0244] Foulcher, Keith, and Tony Day. *Postcolonial Readings of Modern Indonesian Literature.* Leiden, The Netherlands: KITLV, 2002.

[0245] Hamka. *Merantau ke Deli,* 6th printing. Jakarta: Djajamurni, 1966.

[0246] Hill, David T., ed. *Beyond the Horizon: Short Stories from Contemporary Indonesia.* Clayton, Victoria, Australia: Monash Asia Institute, 1998.

[0247] Lubis, Mochtar. *A Road with No End.* Translated by Anthony H. Johns. London: Hutchinson, 1968.

[0248] Nieuwenhuys, Robert. *Mirror of the Indies.* Amherst: University of Massachusetts Press, 1982.

[0249] Pane, Armijn. *Shackles* [Belenggu]. Translated by John H. McGlynn. Jakarta: Lontar Foundation, 1988.

[0250] Pramoedya Ananta Toer. *Child of All Nations*. Ringwood, Victoria, Australia: Penguin, 1984. Originally published as *Anak semua bangsa* (Holland: Manus Amici, 1981).

[0251] ——. *House of Glass*. Ringwood, Victoria, Australia: Penguin, 1992. Originally published as *Rumah Kaca* (Jakarta: Hasta Mitra, 1988).

[0252] ——. *Jejak Langkah* (Footsteps). Jakarta: Hasta Mitra, 1985.

[0253] ——. *The Mute's Soliloquy.* Translated by Willem Samuels. New York: Hyperion East, 1999. Originally published as *Nyanyi sunyi seorang bisu* (Jakarta: Lentera, 1995).

[0254] ——. *Tales from Djakarta: Caricatures of Circumstances and Their Human Beings*. Ithaca, N.Y.: Cornell Southeast Asia Program, 1999. Originally published as *Tjerita dari Djakarta: sekumpulan karikatur keadaan dan manusia* (Jakarta: Penerbit Grafica, 1957).

[0255] ——. *This Earth of Mankind*. Ringwood, Victoria, Australia: Penguin, 1982. Originally published as *Bumi Manusia* (Melaka, Malaysia: Wira Karya, 1981).

[0256] ——. *Tjerita dari Blora.* Jakarta: Balai Pustaka, 1952.

[0257] ——, ed. Haji Mukti. *Hikayat Siti Mariah.* Jakarta: Hasta Mitra, 1987.

[0258] Rendra, W. S. *The Struggle of the Naga Tribe.* St. Lucia, Queensland, Australia: University of Queensland Press, 1979.

[0259] Székely-Lulofs, Madelon. *Doekoen.* Leiden, The Netherlands: KITLV, 2001.

[0260] Utami, Ayu. *Saman.* Jakarta: Kepustakaan Populer Gramedia, 1998.

Language and Linguistics

[0261] Anderson, Benedict R. O'G. "Language, Fantasy, Revolution: Java 1900–1950," in *Making Indonesia: Essays on Modern Indonesia in Honor of George McT. Kahin,* edited by Daniel S. Lev and Ruth T. McVey, 26–40. [0900]

[0262] Anwar, Khaidir. *Indonesian: The Development and Use of a National Language.* Yogyakarta, Indonesia: Gadjah Mada University Press, 1980.

[0263] Artawa, I Ketut. *Ergativity and Balinese Syntax,* 3 vols. Jakarta: Badan Penyelenggara Seri NUSA, 1998.

[0264] Cense, A. A., and E. M. Uhlenbeck. *Critical Survey of Studies on the Languages of Borneo.* Leiden, The Netherlands: KITLV, 1958.

[0265] Echols, John M., and Hassan Shadily. *An English-Indonesian Dictionary.* Ithaca, N.Y.: Cornell University Press, 1975.

[0266] ——. *An Indonesian-English Dictionary,* 3rd ed. Ithaca, N.Y.: Cornell University Press, 1989.

[0267] Errington, J. Joseph. "Continuity and Change in Indonesian Language Development." *JAS* 45, no. 2 (1986): 329–53.

[0268] ——. "His Master's Voice: Listening to Power's Dialect in Suharto's Indonesia." *Crossroads* 15, no. 1 (2002): 1–8.

[0269] ——. *Shifting Languages: Javanese Indonesian Interaction and Identity.* Cambridge: Cambridge University Press, 1998.

[0270] ——. *Structure and Style in Javanese: A Semiotic View of Linguistic Etiquette.* Philadelphia: University of Pennsylvania Press, 1988.

[0271] Grijns, C. D. "Indonesian Terminology and Globalism." *Archipel* 58 (1999): 47–71.

[0272] Hoffman, John. "A Foreign Investment: Indies Malay to 1901." *Indonesia* 27 (April 1979): 65–92.

[0273] Labrousse, Pierre. "La traversée des années 90 par les calembours (plesetan)." *Archipel* 64 (2002): 39–58.

[0274] MacKnight, C. C., and I. A. Caldwell. "Variation in Bugis Mansucripts." *Archipel* 61 (2001): 139–54.

[0275] Maier, H. M. J. "From Heteroglossia to Polyglossia: The Creation of Malay and Dutch in the Indies." *Indonesia* 56 (October 1993): 38–65.

[0276] Minda, D. van, and J. J. Tjia. "Between Perfect and Perfective: The Meaning and Function of Ambonese Malay Su and Sudah." *BKI* 158, no. 3 (2002): 283–303.

[0277] Oetomo, Dédé. "The Chinese of Indonesia and the Development of the Indonesian Language." *Indonesia,* special issue (1991): 53–66.

[0278] Poerwadaminta, W. J. S. *Kamus umum Bahasa Indonesia.* Jakarta: Balai Pustaka, 1976.

[0279] Rahardja, Prathama, and Henri Chambert-Loir. *Kamus bahasa prokem.* Jakarta: Grafiti, 1990.

[0280] Sarumpaet, J. P. *Modern Usage in Bahasa Indonesia.* Melbourne: Pitman, 1980.

[0281] Teeuw, A. *A Critical Survey of Studies on Malay and Bahasa Indonesia.* The Hague: Nijhoff, 1961.

[0282] Tuuk, H. N. van der. *A Grammar of Toba-Batak.* Leiden, The Netherlands: KITLV, 1971.

[0283] Uhlenbeck, E. M. *A Critical Survey of Studies on the Languages of Java and Madura.* The Hague: Nijhoff, 1964.

[0284] Voorhoeve, P. *Critical Survey of Studies on the Languages of Sumatra.* Leiden, The Netherlands: KITLV, 1955.

[0285] Wolff, John U. "Peranakan Chinese Speech and Identity." *Indonesia* 64 (October 1997): 29–44.

[0286] Wurm, S. A., and Shiro Hattori. *Language Atlas of the Pacific Area, Part 2: Japan Area, Taiwan (Formosa), Philippines, Mainland and Insular Southeast Asia.* Canberra: Australian Academy of the Humanities, 1983.

[0287] Zoetmulder, P. J., with S. O. Robson. *Old Javanese-English Dictionary,* 2 vols. The Hague: Nijhoff, 1982.

ECONOMY

General

[0288] Anrooij, F. van, et al. *Between People and Statistics: Essays on Modern Indonesian History.* The Hague: Nijhoff, 1979.

[0289] Arndt, H. W., and Hal Hill, eds. *Southeast Asia's Economic Crisis: Origins, Lessons and the Way Forward.* Singapore: ISEAS, 1999.

[0290] Azis, Iwan J. *The Indonesian Economy and Policy Dynamics in the 1990s.* Washington, D.C.: United States-Indonesia Society, 1997.

[0291 Bastin, J. S. *The Native Policies of Sir Stamford Raffles in Java and Sumatra: An Economic Interpretation*. Oxford: Clarendon, 1957.

[0292] Boeke, J. H. *The Evolution of the Netherlands Indies Economy.* New York: Institute of Pacific Relations, 1946.

[0293] Booth, Anne. *The Indonesian Economy in the Nineteenth and Twentieth Centuries: A History of Missed Opportunities.* London: Macmillan, 1998.

[0294] ——, ed. *The Oil Boom and After: Indonesian Economic Policy and Performance in the Soeharto Era.* Singapore: OUP, 1992.

[0295] Booth, Anne, and Peter McCawley, eds. *The Indonesian Economy during the Suharto Era.* Kuala Lumpur, Malaysia: OUP, 1981.

[0296] Far Eastern Economic Review. *Asia 2002 Yearbook.* Hong Kong: Review Publishing, 2001.

[0297] Hamilton-Hart, Natasha. "Anti-Corruption Strategies in Indonesia." *BIES* 37, no. 1 (April 2001).

[0298] Hatta, Mohammad. *The Cooperative Movement in Indonesia.* Ithaca, N.Y.: Cornell University Press, 1957.

[0299] Higgins, Benjamin. "The Dualistic Theory of Underdeveloped Areas." *Economic Development and Cultural Change* 4 (1956): 99–115.

[0300] Hill, Hal. "The Economy." In *Indonesia's New Order,* edited by Hal Hill, 54–122. Honolulu: University of Hawai'i Press, 1994. [0730]

[0301] ——. *The Indonesian Economy in Crisis: Causes, Consequences and Lessons.* Singapore: ISEAS, 1999.

[0302] ——. *The Indonesian Economy since 1966: Southeast Asia's Emerging Giant.* Cambridge: Cambridge University Press, 1996.

[0303] Hollinger, William C. *Economic Policy under President Soeharto: Indonesia's Twenty-Five Year Record,* Background paper no. 2. Washington, D.C.: United States-Indonesia Society, 1996.

[0304] *Indonesian Economics: The Concept of Dualism in Theory and Practice.* The Hague: van Hoeve, 1966.

[0305] Lewis, Blane D. "The New Indonesian Equalisation Transfer." *BIES* 37, no. 3 (December 2001).

[0306] Lindblad, J. Th. *New Challenges in the Modern Economic History of Indonesia.* Leiden, the Netherlands: PRIS, 1993.

[0307] ——, ed. *Historical Foundations of a National Economy in Indonesia, 1890s–1990s.* Amsterdam: Royal Netherlands Academy of Arts and Sciences, North Holland, 1996.

[0308] Maddison, Angus, and Gé Prince, eds. *Economic Growth in Indonesia 1820–1940.* Dordrecht, The Netherlands: Foris, 1989.

[0309] *Onderzoek vaar de mindere welvaart der inlandsche bevolking op Java en Madoera*, 12 parts in 45 vols. Batavia (Jakarta): Kolff, 1904–1911.

[0310] Palmer, Ingrid. *The Indonesian Economy since 1965: A Case Study of Political Economy.* London: Frank Cass, 1978.

[0311] Pangestu, Mari. *The Role of the Private Sector: Deregulation and Privatization.* Jakarta: CSIS, 1990.

[0312] Papanek, Gustav F., ed. *The Indonesian Economy.* New York: Praeger, 1980.

[0313] Robison, Richard. *Indonesia: The Rise of Capital.* Sydney: Allen and Unwin, 1986.

[0314] Sato, Yuri. "The Salim Group in Indonesia: The Development and Behavior of the Largest Conglomerate in Southeast Asia." *The Developing Economies* 31, no. 4 (December 1993).

[0315] Sutter, John O. *Indonesianisasi: Politics in a Changing Economy, 1940–1955*, 4 vols. Ithaca, N.Y.: Cornell Southeast Asia Program, 1959.

Agriculture

[0316] Allen, G. C., and Audrey G. Donnithorne. *Western Enterprise in Indonesia and Malaya.* London: Allen and Unwin, 1957.

[0317] Bauer, P. T. *The Rubber Industry: A Study in Competition and Monopoly.* Cambridge, Mass.: Harvard University Press, 1948.

[0318] Boomgard, P., and J. L. Van Zanden. *Changing Economy in Indonesia,* vol. 10: *Food Crops and Arable Lands, Java 1815–1942.* Amsterdam: The Royal Tropical Institute, 1990.

[0319] Booth, Anne. *Agricultural Development in Indonesia.* Sydney: Allen and Unwin, 1988.

[0320] Breman, Jan. *Koelies, planters en koloniale politiek: het arbeidregime op de grootlandbouw, ondernemingen aan Sumatra's Oostkust in het begin van de twintigste eeuw.* Leiden, The Netherlands: KITLV, 1992.

[0321] Breman, Jan, and Gunawan Wiradi. *Good Times and Bad Times in Rural Java.* Singapore: ISEAS, 2002.

[0322] Butcher, John G. "The Salt Farm and Fishing Industry of Bagan Si Api Api." *Indonesia* 62 (October 1996): 91–122.

[0323] Clemens, A. H. P., and J. Th. Lindblad, eds. *Het belang van de buitengewesten: economische expansie en coloniale staatvorming in de buitengewesten van Nederlands-Indië.* Amsterdam: NEHA, 1989.

[0324] Dove, Michael R. "Smallholder Rubber and Swidden Agriculture in Borneo: A Sustainable Adaptation to the Ecology and Economy of the Tropical Forest." *Economic Botany* 47, no. 2 (1993): 136–47.

[0325] Eng, Pierre van der. *Agricultural Growth in Indonesia: Productivity, Change and Policy Impact since 1880.* London: Macmillan, 1996.

[0326] ——. "Food for Growth: Trends in Indonesia's Food Supply, 1880–1995." *Journal of Interdisciplinary History* 30, no. 4 (2000): 591–616.

[0327] Fujimoto, Akimi, and Kamaruddin Abdullah, eds. *Highland Vegetable Cultivation in Indonesia: A Multi-Disciplinary Study toward Eco-Farming.* Tokyo: World Planning, 2001.

[0328] Geertz, Clifford. *Agricultural Evolution: The Process of Ecological Change in Indonesia.* Berkeley: University of California Press, 1963.

[0329] Gellert, Paul K. "A Brief History and Analysis of Indonesia's Forest Fire Crisis." *Indonesia* 65 (April 1998): 63–85.

[0330] Gérard, Françoise, and François Ruf. *Agriculture in Crisis: People, Commodities and Natural Resources in Indonesia, 1996–2000.* Montpelier, France/Richmond, Surrey: Cirad/Curzon, 2001.

[0331] Gorcum, K. W. van. *Oost-Indische Cultures.* Amsterdam: de Bussy, 1919.

[0332] Hall, C. J. J. van, and C. van de Koppel, eds. *De landbouw in de Indische archipel,* 3 vols, 4 parts. The Hague: van Hoeve, 1946–1950.

[0333] Hansen, Gary E. ed. *Agricultural and Rural Development in Indonesia.* Boulder, Colo.: Westview, 1981.

[0334] Hart, Gillian. *Power, Labor and Livelihood: Processes of Change in Rural Java.* Berkeley: University of California Press, 1986.

[0335] Kano, Hiroyoshi. *Land Tenure System and the Desa Community in Nineteenth Century Java.* Tokyo: Institute of Developing Economies, 1977.

[0336] ——. "Landless Peasant Households in Indonesia." In *Approaching Suharto's Indonesia from the Margins*, edited by Takashi Shiraishi, 43–73. [0749]

[0337] Lucas, Anton. "Land Disputes in Indonesia: Some Current Perspectives." *Indonesia* 53 (April 1992): 79–93.

[0338] Lucas, Anton, and Carol Warren. "Agrarian Reform in the Era of *Reformasi.*" In *Indonesia in Transition: Social Aspects of Reformasi and Crisis,* edited by Chris Manning and Peter van Diemen, 220–38. [0765]

[0339] Marks, Stephen. "NTT Sandalwood: Roots of Disaster." *BIES* 38, no. 2 (August 2002): 223–40.

[0340] McStocker, Robert. "The Indonesian Coffee Industry." *BIES* 23 (April 1987): 40–69.

[0341] Pearson, Scott, Walter Falcon, Paul Heytens, Eric Monke, and Rosamond Naylor. *Rice Policy in Indonesia.* Ithaca, N.Y.: Cornell University Press, 1991.

[0342] Peluso, Nancy Lee. "Networking in the Commons: A Tragedy for Rattan?" *Indonesia* 35 (April 1983): 94–108.

[0343] Rao, Y. S., et al., eds. *Community Forestry: Socio-Economic Aspects.* Bangkok: Regional Office for Asia and the Pacific, 1985.

[0344] Ruddle, Kenneth, et al. *Palm Sago: A Tropical Starch for Marginal Lands.* Honolulu: University of Hawai'i Press, 1978.

[0345] Setten van der Meer, N. C. van. *Sawah Cultivation in Ancient Java: Aspects of Development during the Indo-Javanese Period 5th to 15th Century.* Canberra: ANU Press, 1979.

[0346] Svensson, Thommy. *Contractions and Expansions: Agrarian Change in Java since 1830.* Gothenburg, Sweden: Historical-Anthropological Project, Gothenburg University, 1985.

[0347] Taylor, Norman. *Cinchona in Java: The Story of Quinine*. New York: Greenberg, [1945].

[0348] Thee Kian Wie. *Plantation Agriculture and Export Growth: An Economic History of East Sumatra, 1863–1942.* Jakarta: LEKNAS-LIPI, 1977.

[0349] White, Benjamin. "'Agricultural Involution' and Its Critics: Twenty Years After." *BCAS* 15, no. 2 (1983): 18–31.

Development

[0350] Ananta, Aris, ed. *The Indonesian Crisis: A Human Development Perspective.* Singapore: ISEAS, 2002.

[0351] Aswicahyono, Haryo, and Mari Pangestu. "Indonesia's Recovery: Exports and Regaining Competitiveness." *Developing Economies* 38, no. 4 (2000): 454–89.

[0352] Barlow, Colin, and Thee Kian Wie. *The North Sumatra Regional Economy: Growth with Unbalanced Development.* Singapore: ISEAS, 1988.

[0353] Booth, Anne. "Development: Achievement and Weakness." In *Indonesia beyond Suharto,* edited by Donald K. Emmerson, 109–35. [0761]

[0354] ——. "Poverty and Inequality in the Soeharto Era: An Assessment."*BIES* 36, no. 1 (April 2000): 73–104.

[0355] Bunnell, Frederick. "Community Participation, Indigenous Ideology, Activist Politics: Indonesian NGOs in the 1990s." In *Making Indonesia*, edited by Daniel S. Lev and Ruth T. McVey, 180–201. [0900]

[0356] Chalmers, Ian, and Vedi R. Hadiz, eds. *The Politics of Economic Development in Indonesia.* London: Routledge, 1997.

[0357] Colombijn, Freek. "A Wild West Frontier on Sumatra's East Coast: The Pekanbaru-Dumai Road." *BKI* 158, no. 4 (2002): 743–68.

[0358] Doorn, Jacques van, and Willem J. Hendrix. *The Emergence of a Dependent Economy: The Consequences of the Opening Up of West Priangan, Java, to the Process of Modernization.* Rotterdam, The Netherlands: Erasmus University, 1983.

[0359] Hill, Hal, ed. *Unity and Diversity: Regional Development in Indonesia since 1970.* Singapore: OUP, 1989.

[0360] Hill, Hal, and Thee Kian Wie, eds. *Indonesia's Technological Challenge.* Singapore: ISEAS, 1998.

[0361] Houben, Vincent J. H., J. Thomas Lindblad, and Thee Kian Wie. *The Emergence of a National Economy: An Economic History of Indonesia, 1800–2000.* Sydney: Allen and Unwin, 2002.

[0362] Humphries, Anne Marie. *Growth Triangles of South East Asia.* Canberra: East Asia Analytical Unit, 1995.

[0363] Lee Tsao Yuan, ed. *Growth Triangle: The Johor-Singapore-Riau Experience.* Singapore: ISEAS, 1991.

[0364] Muizenberg, Otto van den, and Willem Wolters. *Conceptualizing Development: The Historical Sociological Tradition in Dutch Non-Western Sociology.* Dordrecht, The Netherlands: Foris, 1988.

[0365] Murai, Yoshinori. "The Authoritarian Bureaucratic Politics of Development: Indonesia under Suharto's New Order." In *Approaching Suharto's Indonesia from the Margins*, edited by Takashi Shiraishi, 21–42. [0749]

[0366] Nur, Yoslan. "L'île de Batam à l'ombre de Singapour: investissement singapourien et dépendance de Batam." *Archipel* 59 (2000): 145–70.

[0367] Silas, Johan. "Toll Roads and the Development of New Settlements: The Case of Surabaya Compared to Jakarta." *BKI* 158, no. 4 (2002): 677–89.

[0368] Sjahrir. *Basic Needs in Indonesia: Economics, Politics and Public Policy.* Singapore: ISEAS, 1986.

[0369] Smith, Shannon L. *Batam: Politics and Economic Development in Indonesia.* Sydney: Allen and Unwin, 2001.

[0370] Soedjatmoko. *Economic Development as a Cultural Problem.* Ithaca, N.Y.: Cornell Modern Indonesia Project, 1962.

[0371] Tanter, Richard. "Oil, Iggi and US Hegemony: Global Pre-Conditions for Indonesian Rentier-Militarization." In *State and Civil Society in Indonesia,* edited by Arief Budiman, 51–98. [0894]

[0372] Winarso, Haryo. "Access to Main Roads or Low Cost Land? Residential Land Developers' Behaviour in Indonesia." *BKI* 158, no. 4 (2002): 653–76.

[0373] Yoshihara, Kunio. *The Rise of Ersatz Capitalism in South-East Asia.* Singapore: OUP, 1988.

Finance

[0374] Alamsyah, Halim, Charles Joseph, Juda Agung, and Doddy Zulverdy. "Towards Implementation of Inflation Targeting in Indonesia." *BIES* 37, no. 3 (December 2001).

[0375] Ascher, William. "From Oil to Timber: The Political Economy of Off-Budget Development Financing in Indonesia." *Indonesia* 65 (April 1998): 37–62.

[0376] Asher, Mukul G., and Anne Booth. *Indirect Taxation in ASEAN.* Singapore: ISEAS, 1983.

[0377] Azis, Iwan J. "The Nonlinear General Equilibrium Impact of the Financial Crisis and the Downfall of Manufacturing." *Developing Economies* 38, no. 4 (2000): 518–46.

[0378] Boediono. "The International Monetary Fund Support Program in Indonesia: Comparing Implementation under Three Presidents." *BIES* 38, no. 3 (December 2002).

[0379] Boomgaard, Peter. "Buitenzorg in 1805: The Role of Money and Credit in a Colonial Frontier Society." *MAS* 20, no. 1 (1986): 33–58.

[0380] Booth, Anne. "The Burden of Taxation in Colonial Indonesia in the 20th Century." *JSEAS* 2, no. 1 (1980): 91–109.

[0381] Charlesworth, Harold C. *A Banking System in Transition: The Origin, Concept and Growth of the Indonesian Banking System*. Jakarta: New Nusantara, 1959.

[0382] Djiwandono, J. Soedradjad. "Bank Indonesia and the Recent Crisis." *BIES* 36, no. 1 (April 2000): 47–72.

[0383] Editors. "For the Sake of Debt Management: How Was Presidential Decree No. 39/1991 Drafted?" *Indonesia* 54 (October 1992): 149–91.

[0384] Grenville, Stephen. "Monetary Policy and the Exchange Rate during the Crisis." *BIES* 36, no. 2 (August 2000).

[0385] Habir, Ahmad D. "Conglomerates: All in the Family?" In *Indonesia beyond Suharto,* edited by Donald K. Emmerson, 168–202. [0761]

[0386] Heij, Gitta. "The 1981–83 Income Tax Reform Process: Who Pulled the Strings?" *BIES* 37, no. 2 (August 2001): 233–51.

[0387] Hill, Hal. *The Indonesian Economy in Crisis: Causes, Consequences and Lessons.* Singapore: ISEAS, 1999.

[0388] Kenward, Lloyd R. "Assessing Vulnerability to Financial Crisis: Evidence from Indonesia." *BIES* 35, no. 3 (December 1999).

[0389] Linnan, David K. "Insolvency Reform and the Indonesiana Financial Crisis." *BIES* 35, no. 2 (August 1999): 107–37.

[0390] McLeod, Ross. "Crisis-Driven Changes to the Banking Laws and Regulations." *BIES* 35, no. 2 (August 1999): 147–54.

[0391] Mevius, Johan. *Catalogue of Paper Money of the V.O.C. Netherlands East Indies and Indonesia from 1782–1981*. Vriezenveen, The Netherlands: Mevius Numisbooks, 1981.

[0392] Niel, Robert van. "The Function of Land Rent under the Cultivation System in Java." *JAS* 23, no. 3 (1964): 357–76.

[0393] Paauw, Douglas. *Financing Economic Development: The Indonesian Case*. Glencoe, N.Y.: Free Press, 1960.

[0394] Redway, Jake. "An Assessment of the Asset Management Company Model in the Reform of Indonesia's Banking Sector." *BIES* 38, no. 2 (1964): 241–50.

[0395] Shah, A. et al. *Inter-Governmental Fiscal Relations in Indonesia*. Washington, D.C.: World Bank, 1994.

[0396] Sharma, Shalendra D. "The Indonesian Financial Crisis: From Banking Crisis to Financial Sector Reforms, 1997–2000." *Indonesia* 71 (April 2001): 79–110.

[0397] Silver, Christopher, Iwan J. Azis, and Larry Schroeder. "Intergovernmental Transfers and Decentralisation in Indonesia." *BIES* 37, no. 3 (2001): 345–62.

[0398] Wicks, Robert S. *Money, Markets, and Trade in Early Southeast Asia: The Development of Indigenous Monetary Systems to AD 1400*. Ithaca, N.Y.: Cornell Southeast Asia Program, 1992.

[0399] Winters, Jeffrey A. *Power in Motion: Capital Mobility and the Indonesian State.* Ithaca, N.Y.: Cornell University Press, 1996.

Industry

[0400] Aden, Jean. "Entrepreneurship and Protection in the Indonesian Oil Service Industry." In *Southeast Asian Capitalists,* edited by Ruth McVey, 89–101. Ithaca, N.Y.: Cornell Southeast Asia Program, 1992.

[0401] Apkindo. *Directory of the Plywood Industry in Indonesia*. Jakarta: Apkindo, 1985.

[0402] Aswicahyono, Haryo, M. Chatib Basri, and Hal Hill. "How Not to Industralise? Indonesia's Automotive Industry." *BIES* 36, no. 1 (April 2000): 209–41.

[0403] Bailey, Connor. "The Political Economy of Marine Fisheries Development in Indonesia." *Indonesia* 46 (October 1988): 25–38.

[0404] Barr, Christopher M. "Bob Hasan, the Rise of Apkindo, and the Shifting Dynamics of Control in Indonesia's Timber Section." *Indonesia* 65 (April 1998): 1–36.

[0405] Bartlett, Anderson G., et al. *Pertamina: Indonesian National Oil*. Jakarta: Amerasian, 1972.

[0406] Castles, Lance. *Religion, Politics and Economic Behavior in Java: The Kudus Cigarette Industry*. New Haven, Conn.: Yale University Southeast Asia Studies, 1967.

[0407] Erwiza. *Miners, Managers and the State: A Socio-Political History of the Ombilin Coal-Mines, West Sumatra, 1892–1996*. Singapore: Singapore University Press, 2003.

[0408] Hannig, Wolfgang. *Towards a Blue Revolution: Socioeconomic Aspects of Brackishwater Pond Cultivation in Java*. Yogyakarta, Indonesia: Gadjah Mada University Press, 1988.

[0409] Hill, Hal. *Foreign Investment and Industrialization in Indonesia*. Melbourne: OUP, 1988.

[0410] ——. *Indonesia's Industrial Transformation.* Singapore: ISEAS, 1998.

[0411] Hyndman, D. "Melanesian Resistance to Ecocide and Ethnocide: Transnational Mining Projects and the Fourth World on the Island of New Guinea." In *Tribal Peoples and Development Issues*, edited by J. Bodley, 281–98. Mountain View, Australia: Mayfield, 1988.

[0412] Kragten, Marieke. *Viable or Marginal? Small-Scale Industries in Rural Java (Bantul District)*. Utrecht, the Netherlands: Royal Dutch Geographical Society, 2000.

[0413] Marr, Carolyn. *Digging Deep: The Hidden Costs of Mining in Indonesia*. London: Down to Earth and Minewatch, 1993.

[0414] McKendrick, David. "Obstacles to 'Catch-Up': The Case of the Indonesian Aircraft Idustry." *BIES* 28, no. 1 (April 1992): 39–66.

[0415] Poot, Huib, Arie Kuyuenhoven, and Jaap Jansen. *Industralisation and Trade in Indonesia*. Yogyakarta, Indonesia: Gadjah Mada University Press, 1990.

[0416] Robinson, Kathryn May. *Stepchildren of Progress: The Political Economy of Development in an Indonesian Mining Town*. Albany: State University of New York Press, 1986.

[0417] Robison, Richard. "Industralization and the Economic and Political Development of Capital: The Case of Indonesia." In *Southeast Asian Capitalists*, edited by Ruth McVey, 65–88. Ithaca, N.Y.: Cornell Southeast Asia Program, 1992.

[0418] Siahaan, Bisuk. *Industrialisasi di Indonesia sejak hutang kehormatan sampai bantin stir.* Jakarta: Pustaka Data, 1996.

[0419] Tambunan, Tulus Tahi Hamonangan. *Development of Small-Scale Industries during the New Order Government in Indonesia*. Aldershot, UK: Ashgate, 2000.

[0420] Thee Kian Wie. "Competition Policy in Indonesia and the New Anti-Monopoly and Fair Competition Law." *BIES* 38, no. 3 (December 2002): 331–42.

Labor

[0421] Blussé, Leonard. "Labour Takes Root: Mobilisation and Immobilisation of Javanese Rural Society under the Cultivation System." *Itinerario* 7, no. 1 (1984): 77–117.

[0422] Chandra, Siddharth. "The Role of Female Industrial Labor in the Late Colonial Netherlands Indies." *Indonesia* 74 (October 2002): 103–36.

[0423] Hadiz, Vedi R. "Mirroring the Past or Reflecting the Future? Class and Religious Pluralism in Indonesian Labor." In *The Politics of Multiculturalism*, edited by Robert W. Hefner, 268–90. Honolulu: University of Hawai'i Press, 2001.

[0424] ———. "Reformasi Total? Labor after Suharto." *Indonesia* 66 (October 1998): 109–26.

[0425] ———. *Workers and the State in New Order Indonesia*. London: Routledge, 1997.

[0426] Houben, Vincent J. H., J. Thomas Lindblad, et al., eds. *Coolie Labour in Colonial Indonesia: A Study of Labour Relations in the Outer Islands, c. 1900–1940*. Wiesbaden, Germany: Harrassowitz, 1999.

[0427] Jones, Gavin W. "Labor Force and Education." In *Indonesia's New Order*, edited by Hal Hill, 145–78. Honolulu: University of Hawai'i Press, 1994. [0730]

[0428] Knight, G. Roger. "Coolie or Worker? Crossing the Lines in Colonial Java 1780–1942." *Itinerario* 23, no. 1 (1999): 62–77.

[0429] La Botz, Dan. *Made in Indonesia: Indonesian Workers since Suharto*. Cambridge, Mass.: South End Press, 2001.

[0430] Leclerc, Jacques. "An Ideological Problem of Indonesian Trade Unionism in the Sixties: 'Karyawan' versus 'Buruh.'" *RIMA* 6, no. 1 (1972): 76–91.

[0431] Manning, Chris. *Indonesian Labour in Transition: An East Asian Success Story?* Cambridge: Cambridge University Press, 1998.

[0432] ———. "Labour Market Adjustments to Indonesia's Economic Crisis: Context, Trends and Implications." *BIES* 36, no. 1 (April 2000): 105–36.

[0433] Niel, Robert van, ed. and trans. *Coolie Budget Commission: Living Conditions of Plantation Workers and Peasants on Java in 1939–1940*. Ithaca, N.Y.: Cornell Modern Indonesia Project, 1956.

[0434] Reid, Anthony, ed. *Slavery, Bondage and Dependency in Southeast Asia*. St. Lucia, Queensland, Australia: University of Queensland Press, 1983.

[0435] Schiller, A. Arthur. "Labor Law and Legislation in the Netherlands Indies." *Far Eastern Quarterly* 5 (1946): 176–88.

[0436] Tedjasukmana, Iskander. *The Political Character of the Indonesian Trade Union Movement*. Ithaca, N.Y.: Cornell Modern Indonesia Project, 1959.

[0437] Thompson, Virginia. *Labor Problems in Southeast Asia*. New Haven, Conn.: Yale University Press, 1947.

Trade

[0438] Alexander, Jennifer. *Trade, Traders and Trading in Rural Java*. Singapore: OUP, 1987.

[0439] Andaya, Barbara. "The Cloth Trade in Jambi and Palembang Society during the Seventeenth and Eighteenth Centuries." *Indonesia* 48 (October 1989): 26–46.

[0440] Andaya, Leonard Y. "The Trans-Sumatra Trade and the Ethnicization of the 'Batak.'" *BKI* 158, no. 3 (2002): 367–409.

[0441] Barnard, Timothy P. "The Timber Trade in Pre-Modern Siak." *Indonesia* 65 (April 1998): 86–96.

[0442] Barrichello, R. R., and F. R. Flatters. "Trade Policy Reform in Indonesia." In *Reforming Economic Systems in Developing Countries*, edited by D. H.

Perkins and M. Roemer, 271–91. Boston: Harvard Studies in International Development, 1991.

[0443] Chandler, Glen. *Market Trade in Rural Java*. Clayton, Victoria, Australia: Centre of Southeast Asian Studies, 1984.

[0444] Chapman, Ross. "Indonesian Trade Reform in Close-Up: The Steel and Footwear Experiences." *BIES* 28, no. 1 (April 1992): 67–84.

[0445] Fane, George, and Timothy Condon. "Trade Reform in Indonesia 1987–95." *BIES* 32, no. 3 (December 1996): 33–54.

[0446] Fuke, Yosuke. "Used-Clothing Routes: From Japan to Indonesia." In *Approaching Suharto's Indonesia from the Margins*, edited by Takashi Shiraishi, 5–20. Ithaca, N.Y.: Cornell Southeast Asia Program, 1994.

[0447] Garcia, Jorge Garcia. "Indonesia's Trade and Price Interventions: Pro-Java and Pro-Urban." *BIES* 36, no. 3 (December 2000).

[0448] Gerretson, C. *History of the Royal Dutch*, 4 vols. Leiden, The Netherlands: Brill, 1953–1957.

[0449] Heersink, Christiaan G. "Selayar and the Green Gold: The Development of the Coconut Trade on an Indonesian Island (1820–1950)." *JSEAS* 24, no. 1 (March 1994): 47–69.

[0450] Mai, Ulrich, and Helmut Buchholt. *Peasant Pedlars and Professional Traders: Subsistence Trade in Rural Markets of Minahasa, Indonesia*. Singapore: ISEAS, 1988.

[0451] Manguin, Pierre-Yves. "The Vanishing Jong: Insular Southeast Asian Fleets in Trade and War (Fifteenth to Seventeenth Centuries." In *Southeast Asia in the Early Modern Era*, edited by Anthony Reid, 197–213. Ithaca, N.Y.: Cornell University. Press, 1993.

[0452] Miksic, John N. "Traditional Sumatra Trade."*BEFEO* 74 (1985): 423–67.

[0453] Montgomery, Roger, et al. "Deregulation of Indonesia's Interregional Agricultural Trade." *BIES* 38, no. 1 (April 2002): 93–117.

[0454] Pitt, M. M. "Indonesia." In *Liberalizing Foreign Trade*, vol. 5, edited by D. Papageorgiou et al., 1–196. Cambridge, Mass.: Basil Blackwell for the World Bank, 1991.

[0455] Rosner, L. Peter. "Indonesia's Non-Oil Export Performance during the Economic Crisis: Distinguishing Price Trends from Quantity Trends." *BIES* 36, no. 2 (August 2000).

[0456] Steensgaard, Niels. *The Asian Trade Revolution of the Seventeenth Century: The East India Companies and the Decline of the Caravan Trade*. Chicago: University of Chicago Press, 1974.

[0457] Tagliacozzo, Eric. "Trade Production and Incorporation: The Indian Ocean in Flux, 1600–1900." *Itinerario* 26, no. 1 (2002): 75–106.

[0458] Thee Kian Wie. "Indonesia's Recovery: Exports and Regaining Competitiveness." *Developing Economies* 38, no. 4 (2000): 420–53.

[0459] Touwen, Jeroen. *Extremes in the Archipelago: Trade and Economic Development in the Outer Islands of Indonesia, 1900–1942*. Leiden, The Netherlands: KITLV, 2001.

Transport and Communications

[0460] Airriess, Christopher. "Port-Centered Transport Development in Colonial North Sumatra." *Indonesia* 59 (April 1995): 65–91.

[0461] Ammarell, Gene. *Bugis Navigation*. New Haven, Conn.: Yale University Southeast Asian Studies, 1999.

[0462] Beer van Dingstee, J. H. *De ontwikkeling van het postwezen in Nederl. Oost-Indië.* Bandung, Indonesia: Nix, 1933.

[0463] Brooks, Mary R. *Fleet Development and the Control of Shipping in Southeast Asia.* Singapore: ISEAS, 1985.

[0464] Dick, H. W. *The Indonesian Inter-Island Shipping Industry: An Analysis of Competition and Regulation*. Singapore: ISEAS, 1986.

[0465] Gotz, J. F. "Railways in the Netherlands Indies, with Special Reference to the Island of Java." *Bulletin of the Colonial Institute* (1939): 267–90.

[0466] Horridge, Adrian. *Outrigger Canoes of Bali and Madura, Indonesia*. Honolulu, Hawaii: Bishop Museum Press, 1987.

[0467] Mosteller, Dee. "Garuda Bounces from Chaos to Success." *Air Transport World* (November 1980): 32–38.

[0468] Rimmer, Peter J. *Rikisha to Rapid Transit: Urban Public Transport Systems and Policy in Southeast Asia*. Sydney: Pergammon Press, 1986.

[0469] Sartono Kartodirdjo, ed. *The Pedicab in Yogyakarta: A Study of Low Cost Transportation and Poverty Problems.* Yogyakarta, Indonesia: Gadjah Mada University Press, 1981.

[0470] Soegijoko, Budy Tjahjati. "The Becaks of Java." *Habitat International* 10, no. 1–2 (1986): 155–64.

HISTORY

General Histories

[0471] Aveling, Harry, ed. *The Development of Indonesian Society: From the Coming of Islam to the Present Day*. St. Lucia, Queensland, Australia: University of Queensland Press, 1979.

[0472] Benda, Harry J. *Continuity and Change in Southeast Asia: Collected Journal Articles*. New Haven, Conn.: Yale University Southeast Asian Studies, 1972.

[0473] Bourchier, David, and John Legge, eds. *Democracy in Indonesia 1950s and 1990s*. Clayton, Victoria, Australia: Monash University Papers on Southeast Asia, 1994.

[0474] Cribb, Robert, and C. Brown. *Modern Indonesia: A History since 1945*. London: Longman, 1995.

[0475] Dahm, Bernhard. *History of Indonesia in the Twentieth Century*. London: Praeger, 1971.

[0476] Dick, Howard, et al. *The Emergence of a National Economy: An Economic History of Indonesia, 1800–2000*. Honolulu: University of Hawai'i Press, 2002.

[0477] Fox, James J., et al., eds. *Indonesia: Australian Perspectives*. Canberra: Australian National University, 1980.

[0478] Kahin, George McT. *Southeast Asia: A Testament*. London: Routledge Curzon, 2003.

[0479] Kamerling, R. N. J., ed. *Indonesie toen en nu*. Amsterdam: Intermediair, 1980.

[0480] Kroef, Justus M. van der. *Indonesia in the Modern World*, 2 vols. Bandung, Indonesia: Masa Baru, 1954–1956.

[0481] Legge, J. D. *Indonesia*, 3rd ed. Sydney: Prentice-Hall, 1980.

[0482] McVey, Ruth T., ed. *Indonesia*. New Haven, Conn.: Human Relations Area Files Press, 1963.

[0483] ——, ed. *Southeast Asian Transitions: Approaches through Social History*. New Haven, Conn.: Yale University Press, 1978.

[0484] Ricklefs, M. C. *A History of Modern Indonesia*. London: Macmillan, 1981.

[0485] Sartono Kartodirdjo. *Modern Indonesia: Tradition and Transformation, A Socio-Historical Perspective*. Yogyakarta, Indonesia: Gadjah Mada University Press, 1984.

[0486] ——. *Protest Movements in Rural Java*. Singapore: Singapore University Press, 1973.

[0487] Soebadio, Haryati, and Carine A. du Marchie Sarvaas, eds. *Dynamics of Indonesian History*. Amsterdam: North-Holland, 1978.

[0488] Steinberg, David Joel, et al. *In Search of Southeast Asia: A Modern History*, 2nd ed. Honolulu: University of Hawai'i Press, 1987.

[0489] Sutherland, Heather. "Believing is Seeing: Perspectives on Political Power and Economic Activity in the Malay World 1700–1940." *JSEAS* 26, no. 1 (March 1995): 133–46.

[0490] ——. "Writing Indonesian History in the Netherlands: Rethinking the Past." *BKI* 150 (1994): 785–804.

[0491] Vlekke, Bernard H. M. *Nusantara: A History of the East Indian Archipelago*. Cambridge, Mass.: Harvard University Press, 1945.

[0492] Wertheim, W. F. *Indonesian Society in Transition*, 2nd ed. The Hague: van Hoeve, 1959.

[0493] Zainu'ddin, Ailsa G. *A Short History of Indonesia*, 2nd ed. Stanmore, New South Wales, Australia: Cassell, 1968.

Historiography

[0494] Abidin, Andi Zainal. "Notes on the Lontara' as Historical Sources." *Indonesia* 12 (April 1974): 159–72.

[0495] Bahari, Razif. "Remembering History, w/Righting History: Piecing Together the Past in Pramoeya Ananta Toer's Buru Tetralogy." *Indonesia* 75 (April 2003): 61–90.

[0496] Benda, Harry J. "The Structure of South-East Asian History." *JSEAH* 3, no. 1 (March 1962): 106–39.

[0497] Cowan, C. D., and O. W. Wolters. *Southeast Asian History and Historiography: Essays Presented to D.G. E. Hall*. Ithaca, N.Y.: Cornell University Press, 1976.

[0498] Hall, D. G. E. *Historians of South-East Asia*. London: OUP, 1961.

[0499] Houben, Vincent J. H. "Koloniale geschiedenis van Indonesië in de 21e eeuw: meerzijdig en dubbelzinnig." In *Macht en majesteit*, edited by J. Thomas Lindblad and Willem van der Molen. Leiden, the Netherlands: Universiteit Leiden, 2002.

[0500] Kroef, Justus M. van der. "On the Writing of Indonesian History." *Pacific Affairs* 31 (1958): 352–71.

[0501] Levine, David. "History and Social Structure in the Study of Contemporary Indonesia." *Indonesia* 7 (April 1969): 5–20.

[0502] Reid, Anthony, and David G. Marr, eds. *Perceptions of the Past in Southeast Asia*. Singapore: Heinemann, 1979.

[0503] Robison, Richard. "Culture, Politics and Economy in the Political History of the New Order." *Indonesia* 31 (April 1981): 1–29.

[0504] Smail, John R. W. "On the Possibility of an Autonomous History of Southeast Asia." *JSEAH* 2 (July 1961): 72–102.

[0505] Soedjatmoko et al., eds. *An Introduction to Indonesian Historiography*. Ithaca, N.Y.: Cornell University Press, 1965.

To 1400

[0506] Bellwood, Peter. *Prehistory of the Indo-Malaysian Archipelago*, rev. ed. Honolulu: University of Hawai'i Press, 1997.

[0507] Bosch, F. D. K. *Selected Studies in Indonesian Archaeology*. Leiden, the Netherlands: KITLV, 1961.

[0508] Bougas, Wayne A. "Bantayan: An Early Makassarese Kingdom 1200–1600 AD." *Archipel* 55 (1998): 83–123.

[0509] Buchari. "Sri Maharaja Mapanji Garasakan: A New Evidence on the Problem of Airlangga's Partition of His Kingdom." *Madjalah Ilmu-Ilmu Sastra Indonesia* 4, no. 1–2 (1968): 1–26.

[0510] Casparis, J. G. de. *Prasasti Indonesia: Selected Inscriptions from the 7th to the 9th Centuries A.D.* Bandung, Indonesia: Masa Baru, 1956.

[0511] Christie, Jan Wisseman. "Raja and Rama: The Classical State in Early Java." In *Centers, Symbols, and Hierarchies: Essays on the Classical States of Southeast Asia*. New Haven, Conn.: Yale University Southeast Asian Studies Monograph Series no. 26, 1983.

[0512] ——. "State Formation in Early Maritime Southeast Asia: A Consideration of the Theories and the Data." *BKI* 151, no. 2 (1995).

[0513] ——. "States without Cities: Demographic Trends in Early Java." *Indonesia* 52 (October 1991).

[0514] Coedès, G. *The Indianized States of Southeast Asia*. Honolulu, Hawaii: East-West Center Press, 1968.

[0515] Hall, D. G. E. *A History of South-east Asia*, 3rd ed. London: Macmillan, 1968.

[0516] Hall, Kenneth R. *Maritime Trade and State Development in Early Southeast Asia*. Honolulu: University of Hawai'i Press, 1985.

[0517] Hall, Kenneth R., and John K. Whitmore, eds. *Explorations in Early Southeast Asian History: The Origins of Southeast Asian Statecraft*. Ann Arbor: Center for Southeast Asian Studies, University of Michigan, 1976.

[0518] Heine, Geldern, Robert von. *Conceptions of State and Iingship in Southeast Asia*. Ithaca, N.Y.: Cornell Southeast Asia Program Data Paper, 1956.

[0519] Houben, V. J. H., H. M. J. Maier, and W. van der Molen, eds. *Looking in Odd Mirrors: The Java Sea*. Leiden, The Netherlands: Rijksuniversiteit te Leiden, 1992.

[0520] Kulke, Hermann. "Epigraphical References to the 'City' and the 'State' in Early Indonesia." *Indonesia* 52 (October 1991): 3–22.

[0521] Leur, J. C. van. *Indonesian Trade and Society*. The Hague: van Hoeve, 1955.

[0522] Manguin, Pierre-Yves. "Palembang and Sriwijaya: An Early Harbour-City Rediscovered." *JMBRAS* 66,1 (1993).

[0523] ——. "The Merchant and the King: Political Myths of Southeast Asia Coastal Polities." *Indonesia* 52 (October 1991): 41–54.

[0524] Marr, David G., and A. C. Milner. *Southeast Asia in the 9th to the 14th Centuries*. Singapore: ISEAS, 1985.

[0525] McKinnon, E. Edwards. "Early Politics in Southern Sumatra: Some Preliminary Observations Based on Archaeological Evidence." *Indonesia* 40 (October 1985): 1–36.

[0526] ——. "Mediaeval Tamil Involvement in Northern Sumatra, c 11–c 14 (the Gold and Resin Trade)." *JMBRAS* 69, no. 1 (1996): 85–99.

[0527] Miller, James Innes. *The Spice Trade of the Roman Empire, 29 B.C. to A.D. 641*. Oxford: Clarendon Press, 1969.

[0528] Pigeaud, Th. *Java in the 14th Century, A Study in Cultural History: The Nagara-Kertagama by Rakawi Prapanca of Majapahit, 1365*, 5 vols. The Hague: Nijhoff, 1960–1963.

[0529] Reid, Anthony, and Lance Castles, eds. *Pre-Colonial State Systems in Southeast Asia*. Kuala Lumpur, Malaysia: JMBRAS, 1976.

[0530] Robson, Stuart, trans. *De´sawarnana (Nagarakrtagama) by Mpu Prapanca*. Leiden, the Netherlands: KITLV, 1995.

[0531] Salmon, Claudine. "Srivijaya, la Chine et les marchands chinois (Xe–XIIes): Quelques réflexions sur la société de l'empire sumatranais." *Archipel* 63 (2002): 57–78.

[0532] Schrieke, B. "Ruler and Realm in Early Java." In B. Schrieke, *Indonesian Sociological Studies*, vol. 2. The Hague: van Hoeve, 1959.

[0533] Smith, R. B., and W. Watson, eds. *Early South East Asia: Essays in Archaeology, History and Historical Geography*. Kuala Lumpur, Malaysia: OUP, 1979.

[0534] Soemantri, Hildawati. *The Terracotta Art of Majapahit*. Jakarta: Ceramic Society of Indonesia, 1997.

[0535] Soepomo, S. "The Image of Majapahit in Later Javanese Indonesian Writing." In *Perceptions of the Past in Southeast Asia*, edited by Anthony Reid and David Marr. Singapore: Heinemann(Asia)/ASAA, 1979.

[0536] Stutterheim, W. "The Meaning of the Hindu-Javanese Candi." *Journal of the American Oriental Society* 51 (1931): 1–31.

[0537] Verin, Pierre. *The History of Civilisation in North Madagascar*. Rotterdam, the Netherlands: Balkema, 1986.

[0538] Wheatley, Paul. *The Golden Khersonese: Studies in the Historical Geography of the Malay Peninsula before A.D. 1500*. Kuala Lumpur, Malaysia: University of Malaya Press, 1961.

[0539] ——. *Nagara and Commandery: Origins of the Southeast Asian Urban Traditions*. Chicago: University of Chicago, Department of Geography, 1983.

[0540] ——. "Satyanrta in Suvarnadvipa: From Reciprocity to Redistribution in Ancient Southeast Asia." In *Ancient Civilization and Trade*, edited by Jeremy A Sabloff and C. C. Lamberg-Karlovsky. Albuquerque: University of New Mexico Press, 1975.

[0541] Wisseman, Jan. "Markets and Trade in Pre-Majapahit Java." In *Economic Exchange and Social Interaction in Southeast Asia*, edited by Karl L. Hutterer. Ann Arbor: South and Southeast Asian Studies, University of Michigan, 1977.

[0542] Wolters, O. W. *Early Indonesian Commerce: A Study of the Origins of Srivijaya*. Ithaca, N.Y.: Cornell University Press, 1967.

[0543] ——. *The Fall of Srivijaya in Malay History*. Kuala Lumpur, Malaysia: OUP, 1970.

[0544] ——. *History, Culture, and Region in Southeast Asian Perspectives*, rev. ed. Ithaca, N.Y.: Southeast Asia Program/ISEAS, 1999.

[0545] ——. "Restudying Some Chinese Writings on Sriwijaya." *Indonesia* 42 (October 1986): 1–41.

1400–1800

[0546] Andaya, Barbara W. "Cash Cropping and Upstream-Downstream Tensions: The Case of Jambi in the Seventeenth and Eighteenth Centuries." In *Southeast Asia in the Early Modern Era*, edited by Anthony Reid. Ithaca, N.Y.: Cornell University Press, 1993.

[0547] ——. *To Live as Brothers: Southeast Sumatra in the Seventeenth and Eighteenth Centuries*. Honolulu: University of Hawai'i Press, 1993.

[0548] Andaya, Leonard Y. "Cultural State Formation in Eastern Indonesia." In *Southeast Asia in the Early Modern Era*, edited by Anthony Reid. Ithaca, N.Y.: Cornell University. Press, 1993.

[0549] ——. *The Heritage of Arung Palakka: A History of South Sulawesi (Celebes) in the Seventeenth Century*. The Hague: Nijhoff. 1981.

[0550] ——. *The Kingdom of Johor, 1641–1728: Economic and Political Developments*. Kuala Lumpur, Malaysia: OUP, 1975.

[0551] ——. *The World of Maluku: Eastern Indonesia in the Early Modern Period*. Honolulu: University of Hawai'i Press, 1993.

[0552] Blussé, Leonard. *Strange Company: Chinese Settlers, Mestizo Women and the Dutch in VOC Batavia*. Leiden, The Netherlands: KITLV, 1986.

[0553] Boxer, C. R. *The Dutch Seaborne Empire 1600–1800*. Harmondsworth, UK: Penguin, 1973.

[0554] ——. *Francisco Viera de Figueiredo: A Portuguese Merchant-Adventurer in South East Asia, 1624–1667*. Leiden, The Netherlands: KITLV, 1967.

[0555] ——. *The Portuguese Seaborne Empire: 1415–1825*. Harmondsworth, UK: Penguin, 1973.

[0556] Brown, C. C. *Sejarah Melayu, or Malay Annals*. Kuala Lumpur, Malaysia: OUP, 1970.

[0557] Carey, Peter. "Civilization on Loan: The Making of an Upstart Polity: Mataram and Its Successors, 1600–1830." *MAS* 31, no. 1 (1997): 711–34.

[0558] Chaudhuri, K. N. *Trade and Civilisation in the Indian Ocean: An Economic History from the Rise of Islam to 1750*. Cambridge: Cambridge University Press, 1985.

[0559] Graaf, H. J. de. *De geschiedenis van Ambon en de Zuid-Molukken*. Franeker, The Netherlands: T. Wever, 1977.

[0560] Graaf, H. J. de, with Theodore G. Th. Pigeaud. *Islamic States in Java 1500–1700*. Leiden, The Netherlands: KITLV, 1976.

[0561] Haan, F. de. *Priangan: de Preanger-regentschappen onder het Nederlandsch bestuur tot 1811*, 4 vols. Batavia (Jakarta): Baravaasch Genootschap van Kunsten en Wetenschappen, 1901–1912.

[0562] Jacobs, Els M. *Koopman in Azië: de handel van de Verendigde Oost-Indische Compagnie tijdens de 18de eeuw*. Zutphen, The Netherlands: Walburg Pers, 2000.

[0563] Kathirithamby-Wells, J. *The British West Sumatra Presidency 1760–1785: Problems of Early Colonial Enterprise*. Kuala Lumpur, Malaysia: Penerbit University Malaya, 1977.

[0564] ——. "The Inderapura Sultanate: The Foundations of Its Rise from the Sixteenth to the Eighteenth Centuries." *Indonesia* 26 (April 1976): 65–84.

[0565] Knaap, G. J. *Kruidnagelen en Christenen: de Verenigde Oost-Indische Compagnie en de bevolking van Ambon, 1656–1696*. Leiden, The Netherlands: KITLV, 1987.

[0566] Kumar, Ann. "Javanese Court Society and Politics in the Late Eighteenth Century: The Record of a Lady Soldier." Parts 1 and 2. *Indonesia* 29 (April 1980): 1–46; 30 (October 1980): 67–111.

[0567] ——. *Surapati: Man and Legend*. Leiden, The Netherlands: Brill, 1976.

[0568] Lombard, Denys. *Le sultanat d'Atjeh au temps d'Iskanadar Muda, 1607–1636*. Paris: Ecole Francais d'Extreme Orient, 1967.

[0569] Marsden, William. *The History of Sumatra*. Oxford in Asia reprint. Kuala Lumpur, Malaysia: OUP, 1966.

[0570] Masinambow, E. K. M., ed. *Halmahera dan Raja Ampat sebagai kesatuan majemuk*. Jakarta: Leknas, 1987.

[0571] Meilinck-Roelofsz, M. A. P. *Asian Trade and European Influence in the Indonesian Archipelago between 1500 and about 1630*. The Hague: Nijhoff, 1962.

[0572] Moertono, Soemarsaid. *State and Statecraft in Old Java: A Study of the Later Mataram Period, 16th to 19th century*. Ithaca, N.Y.: Cornell Modern Indonesia Project, 1974.

[0573] Noorduyn, J. "Majapahit in the Fifteenth Century." *BKI* 134, nos. 2–3 (1976): 207–74.

[0574] ——. "Makasar and the Islamization of Bima." *BKI* 143, nos. 2–3 (1987): 312–42.

[0575] Raffles, Thomas Stamford. *The History of Java*, 2 vols. London: John Murray, 1817. Reprint, Kuala Lumpur, Malaysia: OUP, 1965.

[0576] Reid, Anthony. *Southeast Asia in the Age of Commerce, 1450–1680*, 2 vols. New Haven, Conn.: Yale University Press, 1988, 1993.

[0577] Ricklefs, M. C. *Jogjakarta under Sultan Mangkubumi 1749–1792: A History of the Division of Java*. London: OUP, 1974.

[0578] ——. *Modern Javanese Historical Tradition: A Study of an Original Kartasura Chronicle and Related Materials*. London: School of Oriental and African Studies, 1978.

[0579] ——. *The Seen and Unseen Worlds in Java, 1726–1749: History, Literature and Islam in the Court of PakubuwanaII*. Honolulu: ASAA with Allen and Unwin and University of Hawai'i Press, 1998.

[0580] ——. *War, Culture and Economy in Java 1677–1726: Asian and European Imperialism in the early Kartasura Period*. Sydney: Allen and Unwin, 1993.

[0581] Robson, S. O. "Java at the Crossroads: Aspects of Javanese Cultural History in the Fourteenth and Fifteenth Centuries." *BKI* 137 (1981): 259–92.

[0582] Schrieke, B. J. O. *Indonesian Sociological Studies*, 2 vols. The Hague: van Hoeve, 1955.

[0583] Tarling, Nicholas. *Anglo-Dutch Rivalry in the Malay World 1780–1824*. Cambridge: Cambridge University Press, 1962.

[0584] Taylor, Jean Gelman. *The Social World of Batavia: European and Eurasian in Dutch Asia*. Madison: University of Wisconsin Press, 1983.

1800–1942

[0585] Abeyasekere, Susan. *Jakarta: A History*. Singapore: OUP, 1987.

[0586] ——. *One Hand Clapping: Indonesian Nationalists and the Dutch, 1939–1942*. Clayton, Victoria, Australia: Monash University, Centre of Southeast Asian Studies, 1976.

[0587] ——. "The Soetardjo Petition." *Indonesia* 15 (April 1973): 81–108.

[0588] Bastin, J. S. *Raffles' Ideas on the Land Rent System in Java and the Mackenzie Land Tenure System*. The Hague: Nijhoff, 1954.

[0589] Baudet, H., and I. J. Brugmans, eds. *Balans van beleid: terugblik op de laatste halve eeuw van Nederlandsch-Indie*. Assen, The Netherlands: van Gorcum, 1961.

[0590] Benda, Harry J. "Christiaan Snouck Hurgronje and the Foundations of Dutch Islamic Policy in Indonesia." *Journal of Modern History* 30 (1958): 338–47.

[0591] ——. "The Pattern of Administrative Reforms in the Closing Years of Dutch Rule in Indonesia." *JAS* 25 (1966): 589–605.

[0592] ——. "Peasant Movements in Colonial Southeast Asia." *Asian Studies* 3 (1965): 420–34.

[0593] Blumberger, J. Th. Petrus. *De nationalistische beweging in Nederlandsch-Indië*. Haarlem, The Netherlands: Tjeenk Willink, 1931, 1987.

[0594] Booth, Anne. "Japanese Import Penetration and Dutch Response: Some Aspects of Economic Policy Making in Colonial Indonesia." In *International Commercial Rivalry in Southeast Asia in the Interwar Period*, edited by Sugiyama Shinya and Milagros Guerrero, 134–64. New Haven, Conn.: Yale Center for International and Area Studies, 1994.

[0595] Breman, Jan. *Control of Land and Labour in Colonial Java: A Case Study of Agrarian Crisis and Reform in the Region of Cirebon during the First Decades of the 20th Century*. Leiden, The Netherlands: KITLV, 1983.

[0596] ——. *The Village in Nineteenth Century Java and the Colonial State*. Rotterdam, The Netherlands: Erasmus University, Comparative Asian Studies Programme, 1980.

[0597] Carey, Peter. "Waiting for the 'Just King': The Agrarian World of South-central Java from Giyanti (1755) to the Java War." *MAS* 20, no. 1 (1986): 59–137.

[0598] ——, ed. *The British in Java 1811–1816: A Javanese Account*. Oxford: Oxford University Press, 1992.

[0599] Chandra, Siddharth. "What the Numbers Really Tell Us about the Decline of the Opium Regie." *Indonesia* 70 (October 2000): 101–23.

[0600] Cribb, Robert, ed. *The Late Colonial State in Indonesia: Political and Economic Foundations of the Netherlands Indies, 1880–1942*. Leiden, The Netherlands: KITLV, 1994.

[0601] Day, Clive. *The Policy and Administration of the Dutch in Java*. New York: Macmillan, 1904.

[0602] Drooglever, P. J. *Vaderlandse Club: totoks en de Indische politiek*. Franeker, The Netherlands: T. Wever, 1980.

[0603] Elson, R. E. *Javanese Peasants and the Colonial Sugar Industry: Impact and Change in an East Java Residency*. Kuala Lumpur, Malaysia: OUP, 1984.

[0604] Fasseur, C. *De Indologen: Ambtenaren voor de Oost 1825–1950*. Amsterdam: Bakker, 1993.

[0605] ——. *The Politics of Colonial Exploitation: Java, the Dutch and the Cultivation System*. Edited and translated by R. E. Elson and Ary Kraal. Ithaca, N.Y.: Cornell Studies on Southeast Asia, 1992.

[0606] Furnivall, J. S. *Netherlands India: A Study of Plural Economy*. Cambridge: Cambridge University Press, 1939.

[0607] Goor, J. van, ed. *Imperialisme in de marge: de afronding van Nederlands-Indië*. Utrecht, the Netherlands: HES, 1986.

[0608] Gouda, Frances. *Dutch Culture Overseas: Colonial Practice in the Netherlands Indies 1900–1942*. Amsterdam: Amsterdam University Press, 1995.

[0609] Haan, F. de. *Oud Batavia: gedenkboek uitgegeven naar aanleiding van het driehonderd jarig bestaan van der stad in 1919*, 2 vols. Batavia (Jakarta): G. Kolff, 1922–1923.

[0610] Hisyam, Muhamad. *Caught between Three Fires: The Javanese Pangulu under the Dutch Colonial Administration, 1882–1942*. Jakarta: INIS, 2001.

[0611] Houben, Vincent J.H. *Kraton and Kumpeni: Surakarta and Yogyakarta, 1830–1870*. Leiden, The Netherlands: KITLV Press, 1994.

[0612] Ingleson, John. *In Search of Justice: Workers and Unions in Colonial Java, 1908–1926*. Singapore: OUP, 1986.

[0613] ——. *Road to Exile: The Indonesian Nationalist Movement 1927–1934*. Singapore: Heinemann, 1979.

[0614] Kat Angelino, A. de. *Colonial Policy*, 2 vols. The Hague: Nijhoff, 1931.

[0615] Knapp, Gerrit J. *Shallow Waters, Rising Tide: Shipping and Trade in Java around 1775*. Leiden, The Netherlands: KITLV, 1996.

[0616] Knight, G. Roger. "The Contractor as Suikerlord and Entrepreneur: Otto Carel Holmberg de Beckfelt (1794–1857)." In *Macht en majesteit*, edited by J. Thomas Lindblad and Willem van der Molen, 190–205. Leiden, The Netherlands: Universiteit Leiden, 2002.

[0617] Knight, G. Roger, and Archur van Schaik. "State and Capital in Late Colonial Indonesia: The Sugar Industry, Braakhuur, and the Colonial Bureaucracy in North Central Java." *BKI* 157, no. 4 (2001): 830–59.

[0618] Laffan, Michael F. "'A Watchful Eye': The Meccan Plot of 1881 and Changing Dutch Perceptions of Islam in Indonesia." *Archipel* 63 (2002): 79–108.

[0619] Locher-Scholten, Elsbeth. "Dutch Expansion in the Indonesian Archipelago around 1900 and the Imperialism Debate." *JSEAS* 25, no. 1 (March 1994): 91–111.

[0620] ——. *Ethiek in fragmenten: vijf studies over koloniaal denken en doen van Nederlanders in de Indonesische archipel 1877–1942*. Utrecht, The Netherlands: HES, 1981.

[0621] McVey, Ruth T. *The Rise of Indonesian Communism*. Ithaca, N.Y.: Cornell University Press, 1965.

[0622] Mrázek, Rudolf. *Engineers of Happy Land: Technology and Nationalism in a Colony*. Princeton, N.J.: Princeton University Press, 2002.

[0623] ——. "Sjahrir at Boven Digoel: Reflections on Exile in the Dutch East Indies." In *Making Indonesia*, edited by Daniel S. Lev and Ruth T. McVey, 41–65. [0900]

[0624] Multatuli [Edward Douwes Dekker]. *Max Havelaar: Or the Coffee Auctions of the Dutch Trading Company*. Amherst: University of Massachusetts Press, 1982.

[0625] Nagazumi, Akira. *The Dawn of Indonesian Nationalism: The Early Years of the Budi Utomo, 1908–1918*. Tokyo: Institute of Developing Economies, 1972.

[0626] Niel, Robert van. *The Emergence of the Modern Indonesian Elite*. The Hague: van Hoeve, 1960.

[0627] Noer, Deliar. *The Modernist Muslim Movement in Indonesia 1900–1942*. Kuala Lumpur, Malaysia: OUP, 1973.

[0628] Poeze, Harry, ed. *Politiek-politioneele overzichten van Nederlandsch-Indië*. Deel I 1927–1928; deel II 1929–1930; deel III 1931–1934, deel IV 1935–1941, 1994. The Hague: Martinus Nijhoff, 1982, 1983, 1989.

[0629] Resink, G. J. *Indonesia's History between the Myths: Essays in Legal History and Historical Theory*. The Hague: van Hoeve, 1968.

[0630] Rush, James R. "Social Control and Influence in Nineteenth Century Indonesia: Opium Farms and the Chinese of Java." *Indonesia* 35 (April 1983): 53–64.

[0631] Rutherford, Danilyn. "Fashioning the Ridiculous: Furnivall's *Leviathan* and Dutch Imperialism in New Guinea." In *Southeast Asia over Three Generations: Essays Presented to B. R. O'G. Anderson*, edited by James T. Siegel and Audrey R. Kahin, 27–46. Ithaca, N.Y.: Cornell Southeast Asia Program, 2003.

[0632] Shiraishi, Takashi. *An Age in Motion: Popular Radicalism in Java, 1912–1926*. Ithaca, N.Y.: Cornell University Press, 1990.

[0633] ——. "A New Regime of Order: The Origins of Modern Surveillance Politics in Indonesia." In *Southeast Asia over Three Generations: Essays Presented to B. R. O'G. Anderson,* edited by James T. Siegel and Audrey R. Kahin, 47–74. Ithaca, N.Y.: Cornell Southeast Asia Program, 2003.

[0634] ——. "The Phantom World of Digoel." *Indonesia* 61 (April 1996): 93–118.

[0635] ——. "Policing the Phantom Underground." *Indonesia*. 63 (April 1997): 1–46.

[0636] Sutherland, Heather. *The Making of a Bureaucratic Elite: The Colonial Transformation of the Javanese Priyayi*. Singapore: Heinemann, 1979.

[0637] Tagliacozzo, Eric. "Kettle on a Slow Boil: Batavia's Threat Perceptions in the Indies' Outer Islands." *JSEAS*. 31, no. 1 (April 1996): 70–100.

[0638] Vandenbosch, Amry. *The Dutch East Indies: Its Government, Problems and Politics*, 3rd ed. Berkeley: University of California Press, 1942.

[0639] Veur, Paul W. van der. "Cultural Aspects of the Eurasian Community in Indonesian Colonial Society." *Indonesia* 6 (1968): 38–53.

[0640] Wilson, Greta O. *Regents, Reformers, and Revolutionaries: Indonesian Voices of Colonial Days: Selected Historical Readings 1899–1949*. Honolulu: University of Hawai'i Press, 1978.

[0641] Witlox, Marcel. "Met gewaar voor lijf en goed: Mekkagangers uit Nederlands-Indië in de 19de Eeuw." In *Islamitische Pelgrimstochten*, edited by Willy Jansen and Huub de Jonge. Muiderberg, the Netherlands: Coutinho, 1991.

[0642] Zwitzer, H. L., and C. A. Heshusius. *Het KNIL, 1830–1950: een terugblik*. The Hague: Staatsuitgeverij, 1977.

1942–1949

[0643] Anderson, Benedict R. O'G. *Java in a Time of Revolution: Occupation and Resistance, 1944–1946*. Ithaca, N.Y.: Cornell University. Press, 1972.

[0644] ——. *Some Aspects of Indonesian Politics under the Japanese Occupation, 1944–1945*. Ithaca, N.Y.: Cornell Modern Indonesia Project, 1961.

[0645] Anderson, David Charles. "The Military Aspects of the Madiun Affair." *Indonesia* 21 (April 1976): 1–64.

[0646] Aziz, M. A. *Japan's Colonialism and Indonesia*. The Hague: Nijhoff, 1955.

[0647] Bahar, Saafroedin, and Nannie Hudawati, eds. *Risalah sidang Badan Penyelidik Usaha-usaha Persiapan Kemerdekaan Indonesia (BPUPKI); Panitia Persiapan Kemerdekaan Indonesia (PPKI)*. Jakarta: Sekretariat Negara RI, 1998.

[0648] Benda, Harry J. *The Crescent and the Rising Sun: Indonesian Islam under the Japanese Occupation, 1942–1945*. The Hague: van Hoeve, 1958.

[0649] Benda, Harry J., et al. *Japanese Military Administration in Indonesia: Selected Documents*. New Haven, Conn.: Yale University Press, 1965.

[0650] Coast, John. *Recruit to Revolution: Adventure and Politics in Indonesia*. London: Christophers, 1952.

[0651] Elsbree, Willard H. *Japan's Role in Southeast Asian Nationalist Movements*. Cambridge, Mass.: Harvard University Press, 1953.

[0652] Frederick, William H. *Visions and Heat: The Making of the Indonesian Revolution*. Athens: Ohio University. Press, 1988.

[0653] Friend, Theodore. *The Blue-Eyed Enemy: Japan against the West in Java and Luzon, 1942–1945*. Princeton, N.J.: Princeton University Press, 1988.

[0654] Fusayama, Takao. *A Japanese Memoir of Sumatra, 1945–1946*. Ithaca, N.Y.: Cornell Modern Indonesia Project, 1993.

[0655] Han Bing Siong. "Sukarno-Hatta versus the Pemuda in the First Months after the Surrender of Japan (August–November 1945)." *BKI* 156, no. 2 (2000): 233–73.

[0656] Harvey, Barbara S. "Diplomacy and Armed Struggle in the Indonesian National Revolution: Choice and Constraint in a Comparative Perspective." In *Making Indonesia*, edited by Daniel S. Lev and Ruth T. McVey, 66–80. [0900]

[0657] Hatta, Mohammad. *The Putera Reports: Problems in Indonesian-Japanese War-Time Cooperation*. Ithaca, N.Y.: Cornell Modern Indonesia Project, 1971.

[0658] Heidhues, Mary Somers. "When We Were Young: The Exile of the Republic's Leaders in Bangka, 1949." In *Making Indonesia,* edited by Daniel S. Lev and Ruth T. McVey, 81–95. [0900]

[0659] Jong, L. de. *Het Koninkrijk der Nederlanden in de Tweede Wereld Oorlog*, deel 11: *Nederlands Indië*. The Hague: Staats-uitgeverij, 1984.

[0660] Kahin, Audrey R., ed. *Regional Dynamics of the Indonesian Revolution: Unity from Diversity*. Honolulu: University of Hawai'i Press, 1985.

[0661] Kahin, George McTurnan. *Nationalism and Revolution in Indonesia.* Ithaca, N.Y.: Cornell University Press/Southeast Asia Program, 1952. Reprint, Ithaca, N.Y.: Cornell University Press/Southeast Asia Program, 2003.

[0662] ——. "Sukarno's Proclamation of Indonesian Independence." *Indonesia* 69 (April 2000): 1–3.

[0663] Kanahele, George Sanford. "The Japanese Occupation of Indonesia: Prelude to Independence." Ph.D. diss., Cornell University, 1967.

[0664] Kurasawa-Shiraishi, Aiko. *Lahirnya tentara Pembela Tanah Air (PETA); Monografi*. Jakarta: LEKNAS/LIPI, 1977.

[0665] Lucas, Anton E. *One Soul One Struggle: Region and Revolution in Indonesia*. Sydney: Allen and Unwin, 1991.

[0666] ——. "Social Revolution in Pemalang, Central Java, 1945." *Indonesia* 24 (October 1977): 87–122.

[0667] McCoy, Alfred W. *Southeast Asia under Japanese Occupation*. New Haven, Conn.: Yale University Southeast Asia Studies, 1980.

[0668] Nasution, A. H. *Fundamentals of Guerrilla Warfare*. London: Pall Mall, 1965.

[0669] ——. *Memenuhi panggilan tugas,* Jilid 2: *Kenangan masa gerilya*. Jakarta: Gunung Agung, 1983.

[0670] Nishijima, Shigetada, et al., eds. *Japanese Military Administration in Indonesia*. Washington, D.C.: Joint Publications Research Service, 1963.

[0671] Nortier, J. J. *Acties in de archipel: de intelligence-operaties van NEFIS-III in de Pacific-oorlong*. Franeker, The Netherlands: Wever, 1985.

[0672] Raben, Remco. *Representing the Japanese Occupation of Indonesia: Personal Testimonies and Public Images in Indonesia, Japan, and the Netherlands*. Amsterdam: Netherlands Institute of War Documentation, 2000.

[0673] Reid, Anthony J. S. *The Blood of the People: Revolution and the End of Traditional Rule in Northern Sumatra*. Kuala Lumpur, Malaysia: OUP, 1979.

[0674] ——. *The Indonesian National Revolution 1945–1950*. Hawthorn, Victoria, Australia: Longmans, 1974.

[0675] Reid, Anthony, and Akira Oki, eds. *The Japanese Experience in Indonesia: Selected Memoirs of 1942–1945*. Athens: Ohio University Press, 1986.

[0676] Said, H. Mohammed. "What Was the 'Social Revolution' of 1946 in East Sumatra?" *Indonesia* 15 (April 1973): 145–86.

[0677] Salim, Leon. *Prisoners at Kota Cane*. Ithaca, N.Y.: Cornell Modern Indonesia Project, 1986.

[0678] Sato, Shigeru. *War, Nationalism and Peasants; Java under the Japanese Occupation, 1942–1945*. Sydney: Allen and Unwin, 1994.

[0679] Schiller, Arthur A. *The Formation of Federal Indonesia, 1945–1950*. The Hague: van Hoeve, 1955.

[0680] Shimer, Barbara Gifford, and Guy Hobbs, trans. *The Kenpeitai in Java and Sumatra*. Ithaca, N.Y.: Cornell Modern Indonesia Project, 1986.

[0681] Smail, John R. W. *Bandung in the Early Revolution, 1945–1946: A Study in the Social History of the Indonesian Revolution*. Ithaca, N.Y.: Cornell Modern Indonesia Project, 1964.

[0682] Smit, C. *Het Akkoord van Linggadjati: uit het dagboek van Prof. Dr. Ir W. Schermerhorn*. Amsterdam: Elsevier, 1959.

[0683] Soerjono. "On Musso's Return." *Indonesia* 29 (April 1980): 59–90.

[0684] Swift, Ann. *The Road to Madiun: The Indonesian Communist Uprising of 1948*. Ithaca, N.Y.: Cornell Modern Indonesia Project, 1989.

[0685] Wehl, David. *The Birth of Indonesia.* London: Rowell and Sons, 1948.
[0686] Zed, Mestika. *Somewhere in the Jungle: Pemerintah Darurat Republik Indonesia: sebuah mata rantai sejarah yang terlupakan*. Jakarta: Grafiti, 1997.

1950–1966

[0689] Anderson, Ben. "How Did the Generals Die?" *Indonesia* 43 (April 1987): 109–34.
[0690] Anderson, Benedict R., and Ruth T. McVey. *A Preliminary Analysis of the October 1, 1965, Coup in Indonesia*. Ithaca, N.Y.: Cornell Modern Indonesia Project, 1971.
[0691] Cribb, Robert, ed. *The Indonesian Killings of 1965–1966: Studies from Java and Bali*. Clayton, Victoria, Australia: Monash University Centre of Southeast Asian Studies, 1990.
[0692] Crouch, Harold. "Another Look at the Indonesian Coup." *Indonesia* 15 (April 1973): 1–20.
[0693] Dijk, C. van. *Rebellion under the Banner of Islam: The Darul Islam in Indonesia*. The Hague: Martinus Nijhoff, 1981.
[0694] Federspiel, Howard M. "The Military and Islam in Sukarno's Indonesia." *Pacific Affairs* 46, no. 3 (1973): 407–20.
[0695] Feith, Herbert. *The Decline of Constitutional Democracy in Indonesia*. Ithaca, N.Y.: Cornell University Press, 1970.
[0696] ——. "The Dynamics of Guided Democracy." In *Indonesia,* ed. Ruth T. McVey. [0482]
[0697] Ghoshal, Baladas. *Indonesian Politics, 1955–1959: The Emergence of Guided Democracy*. Calcutta: K. P. Bagchi, 1982.
[0698] Hanna, Willard A. *Bung Karno's Indonesia*. New York: AUFS, 1960.
[0699] Harvey, Barbara S. *Permesta: Half a Rebellion*. Ithaca, N.Y.: Cornell Modern Indonesia Project, 1977.
[0700] Hindley, Donald. "Alirans and the Fall of the Old Order." *Indonesia* 9 (April 1970): 23–66.
[0701] Hong Liu. "Constructing a China Metaphor: Sukarno's Perception of the PRC and Indonesia's Political Transformation." *JSEAS*. 28, no. 1 (March 1997): 27–46.
[0702] Hughes, John. *Indonesian upheaval*. New York: Fawcett, 1967.
[0703] Jay, Robert R. *Religon and Politics in Rural Central Java*. New Haven, Conn.: Yale University Southeast Asian Studies, 1963.
[0704] Kahin, George McT. "Indonesia." In *Major Governments of Asia*, 2nd ed., edited by George McT. Kahin. Ithaca, N.Y.: Cornell University. Press, 1963.
[0705] Legge, J. D. *Central Authority and Regional Autonomy in Indonesia: A Study in Local Administration 1950–1960*. Ithaca, N.Y.: Cornell University Press, 1961.
[0706] Lev, Daniel S. *The Transition to Guided Democracy: Indonesian Politics, 1957–1959*. Ithaca, N.Y.: Cornell Modern Indonesia Project, 1966.

[0707] McGregor, Katharine E. "Representing the Indonesian Past: The National Monument History Museum from Guided Democracy to the New Order." *Indonesia* 75 (April 2003): 91–122.

[0708] Mossman, James. *Rebels in Paradise*. London: Jonathan Cape, 1961.

[0709] Nasution, A. H. *Memenuhi panggilan tugas*, Jilid 3: *Masa pancaroba pertama*; Jilid 4: *Masa pancaroba kedua*. Jakarta: Gunung Agung, 1983, 1984.

[0710] Pelzer, Karl J. *Planters against Peasants: The Agrarian Struggle in East Sumatra, 1947–1958*. Leiden, The Netherlands: KITLV, 1982.

[0711] Robinson, Geoffrey. "The Post-Coup Massacre in Bali." In *Making Indonesia,* edited by Daniel S. Lev and Ruth T. McVey, 118–43. [0900]

[0712] Subandrio. *Kesaksianku tentang G-30-S.* Jakarta: n.p., 2000.

[0713] Sulistyo, Hermawan. *Palu arit di ladang tebu. Sejarah pembantaian massal yeng terlupakan (1965–1966).* Jakarta: Gramedia, 2000.

[0714] Sundhaussen, Ulf. *The Road to Power: Indonesian Military Politics 1945–1967*. Kuala Lumpur, Malaysia: OUP, 1982.

[0715] Wertheim, W. F. "Suharto and the Untung Coup: The Missing Link." *Journal of Contempoary Asia* 1, no. 2 (1970): 50–57.

Suharto Era (1967–1998)

[0716] Anderson, Benedict. "Old State, New Society: Indonesia's New Order in Comparative Historical Perspective." *JAS* 42, no. 3 (1983): 477–98.

[0717] ——, ed. *Violence and the State in Suharto's Indonesia.* Ithaca, N.Y.: Cornell Southeast Asia Program, 2001.

[0718] Arndt, H. W. "Indonesia—Five Years of 'New Order.'" *Current Affairs Bulletin* 47, no. 5 (1971): 67–78.

[0719] Aspinall, Edward, Herb Feith, and Gerry van Klinken. *The Last Days of President Suharto*. Clayton, Victoria, Australia: Monash University, 1999.

[0720] Berger, Mark T. "Old State and New Empire in Indonesia: Debating the Rise and Decline of Suharto's New Order." *Third World Quarterly* 18, no. 2 (1997): 321–61.

[0721] Bourchier, David. "Crime, Law and State Authority in Indonesia." In *State and Civil Society in Indonesia,* edited by Arief Budinman, 177–212. [0894]

[0722] ——. *Dynamics of Dissent in Indonesia: Sawito and the Phantom Coup*. Ithaca, N.Y.: Cornell Modern Indonesia Project, 1984.

[0723] Bourchier, David, and Vedi R. Hadiz, eds. *Indonesian Politics and Society: A Reader*. London: Routledge Curzon, 2003.

[0724] Bresnan, John. *Managing Indonesia: The Modern Political Economy*. New York: Columbia University Press, 1993.

[0725] Brooks, Karen. "The Rustle of Ghosts: Bung Karno in the New Order." *Indonesia* 60 (October 1995): 61–99.

[0726] Challis, Roland. *Shadow of a Revolution: Indonesia and the Generals*. Sparkford, UK: Sutton Publishing, 2001.

[0727] Crouch, Harold. *The Army and Politics in Indonesia*. Ithaca, N.Y.: Cornell University Press, 1978.

[0728] Emmerson, Donald K. "Invisible Indonesia." *Foreign Affairs* 66 (winter 1987–1988): 368–87.

[0729] Feith, Herbert. "Suharto's Search for a Political Format." *Indonesia* 6 (October 1968): 88–103.

[0730] Hill, Hal, ed. *Indonesia's New Order: The Dynamics of Socio-Economic Transformation*. Honolulu: University of Hawai'i Press, 1994.

[0731] Honna, Jun. "Military Ideology in Response to Democratic Pressure during the Late Suharto Era: Political and Institutional Contexts." *Indonesia* 67 (April 1999): 77–126.

[0732] Hooker, Virginia. *Culture and Society in New Order Indonesia*. Kuala Lumpur, Malaysia: OUP, 1995.

[0733] Jenkins, David. *Suharto and His Generals: Indonesian Military Politics 1975–1983*. Ithaca, N.Y.: Cornell Modern Indonesia Project, 1984.

[0734] Kroef, Justus M. van der. "'Petrus' Patterns of Prophylactic Murder in Indonesia." *Asian Survey* 25, no. 7 (1985): 745–59.

[0735] Liddle, R. William. "Suharto's Indonesia: Personal Rule and Political Institutions." *Pacific Affairs* 58, no. 1 (1985): 68–90.

[0736] McDonald, Hamish. *Suharto's Indonesia*. Melbourne: Fontana, 1980.

[0737] McLeod, Ross. "Soeharto's Indonesia: A Better Class of Corruption." *Agenda* 7, no. 2 (2000): 99–112.

[0738] Mortimer, Rex, ed. *Showcase State: The Illusion of Indonesia's "Accelerated Modernisation."* Sydney: Angus and Robertson, 1973.

[0739] Oey Hong Lee, ed. *Indonesia after the 1971 Elections*. London: OUP, 1974.

[0740] Pabottingi, Mochtar. "Indonesia: Historicizing the New Order's Legitimacy Dilemma." In *Political Legitimacy in Southeast Asia: The Quest for Moral Authority*, edited by Muthiah Alagappa, 224–56. Stanford, Calif.: Stanford University Press, 1995.

[0741] Polomka, Peter. *Indonesia since Sukarno*. Harmondsworth, UK: Penguin, 1971.

[0742] Raillon, François. *Les étudients indonésiens et l'Orde Nouveau: politique et idéologie du Mahasiswa Indonesia (1966–1974)*. Paris: Editions de la Maison des sciences de l'Homme, 1984.

[0743] Ryter, Loren. "Pemuda Pancasila: The Last Loyalist Free Men of Suharto's Order?" *Indonesia* 66 (October 1998): 45–73.

[0744] Saltford, John. "United Nations Involvement with the Act of Self-Determination in West Irian (Indonesian West New Guinea), 1968–1969." *Indonesia* 69 (April 2000): 71–92.

[0745] Sato, Yuri. "The Development of Business Groups in Indonesia: 1967–1989." In *Approaching Suharto's Indonesia from the Margins*, edited by Takashi Shiraishi, 101–53. [0749]

[0746] Schiller, Jim, and Barbara Martin-Schiller, eds. *Imagining Indonesia: Cultural Politics and Political Culture*. Athens: Ohio University Center for International Studies, 1997.

[0747] Schulte Nordholt, N. G. *State-Citizen Relations in Suharto's Indonesia: Kawula-Gusti*. Rotterdam, The Netherlands: Erasmus University, Comparative Asian Studies Programme, 1987.

[0748] Schwarz, Adam. *A Nation in Waiting*. Boulder, Colo.: Westview, 1994.

[0749] Shiraishi, Takashi. *Approaching Suharto's Indonesia from the Margins*. Ithaca, N.Y.: Cornell Southeast Asia Program, 1994.

[0750] Thee Kian Wie. "Reflections on the New Order 'Miracle.'" In *Indonesia Today: Challenges of History*, edited by Grayson Lloyd and Shannon Smith, 163–80. Singapore: ISEAS, 2001. [0763]

[0751] Vatikiotis, Michael R. J. *Indonesian Politics under Suharto: Order, Development and Pressure for Change*. London: Routledge, 1993.

[0752] Watson, C. W. *State and Society in Indonesia: Three Papers*. Canterbury, UK: University of Kent, Centre of South-East Asian Studies, 1987.

Post-Suharto (1998–2003)

[0753] Alisjahbana, Armida A., and Chris Manning. "Survey of Recent Developments." *BIES*. 38, no. 3 (2002): 277–305.

[0754] Amnesty International. *Indonesia: Impunity and Human Rights Violations in Papua*. London: Amnesty International, April 2002.

[0755] ——. *Indonesia: Impunity Persists in Papua as Militia Groups Take Root.* London: Amnesty International, September 2000.

[0756] Baker, Richard W., M. Hadi Soesastro, J. Kristiadi, and Douglas E. Ramage, eds. *Indonesia: The Challenge of Change*. Leiden, the Netherlands: KITLV, 1999.

[0757] Bambunan, Tulus, and Budi Santosa, eds. *Indonesia: The Challenge of Change*. Jakarta: Universitas Trisakti, [1998].

[0758] Budiman, Arief, et al., eds. *Reformasi: Crisis and Change in Indonesia*. Clayton, Victoria, Australia: Monash Asia Institute, 1999.

[0759] Dick, Howard. "Survey of Recent Developments." *BIES* 37, no. 1 (2001): 7–41.

[0760] Dijk, Kees van. *A Country in Despair: Indonesia between 1997 and 2000*. Leiden, The Netherlands: KITLV, 2001.

[0761] Emmerson, Donald K., ed. *Indonesia beyond Suharto: Polity, Economy, Society, Transition*. Armonk, N.Y.: M. E. Sharpe, 1999.

[0762] Feillard, Andrée. "Indonesian Traditionalist Islam's Troubled Experience with Democracy (1999–2001)." *Archipel* 64 (2002): 117–44.

[0763] Lloyd, Grayson, and Shannon Smith, eds. *Indonesia Today: Challenges of History*. Singapore: ISEAS, 2001.

[0764] Malley, Michael S. "Indonesia in 2001: Restoring Stability in Jakarta." *Asian Survey* 42, no. 1 (2002): 124–32.

[0765] Manning, Chris, and Peter van Diermen. *Indonesia in Transition: Social Aspects of Reformasi and Crisis*. London: Zed Books, 2000.

[0766] Peluso, Nancy Lee, and Michael Watts. *Violent Environments*. Ithaca, N.Y.: Cornell University Press, 2001.

[0767] Raillon, François. "De la reformasi à la restauration? Quand le passé sert à relire le présent." *Archipel* 64 (2002): 59–80.

[0768] ——. "Indonésie 2000: le statusquo." *Archipel* 61 (2001): 155–78.

[0769] Schwarz, Adam, and Jonathan Paris, eds. *The Politics of Post-Suharto Indonesia*. New York: Council on Foreign Relations, 1999.

[0770] Selo Soemardjan, ed. *Kisah perjuangan reformasi*. Jakarta: Sinar Harapan, 1999.

[0771] Smith, Anthony L., ed. *Gus Dur and the Indonesian Economy*. Singapore: ISEAS, 2001.

[0772] Strassler, Karen. "Currency and Fingerprints: Authentic Reproductions and Political Communication in Indonesia's 'Reform Era.'" *Indonesia* 70 (October 2000): 71–82.

[0773] Wessel, Ingrid, and Gerogia Wimhoefer, eds. *Violence in Indonesia*. Hamburg, Germany: Abera, 2001.

Regional

[0774] Andaya, Barbara Watson. "From Rum to Tokyo: The Search for Anticolonial Allies by the Rulers of Riau, 1899–1914." *Indonesia* 24 (October 1977): 123–56.

[0775] ——. "Upstreams and Downstreams in Early Modern Sumatra." *Historian* 57 (1995): 537–52.

[0776] Andaya, Leonard Y. "Unravelling Minangkabau Ethnicity." *Itinerario* 24, no. 1 (2000): 20–43.

[0777] Aspinall, Edward. "Sovereignty, the Successor State, and Universal Human Rights: History and the International Structuring of Acehenese Nationalism." *Indonesia* 72 (April 2002): 1–24.

[0778] Barnard, Timothy P. "Texts, Raja Ismail and Violence: Siak and the Transformation of Malay Identity in the Eighteenth Century." *JSEAS* 32, no. 3 (2001): 331–42.

[0779] Barnes, R. H. "Alliance and Warfare in an Eastern Indonesian Principality: Kédang in the Last Half of the Nineteenth Century." *BKI* 157, no. 2 (2001): 271–311.

[0780] Bastin, John. *The British in West Sumatra (1685–1825)*. Kuala Lumpur, Malaysia: University of Malaya Press, 1965.

[0781] Bertrand, Jacques. "Legacies of the Authoritiarian Past: Religious Violence in Indonesia's Moluccan Islands." *Pacific Affairs* 75, no. 1 (spring 2002): 57–85.

[0782] Bouman, J. C., et al. *The South Moluccas: Rebellious Province or Occupied State*. Leiden, The Netherlands: Sijthoff 1960.

[0783] Bowen, John R. *Sumatran Politics and Poetics: Gayo History, 1900–1989*. New Haven, Conn.: Yale University Press, 1991.

[0784] Chauvel, Richard. *Nationalists, Soldiers and Separatists: The Ambonese Islands from Colonialism to Revolt*. Leiden, The Netherlands: KITLV, 1990.

[0785] Chou, Cynthia, and Will Derks. *Riau in Transition*. *BKI*, special issue, 153, no. 4 (1997).

[0786] Cummings, William. "The Dynamics of Resistance and Emulation in Makassarese History." *JSEAS* 32, no. 3 (2001): 423–35.

[0787] ——. *Making Blood White: Historical Transformations in Early Modern Makassar*. Honolulu: University of Hawai'i Press, 2002.

[0788] Davidson, Jamie S., and Douglas Kammen. "Indonesia's Unknown War and the Lineages of Violence in West Kalimantan." *Indonesia* 73 (April 2002): 53–87.

[0789] Dick, H. W. *Surabaya, City of Work: A Socioeconomic History, 1900–2000*. Athens: Ohio University Press, 2002.

[0790] Dobbin, Christine. "Islamic Fervour as a Manifestation of Regional Personality in Colonial Indonesia: The Kamang Area, West Sumatra, 1803–1908." *Archipel* 56 (1998): 295–308.

[0791] ——. *Islamic Revivalism in a Changing Economy: Central Sumatra, 1764–1847*. London: Curzon, 1983.

[0792] Drakard, Jane. *A Kingdom of Words: Language and Power in Sumatra*. Selangor Darul Ehsan, Malaysia: OUP, 1999.

[0793] ——. *A Malay Frontier: Unity and Duality in a Sumatran Kingdom*. Ithaca, N.Y.: Cornell Studies on Southeast Asia, 1990.

[0794] Ebing, Ewald, and Youetta de Jager, eds. *Leadership and Social Mobility in a Southeast Asian Society: Minahassa, 1677–1983*. Leiden, The Netherlands: KITLV Press, 1998.

[0795] Eghenter, Christina. "Towards a Causal History of a Trade Scenario in the Interior of East Kalimantan, Indonesia, 1900–1999." *BKI* 157, no. 4 (2001): 739–69.

[0796] Geertz, Clifford. *Negara: The Theatre State in Nineteenth Century Bali*. Princeton, N.J.: Princeton University Press, 1980.

[0797] Graves, Elizabeth E. *The Minangkabau Response to Dutch Colonial Rule in the Nineteenth Century*. Ithaca, N.Y.: Cornell Modern Indonesia Project, 1981.

[0798] Hadler, Jeffrey Alan. "Places Like Home: Islam, Matriliny, and the History of Family in Minangkabau." Ph.D. diss., Cornell University, 2000.

[0799] Hainsworth, Paul, and Stephen McCloskey. *The East Timor Question: The Struggle for Independence from Indonesia*. New York: St. Martin's Press, 2000.

[0800] Hefner, Robert W. *The Political Economy of Mountain Java: An Interpretive History*. Berkeley: University of California Press, 1990.

[0801] Heidhues, Mary Somers. *Bangka Tin and Mentok Pepper: Chinese Settlement on an Indonesian Island.* Singapore: ISEAS, 1991.

[0802] Henley, David E. F. *Nationalism and Regionalism in a Colonial Context: Minahasa in the Dutch East Indies*. Leiden, The Netherlands: KITLV, 1996.

[0803] *Het drama van de Asmat-Papuas*. Leiden, The Netherlands: INDOC, 1982.

[0804] Hirosue, Masashi. "The Batak Millenarian Response to the Colonial Order." *JSEAS* 25, no. 2 (September 1994): 331–43.

[0805] Irwin, Graham. *Nineteenth Century Borneo: A Study in Diplomatic Rivalry*. Singapore: Donald Moore, 1967.

[0806] Joliffe, Jill. *East Timor: Nationalism and Colonialism*. St. Lucia, Queensland, Australia: University of Queensland Press, 1978.

[0807] Kahin, Audrey. *Rebellion to Integration: West Sumatra and the Indonesian Polity*. Amsterdam: Amsterdam University Press, 1999.

[0808] Kell, Tim. *The Roots of Acehnese Rebellion 1989–1992*. Ithaca, N.Y.: Cornell Modern Indonesia Project, 1995.

[0809] King, Peter. "Morning Star Rising? Indonesia Raya and the New Papua Nationalism." *Indonesia* 73 (April 2002): 89–127.

[0810] Kraan, Alfons van der. *Lombok: Conquest, Colonization and Underdevelopment, 1870–1940*. Singapore: Heinemann, 1980.

[0811] Lindblad, J. Thomas. *Between Dayak and Dutch: The Economic History of Southeast Kalimantan, 1880–1942*. Dordrecht, The Netherlands: Foris, 1988.

[0812] Magenda, Burhan. *East Kalimantan: The Decline of a Commercial Aristocracy*. Ithaca, N.Y.: Cornell Modern Indonesia Project, 1991.

[0813] May, R. J., ed. *Between Two Nations: The Indonesia-Papua New Guinea Border and West Papua Nationalism*. Bathurst, New South Wales, Australia: Robert Brown, 1986.

[0814] Moore, Samuel. "The Indonesian Military's Last Years in East Timor: An Analysis of Its Secret Documents." *Indonesia* 72 (October 2001): 9–44.

[0815] Mote, Octovianus, and Danilyn Rutherford. "From Irian Jaya to Papua: The Limits of Primordialism in Indonesia's Troubled East." *Indonesia* 72 (October 2001): 115–40.

[0816] Osborne, Robin. *Indonesia's Secret War: The Guerrilla Struggle in Irian Jaya*. Sydney: Allen and Unwin, 1985.

[0817] Pelzer, Karl J. *Planter and Peasant: Colonial Policy and the Agrarian Struggle in East Sumatra, 1863–1947*. Leiden, The Netherlands: KITLV, 1978.

[0818] Reid, Anthony J. S. *The Contest for North Sumatra: Atjeh, the Netherlands and Britain, 1858–1898*. Kuala Lumpur, Malaysia: OUP, 1969.

[0819] Robinson, Geoffrey. *The Dark Side of Paradise: Political Violence in Bali*. Ithaca, N.Y.: Cornell University Press, 1995.

[0820] ——. "Rawan Is as Rawan Does: The Origins of Disorder in New Order Aceh." *Indonesia* 66 (October 1998): 127–58.

[0821] Rutherford, Danilyn. "Waiting for the End in Biak: Violence, Order, and a Flag Raising." *Indonesia* 67 (April 1999): 39–59.

[0822] Sartono Kartodirdjo. *The Peasants' Revolt of Banten in 1888, Its Conditions, Course and Sequel: A Case Study of Social Movements in Indonesia*. The Hague: Martinus Nijhoff, 1966.

[0823] Schouten, M. J. C. *Leadership and Mobility in a Southeast Asian Society: Minahasa, 1677–1983*. Leiden, The Netherlands: KITLV, 1998.

[0824] Schulte Nordholt, Henk. *Bali: Colonial Conceptions and Political Changes 1700–1940: From Shifting Hierarchies to "Fixed Order."* Rotterdam, The Netherlands: Erasmus University, Comparative Asian Studies Programme, 1986.

[0825] ——. "The Mads Lange Connection: A Danish Trader on Bali in the Middle of the Nineteenth Century: Broker and Buffer." *Indonesia* 32 (October 1981): 16–47.

[0826] ——. *The Spell of Power: A History of Balinese Politics 1650–1940*. Leiden, The Netherlands: KITLV, 1996.

[0827] Sjamsuddin, Nazaruddin. *The Republican Revolt: A Study of the Acehnese Rebellion*. Singapore: ISEAS, 1985.

[0828] Smail, John R. W. "The Military Politics of North Sumatra: December 1956–October 1957." *Indonesia* 6 (October 1968): 128–87.

[0829] Spyer, Patricia. *The Memory of Trade: Modernity's Entanglements on an Eastern Indonesian Island*. Durham, N.C.: Duke University Press, 2000.

[0830] Stoler, Ann Laura. *Capitalism and Confrontation in Sumatra's Plantation Belt 1870–1979*. New Haven, Conn.: Yale University Press, 1985.

[0831] Sutherland, Heather. "Power and Politics in South Sulawesi, 1860–1880." *RIMA* 17, nos. 1–2 (1983): 161–207.

[0832] Vickers, Adrian. *Bali: A Paradise Created*. Ringwood, Victoria, Australia: Penguin, 1989.

[0833] Warren, James F. *The Sulu Zone 1768–1898: The Dynamics of External Trade, Slavery and Ethnicity in the Transformation of a Southeast Asian Maritime State*. Singapore: Singapore University Press, 1981.

[0834] Watson, C. W. *Kerinci: Two Historical Studies*. Canterbury, UK: University of Kent, 1984.

[0835] Webb, R. A. F. Paul. *Palms and the Cross: Socio-Economic Development in Nusatenggara, 1930–1975*. Townsville, Queensland, Australia: James Cook University, 1986.

[0836] Williams, Michael C. *Sickle and Crescent: The Communist Revolt of 1926 in Banten*. Ithaca, N.Y.: Cornell Modern Indonesia Project, 1982.

[0837] Woelders, M. O. *Het Sultanaat Palembang, 1811–1825*. The Hague: Nijhoff, 1975.

[0838] Young, Ken. *Islamic Peasants and the State: The 1908 Anti-Tax Rebellion in West Sumatra*. New Haven, Conn.: Yale Southeast Asia Studies Monograph Series no. 40, 1994.

[0839] Zed, Mestika. *Kepialangan, politik dan revolusi: Palembang 1900–1950*. Jakarta: LP3S, 2003.

[0840] Znoj, Heinzpeter. "Sons versus Nephews: A Highland Jambi Alliance at War with the British East India Company, ca. 1800." *Indonesia* 65 (April 1998): 97–121.

Biography and Autobiography

[0841] Ali Sastroamijoyo. *Milestones on My Journey*. St. Lucia, Queensland, Australia: University of Queensland Press, 1979.

[0842] Bachtiar, Harsja. "Raden Saleh: Aristocrat, Painter and Scientist." *Majalah Ilmu-ilmu Sastra Indonesia* 6, no. 3 (1976): 31–79.

[0843] Collis, Maurice. *Raffles*. London: Faber, 1966.

[0844] Dahm, Bernhard. *Sukarno and the Struggle for Indonesian Independence*. Ithaca, N.Y.: Cornell University Press, 1969.

[0845] Elson, R. E. *Suharto: A Political Biography*. Cambridge: Cambridge University Press, 2001.

[0846] Goto, Kenichi. "The Life and Death of Abdul Rachman (1906–1949): One Aspect of Japanese Indonesian relationships." *Indonesia* 22 (October 1976): 57–70.

[0847] Hadler, Jeffrey. "Home, Fatherhood, Succession: Three Generations of Amrullahs in Twentieth-Century Indonesia." *Indonesia* 65 (April 1998): 122–54.

[0848] Hamka. *Ajahku: riwajat hidup Dr. H. Abd. Karim Amrullah dan perdjuangan kaum agama di Sumatera*, 3rd printing. Jakarta: Djajamurni, 1967.

[0849] Hatta, Mohammad. *Memoirs*. Singapore: Gunung Agung, 1981.

[0850] Hauswedell, Peter Christian. "Sukarno: Radical or Conservative?" *Indonesia* 15 (April 1973): 109–44.

[0851] Hering, Bob. *Soekarno; architect van een natie; 1901–1970* (Sukarno: Architect of a Nation: 1901–1970). Leiden, The Netherlands: KITLV, 2001.

[0852] ——. *Soekarno: Founding Father of Indonesia 1901–1945*. Leiden, the Netherlands: KITLV, 2002.

[0853] Jarvis, Helen, trans. and ed. *From Jail to Jail: Tan Malaka*, 3 vols. Athens: Ohio University Center for International Studies, 1991.

[0854] Kleden, Ignas. "The Changing Political Leadership of Java: The Significance of Sultan Hamengku Buwono IX." In *State and Civil Society in Indonesia*, edited by Arief Budiman, 349–63. [0894]

[0855] Kohen, Arnold S. *From the Place of the Dead: The Epic Struggles of Bishop Belo of East Timor*. New York: St. Martin's Press, 1999.

[0856] Kumar, Ann. *The Diary of a Javanese Muslim: Religion, Politics and the Pesantren, 1883–1886*. Canberra: Australian National University, 1985.

[0857] Latief, Kol. Abdul. *Pleidoi Kol. A. Latief terlibat G30S*. Jakarta: Institut Studi Arus Informasi, 2000.

[0858] Leclerc, Jacques. "Underground Nationalist Activities and Their Double (Amir Syarifuddin's Relationship with Indonesian Communism)." *Kabar Seberang* 17 (June 1986): 72–98.

[0859] Legge, J. D. *Sukarno: A Political Biography*, rev. ed. Harmondsworth, UK: Penguin, 2003.

[0860] Lev, Daniel S. "In Memoriam: Yap Thiam Hien (1913–1989)." *Indonesia* 48 (October 1989): 107–10.

[0861] Luxfiati, Siti Zainab. *Bung Tomo: Vokalis DPR 1956–1959 (sebuah dokumen sejarah)*. Jakarta: Yayasan Bung Tomo, [1998].

[0862] Malik, Adam. *In the Service of the Republic*. Singapore: Gunung Agung, 1980.

[0863] Moussay, Gérard. "Une grande figure de l'Islam indonésien: Buya Hamka." *Archipel* 32 (1986): 87–111.

[0864] Mrázek, Rudolf. "Bridges of Hope: Senior Citizens' Memories." *Indonesia* 70 (October 2000): 37–51.

[0865] ——. *Sjahrir: Politics and Exile in Indonesia*. Ithaca, N.Y.: Cornell Southeast Asia Program, 1994.

[0866] ——. "Tan Malaka: A Political Personality's Structure of Experience." *Indonesia* 14 (October 1972): 1–48.

[0867] Muchtar, Rusdi, Afadlal, Sumarno, and Dwi Purwoko. *Megawati Soekarnoputri: Presiden Republik Indonesia.* Jakarta: PT Rumpun Dian Nugraha, 2002.

[0868] Noer, Deliar. *Aku bagian ummat, aku bagian bangsa*. Bandung, Indonesia: Penerbit Mizan, 1996.

[0869] ——. *Mohammad Hatta: biografi politik*. Jakarta: LP3ES, 1990.

[0870] Nur El Ibrahimy, M. Tgk. M. *Daud Beureueh: peranannya dalam pergolakan di Aceh*. Jakarta: Gunung Agung, 1982.

[0871] Oshikawa, Noriaki. "Patjar Merah Indonesia and Tan Malaka: A Popular Novel and a Revolutionary Legend." In *Reading Southeast Asia*, edited by Takashi Shiraishi, 9–39. Ithaca, N.Y.: Cornell Southeast Asia Program, 1990.

[0872] Penders, C. L. M., and Ulf Sundhaussen. *Abdul Haris Nasution: A Political Biography*. St. Lucia, Queensland, Australia: University of Queensland Press, 1985.

[0873] Poeze, Harry. *Tan Malaka, strijder voor Indonesië's vrijheid: levensloop van 1897 tot 1945*. Leiden, The Netherlands: KITLV, 1976.

[0874] Pramoedya Ananta Toer and Stanley Adi Prasetyo, eds. *Memoar Oei Tjoe Tat: pembantu Presiden Soekarno*. Jakarta: Hasta Mitra, 1995.

[0875] Rose, Mavis. *Indonesia Free: A Political Biography of Mohammad Hatta*. Ithaca, N.Y.: Cornell Modern Indonesia Project, 1987.

[0876] Rutherford, Danilyn. "Unpacking a National Heroine: Two Kartinis and Their People." *Indonesia* 55 (April 1993): 23–40.

[0877] Simatupang, T. B. *Report from Banaran: Experiences during the People's War*. Ithaca, N.Y.: Cornell Modern Indonesia Project, 1972.

[0878] Soeharto, as told to G. Dwipayana and Ramadhan K. H. *Soeharto: My Thoughts, Words and Deeds: An Autobiography*. Jakarta: Citra Lamtoro Gung Persada, 1989.

[0879] Soewito, Dra. Irna H. N. Hadi, et al. *Chairul Saleh, tokoh kontroversial*. Jakarta: Mutiara Rachmat, 1993.

[0880] Sudarnoto. "A Biography of Ki Bagus Hadikusumo: Early Youth and Education." *Mizan* 2, no. 1 (1985): 78–94.

[0881] Sukarno. *Autobiography, as Told to Cindy Adams*. Indianapolis, Ind.: Bobbs-Merrill, 1965.

[0882] Sumarno. *Megawati Soekarnoputri: dari ibu rumah tangga sampai istana negara.* Jakarta: PT Rumpun Dian Nugraha, 2002.

[0883] Supardi, Imam. *Dr. Soetomo—riwajat hidup dan perdjuangnja*. Jakarta: Djambatan, 1951.

[0884] Swasono, Meutia Farida, ed. *Bung Hatta: Pribadinya dalam Kenangan*. Jakarta: Sinar Harapan, 1980.

[0885] Taylor, Jean Stewart. "Raden Ajeng Kartini." *Signs* 1, no. 3 (1976): 639–61.
[0886] Tjokropranolo. *Panglima besar TNI: Jenderal Soedirman: pemimpin pendobrak terakhir penjajahan di Indonesia*. Jakarta: Surya Persindo, 1992.
[0887] Veur, Paul W. van der. "E. F. E. Douwes Dekker: Evangelist for Indonesian Political Nationalism." *JAS* 17 (1958): 551–66.
[0888] ——, ed. *Towards a Glorious Indonesia: Reminiscences and Observations of Dr. Soetomo*. Athens: Ohio University: Center for International Studies, 1987.
[0889] Yani, Amelia. *Profil seorang prajurit TNI*. Jakarta: Sinar Harapan, 1988.

POLITICS

General

[0890] Alisjahbana, S. Takdir. *Indonesia: Cultural and Social Revolution*. Kuala Lumpur, Malaysia: OUP, 1966.
[0891] Anderson, Benedict. "The Languages of Indonesian Politics." *Indonesia* 1 (April 1966): 89–116.
[0892] ——. *The Spectre of Comparisons: Nationalism, Southeast Asia and the World*. London: Verso, 1998.
[0893] Anderson, Benedict, and Audrey Kahin, eds. *Interpreting Indonesian Politics: Thirteen Contributions to the Debate, 1964–1981*. Ithaca, N.Y.: Cornell Modern Indonesia Project, 1982.
[0894] Budiman, Arief, ed. *State and Civil Society in Indonesia*. Clayton, Victoria, Australia: Centre of Southeast Asian Studies, Monash University, 1990.
[0895] Dick, Howard. "The Rise of a Middle Class and the Changing Concept of Equity in Indonesia: An Interpretation." *Indonesia* 39 (April 1985): 71–92.
[0896] Emmerson, Donald K. *Indonesia's Elite: Political Culture and Cultural Politics*. Ithaca, N.Y.: Cornell University Press, 1976.
[0897] Holt, Claire, et al., eds. *Culture and Politics in Indonesia*. Ithaca, N.Y.: Cornell University Press, 1972.
[0898] Jackson, Karl D., and Lucian W. Pye, eds. *Political Power and Communications in Indonesia*. Berkeley: University of California Press, 1978.
[0899] Lev, Daniel S. "Intermediate Classes and Change in Indonesia: Some Initial Reflections." In *The Politics of Middle Class Indonesia*, edited by Richard Tanter and Kenneth Young. [0905]
[0900] Lev, Daniel S., and Ruth T, McVey, eds. *Making Indonesia: Essays on Modern Indonesia in Honor of George McT. Kahin*. Ithaca, N.Y.: Cornell Studies on Southeast Asia, 1996.
[0901] Liddle, R. William. *Ethnicity, Party and National Integration: An Indonesian Case Study*. New Haven, Conn.: Yale University Southeast Asian Studies, 1970.
[0902] ——. *Leadership and Culture in Indonesian Politics*. Sydney: Allen and Unwin, 1996.

[0903] ——, ed. *Political Participation in Modern Indonesia.* New Haven, Conn.: Yale University Southeast Asian Studies, 1973.

[0904] Mortimer, Rex. "Class, Social Cleavage and Indonesian Communism." *Indonesia* 8 (October 1969): 1–20.

[0905] Tanter, Richard, and Kenneth Young, eds. *The Politics of Middle Class Indonesia.* Clayton, Victoria, Australia: Monash University Centre of Southeast Asian Studies, 1990.

[0906] Willner, Ann Ruth. *The Neotraditional Accommodation to Political Independence: The Case of Indonesia*. Princeton, N.J.: Princeton University Center of International Studies, 1966.

Political Thought

[0907] Anderson, Benedict. *Imagined Communities: Reflections on the Origins and Spread of Nationalism*. London: Verso, 1983.

[0908] ——. "Indonesian Nationalism Today and in the Future." *Indonesia* 67 (April 1999): 1–11.

[0909] ——. *Language and Power: Exploring Political Cultures in Indonesia*. Ithaca, N.Y.: Cornell University Press, 1990.

[0910] Bonneff. Marcel. "La crise indonésienne et l'imaginaire politique javanais." *Archipel* 64 (2002): 3–37.

[0911] Bourchier, David. "Conservative Political Ideology in Indonesia: A Fourth Wave?" In *Indonesia Today*, edited by Grayson Lloyd and Shannon Smith, 112–25. [0763]

[0912] Cribb, Robert. "The Indonesian Marxist Tradition." In *Marxism in Asia,* edited by Colin Mackerras and Nick Knight. London: Croom Helm, 1985.

[0913] Feith, Herbert, and Lance Castles, eds. *Indonesian Political Thinking 1945–1965*. Ithaca, N.Y.: Cornell University Press, 1970.

[0914] Heryanto, Ariel. "The Development of 'development.'" *Indonesia* 46 (October 1988): 1–24.

[0915] Legge, J. D. "Daulat Ra'jat and the Ideas of the Pendidikan Nasional Indonesia." *Indonesia* 31 (April 1981): 151–69.

[0916] ——. *Intellectuals and Nationalism in Indonesia: A Study of the Following Recruited by Sutan Sjahrir in Occupation Java*. Ithaca, N.Y.: Cornell Modern Indonesia Project, 1988.

[0917] McVey, Ruth T. "The Wayang Controversy in Indonesian communism." In *Context, Meaning and Power in Southeast Asia*, edited by Mark Hobart and Robert H. Taylor. Ithaca, N.Y.: Cornell Southeast Asia Program, 1986.

[0918] Mintz, Jeanne S. *Mohammed, Marx and Marhaen: The Roots of Indonesian Socialism*. New York: Praeger, 1965.

[0919] Philpott, Simon. *Rethinking Indonesia: Postcolonial Theory, Authoriarianism, and Identity*. New York: St. Martin's Press, 2000.

[0920] Soediman, Kartohadiprodjo. *Beberapa pikiran sekitar Pantja Sila*. Bandung, Indonesia: Alumni, 1970.

[0921] Tôrnquist, Olle. *Dilemmas of Third World Communism: The Destruction of the PKI in Indonesia*. London: Zed, 1984.

Political Writings

[0922] Aidit, D. N. *The Selected Works of D.N. Aidit*. Washington, D.C.: Joint Publications Research Service, 1959.

[0923] Akhmadi, Heri. *Breaking the Chains of Oppression of the Indonesian People: Defense Statement at His Trial on Charges of Insulting the Head of State, Bandung, June 7–10, 1979.* Ithaca, N.Y.: Cornell Modern Indonesia Project, 1981.

[0924] Bonneff, Marcel, et al., eds. *Pantjasila: trente années de débats politiques en Indoneésie*. Paris: Editions de la Maison des Sciences de l'Homme, 1980.

[0925] Federspiel, Howard M., trans. "Islam and Nationalism." *Indonesia* 24 (October 1977): 39–85.

[0926] Lubis, Mochtar. *The Indonesian Dilemma*. Singapore: Graham Brash, 1983.

[0927] Madjid, Nurcholis. "Islam in Indonesia: Challenges and Opportunities." *Mizan* 1, no. 3 (1984): 71–85.

[0928] Murtopo, Ali. *The Acceleration and Modernization of 25 Years' Development*. Jakarta: Centre for Strategic and International Studies, 1973.

[0929] Natsir, M. *Capita selecta*. The Hague: W. van Hoeve, [1954].

[0930] Notosusanto, Nugroho. *The National Struggle and the Armed Forces of Indonesia*. Jakarta: Centre for Armed Forces History, 1975.

[0931] Semaoen. "An Early Account of the Independence Movement." *Indonesia* 1 (April 1966): 46–75.

[0932] Sjahrir, Sutan. *Our Struggle*. Ithaca, N.Y.: Cornell Modern Indonesia Project, 1968.

[0933] ——. *Out of Exile*. New York: John Day, 1949.

[0934] Soekarno. *Nationalism, Islam and Marxism*. Ithaca, N.Y.: Cornell Modern Indonesia Project, 1970.

[0935] Sukarno. *Towards Freedom and the Dignity of Man*. Jakarta: Department of Foreign Affairs, 1961.

[0936] ——. *Under the Banner of Revolution (Dibawah bendera revolusi)*, vol. 1. Jakarta: Publication Committee, 1966/1959.

Policy Issues

[0937] Alm, James, Robert H. Aten, and Roy Bahl. "Can Indonesia Decentralise Successfully? Plans, Problems and Prospects." *BIES* 37, no. 1 (April 2001): 83–102.

[0938] Aspinall, Edward. "Modernity, History and Ethnicity: Indonesian and Acehnese Nationalism in Conflict." *RIMA* 36, no. 1 (2002): 3–33.

[0939] Aziz, Iwan J. "Intergovernmental Transfers and Decentralization in Indonesia." *BIES* 37, no. 3 (2001): 345–62.

[0940] Bertrand, Jacques. "False Starts, Succession Crises, and Regime Transition: Flirting with Openness in Indonesia." *Pacific Affairs* 69, no. 3 (fall 1996): 319–40.

[0941] Carey, Peter, and G. Carter Bentley, eds. *East Timor at the Crossroads: The Forging of a Nation*. London: Cassell, 1995.

[0942] Columbijn, Freek, and J. Thomas Lindblad, eds. *Roots of Violence in Indonesia*. Singapore: ISEAS, 2002.

[0943] Cribb, Robert. *The Politics of Environmental Protection in Indonesia*. Clayton, Victoria, Australia: Monash University Centre of Southeast Asian Studies, 1988.

[0944] Dake, Christine. *National Integration in Indonesia: Patterns and Policies*. Honolulu: University of Hawai'i Press, 1989.

[0945] Dormeier-freire, Alexandre, and Jean-Luc Maurer. "Le dilemme de la décentralisation en Indonésie." *Archipel* 64 (2002): 255–87.

[0946] Harvey, Barbara S. *The Future of Indonesia as a Unitary State: Separatism and Decentralization*. Alexandria, Va.: CNA Corporation, 2002.

[0947] Kingsbury, D., and H. Aveling. *Autonomy and Disintegration in Indonesia*. London: Routledge, 2002.

[0948] Legge, J. D. *Central Authority and Regional Autonomy in Indonesia: A Study of Local Administration 1950–1960*. Ithaca, N.Y.: Cornell University Press, 1961.

[0949] Mahfud M. D., Moh. "Amandemen UUD 1945 dalam perspektif demokrasi dan civil society." *Civility* 1, no. 2 (2001–2002): 5–27.

[0950] Maryanov, Gerald S. *Decentralization in Indonesia as a Political Problem*. Ithaca, N.Y.: Cornell Modern Indonesia Project, 1958.

[0951] McCawley, Peter. "Some Consequences of the Pertamina Crisis in Indonesia." *JSEAS* 9, no. 1 (1978): 1–27.

[0952] McRae, Dave. "A Discourse on Separatists." *Indonesia* 74 (October 2002): 37–58.

[0953] McWilliam, A. "From Lord of the Earth to Village Head: Adapting to the Nation-State in West Timor." *BKI* 155 (1999): 121–44.

[0954] Mortimer, Rex. *The Indonesian Communist Party and Land Reform.* Clayton, Victoria, Australia: Monash University Papers on Southeast Asia, 1972.

[0955] Otten, Mariël. *Transmigrasi, Myths and Realities: Indonesian Resettlement Policy, 1965–1985*. Copenhagen: International Workshop for Indigenous Affairs, 1986.

[0956] Pabotinggi, Mochtar. "Indonesia: Historicizing the New Order's Legitimacy Dilemma." In *Political legitimacy in Southeast Asia: The Quest for Moral Authority*, edited by Muthiah Alagappa. Stanford, Calif.: Stanford University Press, 1995, 224–56.

[0957] Ramage, Douglas E. *Politics in Indonesia: Democracy, Islam and the Ideology of Tolerance*. London: Routledge, 1995.

[0958] Resosudarmo, Budy R. "Indonesia's Clean Air Program." *BIES* 38, no. 3 (December 2002): 343–65.

[0959] Robinson, Geoffrey. "People's War: Militias in East Timor and Indonesia." *South East Asia Research* 9, no. 3 (2001): 271–318.

[0960] Schulte-Nordholt, Nico. "Indonesia: A Nation-State in Search of Identity and Structure." *BKI* 157, no. 4 (2001): 881–901.

[0961] Sherlock, Stephen. "Combating Corruption in Indonesia? The Ombudsman and the Assets Auditing Commission." *BIES* 38, no. 3 (December 2002): 367–83.

[0962] Sidel, John. "*Macet Total*: Logics of Circulation and Accumulation in the Demise of Indonesia's New Order." *Indonesia* 66 (October 1998): 159–94.

[0963] Sjafrizal. "Some Possible Impacts of Regional Autonomy: West Sumatra Case." *Indonesian Quarterly* 30, no. 1 (2002): 84–94.

[0964] Soesastro, Hadi, Anthony L. Smith, and Han Mui Ling. *Governance in Indonesia: Challenges Facing the Megawati Presidency*. Singapore: ISEAS, 2002.

[0965] Sulistiyo, Hermawan. "Greens in the Rainbow: Ethnoreligious Issues and the Indonesian Armed Forces." In *The Politics of Multiculturalism*, edited by Robert W. Hefner. Honolulu: University of Hawai'i Press, 2001.

[0966] Sundhaussen, Ulf. *Social Policy Aspects in Defence and Security Planning in Indonesia, 1947–1977*. Townsville, Queensland, Australia: James Cook University, 1980.

[0967] Van Klinken, Gerry. "The Maluku Wars: Bringing Society Back In." *Indonesia* 71 (April 2001): 1–26.

Government Institutions

[0968] Anwar, Dewi Fortuna. *Negotiating and Consolidating Democratic Civilian Control of the Indonesian Military*. Honolulu, Hawaii: East-West Center, 2001.

[0969] Barker, Joshua. "State of Fear: Controlling the Criminal Contagion in Suharto's New Order." *Indonesia* 66 (October 1998): 7–44.

[0970] Choesin, Vasta Charmandiva. "The Indonesian Vice-Presidency: Problems in Leadership Succession." *Contemporary Southeast Asia* 11, no. 2 (September 1989): 138–59.

[0971] Crawford, Gordon, and Yulius P. Hermawan. "Whose Agenda? Partnership and International Assistance to Democratization and Governance Reform in Indonesia." *Contemporary Southeast Asia* 24, no. 2 (August 2002): 203–29.

[0972] "Current Data on the Indonesian Military Elite." Regularly published in *Indonesia.* Ithaca, N.Y.: Cornell Southeast Asia Program.

[0973] Evans, Brian, III. "The Influence of the United States Army on the Development of the Indonesian Army (1954–1964)." *Indonesia* 47 (April 1989): 25–48.

[0974] Kammen, Douglas, and Siddharth Chandra. *A Tour of Duty: Changing Patterns of Military Politics in Indonesia in the 1990s.* Ithaca, N.Y.: Cornell Modern Indonesia Project, 1999.

[0975] Kristiadik, J. "Profesionalisme TNI di tengah transisi politik." *Antropologi Indonesia* 25, no. 4 (2001): 19–40.

[0976] Liddle, R. William. "Soeharto's Indonesia: Personal Rule and Political Institutions." *Pacific Affairs* 58, no. 1 (spring 1985): 68–90.

[0977] MacAndrews, Colin, ed. *Central Government and Local Development in Indonesia*. Singapore: OUP, 1986.

[0978] MacDougall, John A. "Patterns of Military Control in the Indonesian Higher Central Bureaucracy." *Indonesia* 33 (April 1982): 89–121.

[0979] Magenda, Burhan Djabir. "Dinamika hubungan eksekutif-legislatif di Indonesia." *Civility* 1, no. 1 (2001): 5–30.

[0980] McVey, Ruth. "Building Behemoth: Indonesian Constructions of the Nation-State." In *Making Indonesia*, edited by Daniel S. Lev and Ruth T. McVey, 11–25. [0900]

[0981] ——. "The Post-Revolutionary Transformation of the Indonesian Army." Parts 1 and 2. *Indonesia* 11 (April 1971): 131–76; 13 (April 1972): 147–82.

[0982] Nasution, Adnan Buyung. *The Aspiration for Constitutional Government in Indonesia: A Socio-Legal Study of the Indonesian Konstituante, 1956–1959*. The Hague: CIP-Gegevens Koninklijke Bibliotheek, 1992.

[0983] Noer, Deliar. *The Administration of Islam in Indonesia*. Ithaca, N.Y.: Cornell Modern Indonesia Project, 1978.

[0984] *Risalah perundingan 1956–1959*, 17 vols. Jakarta: State Printing House for the Secretariat of the Konstituante, n.d.

[0985] Robison, Richard. "Indonesia: Tensions in State and Regime," In *Southeast Asia in the 1990s: Authoritarianism, Democracy and Capitalism*, edited by Kevin Hewison, Richard Robison, and Garry Rodan. St. Leonards, New South Wales, Australia: Allen and Unwin, 1993, 39–74.

[0986] Rohdewohld, Rainer. *Public Administrtation in Indonesia*. Melbourne: Monash University, 1995.

[0987] Said, Salim. *Genesis of Power: General Sudirman and the Indonesian Military in Politics 1945–1949*. Sydney: Allen and Unwin, 1992.

[0988] Shiraishi, Takashi, "Rewiring the Indonesian State." In *Making Indonesia*, edited by Daniel S. Lev and Ruth T. McVey, 164–79. [0900]

[0989] Staff, CSIS. "Indonesia's New Constitution: A Peaceful Reform." *Indonesian Quarterly* 30, no. 3 (2002): 252–62.

[0990] Tjondronegoro, Sediono M. P. *Social Organization and Planned Development in Rural Java*. Singapore: OUP, 1984.

Political Parties

[0991] Brackman, Arnold. *Indonesian Communism: A History*. New York: Praeger, 1963.

[0992] Dake, Antonie C. A. *In the Spirit of the Red Banteng: Indonesian Communists between Moscow and Peking*. The Hague: Mouton, 1973.

[0993] Farram, Stevem. "Revolution, Religion and Magic: The PKI in West Timor, 1924–1966." *BKI* 158, no. 1 (2002): 21–48.

[0994] Hindley, Donald. *The Communist Party of Indonesia 1951–1963*. Berkeley: University of California Press, 1966.

[0995] Madinier, Rémy. "Le Masjumi, parti des milieux d'affaires mussulmans?" *Archipel* 57 (1999): 177–89.

[0996] McVey, Ruth. "Nationalism, Revolution, and Organization in Indonesian Communism." In *Making Indonesia*, edited by Daniel S. Lev and Ruth T. McVey, 96–117. [0900]

[0997] Mortimer, Rex. *Indonesian Communism under Sukarno: Ideology and Politics, 1959–1965*. Ithaca, N.Y.: Cornell University Press, 1974.

[0998] Nishihara, Masashi. *Golkar and the Indonesian Elections of 1971*. Ithaca, N.Y.: Cornell Modern Indonesia Project, 1972.

[0999] Reeve, David. *Golkar of Indonesia: An Alternative to the Party System.* Singapore: OUP, 1985.

[1000] Rocamora, Joel Elisio. *Nationalism in Search of Ideology: The Indonesian National Party, 1946–1965*. Quezon City: University of the Philippines, 1975.

[1001] Tan, Paige Johnson. "Anti-Party Reaction in Indonesia: Causes and Implications." *Contemporary Southeast Asia* 24, no. 3 (December 2002): 484–508.

[1002] Ward, K. E. *The Foundation of the Partai Muslimin Indonesia*. Ithaca, N.Y.: Cornell Modern Indonesia Project, 1970.

[1003] Webb, R. A. F. *Indonesian Christians and Their Political Parties, 1923–1966: The Role of Partai Kristen Indonesia and Partai Katolik.* Townsville,Queensland, Australia: James Cook University, 1978.

Elections

[1004] Antlov, Hans, and Sven Cederroth. *Elections in Indonesia*. London: Curzon Press, 2001.

[1005] Crouch, Harold. "The Army, the Parties and the Elections." *Indonesia* 11 (April 1971): 177–92.

[1006] Feith, Herbert. *The Indonesian Elections of 1955*. Ithaca, N.Y.: Cornell Modern Indonesia Project, 1957.

[1007] Kammen, Douglas. "*Pilkades*, Democracy, Elections and Village Protest in Indonesia." In *Southeast Asia over Three Generations: Essays Presented to B. R. O'G. Anderson*, edited by James T. Siegel and Audrey R. Kahin, 303–29. Ithaca, N.Y.: Cornell Southeast Asia Program, 2003.

[1008] King, Dwight, trans. *"White Book" on the 1992 General Election in Indonesia*. Ithaca, N.Y.: Cornell Modern Indonesia Project, 1994.

[1009] Pemberton, John. "Notes on the 1982 General Election in Solo." *Indonesia* 41 (April 1986): 1–22.

[1010] Pompe, Sebastiaan. *De Indonesische Algemene Verkiezingen 1999*. Leiden, the Netherlands: KITLV, 1999.

[1011] Steijlen, Fridus. "Sutiyoso's Re-Election as Governor of Jakarta." *BKI* 158, no. 4 (2002): 513–27.

[1012] Suryadinata, Leo. *Political Parties and the 1982 General Election in Indonesia*. Singapore: ISEAS, 1982.

[1013] Ward, Ken. *The 1971 Election in Indonesia: An East Java Case Study*. Clayton, Victoria, Australia: Monash University Centre of Southeast Asia Studies, 1974.

[1014] Weatherbee, Donald E. "Indonesia: Electoral Politics in a Newly Emerging Democracy." In *How Asia Votes*, edited by John Fuh-sheng and David Newman, 255–81. New York: Chatham House (Seven Bridges Press), 2002.

[1015] Young, Dwight Y. "The Conduct of the 1999 Election in Sleman, D. I. Yogyakarta: A Case Study (with Voting Results)." *Asian Studies Review* 25, no. 4 (2001): 479–97.

Islam and Politics

[1016] Alfian. *Muhammadiyah: The Political Behavior of a Muslim Modernist Organization under Dutch Colonialism*. Yogyakarta, Indonesia: Gadjah Mada University. Press, 1989.

[1017] Aziz, Abdul, Imam Tholkhah, and Soetarman, eds. *Gerakan Islam kontemporer di Indonesia*. Jakarta: Pustaka Firdaus, 1989.

[1018] Bousquet, G-H., and J. Schacht, eds. and trans. *Selected Works of C. Snouck Hurgronje*. Leiden, the Netherlands: Brill, 1957.

[1019] Bruinessen, Martin van. "Genealogies of Islamic Radicalism in Post-Suharto Indonesia." *Southeast Asia Research* 10, no. 2 (July 2002): 117–54.

[1020] Bubandt, Nils Ole. "Conspiracy Theories, Apocalyptic Narratives and the Discursive Construction of 'Violence in Maluku.'" *Antropologi Indonesia* 24, no. 63 (2002): 15–32.

[1021] Davis, Michael. "Laskar Jihad and the Political Position of Conservative Islam in Indonesia." *Contemporary Southeast Asia* 24, no. 1 (April 2002): 12–32.

[1022] Diederich, Mathias. "A Closer Look at Dakwah and Politics in Indonesia: The Partai Keadilan." *Archipel* 64 (2002): 101–15.

[1023] Federspiel, Howard M. *Islam and Ideology in the Emerging Indonesian State: The Persatuan Islam (PERSIS) 1923–1957*. Leiden, the Netherlands: Brill, 2001.

[1024] Feillard, Andrée. *Islam et armée dan l'Indonésie contemporaine.* Paris: L'Harmattan, 1995.

[1025] ——. "Les oelémas indonésiens aujourd'hui: de l'opposition à une nouvelle legitimité." *Archipel* 46 (1993): 89–110.

[1026] George, Kenneth M. "Designs on Indonesia's Muslim communities." *JAS* 57, no. 3 (August 1998): 693–713.

[1027] Hamayotsu, Kikue. "Islam and Nation Building in Southeast Asia: Malaysia and Indonesia in Comparative Perspective." *Pacific Affairs* 75, no. 3 (fall 2002): 353–75.

[1028] Hasan, Noorhaid. "Faith and Politics: The Rise of Laskar Jihad in the Era of Transition in Indonesia." *Indonesia* 73 (April 2002): 145–69.

[1029] Hefner, Robert W. *Civil Islam: Muslims and Democratization in Indonesia*. Princeton, N.J.: Princeton University Press, 2000.

[1030] ——. "Islam, State, and Civil Society: ICMI and the Struggle of the Indonesian Middle Class." *Indonesia* 56 (October 1993): 1–36.

[1031] Jones, Sidney. "Al-Qaeda in Southeast Asia: The Case of the 'Ngruki Network' in Indonesia." Jakarta/Brussels: International Crisis Group *Indonesia Briefing*, 8 August 2002.

[1032] Laffan, Michael Francis. *Islamic Nationhood and Colonial Indonesia: The Umma below the Winds*. London: Routledge/Curzon, 2003.

[1033] Liddle, R. William. "The Islamic Turn in Indonesia: A Political Explanation." *JAS* 55, no. 3 (August 1996): 613–34.

[1034] Majid, Nurcholish. *Cita-cita politik Islam era reformasi*. Jakarta: Paramedina, 1999.

[1035] Meuleman, Johan Hendrik. "The Role of Islam in Indonesian and Algerian History: A Comparative Analysis." *Studia Islamika* 1, no. 2 (July–September 1994).

[1036] Noer, Deliar. "Contemporary Political Dimensions of Islam." In *Islam in South-East Asia*, edited by M. B. Hooker. Leiden, the Netherlands: E. J. Brill, 1983.

[1037] Peacock, James. *Purifying the Faith: The Muhammadijah Movement in Indonesian Islam*. Menlo Park, Calif.: Benjamin/Cummings, 1978.

[1038] Raillon, François. "The New Order and Islam, or the Imbroglio of Faith and Politics." *Indonesia* 57 (April 1994): 197–217.

[1039] Sidel, John T. "Other Schools, Other Pilgrimages, Other Dreams: The Making and Unmaking of *Jihad* in Southeast Asia." In *Southeast Asia over Three Generations: Essays Presented to B. R. O'G. Anderson,* edited by James T. Siegel and Audrey R. Kahin, 347–81. Ithaca, N.Y.: Cornell Southeast Asia Program, 2003.

[1040] Sjafruddin Prawiranegara. "Pancasila as the Sole Foundation." *Indonesia* 38 (October 1984): 74–83.

Racial and Minority Issues

[1041] Algadri, Hamid. *Politik Belanda terhadap Islam dan keturunan Arab di Indonesia*. Jakarta: Cv Haji Masagung, 1988.

[1042] Anderson, Benedict R. O'G. "Twilight Dogs—Jangled Nerves." *Indonesia* 73 (April 2002): 129–44.

[1043] Blussé, Leonard. "The Role of Indonesian Chinese in Shaping Modern Indonesian life." *Indonesia*, special issue (1991): 1–11.

[1044] Chandra, Siddharth. "Race Inequality and Anti-Chinese Violence in the Netherlands Indies." *Explorations in Economic History* 39 (2002): 88–112.

[1045] Coppel, Charles A. *Indonesian Chinese in crisis*. Kuala Lumpur, Malaysia: OUP, 1983.

[1046] Goss, Andrew. "From Tong-Tong to Tempo Doeloe: Eurasian Memory Work and the Bracketing of Dutch Colonial History, 1957–1961." *Indonesia* 70 (October 2000): 9–36.

[1047] Hefner, Robert W., ed. *The Politics of Multiculturalism: Pluralism and Citizenship in Malaysia, Singapore and Indonesia*. Honolulu: University of Hawai'i Press, 2001.

[1048] Heidhues, Mary Somers. *Golddiggers, Farmers and Traders in the "Chinese Districts" of West Kalimantan, Indonesia*. Ithaca, N.Y.: Cornell Southeast Asia Program, 2003.

[1049] ——. "Indonesia." In *The Encyclopedia of the Chinese Overseas*, edited by Lynn Pan, 151–68. Singapore: Chinese Heritage Centre, 1998.

[1050] "Indonesia." In *Encyclopaedia Judaica*, vol. 8. Jerusalem: Macmillan, 1971.

[1051] Jonge, Huub de. "Discord and Solidarity among the Arabs in the Netherlands East Indies, 1900–1942." *Indonesia* 55 (April 1993): 73–90.

[1052] Kumar, Ann L. "Islam, the Chinese, and Indonesian Historiography—A Review Article." *JAS* 46, no. 3 (1987): 603–16.

[1053] Kwee Tek Hoay. *The Origins of the Modern Chinese Movement in Indonesia*. Ithaca, N.Y.: Cornell Modern Indonesia Project, 1969.

[1054] Lohanda, Mona. *The Kapitan Cina of Batavia, 1837–1942: A History of Chinese Establishment*. Jakarta: Djambatan, 1996.

[1055] Mackie, J. A. C., ed. *The Chinese in Indonesia*. Melbourne: Nelson, 1976.

[1056] Mackie, Jamie. "Towkays and Tycoons: The Chinese in Indonesian Economic Life in the 1920s and 1980s." *Indonesia*, special issue (1991): 83–96.

[1057] Mobini-Kesheh, Natalie. *The Hadrami Awakening: Community and Identity in the Netherlands East Indies, 1900–1942*. Ithaca, N.Y.: Cornell Studies on Southeast Asia, 1999.

[1058] Peluso, Nancy Lee, and Emily Harwell. "Territory, Custom, and the Cultural Politics of Ethnic War in West Kalimantan, Indonesia." In *Violent Environments*, edited by Nancy Lee Peluso and Michael Watts. Ithaca, N.Y.: Cornell University Press, 2001.

[1059] Post, Peter. "The Kwik Hoo Tong Trading Society of Semarang, Java: A Chinese Business Network in Late Colonial Asia." *JSEAS* 33, no. 2 (June 2002): 279–98.

[1060] Rush, James. "Placing the Chinese in Java on the Eve of the Twentieth Century." *Indonesia*, special issue (1991): 13–24.

[1061] ——. "Social Control and Influence in Nineteenth Century Indonesia: Opium Farms and the Chinese of Java." *Indonesia* 35 (April 1983): 53–64.

[1062] Salmon, Claudine, and Denys Lombard. "Islam and Chineseness." *Indonesia* 57 (April 1994): 115–31.

[1063] Somers, Mary F. *Peranakan Chinese Politics in Indonesia*. Ithaca N.Y.: Cornell Modern Indonesia Project, 1964.

[1064] Suryadinata, Leo. *Pribumi Indonesians, the Chinese Minority and China: A Study of Perceptions and Policies*, 2nd ed. Singapore: ISEAS, 1986.

[1065] ——, ed. *Political Thinking of the Indonesian Chinese, 1900–1995*. Singapore: Singapore University Press, 1997.

[1066] Tan, Mély G. "The Social and Cultural Dimensions of the Role of Ethnic Chinese in Indonesian Society." *Indonesia*, special issue (1991): 113–25.

[1067] The, B. A. M., and J. Schijf. "The Chinese Doctors in the Dutch East Indies: Social Mobility among an Ethnic Trading Minority in a Colonial Society." *Indonesia* 53 (April 1992): 33–50.

[1068] Twang Peck Yang. *The Chinese Business Elite in Indonesia and the Transition to Independence 1940–1950*. Kuala Lumpur, Malaysia: OUP, 1998.

[1069] Vuldy, Chantal. "La communauté Arabe de Pekalongan." *Archipel* 30 (1985): 95–119.

[1070] Wibowo, I., ed. *Harga yang harus dibayar: sketsa pergaulatan etnis Cina di Indonesia*. Jakarta: Gramedia, 2000.

[1071] ——, ed. *"Masalah Cina," retrospeksi dan rekontekstualisasi*. Jakarta: Gramedia, 1999.

[1072] Williams, Lea E. *Overseas Chinese Nationalism: The Genesis of the Pan-Chinese Movement in Indonesia, 1900–1916*. Glencoe, IL: Free Press, 1960.

[1073] Willmott, Donald E. *The Chinese of Semarang: A Changing Minority Community in Indonesia*. Ithaca, N.Y.: Cornell University Press, 1960.

[1074] ——. *The National Status of the Chinese in Indonesia, 1900–1958*. Ithaca, N.Y.: Cornell University Press, 1961.

Law

[1075] *Adatrechtbundels*, 45 vols. Leiden, the Netherlands: KITLV, 1910–1955.

[1076] Ball, John. *Indonesian Legal History 1602–1848*. Sydney: Oughtershaw, 1982.

[1077] Benda-Beckman, Keebet von. *The Broken Stairway to Consensus: Village Justice and State Courts in Minangkabau*. Dordrecht, The Netherlands: Foris, 1984.

[1078] Brokx, Wouter. *Het recht tot wonen en tot reizen in Nederlandsch-Indië*. 'sHertogenbosch, The Netherlands: Teulings, 1925.

[1079] Burns, Peter. "The Post Priok Trials: Religious Principles and Legal Issues." *Indonesia* 47 (April 1989): 61–88.

[1080] Cammack, Mark. "Indonesia's 1989 Religious Judicature Act: Islamization of Indonesia or Indonesianization of Islam?" *Indonesia* 63 (April 1997): 143–68.

[1081] ——. "Islamic Law in Indonesia's New Order." *The International and Comparative Law Quarterly* 38 (1989): 53–70.

[1082] Haar, Bernard ter. *Adat Law in Indonesia*. New York: Institute of Pacific Relations, 1948.

[1083] Holleman, J. F. *Van Vollenhoven on Indonesian adat law: selections from Het adatrecht van Nederlandsch-Indië*. Leiden, The Netherlands: KITLV, 1981.

[1084] Hooker, M. B. *Adat Law in Modern Indonesia*. Kuala Lumpur, Malaysia: OUP, 1978.

[1085] ——. *Islamic Law in South-East Asia*. Singapore: OUP, 1984.

[1086] Lev, Daniel S. "Between State and Society: Professional Lawyers and Reform in Indonesia." In *Making Indonesia*, edited by Daniel S. Lev and Ruth T. McVey, 144–63. [0900]

[1087] ——. "Colonial Law and the Genesis of the Indonesian State." *Indonesia* 40 (October 1985): 57–74.

[1088] ——. "The Criminal Regime: Criminal Process in Indonesia." In *Figures of Criminality in Indonesia, the Philippines and Colonial Vietnam*, edited by Vicente L. Rafael, 175–92. Ithaca, N.Y.: Cornell Southeast Asia Program, 1999.

[1089] ——. *Islamic Courts in Indonesia: A Study of the Political Bases of Legal Institutions*. Berkeley: University of California Press, 1972.

[1090] ——. *Legal Aid in Indonesia*. Clayton, Victoria, Australia: Monash University Centre of Southeast Asian Studies, 1987.

[1091] ——. *Legal Evolution and Political Authority in Indonesia: Selected Essays*. The Hague/Boston: Kluwer Law International, 2000.

[1092] Lindsey, Tim, ed. *Indonesia: The Commercial Court and Law Reform in Indonesia*. Sydney: Desert Pea Press, 2000.

[1093] ——. *Indonesia: Law and Society*. Sydney: The Federation Press, 1999.

[1094] Noeh, H. Z. A., and H. A. B. Adnan. *Sejarah singkat pengadilan agama Islam di Indonesia*. Jakarta: Bina Ilmu, 1983.

[1095] Pompe, Sebastiaan. "The Indonesian Supreme Court: Fifty Years of Judicial Development."Ph.D. diss., Leiden University, 1996.

[1096] Ridhwan Indra, H. M. *The Power of the Indonesian Supreme Court*. Jakarta: Haji Masagung, 1994.

[1097] Sabrie, H. Zuffran, ed. *Peradilan agama dalam wadah negara Pancasila: dialog tentang rupa*. Jakarta: Pustaka Antara, 1990.

[1098] Soedirdjo. *Mahkamah Agung: uraian singkat tentang kedudukan, susunan dan kekuasaanny menurut undang-undang nomor 14 tahun 1985*. Jakarta: Medan Saran Press, 1987.

[1099] Southwood, Julie, and Patrick Flanagan. *Indonesia: Law, Propaganda and Terror*. London: Zed, 1983.

[1100] Thoolen, Hans, ed. *Indonesia and the Rule of Law: Twenty Years of "New Order" Government*. London: Pinter, 1987.

International Relations

[1101] Acharya, Amitav. *Constructing a Security Community in Southeast Asia: ASEAN and the Problem of Regional Order*. London: Routledge, 2001.

[1102] Anak Agung Gde Agung, Ide. *Twenty Years of Indonesian Foreign Policy, 1945–1965*. The Hague: Mouton, 1973.

[1103] Anwar, Dewi Fortuna. *Indonesia in ASEAN: Foreign Policy and Regionalism*. Singapore: ISEAS, 1994.

[1104] Arora, B. D. *Indian-Indonesian Relations, 1961–1980*. New Delhi: Asian Educational Services, 1981.

[1105] Bone, Robert C. *The Dynamics of the Western New Guinea (Irian Barat) Problem*. Ithaca, N.Y.: Cornell Modern Indonesia Project, 1958.

[1106] Bootsma, N. A. *Buren in de koloniale tijd: de Philippijnen onder Amerikaans bewind en de Nederlandse, Indische en Indonesische reacties daarop, 1898–1942*. Dordrecht, The Netherlands: Foris, 1986.

[1107] Brown, Colin, ed. *Indonesia: Dealing with a Neighbour*. Sydney: Allen and Unwin, 1996.

[1108] Buchholz, Hans. *Law of the Sea Zones in the Pacific Ocean*. Singapore: ISEAS, 1987.

[1109] Bunnell, Frederick. "American 'Low Posture' Policy toward Indonesia in the Months Leading up to the 1965 'Coup.'" *Indonesia* 50 (October 1990): 29–60.

[1110] Cheah Boon Keng. "The Japanese Occupation of Malaysia, 1941–1945: Ibrahim Yaacob and the Struggle for Indonesia Raya." *Indonesia* 28 (October 1979): 85–121.

[1111] Conboy, Kenneth, and James Morrison. *Feet to the Fire: CIA Covert Operations in Indonesia, 1957–1958*. Annapolis, Md.: Naval Institute Press, 1999.

[1112] Dorling, Philip, ed. *Diplomasi: Australia and Indonesia's Independence: Documents 1947*. Canberra: Australian Government Publishing Service, 1994.

[1113] Efimova, L. M. "New Evidence on the Establishment of Soviet-Indonesian Diplomatic Relations (1949–53)." *Indonesia and the Malay World* 29, no. 85 (2001): 215–33.

[1114] Eldridge, Philip. *Australia and Indonesia: The Politics of Aid and Development since 1966*. Canberra: ANU Development Studies Centre, 1979.

[1115] Gardner, Paul F. *Shared Hopes: Separate Fears: Fifty Years of U.S.-Indonesian Relations*. Boulder, Colo.: Westview Press, 1997.

[1116] George, Margaret. *Australia and the Indonesian Revolution*. Melbourne: Melbourne University Press, 1980.

[1117] Gouda, Frances, with Thijs Brocades Zaalberg. *American Visions of the Netherlands East Indies/Indonesia: US Foreign Policy and Indonesian Nationalism, 1920–1949*. Amsterdam: Amsterdam University Press, 2002.

[1118] Gould, James W. *Americans in Sumatra*. The Hague: Nijhoff, 1961.

[1119] Jones, Howard P. *Indonesia: The Possible Dream*. New York: Harcourt Brace Jovanovich, 1971.

[1120] Jones, Matthew. *Conflict and Confrontation in South East Asia 1961–65*. Cambridge: Cambridge University Press, 2001.

[1121] Kahin, Audrey R., and George McT. Kahin. *Subversion as Foreign Policy: The Secret Eisenhower and Dulles Debacle in Indonesia*. New York: New Press, 1995.

[1122] Kahin, George McT. *The Asian-African Conference, Bandung, Indonesia*. Ithaca, N.Y.: Cornell University Press, 1956.

[1123] Leifer, Michael. *Indonesia's Foreign Policy*. London: Allen and Unwin, 1983.

[1124] Lijphart, Arend. *The Trauma of Decolonization: The Dutch and West New Guinea*. New Haven, Conn.: Yale University. Press, 1966.

[1125] Macintyre, Andrew J. "Interpreting Indonesian Foreign Policy: The Case of Kampuchea, 1979–1986." *Asian Survey* 27, no. 5 (1987): 515–34.

[1126] Mackie, J. A. C. *Konfrontasi: The Indonesia-Malaysia Dispute, 1963–1966*. Kuala Lumpur, Malaysia: OUP, 1974.

[1127] MacMahon, Robert J. *Colonialism and Cold War: The United States and the Struggle for Indonesian Independence, 1945–49*. Ithaca, N.Y.: Cornell University Press, 1981.

[1128] McVey, Ruth T. *The Soviet View of the Indonesian Revolution*. Ithaca, N.Y.: Cornell Modern Indonesia Project, 1957.

[1129] Meijer, Hans. *Den Haag-Djakarta: de Nederlands-Indonesische betrekkingen 1950–1962*. Utrecht, the Netherlands: Spectrum, 1994.

[1130] Mozingo, David. *Chinese Policy toward Indonesia, 1959–1967*. Ithaca, N.Y.: Cornell University Press, 1976.

[1131] Nishihara, Masashi. *The Japanese and Sukarno's Indonesia: Tokyo-Jakarta Relations, 1951–1961*. Honolulu: University of Hawai'i Press, 1976.

[1132] Otterspeer, Willem, ed. *Leiden Oriental Connections, 1850–1940*. Leiden, the Netherlands: Brill, 1989.

[1133] Philpott, S. "Fear of the Dark: Indonesia and the Australian National Imagination." *Australian Journal of International Affairs* 55, no. 3 (2001): 371–88.

[1134] Platje, Wies. "Dutch Sigint and the Conflict with Indonesia, 1950–62." In *Secrets of Signals Intelligence during the Cold War and Beyond,* edited by Matthew M. Aid and Cees Wiebes, 285–312. London: Frank Cass. 2001.

[1135] Poeze, Harry A. *In het land van de overheerser I: Indonesiërs in Nederland 1600–1950*. Dordrecht, The Netherlands: Foris, 1986.

[1136] Posthumus, G. A. "The Inter-Governmental Group on Indonesia." *BIES* 8, no. 2 (1972): 55–66.

[1137] Rix, Alan G. "The Mitsugoro Project: Japanese Aid Policy and Indonesia," *Pacific Affairs* 52, no. 1 (1979): 43–63.

[1138] Schulte Nordholt, Nico G. "Dutch-Indonesian Relations Forty Years after the Transfer of Sovereignty: Some Critical Remarks." *Internationale Spectator* 43, no. 11 (1989): 654–61.

[1139] Sukma, Rizal. *Indonesia and China—The Politics of a Troubled Relationship*. London: Routledge, 1999.

[1140] Tanter, Richard, Mark Selden, and Stephen R. Shalom, eds. *Bitter Flowers, Sweet Flowers: East Timor, Indonesia, and the World Community*. Lanham, Md.: Rowman & Littlefield, 2001.

[1141] Taylor, Alastair M. *Indonesian Independence and the United Nations*. London: Stevens, 1960.

[1142] Uphoff, Elisabeth. *Intellectual Property and US Relations with Indonesia, Malaysia, Singapore, and Thailand*. Ithaca, N.Y.: Cornell Southeast Asia Program, 1991.

[1143] Wal, S. L. van der, ed. *Officiële bescheiden betreffende de Nederlands-Indonesische betrekkingen 1945–1949*, 20 vols. The Hague: Nijhoff, 1971–1996.

[1144] Weinstein, Franklin B. *Indonesian Foreign Policy and the Dilemma of Dependence: From Sukarno to Suharto*. Ithaca, N.Y.: Cornell University Press, 1974.

[1145] Williams, Michael C. "China and Indonesia Make Up: Reflections on a Troubled Relationship." *Indonesia*, special issue (1991): 145–58.

[1146] Yong Mun Cheong. *H.J. van Mook and Indonesian Independence: A Study of His Role in Dutch-Indonesian Relations, 1945–48*. The Hague: Nijhoff, 1982.

[1147] Yoshihara, Kunio. *Japanese Investment in Southeast Asia*. Honolulu: University of Hawai'i Press, 1978.

SCIENCE

Biology

[1148] Backer, C. A., and R. C. Bakhuizen van den Brink: *Flora of Java* [Spermatophytes only], 3 vols. Groningen, The Netherlands: Noordhof, 1963–1968.

[1149] Bakels, Jet. *Het verbond met de tijger: visies op mensenetende dieren in Kerinci, Sumatra*. Leiden, The Netherlands: Research School of Asian African and Amerindian Studies, 2000.

[1150] Balen, S. (Bas) van, and Roy H. Dennis. "Birds of the Danau Senarum National Park." *Borneo Research Bulletin* 31 (2000): 336–60.

[1151] Barlow, H. S. *An Introduction to the Moths of South East Asia*. Kuala Lumpur, Malaysia: Malayan Nature Society, 1982.

[1152] Carcasson, R. H. *A Field Guide to the Coral Reef Fishes of the Indian and West Pacific Oceans*. London: Collins, 1977.

[1153] Hinton, A.G. *Shells of New Guinea and the Central Indo-Pacific*. Brisbane, Australia: Jacaranda, 1977.

[1154] Hoogerwerf, A. *Udjung Kulon: The Land of the Last Javan Rhinoceros*. Leiden, The Netherlands: Brill, 1970.

[1155] Lutz, Richard, Marie Lutz, and Dick Lutz. *Komodo, the Living Dragon*, 2nd ed. N.p.: Dimi Press, 1996.

[1156] MacKinnon, John. *A Field Guide to the Birds of Java and Bali.* Yogyakarta, Indonesia: Gadjah Mada University Press, 1988.

[1157] Payne, Junaidi, Charles M. France, and Karen Phillipps. *A Field Guide to the Mammals of Borneo*. Kota Kinabalu, Malaysia: Sabah Society and WWF Malaysia, 1985.

[1158] Russon, Anne E. "Declining Orangutan Populations in and around the Danau Sentarum National Park, West Kalimantan, Indonesia." *Borneo Research Bulletin* 31 (2000): 372–84.

[1159] Smythies, B. E. "The Bornean Province." In *The Birds of Borneo*. Kota Kinabalu, Malaysia: Natural History Publications, 1999.

[1160] Steenis, C. G. G. J. van. *The Mountain Flora of Java*. Leiden, The Netherlands: Brill, 1972.

[1161 Tsukada, Etsuzo, ed. *Butterflies of the South East Asian Islands*, 2 vols. Tokyo: Plapac, 1982.

[1162] Weber, Max, and L. F. de Beaufort. *The Fishes of the Indo-Australian Archipelago*. Leiden, The Netherlands: Brill, 1953.

[1163] White, C. M. N., and Murray D. Bruce. *The Birds of Wallacea (Sulawesi, the Moluccas and Lesser Sunda Islands, Indonesia): An Annotated Checklist*. London: British Ornithologists' Union, 1986. Includes an excellent bibliography.

Geography, Geology, and Ecology

[1164] Beccari, Odoardo. *Wanderings in the Great Forests of Borneo*. London: Constable, 1989.

[1165] Bemmelen, R. W. van. *The Geology of Indonesia*. The Hague: Government Printing Office, 1949.

[1166] Colombijn, Freek. "Global and Local Perspectives on Indonesia's Environmental Problems and the Role of NGOs." *BKI* 154, no. 2 (1998): 305–34.

[1167] Cribb, Robert. "Environmental Policy and Politics in Indonesia." In *Ecological Policy and Politics in Developing Countries*, edited by Uday Desai. Albany: State University of New York Press, 1998.

[1168] Dam, R. A. C., and S. van der Kaars, eds. *Quaternary Environmental Change in the Indonesian Region*. Amsterdam: Elsevier Science, 2001.

[1169] Donner, Wolf. *Land Use and Environment in Indonesia*. Honolulu: University of Hawai'i Press, 1987.

[1170] Dove, Michael R. "Living Rubber, Dead Land, and Persisting Systems in Borneo: Indigenous Representations of Sustainability." *BKI* 154, no. 1 (1998): 20–54.

[1171] Fisher, Charles A. *South-East Asia: A Social, Economic and Political Geography*. London: Menthuen, 1966.

[1172] Fox, James J. "The Impact of the 1997–98 El Niño on Indonesia." In *El Niño, History and Crisis*, edited by Richard H. Grove and John Chappell, 171–90. Knapwell: White Horse Press, 2001.

[1173] Glover, David, and Timothy Jessup, eds. *Indonesia's Fires and Haze: The Cost of Catastrophe*. Ottawa, Canada: International Development Research Centre, c. 1999.

[1174] Hamilton, W. *Tectonics of the Indonesian Region*. Washington, D.C.: U.S. Government Printing Office, 1979.

[1175] Hardjono, Joan. "Resource Utilisation and the Environment." In *Indonesia's New Order*, edited by Hal Hill, 179–215. [0730]

[1176] Jong Boers, Bernice de. "Mount Tambora in 1815: A Volcanic Eruption in Indonesia and Its Aftermath." *Indonesia* 60 (October 1995): 37–60.

[1177] McCarthy, John F. "Power and Interest on Sumatra's Rainforest Frontier: Clientelist Coalitions, Illegal Logging and Conservation in the Alas Valley." *JSEAS* 33, no. 1 (February 2002): 77–106.
[1178] Neumann von Padang, M. *Catalogue of the Active Volcanoes of the World, Including Solfatara Fields, Part I: Indonesia*. Naples, Italy: International Volcanological Association, 1951.
[1179] Nyhus, P., Sumianto, and R. Tilson. *People, Politics and Village-Level Conservation in Sumatra, Indonesia.* Proceedings of the 1999 AZA Annual Conference, Minneapolis, Minn. Bethesda, Md.: AZA, 1999.
[1180] Simkin, Tom, and Richard S. Fiske, eds. *Krakatau, 1883: The Volcanic Eruption and Its Effects*. Washington, D.C:. Smithsonian Institution, 1983.
[1181] Thornton, Ian. *Krakatau: The Destruction and Reassembly of an Island Ecosystem*. Cambridge, Mass.: Harvard University Press, 1996.
[1182] Tomascik, Tomas, et al. *The Ecology of the Indonesian Seas*, 2 vols. [Hong Kong]: Periplus Editions, [1997].
[1183] Vincent, Jeffrey, Jean Aden, Magda Adriani, Biovanna Dore, Vivianti Rambe, and Thomas Walton. "Public Environmental Expenditures in Indonesia." *BIES* 38, no. 1 (April 2002): 61–74.
[1184] Whitmore, T. C. *An Introduction to Tropical Rain Forests*. Oxford: Clarendon, 1990.
[1185] Whitmore, T. C. *Tropical Fainforests of the Far East*, 2nd ed. Oxford: Clarendon Press, 1984.
[1186] Whitmore, T. C., ed. *The Biogeographical Evolution of the Malay Archipelago*. Oxford: Clarendon Press, 1987.
[1187] Whitten, A. J., S. J. Damanik, J. Anwar, and N. Hisyam. *The Ecology of Sumatra*. Yogyakarta, Indonesia: Gadjah Mada University Press, 1987.

History of Science

[1188] Baas, Pieter. "De VOC in Flora's Lulsthoven." In *Kennis en Compagnie*, edited by Leonard Blussé and Ilonka Ooms, 124–37. Amsterdam: Balans, 2002.
[1189] Beekman, E. M. *The Poison Tree: Selected Writings of Rumphius on the Natural History of the Indies*. Amherst: University of Massachusetts Press, 1981.
[1190] Bergh, Gert D. van den, John de Vos, and Paul Y. Sondaar. "The Late Quaternary Palaeography of Mammal Evolution in the Indonesian Archipelago." In *Quaternary Environmental Change in the Indonesian Region*, edited by R. A. C. Dam and S. van der Kars, 385–408. Amsterdam: Elsevier Science, 2001.
[1191] Boomgaard, P., F. Colombijn, and D. Henley, eds. *Paper Landscapes: Explorations in the Environmental History of Indonesia*. Leiden, The Netherlands: KITLV, 1998.
[1192] Daws, Gavom, and Marty Fujita. *Archipelago: The Islands of Indonesia from the Nineteenth Century Discoveries of Alfred Russell Wallace to the Fate of the Forests and Reefs in the Twenty-First Century*. Berkeley: University of California Press, 1999.

[1193] Knapen, Han. *Forests of Fortune? The Environmental History of Southeast Borneo, 1600–1880*. Leiden, The Netherlands: KITLV, 2001.

[1194] Koninklijke Academie van Wetenschappen. *Science in the Netherlands East Indies*. Amsterdam: De Bussy, 1929.

[1195] Sirks, M. J. *Indisch natuuronderzoek: een beknopte geschiedenis van de beoefening der natuurwetenschappen in de Nederlandsche koloniën*. Amsterdam: Koloniaal Instituut, 1915.

[1196] The, Lian, and Paul W. van der Veur. *The Verhandelingen van het Bataviaasch Genootschap: An annotated content analysis*. Athens: Ohio University Center for International Studies, 1973.

Public Health and Medicine

[1197] Achman, January. *Hollow Development: The Politics of Health in Soeharto's Indonesia*. Canberra: Australian National University, 1999.

[1198] Boomgaard, Peter et al., eds. *Health Care in Java: Past and Present*. Leiden, the Netherlands: KITLV, 1996.

[1199] Hasanbasri, Mubasyir. "Struktur rumah tangga dan perawatan kesehatan lansia di Indonesia." *Populasi* 11, no. 2 (2000): 3–22.

[1200] Hawati, Roosna, et al. *Sketsa kesehatan reproduksi perempuan desa: pengalaman pendampingan*. Jakarta: YPP Press, 2001.

[1201] Hay, M. Cameron. *Remembering to Live: Illness at the Intersection of Anxiety and Knowledge in Rural Indonesia*. Ann Arbor: University of Michigan Press, 2001.

[1202] Jensen, Eric R., and Dennis A. Ahlburg. "Family Size, Unwantedness, and Child Health and Health Case Utilisation in Indonesia." *BIES* 38, no. 1 (April 2002): 43–59.

[1203] Mitchell, David, ed. *Indonesian Medical Traditions: Bringing Together the Old and the New*. Clayton, Victoria, Australia: Monash University Centre of Southeast Asian Studies, 1982.

[1204] Owen, Norman G., ed. *Death and Disease in Southeast Asia: Explorations in Social, Medical and Demographic History*. Singapore: OUP, 1987.

[1205] USAID. *HIV/AIDS in Indonesia and USAID Involvement*. Washington, D.C.: TvT Associates under the Synergy Project, December 2001.

[1206] Watson, Kate. "Searching for Solutions: Indonesia's Response to the AIDS Epidemic." Hons. thesis, University of Melbourne, 1995.

SOCIETY

Anthropology

[1207] Abdullah, Taufik. "Adat and Islam: An Examination of Conflict in Minangkabau." *Indonesia* 2 (October 1966): 1–24.

[1208] Barnes, R. H. *Kedang: A Study of the Collective Thought of an Eastern Indonesian People*. Oxford: Clarendon, 1974.

[1209] Beatty, Andrew. *Society and Exchange in Nias*. Oxford: Clarendon Press, 1992.

[1210] ——. *Varieties of Javanese Religion: An Anthropological Account*. Cambridge: Cambridge University Press, 1999.

[1211] Belo, Jane. *Trance in Bali*. New York: Columbia University Press, 1960.

[1212] Benda, Harry J., and Lance Castles. "The Samin Movement." *BKI* 125, no. 2 (1969): 207–31.

[1213] Boelaars, J. H. M. C. *Head-Hunters about Themselves: An Ethnographic Report from Irian Jaya, Indonesia*. Leiden, The Netherlands: KITLV, 1981.

[1214] Boon, James A. *The Anthropological Romance of Bali 1597–1972: Dynamic Perspectives in Marriage and Caste, Politics and Religion.* Cambridge: Cambridge University Press, 1977.

[1215] Chambert-Loir, Henri, and Anthony Reid, eds. *Potent Dead: The Ancestors, Saints and Heroes in Contemporary Indonesia*. Honolulu: University of Hawai'i Press, 2002.

[1216] Covarrubias, Miguel. *Island of Bali*. London: Cassell, 1937.

[1217] Dove, Michael Roger. *Swidden Agriculture in Indonesia: The Subsistence Strategies of the Kalimantan Kantu'*. Berlin: Mouton, 1985.

[1218] ——, ed. *The Real and Imagined Role of Culture in Development: Case Studies from Indonesia*. Honolulu: University of Hawai'i Press, 1988.

[1219] DuBois, Cora. *The People of Alor: A Social Psychological Study of an East Indian Island*. Minneapolis: University of Minnesota Press, 1944.

[1220] Fox, James J. *Harvest of the Palm: Ecological Change in Eastern Indonesia*. Cambridge, Mass.: Harvard University Press, 1977.

[1221] ——, ed. *The Flow of Life: Essays on Eastern Indonesia*. Cambridge, Mass.: Harvard University Press, 1980.

[1222] Fox, James J., ed. *To Speak in Pairs: Essays on the Ritual Languages of Eastern Indonesia*. Cambridge: Cambridge University Press, 1988.

[1223] Geertz, Clifford. *The Interpretation of Cultures*. New York: Basic Books, 1973.

[1224] ——. *Peddlers and Princes: Social Change and Economic Modernization in Two Indonesian Towns*. Chicago: University of Chicago Press, 1963.

[1225] Geertz, Hildred. "Indonesian Cultures and Communities." In *Indonesia*, edited by Ruth T. McVey. [0482]

[1226] ——. *The Javanese Family: A Study of Kinship and Socialization.* Glencoe, N.Y.: Free Press, 1961.

[1227] George, Kenneth M. "Headhunting, History, and Exchange in Upland Sulawesi." *JAS* 50, no. 3 (1991): 536–64.

[1228] Hatley, Ron, ed. *Other Javas: Away from the Kraton*. Clayton, Victoria, Australia: Monash University, 1984.

[1229] Hefner, Robert W. *Hindu Javanese: Tengger Tradition and Islam.* Princeton, N.J.: Princeton University Press, 1985.

[1230] Heider, Karl G. *Grand Valley Dani: Peaceful Warriors*, 3rd rev. ed.: Harcourt Brace, 1997.

[1231] Hobart, Mark. *After Culture: Anthropology as Radical Metaphysical Critique*. Yogyakarta, Indonesia: Duta Wacana University Press, 2000.

[1232] ——. "Lances Greased with Pork Fat: Imagining Difference in Bali." In *Imagined Differences*, edited by Günther Schlee. Munster, Germany: Lit Verlag, 2002.

[1233] Hoskins, Janet. *The Play of Time: Kodi Perspectives on Calendars, History and Exchange*. Berkeley: University of California Press, 1993.

[1234] Just, Peter. *Dou Donggo Justice: Conflict and Morality in an Indonesian Society*. Lanham, Md.: Rowman & Littlefield, 2001.

[1235] Kahn, Joel S. *Constituting the Minangkabau: Peasants, Culture, and Modernity in Colonial Indonesia*. Providence, R.I.: Oxford: Berg, 1993.

[1236] ——. *Minangkabau Social Formations: Indonesian Peasants and the World-Economy*. Cambridge: Cambridge University Press, 1985.

[1237] Kato, Tsuyoshi. *Matriliny and Migration: Evolving Minangkabau Traditions in Indonesia*. Ithaca, N.Y.: Cornell University Press, 1982.

[1238] Kipp, Rita Smith. *Dissociated Identities: Ethnicity, Religion, and Class in an Indonesian Society*. Ann Arbor: University of Michigan Press, 1996.

[1239] Koentjaraningrat. *Javanese Culture*. Singapore: OUP, 1985.

[1240] Loeb, Edwin M. *Sumatra: Its History and People*. Kuala Lumpur, Malaysia: OUP, 1972.

[1241] Molnar, Andrea Katalin. *Grandchildren of the Ga'e Ancestorys: Social Organization and Cosmology among the Hoga Sara of Flores*. Leiden, The Netherlands: KITLV, 2001.

[1242] Mulder, Niels. *Mysticism and Everyday Life in Contemporary Indonesia: Cultural Persistence and Change*, 2nd ed. Singapore: Singapore University Press, 1980.

[1243] Padoch, C., and N. L. Peluso, eds. *Borneo in Transition: People, Forests, Conservation and Development*. New York: OUP, 1996.

[1244] Palmer, Leslie H. *Social Status and Power in Java*. London: Athlone, 1960.

[1245] Pelras, Christian. *The Bugis*. Oxford: Blackwell, 1996.

[1246] ——. "Patron-Client Ties among the Bugis and Makassarese of South Sulawesi." *BKI* 156, no. 3 (2000): 393–432.

[1247] Peluso, Nancy L. *Rich Forests, Poor People*. Berkeley: University of California Press, 1992.

[1248] Pemberton, John. *On the Subject of "Java."* Ithaca, N.Y.: Cornell University Press, 1994.

[1249] ——. "The Specter of Coincidence." In *Southeast Asia over Three Generations: Essays Presented to B.R.O'G. Anderson*, edited by James T. Siegel and Audrey R. Kahin, 75–89. Ithaca, N.Y.: Cornell Southeast Asia Program, 2003.

[1250] Pollmann, Tessel. "Margaret Mead's Balinese: The Fitting Symbols of the American Dream." *Indonesia* 49 (April 1990): 1–36.

[1251] Probojo, Lany. "Between Modernity and Tradition: 'Local Islam' in Tidore, North Maluku, the Ongoing Struggle of the State and the Traditional Elites." *Antropologi Indonesia* 24, no. 63 (2000): 33–44.

[1252] Rutherford, Danilyn. *Raiding the Land of the Foreigners: The Limits of the Nation on an Indonesian Frontier*. Princeton, N.J.: Princeton University. Press, 2002.

[1253] Sanday, Peggy Reeves. *Women at the Center: Life in a Modern Matriarchy*. Ithaca, N.Y.: Cornell University Press, 2002.

[1254] Schrauwers, Albert. *Colonial "Reformation" in the Highlands of Central Sulawesi, Indonesia, 1892–1995*. Toronto: University of Toronto Press, 2000.

[1255] Schulte Nordholt, H. G. *The Political System of the Atoni of Timor*. Leiden, The Netherlands: KITLV, 1971.

[1256] Shiraishi, Saya. "Silakan masuk, silakan duduk: Reflections in a Sitting Room in Java." *Indonesia* 41 (April 1986): 86–130.

[1257] Siegel, James T. *Fetish, Recognition, Revolution*. Princeton, N.J.: Princeton University Press, 1997.

[1258] ——. *The Rope of God*. Berkeley: University of California Press, 1969.

[1259] ——. *Shadow and Sound*. Chicago: Chicago University Press, 1979.

[1260] Singarimbun, Masri. *Kinship, Descent and Alliance among the Karo Batak*. Berkeley: University of California Press, 1975.

[1261] Snouck Hurgronje, C. *The Acehnese*, 2 vols. Leiden, the Netherlands: Brill, 1906.

[1262] Steedly, Mary Margaret. *Hanging without a Rope: Narrative Experience in Colonial and Post-Colonial Karoland*. Princeton, N.J.: Princeton University Press, 1993.

[1263] Thomas, Lynn L., and Franz von Benda Beckmann, eds. *Change and Continuity in Minangkabau: Local, Regional and Historical Perspectives on West Sumatra*. Athens: Ohio University Center for International Studies, 1985.

[1264] Tol, Roger, Kees van Dijk, and Greg Acciaioli. *Authority and Enterprise among the Peoples of South Sulawesi*. Leiden, The Netherlands: KITLV, 2000.

[1265] Touwen-Bousma, C. *Staat, Islam en locale leiders in West Madura, Indonesië*. Kampen, The Netherlands: Mondiss, 1988.

[1266] Traube, Elizabeth G. *Cosmology and Social Life: Ritual Exchange among the Mambai of East Timor*. Chicago: University of Chicago Press, 1986.

[1267] Tsing, Anna Lowenhaupt. *In the Realm of the Diamond Queen: Marginality in an Out-of-the-Way Place*. Princeton, N.J.: Princeton University Press, 1993.

[1268] Tule, Philipus. "Religious Conflicts and a Culture of Tolerance: Paving the Way for Reconciliation in Indonesia." *Antropologi Indonesia* 24, no. 63 (2000): 92–108.

[1269] Volkman, Toby A. *Feast of Honor: Ritual and Change in the Toraja Highlands*. Urbana: University of Illinois Press, 1985.

[1270] Waterson, Roxana. "Holding Back the Mountain: Historical Imagination and the Future of Toraja-Bugis Relations." *Antropologi Indonesia* 24, no. 63 (2000): 65–81.

[1271] Wouden, F. A. E. van. *Types of Social Structure in Eastern Indonesia*. Leiden, The Netherlands: KITLV, 1968.

[1272] Zerner, Charles. "Signs of the Spirits, Signature of the Earth: Iron Forging in Tana Toraja." *Indonesia* 31 (April 1981): 89–112.

Education

[1273] Abdullah, Taufik. *Schools and Politics: The Kaum Muda Movements in West Sumatra, 1927–1933*. Ithaca, N.Y.: Cornell Modern Indonesia Project, 1971.

[1274] Jones, Gavin W. "Religion and Education in Indonesia." *Indonesia* 22 (October 1976): 19–56.

[1275] Jones, Gavin W., and Peter Hagul. "Schooling in Indonesia: Crisis-Related and Longer-Term Issues." *BIES* 37, no. 2 (2001): 207–31.

[1276] Jones, Sidney. "Arabic Instruction and Literacy in Javanese Muslim Schools." *Prisma* 21 (1981): 71–80.

[1277] Kartini, R. A. "Educate the Javanese." Translated and edited by Jean Taylor. *Indonesia* 17 (April 1974): 83–98.

[1278] Kroeskamp, H. *Early Schoolmasters in a Developing Country: A History of Experiments in 19th Century Indonesia*. Assen, The Netherlands: van Gorcum, 1974.

[1279] Lee Kam Hing. "The Taman Siswa in Post-War Indonesia." *Indonesia* 25 (April 1978): 41–59.

[1280] Oey-Gardiner, Mayling. "Challenging the Indonesian Education System: Basic Education for the New Millenium." *BIES* 36, no. 3 (December 2000).

[1281] Parker, Lynette. "The Quality of Schooling in a Balinese Village." *Indonesia* 54 (October 1992): 95–116.

[1282] *Peringatan 55 tahun Diniyah Putri Padangpanjang.* Jakarta: Ghalia Indonesia, 1978.

[1283] Raharjo, M. Dawam. "The Life of Santri Youth: A View from the Pesantren Window at Pabelan." *Sojourn* 1, no. 1 (1986): 32–56.

[1284] Rodgers, Susan. "Compromise and Contestation in Colonial Sumatra: An 1873 Mandailing Schoolbook on the 'Wonders of the West.'" *BKI* 158, no. 3 (2002): 479–512.

[1285] Skoufias, Emmanuel. "Parental Education and Child Nutrition in Indonesia." *BIES* 35, no. 1 (April 1999): 99–119.

[1286] Suryadinata, Leo. "Indonesian Chinese Education: Past and Present." *Indonesia* 14 (1972): 49–72.

[1287] Taylor, Jean. "Education, Colonialism, and Feminism: An Indonesian Case Study." In *Education and the Colonial Experience*, edited by Philip G. Altbach and Gail P. Kelly. New Brunswick, N.J.: Transaction Books, 1984.

[1288] Tsuchiya, Kenji. *Democracy and Leadership: The Rise of the Taman Siswa Movement in Indonesia*. Honolulu: University of Hawai'i Press, 1987.

[1289] Veur, Paul W. van der. *Education and Social Change in Colonial Indonesia*. Athens: Ohio University Center for International Studies, 1969.

Media and the Press

[1290] Adam, Ahmat. *The Vernacular Press and the Emergence of Modern Indonesian Consciousness*. Ithaca, N.Y.: Cornell Studies on Southeast Asia, 1995.

[1291] Barker, Joshua. "Interkom in Indonesia: Not Quite an Imagined Community." In *Southeast Asia over Three Generations: Essays Presented to B. R. O'G. Anderson,* edited by James T. Siegel and Audrey R. Kahin, 383–96. Ithaca, N.Y.: Cornell Southeast Asia Program, 2003.

[1292] Berman, Laine. "Comics as Social Commentary in Java, Indonesia." In *Illustrating Asia*, edited by John A. Lent, 13–35. Richmond, Surrey, UK: Curzon, 2001.

[1293] Faber, G. H. von. *A Short History of Journalism in the Dutch East Indies.* Surabaya, Indonesia: G. Kolff, 1930.

[1294] Haenens, Leen d', Chantal Verelst, and Effendi Gazali. "In Search of Quality Measures for Indonesian Television News." In *Television in Contemporary Asia*, edited by David French and Michael Richards, 271–93. New Delhi: Sage Publications, 2000.

[1295] Hidayat, Dedy N. "Mass Media: Between the Palace and the Market." In *Indonesia: The Challenge of Change*, edited by Richard Baker et al. [0756]

[1296] Hill, David T. "East Timor and the Internet: Global Political Leverage in/on Indonesia," *Indonesia* 73 (April 2002): 25–51.

[1297] Hill, David T., and Krishna Sen. "Wiring the Warung to Global Gateways: The Internet in Indonesia." *Indonesia* 63 (April 1997): 67–89.

[1298] Kitley, Philip. "Pancasila in the Minor Key: TVRI's *Si Unyil* Models the Child." *Indonesia* 68 (October 1999): 129–52.

[1299] ——. *Television, Nation and Culture in Indonesia*. Athens: Ohio University Press, 2000.

[1300] Kurasawa, Aiko. "Propaganda Media on Java under the Japanese." *Indonesia* 44 (October 1987): 59–116.

[1301] Lindsay, Jennifer. "Making Waves: Private Radio and Local Identities in Indonesia." *Indonesia* 64 (October 1997): 105–23.

[1302] ——. "Television, Orality and Performance. Indonesia's 1999 Elections." *Archipel* 64 (2002): 323–36.

[1303] Nunn, Raymond. *Indonesian Newspapers: An International Union List.* Taipei, Republic of China: Chinese Materials Research Aids Service Center, 1971.

[1304] Oey Hong Lee. *Indonesian Government and Press during Guided Democracy*. Hull, UK: University of Hull, 1971.

[1305] Samuel, Jérôme. "Radios indonésiennes: comment survivre à l'ordre nouveau?" *Archipel* 64 (2002): 289–321.

[1306] Sen, Krishna, and David Hill. *Media, Culture and Politics in Indonesia*. Melbourne: OUP, 2000.

[1307] Soebagijo, I. N. *Sejarah pers Indonesia*. Jakarta: Dewan Pers, 1977.

[1308] Szende, A. *From Torrent to Trickle: Managing the Flow of News in Southeast Asia*. Singapore: ISEAS, 1986.

[1309] Termorshuizen, Gerard. *Journalisten en heet hoofden: een geschiedenis van de Indisch-Nederlandse dagblad pers 1744–1905*. Leiden, The Netherlands: KITLV, 2001.

[1310] Wild, Colin. "Indonesia: A Nation and Its Broadcasters." *Indonesia Circle* 43 (1987): 15–40.

Population

[1311] Boomgaard, Peter. *Children of the Colonial State: Population Growth and Economic Development in Java, 1795–1880*. Amsterdam: CASA, 1989.

[1312] ——. *Population Trends, 1795–1942*. Amsterdam: Royal Tropical Institute, 1991.

[1313] Dorléans, Bernard. "Problèmes d'aménagement urbain et spéculation foncière à Jakarta." *Archipel* 46 (1993): 219–41.

[1314] Gooszen, Hans. *A Demographic History of the Indonesian Archipelago, 1880–1942*. Leiden, The Netherlands: KITLV, 1999.

[1315] Hirschman, Charles. "Population and Society in Twentieth-Century Southeast Asia." *JSEAS* 25, no. 2 (September 1994): 381–416.

[1316] Hugo, Graeme. "The Impact of the Crisis on Internal Population Movement in Indonesia." *BIES* 36, no. 2 (August 2000).

[1317] Hugo, Graeme J., et al. *The Demographic Dimension in Indonesian Development*. Singapore: OUP, 1987.

[1318] Hull, Terence H. "First Results from the 2000 Population Census." *BIES* 37, no. 1 (2001): 103–11.

[1319] Jones, Sidney. *Making Money off Migrants: The Indonesian Exodus to Malaysia*. Wollongong, New South Wales, Australia: University of Wollongong Centre for Asia Pacific Social Transformation Studies, 2000.

[1320] McNicoll, Geoffrey, and Masri Singarimbun. *Fertility Decline in Indonesia: Analysis and Interpretation*. Yogyakarta, Indonesia: Gadjah Mada University Press, 1986.

[1321] Spaan, Ernst. *Labour Circulation and Socioeconomic Transformation: The Case of East Java, Indonesia*. The Hague: Interdisciplinary Demographic Institute, 1999.

[1322] Swasono, Sri-Edi, and Masri Singarimbun, eds. *Sepuluh windhu transmigrasi di Indonesia, 1905–1985*. Jakarta: Universitas Indonesia Press, 1985.

[1323] Tan, Mely G., and Budi Soeradji. *Ethnicity and Fertility in Indonesia*. Singapore: ISEAS, 1986.

[1324] Widjojo Nitisastro. *Population Trends in Indonesia*. Ithaca, N.Y.: Cornell University Press, 1970.

Religion

[1325] Abaza, Mona. *Indonesian Students in Cairo: Islamic Education, Perceptions and Exchanges*. Paris: Association Archipel, 1994.

[1326] Abdullah, Taufik, and Sharon Siddique, eds. *Islam and Society in Southeast Asia*. Singapore: ISEAS, 1986.

[1327] Acciaioli, Greg. "Grounds of Conflict, Idioms of Harmony: Custom, Religion, and Nationalism in Violence Avoidance at the Lindu Plain, Central Sulawesi." *Indonesia* 72 (October 2001): 81–114.

[1328] Aqsha, Darul, Dick van der Meij, and Johan Hendrik Meuleman. *Islam in Indonesia: A Survey of Events and Developments from 1988 to March 1993*. Jakarta: Indonesia–Netherlands Cooperation in Islamic Studies, 1995.

[1329] Boland, B. J. *The Struggle of Islam in Modern Indonesia*. Leiden, The Netherlands: KITLV, 1971.

[1330] Boone, Guus. "Modernism and Mission: The Influence of Dutch Modern Theology on Missionary Practice in the East Indies in the Nineteenth Century." In *Missions and Missionaries*, edited by Pieter N. Holtrop and Hugh McLeod, 112–26. Rochester, N.Y.: Boydell Press, 2000.

[1331] Bowen, John. "A Modernist Muslim Poetic: Irony and Social Critique in Gayo Islamic verse." *JAS* 52, no. 3 (August 1993): 629–46.

[1332] Bräuchier, Birgit. "Cyberidentities at War: Religion, Identity, and the Internet in the Moluccan Conflict." *Indonesia* 75 (April 2003): 123–51.

[1333] Bruinessen, Martin van. "Shari'a Court, Tarekat and Pesantren: Religious Institutions in the Banten Sultanate." *Archipel* 50 (1995): 165–72.

[1334] Castles, Lance. "Notes on the Islamic School at Gontor." *Indonesia* 1 (April 1966): 30–45.

[1335] Coppel, Charles A. "The Origins of Confucianism as an Organized Religion in Java, 1900–1923." *JSEAS* 12, no. 1 (1981): 179–95.

[1336] Dhofier, Zamakhsyari. *The Pesantren Tradition: The Role of the Kyai in the Maintenance of Traditional Islam in Java*. Tempe: Arizona State University Program for Southeast Asian Studies, 1999.

[1337] Dijk, Kees van. "Dakwah and Indigenous Culture: The Dissemination of Islam." *BKI* 154, no. 2 (1998): 218–35.

[1338] Federspiel, Howard M. *Popular Indonesian Literature of the Qur'an*. Ithaca, N.Y.: Cornell Modern Indonesia Project, 1994.

[1339] Geertz, Clifford. *Islam Observed: Religious Development in Morocco and Indonesia*. Chicago: University of Chicago Press, 1968.

[1340] ——. *The Religion of Java*. Glencoe, Ill.: Free Press, 1960.

[1341] Haire, James. *The Character and Theological Structure of the Church in Halmahera, Indonesia, 1941–1979*. Frankfurt am Main, Germany: Peter D. Lang, 1981.

[1342] Hasbullah, Moeflich. "Cultural Presentation of the Muslim Middle Class in Contemporary Indonesia." *Studia Islamika* 7, no. 2 (2000): 1–53.

[1343] Hefner, Robert W. "Islamizing Java? Religion and Politics in Rural East Java." *JAS* 46, no. 3 (August 1987): 533–54.

[1344] ——. "Print Islam: Mass Media and Ideological Rivalries among Indonesian Muslims." *Indonesia* 64 (October 1997): 77–103.

[1345] Hooykaas, C. *Agama Tirtha: Five Studies in Hindu Balinese Religion*. Amsterdam: North Holland Publishing, 1964.

[1346] Howell, Julia Day. "Sufism and the Indonesian Islamic Revival." *JAS* 60, no. 3 (August 2001): 701–30.

[1347] Howell, Julia Day, M. A. Subandi, and Peter L. Nelson. "New Faces of Indonesian Sufism: A Demographic Profile of Tarekat Qodiriyyah-Naqsyabandiyyah, Pesantren Suryala, in the 1990s." *RIMA* 35, no. 2 (summer 2001): 33–59.

[1348] Ibrahim Ahmad, et al., compilers. *Readings on Islam in Southeast Asia*. Singapore: ISEAS, 1985.

[1349] Ichwan, Moch Nur. "Differing Responses to an Ahmadi Translation and Exegesis: The Holy Qur'ân in Egypt and Indonesia." *Archipel* 62 (2001): 143–61.

[1350] Johns, A. H. "Sufism as a Category in Indonesian Literature and History." *JSEAS* 2, no. 2 (1961): 10–23.

[1351] Jones, Sidney. "The Contraction and Expansion of the 'Umat' and the Role of the Nahdatul Ulama." *Indonesia* 38 (October 1984): 1–20.

[1352] ——. "The Javanese Pesantren: Between Elite and Peasantry." In *Reshaping Local Worlds: Formal Education and Cultural Change in Rural Southeast Asia*, edited by Charles F. Keyes, 19–41. New Haven, Conn.: Yale University. Southeast Asian Studies, 1989.

[1353] Kipp, Rita Smith, and Susan Rodgers, eds. *Indonesian Religions in Transition*. Tucson: University of Arizona Press, 1987.

[1354] Madinier, Rémy. "Du temps des chameaux à celui du béton radioactif: les nouveaux usages islamistes du passé." *Archipel* 64 (2002): 145–61.

[1355] Madjid, Nurcholish, *Islam, kemodernan dan keindonesiaan*. Jakarta: Yayasan Paramadina, 1987.

[1356] ——. *Tradisi Islam: peran dan fungsinya dalam pembangunan di Indonesia*. Jakarta: Paramadina, 1997.

[1357] Mulder, Niels. "Aliran kebatinan as an expression of the Javanese worldview." *JSEAS* 1, no. 2 (1970): 105–14.

[1358] Nakamura, Mitsuo. *The Crescent Arises over the Banyan Tree: A Study of the Muhammadiyah Movement in a Central Javanese Town*. Yogyakarta, Indonesia: Gadjah Mada University Press, 1983.

[1359] Nieuwenhuijze, C. A. O. van. *Aspects of Islam in Post-Colonial Indonesia: Five Essays*. The Hague: van Hoeve, 1958.

[1360] O'Connor, Stanley J. "Metallurgy and Immortality at Candi Sukuh, Central Java." *Indonesia* 39 (April 1985): 52–70.

[1361] Peacock, James L. *Purifying the Faith: The Muhammadiyah Movement in Indonesian Islam*. Menlo Park, Calif.: Benjamin/Cummings, 1978.

[1362] Rais, M. Amien. *Islam di Indonesia: suatu ikhtiar mengaca diri*. Jakarta: Rajawali, 1989.

[1363] Reid, Anthony J. S. "Nineteenth Century Pan-Islam in Indonesia and Malaysia." *JAS* 26, no. 2 (1967): 267–83.

[1364] Reuter, Thomas. "Great Expectations: Hindu Revival Movements in Java." *The Australian Journal of Anthropology* 12, no. 3 (2001): 327–38.

[1365] Rodgers-Siregar, Susan. *Adat, Islam and Christianity in a Batak Homeland.* Athens: Ohio University Papers in International Studies, 1981.

[1366] Roff, W. R. "Islam Obscured? Some Reflections on Studies of Islam and Society in Southeast Asia." *Archipel* 29 (1985): 7–34.

[1367] Siegel, James T. "Kiblat and the Mediatic Jew." *Indonesia* 69 (April 2000): 9–40.

[1368] Stange, Paul. "The Logic of Rasa in Java." *Indonesia* 38 (October 1984): 113–34.

[1369] Suryadinata, Leo. "Confucianism in Indonesia: Past and Present." *Southeast Asia: An International Quarterly* 3, no. 3 (1974): 881–901.

[1370] Suwandi, Raharjo. *A Quest for Justice: The Millenary Aspirations of a Contemporary Javanese Wali.* Leiden, The Netherlands: KITLV, 2000.

[1371] Vickers, Adrian. "Hinduism and Islam in Indonesia: Bali and the Pasisir World." *Indonesia* 44 (October 1987): 30–58.

[1372] Wessing, Robert. "Nyai Loro Kidul in Puger: Local Applications of a Myth." *Archipel* 53 (1997): 97–120.

[1373] Woodward, Mark R. *Islam in Java: Normative Piety and Mysticism in the Sultanate of Yogyakarta*. Tucson: University of Arizona Press, 1989.

[1374] ——. "Textual Exegesis as Social Commentary: Religious, Social, and Political Meanings of Indonesian Translations of Arabic Hadith Texts." *JAS* 52, no. 3 (August 1993): 565–83.

[1375] ——, ed. *Toward a New Paradigm: Recent Developments in Indonesian Islamic Thought.* Tempe: Arizona State University Program for Southeast Asian Studies, 1996.

Sociology

[1376] Aragon, Lorraine V. "Communal Violence in Poso, Central Sulawesi: Where People Eat Fish and Fish Eat People." *Indonesia* 72 (October 2001): 45–79.

[1377] Burger, D. H. *Structural Changes in Javanese Society: The Supra-Village Sphere.* Ithaca, N.Y.: Cornell University Southeast Asia Program, 1956.

[1378] Claus, Wolfgang, Hans-Dieter Evers, and Solvay Gerke. "The Formation of a Peasant Society: Javanese Transmigrants in East Kalimantan." *Indonesia* 46 (October 1988): 78–90.

[1379] Collins, Elizabeth Fuller. "Multinational Capital, New Order 'Development' and Democratization in South Sumatra." *Indonesia* 71 (April 2001): 111–34.

[1380] Columbijn, Freek. *Patches of Padang: The History of an Indonesian Town in the Twentieth Century and the Use of Urban Space*. Leiden, The Netherlands: Research School CNWS, 1994.

[1381] ——. "The Politics of Indonesian Football." *Archipel* 59 (2000): 171–200.

[1382] Connor, Linda, and Adrian Vickers. "Crisis, Citizenship, and Cosmopolitanism: Living in a Local and Global Risk Society in Bali." *Indonesia* 75 (April 2003): 153–80.

[1383] Geertz, Clifford. "The Javanese Kiyai: The Changing Role of a Cultural Broker." *Comparative Studies in Society and History* 2 (1960): 228–50.

[1384] Grijns, Kees, and Peter J. M. Nas. *Jakarta-Batavia: Socio Cultural Essays.* Leiden, The Netherlands: KITLV, 2000.

[1385] Jellinek, Lea. *The Wheel of Fortune: The History of a Poor Community in Jakarta*. Honolulu: University of Hawai'i Press, 1991.

[1386] Kato, Tsuyoshi. "Different Fields, Similar Locusts: Adat Communities and the Village Law of 1979 in Indonesia." *Indonesia* 47 (April 1989): 89–114.

[1387] Koentjaraningrat, R. M., ed. *Villages in Indonesia*. Ithaca, N.Y.: Cornell University. Press, 1967.

[1388] Nas, Peter J. M., ed. *The Indonesian City: Studies in Urban Development and Planning*. Leiden, the Netherlands: KITLV, 1986.

[1389] Rotge, Vincent L. *Rural-Urban Integration in Java: Consequences for Regional Development and Employment*. Aldershot, UK: Ashgate, 2000.

[1390] Selo Soemardjan. *Social Changes in Jogjakarta*. Ithaca, N.Y.: Cornell University Press, 1962.

[1391] Shiraishi, Saya. *Young Heroes: The Indonesian Family in Politics*. Ithaca, N.Y.: Cornell Studies on Southeast Asia, 1997.

[1392] Siegel, James T. *Solo in the New Order: Language and Hierarchy in an Indonesian City*. Princeton, N.J.: Princeton University Press, 1986.

[1393] Speyer, Patricia. "Fire without Smoke and Other Phantoms of Ambon's Violence: Media Effects, Agency, and the Work of Imagination." *Indonesia* 74 (October 2002): 37–58.

[1394] Sumarto, Sudarno, Asep Suryahadi, and Wenefrida Idyanti. "Designs and Implementation of Indonesian Social Safety Net Programs." *Developing Economies* 40, no. 1 (2002): 3–31.

[1395] Vel, Jacqueline A. C. "Tribal Battle in a Remote Island: Crisis and Violence in Sumba (Eastern Indonesia)." *Indonesia* 72 (October 2001): 140–58.

[1396] Volkman, Toby Alice et al., eds. *Sulawesi: The Celebes.* Hong Kong: Periplus Editions, 2000.

[1397] Wallach, Jeremy. "Exploring Class, Nation, and Xenocentrism in Indonesian Cassette Retail Outlets." *Indonesia* 74 (October 2002): 79–102.

[1398] Wertheim, W. F. *East-West Parallels: Sociological Approaches to Modern Asia.* The Hague: van Hoeve, 1964.

Women

[1399] Adeney, Frances. *Christian Women in Indonesia: A Narrative Study of Gender and Religion*. Syracuse, N.Y.: Syracuse University Press, 2003.

[1400] Blackburn, Susan, and Sharon Bessell. "Marriageable Age: Political Debates on Early Marriage in Twentieth-Century Indonesia." *Indonesia* 63 (April 1997): 107–41.

[1401] Blackwood, Evelyn. *Webs of Power: Women, Kin and Community in a Sumatran Village*. Lanham, Md.: Rowman & Littlefield, 2000.

[1402] Blussé, Leonard. *Retour Amoy: Anny Tan—een vrouwenleven in Indonesië, Nederland en China*. Amsterdam: Uitgeverij Balans, 2000.

[1403] Brenner, Suzanne A. *The Domestication of Desire: Women, Wealth and Modernity in Java*. Princeton, N.J.: Princeton University Press, 1998.

[1404] ——. "On the Public Intimacy of the New Order: Images of Women in the Popular Indonesian Print Media." *Indonesia* 67 (April 1999): 13–37.

[1405] Budianto, Melani. "Plural Identities: Indonesian Women's Redefinition of Democracy in the Post-Reformasi Era." *RIMA* 36, no. 1 (2002): 35–50.

[1406] Butt, Leslie. "'An Epidemic of Runaway Wives': Discourses by Dani Men on Sex and Marriage in Highlands Irian Jaya, Indonesia." *Crossroads* 15, no. 1 (2002): 55–87.

[1407] Clancy-Smith, Julia, and Frances Gouda, eds. *Domesticating the Empire: Race, Gender, and Family Life in French and Dutch Colonialism*. Charlottesville: University Press of Virginia, 1998.

[1408] Dzuhayatin, Siti Ruhaini. "Gender and Pluralism in Indonesia." In *The Politics of Multiculturalism*, edited by Robert W. Hefner, 253–67. Honolulu: University of Hawai'i Press, 2001.

[1409] Gouda, Frances. "Good Mothers, Medeas, or Jezebels: Feminine Imagery in Colonial and Anticolonial Rhetoric in the Dutch East Indies, 1900–1942." In *Domesticating the Empire: Race, Gender, and Family Life in French and Dutch Colonialism*, edited by Julia Clancy-Smith and Frances Gouda, 236–54. [1407]

[1410] Hellwig, Tineke. "A Double Murder in Batavia: Representations of Gender and Race in the Indies." *RIMA* 35, no. 2 (summer 2001): 1–32.

[1411] Hull, Terence H., Endang Sulistyaningshi, and Gavin W. Jones. *Prostitution in Indonesia: Its History and Evolution*. Canberra: Research School of Social Sciences, ANU, 1995.

[1412] Jones, Gavin W., ed. *Women in the Urban and Industrial Workforce: Southeast and East Asia*. Canberra: ANU, 1984.

[1413] Kipp, Rita Smith. "Emancipating Each Other: Dutch Colonial Missionaries' Encounter with Karo Women in Sumatra, 1900–1942." In *Domesticating the Empire*, edited by Julia Clancy-Smith and Frances Gouda, 211–35. [1407]

[1414] Koning, Juliette, Marleen Nolten, Janet Rodenburg, and Ratna Saptari, eds. *Women and Households in Indonesia: Cultural Notions and Social Practices*. Richmond, Surrey, UK: Curzon, 2000.

[1415] Locher-Scholten, Elsbeth. "So Close and Yet So Far: The Ambivalence of Dutch Colonial Rhetoric on Javanese Servants in Indonesia, 1900–1942." In *Do-*

mesticating the Empire, edited by Julia Clancy-Smith and Frances Gouda, 131–53. [1407]

[1416] ——. *Women and the Colonial State: Essays on Gender and Modernity in the Netherlands Indies 1900–1942*. Amsterdam: Amsterdam University Press, 2000.

[1417] Locher-Scholten, Elsbeth, and Anke Niehof, eds. *Indonesian Women in Focus: Past and Present Notions*. Dordrecht, The Netherlands: Foris, 1987.

[1418] Lont, Hotze. "More Money, More Autonomy? Women and Credit in a Javanese Urban Ccommunity." *Indonesia* 70 (October 2000): 83–100.

[1419] Manderson, Lenore, ed. *Women's Work and Women's Roles: Economics and Everyday Life in Indonesia, Malaysia and Singapore*. Canberra: National Centre for Development Studies, 1983.

[1420] Mellington, Nicole, and Lisa Cameron. "Female Education and Child Mortality in Indonesia." *BIES* 35, no. 3 (December 1999): 115–44.

[1421] Ming, Hanneke. "Barracks-Concubinage in the Indies, 1887–1920." *Indonesia* 35 (April 1983): 65–93.

[1422] Oey-Gardiner, Mayling, and Carla Bianpoen, eds. *Indonesian Women: The Journey Continues*. Canberra: ANU Research School of Pacific and Asian Studies, 2000.

[1423] Pausacker, Helen. "Lovesick: Illness, Romance and the Portrayal of Women in Low Malay Novels from the Dutch East Indies." *RIMA* 35, no. 1 (2001): 43–78.

[1424] Raharjo, Yulfita, and Valierie Hull, eds. *Women in the Urban and Industrial Workforce: Southeast and East Asia*. Canberra: National Centre for Development Studies, 1984.

[1425] Reijs, Jeske, et al., eds. *Vrouwen in de Nederlandse koloniën*. Nijmegen, The Netherlands: Sun, 1986.

[1426] Rodenburg, Jane. *In the Shadow of Migration: Rural Women and Their Households in North Tapanuli, Indonesia*. Leiden, The Netherlands: KITLV, 1997.

[1427] Sears, Laurie J., ed. *Fantasizing the Feminine in Indonesia.* Durham: University of North Carolina Press, 1996.

[1428] Taylor, Jean Gelman, ed. *Women Creating Indonesia: The First Fifty Years*. Clayton, Victoria, Australia: Monash Institute, 1997.

[1429] Widarti, Diah. "Determinants of Labour Force Participation by Married Women: The Case of Jakarta." *BIES* 34, no. 2 (August 1998): 93–120.

[1430] Wieringa, Saskia Eleonora. *The Politicization of Gender Relations in Indonesia: The Indonesian Women's Movement and Gerwani until the New Order State*. Amsterdam: University of Amsterdam Press, 1995.

[1431] Wolf, Diane L. *Factory Daughters: Gender, Household Dynamics, and Rural Industralization in Java*. Berkeley: University of California Press, 1992.

[1432] Zainu'ddin, Ailsa Tomson, et al. *Kartini Centenary: Indonesian Women Then and Now*. Clayton, Victoria, Australia: Monash University Centre of Southeast Asian Studies, 1980.

CURRENT MEDIA

Journals

Antropologi Indonesia, Jurusan Antropologi, FISIP, Universitas Indonesia, Depok, Java Barat, Indonesia.

Archipel, Bureau 732, EHESS, 54 Bd Raspail, 75006 Paris, France.

ASEAN Economic Bulletin, Institute of Southeast Asian Studies (Economic Research Unit), Heng Mui Keng Terrace, Pasir Panjang, Singapore 119614.

Asian Affairs, Royal Society for Asian Affairs, 2 Belgrave Square, London SW1X 8PJ, United Kingdom.

Asian Perspectives (archeology), University of Hawai'i Press, 2840 Kolowalu St., Honolulu, HI 96822, USA.

Asian Survey, University of California Press, Berkeley, CA 94720, USA.

Australian Journal of International Affairs, Australian Institute of International Affairs, Canberra, ACT 2601, Australia.

Bijdragen tot de Taal-, Land- en Volkenkunde, KITLV, Postbus 9515, 2300 RA Leiden, Netherlands.

Borneo Research Bulletin, IEAS, Universiti Malaysia Sarawak, 94300 Kota Samarahan, Sarawak, Malaysia.

Bulletin of Indonesian Economic Studies, Research School of Pacific Studies, Australian National University, GPO Box 4 Canberra Act 2601, Australia.

Contemporary Southeast Asia, Institute of Southeast Asian Studies, Heng Mui Keng Terrace, Pasir Panjang, Singapore 119614.

Critical Asian Studies [formerly *Bulletin of Concerned Asian Scholars*], c/o BCAS, 3693 South Bay Bluffs Drive, Cedar, MI 49621-9434, USA.

Crossroads: An Interdisciplinary Journal of Southeast Asian Studies, Center for Southeast Asian Studies, Northern Illinois University, DeKalb, IL 60115, USA.

Cultural Survival Quarterly, Cultural Survival Inc., Cambridge, MA, USA.

Developing Economies, Institute of Developing Economies, Tokyo, Japan.

Ekonomi dan Keuangan Indonesia, Lembaga Penyelidikan Ekonomi dan Masyarakat, Fakultas Ekonomi, Universitas Indonesia, Kotak Pos 295, Jakarta 10001, Indonesia.

Far Eastern Economic Review, GPO Box 160, Hong Kong.

Flora Malesiana Bulletin, Rijksherbarium, Postbus 9514, 2300 RA Leiden, Netherlands.

Gatra, Gedung Gatra, Jl. Kalibata Timur IV, No. 15, Jakarta 12740, Indonesia.

Indische Letteren, c/o Reggie Baay, Praam 27, 2377 BW Oude Wetering, Netherlands.

Indonesia, Southeast Asia Program Publications, 640 Stewart Avenue, Ithaca, NY 14850, USA.

Indonesia: An Analysis of Economic and Political Trends, Economist Intelligence Unit, 40 Duke Street, London, W1A 1DW, United Kingdom.

Indonesia and the Malay World [successor to *Indonesia Circle*], School of Oriental & African Studies, Univ. of London, Thornhaugh St., Russell Square, London WC1H 0XG, United Kingdom.

Indonesia: Feiten en Meningen, Postbus 4098, 1009 AB Amsterdam, Netherlands.

Indonesian Quarterly, CSIS, Yayasan Proklamasi, Jl Tanah Abang III/27, Jakarta Pusat, Indonesia.

Inside Indonesia, PO Box 1326, Collingwood, Victoria, Australia.

Itinerario, Centre for the History of European Expansion, Faculty of the School of Humanities, University of Leiden, Postbus 9515, 2300 RA Leiden, Netherlands.

Journal of Asian History, Otto Harrassowitz, Postfach 2929, D-6200 Wiesbaden 1, West Germany; Goodbody Hall, Indiana University, Bloomington, IN 47405, USA.

Journal of Asian Studies, AAS, 1 Lane Hall, University of Michigan, Ann Arbor, MI 48109, USA.

Journal of Contemporary Asia, PO Box 592, Manila, Philippines 1099.

Journal of the Malaysian Branch of the Royal Asiatic Society, 130M Jalan Thamby Abdullah, Brickfields, 50470 Kuala Lumpur, Malaysia.

Journal of Southeast Asian Studies (succeeded *Journal of Southeast Asian History*), c/o Department of History, National University of Singapore, 11 Arts Link, Singapore 117570.

Kyoto Review [online]: http://kyotoreview.cseas.kyoto-u.ac.jp.

Masyarakat Indonesia, Biro Pemasyarakatan IPTEK, LIPI, Widya Graha, Jl Jend. Gatot Subroto 10, Jakarta, Indonesia.

Modern Asian Studies, Cambridge University Press, Edinburgh Building, Shaftsbury Rd, Cambridge CB2 2RU, United Kingdom.

Pacific Affairs, University of British Columbia, Vancouver, BC V6T 1W5, Canada.

Panji, Jalan Kemang Selatan Raya, No. 111H, Jakarta 12730, Indonesia.

Populasi: bulletin penelitian dan kebijaksaan kependudukan, Pusat Penelitian Kependuduukan Universitas Gadjah Mada, Yogyakarta, Indonesia.

Review of Indonesian and Malayan Affairs, Department of Southeast Asian Studies, University of Sydney, Sydney NSW 2006, Australia.

Sojourn, Journal on Social Issues in Southeast Asia, Institute of Southeast Asian Studies, Heng Mui Keng Terrace, Pasir Panjang, Singapore 119614.

Southeast Asia Research (SOAS), Turpin Distr. Services, Blackhorse Road, Letchworth, Herts SG6 1HN, United Kingdom.

Southeast Asian Affairs, Institute of Southeast Asian Studies, Heng Mui Keng Terrace. Pasir Panjang, Singapore 119614.

Southeast Asian Studies, Center for Southeast Asian Studies, Kyoto Univ., 46 Shimoadachi-cho, Yoshida, Sakyo-ku, Kyoto 606, Japan.

Studia Islamika, IAIN Syarif Hidayatullah, Jakarta, Indonesia.

Tapol: The Indonesian Human Rights Campaign, 111 Northwood Rd., Thornton Heath, Surrey CR7 8HW, United Kingdom.

Tempo, Gedung Tempo, Jalan Proklamasi No. 72, Jakarta 10320, Indonesia.

Tijdschrift voor geschiedenis, Van Gorcum, Groningen, The Netherlands.

Internet Resources

General

Biro Pusat Statistik: www.bps.go.id. The most useful website for recent statistical data.

International Crisis Group: www.crisisweb.org. The International Crisis Group publishes occasional briefings on Indonesia that are both reliable and informative.

www.Laksamana.net. The best source for up-to-date English digests of current political and economic events in Indonesia.

www.gtzsfdm.or.id. A useful website that gives the most recent news on the course of decentralization.

www.store.eiu.com. The Economic Intelligence Unit's regular economic updates and country profiles.

Environment

The following two websites cover environmental developments in the region and are perhaps the most useful websites on this subject.

Lembaga Ekolabel Indonesia (LEI): www.lei.or.id
Down to Earth: http://dte.gn.apc.org

Human Rights

Amnesty International (AI): www.amnesty.org. AI provides frequent reports on a variety of issues affecting human rights in Indonesia. A list of these publications and their e-mail releases can be accessed via their website.

About the Authors

Robert Cribb is senior fellow at the Australian National University in Canberra and has previously worked in Australia, the Netherlands, and Denmark. His research interests focus on Indonesia and cover political violence, national identity, environmental politics, and historical geography. He is the author of *Gangsters and Revolutionaries* (1991) and the *Historical Atlas of Indonesia* (2000), as well as editor of *The Indonesian Killings of 1965–1966* (1990), *The Late Colonial State in Indonesia* (1994), and (with Li Narangoa) *Imperial Japan and National Identities in Asia, 1895–1945* (2003).

Audrey Kahin received her Ph.D. in Southeast Asian History from Cornell University in 1979. From 1978 to 1995 she was managing editor of Southeast Asia publications at Cornell and coeditor, then editor, of the journal *Indonesia*. She is editor and contributor of *Regional Dynamics of the Indonesian Revolution* (1985), author of *Rebellion to Integration* (1999) and (with George McT. Kahin) *Subversion as Foreign Policy* (1995). Most recently she edited, with James T. Siegel, *Southeast Asia over Three Generations* (2003). She is currently working on problems of integration in Indonesia and a biography of the former Islamic political leader Mohammad Natsir.